RUSSIA'S ISLAMIC THREAT

RUSSIA'S ISLAMIC THREAT

GORDON M. HAHN

YALE UNIVERSITY PRESS
NEW HAVEN AND LONDON

For information about this and other Yale University Press publications, please contact:

U.S. Office: sales.press@yale.edu   yalebooks.com
Europe Office: sales@yaleup.co.uk   www.yaleup.co.uk

Set in Minion by MATS Typesetters, Southend-on-Sea, Essex
Printed in Great Britain by St Edmundsbury Press Ltd, Bury St Edmunds

Library of Congress Cataloging-in-Publication Data

Hahn, Gordon M.
   Russia's islamic threat / Gordon M. Hahn.
      p. cm.
   Includes bibliographical references and index.
   ISBN 978–0–300–12077–6 (alk. paper)
   1. Terrorism—Russia (Federation) 2.   Muslims—Russia (Federation) 3.
   Terrorism—Religious aspects—Islam.   I.   Title.
      HV6433.R9H34 2006
      363.3250947—dc22

                                                                        2006027613

A catalogue record for this book is available from the British Library

10 9 8 7 6 5 4 3 2 1

"The fig tree does not grow in Russia"

—Rafael Khakim(ov), *Gde Nasha Mekka?* (Where Is Our Mecca?)

Contents

Tables

Preface

This book is the first comprehensive examination of Russia's emerging revolutionary jihadist terrorist network and its implications for international security. With the end of the Cold War and especially after 9/11, successive US administrations have shifted ever more research, intelligence, and policy planning resources away from the study of Russia to Islam and traditionally Muslim states. However, with the collapse of the Soviet Union, Russia's Muslims again became an inextricable part of the Muslim *umma* (world community), subject to the influence of its ideological trends and becoming potential recruits and operatives for the Islamo-fascist revolution. Still, Russia's some fifteen million citizens of traditionally Muslim ethnic groups (so-called "ethnic Muslims") remain the world's forgotten Muslims; unduly so. The international security implications of Russia's emerging Islamist network could be profound. Except for Pakistani Islamic fundamentalists and Islamists, none of the world's other radical Muslims live in such close proximity to so many stockpiles of materials and weapons of mass destruction (MWMDs) as do Russia's increasingly Islamist Chechen militants and their growing number of allies in other Russian regions. Moreover, the Chechen-led network's ideology reflects strong antipathy toward the US and its allies and sympathy for the global jihadist movement.

At present, national security and political risk assessments take little if any note of Russia's Islamist jihad: the Chechen-led network's origins, geographical scope, structure, ideology, strategy, tactics, propaganda, and relationship with the international jihadist movement are yet to be properly addressed. The one major in-depth study of Russia's Muslims to date fails to address in any detail their communal (ethnic and/or confessional) mobilization or the jihadist terrorist groups.[1] Studies of the history of the Russo-Chechen conflict and today's Chechen resistance barely touch on Russia's Islamist militants beyond Chechnya's borders, except to note the Chechen jihadists' major terrorist acts in Moscow.[2] There is no book or even major

article focused on the structure, ideology, strategy, operations, and tactics of the
Chechen-led jihadist network, its potential for undermining the Russian state's
stability and territorial integrity, or the mid- to long-term implications for
international security.

This absence is partially explained by the recentness of developments: it was
only in summer 2002 that Chechen resistance forces decided to expand the
war to the entire North Caucasus after their failed August–September 1999
incursion into Dagestan led by al Qaeda operative Abu ibn al-Khattab and his
Chechen associate Shamil Basaev. But there is also a reluctance on the part of
many observers, for ideological and political reasons, to acknowledge that the
Chechen resistance has come under the sway of, and is allied with, the global
revolutionary jihad. Some politicians, analysts, and academics deliberately
foster serious misrepresentations of the situation in Russia's North Caucasus,
arguing that the international Islamist factor is non-existent and that Russian
imperialism is the lone cause of the Chechen war and Islamist terror in Russia.
Some even advise US policymakers to ignore the issue and disabuse themselves
of the "naive and simplistic supposition that the United States and Russia
share a common enemy of 'international terrorism.'"[3] On the other side,
Russian president Vladimir Putin's first instinct after terrorist attacks such as
the horrific taking of hundreds of child hostages at Beslan in September 2004
has been to attribute them solely to "international terrorists" and ignore the
indigenous elements of the Islamist revolutionary movement emerging in
Russia.[4] American think-tanks and the hundreds of thousands of pages
devoted to the Chechnya war have so far spawned no more than a handful of
paragraphs on the North Caucasus jihadi network's Islamist ideology. Not a
word has been written about its rabid anti-Americanism, anti-Westernism,
anti-secularism, or anti-Semitism. This book fills this gaping – indeed,
shocking – void in the universe of Russia-related research.

As is often the case, the reality is considerably more complex than those
involved in the politics of the day are willing to acknowledge. There should be
little skepticism about the presence of internationally tied indigenous Islamists
in Russia. Although the international jihad's influence on the North Caucasus
jihad ought not to be exaggerated, the potential danger it poses to international
security should not be underestimated either. To be sure, the Islamist enemies
of Russia and the West are not exactly one and the same. However, they are
closely allied, virtually identical in their ideology, strategy, tactics, and many of
their jihadist goals, and therefore often work in concert against their enemies.

A basic assumption of the book is that the global jihadi network or any one
of its regional hubs need not be a mass movement to cause great damage to the
US, Russia, or the international community, as 9/11 proved. Basaev, when
asked whether the North Caucasus's network of combat *jamaat* (militant

groups)is a "serious force," pointed out: "Even one person is serious, if he knows what he needs to do and how to do it."[5]

This book is structured as follows. Chapter One explores factors that shape the dynamic of potential political mobilization for Russia's Muslims. Background causes include historical (past conflict between the parties), cultural (authoritarianism, imperialism, extremist nationalism, militarism and militancy, propensities to violence), and structural (ethno-demographics and poverty) factors. Over time the Muslim demographic explosion will tend to multiply the present slow but steady flow of young Muslim males, mostly from the North Caucasus, to Russia's Chechen-led jihad. The most immediate causes of rising "communalism" among Russia's Muslims noted above (the Chechen war, foreign Islamist influences, and Putin's anti-federative counter-revolution) are discussed in detail in Chapters One and Two. Also in Chapter One, I use the theories of nationalism, violence, terrorism, and conflict prevention to demonstrate how these causal factors are combining to spark jihadist Islamism. I also discuss factors that may constrain the development of a mass jihadist movement in Russia, including ethnic, geographic, theological, ideological, and political divisions.

Chapter Two provides a detailed overview of the Chechen war. With the theoretical and causal context established, Chapter Three then looks at the development and nature of Russia's growing Islamist movement and its terrorist revolutionary network of combat jamaats in the period 2002–2005. The following aspects of the network are discussed in detail: (1) the involvement of Chechen and foreign Islamists in the network's establishment; (2) organizational structure and operating principles; (3) ideology; (4) strategy; and (5) tactics and operations. These are compared to the same in the international Islamist movement in order to test the North Caucasus/Russia network's status as a nodal hub within the global jihadist network.

In order to look at these aspects of the network and grasp the capacity of the Ichkeriyan jihadists to "travel" across the diverse ethnicity, culture, and geography of Russia's "Muslim lands," the book's next three chapters are case studies of Islamic and Islamist politics and violence in three of Russia's Muslim republics: Dagestan, Kabardino-Balkariya (KBR), and Tatarstan. These chapters show that there is the expected gradient of decline in the jihadist network's vitality as it moves from the "Vainakh" ethnic dyad in Chechnya and Ingushetiya to Dagestan, to the ethnic Karachai-Balkar- and Circassian-dominated western North Caucasus republics – KBR, Karachaevo-Cherkessiya (KChR), and Adygeya – and outside the Caucasus to Tatarstan, Bashkortostan, and other regions and communities dominated by ethnic Tatars and, to a lesser extent, Bashkirs.

The existence of a strong combat jamaat network in Dagestan, which is home to some twenty different Muslim ethnic groups, indicates that Islamism can trump ethnic differences. Dagestan's Muslims have historically been some of Russia's most devout. The strength of the network there confirms the resurgence of Islam after seventy years of atheist Soviet rule and suggests that re-Islamization can promote Islamism itself among Dagestan's ethnic groups. The spread of the Islamist jamaat network to the KBR is important as it is the geographical and ethno-political gateway to the western-northwestern North Caucasus, which also includes the Muslim republics of the KChR and Adygeya and the Karachai-Balkar and Circassian ethnic Muslim groups. Therefore, the emergence of Islamist cells, jamaats, or a full-fledged network node in the KBR would reflect not only on the jihadist movement's geographical reach but on its pan-Caucasian and pan-Islamic appeal as well.

Tatarstan and Russia's Tatars are for several reasons central to the jihadist movement's prospects for spreading beyond the North Caucasus and becoming a Russia-wide movement. First, it is the region with the largest number of ethnic Muslims, most of them ethnic Tatars. Second, ethnic Tatars are the largest minority in neighboring Bashkortostan and a culturally fraternal people of that republic's second-largest nationality and titular nationality, the Muslim Bashkirs. Third, ethnic Tatars are the largest traditionally Muslim ethnic group in Russia, with large "internal" diaspora urban and rural communities spread across the Middle Volga to Siberia and Moscow, St. Petersburg, and many of Russia's large urban centers. The Tatars' secularization during the Soviet period, their high degree of russification, their traditionally moderate Hanafi form of Islam, and their historical role in the Islamic reform movement ("jadidism" or "new teaching") will test more robustly the appeal of Islamism across Russia's ethnic Muslim groups. Tatarstan is also important for testing to what extent the Putin counter-revolution's recentralization policies are responsible for a new communal politicization, whether ethnic or confessional. Tatarstan's moderate nationalist elite led the fight for the creation of Russia's asymmetrical federative system under President Yeltsin and have the most to lose from Putin's anti-federalist and assimilative policies. For all these reasons, Tatarstan, the politics of Tatar nationalism, and its apparently growing Islamization are critical for understanding Islamism's potential to expand across Russia.

The final chapter addresses how Russia's emerging Islamist movement has already impinged on international security and how it might do so further in the future and offers policy recommendations for addressing Russia's Muslim and Islamist challenge.

Dr. Gordon M. Hahn
Mountain View, California
1 May 2005

Acknowledgements

I would like to thank Jeffrey Bale, Ilan Berman, Fiona Hill, Anatol Lieven, Herman Pirchner, Barry Rubin, Leonard Spector, and one anonymous reviewer for their helpful comments on parts and drafts of the manuscript. Many of the book's pluses emerged as a result of these; all shortcomings fall to the author. I also thank Gary Ackerman, Fredo Arias-King, Charles Blair, Harley Balzer, Walter Connor, Fiona Hill, Mark Kramer, Peter Lavelle, Igor Lukes, Paul Murphy, Herman Pirchner, and John "Pat" Willerton for their encouragement during writing. Last but not least, I thank my wife, Marina, my son, Gordon, my parents, and my father- and mother-in-law, Mark and Karina, for their moral and spiritual support over the years.

Abbreviations

ChRI	Chechen Republic of Ichkeriya
CPSU	Communist Party of the Soviet Union
FO	Federal District
FSB	Federal Service for Security
GRU	Main Military Intelligence Administration
KBR	Republic of Kabardino-Balkariya
KChR	Republic of Karachaevo-Cherkessiya
KPRF	Communist Party of the Russian Federation
MVD	Ministry of Internal Affairs
NChO TOTs	The Naberezhnyi Chelny Branch of the All-Tatar Public Center
OGV	Joint Group of Forces
OMON	Special Purpose Militia Units
ROUD	District Department of Internal Affairs
RSFSR	Russian Socialist Federation of Soviet Republics
VTOTs	The All-Tatar Public Center

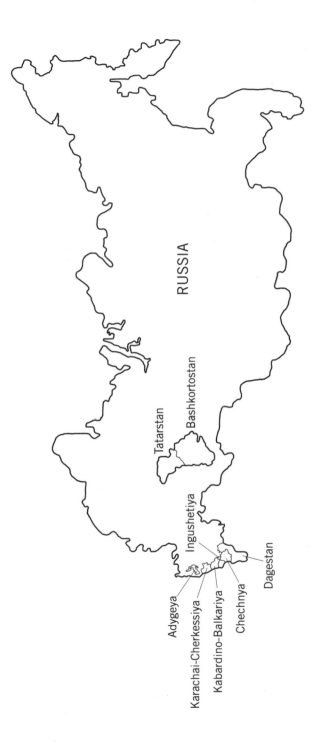

RUSSIA

Bashkortostan

Tatarstan

Ingushetiya

Dagestan

Adygeya

Karachai-Cherkessiya

Kabardino-Balkariya

Chechnya

Russia's Titular Ethnic Muslim Republics

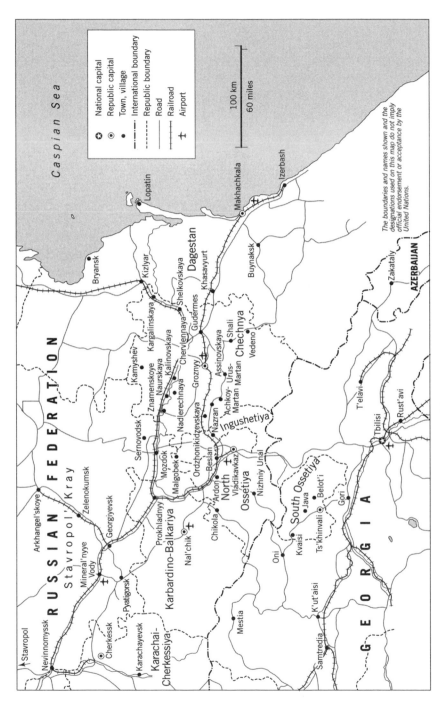

The North Caucasus and its Titular Ethnic Muslim Republics

Legend:

- ⊕ National capital
- ◉ Republic capital
- • Town, village
- — ·· — International boundary
- — — — Republic boundary
- —— Road
- +++ Railroad
- ✈ Airport

100 km
60 miles

Caspian Sea

RUSSIAN FEDERATION

Stavropol' Kray

Karachai-Cherkessiya

Kabardino-Balkariya

North Ossetiya

Ingushetiya

Chechnya

Dagestan

South Ossetiya

GEORGIA

AZERBAIJAN

Stavropol
Nevinnomyssk
Arkhangel'skoye
Cherkessk
Karachayevsk
Nevinnomyssk
Mineral'nyye Vody
Zelenokumsk
Georgiyevsk
Pyatigorsk
Nal'chik
Prokhladnyy
Malgobek
Mozdok
Sernovodsk
Znamenskoye
Naurskaya
Kamyshev
Kargalinskaya
Kalinovskaya
Nadterechnaya
Chervlennaya
Shelkovskaya
Grozny
Assinovskaya
Achkhoy-Martan
Urus-Martan
Shali
Vedeno
Gudermes
Khasavyurt
Buynaksk
Makhachkala
Izerbash
Lopatin
Kizlyar
Bryansk
Ordzhonikidzevskaya
Nazran
Beslan
Ardon
Chikola
Vladikavkaz
Nizhniy Unal
Mestia
Oni
Kvaisi
Java
Belot'i
Ts'khinvali
Gori
Samtredia
K'ut'aisi
Tbilisi
T'elavi
Rust'avi
Zakataly

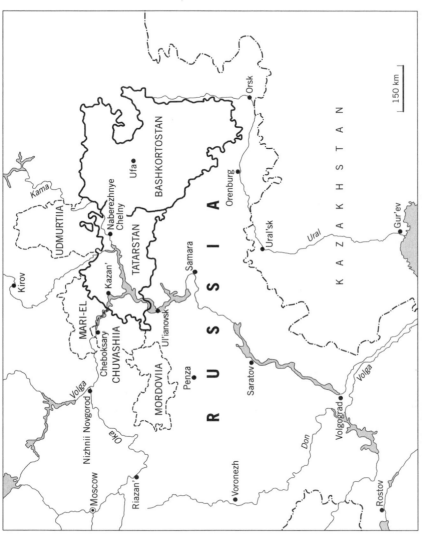

The Titular Ethnic Muslim Republics of Tatarstan and Bashkortostan (Bashkiriya) in the Volga-Urals area of Russia

Chapter One

Russia's Muslim and Islamist Challenge

Russia is experiencing the beginning of an Islamist jihad. Russia's emerging jihadist movement is not limited to Chechnya. A network of terrorists is expanding throughout the North Caucasus – in particular, to the five other titular Muslim republics: Ingushetiya, Dagestan, Kabardino-Balkariya (KBR), Karachaevo-Cherkessiya (KChR), and Adygeya – and could soon spread to Tatarstan and Bashkortostan and beyond. Russia's Chechen-led network of Islamo-terrorists is not only expanding but is becoming increasingly sophisticated and effective, under the influence of al Qaeda and the global jihadist movement. Al Qaeda and its now loose network of affiliates and self-starter cells show the viability of such a model in weak, failing, or failed states. Despite Putin's efforts to recentralize power, Russia remains a weak state, is becoming a failing state, and risks becoming a failed one. A confluence of several immediate causes – the ongoing Chechen war, the growing influence of radicals tied to the international Islamist revolutionary network, and Russian president Vladimir Putin's de-democratizing and anti-federalist counter-revolution – and numerous other background and "structural" causes are leading to a radical re-Islamization of some of Russia's Muslims and the formation of a geographically expanding, ethnically diverse, and flexibly organized terrorist Islamist network across Russia. The emphasis on multi-causality is not an effort to avoid the "rigor of parsimony" in explaining the rise of jihad in Russia. It derives from the study of "great" watershed historical turns and processes such as regime transformations (revolutions and "transitions"),[1] war, and terrorism. Such political phenomena are simply too multifaceted to be explained by a single factor. Complex causality was true for the Soviet collapse.[2] It is also true with regard to the rise of Islamist terrorism in Russia.

THE SOVIET MUSLIM CHALLENGE

The Muslims were an important factor in creating a set of constraints in the late Soviet era that forced the Communist Party leadership to adapt the *perestroika* (restructuring) reforms that in turn precipitated the unraveling of the Soviet monolith. The present Russian leadership, claiming to have learned the negative lessons of liberalization from the Soviet collapse, has opted to move in the opposite direction. Nevertheless, the Soviet collapse may prove to be but the first stage in the dissolution of the centuries-old multi-ethnic Russian empire.

There are parallels and clear points of continuity between the old Soviet Union's Muslim challenge and present-day Russia's Muslim and growing Islamist challenge. In both cases, economic, demographic, and security-related factors linked to the state's Muslim population have played a crucial role in domestic politics. In the Soviet case, such factors certainly helped convince the general secretary of the Communist Party of the Soviet Union (CPSU), Mikhail Gorbachev, to take up first limited economic reforms, then radical political reforms, which led ultimately to the USSR's collapse.

In the late 1970s and early 1980s an emerging contradiction between regime goals and performance began to impinge on the USSR leadership's policy options. The "pre-crisis" situation, as Gorbachev later called it, was signaled by economic stagnation, institutional decay, and ideological delegitimization, and became the basic impetus for his attempt to temper, if not end, the Cold War and embark on *glasnost* (openness) and perestroika. By the 1980s, the international stage had become the scene of simultaneous scientific, techno-logical, information, military, and globalization revolutions, which demanded a high degree of adaptability from societies and states. The USSR was poorly positioned to survive in such an environment. It suffered from sharp contradictions between, on the one hand, its highly centralized "mono-organizational" system that ordered state society, polity, and economy under the strict ideological and political control of the CPSU and, on the other hand, the changing nature and expectations of the Soviet populace and the demands of the "revolutionary" international environment. The Muslim factor played an important, though not primary, role in many of these contradictions.

The scientific-technological revolution required an increase of labor, investment and other inputs into the centrally planned command economy – the Soviet "extensive" model of production and development – or a shift to more efficient intensive capitalist methods of economic development. The USSR was ill-equipped to do the former because of domestic structural constraints that impinged on continuation of the extensive method.[3] Already upon Gorbachev's assumption of power, the decline in the rate of economic growth had reached its nadir with zero increase in Soviet GDP.[4] This economic stagnation was rooted in the inherent inefficiencies of Soviet centralized economic planning, the militarization of the economy, and declining natural-resource, financial, and, especially, labor inputs. Central planning and artificially set prices created distortions in both supply and demand. The militarization of industrial production soaked up as much as 40 percent of the state budget, starving the consumer sector of investment. Moreover, the production of tens, if not hundreds, of crucial consumer and industrial goods was concentrated in single, often enormous industrial plants, usually located in one-company towns. Capital in these plants had to be spent on the provision of social services and housing, responsibilities that in other societies are normally taken up by the private sector, NGOs, and local governments. The isolation of such plants combined with the limited transportation infrastructure and vast expanse of the USSR ensured that supply was tardy and expensive. Since investments from the next year's central budget were based on production quota indicators such as weight and energy consumption, no attention was given either to quality, efficiency, or energy-saving. Inflated production figures further distorted supply, demand, and pricing parameters.[5] In short, industrial production, indeed the entire economy, was extra-ordinarily inefficient and risked collapse.

The Soviet leadership did what it could to prolong its extensive economic development by increasing labor, investment, and energy inputs during the late 1960s and 1970s, but by the late 1970s the uneven geographical distri-bution of production (capacity), ethno-demographics, and population growth, particularly as concerned the Muslim republics, limited the possibilities for increasing the labor inputs without moving the industrial plant to Muslim areas or transferring Muslims to the Slavic heartland. The six Muslim union republics (Azerbaijan, Kazakhstan, Kyrgyzstan, Tajikistan, Turkmenistan, and Uzbekistan) and the RSFSR's autonomous republics (excluding Tatarstan) had been deprived of industrial production in order to limit their political influence as part of the party-state's favoritism toward the country's ethnic Slavic heartland.[6] Economic monocultures were created, particularly in Uzbekistan (cotton) and Turkmenistan (natural gas). At the same time, a policy of "colonial welfarism" was conducted – growing financial subsidies, local control over appointments allowing for "affirmative action" for native Muslims in appointments to local positions of economic and political power, and turning a blind eye to local corruption. These policies further distorted the Soviet economy and halted the integration of these areas into the Soviet system.[7]

Soviet population growth was concentrated among the rural populations of the Muslim nationalities in the Central Asian and Azerbaijan republics. By

1980–1981, Muslim fertility and reproduction rates were two to three times higher than those of European and, in particular, Slavic peoples, the basic cadre of the Soviet party-state. Adjusting the 1979 census for the reidentification of non-Russians as Russians, it was found that ethnic Russians' share of the Soviet population had continued to decline not to the 52.4 percent shown by the official census results but to 50.9 percent, risking their majority status. Indeed, ethnic Russians would make up only 48.5 percent of the population by the Gorbachev era. Estimates held that by 2050 Muslims would constitute just 42.4 percent and ethnic Russians 46.4 percent of the Soviet population. The Soviets' strict internal passport regime prevented sufficient spontaneous migration to industrialized republics, and the regime was reluctant to organize an influx of Muslims to Slavic regions. Moreover, despite incentives such as the promise of high salaries and pension benefits, Soviet Muslims were becoming less and less disposed to move to northern regions to increase manpower in the extraction of oil, gas, iron, coal, gold and diamonds, export of which was the main source of Soviet foreign currency earnings. A concerted social policy aimed at increasing urbanization in order to bring a greater part of the population into industrial production failed in the Muslim (and also largely rural Moldovan) republics, where the faster-growing titular nationalities began instead to undergo ruralization.[8] Low urbanization meant low assimilation, including declining rates of Russian-language knowledge. In short, the Soviet Muslim population, the state's main source for additional labor, was located nowhere near industrial production plants.

A solution would have been to move some of the industrial plants to these more rural republics. But this would have meant the transfer of considerable political power away from Moscow and the Slavs. Greater investment in these regions also would have required reducing investment in the Soviet Union's core industrial plant in the "European," particularly the Slavic, republics, which would have risked alienating the more loyal Slavic peoples and stirring up anti-regime sentiment among the independence-minded Baltic peoples. The Soviets' failure to develop and integrate the Muslim union republics inhibited the implementation of Gorbachev's reforms there. Instead their leaders joined Moscow hardliners in opposition to Gorbachev, further dividing the perestroika-era Soviet elite and facilitating Boris Yeltsin's revolution from above.[9]

Soviet demographics and economics had implications for the USSR's growing imperial burdens and competition with the West. The Muslim peoples made up 24 percent of the Soviet military's conscript pool and 33 percent of actual draftees.[10] Ruralization of the Muslim population worked against the center's assimilative and Russification goals, producing a decline in the number of conscripts who could speak Russian with the proficiency necessary for military service. There was also a decline in the morale and cohesiveness of the army, as Muslim personnel had limited loyalty to the regime, often nil desire to serve, and sometimes suffered brutal hazing at the hands of higher-ranking Slavs. The danger was highlighted for the leadership by the 1979 Soviet invasion of Afghanistan. The initial invasion force, composed of many Central Asian nationalities, had to be reinforced and in part replaced with Slavic forces because of "ethnic Muslim"[11] defections, with growing political costs for the regime as casualties among Russians and Slavs began to mount. This brought home to some Soviet leaders the security implications of these demographic trends.[12]

The imbalances and limitations of Soviet economic and, therefore, military development also were thrown into relief by the war in Afghanistan. Limited infrastructure for water and other supplies in the Central Asian republics, particularly in Uzbekistan, the key border on the war zone, increased the costs of conducting the campaign. As a result, housing, food, and other consumer-goods shortages were exacerbated in the European republics. Moreover, the war highlighted the contrast between Soviet domestic constraints and the demands of the global scientific-technological revolution. At first glance the two sides in the fighting appeared to be rather unevenly matched – a contest between a modern military machine and a poorly armed, rural guerrilla movement – but the contest was made more balanced by US provision of shoulder-held Stinger missiles supplied to the Afghans, underscoring the power of the scientific-technological revolution and the revolution in military affairs.

In 1986, as he pondered economic and political reforms, Gorbachev labeled the Afghan war a "bleeding wound," signaling the rethink that would lead to the Soviets' February 1988 withdrawal and an overall reassessment of the USSR's global role, ideology, and governance system. Indeed, the Soviets' first war with Muslims in decades had crystallized for many the USSR's "macro-structural" dilemma.[13] The Afghan disaster's message of economic and technological backwardness, reinforced by US president Ronald Reagan's military build-up and Strategic Defense Initiative ("Star Wars"), was a major precipitant of reform and the abandonment of the economic development strategy based on central planning.

Russia's present Muslim dilemma is shaped by similar economic, demographic, and military factors. These present Moscow with not only a mid- to long-term Muslim challenge but also a more immediate potential revolutionary Islamist one. In contrast to the Soviet case, however, Moscow's Muslim challenge has already produced a Muslim revolutionary movement – the emerging Islamist movement and the Chechen-led Islamist terrorist network – which is already demonstrating a capacity that could ultimately threaten the integrity of the Russian state.

RUSSIA'S MUSLIM CHALLENGE AND ITS CAUSES

Historical and cultural factors already provide a basis for potential conflict between the Russian state and ethnic Russians, on the one hand, and the country's Muslim population, on the other. Russia's traditionally Muslim ethnic groups ("ethnic Muslims") have been subjected to often brutal Russian/Soviet imperial habits over the centuries.[14] Propensities to violence are prevalent in both the Russian and North Caucasian cultures. These factors certainly create a background against which conflict is possible. But putting aside historical, cultural, and structural causes for the moment, there are at least five other causes of rising communalism, Islamic nationalism, and Islamist terrorism in Russia.[15]

Two intermediate factors – endemic poverty in the North Caucasus and the growing demographic challenge to the ethnic Russian majority – constitute (along with the background causes noted above) the basis of Russia's growing Muslim challenge, which itself further complicates the larger challenge of consolidating the post-Soviet Russian state and federative democracy. These factors and three other immediate causes – the ongoing Chechen war, infiltration of the Chechen militants' revolutionary network deeper into Russia, and Putin's re-authoritarianizing and de-federalizing counter-revolution – are already sparking an Islamist revolutionary terrorist jihad led by Chechen militants.

Socio-economic Deprivation

Although recent research shows that a country's overall level of poverty is not a reliable predictor of terrorism,[16] "relative deprivation" between regions or one communal group and another nonetheless helps explain why some peoples rebel.[17] In Russia there are wide disparities between rich and poor regions and between often more ethnic Russian-populated urban and more non-Russian rural areas within regions, especially in the Muslim republics. Russia's poorest regions are most often those heavily populated by Muslims, the eight so-called titular Muslim republics, especially those in the North Caucasus. The figures in Table 1, culled from official statistics, are probably understated, meaning the picture is even worse than the data indicate. It is no coincidence that the Southern and Volga FOs (Federal Districts),[18] in which all of the titular Muslim republics and almost all of Russia's twenty-one national republics are located, are the poorest in the country; this is a result of Soviet-era policies which sought to confine key industrial assets to Slavic-dominated regions in the RSFSR (Russia's title under Soviet rule), much as was done in the USSR as a whole. However, the data also show the North Caucasus's Muslim republics' economies to be the worst in the country and

Table 1. Socio-Economic Indicators in Russia's Muslim Republics for the First Half of 2005 from Russian Federal Government Data

Governance Unit	Average Monthly Salary in Rubles {Rank in Russia}*	Unemployment Rate**	Capital Investment (Millions of Rubles) {Rank in Russia}	Foreign Investment in Thousands of Dollars {Rank in Russia}
RUSSIA	7,933.3	8.1%	1,252,900.7	16,503,334
SOUTHERN FO	5,377.2 {7/7}	13.2%	99,192.6 {7/7}	445,425 {7/7}
Chechnya	no data	no data	2,218.1 {70/89}	no data***
Ingushetiya	5,319.9 {63/88}	51.2%	475.6 {83/89}	no data
Dagestan	3,569.0 {88/88}	29.9%	6,271.3 {47/89}	no data
KBR	4,311.5 {84/88}	20.9%	2,106.0 {71/89}	no data
KChR	4,507.1 {82/88}	9.1%	1,522.8 {78/89}	no data
Adygeya	4,936.7 {74/88}	16.1%	737.6 {81/89}	609 {67/75}
VOLGA FO	6,079.5 {6/7}	8.0%	192,264.3 {3/7}	693,851 {6/7}
Tatarstan	6,632.0 {41/88}	7.1%	49,566.7 {8/89}	96,695 {15/75}
Bashkortostan	6,287.0 {54/88}	7.2%	27,192.8 {12/89}	11,395 {46/75}

* The first figure is the particular region's positive performance ranking. The second is the total number of regions for which there were data for the particular indicator.
** The unemployment rate was calculated using figures for the working-age population from the October 2002 census (www.perepis2002.ru/ct/html/TOM_07_01.htm). Therefore, the unemployment rates could be slightly higher especially in the North Caucasus with its decades-long higher reproduction rates.
*** The "no data" reported for foreign investment is due to its near-absence in the North Caucasus.

Source: "Osnovnyie pokazateli sotsial'no-ekonomicheskogo polozheniya regionov Rossiiskoi Federatsii v 1 polugodii 2005 goda," www.rg.ru/pril/7/80/95/3867_1.gif, attachment to Tatyana Smolyakova, "Podmoskovnyie vauchera," *Rossiiskaya gazeta*, 7 Sept. 2005, www.rg.ru/2005/09/07/regiony-razvitie.html.

that the Volga area's Muslim republics, Bashkortostan and Tatarstan, are considerably better off. None of the North Caucasus Muslim republics can match the salary, employment, or investment levels in either of the Volga Muslim republics, and all but one (the KChR) have unemployment rates that exceed the national average by between two and six times. At little over $100 per month, the average monthly salary in Dagestan and the KBR is slightly less than half and slightly more than half the national average, respectively. These two republics experienced the most ferocious Islamist terrorist campaigns in 2004–2005 in the world outside of Iraq, Chechnya, and perhaps Moscow. Moreover, even in relatively developed Tatarstan and Bashkortostan, the mostly "ethnic Muslim" villages are considerably poorer than the more Russified cities and fall well below average levels for their respective republic.

The high unemployment rates reflected in Table 1 are of particular concern. When one considers that the real level of unemployment is much higher than the official statistics show and much lower than in ethnic Russian-dominated regions, the situation appears explosive. This is especially true if we take into account that youth unemployment is even greater than overall unemployment rates. Such high levels of joblessness among youth, especially in the North Caucasus where they reach nearly 50 and in some villages reportedly 90 percent, are creating an army of young males with no outlet for their energies. It is no surprise if some of these idle energies are sooner or later expended in armies of Allah. In addition, a demographic explosion among Russia's Muslims and a demographic implosion among ethnic Russians are simultaneously expanding the pool of potential recruits for this army and changing Muslims' expectations about their place in Russian society respectively.

The Demographic Challenge

It is often said that demography is destiny. The Muslim demographic factor already poses a long-term challenge to the Russian state's inter-communal comity and territorial integrity. The immediate shortage of resources in the North Caucasus because of economic backwardness, however, may imbue this demographic shift with a revolutionary dynamic.[19]

Russia's ethnic Muslims are a sizeable minority and continue to have considerably higher birth rates than ethnic Russians (see Table 2). The 2002 census results indicate that there are 14 million ethnic Muslims and they comprise some 10 percent of Russia's population.[20] Moreover, these official figures do not include several very small Muslim nationalities. In addition, several hundred thousand of the 1,457,700 respondents who chose not to identify their nationality were likely from ethnic Muslim groups. So ethnic Muslims probably number 15 million and comprise more than half of Russia's non-Russian population. Thus, if Russia's political system slights minority aspirations for self-determination, it is likely to provoke Muslim communalism which can be translated easily into Islamic separatism and even Islamism by effective radical propaganda.

Tatars are the largest minority in Russia, making up 3.8 percent of the population, 20 percent of the non-Russian population, and over one-third of the ethnic Muslim population. In terms of numbers, they are thus the most dangerous Muslim group for Russia's future. However, a series of factors have so far worked to constrain Tatar nationalism and Tatar Islamic nationalism. In addition to Tatarstan's relative socio-economic well-being, these factors include Tatars' high assimilation rates as reflected in their high rate of urbanization and Russification both inside and outside their home republic. For instance Tatars show a high rate of linguistic assimilation, with 96.1

Table 2. Growth in Ethnic Muslim Populations between the 1989 and 2002 Censuses of the Russian Federation.

Ethnic Group	2002 Population in thousands (%)		1989 Population in thousands (%)		Change in Population from 1989 to 2002 (%)
Russians	115,868.5	(79.82)	119,865.9	(81.53)	−3.45
Non-Russians	27,838.1	(19.18)	27,149.6	(18.47)	+2.53
Muslims*	13,971.0	(9.62)	11,670.5	(7.94)	+19.71
Tatars	5,568.3**	(3.84)	5,552.1	(3.78)	+0.29
Bashkirs	1,673.4	(1.15)	1,345.7	(0.92)	+24.35
Chechens***	1,360.3	(0.94)	899.0	(0.61)	+51.31
Avars	814.5	(0.56)	544.0	(0.37)	+49.72
Kabardins	520.0	(0.36)	386.1	(0.26)	+34.68
Dargins	510.2	(0.35)	353.3	(0.24)	+44.41
Kumyks	422.4	(0.29)	277.2	(0.19)	+52.38
Ingush	413.0	(0.28)	215.1	(0.15)	+92.00
Lezgins	411.5	(0.28)	257.3	(0.18)	+59.93
Karachais	192.2	(0.13)	150.3	(0.10)	+27.88
Laks	156.4	(0.11)	106.2	(0.07)	+47.26
Adygeis	128.5	(0.09)	122.9	(0.08)	+4.56
Balkars	108.3	(0.08)	78.3	(0.05)	+38.31
Nogais	90.7	(0.06)	73.7	(0.05)	+23.07
Cherkess (Circassians)	60.5	(0.04)	50.8	(0.03)	+19.09
Abazins	37.9	(0.03)	33.0	(0.02)	+14.85
Abkhaz	11.3	(0.01)	7.2	(0.005)	+56.94
Kazakhs	653.0	(0.45)	635.9	(0.43)	+2.69
Azeris	621.8	(0.43)	335.9	(0.23)	+85.11
Uzbeks	122.9	(0.09)	126.9	(0.09)	−3.25
Turkmens	33.5	(0.02)	39.7	(0.03)	−18.51
Kyrgyz	31.8	(0.02)	41.7	(0.03)	−31.13
Tajhiks	28.6	(0.02)	38.2	(0.03)	−33.57
TOTAL	145,164.3	(100.00)	147,021.9	(100.00)	−1.28

* This is an underestimate and is explained below.
** Includes Siberian and Crimean Tatars as well as Volga Tatars and excludes so-called "Kryasheny" or Baptized Tatars. It should be noted that there is some reason to believe that forces in Moscow and Bashkiriya may have deliberately deflated the 2002 census numbers for Tatars in executing or counting the results.
*** There may have been some inflation of the Chechen population figures in the 2002 census by Moscow in order to cover up the deaths brought by the two post-Soviet Chechen wars.

Sources: Perepis 2002, "Prilozhenie 5 – Naselenie Rossii po natsional'no prinadlezhnosti i vladeniyu russkim yasykom," www.perepis.ru/ct/html/ALL_00_07.htm, and USSR 1989 Census Results, "Nationality Composition by Union Republics," *Soyuz*, No. 32, Aug. 1990, pp. 12–13, in *JPRS*, 4 Dec. 1990, JPRS-UPA-90-066, pp. 16–19.

percent of Volga Tatars, 97.0 percent of Siberian Tatars, and 99.3 percent of Crimean Tatars able to speak Russian,[21] and there are high rates of Tatar–Russian intermarriage.[22]

Russia's long-term Muslim challenge lies in the high birth rates of its ethnic

Muslim populations as compared to that of ethnic Russians. As Table 2 shows, the number of ethnic Muslims grew by 20 percent between the 1989 Soviet census and the 2002 Russian census. Meanwhile, the country's overall population declined by just over 1 percent, and the ethnic Russian population fell by over 3 percent. Nine of the Muslim ethnicities' population growth reached astonishing levels of over 40 percent, with the Ingush nearly doubling their numbers. Of Russia's twenty-three Muslim nationalities included in published census data, only four declined in size in the inter-census years, a phenomenon explained by an exodus of these groups' members back to their ethnic homelands in Central Asia after the Soviet collapse. This was also the reason for the Kazakhs' small growth. The doubling of the ethnic Azeri population in Russia is a product of group members' fear of residing in a potential war zone, given the ongoing Armenian-Azeri tensions over the Armenian enclave and unrecognized state of Nagorno-Karabakh embedded in Azerbaijan. The ethnic Muslim groups' higher population growth rates mean that the ranks of idle young males, especially in the North Caucasus republics, will be growing.

This problem, however, is not only a long-term one. Already there may be a causal connection between Islamists' growing strength and high population growth rates. Dagestan, the KBR, and Ingushetiya are the republics with the strongest nodes in Russia's Islamist network outside Chechnya. The level of Islamist strength in these republics correlates with both the high levels of unemployment – the highest among the Muslim republics – and very high rates of population growth among these republics' Muslim ethnic groups (Ingushetiya's Ingush, the KBR's Kabards and Balkars, and Dagestan's Avars, Dargins, Kumyks, and Lezgins), which are the highest among Russia's Muslim ethnic groups. These republics' high unemployment rates are, among other factors, a product of high population growth, which is creating a large youth cohort that their weak economies are unable to encompass.

A key reason for the ethnic Muslims' higher population growth rates is their more traditional lifestyle, informed in part by rural custom and Islam. The latter frown upon birth control and women working outside the home. North Caucasus traditions of machismo put a premium on high numbers of children, and rural areas' less characteristically Soviet housing infrastructure (individual houses versus small apartments) better accommodates large families. This traditional way of life is being preserved by the lower level of urbanization in the North Caucasian Muslim republics, leaving the inhabitants less integrated into secular Russian life. The Volga republics of Tatarstan and Bashkortostan have the highest urbanization rates among Russia's Muslim republics, with 74 and 64 percent respectively, followed by the KBR's with 57 percent, Adygeya's with 53 percent, the KChR's with 44 percent, Dagestan's and Ingushetiya's less than 43 percent, and Chechnya's 33 percent. By contrast, 73.3 percent of citizens live in an urban setting across Russia as a whole.[23] Lower levels of urbanization correlated with higher population growth in the North Caucasus, while higher levels of urbanization again produced lower population growth. The urbanized Volga Tatars barely increased in population over the thirteen-year period between censuses.[24] The only real exception to the low urbanization rates in the North Caucasus Muslim republics is the KBR. This is explained by the ethnic Kabards' traditionally closer relationship with ethnic Russians, who form the majority of both the overall and urban population. In Adygeya, only 30 percent of the population comes from ethnic Muslim groups, mostly Adygeis resulting in higher inter-marriage and urbanization rates. Thus, the Kabards (35 percent), and Adygeis (under 5 percent) were the two exceptions among the otherwise rapidly growing ethnic Muslim populations of the North Caucasus between 1989 and 2002. In 2004–2005 the KBR would see one of the fiercest terrorist campaigns of any region in Russia, but Adygeya has so far seen the least Islamist activity among the Muslim republics of the North Caucasus. Still, there is an overall correlation between poor economies, low urbanization, higher birth rates, and stronger Islamist presence across the Muslim republics.

Ethnic Russians show the highest level of urbanization in Russia, which is in part responsible for their precipitous demographic decline and that of the country overall: a population trend that is unprecedented in the industrialized world. However, it is not only the modern urban culture that is stunting population growth. Urban housing dominated by small, typically two-bedroom apartments leaves literally no room for more than one child for families living in cities, and urban families in Russia are overwhelmingly ethnic Russian families.[25] Consequently, by late into the twenty-first century the decline in the ethnic Russian population and the rapid growth among the country's ethnic Muslims together will threaten the ethnic Russians' majority. One estimate has it that by mid-century the ethnic Russian population will have declined to as little as 60 million, as the mortality rate increases with the passing of the much more numerous older generation.[26] The second half of the century, all else remaining equal, should see a further decline of at least 10–15 million. If the ethnic Muslim groups' population continues to grow at the rate it did between the 1989 and 2002 censuses, their numbers will increase to approximately 45 million by the century's end. By that time, therefore, ethnic Muslims will form a plurality and perhaps a majority of Russia's population, and Islam will likely begin to challenge Russian Orthodox Christianity as the country's most widespread religion. Moreover, Russia's Muslim republics will be overwhelmingly ethnic-Muslim. Even Orenburg Oblast, which separates Tatarstan and Bashkortostan from an external border and thus functions as a break on their secessionist aspirations, may approach majority-Muslim status.

At the same time, the relative economic deprivation in Russia's Muslim-populated regions and sub-regional rural districts will approach critical political mass, if the emerging Islamist threat has not already brought matters to a head. The fastest-growing part of ethnic Muslim populations resides in rural confines, and it expresses the greatest resistance to assimilation and integration into Russian society. This is reflected in the lower percentage of these ethnic groups' rural residents who have Russian-language skills compared to those of the corresponding groups' urban residents, as recorded in the 2002 census results.[27]

Moreover, the national and Islamic identity of ethnic Muslim groups in rural areas is likely to strengthen as modernization in the form of globalization and post-industrial technologies penetrates the region. There may be a growing cultural divide between the predominantly secular and increasingly decadent "postmodern" Russian culture and traditional Islam, not to mention its more puritanical Islamist variation. It is becoming increasingly clear that even traditional Caucasian Islam clashes with Russia's urban popular culture, replete with not only the traditional heavy consumption of alcohol but also narcotics abuse, sexual license, and so on. Russia's embrace of post-modernism's hedonism and other forms of excess (particularly among the elite's privileged offspring) is contributing to the Islamist backlash among Muslims. For example, the "provocative conduct" of Sati Kazanova, a native of the KBR and member of the popular, if risqué, female singing trio Fabrika, was condemned by many of the republic's residents as a result of a performance on Russian television. Some declared "a boycott of her family."[28] Such problems are generic to relations between the West and the Islamic world as well. Globalization is exacerbating the reactionary backlash in defense of traditional cultures and lifestyles, while the penetration of technological advances such as the internet into the region facilitates communication between disaffected elements. This friction is particularly felt between the rural and more traditional mountain regions and the more cosmopolitan plains and large cities, especially the Muslim republics' capitals. It is no accident that the "landscapes of jihad" everywhere are the isolated backwaters and refuges of rural, mountainous, and desert areas far removed from the cultural and political centers of modernity.[29]

Re-Islamization and Saturation among Ethnic Muslims

An important break on the mobilization of an Islamic or Islamist revolution would seem to be the divide among Russia's ethnic Muslims between believers and non-believers. It has been estimated that only 3 million (some 20 percent) of Russia's ethnic Muslims are practicing believers.[30] This would seem to impose a real limit on the potential recruits for political Islam, whether of the more moderate or more radical strain. On the other hand, it suggests that, along with population growth, re-Islamization and the formation of a recruitment base for revolutionary Islam in Russia may be far from complete. Indeed, since the ideological liberation begun during perestroika, re-Islamization has proceeded apace. By October 2005, according to the Chairman of the Council of Muftis of Russia (SMR), Ravil Gainutdin, the number of mosques in Russia had grown from a mere 150 as of the Soviet collapse in 1991 to some six thousand.[31] Even in urbanized, secularized, and relatively russified Tatarstan, the number of mosques has increased from a handful to over a thousand, perhaps 1,200, growing at a rate of 50–60 per year.[32]

The number of ethnic Muslims who identify themselves as believers has also grown precipitously, even among more secular and assimilated populations, such as the Tatars of Tatarstan. For example, in the early 1980s, 59 percent of Tatars expressed indifference, and only 15.7 percent declared themselves believers. By 1994 an astonishing 66.6 percent of urban Tatars and 86 percent of rural Tatars declared themselves believers, while 12 and 9.8 percent, respectively, responded that they were wavering. Moreover, data suggest a considerable gap between Tatarstan's native political elite, on the one hand, and other potentially communalism-mobilizing groups within society, on the other. In a 1995 survey only 34 percent of respondents in the political elite declared they were believers (compared to the above-mentioned 1994 figures for urban and rural society), while 62 percent of the creative intelligentsia and 72 percent of working people responded that they were believers.[33] If re-Islamization continues – and it shows no signs of abating – Islamic nationalism and even the Islamist trend are likely to strengthen, especially in combination with continuation of Putin's recentralizing and assimilative policies.

Against the background of a growing revolutionary Islamist insurgency throughout much of the North Caucasus, already capable of bringing terror to Moscow on land, under ground, and in the air, the remaining potential for radical recruitment in society and within the state represents a grave threat to Russia. As Russians are reduced to ever-smaller minorities in Muslim republics dominated by ethnic and, for the most part, believing Muslims, they will feel unwelcome, even fearful. This will only exacerbate the already considerable and rising tensions between indigenous Muslims and the Muslim republics, on the one hand, and the Russian state and ethnic group, on the other hand. The Putin administration's policies suggest that these problems will not necessarily be addressed in such a way as to bring about compromises with or assuage Muslim and other minority communities and sovereignty-minded regions.

Russia's Islamist Challenge

The Chechen Quagmire and Foreign Islamist Revolutionaries

Many of the immediate causes of Russia's burgeoning Islamist movement come from Putin's policies. First and foremost is the often brutal prosecution of the festering low-intensity war in Chechnya. This has led to the Chechens' radicalization under the influence of foreign, jihadist terrorist ideologies and movements funded, inspired, and perhaps still coordinated by al Qaeda. Having lost on the traditional battlefield, the Chechen insurgents have turned increasingly to terrorist methods and to a strategy of expanding the war throughout the North Caucasus and as far beyond as possible. In turn, the Chechen-led terrorist network is facilitating the international Islamists' sustained and growing infiltration into other regions of Russia. This, the second major cause, is at the most fundamental level the result of Russia's geographical proximity to parts of the larger Muslim world, that world's present pre-revolutionary crisis, and the post-Soviet restoration of historical ties between Russia's Muslims and the rest of the umma. The regimes of the Muslim world are clearly under threat from Islamist groups who, in some states, can make a credible counterclaim to sovereignty (for example in Afghanistan, Iraq, Lebanon, and Iran). Moreover, Islamism enjoys considerable support throughtout the Muslim world.

The Chechen quagmire and the foreign Islamist infiltration of the Chechen militants and, therefore, Russia herself are the present-day counterparts to the military and international factors that the Afghan war introduced into the pre-revolutionary Soviet crisis. The expansion of global Islamism may be furthered by the Chechens' turn to a radical strategy of bringing terrorism and war to all of Russia. This course is made possible by modern technologies such as the internet, though in the poverty-stricken North Caucasus limited access to computer technology still constrains this technological engine of the global jihad. Development of the North Caucasus might increase the danger facing Russia by facilitating the spread of the Islamists' message, with the internet performing the function that the introduction of mass print media played in the rise of nationalism.

The third leading cause of expanding Islamist terrorism in Russia is Putin's re-authoritarianizing counter-revolution.[34] As the Chechen war dragged on and terrorism began to mount, the Putin administration responded by transforming Russia from a hybrid regime that was a limited, illiberal "managed democracy" to something altogether more authoritarian.[35] The intermediate level of freedom found in hybrid regimes, regardless of whether they are primarily illiberal democracies or soft-authoritarian regimes, produces the highest risk of generating terrorism.[36]

Consolidated democracies experience comparatively little terrorism, and harsh-authoritarian regimes show only a mid-level risk of terrorism. Although Russia's Muslim republics, including the KBR, tend to be its most authoritarian regions[37] and Putin's counter-revolution has encouraged these regimes to become more firmly authoritarian, they have still not reached a level of authoritarianism firm enough to stamp out terrorist or other forms of opposition. However, by more aggressively and non-surgically cracking down on Muslims across the board and increasingly violating their political, civil, and human rights in many regions, Moscow and the republics' regimes have made many indigenous young Muslims more open to calls for secession and Islamism.

The most malignant aspects of the Putin counter-revolution, especially for some of the Muslim republics and their Muslims, are its de-federalization and assimilative policies. Putin chose to dismantle Yeltsin's strategy for preserving the Russian state's integrity in favor of a more authoritarian, unitary, but still weak and corrupt system.[38] Upon assuming the presidency in May 2000 Putin placed at the top of his agenda the strengthening of the Russian state as a precondition for the successful modernization of the economy and society. This required, in the view of Putin and his closest associates, a turn toward a soft form of authoritarian rule in order to free the central state apparatus from societal interests, including oligarchic business, but more importantly ethno-political regional interests. Besides subduing the financial-industrial oligarchs, Putin increased the power of the executive branch at all levels, subordinated local executives to the federal executive and reintegrated Russia's legal space by bringing most local and regional legislation and constitutions in line with federal laws and the Russian Constitution. Putin's anti-federalist policies in effect dismantled most of the federative asymmetry inherited from Yeltsin, returning legislative power, administration, budgetary funds, and property ownership back to Moscow, eliminating all power-sharing arrangements between the center and the regions, and implementing or attempting to implement a series of assimilative policies that impinged on ethonational minorities, Muslims in particular (see Table 3).

These policies go against the grain of what historical experience, social-science theory, and the ethno-territorial administrative structure that Russia inherited from the USSR recommend for effectively containing communalism in a large multi-communal state with regions defined or predominantly populated by minority communities. A traditional, strictly territorial federalism is unsuited to, indeed was impossible to establish in, post-Soviet Russia because of the country's size, communal diversity, and inheritance of Soviet era ethno-territorial administrative units. Geographically large states are more likely to be multi-national and federative. As Kahn points out, except

Table 3. Putin's Anti-Federative Counter-Revolution

First Wave of Anti-Federative Counter-Revolution

---

(1) the creation of extra-constitutional **federal districts (FOs)** to restore the "executive vertical" – that is, federal control over its agencies located in the regions – but also to coordinate the federal authorities' interference in regional politics, especially elections through the use of administrative resources (police, courts, tax collection, finances, state mass media);

(2) **hyper-centralization of law-making** by requiring regional laws to comply with federal law under a federal constitution which renders federal law supreme in all spheres of life that it chooses to address;

(3) the creation of **a mechanism for "federal intervention"** allowing the president with court approval to remove a regional governor or republican president and call elections to a regional parliament should it refuse to follow court findings that regional executive branch decrees or orders, legislative acts, or constitutions violate the constitution or federal law;

(4) **termination of most, if not all power-sharing treaties** between the federal government and individual regions, ending regional autonomy and official federative asymmetry;

(5) **counter-reform of the Federation Council** from a legislative body composed of elected officials to one of officials appointed by the Russian president;

(6) **recentralization of budget revenues;**

(7) **dissolution of the national autonomous okrugs** and perhaps the national republics, including the titular Muslim republics;

(8) **de facto elimination of consociational minority veto** for region legislatures over federal legislation.

Assimilative Policies

---

(9) **ban on ethnic and religious parties;**

(10) **ban on the use of non-Cyrillic alphabets** in response to Muslim Tatarstan's decision to Latinize the Tatar language;

(11) proposal to introduce a **course on Russian Christian Orthodox "culture"** into Russia's schools;*

(12) an initiative **forbidding Muslim women from wearing the *hijab* (veil)** in passport photographs.*

Post-Beslan Consolidation of the Anti-Federative Counter-Revolution

---

(13) **presidential appointment** rather than popular election of regional **governors and republican presidents** (and perhaps city mayors and district heads);

(14) **elimination of single-mandate district-based seats in the State Duma** and a switch to a full proportional representation or party list voting system.

---

* Policy measures with an asterisk represent initiatives that were defeated or refined because Russia's Muslims mobilized against them.

for China, the largest states in the world (Argentina, Australia, Brazil, Canada, India, Russia, and the United States) are federal.[39] And China, as it reforms economically, has seen decentralization begin to creep into its system of economic governance.[40] The state-building challenge is particularly complex for states that, like Russia, have large and/or numerous minority "identity communities" living in territorial concentrations or national-territorial administrative units. Russia, perhaps more than any other state, needs a sophisticated set of communalism-containment institutions and mechanisms.

It is the largest and one of the most multi-communal countries in the world, with nearly two hundred ethno- and religio-communal groups. Indeed, the Soviet demise recommends federalism to post-Soviet Russia. One of the main institutional factors leading to the demise of the Soviet partocratic regime and state was the considerably non-institutionalized status of Russia in the Soviet Union's ethno-territorial administrative structure.

The decentralization and ultimately the power vacuum created by the end of the perestroika era initially did force Russia to adopt a rather loose system of asymmetric regional autonomy (self-rule, self-governance) in order to assuage special ethno-national aspirations and undercut separatism in Russia's thirty-two national autonomies, including its eight titular Muslim republics.[41] This unique system incorporated a range of measures from the menu drawn up across the globe over the last half-century of experimentation in places like India, Belgium, Canada, Papua New Guinea, Spain, Bosnia-Herzegovina and included elements of asymmetrical ethno-federalism – special authority for some ethno-territorial sub-units within the federation – and consensus-based governance.[42] The distribution of powers between the center and the regions in early post-Soviet Russia was institutionalized neither in the form of a constitution, as in India, nor by specially institutionalized agreements between federal and regional governments, as in Spain.[43] Instead, separate bilateral power-sharing treaties were negotiated over time between the Kremlin, representing the federal center, and eventually forty-six individual regions, most of all with the national autonomies, especially the Muslim republics. In addition, the new system incorporated consensus-based or "consociational" mechanisms of governance with the regions to give them a role in federal governance. This was intended to prevent the ethnic Russian majority extant in an overwhelming majority of regions from frustrating ethno-national minorities seeking to protect their cultural, linguistic, and confessional identities from assimilative policies and/or their territories' natural resources from expropriation by Moscow.[44] Asymmetrical ethno-federalism combined with consensus-building mechanisms, such as the minority veto or grand inter-communal coalition governments, allowed communities sufficient internal self-determination and autonomy for them to opt out of the search for external self-determination through separatism and secession.

The particular mix and design of institutions for any given multi-ethnic state depend on its historical ethno-national and institutional peculiarities, and ultimately on the competition of political ideas and interest.[45] Some mix of the institutions and mechanisms outlined above is usually used in states with concentrated populations of minority communities to guarantee at a minimum these communities' self-determination with regard to language, culture, and religion. At a maximum, they can give such communities some sovereignty in the spheres of economic and political organization and foreign relations. Only a complex system can hold together and effectively manage Russia's complexity – its vast territory, the awkward administrative structure inherited from the failed USSR, and hundreds of divergent ethnic, linguistic, and religious interests. The only viable alternative would be a highly decentralized symmetrical system providing all regions with powers of such importance that national-territorial administrative governance units like the republics would not need to seek special arrangements. However, the Russian elite's political culture seems unlikely to incline it to embark on such a path anytime soon.

Indeed, Putin's de-federalizing counter-revolution moved in the opposite direction by dismantling Yeltsin's developing federative democracy and recentralizing power in Moscow. Attempts by imperial or federal centers to extend "direct rule" over peripheral regions or ethno-federative systems provoke nationalism.[46] This is a result of the provocative effect on communal minorities of having their self-determination and autonomy retracted, especially if such changes mean losing previously hard-won gains. In fact, Putin's tactics are still more provocative. By enacting two contradictory approaches in succession, the Kremlin negated the benefits of Yeltsin's policy and underlined the downsides of Putin's, a sequence that does not contain communalism but exacerbates it. Yeltsin's concessions to the national autonomies highlighted the sense of communal "otherness" among non-Russian national and religious communities and might have risked streng-thening and "over-institutionalizing" communal self-identities.[47] Putin's revocation of Yeltsin's concessions, perceived as discrimination by communi-ties, simultaneously reinforces and offends their self-identities. Moreover, his policies have de-institutionalized inter-communal politics. In essence, Putin abandoned a condition of perhaps some over-institutionalization for one of considerable under-institutionalization of communal politics, driving it underground and potentially onto the streets.

Moscow's attempt to control political developments in the regions has sparked not only the ethno-confessional backlash that is the focus of this book, but also "secular" political instability in the ethnic Muslim republics. In particular, Moscow's recentralization drive has introduced an additional complicating factor into the inter-clan politics that dominate in the Muslim republics, especially those in the North Caucasus. For example, Ingushetiya – the first republic that saw Moscow intervene directly in its politics, a republic populated largely by the Chechens' fellow Vainakh Muslim people, the Ingush, and bordering Chechnya – and Bashkortostan were on the brink of self-described "orange revolutions" in 2005. Soon thereafter Ingushetiya saw an increase in the number of what, for the most part, largely Islamist terrorist acts.

Under Moscow's recentralization drive, a KGB official, Murat Zyazikov, was forced on Ingushetiya as president by the Kremlin in 2003, replacing the popular and independent Ruslan Aushev, who had been a persistent critic of the war in Chechnya.[48] Under Zyazikov kidnappings spread throughout the republic. His opponents and others blamed them on the new president, his brother, and his allies in the security organs. Zyazikov blamed them on Chechen militants. Zyazikov's growing authoritarianism, encouraged by Moscow's soft-authoritarian and recentralizing policies, pushed the opposition to action. Led by Ingushetiya parliamentary deputy Musa Ozdoev, it organized several demonstrations but was prevented from holding one on May Day 2005, which it had explicitly stated would be parlayed into an orange-style revolution. Ozdoev was arrested, and the revolution was aborted.[49] This "secular" instability emerging in Ingushetiya could provide an opening to radical nationalists or Islamists. Indeed, as the Zyazikov administration continued to obstruct and crack down on opposition demonstrations, autumn 2005 saw a spike in the frequency of terrorist attacks in the republic, with thirty in September–October 2005 alone.[50] These coincided with the emergence of two new openly Islamist terrorist organizations, the Khalifat and Amanat groups, in addition to the infamous Ingush Jamaat, which claimed responsibility for many of the attacks.

Thus, by dismantling federalism and democracy, Putin is destabilizing regional politics, providing an additional opening for ethno-nationalism, radical Islam, and Islamist jihadism in Russia. This, in turn, is creating fertile soil for foreign Islamist jihadists to recruit and mobilize through their Chechen allies. In sum, there is much to suggest the road traveled by Russia over the last fifteen years and its present situation will provoke communalist politicization, mobilization, rebellion, and terror both within its borders and further afield.

Although the picture painted here may suggest that an Islamic or Islamist revolution in Russia is inevitable, contingency is an inherent aspect of all great historical events.[51] There are also constraints that may shape, dampen, or mitigate the factors driving growing Russian-Muslim tensions.

CONSTRAINTS ON AN ISLAMIST REVOLUTION IN RUSSIA

The constraints on the mobilization of a mass Islamic/Islamist revolutionary movement consist of diverse cleavages which divide Russia's Muslim community.

Geographically, most of Russia's Muslims are divided between the North Caucasus republics, Tatarstan and Bashkortostan in the Middle Volga and southern Urals areas, the Tatar communities spread across the Volga, Urals, and Siberian Russia, and several large ethnic Muslim communities in Moscow (perhaps two million) and St. Petersburg (a half-million). This geographical dispersion presents coordination problems for the formation of a broad-based Islamic movement and has contributed to socio-economic, religious, and political differences between the populations. As noted earlier, one constraint on the mobilization of Tatar and Bashkir nationalism has been the good economic performance and higher living standards in their titular republics as compared to the destitute North Caucasian republics, which are plagued by difficult mountainous terrain and limited natural resources. Geography also shaped the nature of Islam in the Middle Volga and North Caucasus. It is generally accepted that in areas such as the North Caucasus that were originally Islamicized by Arab conquest, Islam assumed a more rigid, conservative tone, whereas in the Middle Volga, the southern Urals, western Siberia, and former Soviet Central Asia, which were Islamicized through penetration by Arab merchants and diplomatic missions by the Ottoman Empire, Islam took on slightly more flexible forms.[52]

Geography shapes the two mega-regions' somewhat different geopolitical dispositions today as well. In the Middle Volga area, Tatarstan and Bash-kortostan lack external borders and are therefore less able readily to secede and less susceptible to illegal infiltration by radical Islamists and terrorists. The North Caucasus, on the other hand, has porous, mountainous external borders adjacent to countries bordering the centers of Wahhabist and Salafist activity and harboring pro-terrorist sentiment in the Persian Gulf, southwest Asia, and the Middle East. It is twice the distance from the Persian Gulf to Kazan than it is to Grozny.

Ethnically, Russia's Muslims are divided into some forty traditionally Muslim ethnic groups. An example of the ethnic diversity within Russia's Muslim communities is Dagestan. Its population includes some twenty major Muslim nationalities. Its society and polity are so diverse that post-Soviet Dagestan instituted a consensus-based political system which included a joint rotating presidency and other institutional innovations to ensure the representation of the republic's fourteen largest ethnic groups. Still, the republic has been marred by numerous antagonistic relationships between various Muslim nationalities, including between Avars and Dargins, Avars and Akin-Chechens, Avars and Kumyks, Dargins and Kumyks, and Laks and Chechens. Equally important, ethnic Russians as well as perhaps members of other traditionally non-Muslim ethnic groups are converting to Islam in high numbers relative to the past, compounding the ethnic diversity of Russia's Muslim community.

Perhaps the most fortuitous intra-Muslim tension from Moscow's point of view is that between Tatars and Bashkirs. These are relatively large and culturally and religiously fraternal Muslim peoples that, if united in opposition to Moscow, could open a second separatist front. There has been some competition and tension in the history of Tatar–Bashkir relations over identity, language, and even political issues, but for the most part contacts between the two peoples have been marked by friendship and common interest. This was especially true in the late Soviet and early post-Soviet years. These two Muslim peoples and their respective titular national republics, especially Tatarstan, were at the forefront of the movement for sovereignty during the 1990s. Tatarstan president Mintimer Shaimiev forged a constitution declaring the republic "a sovereign state associated with the Russian Federation and a subject of international law"; a Russia-Tatarstan confederation in essence. In February 1994 he engineered the first bilateral federal-regional treaty with Moscow, which gave his republic the most extensive sovereignty of any region. In August, Bashkortostan (Bashkiriya) became the third region (the KBR was the second) to win its own power-sharing treaty with Moscow. Under Putin's drive to rein in regional sovereignty, these two republics were the most resistant to federal- and court-mandated changes to their laws and constitutions.

Moscow appears to have been turning a blind eye to Bashkortostan president Murtaza Rakhimov's "Bashkirization" policies that clearly discriminate against Tatars (and Russians) in order to foment Tatar-Bashkir and Tatarstan-Bashkortostan tensions. Representatives of the Tatar Public Center in Bashkortostan (TOTsB), a branch of the Tatar nationalist TOTs in Tatarstan, and the Tatar Congress have repeatedly appealed to Russia's prosecutor general to challenge the constitutionality of Bashkortostan's language law – to little or no avail. The law in question designates the language of the republic's third-largest nationality, the Bashkirs, as the republic's state language and Russian as its language of inter-ethnic communication. Meanwhile, the language of the republic's second-largest nationality, the Tatars, has no state status. According to the 1989 census, the population's ethnic composition was: Russians – 39 percent, Tatars – 28 percent, and Bashkirs – 22 percent. The 2002 census saw a sudden and suspicious shift, with Bashkirs (25 percent) overtaking Tatars (23 percent).[53] It was left to the US ambassador to Russia, Alexander Vershbow, to challenge Bashkortostan's treatment of its Tatars during his March visit to Ufa.[54]

Similarly, Tatars and Russians demanded for years that federal authorities introduce elections for city and *raion* (district) administration heads and force Rakhimov to give up his power to appoint and fire them. They claimed that Rakhimov was using this and other policies not only to preserve his authoritarian rule but also to "Bashkirize" the republic. The demand coincided with Moscow's drive to bring regional laws into conformity with federal law, which in 2002 required the election of such officials. Moscow in fact was pushing Kazan and other regions to comply with this and other democratic federal norms. However, Rakhimov continued to drag his feet with impunity and conspicuously dared to reiterate his opposition to such elections. Indeed, in 2002 Rakhimov fired numerous ethnic Tatar municipal and raion administration heads. The failure of Moscow to satisfy the appeals suggests that someone in Moscow sees a benefit in having Bashkortostan continue to offend Tatars and perhaps Russians.

The October 2002 census further exacerbated the strains in Tatar–Bashkir relations. The preceding year saw a flood of claims and counterclaims by Bashkirs and Tatars over national identity, origins, and assimilation of one group by another as a whole or in various districts of the republic. Relations between the nationalities' respective intelligentsias seriously deteriorated.[55] Both charged the other and/or Moscow with conspiring to assimilate them in the past and by means of the upcoming census in the present, while each mobilized their ranks to boost "turnout" for the census.[56] Tatar groups then sought to challenge the results in Bashkortostan.

The Tatar–Bashkir disputes have diverted the attention of both Tatar and Bashkir nationalists from what could arguably be regarded as their main and common challenge: Moscow's anti-federalist counter-revolution and heavy-handed policing policies targeting Muslims. The TOTsB leadership warned that mutual efforts to fend off Moscow's encroachments on their autonomy would be impossible until Tatars attained equality in Bashkortostan. Since Shaimiev's ideology of "Tatarstanism" and the constitution hold the republic to be the defender of Russia's several-million Tatar "diaspora", Rakhimov's Bashkirization policy, by driving a wedge between Tatars and Bashkirs, is effectively preventing a Tatar–Bashkir alliance against Moscow.

In the Caucausus as well the Soviet Union's ethno-territorial administrative structure divided and mixed Muslim nationalities in ways that created tensions and conflict between and within them. A prime example is the division of the Muslim Cherkess or Circassian ethnic groups – the Cherkess, Kabards, and Adygeis – across three North Caucasian republics: Kabardino-Balkariya (KBR), Karachaevo-Cherkessiya (KChR), and Adygeya. This included placing Adygeya as an ethnic enclave within Stavropol Krai with no external border with any other region. Similarly, the fraternal Balkars and Karachais were divided between two republics: the KBR and KChR. Another practice that pitted Muslim nationalities against each other was the designation of two Muslim nationalities as the titular dyads of national-territorial governance units, including in two Muslim republics, the KBR and the KChR. There have indeed been tensions between the two Muslim titular nationalities in both.

In these republics, as well as in Dagestan, some ethnic groups have fared better than others politically, often as a result of a democracy deficit preventing ethnic minorities from being able to compete with larger pluralities, or majority groups. Often, an elite dominated by one ethnic group faces off against an opposition dominated by other, often much smaller ethnic groups. The domination of Dargins within Dagestan's political elite has produced an Avar- and Akin-Chechen-dominated Islamist opposition. In the KBR, the more pro-Russian, Kabardin-dominated political elite has given rise to an Islamist terrorist group, Yarmuk, dominated by Balkars. Karachai-Cherkess tensions also have helped shape regime-opposition confrontations in the KChR, both in 1999 and 2004.[57] In these circumstances, the outsiders are more likely to turn to ethno-nationalism, and perhaps radical Islamic nationalism and even Islamism. In this way, although ethnic diversity within Russia's Muslim community inhibits the formation of a mass pan-Islamic movement, it may facilitate the formation of small radical ones. In addition, radical Islamists are aware of this dynamic and have endeavored to recruit across ethnic divides.

Clan cleavages compound ethnic cleavages among Russia's Muslims, especially in the eastern North Caucasus republics of Chechnya, Dagestan, and Ingushetiya. Each republic varies in the way that the hundreds of clans are formed. In Dagestan, village-based *jamaats* (Arabic for "community") or inter-village political structures supersede kinship ties.[58] In Ingushetiya and Chechnya clans are based on more traditional kinship ties.[59] In Chechnya, a complex seven-level system of extended kinship structures translates into competing *teips* which, at the highest level, unite tens or even hundreds of smaller kinship sub-units. It is important to emphasize that, despite divisions along the lines of the teip, the Chechen Islamists have still been able to cooperate in opposition to Russian rule. However, when the Russian threat subsides Chechens and other North Caucasian nationalities have routinely fallen back into often violent infighting, as was seen in the inter-war period of 1996–2000. One way to overcome teip divisions is by the dominance by one or the other of two main competing brotherhoods, Naqshbandiya and Qadiriya, within the mystical Sufi form of Islam that predominates in the North Caucasus. However, in some cases, a Sufi brotherhood is tied to a particular teip is called a *vird*. In fact, various theological differences divide Russia's Muslims.

Theologically, Russia's Muslims are broken up into Shiites, various schools of Sunni Islam, and Sufis, as well as the competing jadidist and Islamist revivals. The pattern of the divisions is such that Islam in the North Caucasus is very different from Islam in Tatarstan, Bashkortostan, and other ethnic Muslim communities outside of the Caucasus. Sunnis predominate in Russia.[60] Shiites are a small minority to be found almost exclusively in the Caucasus, among Azeri Turks and the Azeri diaspora and a portion of Dagestan's small Muslim ethnic group, the Lezgins.[61] The small number of Shiites limits the importance of the Sunni–Shia rift in Russia as it does in most of the Muslim world.[62] Russia's Muslims adhere to only two of the four main

Sunni schools of Islamic jurisprudence, the Hanafi and Shafi *maskhabs*, eschewing the more strict and intolerant Hanbali and Maliki schools. The Hanafi school, founded by Abu Hanifa in Iraq in the eighth century, encompasses the majority of Russia's Muslims. Predominant among the influential Tatars, it is regarded as the most theologically flexible and the most tolerant with regard to other religions and local, including pagan, customs, as well as on issues such as emigration of Muslims to the non-Muslim world.[63] However, in the North Caucasus only Nogais, Balkars, and the majority of Karachais are of the Hanafi school. The Shafi school, which stands between the "liberal" Hanafi and the stricter Maliki and Hanbali, prevails among Russia's Vainakh peoples (Chechens and Ingush), Dagestani peoples (excluding the Hanafist ethnic Nogais), the ethnic Karachais of the Dautskii Gorge, and the few Muslim ethnic Ossetiyans (Digors).[64] The Hanafi school may have had a moderating influence among the Tatars of the Kazan and other khanates in central Russia's Middle Volga, Urals, and western Siberian areas, Kazan, and the several North Caucasus tribes that adopted it.[65] On the other hand, the Shafi school may help explain a certain tendency to adopt more fundamentalist views among Chechens, Ingush, and Dagestan's Dargins, Avars, Kumyks, and Lezgins.

The prevalence of the mystical Sufi form of Islam in the North Caucasus marks another difference between this area's Muslims and those in the rest of Russia. Sufism itself is divided in turn into various orders or brotherhoods (*tariqat* meaning "path leading to Allah"). The Sufi Naqshbandiya *tariqat*, founded in fourteenth-century Bukhara (Uzbekistan), and the Qadiriya *tariqat*, established in twelfth-century Baghdad, dominate Russia's Sufi landscape and have played leading roles in the area's resistance to Russian rule over the centuries. Both of the tariqats existed underground in all the Muslim-populated areas of the Soviet Union but were particularly strong in the North Caucasus republics of Checheno-Ingushetiya and Dagestan, where there were still an estimated 200,000 adepts in the mid-1970s despite decades of Soviet rule.[66] Overall, Sufi brotherhoods appear to have gained in strength in the post-Soviet North Caucasus, especially in Chechnya and Dagestan. According to Dagestan's late nationalities minister Zagir Aukhov, in these two republics there are fifteen Naqshbandiy, five Qadiriya, and five Shaziliya groups.[67] Sufi tariqats of these orders are estimated to compose some 60 percent of Muslim believers in Chechnya, Ingushetiya, and Dagestan.[68]

Jadidism (in Arabic *usul-al jadid*, or the "new method"), a European-oriented Muslim reform movement which swept through the Tatar community in the late nineteenth century, is poised to divide Russia's Muslims further should a revival favored by some leading Muslims come to fruition. Such a revival has been enthusiastically endorsed by perhaps Russia's most influential Muslim, the chairman of the Council of the Muftis of Russia, Ravil Gainutdin,[69] as well as by key political elites and some leading clerics in Tatarstan. Presaged by liberalized visions of Islamic learning by pre-jadidist Tatar Muslim scholars, jadidist thinkers were at the forefront of a Tatar renaissance that aimed to bring Tatars into the contemporary world as both Muslims and a nation, equipped with all the modern tools of science, culture, organization, and social thought. Thus, the late nineteenth-/early twentieth-century Tatar nationalist movement – with its democratic, socialist, and federalist strains – was a direct outgrowth of jadidist thought. Jadidism can be an ideological antidote to both the moderately conservative Islam indigenous to Russia and reactionary Islamist foreign forms.

The penetration into Russia and Eurasia of the Egyptian Salafi revolutionary jihadism and Saudi Wahhabi fundamentalism that produced al Qaeda is a post-Soviet phenomenon, the direct result of conscious efforts on the part of the international jihadist movement and the Saudi Arabian government. The present global jihadist movement, as expressed in the al Qaeda-inspired ideology, is really a mixture of Salafi, Wahhabi, Sufi, and even Shiite influences.[70] Salafism, with its origins in Egypt's revolutionary Muslim Brotherhood, and Wahhabism, Saudi Arabia's strict official theology, have together produced a highly politicized revolutionary Islamist variation on the thirteenth-century mystical professional murderers, the *hashishutyun* or so-called "assassins," but with global political aspirations.[71] The al Qaeda theology/ideology consists of various extremist elements including apocalypticism, messianism, utopianism, totalitarianism, communalism (anti-Semitism, anti-Christianism, anti-Westernism, anti-Americanism, anti-secularism), as well as cultures of violence and martyrdom.[72]

Central to it perhaps is Salafi politics. Salafism is as much a revolutionary political movement as a religious trend, focused initially on the national liberation of Egypt. Sayyid Qutb (1906–66), a founding father of the political Islamist movement, modernized and radically revised the Islamic concept of jahiliya, dividing the world into two irreconcilable camps doomed to a conflict ordained by Allah. Originating in Mohammed's time, *jahiliya* means literally the "(time of) ignorance," that is, the barbarian and pagan period of human history preceding God's revelations written down by Mohammed in the Koran. Qutb claimed that the secular West as well Muslim deviants from "true" Islamic teaching represented a modern jahiliya. Politically, he redefined jihad as revolutionary armed struggle and called for the seizure of power in Muslim countries and the establishment of an Islamic state or caliphate. Muslims are required to fight for Islamic power in order to cleanse the world of jahiliya's remnants. Not only are infidels or non-believers to be fought, but so too are all Muslims who oppose or deviate from Allah's path.[73] An Islamic state, in Qutb's view, was not to be governed by a personalized chief executive, religious or secular, or by specific institutions beyond the rule of God. Rather government would be conducted according to Shariah law as interpreted by the ruling council or *shura* of leading figures, like that which chose Mohammed's successors (and, incidentally brought the umma repeated political infighting and bloodshed).[74]

Wahhabism, rooted in the religious teachings of Saudi theologian Muhammed ibn Abd al-Wahhab (1703–1766), is more of a theology than a political ideology and is founded on a purist, literal interpretation of the Koran and a limited number of verifiable passages (*hadiths*) from the Sunna, a sacred compilation of the Prophet's words and deeds. With the House of Saud's patronage, al-Wahhab implemented a return to the purely Arabian Sunni form of Islam founded by Mohammed at Medina, shorn of all innovations emanating from abroad during the centuries of Islam's expansion. In particular, al-Wahhab introduced a purge of all rituals and holidays devoted to Islamic scholars (*ulema*), teachers (*imams*), or even Mohammed the Prophet. Those Muslims who fail or refuse to comply with al-Wahhab's Islam, in particular Shiites and Sufis, are deemed worthy of death. Indeed, al-Wahhab himself was driven out of an oasis for stoning a woman to death. Some argue that since residual paganism and other local customs among Russia's ethnic Muslims – in particular the Sufi worship of Muslim saints and imams and the ritual Sufi *zikr* of dancing and chanting popular among Chechens and other North Caucasian Muslims – are punishable offenses under Salafism's and Wahhabism's strict code of monotheism, these Islamist trends would have limited appeal among Russia's Muslims.[75] Indeed, tensions between Wahhabis and Sufis have at times exploded into violence.[76]

Organizationally, after the destruction of most of the country's mosques and religious clerics in the 1920s and 1930s, the Soviet authorities established party-appointed, regionally based spiritual boards or administrations of Muslims (*Dukhovnyie Upravlenii Musulman* or DUMs) to control Russia's Muslims. Although underground Sufi brotherhoods and "apartment" mosques, dubbed "parallel" Islam, continued to function, Muslims in Russia saw all open autonomous forms of Islam disappear in favor of the state-controlled "official Islam" subsumed under the party-appointed DUMs. Today, the rift between official and parallel Islam is compounded by openly autonomous unofficial Islamic structures and mosques which refuse to register with the authorities. Complicating the picture still further is the emergence of the revolutionary Islamist combat jamaats.

Moreover, the leading official Islamic organizations are often mutually antagonistic. These include: the Central Spiritual Administration of Muslims (*Tsentralnoe Dukhovnoe Upravlenie Musulman* or TsDUM) of Russia and

European Countries of the Commonwealth of Independent States, headed by mufti Sheik ul-Islam Talgat Tadzhuddin, and the Council of Muftis of Russia (*Sovet Muftiev Rossii* or SMR), headed by mufti Ravil Gainutdin, and the Coordination Center of the Muslims of the North Caucasus (*Koordinatsionnoi Tsentr Msulman Severnogo Kavkaza* or KTsMSK) led by Chairman of the DUM of the KChR and Stavropol mufti Ismail Berdiyev. Although the SMR is ostensibly subordinated to the TsDUM, it competes with it in many regions, especially in Tatarstan and the Volga and southern Urals, where Tatars are prevalent. It has regional allies in the Volga DUM (DUMP) and the DUMs of Bashkortostan, Ulyanovsk, Orenburg, and Mordovia. The KTsMSK is subordinated to the SMR and subsumes the DUMs of the North Caucasus's Muslim republics as well as North Ossetiya and Krasnodar.[77]

The TsDUM and SMR have been involved in a fierce competition for control of regional DUMs, communities, and mosques, as well as for the Kremlin's favor and state funds, in sum, for the leadership position for all of Russia's Muslims. Tadzhuddin and the TsDUM had the upper hand under the Yeltsin administration. However, after the beginning of the US war in Iraq in 2002 Tadzhuddin called for a jihad against Americans, a policy the Kremlin could not support. Tadzhuddin subsequently fell out of favor with Putin, and by late 2002 Gainutdin's SMR had supplanted the TsDUM in the Kremlin's favor. Its leading position was reinforced when Putin appointed Gainutdin, but not Tadzhuddin, to his new advisory Public Chamber in October 2005.

Ideologically, the most obvious divide among Russia's Muslims is that between the pro-Russian DUMs and the revolutionary jihadists. A political conservatism pervades, for the most part, the federation-wide structures (TsDUM, SMR, KTsMSK) and regional-level DUMs. Nevertheless, there are ideological differences and conflicts within the supposed umbrella of the TsDUM.[78] The jadidism and Euro-Islam of the DUM of Tatarstan (DUMT) and, to some extent, of the SMR collides with the TsDUM's Qadimism (traditional Tatar Islam). Also, the DUMT and the SMR lack the KTsMSK's "Eurasianist" orientation. Most DUMs tend to be moderately anti-Western in traditional Russian terms, not jihadist ones. Islamic structures are not particularly divided in their attitudes toward the Russian state (which they support) or toward democracy, the market, and the West (about which they share the traditional Russian reservations).

Various ideological trends and political parties have contended to represent Muslims, and they have split both along the lines of competing political clans and of institutionalized political parties. The first Islamic political parties emerged during perestroika and adopted fairly radical religious agendas. These included the Islamic Rebirth Party, strongly represented in Dagestan, Uzbekistan, and Tajikistan, and, later (under Yeltsin) "Nur" (Light) and the

Party of the Muslims of Russia, which were dominated by Tatars. In 2003 Putin's amendments to Russia's electoral laws disallowed the registration of parties based on religion, ethnicity, and gender. In the December 2003 Duma elections, members of unregistered Muslim parties participated under the umbrella of the Party of True Patriots, which disguised its Muslim base and included prominent Muslim "Eurasianists." In general, however, official political parties play a limited role in Russia's Muslim politics, as they do indeed in overall Russian politics.

Many among Russia's official Muslim clergy ally themselves with Russian nationalists and increasing numbers of state officials and bureaucrats in the Eurasian movement led by Aleksandr Dugin and Aleksandr Panarin, who propose a "holy alliance" between the Christian Orthodox and Islamic (as well as, for some, the Sinese) civilizations against the globalizing, secular American and Western or "Atlantist" juggernaut.[79] Their Eurasian Party includes Russian Orthodox, ethnic Russian Muslim, and traditional "ethnic Muslim" members.[80] The symbiotic relationship between the state authorities and official Islam's top clerics has reinforced the latter's conservatism in relation to the West. Leading Muslim clergy, such as the KTsMSK executive director mufti Shafig-khadzhi Pshikhachev, and Muslim thinkers, such as Geidar Dzhamal and the ethnic Russian convert to Islam and chairman of the Union of Muslim Journalists (SMZh) Dr. Vyacheslav Polosin, frequently espouse Eurasianism's anti-Western and often anti-Zionist ideas on the Dagestan DUM's website, Islam.ru.

Organizations created ostensibly to defend Muslims' rights also include many leading Muslim Eurasianists. Haq, formed in 2004, was ostensibly created to defend Muslims' rights in the wake of Beslan, the rise of public Islamophobia, and the state's harsh security measures. Its leading members include the aforementioned Eurasianists Dr. Polosin and mufti Shafig-khadzhi Pshikhachev. In typical Eurasianist fashion, Haq board member Sergei Komkov told the organization's founding assembly: "Forces antagonistic to Russia as well as to the Muslim world are promoting Islamophobia which serves as one of the levers for Russia's destruction."[81]

CONCLUSION

Russia's Muslim challenge has grown since the Soviet collapse. The lack of economic development combined with a demographic explosion in its Muslim-populated regions is likely to create greater demands on the Russian state to heed the interests of the Muslim community, especially in terms of investment in the North Caucasus economy. If state-Muslim relations remain as they are, the Muslim demographic could transform the current slow narrow stream of young Muslims joining the North Caucasus jihad into a torrential river of jihadist volunteers by mid-century.

At the same time, like the former USSR, Russia has other problems that challenge its stability and that could push it into the category of a failed state over time: a vast and diverse northern territory requiring enormous expenditure on defense, communications, and transport; a large and corrupt bureaucracy opposed to the market mechanisms that might help provide the wealth to meet that expenditure; a reliance on oil and gas revenues in place of structural reforms; the potential nationalist and secessionist aspirations of non-Muslim minorities in, for instance, Karelia, the Volga area, Siberia, and Kaliningrad; and an influx of hundreds of thousands of illegal Chinese immigrants threatening Moscow's hold on Russia's Far East.

At the same time, Putin's counter-revolution is giving rise to more radical political demands. Increased communal politicization among Russia's ethnic Muslims, whether nationalist or confessional in orientation, plays into the hands of domestic and foreign jihadists, who are already feeding on the Chechen quagmire, itself an increasing drain on Russian financial, human, and political resources.

On the other hand, divisions among Russia's Muslims – geographical, ethnic, clan, theological, organizational, and political-ideological – may confound the rise of any mass Muslim or pan-Islamic movement. But such constraints may only partially mitigate the factors driving politicization and mobilization, and Muslims' very inability to produce a broad mass movement capable of inducing the Russian government to enact changes peacefully is likely to frustrate Muslim ethno-nationalists and Islamic nationalists, predisposing some to extremist ideologies and jihad. There is evidence that this is already happening. The constraints on the formation of a mass Islamic/Islamist revolutionary movement may in part explain the emergence of what is to date a small, though growing and effective, underground jihadist terrorist network.

Chapter Two

The Chechen Quagmire and Its Consequences

Foremost among the causes of Russia's strengthening Islamist revolutionary movement is the festering Chechen war. The defeat of the Chechen separatists on the traditional battlefield, combined with the failure of the Russian elite to fashion an effective strategy for resolving the underlying problem, has turned Chechnya into a quagmire. As radical elements under first Chechen president Dzhokar Dudaev (1991–95) and his successors Zelimkhan Yandarbiyev (1996) and Aslan Maskhadov (1997–2005) sought assistance from abroad, they naturally turned to Muslims in an umma increasingly populated by radical Islamic and jihadist movements. At the same time, the Chechens' Sufi jihadist warrior culture, their custom of "blood revenge," the war's decimation of Chechnya and brutalization of the population, and the general absence of a negotiating process combined to turn the Chechens toward Islamist jihadism and its strategy of mass terrorism. Via the Chechen movement, the internet, and other influences, Islamist jihadism is now penetrating other regions in the North Caucasus and beyond.

RUSSIA'S CHECHEN QUAGMIRE

Much has already been written about the Dudaev period and the first Chechen war (1994–96). For our purposes, it suffices to say that Dudaev served the Chechens poorly, and Islam played a role early on in the Russian-Chechen conflict. Beginning with his illegal seizure of power in October 1991, Dudaev opened the door to a renewal of the struggle for power among competing warrior clans that has been the stuff of Chechen history and politics whenever Russian power has been absent or weak. Also, like many Soviet-educated officials, this army general was virtually illiterate in both high political and economic terms. The ensuing economic chaos in Chechnya would play a key role in the ability of the radical Chechen opposition to wreak havoc in the republic. Dudaev's decision to fight the Russian army rather than compromise, as Tatarstan's President Shaimiev and the leaders of Russia's thirty other national autonomies did, led not only to his death in 1995, but to that of tens of thousands of other Chechens in little more than a decade. Dudaev was a fish out of water in his own homeland; he returned from Estonia to a rapidly re-Islamizing near-feudal backwater (with the exception of relatively cosmopolitan Grozny), evenly divided between ethnic Russians and natives from the more peaceable plains clans. Dudaev's economics and finance minister Taimaz Abubakarov reports that Dudaev paid little attention to his ministers' teip allegiances despite the importance of such loyalties in Chechen society and politics.[1]

Although the main themes of this book – the rise of jihadism within the Chechen movement and Russia at large – began to emerge only during the mid-1990s inter-war period, Islam and the threat of jihad played a role in Dudaev's Chechnya as well. Since the eighteenth century Chechen national and teip identities have been deeply intertwined with Islam as a symbol of the "otherness" to Christian Orthodox Russians and as the ideology of resistance to Russian imperial conquest. During the North Caucasus wars of resistance to Russian conquest from 1785 to 1859, devout Islamist teachers such as Sheik Mansur Ushuma, Qazi Mullah, and Imam Shamil played key political, military, and religious leadership roles, including attempting to unite the mountain peoples by the imposition of Shariah law over the region (a move rejected by some Chechen teips). The crushing of Islam under Soviet rule strengthened the identification of Islam with Chechen nationalist aspirations. Nothing evidenced this more clearly than the resurgence of traditional Sufi Islam in the republic with the onset of perestroika and the collapse of Soviet power.

Initially, Dudaev rejected Islam as an ideological foundation of the Chechen independence movement, though he certainly tried to use it, albeit rather clumsily, to persuade Muslim states to support Chechnya's independence and to rally the Chechen people to his cause. The president's salesmanship, not to mention his knowledge of Islamic history, left something to be desired. He was fond of telling foreign Muslim leaders that Chechnya gave birth to Islam, one of several messianic delusions popular among Chechen intellectuals at the time.[2] Some claimed the Chechens were Allah's chosen people destined to liberate the entire North Caucasus from Russian rule, while others saw the nation as an engine of Islamic and even human development.[3] Such ideas contributed to the acceptance of the international Islamists' own messianic ambitions of global jihad by Chechen radicals like former president Zelimkhan Yandarbiyev, warlords Shamil Basaev and Salman Raduev, and Ichkeriyan ideologist Movladi Udugov.

As negotiations with Moscow became bogged down and Dudaev failed to

garner the international community's support for his separatist plans, he tried
to frighten Moscow with the specter of a war in which, he claimed, Chechnya
would ostensibly be able to mobilize one million mujahedin.[4] More
importantly, he quickly relinquished his support for a secular state, seeing
devout Muslims as an important resource of nationalist resistance to Russian
efforts to restore Moscow's control over the republic. In January 1994, he
refused to negotiate regarding Chechnya's inclusion in a "united economic
and legal space" and sought to limit Chechnya's association with Russia to
defense, transport, communications, and cultural ties. This refusal to establish
federal relations by including Chechnya within Russia's legal sovereignty and
economy was actually dictated by plans to introduce elements of Shariah law.[5]
In this way, the Chechens' Islamic orientation indirectly contributed to the
collapse of the agreement with Moscow on Chechnya's place within the
federation. To be sure, there were other economic as well as purely secular
political causes of the talks' collapse. But even some of these were driven by the
history of conflict between Chechens and Russia based on the cultural chasm
between the Islamic and traditional mountain village culture of the Chechens
and the Orthodox Christianity and increasingly secular culture of the
Russians. The Soviet experience in many ways only widened that gulf.

The first post-Soviet Chechen war (1994–96) brought unprecedented
carnage to the republic, with tens of thousands of Chechens as well as ethnic
Russians being killed and vast areas of the republic, including Grozny, being
completely destroyed. After the signing of the Khasavyurt peace agreement in
June 1996 by President Yeltsin and Chechen General Aslan Maskhadov, the
latter was elected president of the republic by a wide margin in January 1997.
However, Maskhadov was faced with the daunting task of reviving a war-torn
land and uniting increasingly politicized teips and warlords who had
established local followings during the war. The new president soon came
under challenge from radical field commanders such as Basaev and Raduev,
who opposed peace with Russia and had begun to develop ties with foreign
Islamists in al Qaeda in order to secure financial and military support for
themselves. Maskhadov was unwilling or unable to crack down on these rene-
gades, who engaged in kidnappings, oil theft, and other criminal activities and
relied increasingly on their foreign Islamist associates for ideological, political,
and financial sustenance. The renegade field commanders, Raduev and Basaev,
moreover, hated each other, and their forces often clashed violently. As the
power of these radical Islamists warlords and criminal gangs grew, Maskhadov
sought to assuage them by adopting strict Shariah law in February 1999. This,
however, did not satiate their growing appetite for power and war with Russia.

In August 1999, Basaev, now closely allied with the Saudi-born Jordanian al
Qaeda operative Abu Ibn al-Khattab,[6] led raids into Dagestan in the hope of

using local radical jamaats there as a base from which to spread the war to the entire North Caucasus. This and a series of five terrorist bombings (four in Moscow) pushed the Russian authorities to renew the Chechen war.[7] Although Russian forces gained control of Grozny, Gudermes, and much of the rest of the republic, the Chechen government and various guerrilla detachments, including Basaev's increasingly Islamist-oriented terrorist detachments, retreated into the southern mountains. From there they have been able to wage a moderately effective guerrilla war against Russian forces by establishing a system of camps and hideouts, conducting raids into the cities, and organizing major terrorist attacks throughout Chechnya and Russia.

Since the beginning of the guerrilla war Putin's policy has consisted of four strands: (1) giving the still unreformed largely Soviet-style army, MVD, FSB, GRU, and loyal Chechen forces freedom in prosecuting the war while overlooking their human rights' violations and economic criminality in order to fulfill his promise to "wipe out the terrorists and bandits in the outhouse"; (2) refusing to negotiate with any Chechens independent of the Russian central elite; (3) exaggerating the level of direct involvement of international jihadists in the Chechen separatist movement in order to underplay the domestic sources of the growing Islamist revolution; and (4) "Chechenizing" the administration and, where possible, much of the fighting in the republic. The further destruction in Chechnya from the second war left many towns, including the capital Grozny, without running water, heat, and electricity and virtually uninhabitable. In addition, unemployment among young Chechen men remains nearly universal,[8] while, as under Yeltsin, meaningful reconstruction aid from Moscow has never materialized, with resources often being diverted by federal and regional bureaucrats. The miserable socio-economic situation in what remains of Chechnya offers fertile soil for radical ideologies, and thus for Islamist recruitment.

Atrocities in the ongoing guerrilla war have been numerous on both sides, mostly involving helpless civilians, both Chechen and Russian. However, the militarily superior side always has greater potential for committing human rights' violations and war crimes. Unsurprisingly, Russia's largely unreformed, unprofessional, and often criminalized military and security forces under the so-called *siloviki* (the power ministries or organs of coercion – MVD, military, FSB, and GRU) have more than played their part in this respect. Russian troops and allied Chechen forces have engaged in systematic abuses, including overly aggressive security sweeps (*zachistki*), summary executions, mass arrests, torture, and rape. Chechen separatists, for their part, have been involved in kidnapping for ransom, preventing civilians from fleeing battle zones, deliberately locating military equipment and forces near civilian residences and hospitals, and more recently conducting mass terrorism and an expanded war throughout the North Caucasus.[9]

Moscow's forced normalization campaign to restore life and order in Chechnya was based on re-establishing an administration of loyal Chechens in 2003. In votes that could in no way be considered free or fair, an official figure of 80 percent elected former chief mufti of Chechnya Akhmed Kadyrov as the republic's president and 90 percent approved a new constitution. However, in April 2004 Kadyrov was assassinated by Chechen rebels. Backed by the Kremlin, Chechen MVD chief Alu Alkhanov was next elected Kadyrov's successor with 73 percent of the votes in a similar ballot. By late 2003 and throughout 2004 Chechnya, like Tatarstan and Bashkortostan, began negotiating a new power-sharing treaty with Moscow, but it still remains unclear just how much autonomous authority the republic will be given.

The Russian government now maintains a permanent large-scale military presence in Chechnya, including the MVD's 46th Brigade, the army's only full division of contract soldiers (*kontraktniki*) – the 42nd Motorized Rifle Division, and some twenty regional military command staffs. Instead of controlled intelligence-gathering and carefully calibrated raids and arrests, *siloviki* persist in heavy-handed and often brutal police operations, including harassment campaigns, kidnapping and murder of "suspects," and sweeping search-and-arrest campaigns. This can only further provoke communalism and extremism among the Chechens. *Siloviki*, in particular the MVD's internal forces and special forces (or OMON), are rotated constantly through the region. As a result troops may be starting to develop a "Chechen syndrome," leading to increases in over-aggressiveness in dealing with ethnic Muslims across Russia. This may have been responsible for the brutal *zachistka*-like raid in Blagoveshchensk, Bashkortostan in December 2004, which led to weeks of demonstrations in Ufa and threatened President Murtaza Rakhimov's regime.

In attempting to "Chechenize" the low-intensity war in Chechenya, Russian *silovoki*, especially the GRU, have relied increasingly on detachments of pro-Russian Chechen fighters, essentially piggybacking on the inter-clan rivalries that have long characterized Chechen politics. These forces, including the Chechen government's police force, numbering 13,000–14,000 men, and Presidential Guard or *Kadyrovtsy*, headed by former Chechen president Akhmed Kadyrov's son, Ramzan, are corrupt, incompetent, and incapable of maintaining order.[10] Most infamous is Kadyrov's Presidential Guard, which has conducted itself like a rampaging army, destroying villages, killing the elderly and children, and raping women at will. Such incidents have continued albeit at a reduced frequency, despite President Putin's claims that acts of this sort would be punished. There are other similar detachments including the

Eastern Battalion led by the elder brother of State Duma deputy Khalid Yamadaev of the pro-Kremlin Yedinaya Rossiya party.[11]

Because of their heavy-handed tactics, Russian and pro-Russian Chechen forces have been unable to establish security, not to mention the promised normalization of life and politics in Chechnya. One of the highest-ranking Russian MVD officers in the North Caucasus, Lieutenant-General Evgenii Abrashin, warned that "the missions assigned to our troops in Chechnya far exceed their capabilities" and that the OGV's "forces are so busy simply trying to ensure their own security" that they "can rarely take measures to go after the resilient guerrillas."[12] Rampant corruption among both civilian and *siloviki* officials goes a long way toward explaining the failure. Chechen police reportedly turn over vital information to Chechen militants, helping them prepare ambushes and terrorist acts, and sometimes join in attacks on Russian troops.[13] For example, in August 2004, two high-ranking police officials in Chechnya were accused of having supplied weapons and explosives to the guerrillas. Additionally, an officer in Kadyrov's Presidential Guard was indicted for providing weapons, explosives, and safe passage to rebel leaders.[14] In September 2004, the procurator-general for the North Caucasus disclosed that two dozen local police had assisted Chechen and Ingush guerrillas in a series of attacks in June on Russian MVD and army posts in Ingushetiya.[15]

The Chechen guerrillas have been effective at using a wide variety of tactics, including large-scale ambushes, detonation of mines and improvised explosive devices (IEDs), anti-aircraft warfare against Russian helicopters and on occasion other military aircraft, and various forms of suicide bombings, utilizing both truck and car bombs, and even female suicide bombers.[16] During the initial conventional military phase of the conflict, rebels shot down numerous Russian helicopters often carrying high-ranking officers from the various *siloviki* using shoulder-launched air defense missiles, anti-aircraft artillery, rocket-propelled grenades, large-caliber machine guns, and small arms. In the first six months of the war alone, militants brought down at least nine helicopters.[17] A series of shortcomings in the organization and management of the *siloviki* has contributed to the Chechens' survival and success: a convoluted command and control structure for Russia's forces in Chechnya incapable of constraining inter-force conflict; rampant hazing (*dedovshchina*); low troop morale; a lack of training in the conduct of anti-guerrilla warfare operations; outdated, worn-out, and scarce equipment; and insufficient flying hours for helicopter pilots before entering the war zone.[18] The Russian *siloviki*'s failings are becoming increasingly apparent across the North Caucasus and much of Russia as the Chechens expand the jihad.

Foreign Islamists and the Jihadization of the Chechen Movement

Both al Qaeda's and official Saudi efforts to spread Salafism and Wahhabism to Russia began under President Dzhokar Dudaev, who was supported in his campaign for independence by the Islamic Path Party, a Chechen branch of the Muslim Brotherhood. Sufism provided fertile soil for the seeds of Islamist jihadism. With the beginning of the 1994–1996 war, the Chechen insurgency started to be radically re-Islamicized. Dudaev provided an opening to Islamists by adopting Islamic-tinged symbolism and propaganda. As the first war festered, Islamists began to gain influence among various elements in the Chechen resistance. By 1995 there were some three hundred "Afghan" Arabs fighting in Chechnya against the Russians. They were joined by mujahedin from Bosnia and Azerbaijan.[19] At the same time, Saudi government-sponsored Islamic charities such as the International Islamic Relief Organization (IIRO), the World Assembly of Muslim Youth (WAMY), the Chicago-based Benevolence International Foundation (BIF), and other Saudi front organizations were active in Chechnya and elsewhere in Russia raising funds for the Chechen resistance and spreading Wahhabist ideas by setting up Islamic educational institutions in Russia and providing opportunities for Russian citizens to study Islam abroad. Chechen diaspora organizations in Turkey and Pakistan engaged in similar activities.[20] Russian sources claim that al Qaeda has funneled $25 million, four Stinger missiles, seven hundred plastic explosive packs amounting to over 350 kilograms, remote detonators, and medical supplies to the Chechen resistance.[21] Although such reports are often exaggerated, that does not discount the fact that considerable assistance has nonetheless been rendered. Basaev himself acknowledged receiving funds from international Islamists for combat and terrorist operations, including $10,000 in 2004. This was probably more likely an exaggeration in the other direction.

In 1996 Osama bin Laden's chief deputy Ayman al-Zawahiri was arrested by Russian law-enforcement bodies as he tried to enter Chechnya. He was then released by the authorities, who were not aware of his true identity. Later, al-Zawahiri articulated his vision for the creation of an expansive southern Eurasian caliphate, arguing that Islamist control of Chechnya and the Caucasus as a whole would fragment Russia and thus weaken an ally of the US in the war on terrorism:

> The liberation of the Caucasus would constitute a hotbed of *jihad* . . . and that region would [then] become the shelter of thousands of Muslim *mujahidin* from various parts of the Islamic world, particularly Arab parts. This poses a direct threat to the United States . . . If the Chechens and other

Caucasian *mujahidin* reach the shores of the oil-rich Caspian Sea, the only thing that will separate them from Afghanistan will be the neutral state of Turkmenistan. This will form a *mujahid* Islamic belt to the south of Russia that will be connected in the east with Pakistan, which is brimming with *mujahidin* movements in Kashmir. The belt will be linked to the south with Iran and Turkey that are sympathetic to the Muslims of Central Asia. This will break the cordon that is struck around the Muslim Caucasus and allow it to communicate with the Islamic world in general, but particularly with the *mujahidin* movement.

Furthermore, the liberation of the Muslim Caucasus will lead to the fragmentation of the Russian Federation and will help escalate the *jihad* movements that already exist in the republics of Uzbekistan and Tajikistan, whose governments get Russian backing against those *jihad* movements.

The fragmentation of the Russian Federation on the rock of the fundamentalist movement and at the hands of the Muslims of the Caucasus and Central Asia will topple a basic ally of the United States in its battle against the Islamic *jihadist* reawakening.[22]

Since then, as Jeffrey Bale notes, the Chechen movement has undergone a transformation similar to that of the Palestinian movement: "the older nationalist elements of the resistance movement have been displaced or supplanted by certain key Islamist commanders and a younger cohort of militant Chechens that has chosen to rally around them."[23] This was a process that gained momentum as Islamic elements were incorporated into the now underground resistance government, the Chechen Republic of Ichkeriya (ChRI) proto-state, and foreign Wahhabists and other Islamic extremists infiltrated the movement, providing finances, guerrilla and terrorist training, and ideo-theological guidance. In April 1997 Shariah courts began issuing "justice" in the republic, organizing trials and televised mutilations and executions masquerading as court-mandated sentences. Under growing pressure from criminalized and increasingly Islamized elements among Chechnya's field commanders, and opposition leaders, in particular Basaev and Raduev, President Maskhadov surrendered his opposition to the formation of an Islamic republic in Chechnya in October of the same year.

Maskhadov was unable to rein in the increasingly lawless and jihadist elements. Basaev, Raduev, and other field commanders used the interlude provided by the Khasavyurt peace agreement to engage in terrorist attacks outside the republic, kidnappings and beheadings of both foreign aid workers and ethnic Russians, and the establishment of camps for the military training and "education" of Islamist jihadists. Criminal activities were used to raise funds to shore up the military and political clout of the increasingly Islamist warlords' fiefdoms in the mounting power struggle sparked by the 1997 presidential elections. The Islamists began first to infiltrate the anti-Maskhadov Chechen opposition, led by Dudaev's interim successor Zelimkhan Yandarbiyev and Salman Raduev, and then the Chechen leadership itself. Basaev, who had already undergone military training in Afghanistan and had developed a relationship with Osama bin Laden, straddled the government-opposition divide. He maintained relationships, though often tense ones, with Yandarbiyev and the mentally unstable Raduev. However, he eventually helped Maskhadov crush the opposition in 1998 and won the post of premier for himself into the bargain. This brought a leading Islamist near to the pinnacle of power in Chechnya for the first time since Yandarbiyev's interim rule.

As Basaev's power increased, largely through the efforts of his foreign benefactors and his own daredevil acts of terrorism, the pro-Islamist element within the Chechen separatist movement grew more substantial. At the same time, Chechnya's Islamists became increasingly embedded in the international revolutionary jihad movement. The 9/11 Commission report and other sources show the considerable ties between al Qaeda and Chechen terrorists in terms of funding, training, and deployment of personnel.[24] There is no doubt that Basaev and other Chechen fighters strengthened their links with al Qaeda during the inter-war period, that several foreign Islamists who until late 2001 had been running terrorist training camps in Afghanistan now came to Chechnya, and that at times during the second war as many as several hundred foreign jihadists were fighting alongside the Chechens. Al Qaeda's Mohammed Atta, the organizer of the September 2001 terrorist attacks in the USA, sought to join the Chechen struggle against Russia in the late 1990s. Atta and several other 9/11 terrorists were on their way to Chechnya when they were ordered by a bin Laden operative to head for the US instead. Two prominent international terrorists, al Qaeda's operative for the North Caucasus, Khattab, and another Saudi-born, Jordanian al Qaeda operative, Abu al-Walid, along with the Afghan-trained Basaev, were responsible for the most horrendous of the early mass terrorist attacks in Russia.

By training Russia's non-Chechen Muslims and spreading the Islamist gospel around Russia, Basaev is now trying to repeat on the Russian scale what bin Laden had achieved on a global one. In 1998, Basaev and Khattab began organizing terrorist structures including the Mazhlis ul Shura of the United Mujahids (Consultative Council of United Holy Warriors), the Congress of the Peoples of Dagestan and Ichkeniya, the Special Purpose Islamic Regiment (SPIR), the Islamic International Peacekeeping Brigade (IIPB), and a group of female suicide bombers – known as the Riyadus-Salikhin Reconnaissance and

Sabotage Battalion of Chechen Shahids. Khattab's goal, if perhaps not yet Basaev's, was the establishment of a North Caucasus caliphate. As a teenager Khattab had fought by bin Laden's side against the Soviets in Afghanistan. He also fought against the former Soviet authorities in Tajikistan; after the Tajik civil war ended he went to Chechnya. By the mid-1990s Khattab had become the *emir* (commander) of al Qaeda's Caucasus operations and was the channel for sending its personnel and funds to the Chechen terrorists. Although Russian forces killed him in April 2002 and his successor al-Walid in 2004, other Arabs have replaced them and have even taken up positions of power within the ChRI leadership.

Thus, there is now a direct link between the international jihad and Russia's Chechen-led jihadist network which facilitates the exchange of personnel, materials, guerrilla tactics, and experience. Russian officers claim that the main reason that Chechen guerrillas have developed great expertise in the use of mines and other explosives is the assistance they have received from foreign Islamists. The US intelligence unit known as the Terrorist Explosive Device Analytical Center (TEDAC), which studies bomb shrapnel from around the world, has determined that an Islamist bomb-making network spreading across Chechnya, Africa, East Asia, and the Middle East appears to be sharing designs and materials for car bombs and IEDs.[25] The Chechen terrorists who seized Moscow's Dubrovka theatre in October 2002 used al Qaeda's communication strategy to the letter, sending a video to the al-Jazeera television station showing a hostage scene replete with Islamist propaganda. The footage showed female suicide bombers wearing Islamic veils in front of a green banner inscribed with the Arabic words "Allahu akhbar" (God is great). Throughout the video the captors used bin Laden's slogan: "We desire death even more than you desire life." International jihadists, like al Qaeda, are now the model for Chechen-led jihadists' terrorist attacks and guerrilla warfare throughout the North Caucasus.[26]

Basaev's IIPB and other Chechen detachments and organizations continue to constitute a loosely organized but tactically flexible force of nearly two thousand highly motivated and well-trained guerrilla fighters and terrorists. In the late inter-war period, the IIPB terrorist training camps began recruiting alienated ethnic Muslims throughout the North Caucasus, providing them with military training and politico-religious indoctrination.[27] The IIPB forged ties with Dagestani Islamists and in August 1999 attempted to establish a bridgehead for the jihad in Dagestan, sparking the second post-Soviet Chechen war.

THE CHECHENS' TURN FROM RESISTANCE
TO JIHADIST TERRORISM

The renewal of the Chechen war in August 1999 allowed Basaev and other jihadists to climb the ladder of power in the ChRI and weaken the more secular and moderate President Maskhadov's hold on power. Maskhadov's position was undermined by the war, which discredited his strategy of maintaining a *modus vivendi* with Moscow under the Khasavyurt agreement that ended the first war. At the same time, the Chechen resistance forces' defeat on the traditional battlefield and their forced retreat into the mountains and forests of southern Chechnya led to a stalemated guerrilla war. Radical Chechens looked for a way out by adopting the more radical ideology, strategy, and tactics of the global jihad after 9/11 when the latter suddenly took on greater appeal in the eyes of many radical Muslims around the world.

The Jihadization of the ChRI Leadership

The turning point in the Chechen resistance movement's radical re-Islamization came at a July–August 2002 expanded meeting of the ChRI government. It was attended by President Maskhadov, Basaev, the other ChRI field commanders, and several foreign al Qaeda operatives and associates. One report claimed that the meeting was conducted in Arabic, with one Abdul-Khalim Sadulaev translating for Maskhadov. The meeting was a *coup d'état* of sorts for the pro-jihad forces. It established a Shariah-based order within the ChRI and the goal of expanding Islamist jihad throughout the North Caucasus. It established a new governing body named the Consultative Assembly, in Arabic the *Madzhlisul Shura* or simply *Shura*, as the top governing body transplanting the ChRI State Defense Committee (Gosudartvennyi Komitet Oborony or GKO) and superseding the Chechen government.[28] Its exact membership remains unclear but it likely includes the heads of the Shura's committees and its emir. Subsequently, President Maskhadov was identified as the chairman of the Shura in official documents, but he never took or was never offered the title of emir. The meeting also adopted amendments to the ChRI constitution. The most important stipulated that the "Madzhlisul Shura is the ChRI's highest organ of power" and that "the Koran and Sunna are the sources of all decisions" that it makes. The Shura's composition, according to another amendment, "is confirmed by the head of state with the agreement of the Supreme Shariah Court." The court is charged with ensuring that the Shura's decisions do not contradict the Koran or Sunna, a principle also enshrined in the amended constitution: "The Madzhlisul Shura is not permitted to adopt decisions that contradict the Koran and Sunna."[29]

The Shura's structure adopted the al Qaeda model, having four committees – military, Shariah, finance, and information. Appointments presumably made or confirmed by Maskhadov in the meeting's wake further reflected the jihadists' progress. Despite the Maskhadov leadership's persistent claims that it did not condone terrorism, long-time, internationally wanted terrorist Shamil Basaev was named head of the Shura's military committee and deputy commander-in-chief of the ChRI's armed forces and was thus given effective command over all the Chechen rebel forces.[30] At the time Basaev was leading the so-called Garden of the Righteous Reconnaissance Brigade of Chechen Martyrs, which was training female suicide bombers who would be deployed in October of the same year in the Nord-Ost theater hostage-taking in Moscow and in several other terrorist acts.

Moreover, several al Qaeda jihadists were appointed to top ChRI military and political offices. One "emir Supyan" chaired the Shura's finance committee. One "emir Kamad" was appointed commander of the northern front, and well-known Saudi-born al Qaeda operative Abu al-Walid was appointed to command the eastern front. The only Chechen nationalists to retain top posts were Doku Umarov and Akhmed Zakaev, who was appointed head of the Shura's information committee. Basaev's chief propagandist and director of the ChRI's 'Kavkaz-Tsentr' website Movladi Udugov was charged to run the foreign information service. One "Bashir" became head of the internal information service. Another al Qaeda operative, Sheik Abu Omar (Mohammed bin Abdallah) as-Saif was appointed the deputy head of the Shura's Shariah committee. Abu Omar, born in Saudi Arabia, spent ten years working with Basaev and Khattab to establish a separate Islamic state in the North Caucasus. He was probably the supreme spiritual authority among the ChRI militants.[31] The most important appointment was of Abdul-Khalim Sadulaev as chairman of the Shura's Shariah committee and head of the ChRI Shariah Court. The holder of these posts, according to the amended ChRI constitution, was now the automatic successor to the ChRI president.[32] In 2004 Maskhadov would appoint Sadulaev as his vice-president, strengthening his position as designated successor. Sadulaev, from all appearances, is a convinced radical Islamist and fits the global jihadist's typical profile.

Sadulaev is young, approximately 36–37 years old.[33] He has had a substantial education, including in religion. He received the latter at home and from Chechen theologians near his native village of Argun (his local familial clan or teip, Ustradoi, is said to have founded Argun).[34] He also studied in Chechnya State University's department of philology. Sadulaev has a good knowledge of Arabic and has completed the *hajj* (pilgrimage) to Mecca once. As imam at an Argun mosque in the mid-1990s, he was reportedly close to the first head of the Chechen Supreme Shariah Court, Shamsudin Batukaev who was meting out harsh Shaviah-based physical punishments at the time. Later Sadulaev was said to be the chief ideologist for Shamil Basaev and Movladi Udugov, and during the inter-war period he organized and conducted popular Islamic programming and sermons on the ChRI's "Kavkaz" TV channel. At the beginning of the second war, he headed the Islamic Jamaat in Argun and the Argun People's Militia, which apparently took part in the August 1999 invasion of Dagestan that helped spark the second war and continued operations in Chechnya through 2001.[35] The extent of his role in military operations and command is still unclear, but it appears to have been limited compared to that of Maskhadov, Basaev, and Ruslan Gelaev.

Sadulaev may have turned to terrorist activities before taking up his place as the top religious figure in the organization. The Russian, prosecutor-general's office claims he was behind the kidnapping of the head of the Médecins Sans Frontières humanitarian mission in 2001. There are reports that he led the "Wahhabi" underground in Chechnya and organized female martyrs (shakhidki) and suicide bombers.[36] Sadulaev may have a deeply personal reason for fighting the Russians. According to the militants' website Kavkaz-Tsentr, in 2003 his wife was killed by Russia forces.[37] This may explain his repeated references in his public statements to the Russians' killing of women and children. At a March 2002 meeting of field commanders, he was identified as a leading Islamic scholar of the Chechen guerrilla forces.[38] In short, Sadulaev has played multiple roles in the movement, but his primary one has been that of Islamist religious and political ideologist.

Sadulaev's rise through the Chechen ranks is sometimes attributed to his value to Maskhadov as an instrument for containing even more radical Islamist commanders such as Basaev, Raduev, and Khattab. A 2002 Chechen-press agency report claimed that Sadulaev's first public appearance involved him making a direct response to charges that Maskhadov had lost control over radical field commanders like Basaev and Gelaev. On that occasion, a March 2002 meeting of field commanders, he stated that Maskhadov was "in full control of Islamic military detachments."[39] However, in March 2004 former ChRI defense minister Magomed Khambiev asserted that Sadulaev was a "Wahhabi emir" whom the radical Islamists had sought to have appointed ChRI president.[40] Islamist pressures reportedly prompted Maskhadov to appoint him as a member of the State Commission on Constitutional Shariah Reform in 1999.[41] The jihadists surely lobbied Sadulaev's appointment in summer 2002 to the posts at the head of the Shura's Shariah committee and Shariah Court. Regardless of Maskhadov's attitude toward the jihadists, their continuing rise to power forced him into a Faustian bargain. Although he was able to retain the support of Basaev's considerable forces and access to al Qaeda funding for the resistance, he associated himself in the eyes of many, certainly the Russians, with the jihadist strategy and terrorist tactics of the Islamists, so paving the latters' way to power after his death in March 2005.

Thus, the last years of Maskhadov's reign were ones of considerable fluctuation in policy driven by the pressures of growing Islamist sentiment within the ChRI leadership and Russian military pressure on the Chechens. Some analysts have argued that the Chechens' expansion of the theater of war beyond Chechnya began only after Maskhadov's demise, with Sadulaev's assumption of power.[42] This view does not stand up to serious scrutiny, however. It is clear that by mid-2004, in addition to having long tolerated if not actually used Basaev's various terrorist operations, Maskhadov also began shifting to the Islamists' strategy of expanding the war beyond Chechnya. This coincided with Sadulaev's rise through the ranks of the ChRI. Although Maskhadov's strategic goal in doing so may have remained Chechen independence, his jihadist colleagues were seeking to establish a North Caucasus caliphate, as reflected in Basaev's August 1999 incursion into Dagestan. In a 1 August 2004 interview Maskhadov supported the creation of a broad Muslim cohort of insurgents for actions throughout the North Caucasus and indeed all of Russia. Seated next to Sadulaev in this joint interview, he warned: "We are capable of carrying out such operations in Ichkeriya, Ingushetiya and Russia, and we will prove it."[43] He also took responsibility for the June 2004 raid into Ingushetiya which led to the deaths of the republic's prosecutor general, the acting MVD chief, and tens of police officers. Maskhadov stated that it was on his own orders that the ChRI Shura set up an "Ingushetiyan Sector" and that "[s]ome 950–1,000 fighters from the Ingushetian, Sunzha, and Achkhoi-Martan sectors, headed by the commander of the western front Doku Umarov, took part in the operation."[44]

Moreover, he would soon reinstate the internationally wanted terrorist Basaev in the post of emir of the Shura's military committee in autumn 2004, just weeks after Basaev's Beslan operation and at a time when one of Basaev's chief projects, the Yarmuk combat jamaat, was wreaking havoc in Kabardino-Balkariya.[45] Indeed, on 3 March 2005, just days before his death at the hands of Russian security forces, Maskhadov claimed that all the combat jamaats in the North Caucasus such as Yarmuk networked by Basaev and involved in numerous terrorist acts were subordinate to him: "I do not think there is a detachment on Chechnya's territory that would ignore my order. In my opinion, there are no such units even on the territories of Ingushetiya, Dagestan, Kabardino-Balkariya, and Karachaevo-Cherkessiya. These are not empty words, but reality. All combat detachments on Chechnya's territory and in neighboring republics are subordinated to the Chechen Resistance."[46] Maskhadov's continued relations with Basaev cast doubt on the sincerity of his denials and those of allies like the London-based ChRI 'foreign minister',

Akhmed Zakaev, of involvement in or even responsibility for the Beslan massacre and other terrorist operations organized by Basaev and his network of combat jamaats.

To be sure, there was a struggle over the ChRI leadership and strategy between the Sufi- and nationalist-oriented Maskhadov and Basaev's more globally-oriented jihadists, but there was obviously a close alliance too. This contradictory dynamic can be seen in the vicissitudes of the February 2005 ceasefire and its aftermath. In a 14 January 2005 decree Maskhadov ordered ChRI forces to observe "a unilateral cessation" of offensive combat actions in Chechnya and beyond for the entire month of February. This was ostensibly intended as a goodwill gesture aimed at opening peace negotiations. However, the ceasefire was announced in two different forms. The decree issued by Maskhadov stipulated that it would apply throughout the entire month. But Basaev issued an accompanying order announcing the ceasefire would hold only through 22 February. Ironically, Basaev's order also noted that Maskhadov's decree proved to the world that all ChRI armed forces were strictly subordinated to the president.[47] In the event there were no terrorist or military operations by the Chechen guerrillas or Islamists during February 2005, which suggests that the ChRI president still wielded at least some authority over both Basaev and the combat jamaat network.[48] At the same time, the fact that Basaev was allowed to deviate from Maskhadov's order underscores Basaev's ability to defy the ChRI president with impunity. Therefore, Maskhadov must be seen as having been indirectly responsible for the Chechens' increasingly jihadist-like terrorism in 2002–2005 owing to his unwillingness or inability to remove or tame Basaev.

Equally contradictorily, there are both benign and malign interpretations of the purpose behind the Chechens' unilateral cessation of hostilities. One interpretation made by pro-Russian sources was that it could have been an attempt to give the Islamist network an opportunity to marshal its resources before launching a fresh wave of guerrilla and terrorist operations. Another possible explanation is that Russian forces had moved in on someone or something important to the Chechens, and the latter sought to stop their operations, at least temporarily. Indeed, one week after Maskhadov's ceasefire term had expired, so did he at the hands of Russian forces. Basaev's high-profile participation in the ceasefire casts doubt on the idea that it was intended to promote the possibility of peace: Basaev had refused to negotiate with the Russians since the beginning of the second war. The date set by Basaev for expiration of the ceasefire, 23 February, was perhaps selected because it was also the date in 1944 on which the Soviet Chechen deportations began. This is regarded by many as the day a genocide commenced against the Chechen people. However, as the former head of the CIA's "Osama bin Laden Unit," Michael Scheuer, notes, it has been standard procedure for Muslims since

Mohammed, and especially for contemporary jihadists, to make offers of a truce or negotiations in combination with threats just before a planned attack.[49] This may be a means of self-absolution. When infidels fail to take up such an offer or are interpreted as having rejected it, the jihadists are justified to attack in accordance with Shariah law. In short, there is a question as to whether the Chechens were really interested in talks with the Russians or were simply gaining time in order to regroup and take an opportunity to regain points lost with the international community as a result of Beslan. Indeed, the Chechens put forward no concrete proposals during the unilateral ceasefire.

Just three days before his death in March 2005 Maskhadov was still speaking as if he were under intense internal pressure. On the one hand, he said that a thirty-minute meeting between himself and Putin could end the war. On the other, he stated that should Putin fail to take up his offer of talks, "mujahedin will stand to the end, and the flames of this war will embrace the whole of the North Caucasus."[50] In the aforementioned August 2004 interview with Maskhadov, Sadulaev outlined the growing Islamist strain in the Ichkeriyan ideology, which now included the goal of creating a North Caucasus caliphate: "God says that all believers are brothers. There are no separate Dagestani people. There are individual Muslim nations in that part of the Caucasus. The nations of the North Caucasus were united until Russia separated us."[51] The implication was clear – the Chechens are fighting to unite the North Caucasus and separate it from Russia. Maskhadov never supported such a policy openly. In summary, on the eve of Maskhadov's death the ChRI's top leadership were divided between nationalists, who sought a Chechen state, and internationalist Islamists, who sought a North Caucasus caliphate as a first step toward broader strategic goals.

Maskhadov's killing on 8 March 2005, days after the ceasefire's conclusion, suggests another possible interpretation. Russian forces suddenly surrounded Maskhadov's basement hideout, and as Russian troops moved through the safe house Maskhadov ordered his guards to kill him to prevent his capture. It is possible that Basaev and the jihadists decided it was time to rid themselves of the constraints, albeit limited, being imposed by Maskhadov. It is well known that many of those in the pro-Moscow forces, such as the Kadyrovites and the Chechen Republic's MVD, are former insurgents. It is also certain that some are moles planted by the ChRI jihadists inside the pro-Moscow Chechen forces in order to facilitate terrorist attacks. Some may even have become double agents. Moreover, we now know that Basaev stayed with Maskhadov in his bunker for several weeks in February 2005 and left only ten days before his death; that is, after Basaev's ceasefire had expired but when Maskhadov's may still have been in force.[52] Indeed, along with the ceasefire announcement Kavkaz-Tsentr posted a photograph of Maskhadov and Basaev seated together and seemingly on friendly terms.[53] Could it be that Basaev ordered moles to tip off the pro-Russian Chechen authorities as to Maskhadov's whereabouts? Does the threat emanating from Basaev explain Maskhadov's twin-track, even schizophrenic policy in the last months and years of his rule? Perhaps relevant here is the history of internal Islamic strife and violence, beginning with continuous succession and power struggles, murders, and internecine warfare after Mohammed's death. For example, it is believed by terrorism experts that Osama bin Laden was behind the assassination of his mentor Abdullah Azzam. Such factional warfare is inherent in the politics of conspiratorial, totalitarian organizations and movements, all the more so when they bear the imprimatur of eternal truth and messianic destiny.

Therefore, although developments under Sadulaev are important, it would be wrong to regard his early steps, as some analysts have, as marking a sharp break or "historic shift" in the Chechens' strategy.[54] The "historic shift" – the consolidation of the militant jihadists' control over the movement and the turn to the goals and tactics of Islamist jihad – actually began under Maskhadov. There was simply a failure by some and a refusal by other Western analysts to recognize it. Before his death Maskhadov had come round to supporting the strategy of expanding the war beyond the borders of Chechnya and to tolerating the idea of taking terrorism straight to Moscow and Beslan. However, Maskhadov's death at the hands of Russian forces and the selection of Sadulaev as ChRI emir and president in March 2005 brought a committed Islamist to the top of the Chechen separatist movement, which gave the jihadists an opportunity to consolidate their hold on power within the ChRI.

The Consolidation of the Islamist Jihadists' Power

Under Sadulaev's leadership the ChRI would nonetheless see a further Islamization of the Chechen "resistance." The Chechen Islamists began to apply the al Qaeda strategy of coopting local Muslim nationalist or Islamic movements into the pan-Islamic jihad by creating a network of jihadist combat jamaats throughout the North Caucasus and even other "Muslim lands" in Russia. The strategy is reminiscent of, if not modeled on, that of the Muslim Seljuk Turks who used hired militia to infiltrate the various independent Muslim sultanates and ultimately reunite the Muslim umma in a single caliphate under the Ottoman Empire from the fifteenth to the early twentieth centuries.

Sadulaev's first organizational measures underscored his radical orientation. Most importantly, he created separate North Caucasus and Dagestan fronts under the ChRI's armed forces, confirming the Chechens' expansion of jihad to the entire North Caucasus. Later, jihadist combat jamaats would be incorporated into these fronts. Sadulaev also disbanded Maskhadov's

Chechen government-in-exile abroad and abolished the roles of foreign plenipotentiaries. In this way, he removed a large part of the relatively moderate Maskhadov elite. In addition, Sadulaev threatened to disband the Chechen parliament as elected in 1997 under Maskhadov, claiming that the overwhelming majority of its members had since transferred their loyalties to Moscow. He was sharply critical of all of Ichkeriya's governmental officials, foreign representatives, and rank-and-file diaspora for their lack of support for the struggle. In particular he accused then ChRI foreign minister Ilyas Akmadov of "total inaction" and of focusing on a "scholarly project" (he presumably meant his Reagan-Fascell Fellowship under the National Endowment for Democracy in Washington) rather than concentrating on working for the ChRI.[55] Sadulaev also expressed his suspicion of the exile community and the West, asserting that they were preparing "Karzais" (a reference to the US-backed Afghan President) for Chechnya.[56]

Accordingly, Sadulaev announced that the future ChRI government would be formed on the principle of the "home factor." Henceforth, only "a minimal number" of ChRI government bodies and organizations would be located abroad and they should "propagandize the ChRI's state policy," assisting only "forced exiles" (*mukhazhir* – an Arabic term for Muslims living under non-Muslim rule) and not simply all Chechens who called themselves "refugees." The new government would be composed of those who possessed "competence, work experience, and allegiance to the cause of Islam and the independence of the Chechen state."[57] It is significant that Sadulaev placed allegiance to Islam before allegiance to the cause of Chechen independence.

Soon Sadulaev's campaign against Maskhadovites and moderates took a new twist. On 8 September 2005 Sadulaev issued an order establishing a commission under the chairmanship of Musa Israilov to examine "economic crimes." It is likely that not only members of the exiled cabinet but also members of the exiled parliament will be targeted by this investigation.[58] Sadulaev then issued a "statement of the presidential administration" which branded the "democratic faction" in the exiled Chechen parliament "saboteurs" and "traitors" and demanded that the Chechen parliament's leadership investigate their activities, warning that "the activity of any political groups or individuals challenging the strategic course of the Chechen state's military-political leadership will be considered state treason with all the ensuing consequences flowing therefrom."[59] All of these moves were clearly intended to isolate Maskhadov's supporters and other relatively moderate Chechens from the ChRI Islamists. They also reflected Ichkeriyan disappointment with the West and signaled that ties with Western governments and NGOs might be cut. Such an attitude was in line with the Chechen jihadists' now open antagonism toward the West and the US. The reason for the Islamist jihadists' consolidation of power lies in this fundamental advantage they have over most Chechen nationalists: they are in Chechnya and control the ChRI's armed forces and jihadist network, while nationalists like Akhmedov and Zakaev live abroad (the former in Washington, the latter in London) and have little influence inside Chechnya any longer.

With the Maskhadovites' decline, the possibility of peace talks with the Russians becomes even less likely than before. Indeed, Sadulaev in one of his first interviews as president stated that the Chechen militants would never again propose talks with the Russians and instead would endeavor to bring about peace by defeating them.[60] Several months later he restated his position by saying that the ChRI would begin peace talks only if they were proposed by the Russians first and on the condition that the pre-war status quo be re-established. That would mean a withdrawal of all Russian forces from Chechnya and the handover of power from the pro-Moscow Alkhanov-Kadyrov government to the ChRI jihadists. At the same time, he stated that the Shura planned to meet soon to discuss peace negotiation terms but that they would be "less acceptable" to the Russian side than unidentified previous ones.[61] Chechen ideologist and propagandist Movladi Udugov reiterated this stance shortly thereafter, renounced Maskhadov's principle of Ichkeriya's "conditional independence" as a starting point for discussions, and defended Basaev by denying that he had ever conducted terrorist acts "in peacetime."[62] Although the nationalists Doku Umarov and Akhmed Zakaev became Sadulaev's vice-president and deputy premier, respectively, both are clearly tainted in Russian and others' eyes by their long association with a terrorist regime. Umarov, moreover, is tainted by his direct involvement in terrorist attacks, and in a July 2005 interview he rejected the possibility of negotiations as long as Putin remained in power.[63]

A Russian-Ichkeriyan accord looks even less likely when one considers the balance of power between the young and perhaps more malleable Sadulaev and the seasoned terrorist mujahid Basaev. It is probable that Sadulaev was as dependent on Basaev's support as Maskhadov in his last years. This was revealed in Basaev's controversial August 2005 Radio Liberty interview in which he stated that when the Shura convened to pick Maskhadov's successor, he had nominated Sadulaev and Sadulaev had nominated him.[64] If Sadulaev were a truly independent leader and the clear senior partner in the venture, he might have been expected to reject or at least qualify Basaev's implied characterization of their parity, but no such statement came from the emir.

Regardless of whether it is Sadulaev or Basaev who really holds the reins in the ChRI at this time, it is evident that the Islamists have taken over the ChRI and are transforming it fully from a nationalist separatist movement to a jihadist revolutionary one tied to the global Islamist terrorist network. Perhaps the best evidence of this is provided by the 2003 and 2004 wave of mounting Chechen-led terrorism, culminating in 2004's summer of terror.

The Turn to Mass Terrorism

The 1–3 September 2004 school hostage-taking in Beslan, North Ossetiya shocked the world. However, this massacre of 332 innocent civilians, including 186 children among over 1,000 casualties, was in fact the logical climax of a years-long bacchanalia of Chechen terrorism during the Putin era. The escalation of terror coincided with the ChRI's jihadization consolidated in 2002. Before Beslan research documented a nearly thirty-fold increase in the number of terrorist acts from 1999 to 2003 (see Table 4). These quantitative data compose the background of what was an equally sharp escalation in the

Table 4. Terrorist Acts Committed in Russia, 1997–2003.[65]

Year	Acts	Arrests
1997	32	10
1998	21	7
1999	20	0
2000	135	24
2001	327	40
2002	360	–
2003	561	–
2004	310	–
2005*	300	–

* For sources on which this estimate is based, see Table 5 below.

scale of terrorist attacks beginning with the al Qaeda-like October 2002 Dubrovka theater seizure, the first Chechen terrorist attack replete with tactics and imagery on the al Qaeda model. In summer 2004 the scale and frequency of mass terrorist attacks escalated throughout Russia, leading up to the Beslan massacre:

- 6 February: A subway train leaving Moscow's Avtozavodskaya metro station exploded, killing more than forty and injuring over 130.
- 9 May: Chechen president Akhmad Kadyrov and six others were killed in a bomb attack at a crowded stadium in the Chechen capital, Grozny. Altogether, fifty-three were injured.
- 15 May: The Moscow–Vladikavkaz passenger train was blown up on the Elkhotovo-Dar-Kokh rail line with no casualties.

- 21–22 June: Over two hundred Chechen and Ingush militants attacked law-enforcement premises in Ingushetiya killing ninety, including Ingushetiya's acting MVD chief Abukar Kostoev, MVD deputy chief Zyaudin Kotiev, and other high-ranking officials.
- 25 July: A senior police officer in a unit fighting organized crime in Chechnya was killed by a car bomb one year after his son was shot dead.
- 15 August: Members of the Chechen-allied Kabardino-Balkariya Islamist Yarmuk combat jamaat engaged in a shootout with security forces in the forest near Chegem in the KBR.
- 24 August: Two Russian Siberian Airlines passenger planes crashed flying out of Moscow, killing all eighty-nine people aboard. Two female Chechen passengers were suspected of having detonated bombs.
- 31 August: A female suicide bomber blew herself up outside Moscow's Rizhskaya metro station, killing nine and wounding fifty-one.
- 1 September: Chechen and Ingush terrorists siezed 1,200 hostages in School No. 1 in Beslan, North Ossetiya. The siege ended in confusion, prompting the terrorists to fire, killing 333, including 186 children.

It is worth noting that the number of attacks actually committed does not provide a full measure of terrorist activity, since it does not include other planned attacks prevented by counter-terrorism operations.[66]

The first effort to expand the war beyond Chechnya after the August 1999 incursion into Dagestan came when militants from the new "Ingushetiya sector," including some 200–450 insurgents, essentially took over the Ingushetiya capital, Nazran, for several hours in June 2004.[67] This attack and the later Beslan tragedy marked the beginning of an apparent cessation, whether by necessity or choice, of mass terror attacks targeting Moscow, and a greater focus on the North Caucasus and other Muslim republics using the network of combat jamaats Basaev was intently building at the time. In an August 2004 interview, Maskhadov himself acknowledged his and the Ingush recruits' direct involvement in the raid by noting his formation of an "Ingushetiya sector."[68] He justified his activities by reference to Ingushetiya President Murat Zyazikov's "war" on the Ingush people, which had "increased the numbers of those who wanted to fight on our side, including among the brotherly Ingushetiyan people."[69] Sadulaev explained the raid's ideological underpinning: "As far as the Ingushetiyans go, we call them and ourselves 'the Vainakhs' [our people] because we are one nation. God says that if your brothers ask for your help, you are obligated to provide help."[70] The raiders who included a good number of ethnic Ingush militants, according to eyewitnesses, seized a large cache of weapons and killed scores of policemen and some civilians.[71] The attack on Ingushetiya provided arms for the terrorists who would conduct the Beslan massacre three months later.

Also, the Chechen-led Islamists probably saw a good opportunity for recruitment and for spreading the war beyond Chechnya, as criticism of President Zyazikov mounted in the republic in response to the increase in the number of kidnappings, the serious rise in crime, corruption, and bribery at all levels of power, and the worsening economic situation. Indeed, the raid succeeded to some extent in further dividing the official Islamic clergy from Zyazikov's pro-Moscow "regime of non-believers," as the mujahedin called it, and at least part of the native Ingush elite. In the raid's aftermath, Magomed Albogachiev called on the president to resign and himself resigned from his position as chief mufti and chairman of Ingushetiya's DUM. Calling the situation in the republic "very tense," he condemned Zyazikov's policies as "against Islam" and "aimed at splitting society and fraught with unpredictable consequences."[72]

An ambitious attempt to incite Christian-Muslim and Ossetiyan-Ingush conflict came with Beslan located in the mostly Christian North Caucasian republic of North Ossetiya.[73] President Putin made no mention of Chechnya in a major speech after Beslan and blamed the tragedy on "the direct intervention of 'international terror' against Russia."[74] To be sure, Basaev's bands were financed from abroad, and Basaev himself acknowledged that two "Arabs" participated in the hostage-taking.[75] However, the truth about the ChRI jihadists at Beslan really lay somewhere between Putin's "international terror" and an act committed by a few radical Chechen militants on the fringes of a just struggle for national independence as described by the Chechens and sympathetic Western commentators.

The ChRI jihadists' motive can be discerned in the ethno-political landscape of North Ossetiya, Ingushetiya, and Beslan. The location of Beslan and North Ossetiya, the area's inter-ethnic and inter-confessional relations, and its recent political history all suggest that the goal was to provoke conflict between the predominantly Christian Ossetiyans and the Muslim Ingush and ultimately Christians and Muslims across the North Caucasus. Beslan is near the "capital" of the small Muslim Digor tribe in North Ossetiya, Chikola. They among others, the Chechens hoped, would be blamed for Beslan by the mostly Christian Ossetiyans. The latter are a particular irritant to Muslims in the Northern Caucasus as they are one of the few North Caucasian nationalities to have largely rejected Islam.[76] They have been, and continue to be, resented by many local Muslims for being a key ally of Russian rule over the North Caucasus since the eighteenth century.[77]

There are other tensions at play in the republic as well. Unidentified elements had detonated an explosion destroying a hundred-year old mosque in 1996 in North Ossetiya's capital of Vladikavkaz. Relations between the republic's Muslims and the North Ossetiya leadership were already extremely tense. Local Muslims had long charged the republic's leadership, then headed by former CPSU Politburo member and Ingushetiya Communist Party boss Aleksandr Dzasokhov, with blocking the development of Islam in the republic.[78] Most importantly, the Chechens' hoped to reignite the Ossetiyan-Ingush war of 1992. This short but bloody conflict left six hundred people dead, and some sixty thousand Ingush were forced out of North Ossetiya into refugee camps in Ingushetiya.[79] Basaev hoped that Beslan would spark Christian Ossetiyan retribution against Muslims, especially the Ingush in North Ossetiya, and that this would in turn spark Ingush attacks on Christians in North Ossetiya and Ingushetiya, reigniting the Ingush-Ossetiyan war.[80] This was also former Ingushetiya president Ruslan Aushev's interpretation of the Chechen strategy.[81] Indeed, the Chechens appeared to be trying to provide Christian retribution against Muslims. During the crisis Basaev announced that several terrorists were Ingush and one was an Osset, and the ChRI ChechenPress website announced the participation of one of its affiliated terrorist cells in the republic, the Ossetiyan Jamaat.[82]

For months after Beslan, tensions between Christians and Muslims and between North Ossetiya and Ingushetiya remained on the brink of violence.[83] Among the Ingush, rumors circulated that the Ossetiyans had organized the crime to provoke pogroms against them.[84] Among the Ossetiyans, rumors were rife that the Ingush knew about the attack ahead of time and had left town *en masse* beforehand. On the evening of 25 September some twenty-eight shells were fired on the Mountain Cadet Corps in Ingushetiya from a forest in the direction of North Ossetiya.[85] By October, there were reports that some Ossetiyans had set up a group called the "Ossetiyan Ku Klux Klan" (*Osetinskii kukluksklan*).[86] On 23 October armed relatives of the Beslan massacre's victims seized the Ingushetiya–North Ossetiya border's Chermen Circle checkpoints on the heavily traveled Kavkaz highway in Prigorodnyi raion, and demanded that the authorities stop all Chechens and Ingush from entering North Ossetiya.[87]

Republican, Muslim, and Russian leaders deserve some credit for speaking out in the immediate aftermath of Beslan to prevent violence, as both Christian and Muslim extremists tried to capitalize on the rising tensions.[88] Nevertheless, the Beslan crisis ultimately scuttled emerging cooperation between the two republics in moving toward a resolution of the conflict over Prigorodnyi raion, the nub of the 1992 war.[89] Anger and frustration in the republic over the failure to prevent and properly investigate the tragedy were "epidemic" toward "Dzasokhov, all the way up to and including President Putin."[90] In 2005 North Ossetiya president Dzasokhov resigned as a result of a continuing storm of criticism for his lack of action during the crisis. In short, although the ChRI jihadists' gambit did not achieve its goal of inciting a larger war, it greatly heightened Ingush-Ossetiyan political tensions.

In 2004–2005 there was a change in the pattern of ChRI jihadist activities from mass civilian terror in Moscow and other locales to attacks on officials and *siloviki* in the North Caucasus. In 2005, attacks in Chechnya decreased even as they increased in the other North Caucasus republics. According to official MVD figures, "only" 69 of the 561 terrorist attacks in 2003 occurred outside Chechnya. But in 2004, some 90 of just over 300 attacks occurred outside Chechnya. In the first ten months of 2005 alone, there were approximately 160 attacks outside of Chechnya in the North Caucasus, with some 110 in Dagestan alone (see Table 5).[91] Whether this was the result of a

Table 5. Terrorist Attacks in the North Caucasus Muslim Republics,
          January–October 2005*

Republic	Estimated Number of Terrorist Attacks
Chechnya	39–100
Ingushetiya	30
Dagestan	110
KBR	20
TOTAL	199–260

* This table does not include the small number of attacks in many other regions of the North Caucasus and elsewhere.

Sources: Chechnya – RFERL Newsline, Vol. 9, No. 236 (20 Dec. 2005). Ingushetiya – author's own count. Dagestan – Dobaev, "Voina na Kavkaz: realii i perspektivy" and author's own count. KBR – author's own rough count.

tactical decision to abandon mass, high-profile terrorist attacks targeting civilians or was dictated by more effective counter-terrorism operations in and around Moscow is difficult to ascertain. While there can be doubt about the motives behind abandoning mass terror against civilians, there can be none about the new strategy of fomenting revolutionary jihad in the North Caucasus and beyond, as the activities of the network of combat jamaats clearly show. This expanding terrorist activity included considerable cross-mobilization from Chechen terrorists to other ethnic Muslims of the North Caucasus. This represents only the tip of the iceberg of potential ethnic and confessional mobilization among Russia's ethnic Muslim nationalities, especially but not exclusively in the Muslim republics of the North Caucasus.

Maskhadov's death appeared to disrupt the Chechen-led Islamist network's activities temporarily. In March 2005, the first presidential decree from

Maskhadov's successor, Sadulaev, confirmed "the unchangeability of the course of the Chechen state" and his command over all fronts and their subdivisions or "sectors" inside and outside Chechnya.[92] Indeed, in a May 2005 interview senior Chechen field commander Doku Umarov, who would soon be named Sadulaev's vice-president and deputy emir, stated that by the year's end Chechen militants would begin small- and large-scale guerrilla-style operations beyond Chechnya, claiming that the resistance had previously refrained from doing so at the late Maskhadov's insistence.[93] Basaev himself promised Russia another "hot summer." There was a mild lull in terrorist activity in the first half of 2005;[94] however, this did not differ substantially from that in early 2004 and probably reflected a combination of the routine post-winter preparatory period and the need to regroup after Maskhadov's death. Late summer and autumn 2005 then saw a spike in jihadist terror throughout the North Caucasus.

RUSSIA'S REACTION TO ISLAMIST TERROR

The rise of Islamist terrorism has probably contributed to the general backsliding on democracy and federalism in Russia under Putin. As the jihadists' campaign of terrorism mounted, culminating in the massacre at Beslan, the Kremlin decided to discard the popular election of regional governors and republican presidents. Officials justified this move by pointing to the risk of radical nationalists or Islamists coming to power in the North Caucasus and, in particular, in Dagestan. In an early July 2005 speech presidential administration first deputy head Vladislav Surkov justified the presidential appointment of regional chief executives by asking: "But would it not be the last straw if Dagestan elected some Wahhabi follower as their governor?"[95]

Putin also called for new legislation to increase security. The Duma quickly prepared amendments to twenty-nine laws related to fighting terrorism, the criminal and criminal procedure codes and the code on administrative infringements of the law. The right to conduct wiretaps and searches without a court warrant was reinstated in cases where terrorism was suspected. Given the anti-democratic instincts of Russian security services, these new rights inevitably reinforced already heavy-handed law-enforcement practices. For example, Moscow police conducted sweeps on 15–16 September, rounding up more than eleven thousand Muslim suspects.[96] Authorities in Moscow Oblast rounded up about 2,500 unregistered Muslims during similar sweeps.[97] The Muslim republics' authorities were particularly aggressive in conducting mosque sweeps and other security measures.

Moreover, Russian nationalists used Beslan to promote draconian measures. Motherland Party and Duma faction leader Dmitrii Rogozin, who supports the dissolution of all of Russia's thirty-two national autonomies, called for direct presidential rule in the republics of North Ossetiya, Ingushetiya, and Chechnya.[98] Prosecutor-general Vladimir Ustinov proposed the detention of the families of hostage-takers, noting the policy could be broadened to include families of all "terrorists," however the term might be defined. The Duma's deputies applauded the proposal as well as Ustinov's comment that the seizure of terrorists' family members should be "accompanied by a demonstration to these terrorists of what might happen to [their families]."[99] Although these measures were not ultimately adopted, their airing created an even tenser public atmosphere as a wave of Islamophobia swept the country.

The Russian political elite's reaction reverberated throughout society. This was no surprise, since societal Islamophobia had already been primed by the Chechen war, earlier terrorist attacks, and a general predisposition to xenophobia. In Beslan's wake, there was a rash of beatings and murders targeting Muslims. For example, Hero of Russia, Magomed Tolboev, a holder of Russia's equivalent of the Medal of Honor and a test pilot from Muslim Dagestan, was beaten by two police officers in Moscow.[100] On 18 September, perhaps as many as fifty skinheads attacked four men from the Caucasus on a Moscow subway train. The attackers screamed ethnic slurs such as "Khach", "Here you go, bitch, for Beslan, for the planes" and "for Nord-Ost and for Riga metro station!"[101] In the most horrific case, Moscow police found the badly mutilated body of a murdered Tajik along with a piece of paper bearing anti-Islamic slogans: "Death to Khaches [derogatory term for Muslim]! Death to Islam!"[102] Islam.ru the website of the Coordinating Center of the Muslims of the North Caucasus (TsKMSK), reported that the frequency of race-based crimes had doubled since Beslan.[103]

There were many incidents of what Islam.ru, dubbed "Avia-Islamophobia"; cases where airplane passengers refused to board flights on which Muslims, including some high-level official clerics, were scheduled to fly.[104] The DUM of Nizhegorod Oblast claimed that discrimination against Muslim women in employment was on the rise, and an Islamic Sunday school director in the region said that "ethnic Russians are not just afraid but hate" Muslim women.[105] Some 79 percent of listeners to the very liberal Ekho Moskvy radio station who contributed to a survey agreed that the spread of Islam in Russia was a threat to its stability.[106]

On the other side, some Muslim social institutions underplayed the reality of the terrorist threat and, like all communal identity groups, emphasized the threat to themselves rather than that hanging over the "other." For example, in response to the arrest of alleged members of the Islamic revolutionary organization Hizb ut-Tahrir in Tatarstan, Bashkortostan and several other regions in the Volga-Urals area, an Islam.ru report seemed to revel in the investigation's problems and quickly switched to a condemnation of Russian law-enforcement bodies' inaction against skinheads, quoting one of their websites: "Russians, a white people, cannot live in their own country, not fearing attacks from some Khaches, Churks [derogatory term for Turks], and other special ones who even from a biological point of view are the lowest race."[107]

The dispute over whether Islam is in any way responsible for terrorism that has gripped much of the world took on a more intensified, vitriolic, and hence polarizing character in Russia after Beslan. A series of media exchanges between controversial publicist and Russian Orthodox Church deacon Andrei Kuraev and Union of Muslim Journalists chairman Ali-Vyacheslav Polosin was indicative of the new tone.[108] Kuraev pegged Islam as the cause of terrorist acts and portrayed Beslan's victims as exclusively Orthodox Christian Russians.[109] Polosin reminded readers that Kuraev had just returned from a countrywide tour with a "Satanic rock group," Alisa, during which, according to Polosin, Kuraev had proclaimed: "Whether in a generation Russia or 'the United Moscow Emirates' will be here depends on you. If in Russian families, in your families, there be only one child, then your grandsons will become a minority in the country, which was once ours. What is to be done so that the cathedral does not become the mosque? Make more Russian children!" Polosin responded: "In Russia at the behest of the 'canonically holy' Archbishop Joseph Volotskii they burned in wooden cages non-Orthodox Christians, forcibly Christianized Tatars and Bashkirs."[110] Calling Kuraev an "Islamophobe," Islam.ru asserted that "despite the official position of the Russian Orthodox Church in regard to the struggle with terrorism . . . many priests have spoken in support of deacon Kuraev's statements."[111]

The Russian media, much of it now state-controlled, also tended to whip up Islamophobia. In a meeting with journalists on 27 October 2004 in Saratov, Council of Muftis co-chairman and DUM Povolzhya (Volga Area) head Mukaddas Bibarsov said that the North Caucasus was developing "on the negative side" because journalists were portraying every criminal episode as a case of Muslim terrorism.[112] According to a content-analysis study by the Sova Center, some of the country's highest-circulation newspapers functioned as anti-Muslim "provocateurs" during and after Beslan. Independent Institute of Communications director Iosif Dzyaloshinskii said scholars had found widespread "subversion of inter-ethnic and inter-religious harmony" in the post-Beslan Russian media.[113]

Growing Russian-Muslim and state-Muslim tensions are interacting with a growing trend among ethnic Russians of disdain for, and willingness to level

Table 6. Comparative Statistics of the Victims of Racist and Neo-Nationalist Violence in 2004 and 2005.

Year	2004		2005	
	Killed	Injured/ Wounded	Killed	Injured/ Wounded
Black-skinned	1	33	2	37
Natives of Central Asia	7	20	8	20
Natives of the Caucasus	14	37	8	42
Natives of the Near East and Africa	4	12	0	6
Natives of the Asia-Pacific Countries (China, Vietnam, Mongolia, etc.)	8	26	2	42
Other people of "non-Slavic appearance"	2	20	0	23
Representatives of youth subcultures and leftist youth	0	4	3	87
Others or no information	10	56	5	109
Total	46	208	28	366

Source: From the Sova Center report on xenophobia in Russia. See Galina Kozhevnikova, "Radikalnyi natsionalizm v Rossii i protivodeistvie emu v 2005 godu," Polit.ru, 9 Feb. 2006, www.polit.ru/ research/2006/02/03/year2005.html.

violence against, ethnic minorities. There is now considerable public support for limits on minorities' civil and political rights. A VTSIOM-A survey carried out in 2003 found that 21 percent of ethnic Russians supported the sentiment "Russia for the Russians" and felt it should have been put into practice long ago, and 32 percent said it should be implemented but within reasonable limits.[114] One out of every four respondents in a 2004 survey felt that the rights of certain minorities should be limited; 60 percent thought that the rights of Caucasian nationalities should be limited, 51 percent – Chinese, 48 percent – Vietnamese, 47 percent – Central Asians, 28 percent – Africans and Jews, and 18 percent – Tatars.[115] Prejudice against the last is perhaps the most dangerous trend for the maintenance of inter-ethnic comity in Russia given its large number of Tatars. Largely ethnic Russian skinhead violence against national minorities, many of them ethnic Muslims, some from the North Caucasus (see Table 6), has reached high levels. To be sure, much of this violence is not directed against Muslims specifically but rather against ethnic groups involved in massive illegal and legal immigration of the kind common in many other countries. Also, the number of attacks on Muslims as such decreased slightly from 2004 to 2005. Nonetheless there were still several brutal high-profile skinhead attacks specifically targeting Muslims in 2005.[116]

The atmosphere of intensified xenophobia and Islamophobia has prompted even official Muslim clerics and other pro-Moscow Muslims to create new organizations and mechanisms for defending Muslims' rights. Several leading Muslim rights' activists formed the organization "Haq" (Justice) to defend Muslims' civil and human rights. Another group formed the Islamic Heritage Initiative. This mobilization may be the first phase of a broader Islamic politicization sparked by the Russian reaction to Islamist terrorism. Such a process could either supplant or feed Russia's jihadist movement.

CONCLUSION

The Chechen quagmire and the ChRI's radical "jihadization" produced a level of terror unknown in Russia since the Stalin era. Moreover, the North Caucasus's revolutionary jihad is likely to continue for the foreseeable future. In turn, jihadist terrorism provided a new pretext for the Russian elite to follow its instinct to recentralize power in times of crisis; an instinct that is stronger in Russian political culture than in the West. The resulting consolidation of Putin's re-authoritarianizing counter-revolution, the police crackdown on Muslims, and the rise in Islamophobia after Russia's 2004 "summer of terror" further alienated many young and some traditional Muslims from the Russian state. Russia's emerging jihad is now undergoing an ominous expansion of the Islamist terrorist network deeper into the North Caucuasus and perhaps elsewhere in Russia.

Chapter Three

Russia's Jihadist Network

The jihadist ChRI has become the central node in an expanding, loosely coordinated network of associated nodes elsewhere in the North Caucasus and beyond. The network consists of a hierarchy of regional sectors, combat jamaats and subordinate terrorist cells. Over the last few years the combat jamaats have become its key organizational unit. The network reaches throughout much of the North Caucasus and, so it appears, into the Middle Volga, the Urals, Siberia, even to Moscow itself. It is dedicated to establishing a North Caucasian or even a Eurasian caliphate on the former "Muslim lands" on Russian territory and is itself connected to the international jihadist movement. The organizational structure, ideology, and tactical operations of the ChRI hub (its affiliated combat jamaats) reflect those of the former global hub, al Qaeda, and the now more independent nodes of the global jihadist movement. Russian analyst Georgii Engelhardt did not exaggerate much when he claimed that Putin's federal administration and its allies, on the one hand, and the ChRI jihadist network, on the other, are now the two most influential political forces in the country.[1] There can be no doubt that they are locked in a vicious and brutal struggle for the hearts and minds of Russia's Muslims and the territories they inhabit.

ORGANIZATION AND STRUCTURE

A Free-Scale Network

Russia's Islamist network, as a Muslim anti-Russian movement, mirrors the flexible but still somewhat disciplined "free-scale network" employed by al Qaeda, consisting of a central hub connecting associated nodes with each other.[2] Its hub is the ChRI leadership, in particular its Shura (see Table 7). This serves as the support center for associated nationalist and Islamist groups, sometimes as the coordinating center for major operations requiring the

Table 7. The ChRI's Leadership Structure in December 2005.

Madzhlisul Shura	Presidency/Government Cabinet
Emir – Abdul-Khalim Sadulaev	President/Premier – Abdul-Khalim Sadulaev
Shariah committee head – Abdul-Khalim Sadulaev	Vice-president – Doku Umarov
Military committee head – Shamil Basaev	First vice-premier – Shamil Basaev
Military committee deputy head – Abu Havs	
Information committee head – Movladi Udugov	Vice premier – Akhmed Zakaev
Financial committee head – unknown	

involvement of several jamaats or cells, as a source of ideological influence and perhaps direction, and as a conduit for weapons, financing and other resources, including those coming from the international network. At the apex of the network is the Shura's emir and ChRI president Abdul-Khalim Sadulaev. The Shura's structure resembles that of al Qaeda, and its establishment at the head of the ChRI in summer 2002 marked the ascendancy of Qutbist/Islamist influence within the Chechen jihadist movement. The al Qaeda Shura's committees for defense, information, finance and Shariah are replicated by the Chechens' military, information, finance and fatwa committees. Just as Osama's deputy al-Zawahiri heads both the Shura and the fatwa committee,[3] so Sadulaev served not only as Maskhadov's vice-president, but also as head of the Shariah Court and the Shura's Shariah committee.

Sadulaev now enjoys an unprecedented concentration of power within the ChRI, at least on paper. Like Maskhadov before him, he holds the offices of ChRI president, supreme commander-in-chief of the armed forces of the ChRI, and emir of the Shura. He also remains in charge of Shariah interpretation as chairman of the Supreme Shariah Court.[4] With his assumption of power a debate began over the ChRI's military organization and political regime. Jihadists began to push for jettisoning the remnants of "infidel" models of government, given the movement's new orientation to create an Islamist state based on the rule of Shariah law. Prior to Emir/President Sadulaev's issuance of decrees reorganizing the ChRI government, Basaev's long-time ally and radical jihadist Movladi Udugov posted an unusually long article on his Kavkaz-Tsentr website on the subject of Islamist state-building. The article, attributed to Udugov's think-tank, the Islamic Center for Strategic Research and Political Technologies, reflected the ideas of its probable author, Udugov himself, and likely those of Basaev too. Udugov argued that in its war "for the establishment of a Shariah state," the new ChRI leadership faced a choice between the two incompatible forms of state organization extant in the Chechen Islamist movement: the infidel form with its elections, parliaments, independent civil courts, governments, and presidents, and the Shariah form, with its emirs, shuras and Shariah courts.[5]

Assessing the reasons for Muslims' failure over the course of a century to re-establish a Shariah-ruled Islamic caliphate after the Ottoman Turkish caliphate's "abrogation" by "the global Zionist conspiracy," the article emphasized the lack of an "Islamic coordinating center," a "Shariah State," to serve as a base for the global jihad against "the world of victorious Satanism." It proposed a strategy of establishing Shariah rule within a small territory and cited successful contemporary examples such as Kelantan in Malaysia, a Turkish village in Germany, a Dagestani collective farm in Kazakhstan during the Soviet era, and the Karamakhi and Chabanmakhi village jamaats which were the focus of an Islamist uprising and Basaev-Khattab's raid in 1999. A key factor explaining the Muslims' failure to re-establish the caliphate, the article concluded, is their tendency to try "to establish the Shariah in a peaceful way" and to borrow the infidels' models of government.[6] But most important are Muslims' deviations from the traditional Islamic, Shariah-determined state-building formula: religion determines the laws that determine state power, which determines the population's subordination, which defines the state's territory. Not a word was mentioned about the need for elections in keeping with even the Iranian model of combining clerical rule with elements of democracy.[7]

A week later, in the 19 August 2005 declaration to the Chechen people in which he announced that there would be changes in the ChRI government, its foreign representatives, and perhaps the parliament, Sadulaev seemed to be responding to Udugov's article. The ChRI emir acknowledged problems resulting from "a kind of political hybrid received from a crossing of Western and Eastern ideologies" in a period of war.[8] However, Sadulaev took only a half-step toward the caliphate model with the changes he implemented (see Table 8). His Western-style "decrees" appointed a new "cabinet of ministers" in accordance with "the ChRI constitution's article 76" and ChRI "laws." Sadulaev himself assumed the post of "chairman of the ChRI cabinet of ministers," which, in addition to his posts of ChRI president and emir of the Shura, further consolidated his power.[9] He also fulfilled his promise to rely on home cadres in the formation of a new cabinet. The membership and functions of the cabinet are characterized by considerably greater transparency than are those of the Shura and presidential administration, about which we are almost totally in the dark. At the same time, he reappointed the arc-Islamist Basaev as head of the Shura's military committee and as deputy chairman of the government and charged him with running the military, security, and police bodies, which include the ChRI National Security Service, an "anti-terrorist center," the MVD, and other coercive and law-enforcement bodies. Although

Table 8. The Known Structures and Personnel of Sadulaev's Cabinet of Ministers
    as of 23 August 2005

Top Leadership
Chairman – ChRI President and GKO/Madzhlisul Shura Emir Abdul-Khalim Sadulaev
First Deputy Chairman – Shamil Basaev
Deputy Chairman – Akhmed Zakaev
Power Ministries Bloc – Shamil Basaev
National Security Service – Director – ChRI Vice-President Doku Umarov
MVD – Apti Sulimkhadzhiev
Anti-terrorist Center – Khalid Idigov
Armed Forces – Shamil Basaev
Socio-Economic Bloc – ChRI Emir, President, Cabinet Chairman Abdul-Khalim Sadulaev
Ministry of Health – Minister Umar Khanbiyev
Ministry of Education and Science – Minister Abdul-Vakhab Khusainov
    First Deputy Minister – Ilman Yusupov
Ministry of Economy and Finance
Information Bloc
Ministry of Information and the Press – Minister Movladi Udugov (website Kavkaz-Tsentr)
Ministry of Communications
Foreign Affairs Bloc – Akhmad, Zakaev
Ministry of Foreign Affairs – Minister Usman Ferzauli
    First Deputy Minister – Ilyas Musaev
Department for Ties with Vainakh Diaspora – Ali Ramzan Ampukaev
Ministry of Social Welfare – Apti Bisultanov
Ministry of Culture – Akhmad Zakaev
    First Deputy Minister – Said-Khusain Alievich Tazbaev

Sources: Sadulaev's decrees "On the Structure of the Cabinet of Ministers of the ChRI" and "On the Composition of the Cabinet of Ministers of the ChRI" in "Ukazy Prezidenta ChRI A.-Kh. Sadulaev," Kavkaz-Tsentr, 25 Aug. 2005, 14:05:31, www.kavkazcenter.net/russ/content/2005/08/ 25/37056.shtml. See also "Prezident ChRI Sadulaev podpisal novyi ukaz i rasporyazhenie," Kavkaz-Tsentr, 11 Sept. 2005, 16:20:57, www.kavkazcenter.net/russ/content/2005/09/11/37432.shtml; "Ukazy Prezidenta Chechenskoi Respubliki Ichkeriya A.-Kh. Sadulaeva," Kavkaz-Tsentr, 26 Sept. 2005, 22:02:57, www.chechenpress.info/events/2005/09/26/01.shtml; "Novyi ukaz Prezidenta ChRI o kadrovom naznachenii," Kavkaz-Tsentr, 28 Sept. 2005, 22:02:57, www.kavkazcenter. net/russ/content/2005/09/ 28/37916.shtml.

the ChRI's armed forces were not among Basaev's named competencies, his other posts, however, suggested he was still second-in-command of the armed forces and of the ChRI overall. Basaev's assignments underscored his central and apparently growing role in the Chechen Islamist movement.

The power of the ChRI's emir/president, though not his influence, within the overall network is limited both outside Chechnya and in some ways even within the ChRI leadership. The wartime conditions prevent the Shura from meeting more than a few times a year. The emir/president is often isolated from powerful field commanders, who are dispersed around the breakaway republic and, in Basaev's case, often travel around the North Caucasus organizing, inspecting, advising, and probably directing the combat jamaats and their activities. Ironically, it appears that the Shura functions in relation to the ChRI government much as Russia's presidential administration does in relation to the Russian cabinet and governmental ministries, bifurcating the executive branch and subordinating the latter's structures to the emirate/ presidential structures. In short, it cannot be said that there is a strict subordination to an all-powerful emir as yet. Although independent ChRI leaders such as Basaev have defied strict subordination, such an approach suits, indeed typifies, a terrorist network.

Similarly, the ChRI Shura functions mostly as a coordinating center for the network's nodes, the combat jamaats inside and outside Chechnya, and not as the apex of a rigorous administrative or command and control hierarchy. Its authority derives from its members, ideological affinity, and access to the international jihad's financial network. The ChRI Shura probably provides some strategic decision-making for an evolving set of republic-level nodes – such as Rabbani's Dagestan front and the Kabardino-Balkariya sector – which in turn serve as hubs coordinating the combat jamaats. The jamaats are themselves likely lower-level hubs for nodes consisting of smaller several-member cells. The relationship between the ChRI and its nodes appears to be much closer than that between the ChRI and al Qaeda or affiliated jihadist nodes around the world.

Command and control in such a network is loose and limited, giving hubs and nodes increasing autonomy the farther one moves away from the coordinating hub. Typically there is less autonomy in the implementation of major or politically sensitive operations having major strategic implications for the overall network.[10] Basaev seemed unwilling to discuss the combat jamaats in any detail in an August 2005 interview but did note their "mobility, autonomy, and independence" to operate within their sector "where, when, and how it is preferable for the group." Combat jamaats are able, in his words, "to work autonomously even for a year."[11] In a March 2004 communiqué posted on the ChRI website Kavkaz-Tsentr, one Musa (probably the KBR-based Islamist Musa Mukozhev) stipulated how best to command and control guerrilla warfare and jihadist terror in terms of Shariah law:

According to Shariah law, groups of mujahedin, depending on the scale and type of scheduled operations planned, should coordinate their actions and notify one another about them whenever possible. If individual combat actions are carried out, coordination is not obligatory. If, however, carrying out a medium-scale operation requires the involvement of a group of mujahedin, they should seek advice from the group's emir, who makes the decision and acts according to the circumstances. Carrying out major operations, which require the participation of two or more groups, is impossible without coordination of actions. Shariah envisages the creation of an advisory body headed by one emir and two of his deputies (*naibs*). The general assembly of the coordination council Shura with the participation of the emirs of the groups or their *naibs* will be held as needed. We are not murderers or bandits. Therefore, the actions of each mujahid should meet the requirement of Islamic law, Shariah. To ensure this, and to resolve controversial issues that might arise, a Shariah oversight body should be created under the coordination council, according to the *kada'u-d-darura* principle [as needed, much as a field court or military tribunal would]."[12]

Although this interpretation comes from a lower-level Islamist structure affiliated with the ChRI and not the ChRI Shura, it probably approximates the ChRI network's practices. Consistent with the idea of a free-scale network, individual local cells are given considerable leeway to conduct smaller operations as they see fit. It is likely that cells know little about each other or their activities. This revolutionary organizational technique well known from the days of the Russian Revolution a century ago, is used across most nodes attached to the ChRI hub and in most international jihadist structures. It prevents penetration by the secret services or the arrest of operatives from exposing other cells or entire jamaats, nodes, and hubs. Therefore, it is only when a "medium-scale operation" requires an entire jamaat's involvement that it is advised that the node's leader or emir should be consulted. Decision-making regarding major operations is given to the ostensibly Shariah-based advisory body or Shura at the hub, consisting at a minimum of an emir and his *naibs* (deputies). Issues requiring such a procedure would include whether to undertake major guerrilla operations and terrorist acts involving more than one jamaat. The fact that the shura is convened on an "as needed" basis (*kada'u-d-darura*) as controversial issues arise, particularly major operational and strategic decisions or Shariah interpretation, underscores the flexibility of the system. Given Sadulaev's religious education and his past experience on the Shura's Shariah committee and in the Shariah Court, he is well qualified to exercise considerable decision-making authority at the center of such a network. On the other hand, to paraphrase something once said about another religious leader, "the emir has no troops," in sharp contrast to Basaev.

The Network's Nodes: The Combat Jamaats
The Arabic word *jamaat* denotes a collection or association of people and does not necessarily imply political or military activities. The benign use of the

term, as distinct from the term "combat jamaat" (*boevyi dzhamaat*), has become common throughout the North Caucasus in the post-Soviet period. Although this testifies indirectly to the growing influence of foreign Islamic thought in the region, it does not in itself reflect radical re-Islamization. However, the term only came into use among the Vainakhs (Chechens and Ingush) when foreign Islamists introduced it with its religious-military connotation of an Islamist jihadist group or community. They and their Chechen associates have now spread this usage to the whole of Russia.[13] The negative connotations of the term in Russia now were reflected in a 21 February 2005 meeting between Russian MVD chief Rashid Nurgaliev and President Putin. When Nurgaliev used the word in reporting on the MVD's siege of the KBR's terrorist Yarmuk combat jamaat, Putin promptly asked his minister not to use "their terminology."[14]

The ethnic Chechen Jordanian Islamist Sheik Fathi brought the term and accompanying structural form into Chechnya in its present military-religious usage when he created a pro-Chechen combat jamaat based on a detachment of militant veterans of wars in the Middle East, Afghanistan, and Tajikistan. It apparently enjoyed substantial foreign funding and thus began to attract fighters from other Chechen detachments. The organizational method of militant jamaats began to expand through Chechen society during the inter-war period, and their radicalism put them in alliance with Chechen radicals like Basaev, Gelaev, and Raduev, and at ideological then political odds with President Maskhadov. Fathi did not publicly criticize Maskhadov, but he did make frequent calls for the Islamization of the Chechen state and in speeches in the mosques criticized the brand of Sufi Islam so popular there. After Fathi's death in 1997, his successor, Abdurrakhman, another ethnic Chechen from Jordan and the religious leader of all of Chechnya's jamaats, directly confronted Maskhadov. In July 1998 his jamaat and others, allied with radical field commander Raduev perhaps with Basaev's support, battled with pro-Maskhadov forces in Gudermes. With the beginning of the second war, the now-numerous Chechen jamaats were reportedly completely subordinated to the ChRI leadership.[15] Maskhadov's former spokesman Mairbek Vachagaev has noted:

Today, in terms of the military resistance, the jamaat units are some of the most powerful military groups in the Chechen resistance movement. It is impossible to ignore their influence, and therefore the statements of any Chechen public figures should always be understood on the basis of this military force. In less than 15 years, jamaats have gone from organizations with just a few members to one of the leading forces on the political and military scene in Chechnya.[16]

In short, the combat jamaats with their emirs, naibs, and affiliated cells are now the military-terrorist organizational form of preference within Russia's Islamist network.

The expansion of the jamaat network beyond Chechnya's borders was organized by radical Islamist field commanders Basaev and Khattab. At present it consists of perhaps as many as thirty combat jamaats across the North Caucasus, not including those within Chechnya, and is built on regional and sometimes more local nodes. The combat jamaats, as in the international

Table 9. Known Islamist Combat Jamaats Active and Based Outside of Chechnya.

Jamaats	Republics/Regions Where Based – Where Active
Ingush Jamaat	Ingushetiya
Khalifat (Caliphate) Jamaat	Ingushetiya
Amanat Jamaat	Ingushetiya
Ossetiyan Jamaat	North Ossetiya
Shariat Jamaat	Dagestan
United Islamic Combat Jamaat "Yarmuk"	KBR – KChR, Moscow
Jamaat Number 3	KChR – KBR, Moscow
Jamagat Jamaat [26]	KChR
Nogai Jamaat	Chechnya – Stavropol, perhaps Adygeya
Islamic Jamaat	Tatarstan – perhaps active in Bashkortostan
Jama'at al-Islami*	Bashkortostan – perhaps active in Tatarstan
Jamaat	Ulyanovsk
Moscow Jamaat (?)	Moscow

* This may be the same jamaat as Tatarstan's Islamic Jamaat (in Arabic *Jama'at al-Islami*).
(?) – This signifies some question about the existence of the listed jamaat.

Islamist network, are supported by non-combatant sympathizers who provide safe houses and logistical support.[17] Engelhardt estimates that the whole combat jamaat network – including combatants, terrorists, and operative supporters providing financial, logistical, and other forms of support – involved 10,000–14,000 Islamists as of late 2004.[18] According to another estimate, this number would include no fewer than four thousand "extremist combatants" or jihadist fighters and terrorists from not only the North Caucasus but also the Volga area and Central Russia.[19] These figures, however, may be as much as twice the real number, especially as regards the Volga and Central Russia.

Making a precise estimate is difficult for a number of reasons: lack of access to the war zone, Chechen secrecy, and the constant movement of fighters to and from the various republics. A general range for the number of jihadists in the North Caucasian Islamist network and even more distant nodes/jamaats can be established by looking at various estimates (see Table 10). Basaev

Table 10. Estimate of the Number of Islamic Jihadist Fighters and Radical Islamists in Russia by Region in 2005

	Number of Terrorist Fighters	Number of Radical Islamists
Chechnya	150–2,500	2,500
Ingushetiya	500	2,000
Dagestan	500–2,000 or more	2,000 or more
KBR	400–500	1,500–2,000
KChR	30–100s	200–2,000
Adygeya	30 (1 jamaat)	30–100s
Krasnodar	0–30 (1 jamaat)	30–100s
TOTAL, NORTH CAUCASUS	2,000–7,000	8,250–11,000
Tatarstan	30 (1 jamaat)	30–100
Bashkortostan	0–30 (1 jamaat)	30–100
Ulyanovsk	0–30 (1 jamaat)	no data
TOTAL, RUSSIA	2,000–5,500	8,500–11,200

Sources: Chechnya – In 2005, there were various estimates made by officials (including Chechen President Alu Alkhanov, Chechen State Council chairman Taus Dzhabrailov, Southern FO presidential envoy Dmitrii Kozak, the North Caucasus Regional Operational Staff Commander Colonel General Arkadii Yedelyev) on the number of militants in Chechnya, ranging from 250–1,500. See "Kadyrov and MVD Disagree on Fighter Numbers," Retwa.org, 18 Jan. 2006, www.retwa.org/ home.cfm?articleId=1699; Paul Tumelty, "Chechnya: A Strategy for Independence," Jamestown Foundation *Chechnya Weekly*, 3 Aug. 2005; and RFERL Newsline Vol. 9, No. 154 (16 Aug. 2005). Ingushetiya – The author has seen no estimates, but the number is unlikely to be considerably less than those for Chechnya and Dagestan. Dagestan – Emil Pain, "Moscow's North Caucasus Policy Backfires," *Central Asia – Caucasus Analyst*, 29 June 2005, and Igor Dobaev, "Terroristicheskie gruppirovki na Yuge Rossii: novyie tendentsii," Evrazia.org, 12 July 2005, http://evrazia.org/modules.php? name=News&file=article&sid=2558; Fred Weir, "Russia Sees Global Jihad on Southern Flank," *Christian Science Monitor*, 25 July 2005; and Vakha Khasanov, "Pobeda rozhdaetsya v soznanii, i lish zatem v deistvii," Kavkaz-Tsentr, 13 July 2005, 00:46:30, www.kavkazcenter.net/russ/content/2005/07/13/ 36053.shtml, cited "local obervers" also estimating more than 2,000. KBR – Andrei Alekseyev, "Est' dannyie o svyazi dzhamaata s Basaevym," *Kommersant Vlast*, No. 39, 3 Oct. 2005, www.kommersant.ru/k-vlast/get_page.asp?page_id=20053930-7. Estimates of Mukozhev's followers numbering 7,000–10,000 are likely gross overestimates (see Chapter Five); "V MVD KBR nedoumevayut, pochemu musul'mane prodolzhayut molit sya u zakrytoi mecheti," Islam.ru, 27 April 2005, www.islam.ru/press/rus/2005-04-27/#8075; Alexander Raskin and Sergei Kuklev, "Chechnya Metastasis," *Newsweek Russia*, No. 1, 14 Jan. 2005; and Charles Gurin, "Authorities Suspect Islamists Murdered Drug Agents in Kabardino-Balkaria," The Jamestown Foundation *Eurasia Daily Monitor*, Volume 1, Issue 149, 17 Dec. 2004, www.jamestownfoundation.org. KChR – According to the KChR MVD, as cited in Ivan Sukhov, "Karachaevo-Cherkesiya: burnaya politicheskaya zhizn', APN, 25 Nov. 2005, www.apn.ru/?chapter_name=advert&data_id=761&do=view_single. Tatarstan, Bashkortostan, Ulyanovsk – See Chapter Six.

claimed in August 2005 that jihadists in Chechnya numbered "several thousand," which would mean presumably at least two thousand.[20] Pro-Moscow Chechen vice-premier and militia commander Ramzan Kadyrov, on the other hand, has claimed there may be as few as 150 militants in Chechnya.[21] Both estimates probably reflect their makers' biases. The truth probably lies somewhere in the middle: approximately 1,000–1,500 jihadist fighters in Chechnya. Basaev's strong influence within the ChRI rests on the large share of the Chechen forces under his command both inside and outside Chechnya. Pro-Moscow Chechnya's senator on the Russian Federation Council Taus Dzhabrailov estimated in August 2005 that Basaev commanded a force of 300–400 fighters.[22] This would mean he controlled at least 20 percent overall but perhaps as much as half of the Chechnya-based armed forces. Being the main power behind the organization of the broader North Caucasus network, Basaev probably had majority support within the overall network. It is also likely that the overwhelming majority of foreign mercenaries were loyal to him. However, the number of such mercenaries has sharply declined from perhaps 1,000–2,000 in 2000 to as few as 200–300 from fifty different countries in 2005.[23] Still, it is clear that Basaev and his allies constitute the backbone of Ichkeriyan military and terrorist forces and the overall combat jamaat network.

The number of recently killed, captured, and surrendered militants can help clarify our picture of the number of jihadists in Chechnya and the larger North Caucasus. There is a caveat which is that the figures come from official Russian sources, and, as with the figures for the current number of active militants, they vary widely. In November 2005, Chechen president Alu Alkhanov claimed "approximately seven thousand former guerrillas" had been pardoned, though without providing a timeframe.[24] Even if this figure covered the entire period since an amnesty program was instituted in 2002 and extended across the entire North Caucasus, it would still represent a rather large, continuously renewed terrorist cadre since most of these 7,000 were replaced as shown in Table 9. It appears that 2005 saw some 300 jihadists killed, 1,200–1,400 arrested, and 49 surrendered.[25] It is likely that jihadists in the combat jamaat network and their active supporters based outside Chechnya now outnumber those based inside. The network's total number of guerrilla and terrorist combatants is probably close to four thousand combatants. Another five thousand accomplices – those providing logistical support such as safe houses and acting as "legs" (nogi) transporting money and supplies – bring the entire network's number to some nine thousand.

Russian security organs' often heavy-handed operations and sweeps, conducted to wipe out the jihadist jamaats, bring only Pyrrhic victories; old jamaats re-emerge in a new place or form, or new ones arise. The Chechen-led network of combat jamaats has spread throughout the North Caucasus and perhaps into Tatarstan and Bashkortostan. According to Dobaev, a combat jamaat is usually composed of many people who cannot return home for various reasons besides religion and politics: they are wanted for criminal activity, have family problems, etc. A jamaat's emir is typically a local resident who is sometimes accompanied by an "instructor-contact" (*instruktor-svyaznyi*), who in many cases is a foreign mercenary. Instructor-contacts are in charge of maintaining weapons, communications equipment, other technology, reserve provisions, and medical supplies as well as conducting reconnaissance and recruiting new fighters. The instructor-contact travels between the jamaat's territory and republic, on the one hand, and the ChRI or even abroad, on the other.[27]

Initially it was unclear where many jamaats fit into the command and geographical structure of the ChRI's forces. In spring 2005 Sadulaev reorganized the "military-political" structure of the ChRI in preparation for the year's campaign. (Winter is usually a downtime for the jihadists because of the mountainous terrain and harsh climate.) His decree provided some clarity the number of fronts was increased from four to six, adding the Caucasus and Dagestan fronts (see Table 11).[28] In Sadulaev's 19 August 2005 declaration to the Chechen people he explained the creation of the extra fronts as being dictated by "the broadening of the theater of combat operations in the

Table 11. Structure of the ChRI Armed Forces and Associated North Caucasus
   Combat Jamaat Network

MARTYR'S BRIGADE 'RIYADUS-SALIKHIN: Emir-Shamil Basaev

EASTERN FRONT: Emir – Akhmad Avdorkhanov, killed by Russian forces on 12 September 2005
(Vachagaev: Chechen and Dagestani jamaats work closely together)
Eastern parts of Chechnya: Emir – Akhmed Avdorkhanov
   Argun Sector: Emir – Islam
   Gudermes Sector: Emir – Abdul Rashid
   Kurchaloev Sector: Emir – Khalid

WESTERN FRONT (Southern raions bordering Georgia): Emir – Doku Umarov
• Sernovodskyi Jamaat: Emir – Abdul Salamov

NORTHERN FRONT: Emir – unknown (Lechi Eskiyev killed in January 2006)

DZHOKARSKII (GROZNYI) FRONT: Emir – Abu Omar as-Seif (killed February 2006)
Northern Sector: Emir – Abdul Rakhman

CAUCASUS FRONT: Emir – Abu Muslim
Ingush Sector
• Ingush Jamaat: Emir – Ilyas Gorchkhanov (killed 13 October 2005)
• Khalifat Jamaat: Emir – Alikhan Merzhoev (replaced Magomed Khashiev killed in October 2004)

- Amanat Jamaat
- Ingush Jamaat "Shariah:" Emir – Khabibulla
- Jamaat "Siddik": Emir-Duka, naib – Abdullakh

Ossetiyan Sector
- Ossetiyan Jamaat: Emir – Aslam Digorskii – perhaps one and the same jamaat as:
- "Ossetiyan Jamaat of Ossetiya 'Kataib al-Khoul'": Emir – Saad

Kabardino-Balkariyan Sector
- Yarmuk Jamaat – three successive emirs (Muslim Atayev-Seifullah, Ruslan Bekanov-Seifullah and Anzor Astemirov killed in 2005)

Karachaevo-Cherkessian Sector
- Jamaat Number 3
- Jamagat Jamaat

Adygei Sector
- Nogai Jamaat
- Unnamed "group of Adygeis": Emir – Marat Teuchezhskii

Krasnodar Sector

Stavropol Sector

DAGESTAN FRONT: – Emir – Ribbani Dzhalilov
Jannat Jamaat (destroyed January 2005): Emir – R. Makasharipov
Shariat Jamaat: Emir – Murad Lakhiyalov (R. Makasharipov killed by Russian forces July 2005)

JAMAATS OUTSIDE THE NORTH CAUCASUS
Islamic Jamaat (Naberezhnyi Chelny in Tatarstan and perhaps Bashkortostan)
Islamic Jamaat (Bashkortostan and perhaps Tatarstan)
Moscow Jamaat (Moscow and KBR)

Sources: "Ukazom Prezidenta ChRI Sadulaeva sozdan Kavkazskii front," Kavkaz-Tsentr, 16 May 2005, 00:54:35 www.kavkazcenter.com/russ/content/2005/05/16/33965.shtml; "Chechenskie separatisty tozhe ukreplyayut svoyu 'vlastnuyu vertikal,'" Kavkaz-Tsentr, 26 May 2005, 09:24:13, www.kavkazcenter.com/russ/content/2005/05/26/34353.shtml; "Obrashchenie Prezidenta ChRI A.-Kh. Sadulaeva k chechenskomu narodu," Kavkaz-Tsentr, 19 Aug. 2005, 16:55:28, www.kavkazcenter.net/russ/content/2005/08/19/36843.shtml; "Shamil Basaev: 'Nalchik atakovalo 217 modzhakhedov,'" Chechenpress.org, 17 Oct. 2005, www.chechenpress.info/events/2005/10/17/02.shtml; "Zayavlenie boitsov osetinskogo Soprotivleniya v svyazi s vzryvami gazoprovodov," Chechenpress.org, 26 Jan. 2006, www.chechenpress.net/events/2006/01/26/11.shtml; *Marat Teuchezhskii ot imeni gruppy musulman adygov, prinyavshchikh reshenie vyiti na Dzhikhad*, "Dzhikhad – eto sredstvo usmireniya zla," Kavkaz-Tsentr, 4 May 2006, 00:49:55, www.kavkazcenter.com/russ/content/2006/05/04/44253.shtml; and "Osetinskii Dzhamaat preduprezhdaet," Kavkaz-Tsentr, 22 April 2006, 13:59:34, www.kavkazcenter.com/russ/content/2006/04/22/43942.shtml.

Caucasus."[29] Sadulaev's transfer of the North Caucasian sectors from the command of the less Islamist Umarov's western front in order to form a separate Caucasus front suggests again the jihadists' growing control over the movement and its direction beyond Chechnya. The Caucasus front is headed by the Sadulaev-appointed emir Abu Muslim. The fronts are further broken down into thirty-five *sektory* (sectors) or *napravlenii* (directions). According to one source, the sectors each contain 100–200 militants, divided into *otryady* (detachments) of ten, each with an emir in charge; the emir further divides the detachments into groups of three fighters.[30] The combat jamaats appear to fall in the command hierarchy between sectors and detachments, being composed of several detachments or groups subordinated to one emir. Although many of the combat jamaats declared their allegiance to the ChRI president and emir, the jamaats in the KBR (Yarmuk Jamaat), Karachaevo-Cherkessiya (Jamaat Number 3), and Ingushetiya (Amanat Jamaat) probably retained significant loyalties to Basaev. Emir Nuraddin, the former emir of the eastern front, was appointed Basaev's deputy on the Shura's military committee in May 2005, suggesting an effort by Sadulaev to check Basaev's power over the jamaats beyond Chechnya's borders.[31] However, Nuraddin was subsequently replaced by al Qaeda operative Abu Havs some time later.

There is considerable qualitative data showing that the expanding jihadist revolution includes cross-mobilization of non-Chechen Muslims by Chechen terrorists – the tip of an iceberg of potential ethnic and confessional mobilization among Russia's ethnic Muslims in their titular republics. Combat jamaats first appeared in the eastern North Caucasus republics of Chechnya, Ingushetiya, and Dagestan. Whereas the names of such jamaats based in Chechnya were previously given little publicity in either official Chechen or Russian sources, they are now being mentioned more frequently in both. A "Sidik Jamaat" was mentioned by Kavkaz-Tsentr in a report on its emir, Abdullakh, when he was killed by Russian forces in December 2005. Earlier, Russian sources had reported the killing of Magomed Vagapov, emir of Goitinskii Jamaat, and Aslan Salamov, emir of Sernovodskyi Jamaat.[32]

The emergence of combat jamaats in Ingushetiya is not surprising; they simply spread from the neighboring Chechens, the Ingushetiyans' fraternal Vainakh people. Besides Dagestan, Ingushetiya probably has the largest number of jihadists and combat jamaats, though the exact numbers are unknown. On 4 June 2005, an analytical article on the jihadists' website Kavkaz-Tsentr asserted with some justification that Ingushetiya, along with Dagestan, had turned out to be among the "most vulnerable" republics in the North Caucasus and that the Ingush mujahedin were proving the most capable.[33] However, the number of terrorist attacks in the republic during the Putin era has not been as great as in some other North Caucasus republics, such as Dagestan. An official Ingush publication counted 5 terrorist attacks in 2000, 9 in 2001, 11 in 2002, 29 in 2003, 19 in 2004, and 6 in the first seven months of 2005.[34] The latter article was clearly intended to show that Ingusehtiya's president, Murat Zyazikov, was more effective in the battle with terrorists in contrast to his counterparts in other North Caucasus republics. As if in answer to this claim, late summer and early autumn 2005 and spring 2006 saw a surge in terrorist attacks in the republic. Previously, Ingushetiyan combat jamaats appeared to serve only as staging venues, providing supply depots and safe houses for operations being planned elsewhere: Beslan, for instance.

Ingushetiya's Khalifat (Caliphate) combat jamaat reportedly "abetted" the forces that seized Beslan's School No. 1. Khalifat's emir, Magomed Khashiev, according to Russian deputy prosecutor general Nikolai Shepel, was in contact with terrorists in the Beslan school by telephone. In October 2004 Khashiev was killed by Russian forces and was replaced as emir by one Alikhan Merzhoev.[35] Khalifat took part in the June 2004 raid by hundreds of Ingush, Chechen, and other Islamist fighters on *siloviki* premises in Ingushetiya's capital, Nazran, and in other localities in the republic. Arab al Qaeda operatives Abu al-Valid and Abu Dzeit helped train and finance Khalifat.[36] According to Ingushetiya's law-enforcement organs, Khalifat was also behind an assassination attempt that injured Ingushetiya premier Ibrahim Malgasov and Nazran's MVD chief Dzhabrail Kostoev. In September 2005, according to the FSB, Russian forces cornered and killed Khalifat's new emir, Merzhoev, in his home in the Ingushetiyan village of Karabulak.[37]

Ingush Jamaat is a large combat jamaat apparently encompassing a series of logistical, support, and small combat jamaats throughout the republic. It was a major participant in the June 2004 raid on police stations in the republic, the Beslan school hostage-taking and massacre, and the October 2005 Nalchik (KBR) raid. Its emir was Ilyas Gorchkhanov until his death during the same Nalchik raid.[38] He was subordinated to one "Akhmad," who was appointed as emir and commander of the ChRI's Ingush sector by Sadulaev in May 2005.[39] The Ingushetiya-based Amanat (Silence) Jamaat emerged in March 2005 and, according to Russian law-enforcement agencies, was assigned the new role of deploying poisonous substances such as cyanide on a mass scale in terrorist attacks. Amanat's leader, Alash Daudov, a former Groznyi raion internal-affairs worker, defected to the pro-Chechen Arab field commanders during the present Chechen war. According to information from Russian security officials, Amanat Jamaat may be one of several combat jamaats in Ingushetiya and Chechnya led by Jordanian al Qaeda emissary Abu Mudzhaid (Mujaid). Amanat was reported by Russian officials to have been behind a series of pre-empted terrorist acts involving suicide bombers and two powerful poisons.[40]

The North Ossetiyan republic's Ossetiyan Jamaat is led by Aslam Digorskii, apparently an ethnic Digor, a Muslim ethnic Ossetiyan sub-group. According to the Chechen separatists' own website, Kavkaz-Tsentr, the Ossetiyan Jamaat participated in the Beslan attack and is subordinated to the Chechen command of President Sadulaev.[41] It appears that North Ossetiya has at least one other jamaat, since Kavkaz-Tsentr reported an October 2005 attack on Chechen "apostates" by a group of mujahedin headed by one "emir Saad."[42]

Dagestan was first home to a series of Islamist jamaats in 1999 which became the core focus of the August invasion of that year into the republic by Basaev and Khattab and upon which they hoped to establish a bridgehead for the foundation of an Islamist North Caucasus caliphate. At present, according to estimates, there are ten or more combat jamaats in Dagestan, many subordinated to a hub jamaat led by Basaev associate and emir of Dagestan Rabbani Khalilov.[43] The Jannat and Shariah jamaats emerged into the open in 2004. Dagestan law-enforcement agencies appeared to have killed Jannat's leaders in Makhachkala in January 2005, but the body of its emir, Rasul Makasharipov, was never found.[44] Jannat was indeed extinguished, but Makasharipov re-emerged in March as emir of Shariah Jamaat. In a March 2005 statement he pledged Shariah Jamaat's allegiance to the emir of Dagestan, Khalilov, and through him to the new ChRI president, Sadulaev, and his battle plan for 2005.[45] Shariah Jamaat was behind tens – perhaps nearly one hundred – attempted and successful assassinations and terrorist attacks in 2004–2005 in Dagestan.[46]

In 2002, combat jamaats began to emerge in the western North Caucasus dominated by the Muslim Circassian ethnic groups – Kabards, Cherkess, and Adygeis – divided across their respective titular Muslim republics, the KBR, the KChR, and Adygeya. The most prominent combat jamaat in the western North Caucasus is the KBR's "United Islamic Combat Jamaat 'Yarmuk,'" discussed in Chapter Five. One FSB general claims Basaev's close associate, the late Khattab, "increasingly withdrew from the Chechens and came increasingly to trust Karachais and Kabards."[47] This suggests that Yarmuk's emergence was part of the international jihadists' strategy of expanding the Chechen war to the western North Caucasus. It may also reflect the al Qaeda practice of recruiting outside the core group or organization for such operations as suicide bombings.[48] Yarmuk's first members were separatist veterans of the 1994–96 Russo-Chechen war trained by Basaev and Khattab. The jamaat was formed during the second war in summer 2002 in Georgia's Pankisi Gorge from among KBR residents who had joined Basaev-allied Chechen separatist field commander Ruslan Gelaev's detachment.[49] By autumn/winter 2004–05, Yarmuk was the highest-profile combat jamaat outside Chechnya and marked the breakthrough of Islamist radicalism and revolutionary jihad into the western North Caucasus.

This expansion took in the KChR and Adygeya as well. In 2000–2001, three "Wahhabite" jamaats in the KChR – Uchkek, Krasnogorsk, and Karachai Jamaats – had to be broken up in police operations.[50] By summer 2004, Jamaat No. 3, built on remnants of the Karachai jamaat, was the main Islamist force and political story in the republic. It is led by KChR resident and ethnic Karachai Achimez Gochiyayev, who has been a close associate of Basaev in organizing terrorist attacks. Jamaat No. 3 members have been implicated in several major terrorist attacks.[51] The only North Caucasian Muslim republic that has not seen much open jamaat activity is Adygeya. Adygeis compose but 26 percent of the population; Russians are the majority. However, in February 2005 Basaev reportedly met with "field commanders" from Adygeya as well as Cherkessk, Krasnodar and Stavropol Krais, and Rostov Oblast to discuss plans for extending the jihad across the entire North Caucasus during the year.[52] Nogai Jamaat has plagued Stavropol Krai most and may now have extended the Islamist network to Adygeya. It was originally formed by Basaev in the first Chechen war and still conducts raids into Stavropol, probably from bases in Adygeya or the KChR.[53] With the proliferation of combat jamaals the Chechens' website Kavkaz-Tsentr boasted in a February 2005 headline: "The North Caucasus Is in the Jamaats' Hands."[54]

For reasons discussed earlier, the emergence of the Islamic jamaats in Tatarstan and Bashkortostan would be a watershed event in the development of Islamism and the extension of the combat jamaat network's reach across Russia. In January 2006, Basaev gave an interview to Kavkaz-Tsentr in which he announced the jihadists' plans to "cross the Volga" in "summer 2006."[55] In fact, the "crossing of the Volga" may have begun much earlier. There have already been signs of combat jamaat and foreign Islamist presence in Tatarstan, Bashkortostan, and other regions with large ethnic Tatar communities, including several terrorist and sabotage attacks in Tatarstan and Bashkortostan (see Chapter 6). In a June 2005 interview ChRI propagandist Udugov noted "the organization of a new combat jamaat in Moscow" itself.[56] Given the frequency of major terrorist operations in Moscow, this is no surprise.

Mobilization and Recruitment

The Ichkeriyan-led jihadist network's methods of "recruitment" remain shrouded in secrecy, but it appears that they are similar to those of al Qaeda in many respects. Its leadership and most effective foot soldiers are Muslim volunteers who seek to join the movement on their own initiative.[57] Al Qaeda never engaged in recruitment of Muslims from above, but rather in essence accepted applications from below.[58] Marc Sageman has shown that even before 9/11 jihadist networks were expanding as a result of the spontaneous mobilization of volunteers driven by social alienation and intra-communal (ethnic Muslim) social, friendship, and kinship ties. Sageman's sample of four hundred terrorists showed that 78 percent of members in a terrorist cell were members of a Muslim group's diaspora typically in a European country, 68 percent had friendship ties to other members of the group, and 75 percent had kinship ties.[59] Coordinating hubs of the global jihad, such as al Qaeda, accept cadres formed on the basis of ties to existing members. Recruits are usually like-minded family members and/or friends, who are devout Muslims and join a jihadist organization as a group.[60] This explains the clusters of certain nationals and relatives at various places and times within such movements: for example, the concentration of Egyptians in the upper echelons of early al Qaeda.[61]

Post-Afghanistan al Qaeda has become an ideology more than an organization. It does not directly train terrorists or carry out terrorist operations so much as fund others' operations. Thus, there is a question as to just how much "al Qaeda central" is involved in cadre selection, not to mention recruitment. It is likely that al Qaeda's network-building procedure is much like that of a grant-giving foundation which agrees to sponsor activities depending on the "quality" of the project proposal and the capabilities of the applicant. After applying and fulfilling the organization's requirements, candidates are awarded membership and take a loyalty oath to the emir or commander. Once inducted, new jihadists are expected to perform and report back in order to continue to receive support.

Russia's jihadist network bears the hallmarks of some but not all of the practices of al Qaeda. The North Caucasus network does not consist of members of diaspora groups. Although there are foreign terrorists, even in key positions, they were already members of the jihadist network before being sent to Chechnya. They are not immigrants who, cut off from their native lands and cultures, have become alienated from their surroundings. The many ethnic Muslim immigrants in Russia from Central Asia and Azerbaijan have not shown up in the ChRI jihadist network. In other respects, however, the ChRI network mirrors much in the al Qaeda movement. In the North Caucasus friendship and kinship ties help mobilize radical Islamists from below. This dynamic is writ large in the local village and clan structure of North Caucasus societies. The spread of radical Islam within individual Chechen teips is well known, but a similar pattern of kinship and social relations exists in much of the North Caucasus. The three Dagestani jamaats that were infiltrated by Wahhabists in 1998–99 to serve as a base for Basaev and Khattab's August 1999 invasion and hoped for 'Islamic Republic' appear a case in point. A key social and political unit in Dagestan is the village jamaat, defined by kinship, social, and local territorial ties alike. These close ties within a relatively small, closed group can facilitate the transformation of the group as a whole into one amenable to joining a radical structure or movement *en masse*. In more atomized, modern social structures, there is perhaps less opportunity for the spread of an ideology across such a group, even where binding family and social ties survivie.

As with international jihadists, Russian-based Islamist terrorists are not particularly more destitute, poorly educated, or pathological than other people in their surroundings. Indeed, members of international jihadist networks tend to be average or well-off within the local context, have more education and higher intelligence, and, aside from their militant political activities, are otherwise relatively "normal" individuals. They do not come from the poorest countries. Three-fourths are from "caring, intact . . . upper and middle class families, and were mildly religious and concerned about their communities." "Three-fourths are either professionals (physicians, lawyers, architects, engineers, or teachers) or semi-professionals (businessmen, craftsmen, or computer specialists)" and "are anchored in family responsi-bilities." Three-fourths are married, and the majority have children. Except for female suicide bombers, they tend to be young men in their mid-twenties; the average age is twenty-six.[62]

Though there is limited biographical data on them, anecdotal evidence suggests that Russia's Islamist revolutionaries and terrorists have similar biographical profiles. The new ChRI president and emir, Abdul-Khalim Sadulaev, certainly fits this profile. Similarly, Yarmuk's core members originally left the KBR on their own initiative to join the Chechen rebels in the first war and the Chechen Islamists in the second. Most hailed from the small Balkar-dominated village of Kendelen, suggesting self-mobilization through family and social ties. The first emir of Yarmuk, Muslim Atayev-Seifullah, was born in 1974 and was by all accounts talented and capable. According to Valery Kanukov, chief prosecutor in the Elbrus district, he was one of the best students in his school and attended Kabardino-Balkariya University. He reportedly distinguished himself in Gelaev's eyes by his exceptional organiza-tional abilities and good physical condition. He was married and the father of two, as was twenty-four-year-old Nur-Pashi Kulayev, the only known survivor among the terrorists at Beslan.[63] Atayev-Seifullah's successors had similar profiles. Dagestani militant Rustam Abdullayev, regarded by some in 2004 as "[t]errorist number one" in Dagestan, also fits the same age and education profile. He was born in 1974, has a higher education and worked in a physics institute under the Academy of Sciences.[64]

The two main motivating factors for jihadist volunteers are the Chechen war, the autonomous mosque and the Muslim community – local, in Russia and global. Yarmuk's and the other jamaats' statements are often more Islamist than those coming from the ChRI leadership. This suggests that their Islamist zeal is being generated internally, communicated through the internet and driven by the perceived relevance and attractiveness of the ideology/ theology itself not only via direct contact with Chechen and foreign Islamists.

IDEOLOGY

Ideology justifies and sometimes even determines a movement's goals and indirectly the strategy adopted to attain its goals. The ideology of the ChRI and its Islamist network is increasingly imbued with the Wahhabi theological foundations and Salafist political tenets of Islamist jihadism: the omnipotence and omnipresence of Shariah law in an Islamic state or caliphate, the rejection of ethno-nationalism and democracy as bases for caliphate-building, the obligation of jihad, and the glory of martyrdom.

Shariah-based State

The essence of the Islamist ideology is that Muslims should do everythng possible to live under Shariah law. Ultimately, this principle dictates the creation of a Shariah law-based state or caliphate wherever possible. Sadulaev has provided an explicit statement on the nature of the caliphate to come: "We are obliged to create here, on our indigenous land, an Islamic state."[65] In his first interview as new emir in July 2005, he stressed the leading and pervasive role Islam would play in the foreseen caliphate: "The Islamic religion should occupy the leading place in the Chechen state."[66] He elaborated on this in his first appeal to the Chechen people:

> Even a small detail in our daily life such as conduct during eating, even that is not forgotten by the religion of Islam. Such is Allah's Law, and we do not intend to deviate from it on our path. Any normative acts and resolutions of the Chechen state will be formulated only on this basis. After Aslan [Maskhadov] (the Martyr, Allah Willing) established Shariah rule in the ChRI, he never issued serious resolutions without first getting the agreement from his advisors who were Shariah legal scholars. Our main goal is to help those under illusions. To send a Muslim brother, who is violating Allah's Law, on the true way or a sister under illusions, a Chechen woman or non-Chechen woman – there is no difference.[67]

The growing role of Shariah is evidenced in both the actions and pronouncements of the ChRI "state" and its militant leaders. Already, at the July-August 2002 broadened meeting of the Shura at which Sadulaev was appointed as head of its Shariah committee and was designated as Maskhadov's successor, the top military and political figures (the field commanders and the members of the ChRI Shura, government, parliament, and local administrations) were required to take an "oath" to Maskhadov. This was an Islamic oath, referred to by the participants in the Arabic as *bayat*, and it was said to remain in force "as long as he Maskhadov observes and defends the Shariat," not as long as he defended Chechnya or observed its constitution.[68]

The ChRI's political and military organization has been increasingly infiltrated by Shariah law. Even earlier, in the 1 August 2004 interview with Maskhadov and Sadulaev, the former acknowledged that all the guerrilla operations in the North Caucasus were undertaken in accordance with Shariah as interpreted by Sadulaev.[69] As noted above, the KBR-based Musa detailed how the jihadist network of combat jamaats and their guerrilla warfare and terrorist operations should be coordinated in accordance with Shariah. In September 2005 Kavkaz-Tsentr website reported that Shariah courts (*kadii*) and investigative groups were being established for all six fronts in the theater of operations of the ChRI "armed forces."[70]

That Shariah law would be enforced in a strictly literal and non-contextualized manner can be gleaned from the statements and writings of Sadulaev and other ChRI leaders. For example, in discussing the appropriate punishment for the accidental death of a child during a mujahedin operation, Sadulaev stressed that Shariah law requires a fine equal to "the value of a hundred camels."[71]

Shariah as Antidote to Democratic "Jahiliya"

In his article "Everything That Does Not Correspond to the Shariah Is Illegitimate," ChRI propagandist Udugov rejects all Western non-Muslim governmental institutions in favour of Shariah-mandated forms of rule, such as the shura.[72] Arguing that the idea of a Shariah-based caliphate is a "counter-weight to the democratic point of view," he explicitly references Qutb and his view that "the modern Western world (despite the presence of God's revelation) continues to be in a state of jahiliya and is imposing this jahiliya on the rest of the entire world." Not only does the West suffer from "the ignorance," but it is mired in the worst form, the "complex" rather than "simple" form of jahiliya, in Arabic *jahlu murakkab*, which "borders on clinical retardation." In this condition, "the head is filled with an enormous amount of intellectual garbage." Rejecting his own past ignorance when he played the infidels' game by heading the ChRI State Commission for Treaty Negotiations with Russia, he praised "the firm position of several authoritative mujahedin and jamaats who did not go for *jahiliya's* delights or political light-headedness, but were prepared for war with the Russian infidels."[73]

In line with Qutb's thinking, Udugov firmly places Shariah law above the Koran and Sunna:

As a matter of fact, they can talk about the Koran and Sunna and talk about it forever, and not only Muslims but even infidels. But the Shariah, it is not simply talking. It is the real and concrete embodiment of the Koran and Sunna into life! It is the real and concrete establishment of Allah's Power on earth! This is the ONLY LAW prescribed to Muslims. Usman ibn Affan, Allah be pleased by him, said: "Power can do that which the Koran cannot." For our democrats let us explain that here under "power" is understood Shariah power . . .

. . . Only the Shariah never changes, because it is not human conjuring, but the Law, granted by God.[74]

Islamists use the Shariah in this way so that the power to establish the rules, institutions, and ultimately the nature of the caliphate will conveniently be left to a small circle of selected jihad leaders and allied Islamic scholars.

Next Udugov specifically denounces three basic Western institutions and principles – international law, democratic rule, and elections:

Truly, we believe in this! And once more we believe in this! And all Muslims believe in this, and they fear those roads that lead to Hell! Therefore, a question naturally arises: What relation to the Sunna, willed to us by the Prophet, . . . or the true caliphs, does the demand to observe "international law," "the rules of the UN," and "democracy" have? And we answer – not any!

Explaining why the jihadists reject international law and democracy, he asserts plainly: "Justice can only be from Allah, and this justice is called the Shariah. All the rest that is thought up by people themselves is only an imitation of 'justice' and from the devil." Reiterating the point, he quotes a hadith from the Sunna where Mohammed urges his followers not to "deviate" from his teachings and those of the "true caliphs," and "not to allow any innovations for each of them is a human invention and in each invention is a delusion and, in some, the road straight to Hell." Decrying Chechen "national democrats," Udugov sums up: "Yes, we confirm that democracy contradicts the Shariah, and therefore we are exactly for the Shariah, and not for democracy."[75]

In a long excursus reviewing the conspiratorial and bloody history of succession struggles since Mohammed's death, Udugov shows rather persuasively that the historical practice of politics under Islam has been anything but democratic. His point is to demonstrate not merely that history holds lessons for the present but that the shura model of concentrated power must be replicated precisely in present and future practice. Udugov concludes:

Such is a short history of the election of the first true caliph. Here it is easily visible that a small group of authoritative companions, agreeing between themselves, elected the caliph and presented him to the rest. The rest in succession, not arguing, not discussing, and not arranging a "referendum," took an oath to this leader. Such is the method of election of a leader approved in Islam, and it is obvious that they elect him not by "universal secret ballot," as our democrats imagine, but a small group of authoritative people of the country or people elects him . . .

Many tribes of Bedouins considered themselves free from any given obligations after the Prophet's death . . . False prophets appeared who tried to drive people from the path [of Allah], and leaders appeared who decided to move away from the religion of Islam. In the present Western terminology, there appeared, so to speak, a "democratic opposition to the 'Medinian clerical regime.'" Abu Bakr, Allah be pleased by him, organized eleven large contingents who brutally suppressed all the heretics.

If the thought has come to someone to call the history of the election of Abu Bakr a "democratic process," this can also be explained by ignorance.[76]

Udugov's views and those of similar Caucasus jihadists run directly counter to the views of some Muslim reformers who argue that not only is there no contradiction between Islamic and democratic principles, but that traditional Islamic thought and practice include elements of constitutionalism and even elections.[77]

Umma over Ethno-National "Apartments"

Pan-Islamism is the ideological foundation of the strategic choice taken to expand the jihad to the entire North Caucasus and beyond. Russia's Muslims, as part of the umma, should be united in a single Shariah-based caliphate and not be seduced and divided by the Western notion of national self-determination. For example, Udugov renounces "nationalism and national apartments,"explicity invoking Osama bin Laden's mentor, Abdullah Azzam. Udugov thus rejects a revival of Chechen statehood, which he regards as having been destroyed during the second Chechen war. He proposes instead that Sadulaev has become de jure and de facto the "imam of the Caucasus" (note – not just the North Caucasus) by virtue of the oaths of loyalty taken to him by the North Caucasus's jihadist combat jamaats.[78]

In sum, the ChRI leadership's traditionalist or Islamist view of Shariah is sharply opposed to the reformist or rationalist view. It is regarded as the product of divine, not human inspiration and should be an integral part of building an Islamic state. Most importantly, these ideological tenets define a revolutionary goal broader than Chechen or even North Caucasus independence: the establishment on any Russian territory where Muslims live of an Islamist caliphate ruled on the basis of the strictest traditionalist interpretation of Shariah law.

There is much in the Salafi and Wahhabi ideologies that may resonate among Russia's ethnic Muslims in both the historical and post-Soviet contexts. Qutb, other Salafists, and even Wahhabis have explained the decline of Islam and Islamic civilization as a consequence of Muslims' abandonment of the true path as originally set forth by their earliest forebears. Similarly, Chechen and other nationalists among Russia's ethnic Muslims, especially in the North Caucasus, are being told and perhaps convinced by ChRI Islamists that their subjugation to Russian rule is a result of their imperfect or incomplete Islamization before imperial Russia's expansion into the Caucasus.[79] The ChRI jihadists' emphasis on Muslims' deviations from Allah's path in the context of a general crisis of values reflected in rampant greed, corruption, and promiscuity in post-Soviet Russian society and culture is a powerful one, even to semi-devout Muslims.

The Culture of Jihad and Martyrdom

Salafists like Qutb hail violent revolutionary jihad and martyrdom as the only way for Muslims to gain self-determination under Shariah law. Today's international jihadists adhere to and promote the militant interpretation of jihad according to which it is one of the Five Pillars of Islam and therefore an obligation for all Muslims. The duty of martyrdom is always paired with the duty of jihad.[80] Similarly, the leader of Russia's Islamists repeatedly issue calls on the internet for Muslims to fulfill their "obligation" to support jihad and are conciously endeavoring to create the Islamist-specific "culture of martyrdom."[81] Using the Arab term for "apostate" (*munafik*), Sadulaev warns Russia's Muslims: "It is possible for one to enter Heaven only in the event that [one] fulfills the will of Allah."[82] What is Allah's will? In his June 2005 "appeal to the people" Sadulaev defined it in a prayer-like homage as jihad and martyrdom:

> The straight way is the true way; this is our way. And we are conducting jihad in order to attain the right to go along this way [of Islam]. . .
> "Allah tests us in order to clarify who has come to believe the truth."
> Allah knows all ours that is secret and manifest. Through trials Allah reveals the true believers for our selves.
> "And to bring out from you the Martyrs."
> To bring them near to Him.
> "And Allah does not love the makers of injustice."
> And Allah says more:

"To cleanse those who have come to believe from you."

Just as they temper and cleanse iron from various admixtures, so Allah cleanses us. Only trials cleanse people.

"Do you really think that you will enter Heaven before Allah distinguishes from among you those who complete Jihad and who endure" . . .

"And those who respond to Allah's call are those He awards."

Of those who keep to Allah's religion

"Not one soul will die, except with Allah's attribution."

If we die it is only according to God's assent.

In such a case what holds us back from the true path? Islamic scholars say that when the enemy steps onto Islamic land, the Muslim should slay [him], but only with the intention of ennobling the Word of God. The jihad of the person who does not know this rule and goes to war with the knowledge that he is defending Muslim land, freeing it from the enemy, will also be accepted by Allah. The Prophet Mohammed, Allah bless him, speaks about this and welcomes it:

"He who is killed defending his honor will be a Martyr. [He] who is killed defending his blood life is a Martyr. [He] who defends property is a martyr."[83]

ChRI-associated, KBR-based Islamists, for example, have searched for legal justifications of jihad in the Koran and Shariah. According to the aforementioned Musa, after Russian forces killed Atayev-Seifullah, first emir of the KBR combat jamaat Yarmuk, all Muslims were required by Shariah law to join in jihad against non-believers. The sin of abstention from jihad, according to Musa, renders a Muslim a non-believer, who having "left Islam" is worthy only of death like other non-believers.[84] Musa interpreted the January 2005 killing of Atayev-Seifullah, his wife, and two-year-old son by Russian troops in terms of jihadist martyrdom: "Emir Seifullah showed a fine example of how a Muslim should defend his family and honor from the Russian aggressors and their loyal dogs. He concluded an advantageous deal and received a great profit which Allah promises those who carry out a true trade in the name of jihad."[85]

Symbolism and Discourse

The semiotics in official communiqués from the ChRI and leaders across its network have begun to signal a fervent Islamist revolutionary élan. There are now repeated incantations to Allah and frequent citations from the Koran and Sunna in statements and declarations. Whereas Maskhadov's Islamic salutations to Allah at the beginning of interviews were typically limited to one line, we now hear statements of the following kind from Sadulaev when he begins an interview:

I run to Allah from the evil of the cursed Satan! In the name of Allah the Compassionate and Merciful! Praise to Allah, the Ruler of worlds! Allah's Peace and Mercy to the best of the prophets, his family, his accomplices, and all Muslims! The Peace and Mercy of Allah to you! I will answer the questions of the correspondent of Radio Liberty Aslan Dukaev, God willing![86]

Caucasus jihadist symbolism is even reidentifying individual Chechens with the Arab Muslim world. Basaev, for example, took an Arab name: "Abdallah Shamil Abu Idris".

The local combat jamaats' statements are also replete with references to Allah, citations from, and extremist interpretations of the Koran and of Shariah law, and the inflammatory language of radical Islam. For example, in justifying the obligatory jihad for all Muslims Musa wrote about the KBR leadership's actions in typical Islamist fashion, lacing his explanation with references to blood and Satan: "All this was accompanied by an uncensored abuse of the Most High Allah and His messenger Mohammed, Allah bless and welcome him. . . . Soon Satan's servants spilled the first blood."[87] Dagestan's Shariah Jamaat likewise includes numerous citations from the Koran in its communiqués to justify its guerrilla and terrorist operations.[88]

The ChRI network does not differ appreciably from the rest of the global jihad in its attitudes toward the US, the West, Israel, and Jewish people. Despite the lack of an open declaration of jihad against the West and the US, Russia's jihadist websites reveal a seething hatred for them. In the end, this aspect of the ideology also shapes the movement's goals and strategy (see Chapter 7).

These theological and ideological trends are likely to strengthen as the changeover from the Dudaev to the Sadulaev generation continues. This development resembles a similar second-generation radicalization of the Islamist orientation that occurred with the ascendancy of bin Laden's al Qaeda after the assassination of Abdullah Azzam.

Theology, Ideology, Rationality, and Jihadist Politics

Despite all the theological histrionics, like its global counterpart Russia's burgeoning jihadist movement is as much a political as a religious phenomenon. Theo-ideology certainly narrows the behavioral and political options open to Islamists. As with other movements that utilize suicide bombings and missions, there is a certain "bounded rationality" operating within it.[89] Even this explanation of seemingly irrational behavior does not capture the reality of the tensions between theo-ideology and political interests. The almost mystical belief in the predestined victory of jihad sits uncomfortably alongside the hard calculations that need to be made about the correlation between political and military forces. Such tension produces some real ambiguities in the political tactics adopted by Russia's jihadists.

For example, under Maskhadov the ChRI wanted to be seen internationally as a potentially reliable state leadership and negotiating partner for the Russians. This required that the ChRI president maintain at least the appearance of tight command and control over the field commanders and that he should publicly condemn Basaev's terrorism even as he supported him with appointments and the like. (Maskhadov surely hoped that Basaev's terrorist campaigns could conceivably turn Russian public opinion against the Kremlin and force it to the negotiating table.) Maskhadov's apparently schizophrenic policies were informed by the contradictions between rising ideology and long-term political calculations and seem to have an echo today. On the one hand, Sadulaev has not ruled out negotiations, but the weight of most of his comments, those of others like Basaev, and the ChRI's jihadist goals and strategy suggest an unwillingness to negotiate a real peace. In one of his first interviews as ChRI president, Sadulaev announced that the Chechen rebels would never again offer to begin peace negotiations and instead would seek to force Russia to offer peace: "Our strategic mission will be to force peace on the Kremlin. . . . The leadership of the Chechen resistance is always open to a real political dialogue with Russia on the basis of the principles put forward by Maskhadov. However, we will never ask the Kremlin for peace again."[90] Udugov has acknowledged that Shariah law permits treaties with infidels, but he and others constantly cite the Koran and Sunna to the effect that twelve thousand Muslim warriors can defeat the world.[91] At the same time, Basaev rejects peace talks once and for all, and the ChRI's websites are filled with talk of spreading jihad across Russia. Thus, not only are there theo-ideological differences among the rising Islamists and the waning Chechen nationalists, there are also disagreements over goals, strategy and tactics.

GOALS, STRATEGY, AND TACTICS

The Islamist ideology of jihad and of Shariah-based life dictates the nature of the goals and much of the strategy of Russia's jihadist network. The supreme goal is the creation of a Shariah-based state or caliphate. The jihadists' pan-Islamist orientation negates ethno-nationalism in favor of a multi-national *umma*. Therefore, the Islamic caliphate is not to be limited to Chechnya or the

North Caucasus. The culture and traditions of jihad and martyrdom exclude peaceful means and instead recommend extreme violence, including against the mujahid's self, in a single-minded focus on attaining jihad's sacred goals.

The Caliphate

Islamist ideology dictates that Russia's jihadists liberate the entire North Caucasus and establish a caliphate in the region. Qutb, Azzam, and bin Laden have preached that all former Islamic lands from the Philippines to Spain going back to the fifteenth century must be liberated from the infidels.[92] The theater of al Qaeda's operations now encompasses, if not the entire globe then certainly a broad swath of "Muslim lands." For Russia's jihadists, correspondingly, the entire North Caucasus, Tatarstan, Bashkortostan, and necessarily, so it seems, other regions in Russia densely populated by Muslims are potential targets. And they are so not only for the Chechens, but for the global jihad, as reflected in al-Zawahiri's geostrategic analysis cited earlier (pp. 36–37). Chechnya is now routinely mentioned in the statements of bin Laden, al-Zawahiri, and other radical Islamists and Islamic clerics. As the ChRI's field of vision extends deeper into Russia, so will that of the global jihad.

Sadulaev has explicitly stated the goals of liberating the Caucasus and establishing an Islamic state there. In his June 2005 address to the Chechen people he emphasized the pan-Caucasus design for the caliphate:

> I greet all the brothers and sisters in the faith, who take pains on the path of Allah for the sake of gaining freedom so that the religion of truth may be established on our much-suffering homeland and there would rule beneficial morals and pure thoughts. . .
>
> The Russian colonizers will have to part with their centuries-long dreams, not only for the subjugation of Chechnya but also of the entire Caucasus. And then, God willing, they will answer for all that they have done here.[93]

The minimum goal of creating a North Caucasus caliphate is increasingly being accompanied by a more ambitious objective: the liberation of all "Muslim lands" on the territory of Russia and the former Soviet Union and the creation of a Eurasian Islamist caliphate. Both of these projects would further the plans of bin Laden and al-Zawahiri to unite contiguous Muslim lands in a restoration of a great Islamic caliphate lost with the 1921 dissolution of the Ottoman Empire. Accordingly, the Chechen jihadists are beginning to spread their jihad not only to the entire North Caucasus, but also into the Volga's Tatar and southern Urals' Bashkir regions.

Moreover, the ChRI jihadists have shown an interest in small, usually Tatar Muslim areas as far away as Siberia, probably to serve as a base for a restoration

of the Muslim khanate there and its unification with the greater caliphate. A
late 2005 article titled "Siberia's Islamic Choice" posted on the ChRI website
Kavkaz-Tsentr revealed the jihadists' new target: "Siberia is beginning to take
the chance to cease being a Russian colony. This process is only just beginning
but in a number of Siberia's regions – Omsk, Tomsk, Tyumen, and Chita
Oblasts – it is very obviously being felt." The authors argue that the "optimal"
path for Siberia's post-Russian development is a "model built on Islamic
principles of inter-communal relations." The "Islamic model of statehood" is
"extra-territorial," in contrast to the Russian and Western models, and the
"main social formation" is not the nation but the Muslim "umma." Moreover,
they propose that the principle in Shariah law according to which a Muslim
jamaat may not subordinate itself to non-Islamic authorities should become
"the main point" in discussions about future social development "on the
territory of the former USSR."[94] Recently, former associates of Chechen emirs
and field commanders have been arrested in Kemerovo and Irkutsk Oblasts in
Siberia, where they may have been sent to establish jamaats with the aim of
implementing a plan outlined by the supposedly "nationalist" ChRI vice-
president Umarov for the creation of three large new sectors, mega-sectors or
zones – Western, Siberian, and Far Eastern – in order to extend war and terror
to Russia's "economic heart."[95]

The Multi-ethnic, Pan-Muslim Political Strategy

The ChRi jihadists' goal of a multi-national caliphate in the North Caucasus and
perhaps elsewhere in Russia determines their tactics. The Chechen Islamists and
their global allies aim to build a broad, Russia-wide, Chechen-led network by
simultaneously expanding both the theater of operations as well as the definition
of the nation from the Muslim Chechen, to the Muslim "Vainakh" (Chechen
and Ingush), to the Muslim North Caucasian, and finally to the pan-Islamic
community in Russia and perhaps global umma. The ChRI jihadists' political
strategy, therefore, has been to denounce "narrow nationalism" and the creation
of "national apartments" in the Russian or even Western style of the nation-
state. Sadulaev has stressed that the "main policy of the Muslims" is the unity of
all Muslims – "Chechen mujahedin, fighters from Kabardino-Balkariya, the
Ingush brother, the brothers of the Cherkess, Turk, Arab, Dagestani, or Russian
[descent] who have accepted Islam" – regardless of nationality.[96] In a 31 August
2005 interview Basaev left no doubt about his plans to expand the jihadist
network to all "Muslim lands" in Russia: "With Allah's blessing, we established
the Caucasian front this year. Next year we will open fronts in Moscow, the
Volga region, and Urals. Jihad is spreading. More and more oppressed nations
understand they should unite their forces to liberate themselves from Rusnya's
yoke."("Rusnya" is a slur used by the Chechens for Russia.)[97]

The ChRI Jihadists' "Expanded War" Military-Political Strategy

In line with this new political outlook, the ChRI has adjusted its military strategy. Sadulaev's first presidential decrees created a new structure for the ChRI's "armed forces" and separate Caucasus and Dagestan fronts. This move institutionalized a change in jihad strategy; one perhaps resulting from a dispute over the utility of using mass terrorism against civilians and the "far enemy" versus that of more targeted attacks against officials and the "near enemy." As in al Qaeda, the "expanded war" doctrine appears to have provoked disagreement within the ChRI leadership, particularly between Maskhadov and Basaev and perhaps between Islamists and nationalists. Disputes in al Qaeda's early days were resolved by violence and in favor of the more radical position. Osama bin Laden broke with his mentor, Abdullah Azzam, over strategy. Azzam thought the jihad's primary target should be the "near enemy," the regimes in Arab and other Muslim countries. Bin Laden, under the influence of the same al-Zawahiri who traveled to Chechnya and sent al Qaeda's emissary Khattab there, began to argue in the late 1980s that the source of the umma's problems and therefore the target of jihad should be Islam's "far enemy," the United States and its allies.[98] With Azzam's demise and bin Laden's rise, al Qaeda turned to targeting the US first and foremost. For Russia's jihadists, Moscow can be considered the "far enemy." Their numerous mass terrorist attacks on civilians in Moscow in 2002–04 signaled a shift to a focus on this internal "far enemy." The mass civilian hostage-taking in Beslan then seems to have marked a partial turn in the direction of the "near enemy," an effort to incite war on local terrain. The more recent shift to attacks almost exclusively on officials, civilian and *siloviki*, in the North Caucasus seems to mark a further strategic shift by the ChRI jihadists to their "near enemy" – the leaders of the "puppet regimes" in the titular Muslim republics. It cannot, however, be ruled out that this shift is born of necessity as a result of more effective counter-terrorism work in and around Moscow on the part of Russia's *siloviki*.

The mobilizational and organizational concomitant of this more recent strategy is to establish and transform small combat jamaats on the basis of either Islamic (ethnic Muslim) nationalist groups or, where possible, already existing purely Islamist feeling in Russia's Muslim republics. The goal is then to transform sentiments in favour of national self-determination and secession into a struggle for a Shariah-based way of life, which is attainable only with full self-determination under an Islamist caliphate. This political strategy is perhaps viable, since people in more traditional societies, not only in Russia but throughout most of the former USSR and the Balkans, tend to equate nationality with religion. The strategy is being applied to all of the North Caucasus ethnic Muslim peoples and increasingly so among the Tatars of the Volga, Urals, and Siberian areas.

In its operations involving the North Caucasus fronts, sectors, and combat jamaats the Chechen-led Islamist network seems to employ the "strategy of the bee," continually rotating them and their targets. As soon as the leader of Yarmuk was killed in January 2005 in the wake of a major wave of attacks in the KBR, an even more ferocious terror campaign was begun in Dagestan by the combat jamaat Shariah. When its leader was killed in August 2005, North Ossetiya and then Ingushetiya started to experience a major increase in terrorist attacks, including ones on Ingushetiya's prime minister and his deputy.[99] This appears to be the "tactic of the bee," as described by Maskhadov, but applied on the strategic level. According to one source, which cites videotape evidence, Maskhadov gave the following tactical instructions to his field commanders: "Here on these two routes . . . at first give them this place, then give them this place here, then this place, that is, change places, then send them from here, then send them there. That is continuously, each day make them work in shifts. One group moves out, and two rest." On another tape, he is reportedly seen stating: "The task is to make one sniper-shot at any form of transport, at any police car, MVD car, armored personnel carrier. One sniper-shot is made and he leaves. The next day, the next group moves in."[100] Whether rotation on the strategic level is dictated by a need to conserve supplies and finances is difficult to ascertain.

There are several advantages to ChRI's expanded-war doctrine. By forcing the Russians to extend the zone of their operations it removes resources from its Chechnya base. The strategy has already served to spread out existing Russian deployments and required additional forces across the North Caucasus. It is also likely to force the Russians to expend greater material and financial resources. There were extra deployments of MVD and FSB personnel to the KBR and KChR in the conduct of sweeps in March 2005. A leaked draft of the Beslan investigation commission's final report included a proposal to expand the "zone of anti-terrorist operations" from the more limited Chechnya war zone to encompass "the republics of Ingushetiya, Dagestan and North Ossetiya."[101] In summer 2005, Moscow had to send several thousand additional MVD troops and special forces to the North Caucasus. In September 2005 the Russian defense ministry announced that it was establishing as a priority the creation of special "mountain forces" in order to conduct operations across the area. This immediately presented a challenge. North Caucasus military district commander Aleksandr Baranov reported a shortage of "special equipment" needed for outfitting the new "high-priority" mountain troops. [102] Two new military bases were also announced, one in the KBR and one in Dagestan, in order to combat the expanding theater of Islamist militants' operations.

In addition, just as al Qaeda has drawn the US into combat with indigenous peoples in lands where mujahedin operatives or associates were active, so the

Chechens, by expanding war and terror outside Chechnya, have drawn the Russians' heavy-handed military and security services into closer contact with ethnic Muslims located across the North Caucasus and potentially the entire federation. Given their less than ginger operational modality, the *siloviki*'s omnipresence increases the likelihood that the Russian state will drive more Muslims toward radicalism. At the same time, the *siloviki*'s frequently brutal exploits can be utilized in the ChRI's domestic and foreign propaganda. ChRI-affiliated websites deftly highlight real and imagined Russian atrocities. ChRI foreign delegations emphasize to their interlocutors abroad that the Russians are "gradually transforming the war into one against all the peoples of the Caucasus" and "genocide against Adygeis, Abkhazis, Balkars, Ingush, Karachais, Kalmyks, Crimean Tatars, Meskhetiyan Turks, and others."[103] Also, by expanding deployment and further burdening the federal budget, such a strategy brings the war closer to all Russian citizens, Muslim and non-Muslim alike. Consequently, the war's popularity has been in steady decline since 1999, when it initially enjoyed strong majority support. By 2003 less than half of Russians supported the war. Opinion polls conducted in 2005 show the lowest support levels yet. Whereas only 24 percent of respondents favored peace talks in November 2000, by October 2002 it was 45 percent, by October 2003 it was 61 percent, and by November 2005 it was 69 percent.[104]

The expansion of the war zone to other Muslim republics also brings into play the Chechen-led Islamists' political strategy of using nationalism among disenfranchised and alienated smaller ethnic Muslim groups to exacerbate inter-confessional tensions in the North Caucasus to drive a wedge between Russia and its Muslims. The ChRI jihadists' political strategy of fomenting inter-communal conflicts upon which they might feed is reflected in many of the areas the jihadists have targeted for military and terrorist operations under the ChRI's expanded-war doctrine.

The ChRI Jihad Network's Evolving Operational Strategy and Terrorist Tactics

The tactic of mass terrorist attacks on civilians has also caused some dispute within the jihadist movement inside and outside Russia. Azzam disagreed with bin Laden's view that civilians, women and children should be targeted in terrorist acts, and was assassinated for his trouble, apparently on bin Laden's orders.[105] Maskhadov's late adoption of the expanded-war strategy and his reluctance openly to support mass terrorism against civilians mark a similar disagreement within the Chechen resistance. Somewhat like Maskhadov, Sadulaev has at times appeared to be torn over the issue of terrorism against civilian targets, simultaneously condemning such acts but defending Basaev and promoting him to higher office. In a July 2005 interview Sadulaev declared that "the ChRI leadership has considered and considers attacks on peaceful citizens, no less women and children, impermissible, including for Basaev." Although this seemed to put some space between Basaev and his new commander-in-chief, the gap was reduced when Sadulaev proceeded to claim that Chechens had never committed terrorist acts against Russians. In raising the question of Basaev's 1995 seizure of the hospital in Budyonnovsk, Sadulaev did not criticize the hostage-taker for his actions but rather the world community for failing to condemn Russia's crude handling of the crisis.[106] Shura information committee chairman and chief Chechen ideologist Movladi Udugov also defended "the volunteer Basaev" in similar terms in a June 2005 interview.[107] More substantively, Sadulaev was unwilling or unable to reverse Maskhadov's decision to reinstate Basaev to the chairmanship of the military committee, which left him effectively in charge of all the ChRI's military detachments. He also appointed him first vice-premier. Yet Basaev continued to signal that he intended to remain a loose cannon. In March 2005 he stated that "neither [Sadulaev] nor anyone else can forbid me, while this war continues, from doing what God permits me to do."[108]

Therefore, terrorists like Basaev will probably be able to resume mass terrorism against civilians with impunity and even with reward within the ChRI jihad.[109] However, the ChRI's shift from mass attacks against civilians to ones against local officials may have been driven by an assessment that the former are counter-productive politically or too costly in terms of personnel and finance. Significantly, there is no known Chechen fatwa from Sadulaev or any other ChRI authority condemning the former practice. Those among the Chechen militants who may be opposed to tactics such as suicide bombings can point to some important interpretations of Islamic law made by less than moderate Islamic leaders to support their point of view.[110] However, Sadulaev inadvertently made clear his approval of terrorist attacks in contradiction of his ostensible rejections of Basaev's favorite tactic. In his "Appeal to the Chechen People," Sadulaev placed the perpetrators of the Dubrovka and Beslan hostage seizures in the same ranks as heroes of the North Caucasus's resistance to tsarist rule.[111] Mass terrorism is an important part of the jihadists' tactical repertoire for breaking the Russian government's will to continue the fight. Thus, it would be unrealistic, despite the lull in 2005, to expect an end to such activities as subway bombings, plane hijackings, and mass hostage-takings.

There are fears that the ChRI jihadist network may turn to chemical and biological warfare. The commander of the pro-Moscow Chechen "Zapad" or "Western battalion," Said-Magomed Kakiyev, claimed in October 2005 that Basaev was abandoning the new tactic of ambushes and improvised explosive devices (IEDs) targeting civilian officials and *siloviki* for a return to large-scale terrorism, but now with a chemical or biological component.[112] Following reports that a special combat jamaat named "Amanat" had been formed to prepare chemical attacks, a series of mysterious mass poisonings or infections occurred in Chechnya and across Russia in late 2005. At the time of writing, these episodes and the strange symptoms involved remained unexplained.

The most important tactics under the strategy of attacking local officials are the hit-and-run ambushes and roadside detonations of hidden IEDs and mines. Such attacks are implemented using the "tactic of the bee," rotating combat jamaats and cells, and are now part of the standard repertoire of the global Islamist jihad, familiar to the international community from their daily use in Iraq. Typically such operations are conducted by rotating squads of three to five militants who place mines or remotely detonate explosive devices laced with shards of metal and other objects to maximize the destruction. Ambushes of police and military vehicles have the drawback of risking great losses among the mujahedin themselves. Like their nineteenth-century forebears and the Afghans in the 1980s, the ChRI mujahedin have become expert in conducting mountain warfare, exploiting the wooded terrain for hiding out and creating storage depots for weapons, food, and medical supplies, and then moving into the towns and cities, often at night, to conduct ambushes and then redeploy.[113] Daytime attacks often target civilian officials and siloviki as they travel between home and work during rush hours. A logical capstone for the new strategy of attacking officials but one that would mark a turn to the "far enemy" could be attempts to assassinate high-ranking officials in Moscow, perhaps Putin himself.

The Mobility of Russia's Jihadist Network
The ChRI jihadist network has shown considerable ability to dispatch its cadres across Russia for the execution of terrorist operations; a skill that should facilitate the formation of combat jamaats far from the North Caucasus. Cooperation between the Chechen guerrillas and the growing number of Islamists from other Muslim republics has led to the dispatch from the North Caucasus of hundreds, if not thousands, of jihadists across the federation for the commission of terrorist acts. Numerous Ingush have been involved in terrorism across Russia. An unnamed jamaat led by Magomed Kodzoev, the self-proclaimed "supreme imam of the Wahhabists of Ingushetiya and Kabardino-Balkariya," saw twenty of its operatives arrested for terrorist attacks in Mozdok and Moscow in 2003. Other Ingush were also part of a brigade of suicide bombers formed by Basaev used in the October 2002 Dubrovka theater hostage-taking in Moscow.[114] The Beslan attack was perpetrated by an ethnically diverse group of terrorists including nine Ingush, ten or so Chechens, a Tatar, a Kabardin, two Arabs, and others.[115]

KBR and KChR residents have turned up as terrorists in other North Caucasus republics, in federal institutions in Moscow, and beyond Russia's borders. All those charged for the 1999 apartment building bombings in Moscow and Volgodonsk were from the KBR and KChR.[116] One out of four men found guilty of organizing the June 2003 suicide bombing at the military base in Mozdok, North Ossetiya that killed nineteen people was from Nalchik.[117] In 2001 another KBR resident, Murat Shavayev, left for Moscow where he would become a Russian justice ministry bailiff and assist ethnic Karachai and KChR Jamaat Number 3 member Nikolai Kipkeev in organizing the explosion near Moscow's Rizhskaya subway station on 31 August 2004.[118] Kipkeev was fingered by an alleged Islamist resident from Rostov Oblast who was detained by Russian law-enforcement organs in May 2005 as the organizer of four explosions at bus stops in the city of Voronezh in 2004 and 2005.[119] KBR and KChR residents were also involved in a series of car bomb explosions in March 2001 in Mineralnyie Vody, Yessentuki, and the KChR that killed twenty-six and wounded 153.[120] In addition, residents of the KBR were allegedly involved in the detonation of a bomb at the military hospital in Mozdok, North Ossetiya on 1 August 2003. Two KBR policemen may have transported the explosives and detonator from the KBR to North Ossetiya.[121] The KBR MVD claimed to have intelligence indicating that residents of the republic participated in the June attack in Ingushetiya.[122] The preponderance of terrorists from the KBR and KChR among those acting outside the North Caucasus in the organization of mass terrorist operations against civilians, particularly in Moscow, bears the fingerprints of the late al Qaeda operative Khattab, who seems to have turned to the Circassian and Balkar-Karachai peoples for support.

Even Tatars have worked for the jihad in places far from Tatarstan. Nizhnekamsk's central mosque, taken over by radicals allegedly with the help of the raion administration head Rishat Abubakirov, produced a female suicide bomber arrested in Moscow in 2006 on her way to St. Petersburg.[123] As noted above, a Tatar from Tatarstan's Islamic Jamaat was arrested near Moscow in 2005 while allegedly planning terrorism. The ability of ethnic Muslims from distant regions to infiltrate major cities despite Russia's strict internal-passport and residence-registration regime is facilitated by massive corruption and perhaps some support from Muslim "diasporas" in Russia's capital cities.

CONCLUSION

Russia has seen the emergence of a functional Islamist network largely based in the North Caucasus. This has the potential to spread war and terror to other parts of Russia. Its ideological influence and network of combat jamaats may spread to Tatarstan, Bashkortostan, and Moscow itself. The extension of the combat jamaats into Dagestan marks the ChRI network's movement beyond the Chechen-Ingush Vainakh dyad into the area's most important and fervently Muslim republic. Its expansion into the KBR opens the road to the entire western North Caucasus dominated by the Circassian and Balkar-Karachai ethnic groups. The activities of these combat jamaats have so far been largely confined to terrorist attacks on officials and *siloviki* inside their own republics, reflecting the noted shift from targeting the "far enemy" in Moscow to the "near enemy" regimes in Makhachkala and Nalchik. The rise of combat jamaats in Dagestan and the KBR reflects some indigenous support for jihadism among Russia's wavering Muslims.

Chapter Four

The Rise of Jihadism in Dagestan

There are three major causes of the rise of Islamism in Dagestan: (1) the revival of the Chechen war;(2) the repeal under Putin's recentralizing counter-revolution of Dagestan's consensus-based political system which had previously contained the republic's multi-ethnic politics; and (3) the federal authorities' retraction of regional autonomy and republic sovereignty, thus reducing the Dagestani leadership's reliance on local voters and increasing its reliance on the Kremlin and a select group of ethnic-based clans. The Dagestani state and society are a complex quilt of ethnic groups and clans under constant risk of being torn apart by ethnic fractiousness, radical Islam, limited de-Sovietization, and high levels of official corruption, crime, and poverty. Although ethnic and elite divisions serve to limit the scale of any radical re-Islamization, as politics in the Putin era show, it does not at all preclude – and in some ways assists in – the development of a more limited but still potentially substantial Islamist threat to the region.

HISTORICAL, ETHNIC, AND RELIGIOUS CONTEXTS

Culturally, linguistically, ethnically, religiously, and even geographically Dagestan is rife with divisions and contradictions. Geographically, it is divided into coastal areas and a larger mountainous region. Its eastern districts slope down to the Caspian Sea along which sits the republic's capital of Makhachkala (referred to by Islamist extremists as "Shamilkala," presumably in honor of the leader of the North Caucasus peoples' nineteenth-century resistance to Russian rule, Imam Shamil, and not Shamil Basaev). The republic borders both Chechnya and the former Soviet republic and largely Muslim-populated state of Azerbaijan.

Historical Overview

Before being colonized by Russia, Dagestan was part of Arab and Turkish empires under which first Derbent and then other areas that are now part of the republic were Islamized beginning in the seventh century.[1] As previously noted, although Russia first came into contact with the North Caucasus in the sixteenth century under Ivan the Terrible, it was only in the second half of the eighteenth century under Catherine the Great that imperial Russia began to penetrate the region's northernmost portions. In the nineteenth century Russia began to expand its rule over the entire Caucasus, including the North Caucasus. Like the other regions of the latter, Dagestan remained unstable throughout much of the period of tsarist rule. St. Petersburg was unable to assimilate or tame its Muslim peoples, despite aggressive and sometimes brutal efforts to do so.

Contrary to a view popular today, it was not the Chechens who put up the strongest resistance to Russian colonization. Dagestan, especially Avariya, along with the southern mountain regions of Chechnya would last the longest and cost the Russian empire the most in blood and treasure.[2] Although one of the reasons for Dagestan's relative success was the republic's forbidding mountainous terrain and the Chechens' more exposed, forward geographic position, the feistiness of the Dagestanis played an important role. This in turn can be attributed in large part to local martial and social traditions reflected in such customs as obligatory "blood revenge" for killings and other physical offenses; traditions which are perhaps stronger among Dagestani than many other Caucasian nationalities, except for the Chechens. Another significant factor was the mountain resistance movement's ever-more religious coloration, as Russian commander of the Caucasus front General Aleksei P. Yermlov reported in 1826.[3] Dagestan's Islamic leaders were the organizers of the resistance to Russian rule and the empire's desire to Christianize, Russify, and modernize all the peoples of the Caucasus. Dagestan's Avars played the leading role in the nineteenth century in the North Caucasus, supported by Dagestan's Dargins, Kumyks, Laks, Lezgins, and Nogais, not to mention the North Caucasus's other major nationalities – the Chechens, Balkars, Karachais, and Circassians. Imams Mansur and Shamil, who sparked and rallied the resistance, were ethnic Avars, the largest ethnic group in present-day Dagestan. After subduing Shamil's forward bases and support areas in Chechnya and Ingushetiya, Russian forces under the command of General Nicholas I. Yevdokimov finally delivered a series of defeats to his forces and seized Dagestan in summer 1859.[4] Shamil surrendered and handed himself over to Russian forces bringing an ignominious end to his twenty-five-year- and the North Caucasus peoples' half-century resistance to the imposition of tsarist imperial rule. Russian rule over the North Caucasus began to be consolidated, and in 1860 Dagestan Oblast was established. The North Caucasus resistance nonetheless was considered one of world Islam's eight great military oppositions to infidel rule and gave Avars and Dagestanis great pride and some stature in the Muslim world.[5]

During the Russian civil war of 1918–21 Muslims of the North Caucasus declared an independent state, the United Mountain Republic. In the course of the fighting the Mountain Republic was incorporated into Bolshevik Russia by force. Lenin's promise to Russia's national minorities of self-determination, a promise specifically made to the Muslims as well, was thus shown to have been merely a tactic for seizing power, not a state-building strategy or philosophy for a brave new world. The Mountain Republic was replaced by the Bolsheviks in January 1920 with the Mountain (Gorskaya) "Autonomous" Republic (GAR) by decree of the Soviet Central Executive Committee on the recommendation of Stalin's Commissariat of Nationalities. Today's Republic of Dagestan, like Chechnya and other Russian national autonomies, is in great part a product of Stalin's perfection of the tsarist regime's policy of "divide and rule." His use of territorial-administrative schemes was said by the Bolsheviks to fulfill their promise of self-determination to minority peoples. In fact, Stalin divided individual ethnic groups and often paired them with others in a highly centralized unitary state, thereby endeavoring to break down nationalities and prevent them from uniting into larger ethnic, linguistic, and religious groups, other than for their ultimate merger (*sliyanie*) with ethnic Russians toward the ostensible creation of a new "Soviet man." Dagestan was the first "autonomous" republic carved out of the GAR. In order to facilitate assimilation, the alphabets of most of the Dagestani and other North Caucasus peoples were Latinized in the 1920s and then Cyrillicized in 1938.

Like the Chechens, Balkars, Karachais, and other North Caucasian ethnic groups, some of Dagestan's nationalities were subjected to Stalin's deportations in 1944. These nearly destroyed the North Caucasian ethnic groups. Their political rehabilitation and return in the 1950s sparked inter-ethnic tensions – in Dagestan between Akin-Chechens and ethnic Avars, Dargins, and Laks, in particular. When Akin-Chechens were returned from Kazakhstan, they were settled in ethnic Avar, Dargin- and Lak-dominated areas where good land was scarce, provoking a backlash against the them.[6] The dislike by many of Dagestan's Muslim peoples, in particular the Avars and Laks, for the Akin-Chechens is one factor that led to the republic's rebuff of Basaev and Khattab's August 1999 invasion. It provides a buffer against Islamism's spread to the republic through Chechen agency, though not a foolproof one. Like the Muslim Central Asian republics, the Autonomous Soviet Socialist Republics (ASSRs) of the Muslim North Caucasus, including Dagestan, were given short shrift when it came to expenditure on socio-economic development. More importantly, the region's Islamic way of life was completely uprooted by Soviet power. Islamic clerics were killed or coopted into official Soviet Muslim spiritual administrations and were made responsible for maintaining Islam's conformity to Soviet ideology and Muslims' allegiance to the regime.

Dagestan did not play a key role in Russia's revolution from above, the Soviet collapse, or the subsequent formation of post-Soviet Russia's asymmetrical federative system. However, Muslim Dagestani elites were the leaders of the late Soviet Union's first Muslim political party, underscoring the strength of the Islamic tradition in the republic. Dagestani Islamic fundamentalist, Akhmad-kadi Akhtaev, was elected chairman of the first Muslim political organization in the USSR since the revolutionary era, the Party of Islamic Rebirth (Partiya Islamskogo Vozrozhdeniya or PIV), founded in Astrakhan in 1989. The latter played a strong role in late Soviet-era politics in Uzbekistan and especially Tajikistan, where a brief civil war ensued in 1992 between a coalition of democratic, nationalist, and Islamic parties, including the PIV, on the one hand, and the remnants of the Soviet regime, on the other. Foreign Islamists played a small part in this conflict. Dagestani Nadir Khachilaev headed the Union of the Muslims of Russia (Soyuz Musulman Rossii) or UMR, which survived well into the 1990s, and small successor parties of which exist to this day. However, the central dynamic of Dagestani politics in the post-Soviet 1990s was not religious but ethnic.

Ethnicity and Identity

There is no Dagestani ethnic group. Rather, the term refers to a group of over twenty nationalities among the republic's indigenous thirty-four ethnic groups, almost all of which are Muslim. Over 90 percent of Dagestan's population belongs to traditionally Muslim ethnic groups. Besides Christian Orthodox ethnic Russians and Ossetiyans, the key exception is the Jewish Tats. All in all, Dagestan consists of over sixty indigenous ethnic groups and representatives of 102 different ethnic groups. Of Dagestan's nearly two million residents, 99.9 percent belong to seventeen nationalities.[7] Avars make up 28 percent, Dargins – 16, Kumyks – 13, Lezgins – 13, Russians – 7, Laks – 5, Tabasarans – 5, and the Vainakh Akin-Chechens – 5 percent of the population.[8] Dagestan's main ethnic groups are divided into three categories according to basic language groups. The Muslim ethnic groups are divided between two of them, adding another cleavage to the republic's communal structure. The Avars, Dargins (both the Kubanchin and Kaitag sub-groups), Lezgins, Laks, Tabasarans, and Chechens belong to the Dagestani-Nakh wing of the Ibero-Caucasian family of languages along with nine other ethnic groups including the Abkhaz, Aguls, Rutuls, Karatins, Andis, and Botlikhs.

The languages of Dagestani Nakh-speaking ethnic groups constitute a majority group within the republic. Those of the Kumyks, Nogais, and Azeris belong to the Turkish group of the Altai family of languages. Those of the Russians, Tats, and the mountain Jews, who speak a Tat-based language related to the Iranian (Farsi) languages, belong to the Indo-European language family.[9]

Inter-ethnic competition for political office, business ownership, and land had been the central dynamic of post-Soviet Dagestan's politics until the Putin era. The plethora of nationalities and languages contained in this single Russian region required a clause in the Russian Federation law "On the Guarantees of the Rights of the Indigenous Small Peoples of the Russian Federation" that gave a special dispensation to the Dagestan People's Assembly to compile a list of nationalities that included its small ethnic groups. Many would otherwise not have met the standard criteria qualifying small peoples for inclusion under the law's terms.[10]

Although ethnicity is an important social and political factor, it is complicated by the village or jamaat structure of social and political ties. In the Dagestani context, a jamaat is a collection of territorially contiguous villages often tied together by clans or *tukhumy*. This is another way in which Dagestan is geographically factionalized and differs from other North Caucasian societies, including Chechnya, the social structure of which is built on communities of less territorially oriented, extended blood and kinship ties known as teips. Most scholars and political analysts agree that the jamaat structure and a tradition of seeking inter-ethnic harmony have in fact combined to produce considerable interethnic comity.[11] However, it would be wrong to assert that in Dagestan identity with one's jamaat is nearly as strong as with one's ethnicity. A survey conducted in the late Yeltsin/early Putin era among Dagestan's nine largest ethnic groups put identity with the jamaat last across all groups. Identity was with Dagestan, Russia, ethnic group, and religion in descending order.[12] All of Dagestan's cleavages notwithstanding, it is important to remember that the Chechens, similarly divided by nine major inter-teip cleavages and tens of clan cleavages, have managed to produce a fairly powerful, united radical nationalist and Islamist movement capable of busying tens of thousands of Russian troops, carrying out sophisticated acts of mass terrorism, and otherwise doing great damage to Russia, while at the same time becoming a node in the global jihadist network.

In some ways, the village jamaats may facilitate the formation of the jihadist combat jamaats. As the main social unit of Dagestan, the village jamaats offer a readymade small social and political unit within which they can spread Islamist sentiments across kinship and social ties. In this way, the village jamaat may obviate the need to base combat jamaats on radical nationalist or separatist movements that might otherwise be fostered among small, potentially outsider groups not assuaged by Dagestan's consociational political system. With Putin's federative counter-reforms requiring the dismantling of that system, the village jamaats supplement the opportunities for proselytizing and networking that nationalism and Islam afford Islamists seeking to infiltrate the region.

When a rift eventually emerged between Muslim followers of the Naqshbandia tariqat, the predominant Sufi order in Dagestan, and radicals tied to Chechen and foreign Wahhabists, it was unclear whether it occurred along ethnic lines to any degree. Although there is no data on the ethnicity of radical Islamist groups in Dagestan, it needs to be stressed that inter-ethnic conflict within Dagestan can provide opportunities for Islamists to play on divisions, using the alienation of outsider groups to recruit.

Islam

Islam entered the North Caucasus with the Arab caliphate's imperial expansion in the middle of the seventh century, a mere two decades after the Prophet Mohammed's death. With Islam's arrival in the region, Dagestan became and remains overwhelmingly dominated by traditionally Muslim ethnic groups and the most important region for Islamic development in the North Caucasus. Derbent is the locale of the oldest mosque in Russia and it was from there that Islam took root throughout the North Caucasus. Islam never fully displaced local pagan customs in the North Caucasus, however, but rather mixed with them (though this was least true in Dagestan). Thus, Islam here yielded before the multi-deism of the mountain peoples and countenanced the praise of saints, a practice frowned upon throughout most of the Muslim world (except among Sufis) as a contradiction of the Prophet's insistence on monotheism. Caucasian wedding and funeral traditions were also incorporated into Islam's corresponding rites. In Dagestan, Islamic discipline was also undermined by customs (*adat*) internal to each village jamaat, which has its own set of customs.[13]

As Russia began to focus its imperial ambitions on the North Caucasus at the beginning of the nineteenth century, mystic Islamic Sufi brotherhoods penetrated Dagestan. The murids (Sufi teachers) of the Sufi brotherhoods served as a network of underground cells which became the basis for the resistance to Russian rule. Despite the military defeat of the North Caucasus resistance and the relative consolidation of tsarist rule, St. Petersburg failed to Russify and Christianize Dagestan's peoples. In the twilight of Russia's tsarist autocracy, there were some 1,700 mosques, 2,311 Muslim schools (*mekteby*), and 400 religious schools (*madrasahs*).[14] Soviet rule witnessed a much more aggressive, indeed self-described "militant," campaign to uproot Islam – and religion in general – from the region. Muslim clerics were killed or brought under the supervision of the state-controlled Muslim spiritual administrations or boards, and pre-revolutionary Dagestan's Islamic infrastructure of mosques and madrasahs was destroyed. By the mid-1980s only twenty-seven mosques remained, and Muslim education, traditions, and practices were largely confined to the home and secret "parallel" Sufi Islam.[15]

The mystical, often secret Sufi tariqats did survive Soviet rule, and as of today there are fifteen registered murid brotherhoods in the republic. The Sufi tariqatists make up 87 percent of the ethnic Muslim population. The most prominent orders in Dagestan are the Naqshbandiya and Qadiriya. Ethnicity divides all forms of Dagestani Islam. Almost all of the fifteen registered murid brotherhoods in the republic are mono-ethnic.[16] The official Muslim spiritual board's division into regional DUMs during the Soviet collapse produced the DUM of Dagestan (DUMD), which became an important political force in the region over the course of the 1990s. However, the DUMD is discredited among some tariqatists as a result of its association with the Soviet regime and its domination by the larger Avar and Dargin ethnic groups. Thus, Kumyks, Laks, and Lezgins have organized their own Muslim spiritual boards.[17] The Muslims of Dagestan for the most part belong to the Shafi maskhab. Ethnic Azeri Turks and one ethnic Lezgin village near the border with Azerbaijan confess Shia Islam and compose 4.5 percent of Dagestan's population. According to one research survey, 85 percent of Dagestanis as of June 2001 regarded themselves as believers, but only 23 percent reported performing all the required rites, with 62 percent saying they performed only some.[18] This leaves room for further re-Islamization.

DAGESTAN IN THE YELTSIN ERA

With Russia's revolution from above and the collapse of the USSR in 1990–91, Moscow's control over its regions was weakened. Many were allowed so much autonomy that they developed sovereign and unique political, economic, cultural, and social orders. At the same time, the revival of nationalism during the Soviet collapse trickled down to the sub-regional level. Dagestan was faced with a number of serious challenges, including: the rehabilitation of the Akin-Chechens and Lezgins exiled under Stalin; Lezgin, Avar, Dargin and Nogai demands for internal territorial self-determination; and even Lezgin demands for external self-determination (state independence or unification with Azerbaijan's Lezgin areas) in a "Lezginistan." Inter-ethnic tensions ran extremely high. In a 1994 opinion survey conducted in Makhachkala, 52 percent of respondents expressed a willingness to take part in an armed conflict in their ethnic group's interests depending on the circumstances, and

20 percent were prepared to do so unconditionally.[19] In response to this disposition among its peoples, Dagestan developed a unique consensual political system under the auspices of Yeltsin's loose asymmetrical federalism.

Dagestan's Inter-Ethnic Consensual Political System

The Dagestan constitution, adopted in 1994, stipulated a grand inter-communal coalition in the executive branch.[20] The leading executive decision-making body in the republic, the State Council (Gosudarstvennyi soviet), was composed of one representative from each of Dagestan's fourteen largest nationalities elected by the Constititional Assembly (Konstitutsionnoe Sobranie or KS), which had the power to amend the republic's constitution. The KS consisted of 242 members, including the 121 members of the republic's parliament, the People's Assembly (Nardonoe Sobranie or NS). A unique electoral system gave each of the fourteen nationalities a level of representation in the NS almost precisely equal to its share of the population.[21] The other 121 delegates to the KS were elected from cities and raions. Each KS member had the right to nominate one of the assembly's members as a candidate for the republic's top executive body, the State Council, with the three individuals from each of the largest fourteen nationalities who received the most votes also being entered on the ballot automatically.[22] The KS members could then vote for any of the candidates to the State Council, regardless of ethnicity. Thus, in order to be elected, candidates to the State Council needed to appeal across ethnic boundaries.[23]

The Dagestan constitution also provided the legal basis for the only unelected regional chief executive (regional governor or republic president) in Russia until the Putin counter-revolution's abolition in 2005 of all regional elections of chief executives. In 2006 Putin appointed a new president of Dagestan under his new presidential power to appoint all regional chief executives, followed by confirmation by the regional parliament, to which new elections could be called should parliament reject the president's nominee. Until 2006, the chief executive in Dagestan, the State Council's chairman, was elected by its fourteen members and, according to the constitution's article 93, could not come from the same nationality for more than one four-year term. However, the ethnic Dargin Magomedali Magomedov, first elected in 1994, did not relinquish office until February 2006, much to the consternation of the plurality-making Avars and other ethnic groups. The grand ethnic coalition established in the State Council was reinforced, however, by the constitution-ally designed convention of appointing representatives from the largest ethnic groups to the other leading council and government offices. Because of the constitutionally mandated ethnic composition of the State Council, the chairman, Magomedov, appointed two representatives of the fourteen largest nationalities as his deputies, one of whom became his long-standing chairman of the cabinet of ministers, ethnic Kumyk Hizri Sheiksaidov.[24] This system appears to have enjoyed significant, if somewhat artificially inflated support from the republic's populace. For example, three plebiscites, on 28 July 1992, 12 December 1993, and 7 March 1999, produced suspiciously strong majorities against instituting a popularly elected presidency: 88, 68, and 75 percent, respectively. The Dargins and Lezgins in particular rejected the move. A majority of the Avars and their frequent allies, the ethnic Laks, on the other hand, supported the change.[25] The Avars have greater interest in such a presidency, since they form a plurality in the republic and enjoy majorities in several key population centers, which puts their co-ethnics in high-profile political offices from which they could launch presidential candidacies.[26]

Limited Inter-Communal Comity

The institutionalization of ethnicity in Dagestan's political and electoral system appears to have helped, along with the strength of identity with the village jamaat, to undercut the aspirations, if not the importance, of ethnicity in Dagestan's politics throughout the 1990s. For one thing, ethnic political machines were able to lobby for linguistic and cultural education for at least the republic's largest ethnic groups. The fourteen largest ethnic groups' languages were given the status of state languages and are used in mass media, schools, science, and culture.[27] Ethnic-based candidacies and ethnic voting districts rendered ethnic issues irrelevant in election campaigns.[28] Although inter-ethnic conflict in fractious Dagestan was contained throughout the 1990s, a period of ethno-national rebirth and economic decline, it did not eliminate it. There were incidents of violence in Dag between the Avars and Akin-Chechens in Kazbekov raion, between Laks and Chechens in Novolak raion, between Dargins and Kumyks and between Avars and Kumyks in Khasavyurt raion, as well as between Avars and Nogais and between Kumyks and Laks.[29] However, there has been no mass violence of the sort that occurred between Ingush and Ossetiyans, for example, and, excluding jihadist terrorism, the intermittent violence has consisted largely of inter-clan election conflict.[30] On the other hand, the ethnic nature of the politics encouraged by the consociational system has fostered the "ethnization" of state structures. Thus, Avars are said to dominate in the MVD and Lezgins in the prosecutor's office.[31] This could provoke inter-ethnic conflict and radicalism that jihadists might be able to take advantage of.

Limited Democratization

Similarly, in tandem with the limited institutional change that occurs under revolutions from above in the short to mid-term, Dagestan's ethnic-based, single-mandate district electoral system stultified party development in the republic. This has helped the old communist nomenklatura (the CPSU ruling class) maintain its power. Thus, the CPSU's successor party, the Communist Party of the Russian Federation (KPRF), and the pro-Kremlin party of then Russian prime minister Viktor Chernomyrdin, the NDR (Nash Dom – Rossiya or Our Home Is Russia), won 55 and 14 percent of the vote, respectively, in Dagestan in the 1995 Duma elections. The republic was much more subservient to the new leadership in Moscow during the December 2003 Duma elections, when the KPRF and Putin's own nomenklatura-based party Yedinaya Rossiya (the election staff of which was led by Dagestani premier Sheikhsaidov) won 18 and 67 percent of the party list vote, respectively. The cleverly titled Islamic electoral bloc, "True Patriots of Russia," finished third with just under 4 percent.[32]

President Magomedov rose to power in Dagestan during the late Soviet era and like many other Party apparatchiks made a smooth transition from the CPSU's cryptic politics, to semi-democratic perestroika politics, to the new post-Soviet Russian regime. Not surprisingly, Magomedov has proved useful to the apparatchik-dominated Kremlin. He has maintained stability in the region and remained loyal to Moscow, regardless of who has held sway there. Magomedov's refusal to step down from the presidency and the Kremlin's continuing support for him negated some of the positives of Dagestan's consociational political system. Magomedov has effectively been in power for two decades, and his political machine has dominated the economy at the expense of the larger Avar ethno-political clan, not to mention the smaller Kumyk, Nogai, Lezgin, and Lak groups. State businesses and offices have been distributed to relatives and allied groups, fostering corruption and crime. For example, the Dagestan company Deneb, which enjoys a monopoly on non-alcoholic drinks, is owned by the President's son.[33]

Thus, throughout the Yeltsin and Putin eras Dagestan has remained one of Russia's most underdeveloped and corrupt regions. Some 80–90 percent of Dagestan's budget is funded from federal coffers. Depending on which figures one chooses to rely on, unemployment in Dagestan ranges somewhere between 20 and 40 percent, with youth unemployment at anywhere between 30 and 60 percent.[34] "Total corruption," as Russian journalist Valerii Vyzhutovich puts it, is perhaps the republic's most serious social problem. It may have grown worse under Putin. Dagestan People's Assembly chairman Mukhu Aliev, an ethnic Avar, claims not one public office in the republic was obtained without payment of a bribe. Reportedly, $450,000–500,000 is the sum required for appointment as a Dagestan government minister.[35]

These downsides may be a necessary tradeoff for avoiding a terrifying cycle of inter-ethnic conflict.[36] Even before Putin, re-Islamization was pushing some politicians to emphasize religious politics as a way of appealing across clans, jamaats, and nationalities.

Re-Islamization

With perestroika, Russia's revolution from above, and the Soviet regime's demise, Dagestan underwent a rapid and uncontrolled re-Islamization. That this took radical forms early on is not a surprise given seventy years of brutal Soviet rule, the local tradition of resistance to Russian rule, the republic's strong Islamic roots, its formerly close ties with a now-revolutionary Islamic umma, and foreign Islamists' penetration into the region. Whereas only twenty-seven mosques remained from Dagestan's Islamic infrastructure by the mid-1980s, the number at the end of 1998 had grown to some two thousand.[37] According to another estimate, by late 2001 there were 1,600 functioning mosques, 17 Islamic universities, 44 additional higher educational institutions, 132 middle school madrasahs, and 245 Koranic schools for students of all age groups. It is estimated that fourteen thousand people were studying in Islamic educational institutions.[38] At the same time, there were more than 3,500 "professional" servants of Islam and more than two thousand imams and mullahs.[39] However, the average religious knowledge and consciousness of ethnic Muslims, whether observant believers or not, remained low, leaving Dagestanis susceptible to radical proselytizers.[40]

During the perestroika era, the spread of radical Salafism or Wahhabism in Dagestan was limited to educational and charitable activities. The revival of ancient ties with the umma facilitated an influx of such organizations from the Near and Middle East. Political divisions in Moscow yielded a policy vacuum in response to this challenge. Although the revival of traditional Sufi Islam in the republic conflicted with the anti-national and foreign Wahhabi theology, younger Dagestani Muslims were naturally open to forms of Islam that rejected established norms and practices. Thus, local youth came under the sway of the Wahhabis' call to liberate Muslims from both the Russian yoke and the clan- and adat-based structures of Caucasus Sufism, albeit in exchange for the at least equally rigid ideology of Wahhabism. The Wahhabis' exotic appearance – long beards *sans* mustaches, shortened trousers, and chadors covering the entire bodies and faces of women – may also have appealed to the more searching or alienated among the youth desirous for "self-expression."

In the second period (1991–99) Dagestan witnessed the expansion and strengthening of foreign Salafist or Wahhabi, Chechen-tied Islamist organizations and the recruitment, training, and indoctrination of new members. Dagestan, replete with latent inter-ethnic tensions and political and economic stagnation, was fertile soil for the radical re-Islamization of indigenous elements, a situation Basaev and his allies sought to take advantage of in August 1999.[41] The third and more violent period of re-Islamization in Dagestan was one of open jihadist terrorism, which reached a new peak in 2005. After regrouping in the wake of the August 1999 incursion and the Russian forces' return to Chechnya, the ChRI Islamists were forced to abandon their policy of expansion by direct invasion. By 2004 they had settled instead on a strategy of supporting a web of indigenous combat jamaats in Dagestan and elsewhere for carrying out an increasingly aggressive campaign of terrorist attacks on the republic's civilian and security officials.

In the course of the 1990s, the politicization of Islam, whether official, autonomous, or extremist-jihadist, became a way for Islamic leaders, Islamists, and others who sought to capitalize on inter-communal difference and tensions to compensate for their weak religious influence over the population.[42] Whereas during the perestroika era initially adherents to the traditional Shafic school and Sufi brotherhoods in the North Caucasus made no effort to gain political power, by the mid-1990s they were running candidates for parliament and playing an active role in Dagestani politics. As with the emergence of the first Muslim parties during the perestroika era, members of Dagestan's Shafi-Tariqat elite were among the founding leaders of post-Soviet Russia's several Islamic parties, in particular a successor party of the Islamic Party of Rebirth (PIV), the Union of Muslims of Russia (UMR) led by members of the ethnic Muslim Lak opposition in Dagestan.

UMR leader Nadir Khachilaev was becoming increasingly powerful, having been elected Dagestan's deputy to Russia's State Duma. He also became more radical in terms of both his Islamic beliefs and Avar nationalism. The UMR's influence grew in Dagestan in the late 1990s, and the party established strong branches in mountain villages. As ethnic Dargin rule dragged on under Magomedov, Khachilaev and his brother, Magomed, led a group of several hundred armed supporters in seizing the government and State Council buildings for several hours on 21 May 1998, after which they fled, were arrested and convicted, and later given an amnesty in return for promising to refrain from further political activities.[43] The Khachilaevs may have been radicalized and even provided with supplies by Basaev and Khattab, but they were not full-fledged Islamists adhering to the doctrines of jihad and martyrdom. Rather, at heart they remained Sufis and were using Islamist elements to seize power from the ethnic Dargin clan of Magomedov. Thus, in Dagestan as elsewhere, Islamists were using nationalists to expand the theater of jihad, while local nationalists were using Islamic nationalism to boost their own appeal in a local inter-ethnic power struggle.

It was not only autonomous Islamic Avars and jihadist elements who were disenchanted with Magomedov. In August 1998, the official DUM of Dagestan (DUMD) called for the resignation of the republic's leadership so that a constitutional successon could begin. The DUMD continued its opposition into the early Putin era when it backed the Islamic Party of Russia (based on the Muslim political movement "Nur"), registered in the republic in May 2001. Among the party's goals were not only nominating candidates for election to public office in Dagestan and elsewhere, but also "the unification of the Muslim umma, raising the spiritual level of society, and . . . the defense of Muslims' interests."[44] In part, this was a reaction to the regime's clan-based and Dargin-based political machine. However, it was also a reaction to the emerging Islamist threat and the sense that the Magomedov leadership could not cope with the coming storm.

By 1998–99 Basaev and Khattab were preparing to establish an Islamist beachhead in Dagestan.[45] Ultimately it was this jihadist infection from Chechnya and abroad, rather than from Islamists indigenous to Dagestan, that sparked state-Islamist, intra-Islamic, and somewhat inter-ethnic conflict in the republic as the Yeltsin era drew to a close. In 1994 the Saudi Wahhabi cleric and missionary Mukhammad Ali had arrived in Dagestan, spreading his puritanical theology until he was removed from the village of Karamakhi and deported from Russia in 1996.[46] One of Ali's protégés and an early chief ideologist of both Dagestani and Chechen Wahhabism was Mullah Mukhammad Bagautdin (or Bagautdin Kebedov) from Kyzylyurt. His "Salafiiun," as they referred to themselves, would establish a presence in no fewer than eleven raions of Dagestan, including Makhachkala where they controlled the Kavkaz Islamic Center. Bagautdin was an associate of Akhmed-kadi Aktaev, who headed a Salafist organization known as "Islamiiya" and published the popular *Znamya islama* newspaper. Bagautdin and Aktaev had worked together toward the founding of the PIV.[47] The majority of Aktaev's followers are said to have been Avars, but also included non-Dagestani peoples such as Kabards and Karachais. He was reported to be relatively accepting of Sufis, Shafis, and Hanafis. Another Wahhabi with a presence in the republic in the 1990s, Sheik Ayub Astrakhanskii, popular among the small Tsumadins ethnic Muslim group, was tolerant of the other Dagestan peoples, including ethnic Russians and Jews. But although he was tolerant regarding ethnicity, he was said to be – typically for a Wahhabi – less welcoming of non-Wahhabi Muslims.

As the Wahhabis grew in numbers, their doctrinaire and totalitarian ideology began to provoke conflict with and between local *virds* (tariqat brotherhoods based on ethnic groups or village jamaats). Sufis and the secular intelligentsia alike began to express concern as Wahhabis endeavored to take control of local mosques, closed local venues for the ritual *zikr* and dismantled monuments to local Sufi mystics. By 1996–97, the Wahhabis had established strong jamaats in the republic's mountainous western villages of Kadar, Chabanmakhi, and Karamakhi, where a series of clashes and retaliatory murders took place between the Wahhabi and tariqatists. That these villages were predominantly ethnic Dargin should have raised alarm bells in Makhachkala and Moscow. In mid-1996 Karamakhi's citizens accused the Wahhabis of the murder of their village head. When the fleeing assassins received a warm reception in Chechnya, Karamakhi organized a series of demonstrations in the district capital of Buinaksk. A May 1997 clash in Chabanmakh took about a dozen lives. The Karamakhi jamaat also became the scene of a conflict in May 1997, when Wahhabis attempted a takeover of a local mosque from the Shafi Sufis. The former, reportedly armed from outside, cordoned off and fortified Karamakhi village. Others left for the hills from where they planned for jihadist guerrilla warfare. The majority of Muslims from Buinaksk raion came armed to the defense of the Karamakhi Sufis. The village remained sealed off and lived under Shariah law, its men wearing long unkempt beards and half-length pants and the women veils, until the Dagestanis' defeated the 1999 Basaev-Khattab jihadist incursion into the area.[48]

The authorities began to criticize Wahhabism publicly and adopt legal measures to pressure its proponents. Dagestan's parliament adopted a law "On the Fight Against Islamic Fundamentalism" which banned Wahhabism and authorized a series of search and arrest operations. By late 1997 the authorities' crackdown had driven Bagautdin out to Chechnya where he took up refuge at the invitation from then interim ChRI president Zelimkhan Yandarbiyev, Basaev, and Khattab. In early 1998 Bagautdin organized the resettlement of hundreds of Wahhabi families from the western Dagestan mountain regions to Gudermes, Chechnya. Bagautdin's forces fought alongside Basaev's mujahedin units against the armed forces of the ChRI loyal to President Maskhadov in Gudermes, a conflict described by Basaev as "a battle between Chechnya and Russia for Dagestan."[49] When in February 1998 Tsumadi, another western highland village, declared itself an independent Islamic republic, Moscow stepped in to prevent a clash between it and the authorities but at the price of leaving the "Tsumadi republic" under Wahhabi control.

At the same time, foreign Wahhabi missionaries and local Dagestani converts working within the ChRI's Islamist wing became increasingly interested in teaming up with the Chechens in order to strengthen their own jihad. Chechnya became the base for political parties and other organizations tied to Basaev and Khattab and working with elements in Dagestan. Such organizations included the Congress of the Islamic Nation (Kongress

"Islamskaya Natsiya"), the Organization of Caucasian Solidarity "Caucasus Dom" (Organizatsiya Kavkazskoi Solidarnosti "Kavkazskii dom"), the Organization of Islamic Unity of the Caucasus (Organizatsiya Islamskogo Edinstva Kavkaza), the All-Russia Cultural Center "Al-Islamiia" (Vsyorossiiskii Kulturnyi Tsentr "Al'-Islamiia"), the Confederation of the Peoples of the Caucasus (Konfederatsiya Narodov Kavkaza), the Congress of the Peoples of Ichkeniya and Dagestan (Kongress Narodov Ichkeniya i Dagestana or KNID), and the Islamic Jamaat of Dagestan (Islamskii Dzhamaat Dagestana). The last two were instruments created by Basaev and Khattab to mobilize forces for their eventual incursion into Dagestan in August 1999. The KNID, founded in April 1998 "to defend the peoples of Dagestan from Russia's encroachment," was openly condemned by Dagestan's leadership, but to no avail. Chechnya president Maskhadov ignored the Dagestan State Council's appeal to disband the organization.[50] Khattab, meanwhile, began to organize an armed Islamic Legion in addition to his already existing Peacekeeping Unit of the Parliament of Ichkeriya and Dagestan.

On 16 August 1998, the predominantly Dargin villages of Kadar, Chabanmakhi, and Karamakhi declared the creation of "a separate Islamic territory" in which Shariah law replaced Russian and Dagestan law.[51] Five days later the intra-Islamic (Sufi-Shafi versus Sunni-Wahhabi) aspect of the struggle was underscored when Wahhabis assassinated DUMD chairman Saidmukhammad-khadzhi Abubakarov, a strong defender of the Sufi brotherhoods and the Shafi school of Shariah jurisprudence predominant in Dagestan and a critic of the extremist Wahhabi branch of the Sunni-Hanbalist school. In November Basaev's NKID virtually declared war on Russia and Dagestan, promising that "the leaders of the Congress will not allow the occupying Russian army to wreak havoc in the land of our Muslim brethren. We do not intend to leave our Muslim brothers helpless."[52] In December 1998, Khattab's forces attacked the North Caucasian military district base in Buinaksk in an effort to forge a salient that would eventually meet up with liberated Tsumadi. The Islamic Jamaat of Dagestan, tied to Dagestani Islamists, whose members referred to themselves in Arabic as "allies of the Sunno and the jamaat" (*akhl sunna va-l-dzhamaa*), declared it necessary to "activate an Islamic draft and conduct jihad against non-belief and all those who embody it."[53] In April 1999, the new "Emir of the Islamic Jamaat of Dagestan," Bagautdin, appealed to "Islamic patriots of the Caucasus" to "take part in the jihad" and report in Karamakhi for duty in his new "Islamic Army of the Caucasus" in order to fight for the liberation of "Dagestan and the Caucasus." Simultaneously, Magomed Tagayev formed the "Dagestani Imam's Army of Freedom Fighters."[54] In short, Dagestan was on the verge of a carefully planned ChRI incursion.

Basaev and Khattab expected a considerable number of internal Dagestani Islamist elements to rally to their side, from a few thousand to perhaps as many as twenty thousand.[55] According to some, the Islamists controlled several mosques and at least fourteen madrasahs. Their communities were concentrated now in villages not only in the border raions of Buinaksk and Tsumada, but in Khasavyurt, Kazbek, Gunib, Karabudakhkent, and Derbent, as well as in Makhachkala, where Wahhabis were reportedly "strengthening" their position.[56] In one survey conducted from March to September 1998, a year before the Basaev-Khattab incursion, there was a slight increase in support for Wahhabis (especially among Laks) and a more marked decline in negative assessments of them (among Avars, Kumyks, Laks, Lezgins, and Russians, but not among Dargins).[57]

The conditions seemed favorable for the Islamists' gambit. On 22 July, there was an assassination attempt on Makhachkala's mayor, Said Amirov, who had played a leading role in the adoption of a new law banning Wahhabism. On the next day, there was an attempt on Chechen president Maskhadov's life. Clearly, the Islamists were ready to make their move and were spoiling for a fight. On 2 August 1999, several thousand Chechen-led Islamist insurgents crossed the Dagestani border *en masse* and sought to rally Muslims around the "Wahhabi" communities in the republic to rise up against the authorities. The fighting, which soon encompassed numerous districts of the republic, would last for some forty-five days.

Bagautdin's fighters attacked villages in Tsumadi raion. Four days later, Basaev led an army of 1,500 Chechen and mostly Avar and Dargin Dagestani Wahhabis into Dagestan and occupied several Wahhabi villages in border raions of Botlikh and Tsumadi, declaring an independent "Islamic State of Dagestan" and war on Russia. Wahhabis in "Avariya" districts (the ethnic Avar-dominated Botlikh and the ethnic Tsumadin Tsumada raions) and the "Kadar jamaat" (consisting of the Karamakhi, Chabanmakhi, Kadar, and Chankurbe villages in Gubin raion) supported the Chechen insurgents.[58] On 16 August 1999, the villages and jamaats of Karamakhi, Chabanmakhi, and Kadar declared a separate "Islamic territory," rejecting the jurisdiction of Dagestan's authorities, and establishing the rule of Shariah law. Fighting in these districts lasted until 27 August; official data claimed sixty-seven people killed and hundreds wounded. Fighting emerged in Buinaksk and other districts as well. In early September an estimated two thousand fighters entered Dagestan's Novolakskii raion in what some security officials claimed was an effort to reach Dagestan's second city, Khasavyurt, and declare an independent Islamic state by rallying the minority Laks and Akin-Chechens to the fight, including the Lak opposition led by the Khachilaev brothers.[59]

Unfortunately for the Islamists and fortunately for Russia, the bulk of the local population distrust Chechens, who led the operation, and so rallied to the side of Makhachkala and Moscow. President Magomedov called on the security services to rally and if necessary arm local village jamaats against the Islamists. Official Dagestani armed elements along with Russian army, MVD, and FSB units were able to repel the invasion, and the first serious Islamist threat to Dagestan was crushed.

If the presence and level of acceptance of Wahhabis were growing at the time of the Chechen Islamists' incursion, why did it fail to rally Dagestanis against the "puppet" Magomedov regime? One explanation lies in strong local sentiment against Dagestan seceding from Russia and against the Chechen rebels, as a survey conducted across Dagestan's ethnic groups indicated at the time. Moreover, when respondents were asked where the greatest menace to Dagestan's stability lay, Russia was rated the least threatening by far, followed by Eastern countries, then by Western countries, while Chechnya was regarded as the greatest threat.[60] There were several sources of Dagestan–Chechen tensions. As noted earlier, Dagestan's Muslim nationalities were in conflict with Akin-Chechens over land issues. Another explanation may lie in the foreign and particularly Chechen mountain warrior agency of Wahhabi proselytizing.

Georgii Derluguian argues that there was a series of structural aspects in Chechen-Dagestani relations creating tensions:

> The demographic expansion of the Chechens, who for several decades have had the highest birth rates in the region; the precarious distribution of power at the top of Dagestan's multiethnic polity and the corresponding distribution of livelihoods (land plots, trading privileges, lesser government sinecures) at the lower levels; and the tendency of Chechen warlords who emerged during the recent wars to forcefully monopolize the lucrative flow of contraband.[61]

Tensions were exacerbated further by a previous incursion into Dagestan in 1995 shortly after the beginning of the first war. Field commander Salman Raduev, the mentally unstable *"enfant terrible* of the Chechen resistance," attempted to seize a Russian airbase and destroy a squadron of helicopters. When the raid failed, Raduev decided to parlay failure into success by repeating Basaev's gambit at Budyonnovsk six months earlier: he seized a hospital and took its patients and staff hostage. Raduev's cruelty inspired a fundamental change in the attitude of a majority of Dagestanis toward their Caucasian neighbors from sympathy to revulsion.[62] Thus, Basaev's subsequent effort to establish a Wahhabi quasi-state inside Dagestan simply raised old fears, which dictated supporting the Russians' effort to repulse the Chechen raid.

The need to suppress the Islamist jamaats' rebellion in 1999 and push back jihadist forces impelled the Dagestani authorities to take measures that, along with the restart of the Chechen war, further shifted the balance of religious, ethnic, and political forces in the republic and would later reignite conflict over Islam. During the incursion, the official Islamic clergy's DUMD introduced and succeeded in getting passed a law banning Wahhabism. The law gave the DUMD extraordinary powers over Islamic affairs in the republic, including monitoring and controlling the programs of institutions of religious study, and providing assessments of religious organizations to the republic's justice ministry for vetting and re-registration purposes. The law also required that branches of the "republic's religious organization" at lower levels should similarly assist lower-level government bodies.[63]

This arrangement between the Magomedov administration and the DUMD allowed the latter to undercut competitors not only among Wahhabis and Islamists but competing official Islamic structures. Consequently, the influence of the DUMD grew substantially. It took on the properties of a state body, closely partnering with the Magomedov leadership and state structures to defend Dagestan from Islamists. However, the DUMD's new "influence," based on access to a corrupt state's administrative resources, should not be confused with real authority. The new arrangement inevitably drove some Muslim communities underground – including traditional tariqatists who sought to function autonomously, which is the custom of the republic's Sufi brotherhoods – and so risked defections from traditional to revolutionary Islam.

Finally, the DUMD's coziness with the "Darginizing" Magomedov regime risked further alienation of Avars. Avar-dominated raions were some of the most active in the Basaev-organized Islamist uprising and incursion. In addition, except for Chechens, Avars showed the lowest rates of trust in Dagestan and allegiance to Russia in an important opinion survey, with only 31.5 percent mentioning the Dagestani leadership among those they would trust in the event of a crisis. Only 52.7 percent of Avars mentioned Russia in their two answers regarding their most important identity references.[64] Thus, it is not surprising now to find that this and other outsider groups contributed a disproportionate number of those Muslims who joined the Islamist combat jamaats that emerged in Dagestan under Putin.

PUTIN'S COUNTER-REVOLUTION AND THE RISE OF ISLAM

Although Dagestan is the most Islamic of Russia's republics and was the most vulnerable to the side effects of war in Chechnya, there was little organized Islamist presence there when Putin first came to power as a result of their rout at the hands of federal and Dagestani forces after with Chechen incursion.

However, many Chechen fighters wounded and "on leave" remained in, or found their way to, Dagestan (and Ingushetiya) as the second Chechen war proceeded, and Putin's counter-reforms re-exposed the republic to the dangers of nationalist or Islamic mobilization.

Dismantling Consensual Rule

Putin's policy of harmonizing regional laws and constitutions forced the effective dismantling of much of the republic's consensus-based political system. When federal prosecutors first asked Dagestan's prosecutor-general Imam Yaraliev to compile an inventory of all articles in the republic's constitution that contradicted basic federal law, Yaraliev appealed to Russia's Constitutional Court, hoping to fend off Moscow's effort to bring Dagestani law into conformity with Moscow's legislation. Eventually, he was forced to produce a list of forty-five such contradictions contained in twenty-five articles. In summer 2000 the People's Assembly amended or repealed many of the offending articles. For instance, it repealed Dagestan's right under the article 65.6 to suspend the enforcement of federal laws that violated "Dagestan's sovereign rights and interests." The authority of power-sharing agreements with Moscow was reduced by an amendment to article 65.8 which had stipulated that the work of federal bodies in Dagestan was regulated "on the basis of agreements" rather than on the basis of the Russian constitution and such agreements. In addition, Dagestan's courts were resubordinated to the federal court system.[65] Similar changes were made in some sixty of Russia's eighty-nine regional charters and republic constitutions.[66]

The most important amendments would revise the electoral system for the People's Assembly. The Dagestan constitutional court defended the latter in a February 1999 decision, basing its ruling on the specifics of Dagestan's complex ethnic and confessional composition, the republic's constitution, and the treaty and agreement basis of relations between Moscow and the regions.[67] However, subsequent changes to federal election laws would force an end to Dagestan's executive and presidential inter-ethnic "grand coalition" as well as its consociational parliamentary system. In 2003, federal election law was amended, requiring that all regional parliamentary elections be held on the model of the federal-level State Duma's mixed proportional-majority system, with half the parliament's seats being filled on the basis of party lists and proportional representation and half from district seats. Amendments to Dagestan's law on elections reduced the number of deputies to seventy-two and established a 10 percent barrier for any party's entry into parliament. Only two other regions in Russia, the city of Moscow and the Republic of Kalmykia, have established a similarly high barrier.[68] Many explained rising inter-ethnic tensions in the republic during summer 2004 by reference to the changes to the constitution and political system, arguing that the Avar opposition would have a real chance of coming to power.[69]

Putin's recentralization and harmonization policy also dismantled Dagestan's grand coalition, since the Russian constitution at the time required the popular election of regional chief executives. The amended Dagestan constitution and election laws scheduled the presidential election for 2006, at which time the coalitional State Council would be abolished. This raised tensions among the leading ethnic groups in the republic, which began to jockey for position. The Kremlin's subsequent (post-Beslan) decision to end elections of regional chief executives and replace them with a system of presidential appointments removed the threat of inter-ethnic tensions during presidential elections but put the onus on Moscow to produce a nominee acceptable to all groups and raised still higher the stakes of the republic's parliamentary elections. The party-based proportional representation system for electing parliament removes the final leg of Dagestan's inter-ethnic consensual system and is likely to benefit larger ethnic groups and disenfranchise smaller ones. This may make the latter groups more susceptible to radical Islamists. Russian appointment of Dagestan's president, with republican parliamentary confirmation, will focus inter-communal competition on the Kremlin.

Moscow will need to cobble together a majority among representatives of numerous competing nationalities, and the confirmation vote may prove an enormously contentious matter. The outcome of the new system will likely be more disenchantment with Moscow among most ethnic groups.

To be sure, Dagestan's consociational system was somewhat discredited among some of the republic's nationalities by President Magomedov's refusal to step down from the rotating presidency of the State Council at the expiration of his first term in 2000 required by law. His refusal to relinquish it seriously violated the consensual basis of the system, especially in relation to the Avar plurality. The ethnic Avar opposition, the Northern Alliance, threatened on several occasions to tip the republic into civil war. As one observer noted, it was not really Dagestan's political system that was the "destabilizing factor" in the republic, but Magomedov.[70] Dismantling Dagestan's consociational system in order to remove Magomedov is a classic case of throwing the baby out with the bathwater, with no guarantee that the new bathwater will be any cleaner. There is a grave shortage of "clean" politicians in Russia, especially in the North Caucasus. As Dagestan expert Robert Bruce Ware put it:

Over the last five years all of the North Caucasian republics have seen a contraction in the circles of economic and political elites that has narrowed both financial access and democratic participation. While this contraction has local causes, it has also been exacerbated, since the spring of 2000, by the recentralization of the federal government, which has strengthened its influence throughout this region. Whereas regional elites were previously bound by their need for a local political base, Moscow's expanded influence has now become the basis for their power and has tended to insulate local elites from local accountability. This has alienated regional and village leaders and other activists who previously constituted the core of local political bases, but who are now finding their roles to be increasingly redundant.[71]

Russian appointment of Dagestan's president, with republican parliamentary confirmation, will focus inter-communal competition on the Kremlin. Indeed, as rumors emerged that the Kremlin was preparing to remove Magomedov, rising ethno-political entrepreneurship appeared to be provoking inter-communal tensions and tearing Dagestan's complex multi-ethnic quilt apart. Simultaneously there was a resurgence of radical Islamist mobilization.

Inter-Ethnic Tensions

Many in Dagestan argue that abolition of the republic's consociational political system is heightening inter-ethnic tensions. Those latter tensions both cut across and at times coincide with the Russian-Islamist strife. This was evidenced by the conflict in Dagestan during summer 2004 between Dagestan State Council chairman Magomedov, an ethnic Dargin, and the mayor of the city of Khasavyurt and chairman of the city branch of Russia's state-owned savings bank SberBank, Saigidpasha Umakhanov, an ethnic Avar and leader of the Avar-Lezgin opposition to Magomedov, the Northern Alliance.[72] Khasavyurt has large Avar, Lezgin, and Chechen (120,000) populations.[73] At the height of the crisis an ostensibly spontaneous 20 August pro-Umakhanov rally in Khasavyurt of some four thousand people reportedly included Avars, Lezgins, Tabasarans, Laks, Russians, and Nogais; missing were Magomedov's closest ethnic allies, the Dargins and Kumyks.[74] The conflict in turn was used by Chechnya's Islamists to gain more leverage over Dagestan's ethnic groups. To be sure, the dispute had Yeltsin-era origins. In 1998, Umakhanov had joined the Khachilaev brothers' assault on the State Council and parliament buildings, and his detachments allegedly included some Chechen "Wahhabis." Thereafter, Umakhanov remained a leading member of the Avar-Lezgin opposition to Magomedov.[75] He played a key role in the formation of an organization ostensibly created to defend Russia's constitution after Putin declared his legal harmonization policy to "reintegrate Russia's legal space." This support for the Kremlin was aimed at portraying Magomedov in Putin's eyes as a regional leader who was inclined to use the Yeltsin-era autonomy to build an independent powerbase at the Russian constitution's expense. At the same time, Umakhanov was laying the ground for his run for the Dagestani presidency with, as he hoped, Moscow's backing.

The crisis was kicked off by Umakhanov with a 29 July 2004 public rally of some six thousand supporters in Khasavyurt's city center. In a speech Umakhanov charged that Magomedov and his clan were behind a series of murders, including those of republic Dagestan's finance minister and chief mufti and the 9 May 2002 terrorist bombing of a parade in Dagestan's seaport of Kaspiisk. Umakhanov demanded Magomedov's resignation and the bringing forward of the date of the presidential elections set for early 2006. Magomedov responded by filing a slander suit against Umakhanov, initiating proceedings to remove him from office and disband the city assembly before calling new city elections and organizing a demonstration of his largely Dargin supporters in Makhachkala on 11 August.[76] Umakhanov then appeared on Khasavyurt television to condemn Magomedov for trying to turn Dargins and Kumyks against Avars and announced that he would lead a march on Makhachkala to demand his resignation.[77]

In the end, Dagestan's city and raion administration heads, Makhachkala's influential mayor Said Amirov, and the Council of Elders under the Dagestan State Council rallied to Magomedov's side. This was in part the result of efforts by future Dagestan nationalities minister Zagir Arukhov, who was rewarded for his troubles by Dagestani jihadists with assassination in 2005.[78] Moscow also took Magomedov's side in the dispute, not wanting to see a pivotal Muslim republic's leader removed from power at the hands of an autonomous opposition group.[79] By 18 August Umakhanov was backing down, having called off his 10 September march on Makhachkala and promised that there would be no violence. He appeared to play to Moscow one more time in an 18 August *Gazeta* interview in which, when asked who should be Dagestan's president, he replied "only an ethnic Russian."[80]

The inter-ethnic tensions between Dargins and Kumyks, on the one hand, and Avars, Lezgins, and Chechens, on the other, represented in the Magomedov-Umakhanov standoff appeared to translate themselves into some Islamization of their political protests. There were reports that demonstrations in support of Umakhanov featured a smattering of Islamic flags.[81] Indeed, Chechnya's Islamists tried to take advantage of the instability produced by the Magomedov-Umakanov/Dargin-Avar conflict. They and/or their Dagestani allies were reportedly passing out leaflets in the republic urging people to support true Muslims against Moscow under the banner of "Islam and jihad."[82] The Chechen militants' Kavkaz-Tsentr website entered the fray, posting an article stressing that the crisis was occurring "[on] the background of the activization of Dagestan's mujahadin, who are calling Dagestan's population to unify around the Shariah and rebuff the provocateurs along with their goal of preventing the inter-ethnic confrontation planned by the Kremlin's puppets."[83] It also posted an article from its "Strategic Information Department" reminding readers that Khasavyurt, which still has a large Chechen population, had been a part of Chechnya until the Bolsheviks transferred it to Dagestan.[84] There was also a piece that "warned nationalistic groups and clans to stop inflaming inter-ethnic hatred in Dagestan for the benefit of the Kremlin regime," implying the need to unite Muslim forces against Moscow. Later the site seemed to change tactics and attempted to aggravate tensions through a posting claiming that Umakhanov was training and arming militants for an attack on Makhachkala.[85]

The specter of an explosive confrontation between Dargins and Avars (and perhaps other groups, in particular the Akin-Chechens) occurring against a background of expanding Islamist activity was not lost on Moscow. Coming on the eve of Beslan, it was a primary stimulant for the Kremlin's decision taken after the school siege to put an end to the popular election of regional chief executives.

As noted, the dislike among many of Dagestan's Muslim and other minorities for Chechens was a factor in the republic's rebuff of Basaev and Khattab's August 1999 invasion. But new Avar-Chechen tensions have recently also created a dynamic that could make Avar nationalism more directly susceptible to cooptation by radical Islam, even Islamism, in opposition to the Russian state. Those tensions emerged in August 2005 in Khasavyurt raion when Avars from the village of Moksob attacked Chechens in Novoselskoe. The clash involved a hundred people and resulted in twenty hospitalizations; though no firearms were used.[86] The pro-Moscow Chechen administration, which just weeks earlier had signed a cooperation agreement with Dagestan's government, offered to help defuse the tensions. It is unclear whether this conflict was ignited by the July sweeps in the Avar village of Borozdinovsk in Chechnya by the pro-Moscow Chechen security force, the Eastern Battalion, which led to the disappearance of fourteen men and forced several hundred people to flee to Dagestan. If so, then Chechens and Avars might in the long run be brought together in opposition to Moscow, opening up Dagestanis further to Islamist propaganda from Chechen jihadists.

Enver Kisriev concluded in the wake of Basaev's 1999 incursion that a sea change in Dagestani politics had occurred and that the Wahhabi threat had effectively been removed.[87] On the first point a sea change had occurred but not of the kind meant by Kisriev. Dagestani feeling in favor of Russia appears to have been significantly weakened by the second Chechen war that followed the August 1999 Chechen incursion into Dagestan. He was wrong about the second matter. The war and Putin's anti-federalist counter-revolution would spark a veritable explosion, of political violence in the republic, driven for the most part not by inter-ethnic or inter-clan tensions but by a mounting Islamist jihad.

THE RISE OF DAGESTAN'S ISLAMIST COMBAT JAMAATS

As Dagestan's inter-ethnic comity dissolved, despite or, more precisely, because of Moscow's growing role in the republic's politics, ChRI jihadists were stepping up their expanded-war strategy. Already burdened by the need to control Dagestan's criminal, inter-ethnic and inter-clan conflicts, the republic's twenty thousand-strong police force, riven by corruption, was unable to deal with the jihadists. In addition, because of the mountainous topography there was no way to seal the border between the two republics, which has facilitated contacts between Chechen and Dagestani Islamists. There were now some ten or more Islamist combat jamaats operating on Dagestani territory, incorporating perhaps some two thousand jihadist fighters. There are so many Dagestani jihadists that according to the Carnegie Moscow Center's Alexei Malashenko, there is a "popular view" that most militants fighting in Chechnya are not Chechens but Dagestanis.[88] Indeed, by 2005 Dagestan was under siege, with terrorist attacks occurring on average once every three days.

Initially, after the failure of the Islamist village jamaats and Basaev's August 1999 incursion, Dagestan's radical jihadists kept their heads low. However, Rappani Khalilov, a key cog in the Chechen Islamist network and close associate of Basaev, has remained at large for years and was reportedly still running terrorist training camps in the republic.[89] He claimed responsibility for numerous terrorist attacks and was also suspected of organizing the May 2002 Kaspiisk terrorist attack, in which forty-two were killed and more than 150 injured when a mine exploded in the middle of a parade during celebrations commemorating the Soviet victory in World War II over fascism.

Khalilov was thought by some to have been killed in 2003 but no body was ever found. He soon re-emerged and he remains emir of Dagestan's combat jamaats. Terrorism persisted and increased in Dagestan in 2004–2005. In 2004, a leaflet signed by Khalilov claiming responsibility for several terrorist attacks in 2003 circulated in Dagestan.[90] In the absence of a body, federal prosecutors continued to act on the assumption that he was alive and hiding in Chechnya.[91] In April 2004, Basaev ended the mystery, appointing Khalilov as emir of the new "Dagestan front." In March 2005, the 'Shariah' combat jamaat pledged its allegiance and that of all other combat jamaats in Dagestan to both Khalilov and Sadulaev. Hence, Khalilov is still alive and, although perhaps physically disabled, still able to coordinate the activities of combat jamaats operating on Dagestani territory through his deputy Shamil Abidov (a.k.a. Abucv). On the other hand, a Russian MVD spokesman's statements suggest that some top police authorities believe Abidov is now an independent actor, running his own network.[92] It appears that Khalilov, even if he did not found, certainly has controlled Dagestan's two most notorious combat jamaats in recent years – Jannat (meaning "Paradise" in Arabic) and Shariah, established in 2002–2003. Through Khalilov and Basaev, these jamaats are linked to Russia's Islamist hub – the ChRI "government."[93]

Jannat Jamaat

In 2003–2004 the Jannat Jamaat played the leading role among Dagestan's combat jamaats. In 2003, it emerged from the shadows to claim responsibility for a series of assassinations, terrorist attacks, and sabotage operations, so expanding the range of "legal" terrorist-combat targets. It was led by emir Rasul Makasharipov, a close associate of Basaev and the late al Qaeda operative Khattab. Born in 1971, well-educated, and having begun terrorist activities in his mid-twenties, Makasharipov (known as "Muslim") fits the typical profile of Salafist revolutionaries. According to a Shariah Jamaat internet posting, he was one of only two mujahedin operating in Dagestan several years back.[94] He reportedly surrendered to the Russian authorities in 2000 and was sentenced to six-and-a-half years in prison for membership of an "illegal armed formation," but he was amnestied after serving a year. In 2002, he set up Jannat.[95] Makasharipov is reported to have been Khattab's translator and to have spoken fluent Arabic;[96] hence, the Arabic name of the combat jamaat and its sub-units or special detachments.

Jannat is said to have been responsible for the killings of some thirty Dagestani police officers and appeared to be behind a series of assassination attempts against various officials. Most of Jannat's attacks targeted those connected with the fight against "Wahhabism" (Salafists or other Islamists), primarily *siloviki*. A rash of assassinations of Dagestani officials began after Beslan and included an attempt on the life of the mayor of the northern town of Buinaksk, Abakar Akaev, who escaped uninjured. He was returning from a meeting with the Dagestan prime minister, Atai Aliev, and the commander of the North Caucasus military district, Colonel General Aleksandr Baranov.[97]

Jannat carried out the 30 September 2003 murder of five Dagestan MVD employees[98] as they drove to work together in Khasavyurt. Russian deputy Prosecutor-general Vladimir Kolesnikov suggested that Jannat had killed the officers for investigating Jannat.[99] In March 2004 Khalilov issued a statement, distributed in leaflet form throughout the republic, claiming responsibility for the wave of terrorist attacks in Dagestan and warning *siloviki* that "participation, whether direct or indirect, in the war against Muslims makes them enemies and retribution will inevitably catch up with them."[100] Jannat officially claimed responsibility for several assassination attempts against MVD officers in December 2004 as well.[101] It was also reportedly the force behind the 9 May 2003 explosion in Kaspiisk, and likely behind four explosions on 5 April, 24 May, and 8 December 2004 that damaged the gas and oil pipelines running through Dagestan.[102]

In early January 2005, an additional five thousand federal special-forces troops were deployed in the republic in response to a rise in kidnappings. Shortly afterward Dagestan law-enforcement agencies appeared to have killed Jannat's leaders in Makhachkala when a heavily armored tank was used to raze a building in which Makasharipov and several of his naibs were holed up, but the body of Jannat's emir was never found.[103] This marked the second time Makasharipov had narrowly escaped being killed or captured by Russian law enforcement.[104] On 2 February 2005 unidentified militants murdered Dagestan MVD first deputy chief Magomed Omarov in a drive-by shooting and tried to kill Alisultan Alkhamatov, acting head of the Khasavyurt raion administration.[105] In March militants killed a raion MVD chief.[106] The same month a communiqué from Shariah Jamaat appeared on *Kavkaz-Tsentr* signed by its new emir, the missing Makasharipov.[107] The Shariah combat jamaat stepped up its activities, beginning a veritable war in Dagestan.

Shariah Jamaat

Shariah likely incorporated what remained of Jannat. Emir Makasharipov's 14 March communiqué declared Shariah's allegiance to Khalilov, Sadulaev, and the ChRI network's jihadist cause. From then until Makasharipov's death four months later, Shariah would maintain the highest profile among Dagestan's combat jamaats; indeed, among all combat jamaats outside Chechnya. In addition to mounting an aggressive campaign of violence, it used the Chechens' websites effectively to make statements, much as the KBR's Yarmuk combat jamaat would do (see Chapter 7). The granting of access to such sites suggests the ChRI Islamist network's strong support for particular combat jamaats' activities.

Structure

Shariah Jamaat's subordination to the ChRI Islamists' coordinating hub was unmistakable in Makasharipov's 14 March 2005 internet statement, which mourned Maskhadov's death and pledged loyalty to his successor, Sadulaev. The document specified the chain of command from Sadulaev to Khalilov to Dagestan's local jamaats: "The Islamic Jamaat of Dagestan 'Shariah' and all other combat units headed by Emir of Dagestan Rappani Khalilov pledge their loyalty to the new Emir of the Caucasus and Muslims of Russia Sheik Abdul Khalim" (i.e. Sadulaev). It also pledged to fulfill Sadulaev's plan for 2005 in fighting "the Russian occupiers and the Dagestan puppet regime."[108] Shariah's own structure includes a shura with at least one substructure, an information department.[109] Its basic cells consist of autonomous groups of usually three militants, who know only each other; that is, they do not know members of other cells.[110] Shariah's cells may be its designated "special sub-units" or detachments (*spetspodrazdelenie*), which atypically are given names. Two were identified in a communiqué posted on the Chechen rebels' website Kavkaz-Tsentr as "Dzhundullakh" (Soldiers of Allah) in Khasavyurt and "Seifullakh" (Swords of Allah) in Buinaksk (which was given its nineteenth-century name, "Temirkhan-Shura" by the rebels).[111] Shariah Jamaat has also mentioned sectors or theaters (*napravleniya*) of operations under its command, announcing, for example, the appointment of the deputy of an unidentified emir Seifullah, one Sheikh Abdulla Dzhengutaiskii, as the new emir of the "Temirkhan-Shura theater."[112] Groups of Dagestanis of Chechen and Avar nationality especially, but also of other nationalities, are defecting to the Chechens in groups of 2–3 or 10–15, according the Dagestan MVD chief Aldigirei Magomedtagirov.[113] These groups may return to Dagestan as combat jamaats. In this way, the "recruitment" pattern resembles that based on social ties extant in the international network.

Ideology

Shariah Jamaat's ideology is strongly Islamist, as evidenced by the style and contents of its official communiqués, which are laced with references to the Koran, Sunna, and sayings of Mohammed. Thus, Shariah Jamaat begins its statements, in particular those internet postings claiming responsibility for its terrorist operations, by exclaiming to Allah: "In the name of God, the Compassionate, the Merciful! Thanks to God, Lord of the worlds, peace and blessings to the Amir of all the mujahedin, the Prophet Mohammed, his family and followers, and all who have followed them in a jihad to the Day of Judgment!"[114] Russian "occupation" forces are referred to as "*kafiry*" (Arabic for "infidels" or "non-believers").[115] Offensive jihad is the openly stated goal: "The relentless destruction of ideological opponents – this is Sunna! . . . we say to you, loathsome lackeys of Satan: We have no weaknesses, we soldiers of Allah, and having begun on the path of jihad, we have sacrificed our lives, property, shelter, families, and relatives in exchange for HEAVEN!"[116]

The Salafists' mystical belief in martyrdom is a central aspect of the Dagestan's jihadist network node, just as it is for the ChRI hub and the larger international network. Thus, in a 12 July 2005 internet posting the Shariah

Jamaat praised the martyrdom of its slain leader and two of his fellow *shakhids* (martyrs):

> Our brothers have left for our Master with dignity as is suited for real Muslims and men. We are happy for them. They (Allah willing!) are in the Gardens of Paradise! "Do not speak about those who were killed on Allah's path as if they are dead. No! They live, but you do not feel it" (Koran 2:154). "And if you are killed or die on Allah's path, then forgiveness and mercy from Allah are better than what they can gather from worldly goods" (Koran 3:157).[117]

In another internet message it declares:

> The death of our mujahedin is the departure to a better world, in paradise (Allah willing!), this is the mercy of Allah. Each of us desires to become a martyr, fighting for the sake of the elevation of Allah's word.
> "Truly Allah has bought from believers their lives and property in exchange for Paradise. They fight on Allah's path: they kill and are killed. The truly given promise from Him is in the Torah, the Old Testament, and the Koran. And who is more faithful in his promise than Allah! Rejoice in your trade which you have with Him. This is a great success!" (Koran 9:11).[118]

In the same vein, Shariah Jamaat's missives show a fondness for the similarly mystical notion that Allah's support for its jihad will overcome all disadvantages in numbers and technology. The following verses from the Koran are frequently cited:

> "How many ranks, few in number, have defeated numerous ranks with Allah's blessing! Truly, Allah is with the patient (Koran 2:249)."
> "Allah has all that is great, as does His Messenger and believers, but the hypocrites do not know this." (64:8)[119]

Quoting the often-cited Salafi-Wahhabi Koranic verse, one Shariah Jamaat communiqué declares:

> Allah is showing us His signs. He sows fear, horror, and panic in the infidels' hearts, and they throw against one mujahid hundreds of their trained soldiers and heavy weapons.
> "This is because Allah is the protector of those who believed, and the infidels have no protector" (47:11).

"Say: There befalls to us only that which Allah assigns to us, and He is our protector, and let the believers put all their hope in Allah. Say: you [infidels and traitors] do not expect for us anything besides the two best outcomes [victory or the marty's death on Allah's path]. We also expect for you what Allah is sending to you: punishment for Himself or by our hands. Wait and we will wait with you" (9:51).[120]

Shariah expresses the Salafists' emphasis on jihad not simply against non-believers but against Sufi "polydeists" (*mnogobozhniki*) in its 9 April 2005 message, quoting a verse from the Koran frequently cited by Salafists: "Kill the polydeists everwhere you find them, sieze them, fight them, and set up ambushes against them in every place" (9:5).[121] Shariah leaders have stated explicitly in Arabic that the jihad is now obligatory (*farz-ul'-'ain*) for all Muslims, but they undercut Muslim unity by declaring their emnity for "these local (hypocrites), Sufis, little tariqatists, and murids," all in fact but "the community of Sunnis."[122]

Shariah Jamaat's political ideology is reflected in the nature of its main demands. Most prevalently, the Dagestani terrorists call for the withdrawal of Russian troops from Chechnya and the establishment of Shariah law in Dagestan.[123] This suggests that Shariah Jamaat's real goal is the establishment of the North Caucasian caliphate desired by the ChRI leadership. Shariah's official communiqués always emphasize Islam and the establishment of Shariah law over the independence of Dagestan. For example, its internet posting claiming responsibility for the May 2005 assassination of a Dagestani minister called the victim "the main ideologist of the struggle against Islam and the establishment of Shariah law in the North Caucasus."[124] The emphasis here is on Islamist goals("Islam and the establishment of Shariah law," not independence from Russian rule) and Caucasus-wide (the North Caucasus is mentioned, not Dagestan). Another statement emphasized service to Islam first and to a free Dagestan only second: "Cease serving the non-believer authorities which have abused your predecessors and replaced the Shariah with their Satanic laws! Repent and stop your work, and we guarantee your security. When we restore the authority of Allah (God willing), you can honestly work at your posts, guarding Allah's law and really defending your people and a free Dagestan!"[125] This emphasis on the primacy of Shariah law is central among Salafist jihadist movements and organizations the world over.[126] Practically, this would mean the institution of a puritanical social and cultural order of the Salafist-Wahhabi type.

Shariah Jamaat's leaders have expressed their open disdain for any secularism. Its Lakhiyalov laments on videotape: "It matters little that they pervert Allah's religion?! It matters little to you that here we cannot live according to Shariah law?! It matters little to you that they walk around, you look at these undressed women, naked?!"[127]

Strategy

Shariah's strategy for defeating Dagestan's authorities is to drive police and other members of the *siloviki* from their posts by targeting them in terrorist attacks. Shariah Jamaat appears to have expanded the definition of those subject to terrorist attack to cover not only those involved in the authorities' efforts to root out Islamists but all who work in the *siloviki*. In March 2005 it set off what it called a "warning" explosion in Dagestan's capital, Makhachkala. The explosion was accompanied by an internet statement claiming that Shariah was limiting its targets to those directly or indirectly participating in the battle against the mujahedin and urging all those serving the Dagestan authorities to abandon their places of work and promising them immunity if they did so; a tactic used by Yarmuk as well.[128] Shariah Jamaat also warned all Dagestanis to avoid the premises of Russia's *siloviki* and proximity to police and officials, as more attacks were planned.[129] In a later communiqué in May, it stated that the amnesty for defectors from the "infidel" regime would last until September and that the names of the "many" *siloviki* who were supposedly requesting protection under the amnesty were being entered into a database and forwarded to Shariah's sub-units.[130]

However, Shariah seemed to lose patience quickly. On 9 April 2005 it claimed responsibility for at least seven terrorist attacks on MVD and police officials and workers in late March and early April and said that these were a last warning to "all workers of so-called 'law-enforcement' bodies." It issued a very clear explanation of the "reasoning" behind its strategy and the broadening of its range of "legal" combat targets in a "final warning" based on its reading of the Koran:

Our goal is to replace the authority of the non-believer and establish the authority of Allah. You stand as an obstacle in our path, defending with weapons in hand the non-believer's system, which is fighting against the laws of Allah, your Creator, and is guilty of the abuse and enslavement of your predecessors! It is also using you as cannon fodder, sheep, and slaves for the defense of their satisfying life and unlimited power.

From the very beginning of the active phase of jihad in Dagestan we, hoping for your reasonableness, abstained from your purposeful destruction, though we had all the opportunity and full right to this as given by Allah. Strictly targeted acts of revenge were undertaken by us against the more zealous enemies of Allah and Muslims, but you did not appreciate our good will and attitude toward you.

Instead of sincerely repenting before Allah and leaving your dog's work, you all started to fight against us together, hoping on the basis of your greater numbers.

But you forgot about the words of the Most High . . .

After this, a decision has been taken by us for your purposeful destruction . . .

Up until now we abstained from destroying workers of the traffic police, showing them tolerance and mercy, but they turned out so stupid and short-sighted that they also joined the war against us . . . After this an order was issued to all combat sub-units of the Islamic Shariat Jamaat to regard all traffic police as legal military targets subject to destruction.

We speak openly and do what we say.[131]

There is no independent confirmation of Shariah's subsequent claims that many policemen and other law-enforcement and security workers have "repented and left their work."[132] By June 2005 the Chechen rebels' *Kavkaz-Tsentr* website was claiming that Dagestan's militia and police were despised by the population and that some 1,500 militia, police and other "workers of the puppet structures" in the city of Buinaksk alone had tendered their resignations.[133] Dagestani authorities were already reported by more objective sources to have been disorganized and weak in responding to what was referred to openly now as "daily" murders of officials and citizens.[134] The few actions being taken, sweeps of districts and unfocused arrests, were said to be being used by the secular, ethnic Avar-led opposition for political purposes. A Russian State Duma deputy and a district administration deputy head from the opposition to Dagestan president Magomedov appealed for the release of two people arrested for the murder of the republic's pension fund minister.[135] This underscores how easily secular political battles, whether inter-ethnic or not, could be exacerbated by the Islamist threat and vice versa.

Operations, Tactics, and Propaganda

After Beslan there was a small spike in Islamist activity in Dagestan. Russian troops in the republic were put on high alert. Rumors were rife that some or even most of the Beslan terrorists were from Dagestan and that retribution from Cossacks and/or "federals" was imminent. People in the republic reportedly "fear the official vehicles more than the trucks and other vehicles of the Chechens, their Dagestani friends, or individual bandit gangs. . . . The officials from the Russian government come during the day, but the others come through after midnight."[136] On 2 November 2004, new Southern FO presidential envoy and former Russian presidential administration deputy head Dmitrii Kozak arrived in Makhachkala and initially commented:

"Nothing unusual that would distinguish the North Caucasus from the rest of Russia happens here."[137] He was to experience a rude awakening. By spring 2005, Shariah Jamaat had begun a small war in Dagestan that went far beyond Russia's "routine" police criminality.

The scale of the Jannat and Shariah offensives was impressive (see appendix – "Chronology of Mounting Terrorism in Dagestan, 2002–2005", p. 241). The number and sophistication of attacks committed by Jannat and Shariah would in fact constitute the most aggressive and effective local terrorist campaign in post-Soviet Russia, excluding Russian war crimes and jihadist terrorism inside Chechnya. In 2004, Dagestani Islamists executed some thirty operations of a terrorist nature, eighteen in the capital Makhachkala and six in Khasavyurt. In 2005, there was a sharp rise in the terrorist campaign in the republic, with seventy terrorist explosions, including forty in the capital in the first six months.[138] Dagestan's MVD chief reported just before the demise of the rather short-lived Jannat Jamaat that it had been responsible for the killing of twenty-nine members of its department for fighting extremism and criminal terrorism, including its chief, Akhberdilav Akilov.[139] The Dagestan MVD deputy chief estimated at about the same time (January 2005) that Makasharipov and his "group" had been directly involved in killing at least thirty members of staff of Dagestan's internal affairs ministry.[140] *Kavkaz-Tsentr* itself reported that whereas thirty-seven "collaborationists" were killed in 2004 by the mujahedin, in the first five months of 2005 there had already been twenty killings.[141] This, oddly enough, was a gross underestimate. On 4 July Dagestan MVD chief, Aldigerei Magomedtagirov, summed up the results of Dagestan's small-scale war, stating that there had been sixty-eight terrorist attacks in the republic, including forty in the capital Makhachkala, in the first half of 2005, involving the killing of some thirty police officers.[142] As *Kavkaz-Tsentr* boasted in an article titled "The Pigs Squeal, But Jihad Proceeds," this comes to slightly more than one terrorist act on average every three days.[143] Over the course of 2003–05 tens of special security and military forces were also killed, and hundreds from the various *siloviki* as well as some civilians were injured (see Appendix).

Dagestan's Islamist jihadists have been quite resourceful in their operational tactics and propaganda. Shariah Jamaat has deployed several types of attack, including drive-by shootings, roadside mines and improvised explosive devices, the detonation of car bombs near buildings, as well as an innovative "air attack." One study that examined the types of attack conducted in the republic from 1991 to 2005 claimed that the bulk occurred in summertime, especially in August between 7 and 9 o'clock in the morning and 6 and 8 o'clock in the evening – that is, during rush hours. Half of the terror attacks involved the placing and detonation of explosives, one in four involved automatic weapons fire and grenades, and the remainder involved automobile bombs. Half of the attacks targeted high-ranking officials, one-third targeted parliamentary deputies of various levels of seniority and law-enforcement officials, and the remainder were made against servicemen and their families.[144] Shariah appears to be effective at cultivating informers inside law-enforcement agencies. In early spring 2005 security forces found that guerrillas killed on the outskirts of Makhachkala were in possession of execution lists with some 140 names of officials in the republic's MVD and prosecutor's office.[145]

Shariah Jamaat claimed responsibility for a March "warning" explosion and several daring operations in April and May in and around Dagestan's capital, Makhachkala, as well as for detonating two explosive devices on 13 April that killed two law-enforcement officers and wounded six others. One of these went off not far from an atomic energy station. A third explosion was also registered in the capital not far from traffic police headquarters.[146] On 22 April Shariah Jamaat blew up a bus "overfilled" with policemen, resulting in an unknown number of casualties.[147] The group's explosive devices are simple but effective and similar to those used by Islamist jihadists throughout the world. For example, in an August 2005 operation it remotely detonated an explosive device consisting of ammonium nitrate and aluminum powder mixed with shards of metal materials and placed in a large plastic bottle.[148]

Shariah's militants also set the Makhachkala prosecutor's building ablaze on 15 April; an operation worthy of particular attention. They detonated incendiary devices thrown on the roof of the building engulfing the interior in flames. Shariah was particularly bold in detailing the execution of this "air attack" and the gory results, down to how many kilograms of explosives (21) and "special" inflammatory substances (10) were used. The operation killed at least six and left many more in the building with contusions and serious burn injuries. The resulting fire almost completely gutted the interior. Shariah appears to have had inside assistance. The description of the fiery and bloody aftermath in its website posting was fairly detailed, suggesting a continuing on-site presence after the blasts. Shariah also had detailed information, apparently from the republic prosecutor's offices, claiming that seventy-four out of ninety investigations and cases against "so-called 'Wahhabis'" were being processed in this department.[149]

The operation with the greatest potential political consequences was the 20 May 2005 assassination of Zagir Arukhov, the minister of nationalities, information, and foreign relations. As noted above, Arukhov was the architect of the truce between Dargin and Avar groups after the standoff between President Magomedov and Khasavyurt mayor Umakhanov. He was also the force behind a new strategy after 2003 of attempting to halt the rise of Islamism by winning over, rather than repressing, radicals. This policy gave amnesty to several leaders of the Salafist jamaats in Botlikh raion tied to Basaev and the August 1999 Chechen Islamists' raid into Dagestan.[150] However, Shariah Jamaat referred to him as "the main ideologist of the struggle against Islam and the establishment of Shariah law in the North Caucasus" in its internet posting on *Kavkaz-Tsentr* claiming responsibility for his assassination.[151] Arukhov's death at the hands of the very Islamists whom he had argued could be undermined by cooptation rather than by authoritarian crackdown is likely to have strengthened the hand of those who favor more aggressive police action to root out jihadist terrorism. Indeed, in a July 2005 trial of two jihadists for the 9 May 2002 bombing of the Victory Day military parade in Kaspiisk in which reportedly insufficent evidence was produced for a conviction, the defendants were nonetheless sentenced to eighteen and eleven years respectively for membership of a terrorist organization.[152]

Arukhov's assassination was a sophisticated operation which used mobile telephones to detonate a bomb. The building suffered considerable damage, and some sixty occupants had to be evacuated and taken to hospital.[153]

Shariah Jamaat has taken full advantage of the only media resource available to it – ChRI jihadist websites such as *Kavkaz-Tsentr* – in order to advertise itself and its activities. Such web postings serve two purposes: they sow psychological terror facilitate recruitment by encouraging defections from the pro-Russian secular regime to Islamist jihad. Thus, on 4 June 2005, *Kavkaz-Tsentr* carried a piece of strategic analysis asserting with some justification that Dagestan and Ingushetiya had turned out to be the "most vulnerable republics in the North Caucasus." The author boasted that a "full-scale war" was being waged against "the coercive pillars of the puppet Makhachkala regime," that "hundreds" were leaving the republic's *siloviki*, and that during 2004 and the first five months of 2005 not one mujahid had been captured by Dagestani security forces.[154] The new goal of a Caucasus caliphate, the strategy of expanding the jihad, and the Islamist ideological impetus behind them were articulated clearly in a Shariah internet posting claiming responsibility for some six attacks in late May and early June:

"Glory to Allah, our ranks and the territory of the jihad are continuously and inevitably expanding, and more and more young people are joining the jihad, sincerely desiring the elevation of Allah's word. We call on all Muslims to fulfill the duty before the Almighty and come forward, while it is still not too late, and enter on Allah's path in deed, fighting for His path, if you consider yourselves Muslims! The help of Allah is always near. Victory or Paradise!"[155]

Shariah is perhaps unique among combat jamaats in Russia in its use of symbolism in its propaganda, in particular in its renaming cities and streets usually in honor of "shakhids."[156]

The Response of the Republican and Federal Authorities

As the republic was engulfed in this wave of terrorism, the ethnic Avar opposition began to reassert itself by attacking the ethnic Dargin-dominated Magomedov administration. Khasavyurt mayor Saigidpasha Umakhanov told the international news agency Reuters: "There are attacks on police, terrorist acts, attacks on deputies and ministers . . . The government has seized the whole republic, so as to divide up all the money for itself. Well, for the people that is a problem . . . . The government is fighting the people."[157] Much as the Islamists use ethno-nationalism as a basis for recruiting potential extremists, Umakhanov used the Islamists' siege of the republic and the authorities' at times near-helplessness in combating the terrorists as an opportunity to play the ethnic card in his struggle for power. At the peak of the campaign, he openly complained of what he claimed was a disproportionate unemployment rate "far above" the republic's average among his constituency, the ethnic Avars, implying that the Dargin-dominated authorities led by Magomedov were to blame. He followed this charge with a call for the appointment of an ethnic Avar to head the republic.[158]

Republican and federal authorities were deeply concerned by the situation and took measures to address the growing security threat. In June some four thousand members of the security forces were transferred to Dagestan from neighboring regions. Additional MVD troops were also sent from Karachaevo-Cherkessiya, Kabardino-Balkariya, Krasnodar Krai, and Kalmykia.[159] On 11 June federal and regional police, security officers, and reportedly even army units began an intense sweeping operation, conducting house-to-house searches for jihadists in Makhachkala, Khasavyurt, Buinaksk, Kyzlar, and mountain districts such as Botlikh and Tsumada where Islamists had previously established strongholds.[160] The Russian government's official daily paper published commentary decrying and lamenting Dagestan's "systemic crisis," its "Ichkerization," and the "complete paralysis" of its leadership.[161] In mid-July, President Putin visited the republic and affirmed: "We will strengthen our position in Dagestan. We are aware of the local situation, so we should and will resolve this problem."[162] At the same time, he dispatched to Dagestan detachments of Russia's special forces, the famous *spetsnaz*, accompanied by federal and regional officials' denials that the deployment had taken place.[163]

It became indisputable, however, when on 1 July Shariah Jamaat detonated two explosive devices below three trucks in Makhachkala killing at least ten and wounding at least twenty-one members of the *spetsnaz* from the "Rus" unit along with fourteen civilians.[164] On 4 July, the chief of the MVD in Dagestan, Aldigerei Magomedtagirov, announced the removal from office of the Internal Affairs chiefs of Malshochko and three of Dagestan's districts for incompetence in the battle against terrorism. President Magomedov acknowledged: "The situation in the republic is getting worse, far more difficult."[165] The Dagestani authorities were clearly demoralized and in retreat. The combination of Islamist terror and criminal, inter-ethnic, and inter-clan violence was simply overwhelming local law-enforcement resources, and the terrorists were feeling increasingly confident.

In a note to the MVD, Shariah Jamaat emir Makasharipov warned: "I will fire them all, but those who stay, I will kill."[166] However, Shariah's 1 July attack on the *spetsnaz* unit sparked an unprecented manhunt involving searches of over 150 locations by hundreds, if not thousands, of Russian and Dagestani internal troops and police.[167] On 6 July law-enforcement forces laid siege to a house in Makhachkala for fifteen hours in what was reported to be a "full-scale battle" between Shariah Jamaat and security forces. Eventually, the authorities had to resort to the use of tank fire and destroyed the house. Initial accounts indicated that one of the five dead militants was Makasharipov. This time the reports of the emir's death were not premature. Kavkaz-Tsentr, which posted news of the ongoing battle several times in the course of the day, announced that he had become a "martyr" in mid-evening.[168] Dagestan's FSB chief claimed Makasharipov and "Jannat" (*sic*) were planning a Beslan-like school siege.[169] There were other Russian successes in the battle with Dagestan's jihadists. On 17 May it was reported that a senior Arab guerrilla fighter called "Jarah" had been killed in the village of Solnechnoye outside of Khasavyurt by a combined unit of FSB and MVD officers. Two days earlier, Denilbek Eskiyev, an emir in Gudermess raion where many operations in Dagestan had originated, was shot dead in the Chechen village of Gerzel-Aul on the border with Dagestan.[170] However, anti-terrorist successes have been largely the result of operations conducted by federal special forces such as *spetnaz* or rapid-reaction forces, and these have been so heavy-handed – recall the use of a tank to destroy a home occupied by Makasharipov's men in January 2005 – that they have also stirred resentment among the population.[171]

Moreover, the elimination of Makasharipov and other emirs did not substantially reduce the innovativeness and effectiveness of Shariah's operations. There were soon several attacks similar to those conducted by Shariat earlier. Indeed, the authorities' apparent successes seemed but Pyrrhic when on 2 July, the Shariah Jamaat posted a communiqué on *Kavkaz-Tsentr* announcing that in accordance with ChRI president and emir Sadulaev's call to shift the war onto Russian territory it was sending terrorists to Moscow to conduct "sabotage operations" in an operation dubbed "Stab the Pig's Heart as much, If Not More."[172] It is likely this was a response to Makasharipov's death and the ChRI's recognition of the effectiveness of Shariah's jihadist operations. Shariah's missive seemed to threaten terrorist attacks against civilians:

> We warn all Russian occupiers arriving in Dagestan for the implementation of their punitive and military "measures" – our land will burn under your feet and you will nourish our land with your blood! The more of you we destroy, the closer we will be to our Master, and we will do everything to deserve His satisfaction [with us]. Do not think your punitive expeditions and raids by your so-called "*spetsnaz*" and "squads" on our land will go without an answer and consequences for your families, wives, and children, even if you can return back home alive . . . We will come for you in Russia and reach you in your own homes! If necessary we will attack you and destroy you with your children and wives, as you attack us and kill ours. The Prophet Mohammed's (Allah bless and welcome him) fellow fighters asked him what if during their attacks on infidels it happens that they kill the infidels' children, and the Prophet answered: "They are of them" (according to Al-Bukhari). The Supreme Allah says in the Koran: "Fight with them just as they fight with you."[173]

In a 12 July posting Shariah Jamaat announced that its shura had appointed one Shamil Kulinskii as Makasharipov's successor and had adopted a change in its jihadist tactics inside the republic. Charging Russian forces with ignoring their "tolerance," "warnings," "kindness," and "mercy," with storming its members' homes when women and children were there, killing the eighteen-year-old nephew, and kidnapping the wife of the owner of the building where Makasharipov lived, it declared that in response it would henceforth use the following methods of "jihad against the infidels on the territory of Dagestan":

1) Carrying out attacks on the housing of infidels and traitors by all available means and forces even if there might be women and children in them. His associates asked the Prophet (peace to him and blessing) what if it happens that they kill children during their nighttime attacks on infidels, and he answered: "They are of them." (From Al-Bukhari),
2) Destroying the infidels' adult relatives. "Fight them, as they fight you" (Koran)
3) Kidnapping the infidels' wives and daughters.[174]

Then, after a hiatus of some six weeks in the aftermath of Makasharipov's death Shariah Jamaat re-emerged to claim responsibility for a series of terrorist attacks. With its usual Koranic-style salutation in a 25 August *Kavkaz-Tsentr* posting, it claimed responsibility for five attacks on *siloviki* and traffic policemen in the three previous weeks, including the destruction of a traffic police patrol post in Makhachkala, the explosion of car filled with "infidel" traffic police, the "execution" of a Levanshinskii ROVD officer, and attacks on a foot patrol and busload of Russian "infidel-occupiers." The total number of casualties, according to Shariah, was five dead and twenty-nine wounded, with no losses among the "mujahedin." Shariah claimed that the Islamist ranks no longer amounted to just two mujahedin (Makasharipov, alias "Muslim," and one identified as "Idris") as they had two years before, or twenty-five, but "many more" and were growing thanks to an increasing number of defections from the *siloviki* and from among the "pure and sincere youth." Support from inside the FSB, MVD, and the procuracy was said to be of three kinds: voluntary, driven by fear, and from those who pretend to see nothing and simply look the other way.[175]

Thus, while there have been Russian successes in combating Dagestan's jihadists, the movement survives. Just as in Chechnya there have been limited strategic gains while the Islamists have grown in number. The "scorecard" is further balanced by the jihadists' successes in killing and wounding hundreds of military, security, and police officials as well as civilians. Shariah Jamaat estimated in July 2005 that since 2003, Dagestan's low-intensity guerrilla war had resulted in nineteen mujahedin becoming martyrs and "around three hundred infidels" having been "destroyed and sent to Hell (Allah willing!)"[176] As noted in the previous chapter, 2005 would end with over one hundred terrorist attacks having been committed in Dagestan during the year.

CONCLUSION

Under the pressures of the renewed Chechen war and Putin's re-authoritarianizing counter-revolution Dagestan has been transformed from a surprisingly stable polity into one experiencing full-scale low-intensity Islamist guerrilla warfare. Indeed, at the peak of Shariah's campaign of terrorism in summer 2005, Southern FO presidential envoy Dmitrii Kozak published a report very different in tone from his claim weeks earlier that the situation in Dagestan was not very different from that in other regions of Russia. It concluded that the isolation, unpopularity, and corruption of clan-based elites "could lead to the emergence of a macro-regional socio-political and economic crisis" in all the North Caucasus republics and part of Stavropol Krai and predicted, according to a *Moskovskii komsomolets* reporter who obtained a copy, "a sharp growth of radicalism and extremism and an increase in the gap 'between constitutional democratic principles and the processes that are actually occurring.'"[177] In fact, the Kremlin was lagging well behind the pace of events, and not only in Dagestan. Since 2003 the Chechen militants had found more fertile soil for spreading their separatist jihad to the western North Caucasus – Kabardino-Balkariya.

Chapter Five

The Rise of Jihadism in
Kabardino-Balkariya and the
Western North Caucasus

The spread of the Islamist jamaat network to Kabardino-Balkariya (KBR) is strategically important as the republic is the geographical and ethno-political gateway to the western-northwestern North Caucasus.[1] This area encompasses three Muslim republics – the KBR itself, Karachaevo-Cherkessiya (KChR), and Adygeya – and two key ethnic Muslim groupings, the Circassian and Balkar-Karachai. The KBR is the easternmost of these three republics and, therefore, buttresses the rest of the western North Caucasus from the eastern Vainakh and Dagestani areas. The KBR's titular Kabardins are a sub-group of the Circassian ethnic group, as are the KChR's Cherkess and Adygeya's Adygeis.[2] In addition, the KBR's other titular nationality, the ethnic Muslim Balkars, are closely related linguistically and culturally to one of the KChR's two titular Muslim ethnic groups, the Karachais. The KBR is the key republic for the Circassians. It is the only one of the three noted republics where a Circassian ethnic group, the Kabards, constitutes a plurality. The Cherkess in the KChR and the Adygeis in Adygeya are minorities, 10 and 26 percent, respectively. The emergence of Islamist cells, jamaats, or a full-fledged network node in the KBR reflects both the jihadist movement's geographical reach and its potential pan-Caucasus and pan-Islamic appeal. The ChRI's expansion into the KBR is a *fait accompli.*

ETHNIC, HISTORICAL, AND RELIGIOUS BACKGROUND

The Muslim Kabardins and Balkars form a majority of the KBR's population.[3] Kabardins account for nearly 50 percent of the KBR's population, ethnic Russians 32 percent, and the Balkars 10 percent. The Kabardins and Balkars are distinct ethnic groups linguistically and culturally, with somewhat varying historical experiences particularly in relation to Russia and ethnic Russians.

The incorporation of ancient Greater Kabardiya into the Russian Empire came as it did for many other peoples – under threat of forced conquest and subjugation. It has been celebrated by the Soviet and, more recently, Putin's Russian state as the "voluntary unification" of Kabardiya with Russia.[4] Indeed, of all the North Caucasian Muslim peoples, Kabardins most easily succumbed to the expansion of Russian imperial rule. In the mid-sixteenth century, in the wake of Ivan the Terrible's defeat of the Golden Horde, his seizure of Tatar Kazan, and the incorporation of the Kazan khanate into Russia, many Kabard princes sought favor from the Moscow state and were coopted.[5] Ivan married a Kabard princess, and many Kabard princes entered the Russian state service. A significant number converted from Islam to Orthodox Christianity and later resisted the penetration of Islamic Sufi brotherhoods into the region, thereby distinguishing the western from the eastern North Caucasus. Some were even willing to make Kabardiya a protectorate of Moscow. Kabardiya signed a corresponding treaty with St. Petersburg in 1657.

Kabardins, unlike their co-titular Balkars and ethnic brethren Adygeis, did not join the resistance to Russian conquest from 1824 to 1856, led by the ethnic Avar Shamil, or the 1920–21 Dagestani-Chechen revolt against Bolshevik rule. The Balkars have a significant history of resisting Russian rule. For all these reasons, the national consciousness of the Balkars, Karachais, and other North Caucasian peoples of Dagestan, Ingushetiya and Chechnya is distinct from that of the Kabardins on the issue of North Caucasian solidarity and the historical struggle for self-determination and independence from Russian rule. We may even speak of a certain historical resentment toward the Kabardins (as well as the largely Christian Ossetiyans) among the other North Caucasian peoples, especially the Balkars, for facilitating Moscow's imperial rule over the North Caucasus.[6]

The modern KBR, like Dagestan and most of Russia's other national autonomies, is a legacy of Stalin's policies. Following Dagestan, Kabardiya was separated from the GAR (Mountain Autonomous Republic) on 21 September 1921 and established as an "Autonomous oblast" (AO). In 1922 the Balkar and Karachaevo-Cherkessiya AOs were carved out of the GAR. On 16 January 1922 the Kabard and Balkar AOs were joined to form the Kabardino-Balkariya AO. With the USSR's adoption of the new Stalin constitution in 1936, Kabardino-Balkariya was "upgraded" to an "Autonomous Soviet Socialist Republic" (ASSR). After the 1944 deportation of the Balkars, it was renamed the Kabardiniyan ASSR and territorially reconfigured with the transfer of the agriculturally rich lands of Kurinskii raion to North Ossetiya. With the Balkars' rehabilitation and return to the region under Khrushchev in January 1957, it again became the Kabardino-Balkariya ASSR. However, it was again reconfigured with the separation of the Nogai steppe and its distribution among Dagestan, Checheno-Ingushetiya, and Stavropol Krai. The loss of this important economic region caused some dissatisfaction among Kabardins and Balkars and created a potential for territorial disputes between the KBR and its neighbors.[7] For this and other reasons, the KBR and the other North Caucasian national autonomies inherited by Russia from the USSR are regarded by many as artificial, arbitrary, and ultimately illegitimate territorial constructs.

The initial pairing of the Kabardins with the Balkars was dictated by the regime's goal of dividing large and more aggressive Circassian groups from one another. The Kabardins, Cherkess, and Adygeis can be regarded as one and the same Circassian people, speaking closely related dialectics and sharing two literary languages (Kabardin and Cherkess). These, like the tongues of the majority of the twenty or so largest ethnic Muslim peoples of the North Caucasus, belong to the Ibero-Caucasian linguistic group.[8] The Kabardins of the KBR were separated from their ethnic kin by locating the Cherkess in the KChR. "Adygei" is the name used by all three of Russia's Circassian groups.[9] Kabard nationalism in the Soviet era was limited in scope, falling short of a broader Circassian nationalism. In the late 1980s and early 1990s there was a movement to refashion a "Great Adygeya" (Circassia) and reunite the Circassians including the Abkhaz in Abkhazia (in Georgia) in a single national-territoral governance unit. This included schemes such as resettling the Balkars from the KBR in the KChR or the Cherkess from the KChR in the KBR.[10] This mobilization of a broader Circassian nationalism remained aloof of pan-Turkic and pan-Islamic nationalism.[11] However, an Islam-dominated nationalism could overcome territorial and ethnic divisions.

The historically more rebellious Balkars in the KBR and the Karachais of the KChR were also divided from each other by the Soviets. Some 90 percent of Russia's Balkars live in the KBR, a slightly lower-level concentration than that of Russia's Kabardins, who are to be found almost entirely in the KBR.[12] The small Balkar ethnic group, however, still makes up only 10 percent of the KBR's population. The Balkars and Karachais, sometimes referred to as the "Alans" or "mountain Turks," are close in culture, belong to the Turkic linguistic group, and are ethnically related to Adygeis, Ossetiyans, and Turks.[13] Ironically, the Kabardins spread Islam to the Balkars, who imbibed the faith more deeply than the Kabardins themselves.[14]

Like the Chechens, but unlike most Circassians, the Balkars (and Karachais) were deported to Central Asia during World War II. On 8 March 1944 the Soviet NKVD sent east 37,713 Balkars, of whom 52 percent were children and 30 percent were women. By 1948 the exiles' ranks had been reduced by 28 percent as a result of disease, starvation, and repression.[15] Although Stalin's charge that these groups collaborated with the Nazis has some foundation, some defections were to be expected given his own regime's brutality. Nevertheless, the North Caucasian revolts during the war preceded and were not necessarily dictated by the German offensive into the area. German military governors in the North Caucasus won over locals by returning collectivized land to them and staffing administrations with Kabardins, Balkars, Cherkess, and Karachais. In this way, they won sufficient support to form North Caucasian military units under German command.[16] In 1957 Khrushchev rehabilitated the deported Balkars along with the Chechens, other North Caucasian nationalities, and the Crimean Tatars. Beginning in 1965 and continuing through 1969, the Balkars and others were returned to their native homelands.

The Balkars', Karachais', and non-Kabard (Adygei and Cherkess) Circassians' historically strained relationship with Russia makes the Kabardins a linchpin in North Caucasian politics and in the Circassians' relationship to Russia as a whole. Conservative political analyst Aleksandr Tsipko's remarks from 2000 reflect Russia's special reliance on the typically loyal Kabardins: "The leader of Kabardino-Balkariya is also the leader of all the Adygei people in the North Caucasus, and the fragile national consensus on Russia's southern border depends on the loyalty shown towards Moscow by this, the largest ethnic group in the region."[17] All of this makes the KBR a pivotal piece of the puzzle for political stability in the North Caucasus.

There is another important difference between the Kabardins and Balkars. The former (along with the Kumyks, some Avars, some eastern Cherkess, and the culturally close Ossetiyan Digors) come from the smaller number of North Caucasian ethnic groups that have societies that, according to Bennigsen and Wimbush, are more "aristocratic" than "democratic" in class structure. The Balkars (and Karachais), on the other hand, hail from more democratic and clan-based societies, as do the Chechens, Ingush, and a majority of the Dagestani and Adygei tribes.[18] It will be recalled that it was the Kabard princes who acceded to Russian rule. So traditional hierarchical divisions rather than historical legacy suggest the possibility of a split in attitudes between the higher and lower classes of Kabard society with regard to separatism. This could bolster any Balkar opposition to the Moscow-loyal elite in Nalchik. As we shall see, a contemporary KBR Islamist group appeared to include both Balkars and Kabardins.

The Roots of Islam in the KBR

The first waves of Islam's expansion through Arab conquest (600–800 A.D.) and the trade routes of the fur and silk roads (800–1200 A.D.) did not touch the North Caucasus or the central eastern areas of the present-day KBR. Islam first penetrated into the region through the Nogai khanate's expansion into Kabardiya in the late fourteenth or early fifteenth century and expanded among the Kabardins, Balkars, Karachais, and the eastern Cherkess. The Muslim Crimean khanate's activities brought Islam to the entire Cherkess, western Ossetiya, and farther southwest to Abkhazia (a secessionist republic of present-day Georgia) and further entrenched it among the Kabardins, Balkars, and their neighbors.[19] The Ottoman Empire played a central role in Islam's spread among the Circassian. Mass conversion of the Kabardins and Balkars began in the 1840s, on the eve of the region's conquest by Russia, which sparked an exodus of Alans as well as other North Caucasus peoples. Tens of thousands of Alans moved to the Ottoman Empire.

The Kabardins, like all the tribes, are Sunnis of the Hanafi school. But Islam sunk shallower roots among the peoples in the territories of the present-day KBR, especially among the Kabardins, than among the ethnic Muslim groups of Chechnya and the rest of the North Caucasus. Many Kabardins, for example, remain polytheists. Many Kabardins continue to worship the pagan god Tkhawich alongside the Muslim deity. Soviet power uprooted Islam among the Balkars and especially the Kabardins. By the post-Stalin period all of the few remaining mosques were located in the KBR's predominantly Balkar-populated Bakshan raion. Residual pagan customs and North Caucasian traditions, ceremonies, and the like are a potentially useful ally of traditional Islam against the KBR's Islamists. Although remnants of pagan beliefs and local customs (*adat*) can be found among all of Russia's ethnic Muslims, such beliefs intermixed with Islamic elements to produce uniquely North Caucasian and more narrowly ethnic-based customs tied to, but separate from, Islam. Together they constitute a formidable antidote to outsiders proselytizing. Residual pagan customs are most prevalent among Kabardins and the largely Christian Ossetiyans.[20]

Radicals propose a de-ethnicized pan-Islamic ideology which demands that purely "fundamentalist" traditions should replace the remnants of North Caucasian tribal and ethnic customs. The local *adat* put a break on radical Islamicization, because the Islamists reject them as heretical and punishable, by death. This inclines many Kabardins and some other Muslims against Wahhabist teaching. Indeed, some local councils of elders have mobilized to protect youth from the influence of Islamist "pseudo-religious extremism," with some urging by the authorities. In the largest high-mountain settlement in the KBR, Verkhnyaya Balkariya, the Council of Elders and the village's imam, Mukhamed-khadzhi Tsikanov, took on this responsibility.[21] This is an important front for the authorities, clerical and state alike, in their struggle with Islamism, for should the radical Islamists take control of such isolated areas, they would be difficult to dislodge.

Consistent with the Kabardins being the least Muslim of the North Caucasian major Muslim groups, there was no Sufi activity in the Circassian west of the region until after World War II. Today there is still less such activity and fewer mosques than in the rest of the western North Caucasus. However, one of the Qadiriya brotherhoods, the highly secretive "Vis Haji," founded in the 1950s in response to the deportation of Chechens and Ingush to Kazakhstan, was active in Kabardiya as well as in Checheno-Ingushetiya, northern Dagestan, and Muslim Ossetiya in the 1980s.[22]

As in all the Muslim republics and elsewhere where ethnic Muslims reside in Russia, there has been a precipitous growth in the Islamic faith. In the mid-1980s Bennigsen and Wimbush calculated there were no more than ten mosques in all the Kabard, Adgyei, and Cherkess territories combined.[23] The number of Islamic communities in the KBR had reached one hundred by the late 1990s. There were ninety-six working mosques by 2001, and mosque-goers were increasingly young, aged 14–35 for the most part.[24] By 2005, there were 122 Muslim organizations, 180 mullahs, and probably over a hundred mosques.[25] A growth in the number of Islamic educational institutions has also been seen. The first madrasah in the KBR was built in Nalchik in 1991. In 1993 it was upgraded to an "Islamic Institute," and began to train young men for the clergy. In the first class of 130 students there were not only Kabardins and Balkars but Uzbeks and Turks as well. There was some foreign involvement in the early post-Soviet growth of Islam in the KBR. The Nalchik school and institute received money from the Saudi Arabian philanthropic foundation "Salvation." The Saudis also funded a branch of their international organization for the salvation of Islam, "Daugat," in Nalchik. By the mid-1990s some hundred KBR students were studying abroad in Saudi Arabia, Egypt, Syria, Jordan, and Turkey.[26]

More importantly, the number of mosques and Muslim religious communities not registering with the justice ministry is growing, undermining official Islam's position and bolstering the recruiting prospects of radicals.[27] This is a sign of growing alienation from official Islam, the local DUM, and state authorities. Unofficial and unregistered mosques as well as independent madrasahs have become the venues for so-called "young reformers," who emerged in the 1990s in the KBR and elsewhere in the northwest and central Caucasus. These young imams have set about organizing propaganda supporting a so-called "Islamic ideology" in general education and sports schools, and forming a contingent of literate proselytizers for spreading their ideology. Core tenets are that "Shariah law is more just and incorruptible than Russian law" and that it should be used as a way of supplanting Russian ways of life among the mountain peoples of the North Caucasus.[28] The introduction of Shariah law in place of Russian law presupposes, realistically, an independent KBR or North Caucasus state or caliphate.

Socio-economics and Demography

The KBR's population is poorly integrated into Russian society for many reasons. The KBR – like the other Circassian (KChR and Adygeya) and North Caucasian republics (Chechnya, Dagestan, and Ingushetiya as well as titularly Buddhist Kalmykia) – is largely rural, with a significant portion of the population living in inaccessible high-mountain regions that pose a considerable challenge to economic development as well as law enforcement. In 2002, 43.4 percent of the population lived in rural areas, continuing a trend of increasing ruralization due to higher birth rates in these regions. Unemployment among Balkars, especially in the republic's mountainous regions, can be as high as 80–90 percent, creating an environment upon which criminality and radicalism can feed.[29] The largely Kabard-Balkar Muslim majority has been growing rapidly, just as the Muslim share of the overall RSFSR population is increasing.[30] The KBR's recent population explosion, from under 792,000 in 2000 to 901,000 thousand in 2002, contrasts sharply with overall ethnic Russian and Russian Federation declines. The trend in the KBR is part of an overall Russian-Muslim demographic shift that is set to drive Russia's growing Muslim challenge in future decades.[31]

At the same time, the population imbalance between Kabardins and Russians, on the one hand, and Balkars, on the other, along with differences between Kabardins and Balkars regarding their attitude toward Russian rule and Islamic identity translate themselves into inter-ethnic tensions between the KBR's two Muslim titular nationalities. According to Kappeler and Chervonnaya, the Balkars see all Circassians "not as Muslim brothers, but [as] an antagonistic ethnic group."[32] The Balkars, a distinct minority composing 10 percent of the KBR's population, could direct their frustrated nationalism against both Russians and Kabardins. There is no doubt that some Kabardins and Balkars aspire to self-determination separate from each other. Such cross-cutting was clearly the predominant element in KBR inter-communal politics during the Yeltsin era.

KABARDINO-BALKARIYA UNDER YELTSIN

Under Yeltsin's ad hoc asymmetrical federative system, the KBR, like many regions, had considerable autonomy in its internal and external affairs. This situation was a product of the strength of regional demands for autonomy and of resistance to Moscow's centralizing instincts. As early as 1991 the KBR elite, along with Chechen, Tatarstan, Bashkortostan, and Kalmykian elites, generated a powerful backlash against Yeltsin's efforts to appoint presidential representatives.[33] At the same time, President (then also KBR Communist Party first secretary) Valerii Kokov, a native Kabard, maintained his power by walking a tightrope between competing groups in both the republic and Moscow during the USSR's demise and Russia's revolution from above. Also, like most regional leaders, especially those of the national republics, Kokov was a former CPSU apparatchik: no reformer. He supported the August 1991 coup plotters against Gorbachev and Yeltsin and sought autonomy from Moscow in order to protect his and the KBR nomenklatura's power from the democratizing Yeltsin.

The nationalist opposition in the KBR during the upheavals of the late perestroika era was based in the Assembly (from 1991 the Confederation) of Mountain Peoples of the Caucasus (Assembleya/Konfederatsiya Gornykh Narodov Kavkaza or KGNK). The KGNK united then Chechen nationalists, like Zelimkhan Yandarbiyev and Shamil Basaev, and nationalists of other ethnic Muslim groups of the North Caucasus. Its first president was the KBR's ethnic Kabardin scholar Musa Shanib. Its goal was to establish a united North Caucasus state stretching from Georgia's autonomous region of Abkhaziya on the Black Sea across the entire North Caucasus to Dagestan on the Caspian Sea. The organization was founded on the periphery of the North Caucasus in August 1989, in Sukhum, Abkhaziya, as it moved towards war with backing from Moscow against an increasingly neo-fascist regime in Georgia headed by Zviad Gamsakhurdia. When war broke out in 1992 young men from across the North Caucasus including Chechens like Basaev but even more so the Abkaziyans' ethnic and linguistic Circassian cousins – Kabards, Cherkess, and Adygeis – headed to support the Abkhaz bid for independence. In addition to acquiring valuable military experience, many North Caucasus ethno-nationalists like Basaev had already began to turn to a more radical Islamic nationalism during the Georgian–Abkhaz war.

Although this was not true of Shanib, he did employ his status as head of the KGNK and its resources to establish the Kabardin National Congress (KNK). It became the core of the nationalist revolutionary movement in the KBR opposing the crumbling local communist regime there headed by Supreme Soviet Chairman Valerii Kokov. The more irreconcilable opposition of ethnic Balkar nationalists was much smaller. With the Soviet regime split and the failed August 1991 hard-line coup against the reformist, but mutually antagonistic Gorbachev and Yeltsin in Moscow, the source of the KBR communists' power evaporated. The coup itself brought thousands of oppositionists to the central square in Nalchik where they began a hunger strike demanding the dismantling of the Kokov regime, but Kokov and his closest government companions had already fled the capital unbeknownst to the nationalists. When the opposition finally lost patience and stormed the government buildings, they found the president's and other offices abandoned. But instead of seizing power, the KNK requested the government's return and the conduct of free and fair elections for KBR president in January 1992. It appears that the Kabardin opposition was unwilling to act aggressively against the Kabardin-dominated elite because many of the latter had defected, and still maintained ties to the former. They were also likely trying to gauge how the post-coup contest between Gorbachev and Yeltsin in Moscow and the fate of the Soviet state would play out before taking the risk of seizing power illegally. In addition, they may have feared that a split in Nalchik among the Kabardins would facilitate the Balkar secessionists, much as the split in Moscow was facilitating the secession of the union republics. Kokov, using his post as Supreme Soviet Chairman, mobilized the local nomenklatura to get out the vote in a desperate bid to save the ruling elite from retribution should the opposition come to power. Kokov won the presidential election and the local elite holds power to this day, despite another scare months later driven by the stormy events in Chechnya.

After Djokar Dudaev seized power in Chechnya in fall 1991 and the Ingush-Ossetian and Georgian-Abkhaziyan wars heated up, nationalism re-ignited in the KBR. Some 1,500–2,000 Kabardin recruits went to Abkhaziya to fight alongside Basaev's Chechen units in support of the Abkhaz cause. In August 1992 the Kabardin opposition and Balkar movement for secession re-emerged, but this time the Kokov regime, instead of fleeing Nalchik, ensconced themselves in the government's key buildings and armed themselves. Opposition forces brought oil tanker trucks into the central square and threatened to blow up the government buildings and burn all those inside. At this point Shanib, who had been arrested trying to buy weapons in Chechnya from Dudaev, escaped and was given a hero's welcome on the square, where he called on those present to continue their struggle but only after they had helped their Abkhaz brothers achieve independence. When the Kabardin Abkhaz volunteers returned home in late 1993 and early 1994, they found that Kokov had reconsolidated nomenklatura power with Yeltsin's support lent in return for Kokov's support in Yeltsin's victorious 1993 battle with the Russian Congress of People's Deputies. The threat of secession represented by the KBR's first ethno-nationalist revolutionary waves of 1991 and 1992 was used deftly by Kokov to wrest concessions from Yeltsin, who was convinced by Kokov that he and his Kabardin allies were the only guarantors of stability able to stave off the republic's radicals.[34]

As a result of negotiations over Yeltsin's 1992 Federation Treaty, which the KBR signed, the anti-reformist Kokov won, merely having to amend the republic's Soviet-era constitution rather than adopt a new one. For his part,

Yeltsin re-emphasized the policy of Soviet reformers (Khrushchev and Gorbachev) of redressing Stalin's deportations during World War II. On the fiftieth anniversary of the Balkar and Kabard deportations, Yeltsin acknowledged and apologized for the "historical injustice" and issued a decree on rehabilitation that included special pensions and other state financial support for the groups' cultural rebirth and development.[35]

As a consequence, on 1 July 1994 the KBR became the second Russian region to sign a bilateral power-sharing treaty with Moscow.[36] This gave the KBR somewhat less autonomy and sovereignty than Tatarstan and Bashkortostan, but as many similar powers and privileges. Altogether, the KBR's treaty enumerated twenty-three competencies under exclusive KBR jurisdiction, whereas Tatarstan's treaty gave Kazan only fifteen and Bashkiriya's treaty gave Ufa only eighteen. However, Tatarstan was referred to in its treaty as "a state united with the Russian Federation" that conducted its own international affairs, while the KBR was defined as "a state in the Russian Federation" without the right to conduct international affairs.[37] The KBR was afforded "the full panoply of state (legislative, executive, and judicial) power on its territory outside the limits of the competence of the Russian Federation and the joint competence" of Russia and the KBR, which offered the KBR considerable temporary sovereignty, as many spheres had still not been addressed in Russian law. The KBR was also given the power to declare a state of emergency on its territory but only on the basis of Russian Federation legislation (an area of Russian law that would remain unsettled for years to come), and full control over all natural resources and state property. Finally, the territory and status of the KBR were declared inviolable and could not be changed without the KBR's agreement, giving the Kabardins some protection against Balkar secessionism.

The treaty's articles 3.1 and 3.4 gave the KBR full power over the adoption and amendment of the republic's constitution and over the structure of its governmental bodies.[38] The KBR deployed (like the KChR, but to a lesser degree than Dagestan) a consociational power-sharing arrangement that formed a grand "inter-communal coalition." The offices of president, vice-president, and premier were divided up according to nationality after elections. If a Kabard won the presidency (as ethnic Kabard Valerii Kokov has twice done in the post-Soviet era), then the vice-presidency would be given to a Russian, and the premiership to a Balkar. Also, all three groups' languages were given and still have the status of a state language. These measures were necessitated in part by the Soviet legacy and the unbalanced titular diarchy, with Balkars composing only 10 percent of the population. The KBR's Yeltsin-era consociational system was a way to ensure that the small Balkar community would have a share of power commensurate with its status as a titular nationality. It certainly helped limit tensions between the communal components of the KBR's multi-ethnic society throughout the 1990s. By the end of the decade there was very little inter-ethnic tension, let alone evidence of political Islam.

As the USSR and Russian Federation crumbled under the "parade of sovereignties" in 1991–92, representatives of the KBR's Kabard, Balkar, and smaller Karachai minorities repeatedly declared their secessionist intentions. The bidding contest between Gorbachev and Yeltsin for the support of the RSFSR's national autonomies led to an April 1991 law on the rehabilitation of oppressed peoples, which many representatives of those ethnic groups construed as a green light for demanding autonomy and even secession. In the early 1990s Kabard nationalists founded the Congress of the Kabard People, which declared its support for the idea of a "Great Kabardiya" and began to liaise with other political organizations in the KBR with the goal of coming to power.[39] The Balkars and Karachais launched a campaign for autonomy as well. In February 1991 RSFSR Chairman Yeltsin offered a bill to the Russian Supreme Soviet that provided for the restoration of the Karachai Autonomous Republic within the RSFSR. The predominantly ethnic Cherkess leadership of the KChR, however, scheduled a referendum for March 1991 in which a majority of the KChR's voters backed the status quo as endorsed by the KChR leadership. Subsequently, in November an unofficial Balkar National Congress issued an ignored appeal to the KBR Communist Party leadership to support its demands for a Balkar autonomous region.

Thus, most Balkar voters boycotted the 22 December 1992 election of the KBR first president but voted overwhelmingly a week later for "national sovereignty" within the RSFSR in an unofficial referendum. Communist Party first secretary and newly elected KBR president Valerii Kokov regarded the ballot as unconstitutional.[40] Throughout 1992 the republic was on the verge of mass inter-ethnic conflict, with competing Kabard and Balkar nationalist demonstrations frequently being held in close proximity and occasionally leading to scuffles. Many believe that civil war was averted when the force of an exploding grenade thrown by a member of one group of demonstrators at the other was intentionally absorbed by a courageous policeman, Adalbi Shkhagoshev, who lost both his hands in the incident.[41] In a 1994 referendum, 90 percent of Balkars voted for staying in the KBR. Until late 1996 Balkar nationalism was assuaged in part by a consociationalist approach to political appointments: President Kokov's premier was a Balkar, and the speaker of one house of the KBR parliament was a Balkar, the speaker of the other a Kabard.

The downside of the consensus between Nalchik and Moscow was the preservation of the partocratic nomenklatura's authoritarian form of rule. In essence, in exchange for stability in the KBR, Moscow looked the other way as

President Kokov resisted political and economic reform. Kokov maintained Soviet-style pseudo-elections: in 1992 and 1997 he was elected with 99 percent of the vote and no competitors, and in 2002 with 87 percent and some competitors.[42] The titular Muslim republics have consistently ranked as the least democratic of Russia's eighty-nine regions and the KBR has consistently ranked near the bottom in various ratings of freedom and democracy.[43] In many ways, the more authoritarian form of rule maintained in the KBR (and in many of Russia's other national republics) throughout the Yeltsin years presaged the direction Russian politics would take with Putin's rise to power, including many of its specific soft-authoritarian methodologies. Kokov (and many other leaders, especially in the titular Muslim republics) foreshadowed Putin by appointing local administration heads, which at the time was a violation of Russia's constitution, and by controlling appointments to the republic's Judicial Qualifications Commission which examines judges' qualifications. He significantly coopted many social organizations, including the important Circassian movements, the International Cherkess Association and "Adyge Khase".[44]

When the National Congress of the Balkar People (NCBP) resumed operations in 1996 it was headed by retired army lieutenant-general and former commander of the Transcaucasus military district Supyan Beppaev. Beppaev had been accused by the authorities of selling weapons to the Georgians in the early 1990s and in fact had close ties with Chechen president Dzhokar Dudaev, who reportedly urged Beppaev in a telephone conversation to declare an independent Balkar state in order to instigate a war of national liberation throughout the North Caucasus.[45] The NCBP convened a congress of the Balkar people in November 1996 to decide whether to call for the return to Balkar control of the four districts transferred to Kabardiya in 1957 and for the creation of the office of KBR vice-president to be set aside for an ethnic Balkar, or to demand the creation of a Balkar republic separate from the KBR. Delegates voted for the second option. On 17 November the congress unilaterally declared a Balkar Republic, elected a State Council as its temporary government under the chairmanship of Beppaev, and appealed to President Yeltsin to support their actions.[46] Two days later the KBR procurator's office opened a criminal case against the Council's leaders, and the KBR parliament banned it. In Moscow, Russian justice minister Valentin Kovalev denounced the congress's declaration as unconstitutional, and the State Duma sent a delegation to the republic.[47] KBR police began cracking down on the congress with mass arrests. Beppaev backed down, resigning his post and appealing for other delegates to repeal the demand for a Balkar republic. The majority rejected his appeal, and the congress, the Balkar national party "Tere," and other Balkar national organizations were banned, and some of their leaders arrested and tried.[48]

In 1997, another inter-ethnic crisis developed between Balkars and Kabardins when the formers' nationalists again announced plans to establish a separate republic of Balkariya. Chechen rebel commanders offered military assistance.[49] Coercion would be necessary, since in order to fashion a Balkar-dominated territory many isolated Balkar enclaves would need to be ethnically cleansed or fully subdued. Clearly, the Chechens were endeavoring to play on the inter-ethnic rivalry between the KBR's titular Muslim nationalities, and Muslims' resentment of their co-religionist Kabardins' relative acceptance of Russian rule.

The Kabardins' own nationalist organization, "Adyge Khase," remains a significant, if less political force. It claims a membership of five thousand and the support of many more, and limits its activities to the fight for the preservation of "Adygei" (Circassian) culture, language, traditions, and contacts with the five million-strong Circassian diaspora.[50] This is a key area of conflict. Kabard journalist Sultan Akhov claims that half of young Kabardins living in the capital, Nalchik, cannot speak Kabard.[51] Kabardin nationalists also differ from Balkar nationalists over which separated territories should be repatriated to the KBR from other North Caucasus regions.[52] Federal prosecutor in the KBR Yurii Ketov claimed in December 2004 that the idea of partitioning the republic along ethnic lines, though impractical, remains popular.[53] All this underscores the Muslims' historical problem of having been divided along ethnic lines, which hampers their overall quest for self-determination and equal rights within Russia. In this atmosphere, it is not surprising that many pro-Russian Cossacks insist on their status as a separate ethnic group and want the transfer of their compact territory of residence to Stavropol Krai.[54]

Inter-ethnic competition for leadership in Muslim republics like the KBR does not negate the appeal of the pan-Islamic idea under emerging Muslim radicalism.[55] To the contrary the outsider role in KBR politics for which the badly outnumbered ethnic Balkars are destined as a result of Putin's counter-reforms could incline them to seek ideological sustenance and revival in radical Islamist ideas. They could very well begin to perceive fellow Muslims such as the Kabardins who fail to meet Islamist standards as another "other." Islam could also attract some support from more radical elements among the Kabard "winners." A fight by both Kabardins and Balkar nationalists against assimilation by the dominant ethnic Russians may unite them and reinforce any common Islam-dominated nationalism. However, under Yeltsin the outnumbered Balkar movement for self-determination remained a nationalist one, and inter-ethnic Kabard–Balkar tensions were the central aspect of inter-communal politics in the KBR.

Indigenous radical Islam in the KBR was minimal under Yeltsin. In 1996 a radical Islamist leader, one A. Kozdokhov, declared himself emir of the KBR and claimed he could muster some six hundred armed militants. Although Kozdokhov's threat never materialized, as chief mufti of the KBR Shafik-khadzhi Pshikhachev notes, this was the first appearance of "Wahhabis" and of secret Islamist structures in the republic.[56] It was only with the onset of the Putin era that Muslims influenced from outside the KBR and Russia were able to build a more indigenously based movement of Islamists and ultimately violent jihadists in the KBR.

KABARDINO-BALKARIYA UNDER PUTIN

The Putin era has seen a growth in both Balkar nationalism and extremist Islamism, with inter-ethnic conflict being eclipsed by armed conflict between Muslim radicals and the authorities. Under Putin Kokov's authoritarian regime would be given greater freedom to stamp out the potential Islamist infection from Chechnya, while the population would lose many political, civil, and human rights as a result of the Russian president's authoritarian counter-reforms. Together these developments alienated young Muslims from the Russian state and its puppet apparatus in the KBR, pushing them away from the regime's allies within "official Islam" toward more independent and often more extremist forms of the religion. This led to the formation of militant, terrorist Islamist organizations on the republic's territory in mid-2004. Yet as late as July 2004, law-enforcement officials thought that the Islamists' prospects in the KBR were rather poor as compared to Chechnya and Ingushetiya. They argued that "there are more than enough forces and resources in the republic to suppress such actions, and the special services' operational apparatuses there work better."[57]

Putin's legal harmonization policy forced the KBR, like some sixty other regions, to bring its constitution (and numerous laws) into conformity with the federal constitution. Amendments adopted on 19 July 2001 saw the KBR's consociational inter-ethnic coalition system repealed, though nothing prevents the leadership from continuing to employ it extra-constitutionally. In addition, the amended constitution now stipulated that federal laws have precedence over republican laws. Although the power to curtail citizens' rights was described in the amended KBR constitution as a purely federal one in conformity with the Russian constitution, the KBR authorities limited the ability of Muslims to worship freely and even closed mosques.[58] In addition, the Putin administration refused to renew the Yeltsin-era power-sharing treaty with the KBR, which expired on 1 July 2004, and there has been no word as to whether a new one will be negotiated (as with Tatarstan and Chechnya). With this, the KBR's power over its internal affairs was effectively stripped of any real meaning, because the Russian constitution gives regions authority only over those spheres of activity not covered by the exhaustive list of powers given in the constitution's articles 71 and 72. Since the 1994 treaty, federal legislation has filled the legal vacuum that existed in Russia after the Soviet state's demise. Also, Moscow refused to appoint anyone from either titular nationality as its federal inspector.[59]

Moreover, the limited democratization of the Yeltsin era, which was particularly limited in the KBR, has been further constrained. President Kokov has now been the republic's leader for two decades. Early on, he used his position on the federal advisory State Council to keep a step ahead of Putin's efforts to strengthen the "executive vertical," heralding the latter's post-Beslan counter-reforms,[60] but the KBR leadership was soon forced to submit to increasingly stringent political demands from Moscow under Putin's more authoritarian rule, with no compensating economic benefits in return. At a November 2002 council session Kokov supported the termination of mayoral elections, arguing that "the people had not yet matured to such a democratic level."[61] With the formation of the state-supported, pro-Putin Yedinaya Rossiya (or YeR) party, Kokov went to embarrassing lengths to show his submission to Moscow. Because the YeR backed the chairman of the KBR legislature, Zaurbi Nakhushev, during the 2003 State Duma elections, Kokov renounced his opponent abovementioned republican hero Shkhagoshev whom he had once called his "son." Like apparatchiks across the country who joined the YeR nearly *en masse* and were subsequently backed by the enormous administrative resources of the state (federal and regional), Nakhushev defeated Shkhagoshev in what was perhaps the most fraudulent of the 225 single-mandate district races in the 2003 Duma elections.[62] In the party list race involving forty parties Kokov delivered to Putin 77 percent of the vote for the YeR.[63] In the March 2004 presidential election he served Putin with 96.5 percent of the official vote tally in the KBR. Of eighty-nine regions, only Ingushetiya, led by a former KGB operative, produced a larger majority.[64] Thus, Kokov is viewed increasingly as Moscow's repressive puppet.

Meanwhile, poverty, alcoholism, crime, and corruption remain the hallmarks of Kokov's KBR. In November 2001, only Dagestan had a lower average monthly salary than the KBR among Russia's regions with significant Muslim populations, and the KBR had one of the lowest percentages of unemployed receiving benefits.[65] In 2002, the average wage in the republic was only 1,600 rubles per month, half the national average.[66] On the other hand, according to some reports, an elite 10–20 percent of the population have an income "that exceeds all imaginable norms." Kokov's elite – ministers, deputy ministers, and other apparatchiks – lives in an exclusive Nalchik district known as the "noble nest."[67]

Yet this elite has miserably failed in helping the republic negotiate the transition to a market economy. A major failure was its management of the republic's key enterprise, the non-alcoholic beverage plant "Mineralnyie Vody." It was once a major budget contributor, but debts forced it into bankruptcy. It squandered a $75 million loan for renovation and capital repairs, which some experts believe was enough to build two such enterprises from scratch. The republic's government appointed the president of an American firm to run the plant, but he is now wanted for embezzlement. Moreover, the entire defense industry collapsed, and a scheme to combine profitable republic enterprises with unprofitable ones produced no results.[68] Thus, the KBR is a "super-recipient" region in the federation's budgetary system, taking out several times more than it puts in, funds which are then lost by corruption and diversion to favored clans.

The poor economic situation and the lack of opportunities are driving young people out of the region to find simple service jobs elsewhere. The miserable socio-economic situation has also led to a growth in alcoholism, drug addiction, and prostitution. The DUM's inability to resolve these problems plays into the hands of alternative Muslim structures: the jamaats. According to one KBR source, the majority of those turning to jamaats are young people ranging in age from fourteen to twenty-five.[69] Youth's natural predilection to reject its elders' allegiances is exacerbated in such harsh conditions.

In a February 2001 article, Kokov painted a very whitewashed Potemkin village-like picture of the socio-economic situation in the KBR. Using the old Soviet-era indicator, physical volume, he asserted that in 2000 the KBR's industrial production increased by a factor of 1.5. He went so far as to claim (falsely) that the KBR was one of Russia's ten or so donor regions. Kokov also endorsed Putin's "strengthening of the vertical of power" without reservation, unlike many other regional leaders. Most ironically, he boasted that he had secured the KBR's borders and strengthened its passport regime in order to control entry to the republic. He held the KBR up as a model of stability in a stable North Caucasus: "It is necessary to explain, given the newspapers' pages and television screens, that there is no frontal war in the Caucasus today. The North Caucasus is regarded in the whole world as a region ablaze, but it is unstable only in Chechnya."[70] When RTR, the Russian state TV, aired a documentary film called "Caucasian Cresent" in autumn 2000 which claimed that Wahhabism was taking hold in both the KBR (particularly in Tyrnyauz, a town west of Nalchik) and the KChR, Kokov and KChR president Vladimir Semenov complained to Putin that their republics had been "slandered" and appealed to federal prosecutors to bring those responsible for the broadcast up on charges of inciting inter-ethnic conflict. The film sparked popular protests in the KChR and Adygeya.[71] Oddly, Kokov had earlier blamed a series of bombings in government buildings in Nalchik on Wahhabis.[72] The incident underscores the tendency of regional leaders to put forward a good, if false, face to Moscow and its emissaries. Three years later the KBR would be facing an undeniable jihadi threat, be put on emergency alert, and witness repeated armed clashes between law-enforcement organs and an indigenous radical Islamist combat jamaat.[73]

In return for providing support and apparent stability, the Putin regime has backed Kokov, as it has all corrupt and incompetent regional leaders so long as they toed the Kremlin line and prevented an explosion of communal violence. Kokov was on the second seven-member presidium of the advisory Russian State Council.[74] When President Putin traveled to the October 2003 Organization of the Islamic Conference (OIC) summit, he surrounded himself with an impressive delegation that included, among other "Muslim leaders," President Kokov.[75] As a result, Kokov often appears near the top of rankings of the most influential regional leaders.[76] Ironically enough, Kokov's profile rose just as radical Islam began to gain a foothold in the KBR. Soon not only Kokov's, but Moscow's, hold over the North Caucasian republic was cast in doubt.

THE CONTEST FOR ISLAM IN KABARDINO-BALKARIYA

The KBR has witnessed a growing differentiation in the structure of Islamic politics under Putin: official or "traditional" Islam; autonomous and often radical Islamic communities (jamaats); and extremist Islamist combat jamaats, most notably the ChRI-allied, terrorist Yarmuk Jamaat. The second orientation consists of groups of mostly young believers who have rejected the traditional Islam of their parents and grandparents who are sanguine about the official Islamic clergy's support of, and cooperation with, Russian and local KBR authorities. Both radical Muslims and extremist Islamists are critical of official Islam, and the radicals appear to be the cadre pool and perhaps logisticians for the Islamists.

Official Islam: The Spiritual Board of Muslims

Official Islam in the KBR as elsewhere in Russia is caught between Russia's increasingly authoritarian, corrupt, and criminalized state and regime, on the one hand, and radical Muslims and Islamist terrorists, on the other. The KBR DUM, headed by mufti Shafik-khadzhi Pshikhachev, has been forced in the growing crisis to seek support from the authorities in cracking down on Islamists, and simultaneously to criticize them for overzealousness in doing so. At the same time, there has been tension between the authorities and official Islam, as the former seek to control and limit Islam's development even as they acquiesce in assisting that development in order to insulate traditional Islam from Islamist infiltration. For example, when the KBR authorities handed over the building of the DOSAAF (the Soviet-era Voluntary Organization for Assistance for the Soviet Army and Navy) to the Muslim community for its transformation into a "Spiritual Center" and central mosque for the KBR DUM in Nalchik, a major scandal erupted between the parties over the financing, which included money from a gaming baron in the republic.[77] The financial failure of the bank holding the funds for the work led to an official investigation, which to some extent discredited the KBR's then chief mufti and the KBR DUM as a whole.[78] Radicals and Islamists have sought to play up such incidents in their efforts to discredit the DUM. Some imams called on mosque-goers to boycott Nalchik's central mosque in the wake of the authorities' closing of many other KBR mosques.[79] The KBR DUM's new central mosque was also harshly criticized by the jihadist Yarmuk Jamaat as "built by the enemies of God to control Muslims."

> Even a person unfamiliar with Islam understands that the new central mosque built with the support of the godless authorities, on whose orders crosses are shaved out on the heads of believers and during whose rule it is not considered a sin to swear at God and his Prophet (may God bless and welcome him), better fits the description of the "mosque of harm and disbelief." [80]

The KBR DUM has cooperated with the authorities because they are its best source of funding and its only protection from the radicals' wrath. Therefore, even though the radical Islamists impugn official Islam's DUMs for lacking independence from the state and assisting the Russian authorities' and their local allies' alleged suppression of Islam, official Islam's clerics continue to seek state support in order to compete with the radicals for the hearts, minds, and souls of believers. The imam of the KBR's DUM (as well as those of the KChR and Adygeya) even requested in January 2005 that his salary be established, if not paid, by the state as is already the case for imams of the DUMs of Ingushetiya, Chechnya, and less transparently in Dagestan.[81] At the behest of the Russian authorities, the KBR DUM even inspected the ranks of local Muslim clerics through "attestations" regarding their knowledge of Islam in order to weed out extremists.[82]

While neither official, traditional, or more moderate forms of Islam are not taught in state schools, and independent and official madrasahs remain strapped for cash, radicals who receive funding from abroad ignore the strictures of the state in order to propagandize their extremist interpretation of Islam underground. The KBR DUM struggled to win a compromise after the federal education ministry attempted to impose a course on Russian Orthodox culture on Russia's primary schools, a policy that was substantially watered down throughout Russia as traditional Muslims mobilized to fight the measure. Initially, the KBR's Cossack community in Prokhladnensk and others adopted decisions to introduce the subject by September 2003.[83] By August 2004, however, the KBR government approved a new course on "The History and Culture of the Religions of the Kabardino-Balkariya Republic" backed by the KBR DUM together with the Russian Orthodox Church.[84]

The closure of mosques and other measures taken by the authorities in 2003 and 2004 in order to fight the growing Islamist threat created considerable tension between KBR and DUM bodies. When Muslim clerics complained, state officials largely ignored their pleas and KBR law-enforcement organs, in the person of KBR prosecutor-general Yurii Ketov, asserted that "in all the history of Islam's existence in Kabardino-Balkariya there has never been a more preferential attitude toward this religion on the part of the authorities and state than there is today."[85]

On the other side, radicals and Islamists were able to criticize the KBR DUM's cooperation with the authorities as a betrayal of the nation and a blasphemy against Islam. The spokesman of the autonomous and radical Muslim Initiative Group of Kabardino-Balkariya, one "Musa," (likely Musa Mukozhev, discussed below) was careful in a March 2005 statement to discredit the official Muslim administrations and chief muftis, like the DUM KBR and its leader, declaring that they "have no basis in Islam and were contrived by the enemies of religion to control Muslims."[86] He further asserted that the 2004 elections of the DUM KBR leadership were controlled by the authorities, who permitted only those it wished to enter the assembly hall set aside for the election meeting and barred journalists. Musa also condemned new DUM leader Pshikhachev for not only "not objecting to but approving the actions of Satan's associates" – that is, the KBR and Russian leaderships. He charged that Pshikhachev only differed from his predecessor (described as "a KGB agent" with lists of Wahhabis for the police to arrest) in possessing a diploma from Syria. He further charged Pshikhachev with assisting "non-believers" in dividing Muslims as they have done "since Mohammed's time," claiming that the official mufti had cynically approved the closure of other Nalchik mosques in order to herd Muslims to his central mosque and "raise 'the authority of the DUM.'"[87] Thus, Musa charged, the KBR DUM did greater harm to the KBR's Muslims than did non-believers.[88]

Musa subsequently attacked the efforts of the KBR authorities and official clergy to root out Islamists: "That these barbarous actions were not committed by bands of skinheads or fascist aggressors but by those who call themselves 'traditional Muslims' causes concern. These are the same ones who are buried after their death in accordance with Muslim rites in Muslim cemeteries."[89] It is probably true that some imams of official Islam play a role in the roundups of alleged radical Islamists. Indeed, at a meeting of the DUM of the Republic of Adygeya and Krasnodar Krai (DUM RA KK), the rector of the Abu Khanify Cherkessk Islamic Institute, Ismail-khadzhi Bostanov, practically acknowledged as much noting that "every day the authorities ask us for some radicals."[90]

Indeed, the KBR DUM seems confused about how forcefully and directly to confront the radicals, at once exaggerating and downplaying the Islamist revolutionary threat. Like all DUMs, it is engaged in a competition for souls with other official Islamic clergy and has used the charge of Wahhabism to undercut rivals. Yet after Yarmuk Jamaat had already emerged as a force in the republic, KBR DUM leader Pshikhachev acknowledged having initially discounted it, stating that he only began to believe in its existence after the 14 December 2004 attack on the FSKN anti-narcotics agency's headquarters in Nalchik.[91] Official clerics are at times understandably hesitant to defy the radicals openly. The Ingushetiya.ru website posted on 16 December a statement from probably traditional Muslim clerics in the KBR – condemning the Nalchik attack:

> We want to declare that you, "Yarmuk," have nothing at all to do with Islam and the republic's Muslims. . . . You act according to your personal motives and do not consider the opinions of the Islamic population. Thus your words are not valid among Muslims. For us, you are simply bandits. Last night, four brave Muslims who were fighting against the spread of narcotics were murdered. With that you committed a grave sin – the killing of a Muslim for the sake of personal gain . . . . We know who you are and will look for you until the end of your days.[92]

However, the vague signature appended to the message – "the Muslims of Kabardino" – betrayed the authors' fear before the militants. In such circumstances, the KBR DUM's position risks becoming untenable in the face of growing polarization between an increasingly authoritarian Russian state and an increasingly autonomous, alienated, and thus radicalized Muslim society.

Unofficial, Autonomous Islam

Radical Islamists emerged in the KBR under much the same confluence of immediate factors discussed in the case of Dagestan: the Chechen war, Putin's de-democratizing and de-federalizing policies, and some foreign Islamist influence, most importantly through Chechen intermediaries. That such a movement emerged in such a robust and virulent form despite the shallower roots of Islam in the region, especially among the Kabardins, should be of deep concern to Moscow. As in Dagestan and elsewhere in Russia, the KBR's Islamic revival began in the late 1980s and early 1990s with perestroika and the collapse of the Soviet regime. In the early 1990s, many students from the KBR went to study in Egypt, Jordan, Saudi Arabia, and Syria. When Islamic charitable organizations such as the All-World Assembly of Islamic Youth "An Nadva," the Saudi Arabia-funded missionary organization "Dawa," and the "Salvation" international aid and missionary organization began to set up branches in the region, the KBR DUM assisted them in their contacts with the republic's now more than 130 Muslim communities.[93]

Two local Muslims, Musa Mukozhev and Anzor Astemirov, became students of the Dagestani Wahhabi teacher Ahmad-kadi Akhtaev, himself a product of foreign Wahhabi proselytizing. In 1993 Mukozhev founded the Kabardino-Balkariya Islamic Center. It was soon shut down by the authorities, suspected of being a center for teaching Wahhabism. In fact, it was a front for a "new Muslim" movement of young self-described Salafists brought together from mosques around the KBR into an Islamic jamaat at times called the Initiative Group of the Muslims of Kabardino-Balkariya (IGMKB), at other times the Jamaat of the Muslims of Kabardino-Balkariya (DzhMKB).[94] This autonomous jamaat of Salafists grew out of small groups within the mosques of local Muslim communities, which modeled themselves on emerging Chechen jamaats.[95] The IGMKB and the outwardly non-violent DzhMKB became the leading autonomous Islamic and soon opposition structures in the KBR.

The jamaat adhered to the fundamentalist interpretation of Islam proposed by Mukozhev in opposition to the popular Islam shaped by local customs. It asserted that Islam in the KBR should start with a clean slate, shorn of its traditional pagan and *adat* elements, and develop an Islamist orientation modeled on that of the community established by the Prophet Mohammed in Medina.[96] Mukozhev and his followers were highly critical of the DUM's ties to the KBR authorities and official imams' practice of accepting believers' contributions in return for performing rituals, including local *adat* wedding and funeral customs, frowned upon by fundamentalists and Islamists. Mukozhev's jamaat developed links with the Chechen separatists of the first war and the ChRI Islamists of the inter-war period and second war.[97] In 1996, Mukozhev himself became one of the leaders of Basaev's Congress of the People of Chechnya and Dagestan and formed a shadow government with the stated goal of replacing the KBR regime by peaceful means.[98] He was careful not to support the Chechens or declare jihad in the KBR openly and instead provided support to the ChRI and "underground combat jamaats" preparing for war in the KBR and KChR.[99]

When the republic's authorities closed a large mosque in Nalchik to build the new central mosque under the KBR DUM's control in 1997, Mukozhev as the new imam of the Volny Aul mosque criticized the DUM's acceptance of state funds for such a project. In 1999 he established the Kabardino-Balkariya Institute for Islamic Studies (KBIIS).[100] Future combat jamaat emir Astemirov also worked there,[101] although it was headed by another close Mukozhev associate, Ruslan Nakhushev, whom some in the KBR MVD regard as the republic's "Number One Extremist."[102] Nakhushev headed a jamaat whose members dressed in traditional Islamist garb, wore beards, and, in response to later mosque closures, would peform their *namaz* (daily prayers) openly on the streets of Nalchik.[103]

With the second Chechen war, the ChRI leadership began to lobby Mukozhev aggressively for support in their efforts to expand their jihad to the entire North Caucasus. This led to disagreements between those who favored initiating jihad in the KBR and those who wanted to continue the policy of providing covert support for the ChRI. Mukozhev apparently held to the latter policy. In February 2001 he told Professor Mikhail Roshchin of the Russian Academy of Sciences that the republic's Muslims would "need at least twenty years for serious progress." Whether this was traditional Islamic dissembling (*taqqiyah*) in relations with non-believers is impossible to know. At the same time, Mukozhev added that although Muslims were patient, "they could eventually explode."[104] Mukozhev operated openly until summer 2005. Meanwhile the authorities refrained from accusing Astemirov and Nakhushev of any terrorist activities until 2005. This supports the claims of Astemirov that the DzhMKB included people who occupied official positions in the KBR.[105]

By 2004, according to one account, Mukozhev, now the unofficial "emir of Muslims of Kabardino-Balkariya," was leading some forty Islamic communities across the KBR which encompassed more than ten thousand well-organized followers.[106] The chief of the KBR MVD's religious extremism department, Beslan Mukhozhev, gave perhaps more realistic figures in October 2005 of 1,500–2,000 members spread across some twenty affiliated jamaats covering every district in the republic.[107] Therefore, Mukozhev's DzhMKB was probably able to provide an indigenous cadre base for militant Islamists' recruitment into combat jamaats and function as their political arm. The DzhMKB is known to have produced at least one Islamist who ended up at Guantanamo for fighting US forces in Afghanistan.[108] Astemirov himself was the alleged organizer of the attack on the FSKN building in Nalchik in December 2004 by the most renowned KBR combat jamaat, Yarmuk.[109] Astemirov would also be accused as the Yarmuk combat jamaat's new emir of leading the October 2005 raid into Nalchik by over two hundred Chechen and indigenous jihadists.

As the popularity of independent radicals like Mukozhev and Nakhushev grew and reports began to appear that Basaev was visiting the republic, the KBR authorities became increasingly convinced that Islamist-inspired terrorism was in the offing. Beginning in summer 2000 the official Muslim clergy as well as law-enforcement officials began warning of a radical "Wahhabi" presence, by which they meant jihadi terrorists. Indeed, precursors of Yarmuk already existed in Mukozhev's IGMKB and DzhMKB. Mukozhev was likely the same "Musa" whose statements as "spokesman" for the IGMKB have been cited elsewhere here and were curiously compatible with Yarmuk jihadist communiqués at the time.

The authorities responded to the growing threat in ways that further alienated young rank-and-file Muslims and certainly drove some into Mukozhev's and the jihadists' arms. Local Islamic leaders also complained of growing oppression in the KBR. In June 2002 the administration of the city of Chegem, a district capital five kilometers from Nalchik, issued an order banning, among other things, Islamic prayers in mosques except on Fridays from noon until 3 pm. Other city administrations began to emulate Chegem. For example, Nartkaly replaced one mosque's imam, using pressure on relatives to force them to convince him to step down.[110] In September 2003 the KBR's MVD (regional MVDs were strictly subordinated to the federal MVD by this time in line with Putin's counter-reforms) began closing mosques across the republic. Those mosques that were not closed were allowed to open for only 15–20 minutes daily. The KBR's MVD started issuing lists of suspected Islamists and began security sweeps of mosques during Friday prayers. On one occasion over a hundred were detained.[111]

In early 2004 the KBR government issued a decree permitting Muslims to go to mosques only on Friday and limiting prayers to forty minutes.[112] In addition, President Kokov set up commissions tasked with holding meetings in every town and village in the republic at which parents and relatives of alleged "Wahhabis" were told to encourage their young to shave off their beards, stop visiting mosques, and pray at home, or suffer serious measures.[113] However, according to a representative of the terrorists, although republican officials threatened to "repeat 1937," (to all Russian citizens, a clear allusion to Stalin's Great Terror) the residents of some villages and cities "rebuffed the non-believers and chased them in shame from the assemblies."[114] At the same time mosques were being closed, the DUM KBR moved against imam Z. Tilov, a leading opponent of the collection of contributions for clerical services, prompting bitter recriminations from the local community and the "new Muslims" alike.[115] This may have given Mukozhev a sense that the KBR's Muslims had been pushed to the limit and were ready to react.

The older generation in the KBR, as in other Muslim republics, for the most part seems to have continued to support the local official DUM. However the intensified restrictions and police pressures drove the young increasingly into Mukozhev's embrace, further dividing Muslims' loyalties along generational lines.[116] Mukozhev and Nakhushev's own research institute issued a report in June 2002 based on an "ethnographic expedition," which concluded:

> Coercive and administrative methods for solving problems of Islamic fundamentalism can reverberate as intolerance toward the Russian state, the state-forming ethnic group, and the Russian Orthodox religion. In these conditions it is not excluded that a significant portion of young Muslims will be imbued with the thought that full freedom of religion will be possible only in an Islamic state . . . . In the absence of alternatives, separatism can take on a religious guise and, under a sharp deterioration of the ethno-political situation in the region, the form of military jihad.[117]

The aforementioned Musa – likely Mukozhev – recounted the authorities' measures in his later official pronouncements justifying the call to jihad:

> Since fall 2003 war has been declared against Islam and Muslims in the republic. Hundreds of Muslims were subjected to physical violence and humiliation with regard to their religious sensitivities. They dragged them from mosques, beat them, and shaved crosses on their heads. All this was accompanied by an uncensored abuse of the Most High Allah and His messenger Mohammed, Allah bless and welcome him.[118]
>
> Attempts to call the guilty to answer by way of petitioning the judicial organs and monitoring organs produced no results. Hundreds of appeals from victimized citizens have been left without answer . . . .
>
> Taking advantage of the lawlessness, the militant atheists went further. The next step was the closing of all mosques in the city of Nalchik and several mosques in other districts in the republics. Seeing that Muslims did not undertake any adequate response even to this coercive interference and instead continued to console themselves with empty hopes for a good outcome of the issue, the enemies of Allah switched to the physical destruction of Muslims. They openly threatened those who did not submit to their deceptions. In almost all of the population centers assemblies of local residents were organized in the course of which representatives of the ruling elites, with the participation of prosecutors and the MVD, openly threatened the families of Muslims who visit mosques with physical reprisals and promised to "repeat 1937." "Now no one will be ceremonious with you, and people will simply disappear without a trace," they said . . . . Soon Satan's servants spilled the first blood. They beat to death Khasanya settlement resident Rasul Tsakoev.[119]

The increasingly common negative perception of the state authorities and official Islam among both cautious radicals and violent terrorists suggests there was already a *modus vivendi* between these two orientations prior to Yarmuk's emergence as an openly jihadist combat jamaat. Indeed, it was reported early on that the followers of Mukozhev and Nakhushev admired Yarmuk when it exploded onto the KBR political scene in 2004.[120] Others suggest that the Kokov regime's aggressive crackdown on Muslims and the closing of mosques sparked a split within the DzhMKB, with peaceful radicals turning into violent extremists and so producing the "United Islamic Combat Jamaat 'Yarmuk.'"[121]

The Rise of 'Yarmuk'

In late 2004 and early 2005, the highest-profile combat jamaat outside of Chechnya (and therefore the jamaat about which we have the most information) was to be found in the KBR. The rise of Yarmuk was a direct result of the Chechen war and ChRI financial support. In early 2001 KBR MVD chief Khachim Shogenov claimed there were already some 300–400 militant Muslims in the republic, half of whom had undergone guerrilla warfare training and fought against the Russian army in Chechnya. Some reportedly fought in a Kabardin branch of the Ichkeriyan armed forces organized by the notorious Khattab under Basaev's command.[122] Reportedly, over fifty returned to the republic after the war.[123] By mid-2001 Russian security forces were said to have uncovered Islamists' plans to seize power by force in both the KBR and KChR.[124]

The growing regime–Muslim tensions within the KBR seem to have encouraged the Chechens to recruit there. In August 2003, police were alerted to Basaev's presence in the KBR village of Baksan. Special police and FSB units surrounded his hideout, but he managed to escape. In the process Basaev was wounded in both legs and his nephew Hadim, who was also chief of Basaev's personal guard, blew himself up while attacking the local police chief. Rumor had it that Basaev was in the KBR to form a local network of underground Islamic combat jamaats.[125] During this visit he put his imprimatur on the indigenous Yarmuk Jamaat. The claim by one FSB general that Basaev's close associate the late al Qaeda terrorist Khattab "increasingly withdrew from the Chechens and came increasingly to trust Karachais and Kabardins" suggests that Yarmuk's emergence was part of a Chechen-, even al Qaeda-supported strategy to expand the war to the western North Caucasus Muslim republics.[126]

According to the KBR MVD, Yarmuk was formed in summer 2002 in Georgia's Pankisi Gorge by KBR residents who had joined the Basaev-allied Chechen separatist field commander Ruslan Gelaev's detachment there. Its original members are said to have hailed from the village of Kendelen (population six thousand) in the mountainous Balkar-dominated Elbrus district. Kendelen is one of the poorest villages in Kabardino-Balkariya, with 99 percent of working-age adults considered unemployed and surviving on subsistence farming.[127] Gelaev reportedly appointed a Kendelen inhabitant Muslim Atayev, to form Yarmuk because he enjoyed great authority among local young Muslims as the military emir of a jamaat known as the Kabardino-Balkariya Battalion that fought in Chechnya. By all accounts talented and capable, Atayev took the name Seifullah and would lead Yarmuk until his death at the hands of the Russian security services in January 2005.[128]

Atayev-Seifullah recruited some thirty like-minded Muslims, some of whom had taken part in fighting against Russian forces in Chechnya and undergone sabotage training in Khattab's camps. In November 2002, as part of Gelaev's detachment, they crossed the Georgian-Russian border and joined battle with federal forces in the region of Galashki in Ingushetiya. When Gelaev's unit returned to Chechnya, Atayev-Seifullah's unit was ordered to the KBR where it was to go into hiding, try to strenghten itself with new recruits and weapons, and await further orders. A core of eleven Yarmuk members led by Atayev-Seifullah returned to the republic together, while the others followed on individually to avoid detection. Atayev-Seifullah developed new ties among the local radicals, probably Mukozhev and his cohorts, and through them managed to contact Basaev, with whom, according to one report, he met in Baksan during summer 2003. Yarmuk is said to have subordinated itself to the Chechen field commander at that time.[129] Since, it has repeatedly used the Chechens' websites to issue its propaganda as well as to express its solidarity with the Chechen militants, mourning and hailing Ichkeriya president Maskhadov after he was killed by Russian law-enforcement organs and congratulating his successor, Sheik Halim Sadulaev.[130] Yarmuk is reportedly well trained and expert in targeted shooting.[131]

Having emerged from the predominantly Balkar Elbrus raion, Yarmuk may contain more Balkars than Kabardins,[132] but it also appears to reach out actively to non-Balkars. Yarmuk published a letter on 19 December 2004 from a group of Kabardins supporting its activities. In addition it praised Atayev-Seifullah's ethnic Russian wife, Olesya, as a martyr for fighting Russian forces to the death during the siege in which her husband was also killed.[133] The multi-ethnic character of the Islamist movement was confirmed when Atayev-Seifullah was succeeded by a Kabardin who also took the name Seifullah).

Some Russian officials claim that Yarmuk has links to the al Qaeda network, but these can only be regarded as indirect ties via Basaev and the ChRI. However, Russian MVD chief Rashid Nurgaliev, a Tatar by nationality, has now branded the KBR a "breeding ground for Wahhabis."[134] The Russian authorities' use of this term as a broad-brush description for Islamists in Russia is off the mark. Also inaccurate is the view that Yarmuk and the ChRI's other jihadists limit themselves to "defensive jihad," "moral revolution," and "personal reasoning and exercise of judgment."[135] This underestimates the growing influence of extremist international Islamism, Wahhabite or otherwise, in the North Caucasus. Yarmuk's Islamists are self-declared Salafists, who prior to their radicalization would have been adherents of the Hanafite interpretation of Shariah law traditional in the North Caucasus, not the Hanbalite legal school followed in Wahhabite Saudi Arabia. Like the ChRI and al Qaeda jihadists, their views are likely a mix of various Islamist tendencies. Yarmuk's ideology, strategy, and some of its goals bear a striking resemblance to those of al Qaeda and Iraq's al-Zarqawi, including their constant invocation and extremist interpretation of Shariah law.[136]

Yarmuk's Islamist goals can be ascertained from its name, which is borrowed from a river that forms the border between Israel and Jordan and that was the site of one of the greatest military victories in Islam's history of expansion into non-Islamic lands. In 636 A.D., a mere four years after the Prophet Mohammed's death, one of his closest companions, Khalis ibn Walid, led a force of twenty thousand Muslim troops to victory over some forty thousand troops of the Byzantine Empire that included Slavs, Armenians, and Ghassanids. Such a symbol has little to do with "defensive jihad" or the Caucasus, no less the KBR.

Yarmuk and its allies' statements are replete with references to Allah, citations from the Koran and Shariah law, and the attendant language and ideology of internationalist jihad. Musa described the death of Yarmuk's Atayev-Seifullah, his wife, and two-year-old son in terms of jihadist martyrdom: "Emir Seifullah showed a fine example of how a Muslim should defend his family and honor from the Russian aggressors and their loyal dogs. He concluded an advantageous deal and received a great profit which Allah promises those who carry out a true trade in the name of jihad." With Atayev-Seifullah's death, according to Musa, all Muslims were now required by Shariah law to join in jihad against non-believers. The sin of abstention from jihad, he said, renders Muslims non-believers, who having "left Islam" are worthy only of death like original non-believers.[137] Musa has also stipulated how best to organize jihadist terror and conduct partisan or guerrilla warfare, basing his instructions on Shariah law.

On 18 August 2004, Yarmuk emerged from the shadows.[138] Armed with automatic weapons and grenade throwers, eight militants engaged as many as four hundred members of the security forces equipped with armored vehicles and two helicopters for eight hours in forests near Chegem. Six managed to escape.[139] The connection between re-authoritarianization and the rise of jihadism is suggested by the fact that the Chegem authorities had been most aggressive in interfering in the work of local mosques and otherwise restricting Muslims' rights. The Chechen connection to Yarmuk was confirmed when the separatist website *Kavkaz-Tsentr* posted the combat jamaat's declaration regarding its first battle in "the war that Putin unleashed in Chechnya" which was now "taking on the nature of a national liberation fight by the Caucasus nations for their freedom", and expanding. "Now the mujahedin have started active military operations in Kabardino-Balkariya", Yarmuk announced.[140] On 23 August, the same ChRI website posted another message from "the information centre of the Kabardino-Balkariya Yarmuk Jamaat," reading:

> We wish to inform everyone that today, by favor of God, the Kabardino-Balkariya "Yarmuk Jamaat" has been established. Units of the jamaat have been deployed on the territory of Kabarda-Balkariya and are starting to carry out their combat tasks according to the requirements of a jihad. We want to state that "Yarmuk" fighters took part in a recent combat operation in Chegem district . . . . We are mujahedin! We are the soldiers of God! We are not fighting against peaceful citizens, never mind peaceful guests. We are not fighting women and children as the Russian occupation forces are doing in Ichkeriya. We are not blowing up inhabitants in their sleep, as the Russian FSB is doing.
>
> We wish to state that terrorist acts which may occur in the Republic of Kabardino-Balkariya against innocent civilians are the work of the Russian FSB and the Kabardino-Balkariya interior ministry. We are fighting against tyrants and parasites who have placed the interests of their mafia clans above the interests of their own peoples. We are fighting those who are growing fat at the expense of the impoverished and intimidated people of Kabardino-Balkariya who have been brought to their knees. We are fighting the occupation forces and aggressors who have seized Muslim land and are playing master over it . . . .
>
> Citizens of Kabardino-Balkariya! Your apologies for rulers, who have sold themselves to the occupation forces, have reached the point where drug-dealing, prostitution, poverty, crime, debauchery, drunkenness, and unemployment are rife in our republic. Their depraved policy has divided our daughters and sisters and led them on a path of depravity and permissiveness. Together with their Moscow masters and their criminal and unjust rule, they are provoking ethnic discord in the Kabardino-Balkariya Republic. On their orders they are abducting and torturing Muslims of the Kabardino-Balkariya Republic, closing our mosques, and preventing in every way possible the spread of the Islamic religion, the religion of truth and justice. Probably for the first time in Islam's 1,400-year history, a

mosque has been built which they have called not a mosque, but some sort of building of the Spiritual Board of Muslims of the Kabardino-Balkariya Republic. This means that the ordinary Muslims of the republic cannot enter the mosque without special permission! With their consent, over 200,000 Muslims of Ichkeriya have been annihilated, and 50,000 children have become orphans. On the Day of Judgment you [the Russians and their puppets] also will pay for this genocide.[141]

Clearly, the militants' call to arms sought to capitalize on the alienation created by the crackdown in the KBR.

In September 2004, days after Beslan, the KBR was thrown into panic by what appeared to be a Yarmuk-sponsored article on the Kavkazweb site: "End of the World: How Chechen Separatists Are Planning to Destroy Kabardino-Balkariya and Karachaevo-Cherkessiya," which warned that Basaev, who had already claimed responsibility for Beslan, would soon do the same thing at Nalchik's School No. 2 and that this would lead to an inter-ethnic North Caucasus war with the loss of tens of thousands of lives. In reponse, the KBR MVD offered a reward for information about Yarmuk members.[142]

All this, coming on the eve of Putin's post-Beslan call for emergency institutional reforms and security measures, prompted regional authorities to further tighten the screws on Muslims, resulting in more consternation in the religious community. KBR prosecutors demanded stepped-up investigations of alleged Wahhabis, checking local officials' compliance with the demands of the law "On Counteracting Extremist Activity."[143] In mid-September, Nalchik administrators decided to limit the city to one working mosque.[144] The authorities had already ordered the halt of construction of six mosques for each of the city's six districts a month earlier. The new announcement was met by representatives of KBR's DUM with complaints about the unjustified closure of mosques and police pressure on believers who were not involved in extremism.[145] Indeed, the KBR security organs' aggressiveness quickly led to tragedy. On 27 September, an apparently innocent young man was detained by police on suspicion of participating in radical Islamic groups and beaten to death.[146] By February 2005, there were reports of the detainment of children at checkpoints and roadblocks in the KBR.[147]

In October 2004, Russia's FSB chief Nikolai Patrushev stated that Russia's public enemy Number 1, Basaev, had been sighted again in the KBR.[148] It was perhaps not just a coincidence that winter 2004–2005 saw more daring Yarmuk operations. In early December, it attacked a representative of the FSNK and the chief of a strict-regime penal colony in the KBR.[149] On the evening of 13–14 December 2004 Yarmuk executed its boldest operation when it raided the Nalchik headquarters of the FSNK, killing four, including three police officers, seizing 182 pistols of various kinds and 79 assault and sniper's rifles.[150] Most disconcerting for the authorities was the evidence that Yarmuk received assistance from someone inside the FSNK.[151] The organizer of the attack, Anzor Astemirov, and two associates fit the typical age profile of Islamist recruits, ranging from twenty-five to twenty-eight years old. However, unlike many others, Astemirov had attended a higher-education religious school – in Saudi Arabia.[152] Claiming responsibility for the attack, Yarmuk declared in an internet posting that the "doors of jihad" would close in the region only when Shariah law is established and when the "occupied land belongs to our peoples." Jihad was declared specifically in the KBR, KChR, and Adygeya.[153] Thus, Yarmuk is part of the Islamist network's broader strategy of spreading jihad to the three western North Caucasus Muslim republics through the Circassian (Adygei-Cherkess-Kabardin) tribes which populate parts of each.

In late January 2005, Russian law-enforcement organs tracked down and killed Yarmuk leader Atayev-Seifullah and six accomplices in a three-day siege of an apartment complex on the outskirts of Nalchik. During the siege the militants reportedly tried to shoot at a passenger aircraft at the local airport, forcing the cancellation of all flights. Russian deputy interior minister Arkadii Edelev told journalists that two to four of the seven terrorists killed were female suicide bombers being prepared for acts of terrorism.[154] During the siege a Yarmuk internet message on the Chechen rebels' website declared that jihad was "now mandatory for every Muslim in the [North] Caucasus."[155] Two subsequent appeals asserting Muslims' obligation to join the jihad against Russia, posted on the same website and written by "Musa," were signed by the IGMKB.[156] This suggests that the IGMKB and JMKB were covers for Musa Mukozhev's involvement in Yarmuk and served as a recruiting pool for Yarmuk. The relationship between IGMKB/JMKB and Yarmuk could be more direct, with Yarmuk simply being the military wing of the former organizations.

Yarmuk quickly bounced back from this first setback, announcing that it had selected a new emir and adopted operational plans for the KBR and the entire North Caucasus in 2005.[157] On the Chechen insurgents' website *Kavkaz-Tsentr* Yarmuk promised to target the children of the MVD and FSB in retaliation for the killing of Atayev-Seifullah and his family. It declared its strategic aim: to break Russia's two "pillars" in the North Caucasus: Nalchik and Vladikavkaz, North Ossetiya.[158] Yarmuk's new emir, Rustam Bekanov, also renamed Seifullah, was identified as a former naib of Atayev-Seifullah's and an ethnic Kabard from Chegem.[159]

Nevertheless, Yarmuk continued to suffer losses. On 18 and 19 February, Russian security forces killed two more Yarmuk members in another apartment seige, apprehended three others, including two females, and uncovered sixty-nine detonators elsewhere in Nalchik. Commenting on these successful operations at a government meeting on 21 February, President Putin ordered Russian MVD chief Rashid Nurgaliev to "be tougher" in cracking down on militants in the Caucasus.[160] On 15 March, three powerful and ready-to-use explosive devices (36 kilograms) were seized on the outskirts of Nalchik.[161] To this day, Yarmuk has still not succeeded in carrying out a terrorist attack against civilians, as far as we know.

The KBR authorities ratcheted up the pressure. In mid-March a heavy police and military presence was established in Elbrus district. Major security exercises against terrorist threats were conducted in mid-April involving joint operations by FSB, MVD, and Emergency Situations Ministry (MChS) forces.[162] In late April, Russian forces found and killed Atayev's successor, Bekanov-Seifullah, along with three other militants, beheading Yarmuk for the second time in 2005. Russian media declared Yarmuk finished.[163] Two suspects detained by police during the operation claimed that Basaev was dissatisfied with Yarmuk's supposed inactivity and was demanding terrorist acts.[164]

Rumors of Yarmuk's death proved premature, despite early indications. Unlike in the aftermath of the death of Yarmuk's first leader, Atayev-Seifullah, Bekanov-Seifullah's killing was not followed by a web posting announcing the selection of a new emir, suggesting that it may have been destroyed or at least seriously disrupted. Given the number of extremists thought to be in the KBR, the failure of Yarmuk to survive or to be succeeded by a new high-profile jamaat suggested that the threat of Islamism or at least of organized revolutionary Islamist fighters had been overestimated. It cannot be excluded that Basaev and/or Sadulaev simply were not able to determine quickly which Islamist they wanted to approve as the new leader of their top KBR associate jamaat.

The Chechen Islamists' website carried several postings that seemed designed to imply that Yarmuk had survived. A 7 June 2005 message noted an increased presence of security forces in Elbrus, seemingly in response to previous Yarmuk postings warning people to stay away from the resort as it was "located in the combat zone" and MVD militia there as elsewhere were targets of the mujahedin.[165] A 5 June posting "To the Mujahedin of Kabardino-Balkaria," calling for a "jihad of the sword" and condemning Russia's official Islamic clergy for assisting Moscow in "resisting the rebirth of Islam in the Caucasus, Central Asia, the Volga, the Crimea, and the Urals and its natural import into Russia," declared itself inspired by the IGMKB appeal "Jihad Is Obligatory for Muslims of Kabardino-Balkariya" without any mention of Yarmuk.[166] This perhaps reflected a competition for which the prize of being ordained by Basaev as the KBR's leading combat jamaat, and access to funds and websites. Scattered but unclaimed terrorist attacks occurred in summer 2005. The relative lull may have been connected with the flight of Mukozhev abroad or with some of his closest associates into the mountains in fear that Russian security forces were now after them as much as Yarmuk. In the summer Mukozhev disappeared from public view and was thought to have abandoned open Islamic activity for underground jihadist warfare, perhaps in cahoots with Yarmuk. One source claimed he had fled to one of the Arab states.[167] The correlation between the comparative terrorist inaction and Mukozhev's disappearance seems to confirm the tie between the DzhMKB and Yarmuk. Indeed, on 3 October the Moscow journal *Kommersant-Vlast* published an interview in which a top KBR MVD official said that there were preliminary indications that Mukozhev's JMKB had received $16,000 from Basaev during his 2003 visit to the republic and had authored many of Yarmuk's internet communiqués.[168] Eventually, it became clear that Yarmuk, though crippled, was still active, though at a lower level.

The pool of potential militants appeared to be continuing to grow in large part thanks to the Kokov administration's heavy-handed policies. In mid-April 2005, the KBR MVD was included in events destined to alienate Muslims further and increase Yarmuk's recruitment opportunities. Nine female Muslim students were detained for reading the Koran on the premises of Kabardino-Balkariya State University. Reports suggest that during their detention they were forced to lift up their dresses and endure questions from militia regarding Muslim sex practices. The next day, the university's deans announced that group readings of the Koran were now banned on campus.[169] Later, a pregnant Muslim woman was beaten near her home by police because she was wearing a hijab. Islam.ru characterized the human-rights position of the KBR's Muslims as "critical."[170] Another Muslim was forcibly removed from her place of work and brought to police headquarters in Nalchik where she was reportedly mistreated, prompting her to file a lawsuit.[171] In August 2005, four hundred KBR residents appealed to President Putin for permission to emigrate because of the deteriorating situation in the republic.[172]

In September Kokov, likely under Kremlin pressure, resigned the presidency, citing health problems and the need for younger leaders. He was succeeded by a Moscow-based, ethnic Kabard businessman, Arsen Kanokov, a deputy in Russia's State Duma. In his first official statement as president Kanokov announced that the Kokov administration's closing of local mosques and alienation of the KBR DUM had been mistakes, signaling perhaps an abandonment of the more repressive measures that had helped stoke the fires of Islamist revolution in the republic since 2004.[173] However, the Islamists soon indicated that they were in no mood for compromise.

On 13 October 2005 Yarmuk participated in and perhaps led a major raid on Nalchik by KBR, ChRI, Ingush, and other mujahedin forces. The mujahedin attacked at least eight sites, including the airport, the FSB, MVD, and FSKN headquarters, and School No. 5. There were varying reports about the size of the force ranging from fewer than a hundred to several hundred. Basaev claimed the raid involved 217 mujahedin and that he took part in its planning.[174] Many in the KBR claim that Basaev came to Nalchik just before the raid handing out bribes of $100 and weapons to teenagers, and then pointing them in the direction of Russian troops and police. More disconcerting for the Russian authorities is the claim by some official sources that the majority of the attackers were in their early to mid-teens and indigenous to the KBR and that an apparently much larger operation had been foiled, forcing Basaev's jihadists to move prematurely. Russian MVD chief Rashid Nurgaliev claimed that discovery of a cache of tons of explosives and weapons on 10 October had forced the operation to take place earlier than the planned 4 November date which marked the end of Ramadan.[175] Basaev referred to a leak which had tipped off Russian forces.[176] He appeared to be referring to the 8 October arrest by police of a man who claimed he had been asked by a leading Yarmuk member to obtain a map of Nalchik airport for a terrorist attack he was planning.[177] It turned out that Mukozhev's ally and new Yarmuk emir, Anzor Astemirov, had led the Nalchik raid. An official warrant was finally put out for Mukozhev, and Nakhushev was summoned to report to security headquarters for questioning in connection with the raid, after which he disappeared.

Reports on the number of casualties on both sides varied. Official Russian sources claimed 91 mujahedin had been killed, over 40 captured, with 33 federal troops and 12 civilians dead and over 100 hospitalized. Basaev claimed only 41 mujahedin had been killed, while the death toll on the Russian side was 140, with 160 more wounded. Yarmuk claimed "around 40" mujahedin had been killed.[178] While expressing regret for the deaths of civilians during the Nalchik raid, ChRI emir/president Sadulaev praised the operation and declared: "May Almighty Allah help us liberate and unite the entire Caucasus!"[179] Basaev's ChRI coordinating hub, the KBR's Yarmuk Jamaat, and Dagestan's Shariah Jamaat put out similar propaganda messages. They denied that their jihad was driven either by poverty, bad Kremlin policy, or inter-clan rivalries in the republics. Each stressed instead that it was driven by fervent Islamic faith and a desire to establish a state based on Shariah law.[180] This suggests an increasingly sophisticated and better-coordinated communications and propaganda system within the network. On the other hand, Basaev's reliance on teenagers suggests that Yarmuk's pool of recruits is more limited than in other North Caucasus republics. Nevertheless, Yarmuk remains the "main" terrorist jamaat in the KBR, though there may be others.

ETHNO-NATIONALISM AND THE ISLAMIST THREAT IN THE WESTERN NORTH CAUCASUS

The nexus between nationalism and Islamism is more likely to be strengthened from below or by the efforts of the Chechen-led Islamists, rather than from above in the form of elite-led secession. All the same, important or even critical defections by republican or clerical leaders to a nationalist or Islamist opposition are possible. Putin's centralization policies could be accelerating such a process in unexpected ways. For instance, as soon as the Kremlin began to push for the merger of regions in 2002, the KBR parliament characterized the idea as dangerous. One deputy warned that its authors "do not understand that they may wind up with 89 Chechen Republics."[181]

Indeed, events in the KBR clearly demonstrate the connection between ethno-nationalism and Islamism and the potential of the former to become a platform for the latter's growing influence within society. Balkar nationalism is perhaps more easily converted into Islamic nationalism than Kabardin nationalism, as became clear with the KBR authorities' response to the Yarmuk threat.[182] President Kokov attempted to take control of the profitable Balkar-dominated ski-resort district of Elbrus, sparking a new wave of Balkar nationalist mobilization. Kokov's recentralizing methods were reminiscent of the federal authorities' new approach to the regions after the renewal of the Chechen war and Beslan. According to the London-based pro-Chechen website *Chechen Press.org*, on 4 March 2005 the KBR government assembled the village administration heads of Elbrus raion and demanded they sign a pledge "not to support Wahhabites and take all responsibility for their activity." They reportedly threatened Elbrus administration head Khizir Makitov personally, if he did not maintain loyalty. On 10 March, according to the same source, North Caucasus Military District (VO) and MVD Special Designation Militia Units (OMON) forces began a major sweeping operation in the district. Armed officials of the law-enforcement organs were omnipresent in Elbrus district, and armored personnel carriers were located at almost every traffic light in the town of Tyrnyauz, a suspected radical stronghold.[183]

At the same time, a new law "On the Status and Borders of Municipal Formations in the KBR" adopted in early March further heightened tensions. The law transferred the ski-resort town of Prielbrusye and its revenues from the jurisdiction of Balkar-dominated Elbrus to the capital Nalchik, 120 kilometers away. This suggests that Nalchik suspected the loyalty of the Balkar-dominated area and feared it could be a source of funding for the Elbrus-originated Yarmuk.[184] The law also incorporated four districts adjacent to Nalchik into the capital. The two that were predominantly Kabard-populated remained calm. However, the two predominantly Balkar-populated districts, in addition to Elbrus, became support bases for a revived movement to form a Balkar republic separate from the KBR. Artur Zakoev, the former head of the Khasan village administration, one of the two Balkar-dominated villages (the other was Belaya Rechka) to be incorporated into Nalchik, organized an initiative committee to oppose the reforms. On the evening of 14 May, Zakoev was murdered. Then the committee lost two appeals in the KBR's courts, which effectively scuttled the Balkars' hopes of blocking the law.[185] On 28 May, more than a thousand demonstrators went onto Nalchik's central square to condemn Zakoev's assassination and to call for a Balkar Republic separate from the KBR, including the transfer from Kabard to Balkar jurisdiction of four districts that had belonged to Balkariya until 1944.[186] Significantly, the demonstrations also condemned the arbitrariness of MVD anti-terrorist operations.[187]

In late May President Kokov appointed one Osman Kurbanov as his "representative" or inspector in Balkar-dominated Elbrus; the first time the KBR had appointed an envoy to any raion in the republic.[188] This did not sit well with Balkars. On 3 June the ethnic Balkar National Council requested a meeting with Kokov and Southern FO envoy Kozak to challenge the appointment, claiming that Kurbanov had criminal connections and had helped ruin a key enterprise in Tyrnyauz, while Elbrus residents held a meeting outside the Tyrnyauz administration building. As tensions mounted, KBR prosecutor Yurii Ketov wrote to Elbrus raion administration head Khizir Makitov, blaming him for the rising tensions in the district. Makitov claimed that the authorities in Nalchik were pressuring him to step down before the end of his second term.[189]

At the same time, the Balkar-Karachai nationalist but Islamic-oriented movement "Jamagat" is now perhaps tied to the Islamist jamaat, the Balkar-Karachai "Jamagat Jamaat." The latter supports terrorism on its website Camagat.com, which re-emerged after a hiatus in summer 2005 touting the causes of Karachais, Balkars, and the ChRI, and praising recent attacks on local MVD officers and police.[190] Thus, a faction of the Balkar-Karachai nationalist movement has been radicalized and is allying itself with the Chechens' increasingly Islamist expansionist cause. Importantly, the Balkar-Karachai connection strengthens KChR ties to the ChRI Islamist network beyond the formerly very active Jamaat Number 3. The KBR's new Balkar crisis, still unresolved at the time of writing, underscores how the Islamist threat interacts with inter-ethnic tensions and boosts Islamists' prospects for destabilizing the region in the hope of sparking jihad across the North Caucasus.

Islamism and Ethno-Nationalism in Karachaevo-Cherkessiya and Adygeya

The rise of Islamism and ethno-nationalism in the KBR is even more significant as it occurs against a background of increased inter-ethnic tensions in other western North Caucasian republics of the Muslim Circassian and Balkar-Karachai peoples, the KChR and Adygeya. These tensions could lead to instability that would inevitably redound to the benefit of the Ichkeriyan-led North Caucasian jihadist network.

Karachaevo-Cherkessiya

Although the KChR's most important political divide is that which runs between the republic's titular ethnic groups, the Karachais and Cherkess, the republic has also seen an upsurge in indigenous and Chechen-led insurgents' presence under Putin.[191] Excluding Yarmuk, the first and most significant combat jamaat in the western North Caucasus emerged in the KChR, first under the name "Karachai Jamaat" then "Jamaat Number 3." Not surprisingly, it was led by another Basaev associate, ethnic Karachai Achimez Gochiyayev. He and Jamaat Number 3 were involved in several terrorist incidents in Moscow, including the February 2004 subway bombing. By summer 2004 Jamaat Number 3 was showing signs of growing activity and collusion with Chechen-based guerrillas. However, by 2005 it seemed to have ceased operations.

In summer 2004 rumors of possible terrorism in the KChR yielded to significant jihadist terrorist activity. To address the threat KChR president Murtaza Batdyiev issued a July decree establishing a "Frontier Zone" in Karachayevsk, a mountainous region populated largely by the Karachai ethnic minority and thought to be a stronghold of Islamic and separatist groups.[192] In early August an internet article headlined "Basaev Has 'Ordered' Karachaevo-Cherkessiya" suggested that the ChRI jihadist had planned a raid on a police station in the republic following the scenario of the June raid on Ingushetiya and the October 2005 raid on Nalchik. Police were put on alert and armed reinforcements arrived, fanning rumors that militant groups had already entered the republic. On 12 August KChR MVD chief Aleksandr Obukhov gave a press conference to deny these rumors, but he acknowledged that the security situation in KChR was complicated as it was throughout the Southern FO.[193]

Days later checkpoints were set up in an effort to identify "adherents of Wahhabism." Operation "Anti-Terror Whirlwind" also included soldiers checking caves and looking for Wahhabi guerrillas' weapons stores. In vehicle searches "banned books . . . in Arabic," twenty-nine copies of a "Wahhabi" interpretation of the Koran, were reportedly confiscated. Head of the Karachayevskiy district MVD Boris Mamayev claimed the republic had "around twenty-nine people who are sympathetic [to extremism]" and that they were being interrogated, fingerprinted, and photographed.[194] The detainees reportedly told police that the extremists had a three-phase plan of action: (1) the expansion of Wahhabism; (2) the consolidation of the Wahhabite ranks; and (3) jihad.[195] A month later, on the night of 20 September, three armed militants fired on guards at the Zelenchuk hydroelectric complex, which provides about 20 percent of the republic's electricity.[196] On the first day of the Beslan hostage-taking, a shootout took place in the center of the KBR capital Nalchik when notorious ethnic Kabardin terrorist and KChR resident Dagir Khubiev was told by police to pull over and responded by shouting "Allah akbar!" The subsequent shootout ended in his death. Khubiev has been linked to Jamaat Number 3.[197]

The jamaat's leader, Achimez Gochiyayev, was implicated by investigators in two of the three August 1999 Moscow apartment bombings that killed hundreds and helped reignite the war in Chechnya. Five years later, investigators charged that Gochiyayev and Jamaat Number 3 were involved not only in the 6 February 2004 Moscow subway suicide bombing but in most of the acts that composed Russia's 2004 summer of terror, including the bus-stop bombings, both aircraft bombings, and the explosion near the Rizhskaya subway station one day before the Beslan hostage taking.[198] The ethnic connections between the KChR's Karachais and the KBR's Balkars are reflected in ties between the two republics' jihadists, including their premier terrorist jamaats. In Russian MVD chief Nurgaliev's February 2005 report to Putin on the battle against the KBR-based Yarmuk combat jamaat, he stated that a "Karachai jamaat" had ordered the KBR jamaat to begin terrorist operations.[199] One of two alleged trainee suicide bombers killed with Yarmuk leader Atayev-Seifullah in January as well as several militants detained later in the KBR were KChR residents.[200] The new Balkar-Karachai Jamagat Jamaat marks another KBR–KChR jihad connection.

As Jamaat Number 3's activity levels declined, secular and ethno-national political tremors shook the republic. In October–November 2004, the KChR was rocked by mass opposition demonstrations and stormings of President Murtaza Batdyiev's offices after his son-in-law was suspected of involvement in the murders of seven people, including the son of one of the leaders of the parliamentary opposition, in a dispute over the ownership of the republic's largest enterprise, Kavkaz Cement. Presidential envoy Dmitrii Kozak was forced to make several trips to the republic to prevent the opposition's seizure of power by force. At first glance the problem seemed to be a case of ethno-political conflict, if not inter-clan violence, rather than one connected with Islam. Karachais like President Batdyiev and his former top ally, the first deputy premier and KChR MVD chief Ansar Tebuev, dominated the KChR authorities. Karachais make up 33 percent of the KChR population, Cherkess 10 percent, and Russians 42 percent. Like the KBR and Dagestan, the KChR had implemented a power-sharing inter-communal coalition scheme for the republic's top leadership positions – the offices of KChR president, premier, and People's Assembly chairman were shared out among the different groups, which helped contain inter-ethnic tensions during the 1999 KChR presidential elections. When Batdyiev, an ethnic Karachai, won the 2003 election, a Cherkess was appointed government chairman and the Russian parliaments chairman. However, as a result of Putin's legal harmonization policies, the institutionalization of this consociational form of grand inter-ethnic coalition in the republic's constitution was prohibited, with Karachais coming to dominate the elite as a result.[201]

However, there may also have been a connection between this conflict and rising Islamism. The bodies of the victims in the Kavkaz Cement murders were found near a mountain village outside Karachaevsk, a reported terrorist refuge and center of the former Karachaevsk Jamaat.[202] Weeks prior to the murders, deputy premier and MVD chief Tebuev, who had been leading efforts to root out not only criminal elements but also radical Islamists in the republic, was gunned down.[203] Tebuev led counterterrorism investigations and operations against Islamist and Chechen militant fundraising and recruiting activities, including those of Jamaat Number 3's Gochiyayev, a close aid of Chechen militant leader Shamil Basaev. Gochiyayev repeatedly threatened Tebuev. At a government session on 28 September Tebuev warned that radical Islamism was being preached to young people in the republic's mosques: "There is not one mosque in Karachaevo-Cherkessiya where our old men can go anymore – they are simply not admitted. Our imams are being pushed out of the mosques. They are afraid to go there. They command no respect, and no one listens to them. They are not needed."[204] The believed use of an assault rifle and the destruction of a vehicle in the execution of Tebuev's assassination are consistent with the methods of Chechen militants rather than criminal groups. Some evidence points to jihadist members of the ethnic Cherkess diaspora in Jordan, perhaps working with Chechen militants. Cherkess jihadists, thought to be financing Islamist militant groups in the Caucasus, had reportedly gained control of the Cherkessk Chemical Plant, the KChR's largest industrial enterprise, and Tebuev was leading the investigation into this affair at the time of his assassination.[205] All of this may suggest an Islamic connection to the Kavkaz Cement murders. Some locals and relatives of the victims certainly believed that Tebuev's assassination was tied to that crime.[206] Thus, there is some evidence for suspecting a nexus connecting the business dispute, inter-ethnic tensions, and regime-Islamist conflict in the KChR.

Another development has been the recent re-emergence of Karachai,

Abazin, and Nogai nationalism in the KChR, as the republic's authorities have attempted to centralize power in reponse to the Islamist threat, much as Moscow has on the federal level. In June 2005 the KChR passed a new law redefining districts in parts of the republic which involved transferring ownership of what had been ethnic Abazin lands to a neighboring ethnic Karachai village, sparking objections and protests by local Abazins. On 29 June the Abazin national movement, "Abaz," organized a mass demonstration in the central square of Cherkessk, the KChR's capital. It demanded that the federal authorities step in to prevent the law from coming into force.[207] Some protesters occupied the parliament building and only agreed to leave on 1 July after a telephone conversation with the Southern FO envoy Kozak, who met their demands by issuing an official statement condemning the law as "insufficiently thought through" and calling for its suspension. On the same day Kozak met in Moscow with representatives of the Abazins and the KChR government, including KChR premier Alik Kardanov, to discuss the dispute.[208] A week later the KChR parliament annulled the law and created national districts within the KChR for the Abazin and Nogai minorities.[209] On 2 July some six hundred ethnic Karachai delegates, led by KChR parliamentary deputies, in particular the former head of the Karachaevskii district Islam Krymshamkhalov, convened a conference and established a national association – the Congress of the Karachai People (KKN) – to unite Karachais and Balkars, preserve peace, and battle economic problems in the republic. Krymshamkhalov, expected to be elected the KNN's chairman, is reported to believe that peace in the republic can only be achieved by uniting its peoples on the basis of Islam.[210]

Adygeya

Putin's centralization policies sharply polarized center-periphery relations with the small Muslim republic of Adygeya, something which could also play into the hands of Chechen-led Islamists who already have their eyes on the enclave which is surrounded by ethnic Russian-dominated Krasnodar Krai. Ethnic Russians make up 70 percent of Adygeya's population to the Adygeis' 26 percent. Under Yeltsin there was a marked favoritism toward Adygeis in political appointments and the design of political institutions, a problem not redressed to the Russians' satisfaction in the early years of the Putin era. Thus, in league with local ethnic Russian Union of Slavs, the Kremlin began to push for the merger of regions in 2002. Both the KBR and Adygeya objected.[211] On 22 April 2005 some ten thousand mostly Adygei demonstrators went into the streets after plans were announced to merge the Muslim republic with Krasnodar Krai. A Committee to Protect the Status of the Republic of Adygeya and a League of Social Unions were immediately formed.[212]

Intermittent Adygei and Russian demonstrations and counter-demonstrations continued throughout the remainder of 2005. In December the ethnic Russian Union of Slavs convened a congress which issued a resolution calling for Adygeya's merger with Krasnodar and the holding of a referendum to decide the issue.[213] Adygei and Cherkess communities from across the North Caucasus responded during a February 2006 congress by warning Moscow that, should it abolish Adygeya's autonomous status, they would propose unifying all Russia's historically Circassian lands – Adygeya, Kabarda, Cherkessiya, and Shapsughia – to create a far larger Adygei-Circassian Republica.[214]

Demonstrations renewed and tensions continued between the Adygeya leadership and Moscow. When the March parliamentary elections in Adygeya produced a majority for the Kremlin's Ydinaya Rossiya party, making a referendum on Adygeya's merger with Krasnodar Krai likely, the republic's Cherkess Congress along with the KChR's Cherkess organization and the KBR's "Adyghe Khase" – appealed to Council of Europe's secretariat for the Framework Convention for the Protection of National Minorities to issue a condemnation of any such move. In April Adygeya president Khozrot Sovmen resigned as tensions grew with the new parliament and presidential envoy Dmitrii Kozak, who continued to back Adygeya's merger with Krasnodar. Both Sovmen and the ethnic Circassian Cherkess Council and "Adyghe Khase" criticized Kozak and the proposed merger.[215] On 10 April, the Cherkess Council and "Adyghe Khase" adopted a statement expressing support for Sovmen, reaffirming the Circassians' rejection of the merger plan and warning that its implementation could have catastrophic consequences not only for the North Caucasus but for all of Russia. They further announced that a congress of all Circassian peoples had been scheduled for 21 May. The congress as well as numerous Adygei, Cherkess, and Kabard national movements have strong support from émigré communities in Turkey, the United States, and elsewhere.[216]

The joint Circassian (Adygei, Cherkess, and Kabard) opposition to the plan to merge Adygeya with Krasnodar raises the ominous specter of a broad Circassian mobilization which could destabilize all three of the western North Caucasus Muslim republics. The foreign émigré element supporting the Circassians also risks an overreaction from an increasingly xenophobic *siloviki* faction in the Kremlin that suspects the hand of the US and the West behind every domestic problem. Furthermore, all this has been accompanied by a rise in state reprisals against Muslims in Adygeya in the aftermath of the October 2005 Yarmuk-Basaev-backed revolt in Nalchik. In 2006 Adygeya Republic authorities began carrying out search operations and mass arrests of those attending traditional Friday prayers at mosques.[217] In March, the first combat jamaat to declare itself openly in Adygeya emerged.[218]

CONCLUSION

Despite killing successive Yarmuk emirs, radical Islamists and Yarmuk remain active in the KBR. Putin's re-authoritarianizing counter-revolution, the ongoing Chechen war, and the post-Beslan crackdown on real and imagined Muslim extremists by unreformed regional leaders and security organs have intensified the radicalization of the KBR's Muslims. That radicalization, combined with Chechen recruitment and training in the region, has in effect brought the KBR's radical Islamists into alliance with the international Islamist jihadists. Depending on how one interprets the data, the number of militant Islamists joining the Yarmuk and Mukozhev-Nakhushev jamaats appears to be growing. Estimates in 2001 put the number of Islamists in the KBR at 400–500; by September 2004, the KBR MVD's database was said to list 389 participants in "illegally armed formations," including 71 Nalchik residents, and it was reported that that criminal groups were attempting to "use the ideology of Islam as cover" and creating "Wahhabi" jamaats in KBR prisons.[219] At the same time, however, Southern FO prosecutor Nikolai Shepel said the number of radical Islamists in the KBR was fluctuating between five hundred and two thousand.[220]

As long as the Chechen insurgency festers and Putin endeavors to run a hyper-diverse Russia from Moscow and use the unreformed *siloviki* as his main instrument of control, the Islamist infection will deepen across the North Caucasus republics as well as in Stavropol and Krasnodar Krais. Yet the president persists in centralizing. In March 2005 legislation was introduced to the KBR parliament entitled "On the Rejection of Sovereignty" and "On Amendments to the KBR's Constitution" which stipulated the removal of all articles regulating the division of authorities between the KBR and Moscow and turning over this authoritiy exclusively to Moscow.[221] Similarly, tense relations between federal and republican authorities, on the one hand, and official Islamic clergy and rank-and-file Muslims, on the other, are sure to continue driving young Muslims in the direction of more radical political forms of Islam.[222]

Authoritarian repression of Muslims' rights in the KBR is producing what Thomas De Waal aptly termed "a small model of Uzbekistan" – a harsh authoritarian regime holding a simmering population and Islamist movement barely at bay.[223] Shortly after this observation was made, sultanist Uzbekistan saw a revolt sparked by the authorities' apparent overreaction to a radical Muslim movement. President Islam Karimov's decision to fire on thousands of demonstrators, killing hundreds, means the cycle of alienation and radicalization is likely to continue. This is a possible harbinger of things to come in the KBR and its sister republics, the KChR and even Adygeya, where conditions are increasingly similar to those in the KBR.

Chapter Six

Tatarstan and the Tatars:
Nationalism, Islam, and Islamism

By dint of sheer numbers and economic power, Tatarstan and Russia's Muslim Tatars represent the greatest potential danger to the future of the Russian federal state. Tatars are Russia's second largest nationality, and those outside their homeland of Tatarstan constitute an influential internal diaspora. Given Tatars' high rates of urbanization, Russification, secularization, and allegiance to the more moderate Hanafi school of Islam, the legacy of the nineteenth-century Islamic reform movement known as jadidism, and Tatarstan's geographical distance from the North Caucasus and its comparatively sound socio-economic performance, Tatars and Tatarstan will be an important test of the capacity of the Islamist movement and ChRI network to "travel" across ethnicity and territory.

The chief defining factor of Tatar nationalism in the post-Soviet era has been Tatarstan's quest first to win and then to preserve the republic's autonomy within the Russian Federation. Islam has so far been a secondary factor. As Russia's leading republic with a Muslim titular nationality, Tatarstan's "return to Russia's legal space" was pivotal not only for the fate of federalism in Russia but for inter-ethnic and inter-confessional relations in Tatarstan and perhaps for internal Tatar diaspora communities. With the end of autonomy after Putin's federative counter-reforms, there is a real possibility that the quest for internal self-determination will be abandoned by many Tatars in exchange for the more radical agendas of extreme nationalism and Islamism. Although Tatarstan lacks an external border, frustrated nationalism and a strong will to self-determination might lead to secession or destabilization of state and society. The Tatars of the Volga and elsewhere refer to a past of Tatar statehood, which drives much of Tatar nationalism.

The other major factor in Tatar nationalism is Islam, which is a central (though not necessarily the primary) component in Tatars' sense of identity, setting them apart from the Russian Christian Orthodox "other."[1] Tatars' allegiance to the more moderate Hanafi school of Islam and the legacy and revival of the jadidist movement may predispose them to a more moderate nationalist communalism. However, the close identity of Tatar nationalism with Islamic culture and religion and the radicalizing Islamic umma both inside Russia and abroad hold the potential for a more Islamic brand of nationalism and even Islamism to develop. The Russian domestic context in which Tatars currently find themselves may strengthen the impetus toward radicalism. Putin's anti-federalist counter-revolution, the atmosphere created by the ongoing Chechen quagmire, and the infiltration of foreign and perhaps Chechen Islamists could transform Tatars' secular nationalism over the mid- to long term. Should Tatar nationalism become subordinate to Islamist goals, an Islamist-led revolutionary war could well destroy the Russian state as we know it.

HISTORICAL BACKGROUND

Tatar nationalism has roots in a tradition of self-mobilization, a historical pattern of independent Tatar statehood (in particular the Islamized Kazan khanate of the fifteenth and sixteenth centuries), and a national identity tied to moderate and secularized forms of Hanafi Islam. Before and during the Kazan khanate the Tatars were also a major military and ethno-confessional component of Genghis Khan's Mongol hordes that swept across Eurasia.[2] Kazan was conquered and converted to Orthodox Christianity by Ivan the Terrible in 1552. Thus, the loss of Tatar statehood and self-determination is directly tied to Russian imperialism. Under the Russian yoke, Tatars' identity with Islam was strengthened by imperial efforts to convert Muslims and communist efforts to destroy Islam. There is a Tatar tradition of revolt against Russian rule. The tsars' attempts to convert and assimilate Muslim Tatars to Russian Orthodox Christianity, and to discriminate against them when they failed, provoked numerous Tatar uprisings to throw off Russian rule; Tatars' also participated in numerous peasant revolts with no distinct ethno-national goals.[3] Indeed, over the centuries, Tatar nationalist uprisings have often begun as peasant revolts sparked by socio-economic circumstances rather than cultural, national, or religious issues.[4]

In the late nineteenth century Tatars were heavily influenced by the secularizing and moderate "jadidist" Islamic modernization movement and educational system. Although the initiator of the movement was a Crimean Tatar, the Volga or Kazan Tatars quickly became its driving force. Indeed, jadidism was presaged by Kazan Tatar Islamic reformers of the eighteenth and nineteenth centuries, such as Abd ar-Rakim Utyz-Imyani al-Bulgari (1754–1834), Abu Nasr Kursavi (1776–1812), and Shigabutdin Mardzhani (1818–1889), as well as by more secular Muslim Tatar thinkers including the

Crimean Tatar Ishmail bei Gasprinskii. These reformers laid the groundwork for jadidism's transformation from an educational reform movement into a much broader political and Islamic one tied to Tatar nationalism.[5]

Utyz-Imyani and Kursavi rejected the "closing of the gate" to "absolute *idzhtikhad*," that is, the end of the free interpretation of Shariah law regarding issues that the Koran and Sunna (sayings of the Prophet Mohammed) do not address in favor of submission to the reasoning of Islamic legal scholars (*ulema*) based solely on their reading of previous Koranic interpretations and legal consensus (*idzhma*). It was the rise and establishment of four major maskhabs of Islamic jurisprudence and Koranic interpretation from the twelfth century that closed the gate to *idzhtikhad.* Other interpretations on basic issues of faith became impossible outside their typically tight strictures. Reformers like Utyz-Imyani and Kursavi held that such cases should be decided by seeking renewed opinions from recognized Islamic scholars and jurists, putting aside the four schools' petrified Shariah interpretations.[6] Kursavi went even further, proposing what amounted to a revolution for the umma. His first studies of Islamic law and Koranic interpretation as a student in Bukhara ended in the muftiat's issuance of a death sentence against him and his flight back home to Kazan. He had opposed the Bukhara Islamic scholars' efforts to identify Allah's attributes, which culminated in a bitter dispute over whether these amounted to seven or eight. Kursavi argued that their efforts presumed an authority which violated Allah's transcendence and man's right freely to determine his understanding of God's existence. Such an understanding could only be attained by the close study of the Koran, not by submission to interpretations made by *ulema.*[7] Kursavi then sought to "open the doors of *idzhtikhad*" by arguing that the interpretation of Sharia law, though based on the texts of the Koran, Sunna, and idzhma, should take into account "conditions" or living context. Moreover, such interpretations could be undertaken not only by recognized legal scholars but by anyone with sufficient knowledge in the relevant religious disciplines. In addition, he called for the spreading of the knowledge of the sacred texts and legal opinions as far as possible among Muslims; that is, Kursavi was urging the democratization of the holy texts' interpretation. Most importantly in political terms, literal interpretations of the Koran made outside of time and context, according to Kursavi and later jadidists, made it difficult for Tatars to make their way in the modernizing world of late nineteenth-century Russia and therefore should not be the basis for the development of Islam for Tatars.[8]

In support of Kursavi's call for a spreading of the knowledge of the religious and legal texts, Shigabutdin Mardzhani said that practical reforms needed to be made in the curriculum and teaching methods in the madrasahs.[9] The stage was set in the 1870s and 1880s when Ismail bei Gasprinskii, the father of jadidism, established a new model school in Crimea and came to Kazan to spread his educational reforms among the Volga Tatars. His proposals resonated with the changes called for by Kazan's Islamic reformers. This confluence of ideas produced a Tatar reform and enlightenment movement which culminated in a modernizing Tatar nationalist movement. The jadidists' modernization of education in Kazan Gubernia's Tatar schools and madrasahs provided not only for religious lessons but put a premium on the study of the natural and social sciences and of Russian and Arabic as well as the Tatarization of the curriculum and pedagogy (not just teaching of, but teaching and learning in the Tatar language).[10]

The jadidists not only transformed religious education in Kazan and other parts of the Turkic-speaking Muslim world, they also began to secularize and rationalize Islam, making Tatars some of the most modern Muslims of their day. They engaged in and, in many ways, won an ideological battle for the control of mosques and madrasahs with the conservative "Qadimists", (*qadim* means "old"), who insisted that "all that is old is good."[11] Qadimists "defended medieval particularism and obsolete traditions, attacked the reform and enlightenment movement, and preserved the soil for religious fanaticism." Indeed, Qadimist leader Ishmukhamed Dinmukhamed called the jadidists "members of Satan's party."[12] The jadidists built on twelfth-century Islamic teacher Ibn Rushd's idea of "bifurcated truth." Tatar jadidist cleric and Mardzhani follower Sh. Kultyasi set out a strict division between the worlds of religion and science. Shariah law, informed by idzhma as in its early, more fluid form, was given the spheres of religion, moral and ethical education, and the regulation of interpersonal relations. "Explanation of the nature of reality, the large and small bodies in it, their order, and the resolution of controversial questions of the universe" were the realms of science.[13] Kultyasi and others emphasized science as the key to the understanding of earthly causality and castigated the Qadimists for stunting Muslims' initiative by attributing all phenomena to Allah.[14]

The political implications and consequences of jadidism are the subject of some dispute. Some regard it as an essentially apolitical movement, while others see it as generally nationalist or ethno-political in orientation.[15] There is no doubt that jadidism had important ethno-political implications and consequences that went far beyond the concerns of simple education reform. Those implications became the very core of the late nineteenth- early twentieth-century Tatar national movement. For the Tatar intelligentsia then and now, jadidist transformations "touched on socio-economic, family household, and cultural-ideological relations," including equal rights for women, the spreading of cultural and educational institutions, the development of Tatar press, literature, art, scholarship and science. For some these goals were part of a democratic agenda, for others they were part of a socialist one. For all they were aimed at ending the Tatars' colonial subordination to St. Petersburg and the attainment of Tatar equality with Russian and European civilizations.[16]

The nationalist Tatar intelligentsia led the way. It included Tatar pedagogues, writers, historians, journalists, and entrepreneurs, but also jadidist Islamic scholars.[17] The jadidists' expanding control of theological and religious schools meant that by the early twentieth century Kazan's young jadidist intellectuals and mullahs were playing a leading role in disseminating among Tatars and other Muslims in Russia the newest trends in secular Russian and thus Western social thought (capitalist, democratic, nationalist, and socialist), building support for constitutionalism, parliamentarianism, and ethno-nationalism, though not separatism.[18] The jadidists' Tatar nationalism included both democratic and reformist Islamic strains, since the religious and secular intelligentsia alike recognized the central place of Islam in Tatar identity. This was reflected in jadidists' mixing of Tatar nationalist, Islamic, and even pan-Turkic ideas. According to the jadidists' vision, a constitutional monarchy of the kind promised but never delivered by Tsar Nicholas II after 1905 would give Tatars political and civilizational equality with Russians if combined with a federative or quasi-federative Russian state, and Islam would attain equal rights, even equal influence with Russian Christian Orthodoxy. Both Gasprinskii and prominent Kazan jadidist G. Gazizi supported the reform of the Tsarist empire into "a federation or, in the worst case, a form of autonomy for the indigenous peoples."[19] Gasprinskii also supported the unification of all Turkic peoples under Russian rule.[20]

In sum, when Russia entered upon its tortuous path to modernity, the jadidist enlightenment and the evolution in Tatar Islamic and social thought had prepared Kazan's Tatars to be able to take the fullest advantage of Russia's opening to the modern industrialized Western world with all its various "isms." In the end, both Russia and Kazan would be sidetracked by a Bolshevik minority who fought their way to power and imposed a cruel, radical answer to the dilemmas of modernization. The death knell for Tatar nationalist aspirations under Soviet rule was sounded with the arrest and murder of Tatar Bolshevik leader Sultan Galiev, whom Stalin disposed of for insisting on the "national deviation" of pushing for union republic status outside the RSFSR in the 1930s.

With the failure of the Soviet experiment, an opening emerged for a jadidist revival and a second Tatar renaissance. In the post-Soviet era, for the most part Tatars have readopted the moderate nationalism and Islam of their grandfathers and great-grandfathers. Although a revival of jadidist reform Islam could impinge on the appeal of radical Islam, it would inevitably produce a nationalist upsurge as well, providing a foundation for radical Islamists to build on, especially in an atmosphere of contracting democracy, federalism, and tolerance. Although some Islamic leaders in Tatarstan today consider re-Islamization a precondition of a real revival of jadidism, many political leaders, including President Shaimiev's top political advisor Rafael Khakimov, think the two can and must be revived simultaneously to avoid radical re-Islamization.[21] Even traditional Muslim Tatars, being of the Hanafi school, tend to be less influenced politically by their faith.[22] That said, as Tatars' dream of autonomy is deferred, blocking their ethno-national aspirations, the potential for mass communal politicization tinged with some radical re-Islamization (perhaps originating from outside Tatarstan) could be actualized. Tatars could first be ethno-politically radicalized and then begin to delve further into their history and religion, increasing the opportunities for interpretation and manipulation of both ethno-political entrepreneurs and extremist Islamic proselytizers seeking to make political capital out of inter-ethnic tensions. It ought not to be forgotten that it was only after the independence of nationalist Dzhokar Dudaev's regime was threatened in 1994 by opposition forces backed by Moscow that the Chechen dictator turned to Islam to rally new forces to his cause.

THE RISE OF INSTRUMENTALIST NOMENKLATURA TATAR NATIONALISM

In the perestroika years, Tatarstan, like many other republics, experienced a nationalist revival. The Russified and secularized communist nomenklatura in Tatarstan, led by Communist Party of Tatarstan first secretary and Supreme Soviet chairman Mintimer Shaimiev, retained a hold on power locally, while endeavoring to negotiate the political waves induced by bitter factional infighting in Moscow, the resulting weakening of Gorbachev's reformist Soviet regime, and the ultimate collapse of the Soviet state.[23] The Tatar nomenklatura, in particular Shaimiev himself, supported the hardline communist coup against Gorbachev in August 1991, only then to realign itself with Yeltsin after he emerged the victor. Indeed, Shaimiev had reportedly supported the August coup because its leaders promised him that Tatarstan would be given union republic status outside the RSFSR.[24]

Pushed by the nationalist opposition and personal considerations of power, the Tatarstan leadership drove the movement for the formation of a loose asymmetrical federative system in Russia that would leave the regions with considerable political, economic, and cultural autonomy. In negotiating with Moscow Shaimiev, deftly promoted and pointed to the threat from radical Tatar nationalists in order to convince the Kremlin to decentralize power. The republican leadership cooperated with moderate nationalist organizations such as the All-Tatar Public Center (Vse-Tatarskii Obshchestvennyi Tsentr or VTOTs), the All-World Congress of Tatars and the Idel-Ural Assembly in coordinating the activities of the Tatar national movement inside the republic and with similar movements throughout the Volga mega-region including in Mari El, Chuvashia, Udmurtia, and Bashkortostan. Shaimiev's top political advisor Rafael Khakimov was the author of the first VTOTs program and chief ideologist of Shaimiev's policies.[25] Khakimov remains both Shaimiev's top political advisor and a member of the editorial board of the Idel-Ural Assembly's newspaper *Tatarskie krai* to this day. He argued then that Russia's collapse was inevitable and its borders illegitimate. Either an enlarged Tatarstan should be recognized as an integral part of a centuries-long, joint Tatar-Russian project with its origins on the post-Kievan Rus state – a Russian federated state – or a looser entity should emerge with Tatarstan being part of a more amorphous "Russian space."[26]

In the end, Shaimiev decided he could negotiate a power-sharing treaty with Moscow and through a mixture of subterfuge and repression was able to marginalize Tatarstan's extreme nationalists. In particular, he split the moderate camp by pushing through the Tatarstan Supreme Soviet a declaration of sovereignty and began negotiations with Moscow that delivered a great deal of autonomy for the republic, both on paper and in the real political and economic life of the republic.

This is not to say, as some do, that the emerging nationalist revolution in Tatarstan during the 1990s could not have threatened the Russian state.[27] Indeed, between 1987 and 1993 there were 142 mass demonstrations in Tatarstan focused on nationalist demands. In October 1991, as many as twenty thousand protesters gathered before the Supreme Soviet to demand the adoption of a declaration of independence.[28] Radical nationalists, influenced by pan-Islamic nationalism, such as the radical nationalist Ittifak movement's leader Faizulla Bairamova, demanded not only Tatarstan's independence but the incorporation of lands of the former Tatar khanates in the Urals and Siberia, including the regions of Tyumen, Samara, Saratov, Astrakhan, and, most significantly, Orenburg, which would give a united Tatarstan-Bashkortostan state an outlet to Muslim Central Asia.[29] In the cities of Naberezhnyi Chelny and Kazan radical Tatar nationalists began the process of forming the embryo of a national army under the guise of a national guard.[30] In fall 1991 Shaimiev used the MVD to disarm and arrest 623 extremist Tatar nationalists. October raids turned up 742 weapons.[31]

Along with repressive measures, more subtle instruments were deployed to defuse radical nationalism. Shaimiev succeeded in splitting or marginalizing radical Tatar nationalist groups such as Ittifak and VTOTs, that favored secession from Russia, by offering Tatars sovereignty, a referendum to approve such a goal, and negotiations with Moscow to achieve it. This two-track strategy ultimately won a high degree of autonomy for the republic. On 21 March 1992 Tatarstan's referendum on soverignty that resulted in a 63 percent vote in favor of the declaration of sovereignty, and 37 percent against. While actual support for Tatarstan's independence was low compared with that for the more modest goal of internal self-determination, the disunity in Moscow and the more serious threat in Chechnya served to obviate confrontation between Kazan and the Kremlin. A divided Moscow could not afford a fight on two fronts. A unified Russian elite, such as that which prevails in Moscow today, would have been more confident in confronting re-emerging Tatar separatism.

The March 1992 referendum gave Shaimiev a popular mandate to negotiate a power-sharing treaty with Moscow. With the radicals' defeat in 1991–92 and the practical Tatar nomenklatura and moderate nationalists working toward similar goals, Tatarstan (like Bashkortostan) was able to forge a loose confederal relationship with Moscow, leading the way in building the Russia Federation's treaty-based "official asymmetry." As the negotiations dragged on, the Tatarstan leadership highlighted for Moscow the potential for a second Chechnya in Tatarstan. In 1993 Khakimov published a book in which he argued that Russia's various national minorities were proceeding on the assumption that the Russian Empire had not been fully dismantled with the collapse of the USSR and that they were destined to create their own ethno-territorial states. Khakimov seemed to warn that a violent final dissolution of the Russian Empire might be unavoidable, noting: "It is necessary to prepare for harsh times. . . . Empires do not die out quietly. When collapsing, they stink.'"[32]

In the end, that specter, along with Kazan's more flexible and sophisticated approach to finding an institutional solution to the vexing problem of its internal self-determination within the Russian Federation, prevented or at least postponed conflict. In February 1994, after two years of difficult negotiations, Kazan signed the first bilateral federal-regional treaty with Moscow. According to article 11.3 of Russia's 1993 constitution, such treaties could redistribute the joint federal-regional competences and powers listed in article 72. However, the Moscow–Kazan treaty went further, handing over solely federal powers to Kazan and stipulating that the republic was "a state united with the Russian Federation" as opposed to a subject of the federation. The republic's relationship with Moscow, the treaty continued, was based upon not only the treaty and Russian constitution but also the 1992 Tatarstan constitution. The latter stipulated that Tatarstan was a "sovereign state," an independent subject of international law, and merely "associated with" Russia.

Moreover, Tatarstan's founding document boldly violated the federal constitution by declaring the supremacy of republican law over its federal equivalent in the event of contradictions. Subsequent agreements with Moscow gave Kazan even more rights, including to 75 percent of the tax revenues collected on its territory, 50 percent more than allowed to most other regions, particularly the twenty-six that never signed a power-sharing treaty or agreement with Moscow. Based on the treaty and the constitution, Tatarstan moved aggressively to fill the legal vacuum left by the USSR's collapse, adopting thousands of regional laws, executive directives, and the like. These would soon be construed as violating federal laws and the Constitution, once federal legislation was adopted that differed from regional law, and Moscow decided to stand on clauses in the Constitution that gave precedence to federal laws over regional laws rather than on a division of sovereignty and the bilateral power-sharing treaty.

Eventually, forty-five regions, mostly the national autonomies, would follow Kazan's example and sign power-sharing treaties and agreements, though none would achieve the degree of sovereignty won by Kazan. The first two to follow were, incidentally, also titular Muslim republics, the KBR and Bashkortostan, and each received broad autonomy. Thus, Tatarstan had not only won for itself a nearly confederal status with Russia but it had led Russia's first successful democratically oriented, federalist movement, which became an integral part of Russia's revolution from above.

Islam's central place in Tatar national identity, even if not so much religious as cultural, dictated that Tatarstan's political elite also address the religion's role in the republic and even in Russian society more generally. Just as the Tatarstan model propagated a moderate vision of Tatar nationalism and self-determination embedded in Russian history, it also embraced a "usable past" of reform Islam, jadidism, to contain any emerging Islamic nationalism. At the same time, the close connection between national identity and Islam means that radical nationalism – that is, most of the nationalists outside of the more moderate and instrumentally nationalist Tatar nomenklatura or political elite – rejects moderate Islamic trends.

The most radical Tatar nationalist movement, "Ittifak," led by Faizulla Bairamova, has espoused a radical Islamic nationalism, unlike the VTOTs, which has been comparatively moderate at least until recently. Ittifak's 1996 "Canon of the Tatar People" proselytized a xenophobic view of a "Jewish-Christian civilization" that was alien to Tatar civilization and could be repelled only by "true" Islam and "pure" nationalism.[33] Ittifak's December 1997 Fourth Congress more explicitly rejected moderate nationalism and openly declared jihad:

We come out against those representatives of the Tatar intelligentsia, who want to supplant the Koran with such tendencies as jadidism, Sufism, and "Euro-Islam." It is a national liberation struggle which we are leading against the Russian Empire, and we declare from now on a jihad aimed at throwing off the domination of the unbelievers . . . . We are Muslim nationalists, and we are beginning a struggle for the creation of an Islamic state in Tatarstan.[34]

This potential extremist threat had informed the Tatarstan political elite's willingness to supplement secularism with Euro-Islam and jadidism. Thus, Shaimiev's advisor, Rafael Khakimov, has become Tatarstan's leading ideological patron of a jadidist revival. He wrote what can be regarded as the neo-jadidists' manifesto in 2003, *Gde nasha Mekka?*, which openly criticized both traditional Islam in Tatarstan and Russia and Islamist extremism and called for Islamic reform along jadidist lines. The jadidists' prescriptions, according to Khakimov, will allow re-Islamization of Russia's Tatars to advance rather than hinder Tatarstan and ethnic Tatars' modernization and secure a worthy place for them in a rational, globalized, high-tech, democratizing world.[35] Khakimov declares: "I live in Tatarstan and do not want to be like an Arab of the Middle Ages," emphasizing jadidism's nationalist orientation and liberal interpretation of Islamist teaching. His emphasis is on the Koranic writings of the Mecca period "aimed at all peoples" of all times. There are "no differences in the rights of men and women," the use of force is banned for conversion to Islam, and a tolerant attitude to peoples of all religions is clearly expressed. Khakimov's Koran is one where tolerance is written: "O people, We created you as men and women; We divided you into nations and tribes so that you would know one from the other." The writings of the Medina period, in Khakimov's jadidist view, stand in stark, negative contrast to those of the Mecca period. They are much less relevant to Islam, as they were composed mostly for the Arabs of the seventh century in the context of an Islam fighting to expand its influence militarily across the world. This explains, for jadidists and Islamic reformers alike, calls in the Medina-era *ayats* (verses) for Muslims to fight non-Muslims wherever they are encountered and to place men above women.[36]

Khakimov rejects the conservatism of the official Muslim clergy much as he does the Muslim nationalists' extremism. His views implicitly run counter to the preference among many in the official Islamic clergy for traditional Tatar Islam oriented on the Hanafi school, on the grounds that the latter lacks jadidism's interest in the development of the Tatar nation. Indeed, Khakimov has criticized explicitly the official Muslim clergy for a lack of knowledge regarding leading jadidist intellectuals and theologians such as Kursavi,

Mardzhani, and Musa Yarulla Bigiev (1875–1949).[37] He has also castigated the official clergy for ignoring the development of the economy and Tatar culture.[38] In *Gde nasha Mekka?*, Khakimov supports the jadidists' desire to open the gates of *idzhtikhad*. This "allows taking into account the evolution of society, offering a contemporary interpretation of Islamic norms," "brings East and West closer," and is a "source of liberal thinking."[39] Like the nineteenth-century jadidists, Khakimov supports the right of not only every Islamic scholar, but every Muslim, to his or her own interpretation of the Koran, so undermining the power of the official clergy.[40]

For Khakimov, Tatars in Russia should not seek the establishment of Shariah law, but like Muslims in Turkey should learn to live in a secular state and transform Russia into a fully multicultural, democratic federation:

> The shariah does not function in Russia, and Orthodox Christians comprise the majority of the population. Muslims should settle into this way of life . . . . This country is no worse and no better than Muslim states, it is simply different. This is our fate and our destiny – to work out the experience of the true path in these conditions. We cannot be made a Saudi Arabia, and we can hardly become Christian Europe. We are as we are. The date tree does not grow on Russian soil.[41]

Secularism and jadidism, according to Khakimov, will allow Muslim Tatars to leave the world of traditional Islam in which "any new idea is immediately regarded as heresy" and advance into the modern world where the individual is equal to the jamaat.[42] On the world stage, the Tatars' enlightened Islam will allow them to be a bridge between East and West, on the border between which it is the Tatar nation's fate to be situated both geographically and culturally and where they have built their own "sub-civilization."[43] Tatarstan's reform Islam, industrial base, and human capital and the meeting of the Islamic and Western worlds put Tatars in a good position to play a leading role not only in the Turkish and Muslim worlds but also to fulfill their global "task" and "destiny":

> For the Tatars salvation is in the future, not the past. And our path to progress was begun by the jadidists, who following the Prophet's testament began the reform of Islam. We should continue it, relying on all that is of value and has been developed by mankind.
>
> Europe has always been a source for us, from which we took wisdom and knowledge. It remains so even now. Our task is not building fences separating Tatars from other peoples and not locking ourselves away on an artificial ethno-confessional reservation, but the creation of bridges

between the various religions, between the various understandings of Islam, and between Islam and Christianity. Our mission is the spreading of tolerance which can strengthen all mankind with common ties.[44]

Khakimov's views have been attacked by conservative Islamic clerics and Muslim intellectuals from both inside and outside Tatarstan. For example, radical Islamic intellectual Geidar Dzhamal assailed the title of *Gde nasha Mekka?*, calling it blasphemous, and asserted that by using it Khakimov had expelled himself from the ranks of Muslims.[45] Mufti Mukaddas Bibarsov, chairman of the DUM of the Volga Area (Privolzhya) disparaged secular theoreticians of jadidist reformism like Khakimov, who acknowledges he is not a practicing Muslim believer, as akin to "eunuchs who attempt to talk about family life."[46] Although DUMT Chairman Gusman Iskhakov has not challenged Khakimov's jadidism, his deputy, Gurman Valiulla Khazrat Yakupov, issued an erudite defense of Tatars' traditional "Qadimist" Hanafism in September 2003, arguing that traditional Islam had not been a hindrance to modernization in Malaysia and therefore would not be in Tatarstan.[47] Some of Khakimov's harshest Muslim critics are anti-Western, pro-Moscow, and Eurasianist in their theological and geopolitical orientation. The Dagestani DUM-sponsored website Islam.ru carried a series of articles attacking Khakimov's work, criticizing the neo-jadidist trend within the Tatarstan political and religious elite, and defending Qadimism.[48]

Tatarstan's official clergy is considerably less jadidist in orientation than the Tatar intelligentsia and allied elements within the Shaimiev administration. At the same time, it is still in its infancy, being less than a decade old, and it is constrained by its financial dependence on the Shaimiev regime.[49] Therefore, its confessional, ideological, and political orientations – like those of the Tatar people – are still in their formative stages. Yet already there is a significant jadidist strain in some of its policies. DUMT chairman has designated as an "urgent issue" the "religious education and enlightenment of all levels and strata of the population for the formation of a civilized understanding of Islam and securing the continuity of its spiritual evolution."[50] The DUMT has encouraged the reintroduction of the "new" method in the republic's madrasahs and sponsored, along with the Institute of History of the Tatarstan Academy of Sciences (where Khakimov is a leading force) and official Islam's Council of the Muftis of Russia, the establishment of the Russian Islamic University (RIU) in Kazan. The RIU, which Iskhakov calls a "powerful scientific educational center" and to which, in Khakimov's words, "falls the enormous responsibility of giving meaning to and spreading the experience of jadidism," offers both religious and secular education in the jadidist tradition.[51] The DUMT-affiliated publishing house Iman, in an effort to restore the Tatar legacy of social thought and revive the various Tatar literatures banned during the Soviet era, has given a prominent place to the late nineteenth- and early twentieth-century jadidists' works. However, much remains to be done in returning these works to Tatars. The DUMT also publishes a scholarly journal, *Mir Islama*, which promotes scholarly studies of the jadidist movement, Tatar national identity, and Islamist theology. Also, the chairman of the influential Council of Muftis of Russia, Ravil Gainutdin, an ethnic Tatar, has embraced jadidism.

The Tatar people, intelligentsia, and clergy are just beginning to rediscover their Islamic roots. Indeed, Khakimov has taken them to task for failing to read the leading jadidist texts.[52] One reason, however, is that many are no longer available, removed from history by the Soviet regime.[53] Nevertheless, with or without official support, historians, writers, journalists and poets over time will inevitably unearth much of the material buried by seven decades of Soviet rule.

The failure of Shaimiev's moderately nationalist nomenklatura-led regime to defend Tatarstan's sovereignty and unite Tatars around the republic-homeland during Putin's anti-federalist counter-revolution risks discrediting moderate reformist jadidism as much as it does moderate Tatar nationalism. Thus, there is the danger that re-Islamization will occur in a political context that increasingly favors more radical Tatar nationalism and the Islam of people like Bairamova or, as we have seen in other Muslim republics, "new Muslims" and Islamist jihadists.

THE FAILURE OF INSTRUMENTALIST NOMENKLATURA TATAR NATIONALISM

Putin's counter-revolution has had a more profound effect on Tatarstan than on perhaps any other region because of the loss of Kazan's sovereignty and autonomy and the post-Soviet ruling Tatar nomenklatura's huge political stake in them. Tatarstan's status as "a subject of international law" and "sovereign state" "associated" with the Russian Federation established much of Shaimiev's and the Soviet-era Tatar nomenklatura's political legitimacy. Years of promoting itself as the champion of asymmetrical federalism and regional autonomy reinforced the regime's initial legitimacy after it won the republic's 1992 referendum on Tatarstan's declaration of sovereignty. Sovereignty and autonomy, asymmetrical federalism, and moderate nationalism and Islam became the tenets of Tatarstan's official ideology. These institutional arrangements contained Tatar nationalism, marginalizing nationalist and Islamic radicals and thus preserving the Soviet nomenklatura's hold on power. Tatar nationalism was supplanted by Shaimiev's multi-ethnic, multi-confessional "Tatarstanism," based on the notion of ancient Muslim Tatarstan's (or the Kazan khanate's) instrumental role in Russian history and its right therefore to a special place in Russia and a unique degree of autonomy from Moscow. Putin's anti-federalist counter-revolution under-mined Tatarstan's popularly mandated status and thus Shaimiev and the increasingly ethnic Tatar ruling elite's political standing in the republic.

The Shaimiev regime's stake in defending its sovereignty was strengthened by the dividends it brought in terms of control over the republic's natural resources, state property, and finances. Shaimiev, in a more careful and restrained manner than Bashkortostan's President Murtaza Rakhimov, created a state capitalist system with all of the attendant maladies of cronyism and state oligarchy now extant in Moscow and the rest of Russia. Shaimiev also used more progressive approaches like land reform to strengthen the region's independence from Moscow. As one of only three regions (Samara and Satarov are the others) to have legalized the sale and purchase of land, Tatarstan has thus given its inhabitants a stake in the republic's sovereignty. Shaimiev's insistence on Tatarstan's sovereignty and control over all land and natural resources on its territory was a major, if not the main, target of Putin's anti-federalist counter-revolution.

Putin's Counter-revolution and Tatarstan's Resistance and Retreat

Many national republics, in particular several titular Muslim ones, put up some, often purely bureaucratic, resistance to Putin's recentralization, especially the "harmonization" of their constitutions with the federal constitution. But Tatarstan led the way with a more significant though ultimately doomed effort to defend regional autonomy.

Shaimiev's administration relied mostly upon bureaucratic obstructions, court battles, and horse-trading on the margins rather than open political resistance. With the Islamist threat extant in Russia and around the world and the renewed Chechen war, there was no political will in Kazan to call radical nationalists onto the streets as in the early 1990s in order to protect Tatar sovereignty. The cautious Shaimiev administration had little choice but to back down repeatedly in a forced retreat before Moscow's assault on Tatar sovereignty. Tatarstan thus saw its constitution amended and stripped of clauses supporting autonomy and sovereignty. In addition, hundreds of laws and other normative legal documents were repealed or amended, and the Russia–Tatarstan power-sharing treaty was renounced by Moscow. In addition, numerous assimilation policies were implemented that impinged on Tatars' established religious, cultural, linguistic, political, and civil rights.

With his close ally, speaker of Tatarstan's legislature (called the State Council) Farit Mukhametshin, Shaimiev led Tatarstan's executive and legislative branches in efforts to block or delay Putin's anti-federalist counter-revolution in Tatarstan. For example, in 2001–2002 the Tatarstan State Council twice recessed early for the summer when the Kremlin pressed it to amend its constitution. In addition, from 2000 to 2004 Tatarstan filed several suits and tens of appeals in the Russian and Tatarstan courts to salvage clauses in its constitution that formed the legal basis of its sovereignty and autonomy. Tatarstan fought several victorious legal battles in what ultimately proved Moscow's triumph in the overall constitutional war. With Putin's increased control over both federal and regional prosecutors and constitutional and supreme courts, Tatarstan's authorities could only delay rather than repel federal efforts to amend its constitution and laws to suit Moscow's desires.

Shaimiev was at times confrontational. In November 2000, when Chuvashia president Nikolai Fedorov appealed to the constitutional court against Putin's federal intervention powers, Russian justice minister Yurii Chaika was dispatched to Kazan to secure a written pledge from Shaimiev that he would bring the republic's constitution and laws into harmony with federal law. However, Shaimiev refused to comply and said negotiations would need to continue.[54] He suggested several times that the federal government would have to bring some of its own laws into conformity with the Russian constitution and that it had much to learn from regional law, especially his own "Tatarstan model." Shaimiev's call for federal use of good regional laws was to some extent heeded by the center.[55] However, under no circumstances were the regions to be granted institutionalized power to participate directly in federal law-making. Thus, on 17 July 2001, as the legal and constitutional harmonization policy continued to be pressed by Moscow, Shaimiev issued a not so veiled warning to the Kremlin, stating that Tatarstan and Chechnya had been the only republics not to have signed the old 1992 federation treaty and that the "federal center needs to pay more attention to this fact."[56] In the context of the renewed Chechen war, this was a strong statement.

Seven months after the founding of the federal intervention mechanism (which marked the beginning of the harmonization process to reintegrate Russia's legal space) and approaching two years after the June 2000 deadline by which regions were to have harmonized their constitutions and charters, some regions' laws and constitutions were still in violation of federal norms, in particular those of Tatarstan. According to first deputy prosecutor general Yurii S. Biryukov, some republics were "trying to drag out the review of [federal] protests and representations" against regional laws and constitutions and had "ignored" federal laws and Russian constitutional court decisions requiring them to harmonize their constitutions and laws with their federal counterparts.[57] "[S]everal clauses in the constitutions of the republics of Altai, Adygeya, Bashkortostan, North Ossetiya-Alania, and Tatarstan," including key clauses "on the state sovereignty of the republics, the supremacy of the laws [of the republic] and of the rights to stop the application of legal acts of the Russian Federation on their territories, the status of the republics as subjects of international law, the right to the use and disposition of natural resources on the territories of the republics," remained in violation. Biryukov warned, under the then new federal intervention mechanism, that if regional authorities failed to amend acts found by the courts to be in violation of federal norms within six months, then "the president has the right to issue a warning which will have started the procedure" for removing any offending regional chief executives or disbanding any offending regional legislature."[58]

Throughout 2001 and early 2002 President Shaimiev and Tatarstan's State Council brainstormed on how to amend the constitution in accordance with Moscow's demands but still retain some of the constitutional and legal basis for Tatarstan's sovereignty. In January 2001 Shaimiev told Moscow that the harmonization process could not be completed until after the Tatarstan presidential election set for March 2002.[59] After Shaimiev's easy re-election, deputy prosecutor general for the Volga FO Aleksandr Zvyagintsev renewed pressure on Kazan in June, pointing out that all fifteen of the Volga FO's regions had brought their constitutions into conformity with federal norms, except for two: the two lone Muslim republics, Tatarstan and Bashkortostan.[60]

Shaimiev sought to preserve his legitimacy by offering Moscow compromises, alternatives, and supplements to Putin's counter-revolution. First, he proposed the joint federal-regional jurisdiction of the spheres outlined in article 72 of the Russian federal constitution be eliminated and its competencies divided up between the center and the regions. This suggestion had gained currency among some Russia officials and scholars.[61] Second, he suggested a federal-regional consensus-building mechanism, a type of "minority veto," for the regions' participation in the federal legislative process. It would have given each Federation Council member a "delaying veto," forcing a second review of any piece of legislation touching on issues of national minority rights under review in the Federal Assembly's upper chamber, institutionalizing the regions' right to propose amendments.[62] Shaimiev's consociational mechanism would have been more robust than the Yeltsin-era reconciliation mechanism that Putin soon moved to weaken.[63] Not surprisingly, after the Kremlin got a look at Shaimiev's proposals, set to be delivered in a speech to the 20 February 2001 session of the new advisory State Council (made up of the regions' governors or presidents and created to compensate for their removal from the Federation Council), Putin changed the meeting's agenda to land reform. By the State Council's March session, membership of its presidium had been "rotated," Shaimiev lost his seat, and his proposals were removed from the agenda.[64]

In spring 2002, Kazan acquiesced. The 10 May 2002 amendments changed almost all of the 1992 constitution's 130 clauses, including the most controversial article, 1.1, which stated that "Tatarstan is a subject of international law and a state associated with the Russian Federation."[65] The replacement article deprived Tatarstan of its international status, redefining the republic as a state "united with" and "a subject of the Russian Federation."[66] By this Tatarstan recognized its membership in the federation. However, Moscow remained dissatisfied with this and numerous other articles, including the amended article 16.1: "The land, its minerals, water, forest and other natural resources, animal and plant world are used and protected in the Republic of Tatarstan as the basis of the life and activity of the people."[67] Thus, immediately after the amendments came into force, deputy prosecutor general for the Volga FO Aleksandr Zvyagintsev protested against fifty-two of the articles, including those on sovereignty, citizenship, and several spheres which he said belonged solely to federal competence: the activity of economic enterprises, consumer rights' protection, war and peace, national security, criminal and criminal procedure law. When Zvyagintsev submitted his complaints to the Tatarstan State Council, the parliament immediately decided to break early for the summer, again delaying the process.[68]

In January 2003, in an apparent compromise, Zvyagintsev reduced the number of clauses in the Tatarstan constitution against which his complaints were directed to thirty-seven. Most importantly, he withdrew his challenge to the clause giving the republic the status of a "state" (*gosudarstvo*).[69] A hiatus in Moscow's efforts to rein in Kazan then ensued. The Kremlin needed to secure the support of Tatarstan's party of power Tatarstan – New Century (Tatarstan – Novyi Vek or TNV) for Yedinaya Rossiya (United Russia) and for Putin himself in the 2003–04 federal parliamentary and presidential elections. The truce brought Moscow high dividends. The Tatar president lavishly applied Kazan's administrative resources to secure victories for Putin and Yedinaya Rossiya, with Shaimiev becoming one of the party's three vice-chairmen. In the December 2003 Russian State Duma elections Yedinaya Rossiya won all five single district seats and 60 percent of the party vote. In the Tatarstan State Council election, it won 80 percent of the seats, and in the March 2004 Russian presidential election Shaimiev secured Putin 83 percent of the vote.

However, the benefits were considerably fewer for Kazan, especially Tatar nationalists. Moscow's war on Tatarstan's constitution resumed days after Putin's easy re-election. Tatarstan's battle for sovereignty came to an ignominious end on 31 March 2004, when Tatarstan's Supreme Court upheld Zvyagintsev's objection to the relevant clause, among others. The federal prosecutor in Tatarstan, Kafil Amirov, an ethnic Tatar, added insult to injury when he declared his full support for the Tatarstan court's decision.[70] Tatarstan's authorities now had three months to amend the constitution or face a presidential warning and possible disbandment of the Tatarstan State Council and/or the removal from power of president Shaimiev. However, as of mid-2005 Tatarstan had still not complied as its fraternal Muslim republic, Bashkortostan, had been forced to do. In April 2006, prosecutors were still appealing against parts of the court decisions.

Kazan began looking carefully at Moscow and the Kremlin's efforts to normalize the situation in Chechnya by granting it some measure of autonomy. In Tatarstan's Supreme Court in the March 2004 case, its representative argued that the Venice International Commission, not to mention Moscow, had approved of the new Chechen constitution backed in a republic referendum and enacted in 2003. The Chechen constitution's first article reads just like the Tatarstan constitution's sovereignty clause that had been challenged by federal prosecutors and the courts.[71] In the context of Tatarstan's long retreat Chechnya's constitutional success was a bitter pill for Kazan to swallow.

The Tatar intelligentsia and the nationalist opposition began to wonder aloud whether Tatarstan had made the right choice in compromising with Moscow in the mid-1990s. In a 21 March 2003 article, the capital's influential daily newspaper *Vechernyaya Kazan* signaled Tatar consternation over Chechnya's relative gains. Pondering Kazan's lost sovereignty, it ruminated: "It is impossible to buy sovereignty . . . it can only be taken by force of opinion, as it was in Tatarstan in the early 1990s, or by force of weapons . . . as is occurring now in Chechnya. . . . Sovereignty exists only as armed sovereignty . . . this thesis is universal." Even a compromise on "limited sovereignty" would be possible only "if the region demonstrates sufficient ability to arm itself so that the authorities in the center recognize that the costs of 'forced disarmament' of such a region are unacceptable." The article concluded that "the abrogation of Tatarstan's sovereignty is an automatic result of its leadership's policy." In its next issue the Tatarstan government's newspaper, *Respublika Tatarstan*, also noted the contradiction inherent in Moscow granting sovereignty to Grozny as it took it away from Kazan. In July 2002 Tatar State Council chairman Farit Mukhametshin decried the center's "dual approaches and standards."[72] The moderate Shaimiev regime's loss of legitimacy resulting from its failure to salvage Tatarstan's sovereignty constitution can only play into the hands of more radical forces.

The constitution, however, was not the only victim of Putin's counter-revolution in Tatarstan. Putin's legal harmonization process also encompassed thousands of laws and tens of thousands of governmental directives, orders, and instructions nationwide.[73] In 2003 Tatarstan published what was clearly an incomplete list of sixty laws harmonized with federal law in 2000–2001 alone.[74] Tatarstan's autonomy was further restricted by Putin's dismantling of asymmetrical fiscal federalism. Yeltsin's inter-budgetary system allowed Moscow to buy off potentially destabilizing national autonomies, most importantly those with large "Muslim" populations like Tatarstan and Bashkiriya. Hence republican presidents were more easily able to marginalize radical nationalists by the mid-1990s, because relative socioeconomic strength reduced inter-ethnic competition for resources and, in tandem with concessions from Moscow on sovereignty and other issues, assuaged nationalist aspirations. The risks of seceding seemed prohibitive, given the fiscal and other rights won in treaties and agreements with Moscow.[75] But Putin's centralization of tax revenues has substantially drained regional coffers. The Kremlin initially tried to preserve some fiscal asymmetry by compensating autonomy-minded republics like Tatarstan through the financing of federal socio-economic development programs. Thus, for 2002, Kazan was promised financing for its socio-economic program that exceeded by a factor of ten the funds for all such programs in the Far East FO regions put together.[76] Such imbalances will not suffice to fully compensate regions for the revenues lost by the centralization of tax revenues, and at the same time they will anger governors of "Russian" regions and increase the chances of inter-ethnic competition for resources.

Republican leaders such as Shaimiev complained that budgetary and overall centralization left them with all the responsibility for governing but no resources to do it with. Such grievances were further heightened by legal amendments in 2004 that put all natural resources under federal control once again and allowed for the removal of governors who let economic crises develop in their regions. In 2005 Southern FO presidential envoy Dmitrii Kozak proposed offering socio-economic development programs only to the poorest regions, a category into which Tatarstan does not fall. Finally, the plan to redistribute competencies between the federal, regional, city, and local governments by increasing finances of local government while leaving federal coffers largely untouched means a further constricting of regional budgets. This will leave regional governments in republics like Tatarstan with fewer funds not only for social and economic projects but also for important cultural, linguistic, and religious projects, so strengthening the assimilative effect of other Putin policies.

Putin's assimilation policies also impinge on the status of Tatarstan and Tatars more than on any other Muslim republic or ethnic group. The ban on ethnic and religious parties reduces Tatars' ability as a group to influence Russian or regional politics and neutralizes Khakimov's call in his long programmatic article "Kto Ty, Tartarin?" ("Who Are You, Tatar?") for the creation of a Russia-wide Tatar political party "not connected with the federal authorities," an intended slap in the face for Tatarstan's party of power, the TNV, which has, in effect, been incorporated into the Kremlin's Yedinaya Rossiya.[77] Any Russia-wide Muslim party is likely be dominated by Tatars, given their status as the largest ethnic Muslim group. Regionally, large Tatar diaspora communities in numerous regions have thus been deprived of the opportunity to play a significant role in local politics.

Tatars along with some other Muslims were effective in fighting off some of the Kremlin's Putin-era assimilative initiatives. A group of Tatar women successfully turned back the MVD's attempt to prevent Muslim women from wearing the hijab or headscarf in their passport photographs, and Tatarstan's leadership opposed and helped weaken the Russian education ministry's effort to impose mandatory courses on Orthodox Christian culture on schools. Tatarstan also forced Moscow to allow the republic's residents a page in their Russian internal passports designating their nationality, something denied to Russian citizens in all other republics. Some Kremlin policies appear to have targeted Tatars specifically. Most importantly, June 2002 amendments to the federal language law prohibiting the use of any script other than Cyrillic rendered illegal Tatarstan's 1999 decision to support the gradual transition to a Latinized Tatar-language script. Karelia was the only other region to adopt such a policy. Shaimiev and other Tatar leaders have condemned the Duma's decision and have filed suit in Russia's Constitutional Court and the International Human Rights Court in Strasbourg.[78]

As Tatarstan's elite retreated in the face of Moscow's onslaught, President Shaimiev's top political advisor Rafael Khakimov, a key architect of Kazan's emerging Tatar national ideology, issued a desperate plea to Tatars. In a seminal article entitled "Who Are You, Tatar?," signed "Khakim" without the Russian-language "ov" suffix, he called for unity and outlined a plan for rallying Tatars across Russia to defend their right to self-determination and Tatarstan's sovereignty and autonomy. Castigating Moscow's continuing efforts since Stolypin's time to divide the Tatar nation, he asserted that not only were Siberian, Kryasheny (ethnic Tatars baptized into Russian Orthodoxy), and other Tatar communities across Russia inalienable parts of the Tatar nation, but so also were Bashkirs, Nogais, and other Turkic-speaking minorities. Khakimov then scolded Tatars for their tendency to consume their energies in infighting. Indeed, the numerous different ideological tendencies within the Tatar nationalist movement, briefly discussed here – instrumental nomenklatura nationalists (Tatarstan's political elite), democratic nationalists (for example, Farukshin), radical secular nationalists (the moderate wing of the All-Tatar Public Center and the Tatar youth organization "Azatlyk"), moderate Islamic nationalists of the All-Tatar Public Center's radical wing, and radical Islamic nationalists like Bairamova's Ittifak – explain much of the recent impotence of the Tatar national movement.

Arguing that Russia was mistaken in attempting to stand between East and West, Khakimov insisted that the Tatars' task was not to secede from Russia but to help transform it by continuing their historically "unbroken movement from the East to the West," taking Russia with them. He argued that Tatars were bound to this task as cofounders of the Russian state, which arose from a de facto Russian-Tatar union during the time of the Golden Horde. According to Khakimov and a growing number of Tatar intellectuals, this imperial enterprise was largely Tatar in inspiration and historically progressive. Since Russia was a joint Russian-Tatar Eurasian project, he insisted, Russia was doomed if it failed to develop its democracy and preserve asymmetrical federalism. Thus, Tatarstan's championing of divided sovereignty and regional autonomy helps to preserve rather than undermine Russia's inter-communal comity, political stability, territorial integrity, and ability to modernize. In order to defend Tatar self-determination and Tatarstan's sovereignty, Khakimov proposed a series of measures to rally Russia's Tatars around the republic to defend it against Moscow's recentralization drive: (1) the development and defense of the Tatar language as one of two motors to strengthen Tatar national identity and unity; (2) the revival of jadidism as the second motor to drive Tatars' and Tatarstan's enlightenment and moderniza-tion; (3) the transition of the Tatar language from the Cyrillic to the Latin alphabet to meet the demands of globalization; (4) increased Tatarstan investment and activity by Tatar national cultural autonomies across the country in rallying the internal Tatar diaspora to a common "Greater Tatarstan" movement; and (5) the development of Tatar mass media, including an international Tatar university and television channel and a Tatarstan internet system.[79]

Although Khakimov's cry had little immediate effect, it provided a program for moderate Tatar nationalists. Similar cries and small steps toward carrying out Khakimov's initiatives came from other Tatar intellectuals, especially historians. Tatarstan's perhaps most noted historian, Damir Iskhakov, formed a commission under the World Tatar Congress to help find funding for Khakimov's agenda but also lamented that since the mid-1990s Tatars "had lost momentum" and "begun to be transformed into a divided nation."[80] As Putin's Thermidorian juggernaut continued in its progress, the Tatar intelligentsia's leading weekly newspaper, *Zvezda Povolzhya*, would publish an editorial titled "Retreat."[81]

Retreat was soon followed by surrender. Putin's post-Beslan proposal for the presidential appointment of regional chief executives required an official response from regional governments. Khakimov signaled Kazan's dissatis-faction, stating that "forces that would like to put an end to democracy and federalism" but "do not have enough resources" are at work and that "the negative consequences of liquidating federalism are too great."[82] Other Tatarstan officials expressed more open disagreement with Putin's counter-reforms. The chairman of the Tatarstan State Council's economy, investments, and entrepreneurship commission, Marat Galeev, warned that "Tatarstan will not reconcile itself to the full loss of statehood."[83]

Tatarstan, along with a few other regions, attempted to limit the presidential powers of appointment and proposed various amendments, but with little effect. Given the significant negative reaction to Putin's counter-reforms, Shaimiev certainly needed to challenge the Kremlin's gambit and win some sort of compromise for Kazan. State Duma deputy from Tatarstan Oleg Morozov said that Shaimiev would propose that regional chief executives be given the authority to appoint mayors in their regions, a step that would compensate regional leaders for power lost to Moscow at the expense of local government and democracy.[84] Tatarstan State Council chairman Farit Mukhametshin said at a 13 October 2004 meeting with visiting officials of the parliamentary assembly of the Council of Europe that the legislative chairmen of the Volga FO's regions had offered amendments that would require the president's nominees to be residents of the region they would head.[85] The Tatarstan State Council's committee on state-building and local self-government proposed that Putin should be required to choose candidates for regional leaders "taking into consideration the historical, cultural, economic, and social peculiarities of each region" and promised deputies that it would propose limitations on presidential power to dissolve regional parliaments that reject the president's nominee for the post of regional leader more than twice.[86]

Two days later, on 25 October, a plenary session of the Tatarstan State Council met to address Putin's proposals. It described his counter-reforms as "a coup d'état."[87] At least nine of its deputies rose to question or oppose them outright. Chairman Mukhametshin proposed that legal amendments should be put forward both to address the "representation and system for the formation" of the emasculated Federation Council and the advisory Council of the Regional Legislative Heads, and to give regional chief executives "sufficient powers" over the activities of federal structures on their territories. He promised that Tatarstan would introduce changes to Putin's proposed amendments and "on principle defend" them "so that the voice of Tatarstan is heard."[88] Then President Shaimiev, whose attendance underscored the importance of the session, became the first regional leader to oppose openly any aspect of Putin's proposed post-Beslan counter-reforms. Although he supported Putin's proposal for the presidential nomination of regional governors and presidents, he criticized the proposal to give Russia's president the power to disband any local legislature that twice declines to approve his nominee for the post of regional chief executive. Shaimiev argued that "parliaments are elected by the people" and "we should not accept under any circumstances any possibility of disbanding our parliament." He stressed that local legislatures should have the right to express their views on the candidates for governor.[89]

In a 10 November interview Shaimiev stated he could not support or see how a legislative body such as the Duma or its majority Yedinaya Rossiya faction (which he co-chaired) could approve amendments to allow the disbanding of regional legislative bodies and noted that the latter, violated the Russian Constitution's article 85 which stipulates conciliation procedures between federal and regional governmental bodies in the form of joint federal-regional committees, when disputes arise.[90] In the end, Tatarstan's State Council in a purely advisory vote approved changes allowing Russia's president to appoint regional leaders by a vote of fifty-seven in favor to nineteen against, with three deputies abstaining.[91] However, Tatarstan continued to stall. Although the bill establishing the presidential appointment of regional chief executives was signed into law by Putin in December 2004 without any significant amendments, by March 2006 the Tatarstan State Council had still not gotten round to amending the republic's constitution to reflect this change. Moreover, Tatarstan had still not amended the constitution in accordance with prosecutors' continuing protests of the non-constitutionality of clauses on Tatarstan citizenship and Tatarstan's right to conduct foreign policy and foreign economic relations.

The *coup de grâce* of Moscow's assault on Tatarstan's sovereignty came with the Kremlin's move to re-negotiate and, with some regions, nullify bilateral federal-regional power-sharing treaties. Putin's 2003 law "On the General Principles for Organizing Legislative and Executive Organs of State Power in the Russian Federation Subjects [Regions]" provided for a two-year period in which to amend existing agreements. Along with regional autonomy and divided sovereignty, the 1994 Moscow–Tatarstan bilateral treaty had provided for its control over all natural resources and property located on its territory. Like most of the treaties that were negotiated after it, it was found to contain numerous violations of the federal constitution: more than any other, according to one expert at least nineteen.[92] The treaty's introduction, which referred to Tatarstan as a "state united with" the Russian Federation, still seemed to suggest a confederation of two sovereign states rather than Tatarstan's existence within a single federal state.[93] Article 2.6 gave Tatarstan authority over "issues of the ownership, use, and disposal of land, minerals, water, timber and other natural resources, as well as state enterprises, organizations, and other movable and immovable real estate under state ownership located on the territory of the Republic of Tatarstan."[94] This contradicted the federal constitution's article 72.1a, which placed these spheres under joint federal-regional jurisdiction. With the treaty no longer in force and Putin-era legislation putting all natural resources under federal control, Tatarstan would lose control over its resource base.

Consternation in Kazan over Chechnya's new constitution and apparent sovereignty inclined Moscow to coordinate negotiations with the only regions apparently being considered for new power-sharing treaties as of 2005 – Chechnya and Tatarstan. The Kremlin requested that Tatarstan's treaty not be hurried or forced to completion before the signing of the Moscow–Chechen treaty. At the same time, it created a law requiring that all future power-sharing treaties, including the new Russia–Tatarstan one, be adopted as a federal law and pass through both houses of the Russian Federal assembly, now fully under Moscow's control. Although this would give Moscow a clear upper hand in negotiations, Kazan agreed.[95]

Despite efforts to coordinate the Chechen and Tatarstan treaty negotiations, concerns similar to those that arose over the two republic constitutions' sovereignty clauses emerged again over the relative outcomes for the two republics' treaties. For example, writing in *Nezavisimaya gazeta* in January 2005 democratic-nationalist Tatar political scientist Midkhat Farukshin argued that signing a bilateral power-sharing treaty between Moscow and Chechnya could result in an explosion of separatism in other national republics. If Chechnya was given the right to manage its natural resources, especially its oil, Farukshin reasoned, every Russian region would demand a similar treaty, basing its claim on the Russian constitution's principle of equal rights for all federation subjects. Similarly, he reiterated that the principle of republican sovereignty contained in the March 2003 Chechen constitution contradicted the June 2000 Russian Constitutional Court ruling under which sovereignty was declared indivisible and the Tatarstan constitution's sovereignty clause was ruled unconstitutional.[96] The extent of Kazan's retreat in defending the treaty's sovereignty-making power was made clear when the 15 February 2005 anniversary of the signing of the first Moscow–Tatarstan bilateral treaty was completely ignored by Shaimiev and the authorities in Kazan.[97]

In addition, the new treaty was being negotiated in the context of a new balance of power between Moscow and the regions that favored Moscow, given Putin's new right to appoint regional chief executives. Despite Putin's likely preference for reappointing Shaimiev (as he would in 2005) in light of his popularity and sound record in managing the potentially troublesome republic, the Russian president held the trump card, the option of threatening

Shaimiev with removal from office.[98] From initial reports on the draft treaty approved by Tatarstan's State Council in October 2005, Kazan failed in its attempt to insert a statement on the republic's state sovereignty but may have managed to preserve some rights in the use of the republic's natural resources and state property, the conduct of foreign economic affairs, and the requirement that the Tatarstan president speak both Russian and Tatar.[99] For "domestic" purposes Shaimiev also secured the right of Tatarstan residents to have a special insert in their internal passports designating their nationality. Thus, the republic appeared to have preserved a small sphere of autonomy confined to cultural matters and its natural resources and state property.

The success of Putin's anti-federalist counter-revolution exposes Shaimiev's inability to protect the republic's autonomy or the sinecures of key members of the Tatar elite. If in August 2003 *Zvezda Povolzhya* published a lead editorial titled "Retreat"; in late 2004 an appropriate title for an editorial was "Surrender." Except for a few sops to Tatar autonomy in a much less robust power-sharing treaty, there is little if anything left of Tatarstan's autonomy or the Russian federative system forged by Shaimiev in the early 1990s. The Shaimiev administration's failure to defend Tatarstan's sovereignty in the face of Putin's counter-revolution is likely to undermine the political viability not only of the Tatarstan model's moderate Tatar nationalism, but also of its efforts to contain radical Islam through a revival of Tatar jadidism.

THE LIMITED MOBILIZATION OF THE MODERATE TATAR NATIONALISTS

Putin's policies and Kazan's submission to them produced considerable pressure on Shaimiev from nationalists of all stripes to protect Tatar sovereignty. As soon as Putin's counter-revolution began, moderate Tatar nationalists began mobilizing, but the nomenklatura nationalists' domination of the Tatar political scene since the mid-1990s left the movement pale in comparison to the early 1990s. Still, in late 2001 the moderate nationalist VTOTs, which always has conditioned its support of Shaimiev on his continued defense of Tatar sovereignty,[100] was able to muster a two thousand -strong demonstration. Demonstrators reportedly chanted anti-Russian slogans in addition to calling for independence from Moscow. As the implementation of Putin's federative counter-reforms peaked in 2002, leading to the amended Tatar constitution in May, the VTOTs organized a series of organizations to defend Tatarstan's sovereignty. When federal prosecutors again challenged the amended Tatar constitution over clauses that still referred to Tatarstan as a sovereign state, President Shaimiev was forced to hold a closed meeting with the leaders of the VTOTs and Tatar civic and political organizations on 31 July 2002. They reportedly discussed possible cooperation between regime and opposition in defending Tatarstan's sovereignty;[101] a hint that Kazan was considering a renewal of the early 1990s tactic of supporting the opposition in order to frighten Moscow. However, to date there have been few signs of any such cooperation.

There have been signs of radicalization among moderate nationalists, however. In February 2003, a VTOTs congress convened to discuss "ways of preserving the Tatar people in conditions of forcible harmonization of the Tatar constitution with the federal one." Participants criticized Tatarstan's leadership for its failure to defend Tatars' rights. VTOTs chairman Rashit Yagafarov stated that the worsening political situation is making it difficult to promote Tatar, Muslim, and Turkic unity and might force the VTOTs underground. Delegates even warned of turning Tatarstan into a second Chechnya. One VTOTs official warned that if the pressure from Moscow continues, it will lead to "extreme measures." Asked what he meant, he replied: "Well, look at what happened in Chechnya." In the congress's lobby, a book entitled *The Jihad of the Tatar People* and photographs of Tatar nationalist leaders with Chechen field commanders were sold to congress delegates.[102]

One dilemma facing moderate Tatar nationalists is the apparent contradiction between democracy and Islam, which leading members of the Tatar intelligentsia and political elite like Rafael Khakimov have tried to resolve by promoting jadidist reform Islam. Putin's post-Beslan package of anti-terrorist measures, in particular the end of popular elections of regional chief executives, forced moderate Tatar nationalists to focus on the issue of democracy, rather than just federalism and regional autonomy. Yagafarov charged: "The central authority does not need the voice of the people. A majority of Tatars will be dissatisfied with such innovations, and it will set in. We of course strive toward democracy in our souls, but it seems that we should say goodbye to democracy."[103] Tatar democratic-nationalist chairman of Kazan State University's political science department, Professor Midkhat Farukshin, said Putin's proposal marked "a step backward in democratic development and a further reduction of federalism."[104] Simultaneously, popular Tatarstan journalist Lev Ovrutskii published a new book, *When Republics Were Great*, which discusses what he terms "a crossroads on the development of federalism." In a 15 October interview Ovrutskii, an ardent "Kazan federalist" and critic of Tatarstan President Shaimiev's failure to defend the republic's autonomy, said that President Putin's post-Beslan counter-reforms "frightened" him and that people would start to "organize public resistance." Ovrutskii stressed the federalists' failure to create an appropriate political culture in the country: "[W]e, the current generation of Kazan federalists," he said, needed but failed to convince even "a Bryansk peasant . . . that everybody, including himself, gains from Tatarstan's sovereignty and federative relations."[105] Editor-in-chief of *Zvezda Povolzhya* Rashit Akhmetov wrote that the proposal violated Tatarstan's constitution and would lead to an abrogation of Tatarstan's presidency, noting that Putin had said upon coming to power that "there should be only one president in Russia."[106] Akhmetov editorialized on 21 October for holding a referendum in Tatarstan on whether regional leaders should be elected by a direct public vote or appointed by the Russian president. He argued that the republic's "party of power" Tatarstan – Novyi Vek, which had allied itself with the Kremlin's party Yedinaya Rossiya in the December 2003 elections to the federal State Duma, should introduce the referendum proposal and that forces across the republic's entire political spectrum – communists, nationalists, democrats – should unite to defend the right to popular election of the republic's president. He added that if Shaimiev fought for a referendum, he would attain the stature of Alexander Dubcek after the 1968 Prague Spring.[107] Tatar leaders outside the republic also objected to Putin's proposals. At a 17 September meeting of the executive committee of the Congress of Tatars of Bashkortostan sociology professor Jewdet Gyilaetdinov said Russian authorities preferred restricting democracy to examining the reasons for terrorism, reminding participants that over 200,000 civilians had been killed in Chechnya, including 35,000 children.[108]

There was an impetus, albeit still unrealized, to organize a broad anti-federal opposition front that included Tatar nationalist forces like the VTOTs and democratic forces. Within a month of Putin's announcement of his proposals Kazan's nationalist, federalist, and democratic forces did mobilize but separately. The annual VTOTs-led demonstration of an estimated three hundred people was held on 15 October 2004 in Kazan to commemorate the defense of the city against the Muscovite forces of Ivan the Terrible in 1552. Although the same anniversary demonstration in 2003 was reported to have drawn seven hundred more participants, it had addressed mostly economic and symbolic nationalist issues.[109] The 2004 demonstration raised the Tatar nationalists' traditional grievances, but issues of Tatar nationality, Islam, and, to a lesser extent, democracy were also aired. Demonstrators demanded the restoration of the 1992 Tatar constitution and "equal rights in relations with Russia within the framework of a potential Eurasian confederation." Speakers leveled the usual accusations against Moscow of depriving the Tatars of their statehood, script, and economic independence. A resolution demanded a halt to "predatory payments" and "colonial taxes" under the revenue transfer system in inter-budgetary relations with the Moscow Kremlin. Participants also appealed to the republic's leadership to "defend the interests of the Tatar people" and called for immediate steps to commemorate the city's sixteenth-century battle with Ivan the Terrible by erecting a monument to the city's defenders near the Kazan government headquarters. Islam related issues were also raised. Speakers criticized the recently negotiated return of the Kazan Mother of God icon to Tatarstan from the Vatican, saying that the placement of a Christian Orthodox symbol in Kazan reaffirmed "the colonial enslavement and humiliation of the Tatar people." The demonstration ended with a march on Kazan's Kremlin, where participants said a Muslim prayer in memory of Kazan's defenders of 1552.[110] At the same time, the issue of democracy emerged in a resolution that warned that Putin's counter-reforms were a "direct path to dictatorship."

A separate demonstration was organized by Airat Sharipov, a Tatar businessman and, supporter of federalism and democracy. Sharipov, the leader of the Sozidaniye political association, organized a Committee for Defense of Democracy and called on Kazan residents to join a 23 October demonstration to safeguard their right to elect regional leaders. The Committee was joined by popular journalists Lev Ovrutskii and Rimzil Valeev, Professor Midkhat Farukshin, and political-science researcher Vladimir Belyaev.[111] The demonstration drew anywhere from fifty to four hundred people, including local communist activists and several VTOTs leaders.[112] A draft resolution charged that "refusal to let the public elect regional leaders contradicts the principles of federalism and democracy and means that Russia is turning into a unitary state." The democratic element in the new Tatar coalition was explicitly spelled out by Sharipov, who stated that the 23 October demonstration was aimed "at defending people's right to elect the head of the republic, democratic achievements, civic rights and freedoms, and the constitution."[113]

This embryonic alliance of democrats and moderate nationalists could be a powerful force in Tatarstan, as could other such coalitions elsewhere in Russia. As much social-science research shows, intellectuals shape a nation's historical "myth" and are therefore pivotal in the development of nationalist movements. However, in Russia today such coalitions would need the support of similar elements within the state apparatus if they are to be effective, since they often lack resources. This could change, however. There are many successful Tatar businessmen inside and outside of Tatarstan, and there is a tradition of them contributing to the Tatar nationalist movement.

Although some within the moderate republic-wide VTOTs were inclined to support a democracy-oriented nationalist mobilization, others appeared to be moving in a more radical direction, producing a split that risked strengthening the radical element within the movement and the republic. Even before Beslan, a major radical-led challenge to the moderate VTOTs chairman, Rashit Yagafarov, had already emerged. Tensions peaked in August 2004, and Yagafarov, facing intense criticism, said he would resign. Although the 18

September VTOTs plenum in Kazan re-elected him, a major split occurred. Of the forty members present at the plenum, a slim majority of twenty-two voted for Yagafarov, and another seven backed its decisions by proxy. Several opposition-led organizations from the Aznaqai, Chally, Chistai, Yashel Uzan, and Kazan branches, headed by radical Tatar nationalist Zaki Zainullin, held an alternative plenum. Even the moderate Yagafarov-led plenum adopted a resolution protesting against the dissolution of Russia's federative system and infringements on social rights and religious feelings.[114] By November 2004, the VTOTs was debating whether or not to go "underground," perhaps implying a turn to violence.[115] The radicalization of the VTOTs culminated in the April 2005 election of a new chairman, Talgat Bareyev, who immediately announced a shift in policy to the position of the early 1990s favoring the "full independence of Tatarstan from Russia." Criticizing Putin's Russia for becoming a "fictional federation" and "police state," he declared Tatarstan to be Russia's "internal near abroad" and called for demonstrations in summer 2005 in support of independence on the "model of San Marino or the Vatican."[116]

RADICALIZATION OF THE RADICALS

While most of the moderate nationalists seem to have little connection with political Islam, much less with radical Muslims or Islamists, a careful look at the radicals reveals a different picture. The VTOTs branch in the city of Naberezhnyi Chelny (NChOTOTs), led by the mercurial Rafis Kashapov, is becoming ever more radical, even extremist. Naberezhnyi Chelny is Tatarstan's second largest city and the home of the increasingly troubled "KamAZ" truck and tractor plant. The city has been a hotbed of Tatar nationalist opposition and is a potential hotbed of radical Islam. It was radical elements in Naberezhnyi Chelny, along with others in Kazan, who began forming the embryo of an army under the guise of a national guard during Russia's revolution from above and the Soviet collapse.[117] In fall 1992 the city was the scene of a brief Tatar nationalist uprising put down by Shaimiev. Although as of 1993 only 30 percent of the city's Tatars were Muslim believers, 43 percent of them also considered Tatar national rebirth impossible without an Islamic revival. Moreover, the city can be regarded as a center of "national radical opposition" both to nomenklatura nationalists of "centralist Kazan" and to the self-organized and moderate nationalist VTOTs.[118] There is now evidence of both indigenous and foreign Islamist elements in the city.

The NChOTOTs has been the most aggressive organization in the republic on issues related to Islam in recent years and the focus of much conflict with ethnic Russians and law-enforcement bodies. In spring 2003, NChOTOTs activists tried to destroy the foundation that had been laid for a Russian Orthodox Church in the city. Three elderly women were arrested for the crime, but it is doubtful that they really could have been responsible. It was suspected that young men did the work and then fled the scene, leaving the authorities only the babushkas to prosecute. Months later, vandals attacked the NChOTOTs headquarters, destroying Tatar national symbols and injuring several members, including Kashapov, who was hospitalized. Soon after his release, he was arrested for the NChOTOTs' alleged distribution of literature inciting inter-ethnic antagonism. Kashapov was eventually acquitted in April 2004, and the court demanded that the authorities apologize to him.

However, five days after Beslan Naberezhnyi Chelny's city court complied with the Tatarstan justice ministry's early August request that the NchOTOTs be liquidated. The ministry filed the petition arguing that the NChOTOTs had failed to re-register before 1 July 1999 as required by a 1995 law on public association. However, the federal law "On Public Associations" explicitly states that branch organizations do not need to be registered.[119] Nevertheless, a representative of the republic-level VTOTs claimed that the NChOTOTs had repeatedly tried to register, but each time its documents were returned for minor technical reasons.[120] In October Tatarstan's Supreme Court rejected a VTOTs appeal and upheld the earlier Naberezhnyi Chelny city court verdict. VTOTs leaders said they would appeal in Russia's Supreme Court and, if necessary, go to the European Court of Human Rights.[121] That the deadline had passed over five years before and the court responded with unusual rapidity suggests the move was dictated by Moscow in response to Beslan and part of Putin's overall tightening of the screws on independent organizations as terrorism grew.[122] In response to its loss of registration, the NChOTOTs issued a defiant statement asserting that it was still in operation despite the court's "illegal" ruling "adopted under pressure." The statement lambasted the authorities' "information war" and the Russian security forces' "psychological terror" against the NChOTOTs and asked all in Tatarstan "to raise their voice against the campaign of lies and slander . . . illegal political terror, as well as the illegal political investigation . . . in relation to the NChOTOTs and its leader Rafis Kashapov."[123]

There is evidence that over the last year or so inter-confessional tensions have been mounting in the republic, and in Naberezhnyi Chelny in particular. An August 2004 NChOTOTs statement listed numerous, largely unpublicized attacks on Muslim mosques, Christian Orthodox churches, and other religious sites in Tatarstan: "The arson of a mosque in Elevator Hill, the beating of the imam of the Makhallya Tufan Mosque, the burning of a tractor at the construction site of the Sobornyi mosque, the smashing of windows of the New City mosque (the Ak mosque), and the beating of a guard at the Tauba mosque construction site, and others. Besides this in Chelny at the Orthodox cemetery they chopped up and burned several crosses . . . . The wooden part of an assistance center in a church in Orlovka village was set on fire and burnt . . . . The wooden foundation of a church was set on fire."[124]

Although the "terror" label applied by radical nationalists to the state's efforts to rein in Islamists is an exaggeration, it is true that there is growing surveillance and harassment not only of suspected extremists and radical organizations but also of moderates, which is creating an atmosphere of fear in parts of what was formerly a calm Muslim republic.[125] In a September 2005 press conference after the completion of Kazan's millennium anniversary celebrations, more moderate central VTOTs leaders condemned the Tatarstan leadership for surrendering to Moscow's authoritarian counter-revolution and having enriched themselves in the period of broad autonomy. They charged that they, like everyone else in the republic, were now afraid to utter the word "sovereignty" which not long ago had been repeated on the republic's official media day and night. *Novaya gazeta*'s Boris Bronshtein discovered perhaps the reason for the growth in such fears. When he left the press conference, he was confronted by a plainclothes MVD officer who asked him if he had attended the press conference and requested his full name.[126] A month later an amendment was introduced to the Tatarstan State Council that would remove references to the republic's sovereignty from the law establishing the state holiday that commemorates Tatarstan's 1992 declaration of sovereignty.[127]

Not surprisingly, much of the nationalist Tatar intelligentsia that once supported Shaimiev is now engaged in deep soul-searching about the rapid repeal of Tatarstan's self-rule. Their disappointment is expressed in *Zvezda Povolzhya*, an independent weekly newspaper that reflects the thinking of the moderate nationalist, democratic Tatar movement. A typical piece of analysis on the fate of Tatar self-determination ran: "In the new conditions Tatarstan's refusal of the role of active player on the Tatar socio-political field, which will transform it into a passive registrar of what is happening, evokes serious reflection and poses the following question: to what extent and under what circumstances can Tatarstan emerge as the ethno-national nucleus [of the Tatar nation] in the future?" Its conclusion struck a note that by now should be familiar to the reader of this book but a new one for post-Soviet Tatarstan: Tatar nationalism among the young "is now taking on more of a Muslim color."[128]

Such a trend would explain, along with the demise of Tatarstan sovereignty, why the NChOTOTs and perhaps others are being seduced by the Chechens' efforts to mix nationalism with internationalist Islamism. In May 2005 the

VTOTs, in particular its radical branch in Naberezhnyi Chelny, began posting statements on Chechen resistance websites. The NChOTOTs issued a statement in May 2005 that was approved by the central VTOTs leadership and sent to the Chechen resistance's website Chechenpress.com rejecting the idea that the resignation of the North Ossetiya president, which it viewed as having been engineered by Moscow, should be repeated in Tatarstan. In particular, it condemned Moscow's demand that the Russian flag replace the Tatarstan flag atop all state office buildings. Its tone was particularly harsh and read in part:

> All this shows that today's Moscow chauvinists have surpassed their Soviet forebears and do not recognize any reasonable frameworks. It is possible to believe that they have absolutely lost all reason and are falling into the abyss of fascism. We need to say: Collect yourselves, misters! It is impossible to go this far. You will fall! Your excessive meddling has led to disintegration of the union; do you also want disintegration of Russia? We demand: Hands off the post of presidents in national republics, their flags, their hymns and their arms! Leave them alone![129]

In late May 2005, NChOTOTs chairman Rafis Kashapov wrote an article for the ChRI Islamists' website *Kavkaz-Tsentr*.[130] Although it addressed a theme which could be construed as a purely nationalist one – Russia's new holiday celebrating victory over the Kazan-based Turkish khanate of the Golden Horde at the Battle at Kulikovo in 1380 – the fact that it was written specially for a medium which routinely publishes calls for jihad against Russia (and the US) marked a new departure for radical Tatar nationalists. Kashapov subsequently posted other articles on *Kavkaz-Tsentr*, including an October 2005 letter commemorating those who perished in the defense of Kazan on 15 October 1522 after a forty-one-day siege of the city by Ivan the Terrible's Russian forces.[131]

Another Tatar and, more interestingly, a leading Tatarstan mufti, Iskhak Lotfullin, posted a series of six articles on *Kavkaz-Tsentr* titled "In the Empire's Smothering Embrace." Lotfullin leads a group of Kazan muftis opposed to DUMT chairman Gusman Iskhakov.[132] In the first two installments, Lotfullin traces "the Russian empire's genocide against the Tatar people" or Russia's imperial legacy going back to the fourteenth century, without making any mention of the part played across the centuries by the Tatars and Tatar-dominated khanates. One-sided historiography is often not only a sign of ethno-political mobilization, but also of the aggressive nationalism of the kind propagated by extremists, including Islamists. Lotfullin's fourth installment closes by recommending that the only way to avoid the "death of the Tatar people" is "the rebirth of its national culture and spiritual values formed around Islam." Elaborating in his fifth installment, the mufti seems to condone violent jihad: "Speaking of Tatar Muslims' jihad, it is impossible to present it *only* as a purely external struggle against the oppressive believers of other faiths against Islam. No, Jihad for Tatars is *also* a struggle against their own shortcomings and weakness in faith." In his final installment Lotfullin puts part of the blame for the transgressions against all Russia's Muslims on the Russian Orthodox Church and in strong language raises the Chechen cause: "Crosses on Orthodox churches in Russia are still placed over an inverted crescent, and Russian tanks with crosses on their sides and blessed with the 'holy water' of army priests then swim in the blood of the peaceful population of Ichkeriya!"[133]

These propaganda efforts marked the first open signs of cooperation between Tatar nationalist, even Islamic, and Chechen Islamist groups. Moreover, not only have Tatars initiated ties with the ChRI terrorists' sites, but in turn the latter have begun to publish propaganda on the subject of Tatarstan, Bashkortostan, and Tatar communities.[134] This has been followed by police claims that a Tatar combat jamaat, the Islamic Jamaat, has emerged in Nabereznyi Chelny and the arrest of numerous Tatarstan residents reportedly engaged in sabotage and terrorist activities.

THE EMERGENCE OF ISLAMISTS ON THE VOLGA

There have been numerous claims that "Wahhabism" is making inroads among Volga Muslims and Tatar communities since Putin's rise to power, but there had been little in the way of even alleged sabotage or terrorist activity until 2004–2005. In 2001 the chairman of the Ufa-based moderate Islamic TsDUM, Talgat Tadzhuddin, acknowledged he had twice met with one of Osama bin Laden's brothers. Tadzhuddin has been vociferous in accusing the leader of Russian Islam's less traditional wing, chief mufti of the Muslim Spiritual Board of Asian Russia Rafael Galiullin, of supporting Wahhabism. Tadzhuddin subsequently appealed to Putin to "cleanse" Russia of Wahhabite influence, something he argues has led to takeovers of mosques in Penza, Ulyanovsk, and Moscow and instability among Muslims in Sverdlovsk. Kirov Oblast's chief mufti asked for help in building educational institutes to counter the growing influence of Saudi-trained radical Wahhabi teachers in the region's southern districts. In 2002 Volga FO presidential envoy and former Russian premier Sergei Kirienko expressed similar concerns over growing Wahhabi influence in Tatarstan. Chechnya administration head Akhmad Kadyrov warned in 2002 that Wahhabis were developing great influence in Tatarstan and central Russia. While some of these claims may be a function of an internal Islamic power struggle or arise from other political motives, it is likely that at least some are based on reliable information. There are also claims that some Tatars have at least limited connections to Chechen separatists and international terrorists. NChOVTOTs leader Rafis Kashapov claimed there were at one time two units of some seven hundred Tatars each fighting alongside the Chechens against Russian forces. The NChOVTOTs reportedly approached numerous (according to some reports, hundreds of) volunteers for the Taliban's post-9/11 jihad for help in getting to Afghanistan to fight against the US. When eight Russian citizens turned up among detainees at Guantanamo in January 2002 for alleged participation in Taliban and al Qaeda activities against the US, it emerged that two were residents of Tatarstan and two others were ethnic Tatars.

Concrete evidence of Islamists in the region started to emerge in 2002, when the first Islamist organization, the Islamic Committee of Naberezhnyi Chelny, appeared in the republic, and its newspaper *Muvakhkhid* began to circulate freely about Tatarstan's second city.[135] However, it was in the wake of the Beslan massacre and Basaev's August 2005 claim that the ChRI network would spread to the Volga area "next year" that foreign and then indigenous Islamists were suddenly uncovered along the Volga and in more distant Tatar communities.

Beslan had immediate repercussions in Tatarstan when Russia's deputy general prosecutor for the Southern FO, Sergei Fridinskii, stated that while there was no evidence to support earlier official Russian statements that Arabs or Africans had been among the terrorists, the "multi-ethnic" operation involved Tatars in addition to Chechens, Kazakhs, and Koreans. This claim raised official and unofficial eyebrows in Kazan. According to Kazan daily *Vechernyaya Kazan*, the Tatarstan leadership frantically sought to clarify the information with the republic's MVD and FSB, but to no avail.[136] At a 10 September session of the Tatarstan Security Council, Tatarstan FSB chief Dinar Khamitov rejected Fridinskii's claim that Tatars were among the hostage-takers in Beslan. President Shaimiev demanded that those responsible for spreading this apparently false information be punished "regardless of their rank."[137] However, at the same session, Khamitov painted a picture of a republic under real threat of terrorist infiltration. He warned that "the foreign ideologists of terrorism are looking at several regions including Tatarstan as a base for the creation of orthodox Islamic centers and the incitement of inter-ethnic and inter-confessional antagonism," and that Tatarstan was the target of "emissaries of various foreign religious public organizations, the activity of which carries an expressed extremist character, [who] occasionally visit the republic." He said that the FSB had tracked and expelled numerous such emissaries from Tatarstan and Russia over the last few years. Moreover, Khamitov claimed that the Islamic revolutionary organization Hizb ut-Tahrir Islami had stepped up efforts in the republic since early 2004 to recruit fighters for the Chechen separatists. First deputy interior minister Renat Timerzyanov warned that "nobody should be under the delusion that a stable situation exists in Tatarstan," adding that the republic had long been an object of extremist and Wahhabist organizations' attention. He singled out the Tatarstan city of Almetevsk, where "supporters of Wahhabism feel perfectly comfortable," and the leader of the Almetevsk mosque, "Wahhabism supporter" Nadir Aukhadiyev, as being of "special concern." He also noted problems in the rural Kukmor, Argyz, Chistopol, and Nurlat raions.[138]

Media outlets in Moscow and Kazan painted an even more dire picture of the security situation in Tatarstan as laid out in Khamitov's report. *Respublika Tatarstan* suggested that one cause was local police's prior indifference and cited Tatarstan MVD deputy chief Timerzyanov complaining that the republic's security organs "up until the present time treated these phenomena flippantly." A portion of the Tatarstan Security Council session broadcast on Kazan's *Efir TV* showed President Shaimiev asking Timerzyanov why, if imam Aukhadiyev supported Wahhabism, he was still working at the mosque. Timerzyanov responded that this point of view was "still debatable," to which Shaimiev answered: "And when will we recognize [Aukhadiyev's Wahbabism]? When something else happens?"[139]

Nezavisimaya gazeta's Vera Postnova, disliked by the Tatarstan leadership for her supposedly "alarmist" reporting about Islamists in the republic, wrote that in addition to the aforementioned districts regarded by Khamitov as infiltrated by Islamist recruiters for the Chechen cause, the FSB chief had also mentioned the Tatar industrial and oil centers of Naberezhnyi Chelny and Nizhnekamsk. Khamitov focused special attention on Chelny's Yoldyz Islamic school. One of its graduates reportedly took part in the 1999 apartment-building bombings that in part sparked the second post-Soviet Chechnya war. In 2000, Yoldyz was deprived of its license, purged of Islamic teachers for their proselytizing of Wahhabist ideas, and re-registered as an Islamic school for girls. However, Khamitov apparently reported that it had illegally continued radical proselytizing and was now training "black widows" (widows of Chechen militants or victims of Russian brutality who turned *shakhidki*) in the most effective use of explosive-laden vests or belts in suicide terrorist acts.[140] Postnova commented that Yoldyz might now be closed down altogether, driving its organizers underground, where, she said, many radical Islamic schools were already operating. She also reported that many of these were under the wing of the former DUM deputy chairman, the influential theologian and now radical Islamic sect leader Narsulla babai Samatov, who was quoted as saying: "I am against the Wahhabis, but I am against the mullahs and muftis even more because there should not be any intermediaries between Muslims and the Most High."[141] Khamitov also noted problems at Nizhnekamsk's central mosque, which had been taken over by Wahhabis with the help of the raion administration head Rishat Abubakirov.[142] According to Postnova, that mosque produced the female suicide bomber arrested in Moscow in 2004 who was allegedly on her way to execute an attack in St. Petersburg.[143]

Khamitov's report and the attendant press commentaries sparked a harsh rebuke from local Muslim leaders. Imam of the Volga Area DUM Mukaddas Bibarsov carefully aimed his words not at the *siloviki* but at Postnova who, he claimed, "always loves to lay it on thick." Similarly, Naberezhnyi Chelny's leading mufti Alfas Gaifullin condemned *Nezavisimaya gazeta* and other publications which had reported that female suicide bombers were being trained at the Yoldyz Islamic school. He also asserted that the police charges of extremist religious activities in the city "were not sufficient to comment on" and that the Yoldyz as well as Darussalyam religious schools were no longer active. He also noted (as Postnova had) that the former Yoldyz premises would soon be reopened as an institution affiliated to Moscow's Russian Islamic University.[144]

DUMT deputy chairman Valiulla Yakupov also expressed doubts about the veracity of the claims made by the republic's *siloviki* at the Tatarstan Security Council, though he made similar charges himself. He strongly criticized the "selectivity" of the security organs' activities and the corruption of officialdom. Yakupov tellingly noted that Tatarstan's education ministry was responsible for licensing all madrasahs: "Then this ministry, as well as the Tatarstan Republic's Council for Religious Affairs and MVD, conducts inspections several times a year in each religious study institute. In 'peace' time no violations of any kind are discovered, but just as soon as a terrorist act occurs they immediately remember about the Wahhabis and their allies."[145] Yakupov also blamed corrupt state officials for the spread of extremism because they often banned madrasahs that distributed reliable information about Islam and licensed others that did not.[146]

Here, Yakupov's remarks pointed to some very real problems. The eternal arbitrariness of Russian police and bureaucrats persists. As shown in previous chapters, Russia's far from democratized security organs sometimes manufacture "extremists" in order to give the impression of efficiency. Giving such officials increased powers to solve the problem of terrorism without the appropriate legislative and judicial checks and balances in place risks greater alienation, expanding the potential pool of recruits for the combat jamaat network.

FOREIGN ISLAMISTS, COMBAT JAMAATS,
AND TERROR AMONG THE TATARS

As noted above, Basaev promised that combat jamaats would expand into the Volga area, suggesting, along with other evidence presented here, that the ChRI Islamist network is set to spread to Tatar communities in Tatarstan, Bashkortostan, and elsewhere. Although at the time of writing there still is no clear Basaev connection in Tatarstan and Bashkortostan, there are signs of the emergence of at least one "Islamic Jamaat" in these republics. In May 2005 Russian MVD operatives detained in the town of Zelenograd near Moscow a twenty-year-old terrorist suspect named Sogayunov, who was said to be a member of the "Islamic Jamaat" based in the Tatarstan Republic's second city, Naberezhnyi Chelny, the haven of radical Tatar and Islamic nationalism. He was charged with planning arson and bomb attacks to coincide with the international celebrations on the sixtieth anniversary of victory in World War II. Whether foreign leaders were being targeted is unknown. The MVD in Tatarstan claimed Islamic Jamaat was also planning terrorist attacks for Kazan's thousandth-anniversary celebrations in July and August 2005.[147]

There also have been alleged sabotage attacks on oil and electricity infrastructure and attempts to commit other terrorist attacks in Tatarstan. In late April 2005, Timur Ishmuradov and Ravil Gumarov, two of the three ethnic Tatars (and four Tatarstan residents) among the eight "Russian Taliban" from Guantanamo Bay, were detained for possession of firearms and explosives and for executing a gas pipeline explosion on 8 January 2005.[148] In August they were indicted on charges of "terrorism." Although investigators determined that they were members of a criminal not religious group, they added: "The actual objective was to destabilize the situation in the republic, drawing away law-enforcement bodies from probing into activities of Hizb ut-Tahrir, which is banned in Russia."[149] On 1 June, while Ishmuradov and Gumarov were in detention, a power line's support tower was destroyed by an explosion in Tatarstan.[150] In August, two other "Russian Taliban" and Tatarstan residents, Airat Vakhitov and Rustam Akhmyarov, were arrested in Moscow for planning terrorist attacks in Tatarstan.[151] The Chechens' website *Kavkaz-Tsentr* took particular exception to Vakhitov's autobiography as he told it to the Russian press, since it implicated the ChRI with the al Qaeda network. Vakhitov's suggestion that he ended up in Afghanistan after being kidnapped from a Chechen wedding and spirited away to Khattab's "Kavkaz" training camp in Serzhen Yurt, Chechnya for indoctrination, and that "Kavkaz" was run by Arabs – a well-established fact – drew scorn from *Kavkaz-Tsentr*, which concluded that Vakhitov must be a FSB operative.[152]

In October, Tatarstan MVD officials brought charges against three

Tatarstan residents, including a twenty-three-year-old from Kukmoro raion and an alleged member of an "organized criminal group" that had begun to carry out some thirteen planned sabotage attacks, including six in Tatarstan. According to the MVD, the group had been ordered by "the leaders of the illegal bandit formations in Chechnya" to commit "a series of terrorist acts" and had received from them "weapons, technical instructions, and the necessary components for preparing explosive devices." The goal of the group was described as the creation of "an Islamic state in the Volga area connected to Central Asia and the North Caucasus."[153] A week before charges were filed against the Kukmoro resident, three other defendants charged with one of the previous sabotage attacks were acquitted by a Tatarstan court which ruled that their confessions had been beaten out of them.[154]

In Bashkortostan a low-profile radical, if not actually terrorist, combat jamaat, also identified by the name "Islamic Jamaat," is reported to be handing out extremist literature; the two Islamic Jamaats could actually be one and the same organization.[155] At the same time that Tatarstan's Islamic Jamaat was alleged to be planning terrorism, Bashkortostan was reported to be a target of saboteurs, and an attack was barely pre-empted.[156] The emergence of radicalism in the Volga area also could be related to its possible recent infiltration by foreign radical Islamist elements.

Islamists in the region would be helped by nationalist or other forms of instability, not only in Tatarstan, but in Bashkiriya too, where in fact Tatar-Bashkir tensions have been on the rise, as noted in Chapter One, and where the regime of President Murtaza Rakhimov appeared on the brink of an "orange revolution" in April 2005. Indeed, the crisis was sparked by the growing authoritarianism of the predominantly ethnic Bashkir government; something encouraged by Moscow's recentralizing policies. Rakhimov, an ethnic Bashkir, has conducted a Bashkirization policy in appointments and on cultural issues, alienating Russians and Tatars who form the backbone of the opposition. The Bashkirs' 21 percent of the population to the Russians' 42 and Tatars' 28 percent has not stopped Rakhimov from opposing Tatars' efforts to have their language given official state status like Bashkir and Russian.

The would-be revolution was sparked by police brutality during the arrest of as many as one thousand young men in the city of Blagoveshchensk in December 2004. Hundreds claimed to have been beaten in the police rampage, and there were even reports of rape.[157] At a 27 December press conference in Moscow "For Human Rights" head Lev Ponomarev said that the "Chechenization of Russia is taking place."[159] It should be noted that MVD troops from Russia's regions are rotated through Chechnya on a regular basis, including those from Bashkortostan. It cannot be discounted that these events, in particular the harshness of the police crackdown in Blagoveshchensk, were driven by the growing distrust between the "Chechenized" police and ethnic Muslim communities. Demonstrations escalated throughout winter and spring 2005, and a final wave of mass meetings was set to begin on 1 May. The revolution, however, fizzled out under police pressure, when the Bashkir FSB called in the movement's leader for interrogation on May Day eve. He soon announced that the opposition was postponing its activities.

Moscow's support for Rakhimov has survived despite the Bashkir president's stubborn resistance to his efforts to seize control of the republic's assets, especially its oil and chemical complex, his Bashkirization policies, and his reluctance in "harmonising" the republic's constitution and legislation. With Putin's recentralization policies Moscow's prospects for regaining control over the region appeared to improve. Bashkortostan was the third Russian region, behind Tatarstan and the KBR, to sign a power-sharing treaty with Moscow in the wake of the Soviet collapse. By this and other means Bashkortostan obtained great freedoms for itself, second only to those secured by Tatarstan. President Rakhimov was allowed to retain great power for himself, and his family. His son, Ural, became Bashkortostan's chief state oligarch, running the state oil and chemical industry that Moscow has long sought to get its hands on. In the 2003 Bashkortostan presidential election, forces in Moscow undertook a half-hearted attempt to challenge Rakhimov, forcing him into a runoff round. At the time of the Blagoveshchensk crisis and would-be orange revolution, a political scandal emerged involving an attempt by deputies in the Bashkir State Assembly tied to Ural to remove his father's trusted premier from power. Although Rakhimov was able to put down the "revolution from above" and although Moscow's role in Ural's betrayal is unclear, it is clear that Rakhimov's position both in Ufa and among some factions in Moscow is weakening. However, as in the other Muslim republics, the Kremlin would be stepping into a minefield that risks sparking Bashkir nationalism should it attempt to remove the president. Meanwhile Tatar nationalism is being fed by the Tatars' third-rate status in Bashkortostan.

Beyond the Volga area's two titular Muslim republics, there is some evidence of combat jamaat activity in non-Muslim regions with significant Tatar minorities. Ten members of a group calling itself "Jamaat" were arrested in 2003 in Ulyanovsk Oblast.[159] They set up a mosque in an apartment, advocated Wahhabism, and distributed extremist literature. Jamaat's eight members included residents not only of Ulyanovsk, but also of Tatarstan, Chuvashia, and Dagestan. In December 2005 they were found guilty of "banditism," kidnapping, illegal possession of firearms, ammunition, and explosives, and actions aimed at inciting inter-ethnic hatred and religious antagonism.[160] According to prosecutors, Jamaat worked to share experience and train jihadist groups in other Tatar-populated regions including

Bashkiriya, Mordovia, Saratov, and Nizhny Novgorod, and "staged public actions aimed to instigate hatred against the unfaithful."[161] There have been reports of Tatar diasporas outside the Volga area producing Islamist radicals as well. In December 2005, the newspaper *Izvestiya*, claimed in a controversial report that the largest Tatar community outside Tatarstan in Russia, in Penza Oblast's village of Srednyaya Elyuzan, had seen four of its seven mosques taken over by "Wahhabis."[162] The charge was refuted by the mosques' imams and the two competing local official Islamic organizations of the TsDUM and United Spiritual Board of Muslims (EDUM) and questioned by Tatarstan president Shaimiev, who sent a team of journalists to investigate.[163] Subsequently, the Penza MVD brought charges of extremism and incitement of inter-communal antagonism against one madrasah.[164]

FOREIGN ISLAMISTS AMONG THE TATARS: HIZB UT-TAHRIR ISLAMI

The link between Taliban- and al Qaeda-tied international terrorists, on the one hand, and the Chechens' radicalization and the expansion of its associated Islamist network, on the other, shows the dangers brought by even the weakest infiltration by foreign Islamists into a region. Given Tatars' ostensible moderation in their nationalism and Islam, less radical imported brands of Islamism might be more effective there than the indiscriminately violent forms of Islamo-fascism seen elsewhere.

Indeed, in 2004 a new Islamist force from abroad appeared to have arrived in some strength in Tatarstan and other Tatar-populated regions. In the wake of Beslan, Russian security forces suddenly made a rash of arrests of alleged Islamists from the Muslim revolutionary organization Hizb ut-Tahrir Islami (the Islamic Liberation Party or HTI) in at least nine of Russia's regions. Hizb ut-Tahrir was founded in 1953 in Jordan, expanded to some forty countries including Central Asia in the early 1990s, and is now apparently based in London.[165] Unlike other revolutionary Islamist organizations, it claims to seek the establishment of a south Eurasian caliphate through non-violent means. However, although it originally rejected jihad, more recently it has declared one against the United States. It appears that while its members do not undertake terrorist attacks themselves, they do encourage others to engage in them.[166] Russian investigators' conclusions about the specifics of the January 2005 gas pipeline explosion in Bugulma, Tatarstan mentioned above – that Ishmuradov and Gumarov were members of a criminal rather than a religious group but that the objective was to stop law-enforcement organs from pursuing Hizb ut-Tahrir – fits this profile.[167] Estimates are that it has 5,000–10,000 core members with even more supporters, including

5,000–10,000 operating in Turkey, Syria, Pakistan, and Indonesia. Its presence in the post-Soviet space had until recently been confined to Central Asia.[168] Recently, Colonel Begejan Akhmedov from Kyrgyzstan's National Security Service (SNB) stated that HTI has three thousand supporters in Kyrgyzstan and ten thousand in Central Asia, and it has been reported that cells in Central Asia were developing their ties with Russia-based supporters.[169]

Although Russia's Supreme Court ruled it a terrorist organization and banned it in Russia in 2003, Hizb ut-Tahrir had shown little prior presence in Russia. The bulk of the nearly two hundred alleged members arrested in fall-winter 2004–05 were detained in Tatarstan and Bashkortostan. The Tatarstan FSB also reported that this was one of two groups of Islamist extremists uncovered in the republic and that twenty suspects had been detained. The arrests also uncovered explosives and written materials that indicated intent to commit a terrorist act.[170] Of the twenty arrests in Tatarstan in autumn 2004, fourteen were made in Naberezhnyi Chelny.[171] Others were made in Samara, Nizhegorod, Ulyanovsk, Chelyabinsk, Irkutsk, Tyumen, and Khantsy-Mantsiiskii Autonomous Okrug; all regions with significant minorities of Tatars and, in some cases, Bashkirs.[172]

It seems unlikely that such a substantial Hizb ut-Tahrir infiltration into Russia occurred in the less than two-month period between Beslan and the spate of arrests. This would suggest a longer-term buildup unbeknown to or ignored by Russia's *siloviki* starting in summer 2004 along with, but not likely connected to the wave of terror. Muslim and human rights activists have claimed that the charges are trumped up. However, some of the arrests appear to be legitimate. In a sense, it makes little difference. Whether there is genuinely an extensive presence of Hizb ut-Tahrir operatives in Russia or innocent Muslims have been arrested on false charges, neither bodes well for the future of relations between the Russian state and its Muslims. The arrests its sparked some protests, and Uzbekistan's heavy-handed treatment of alleged Hizb ut-Tahrir members with the resulting violent uprising in Andizhan in May 2005 may have softened the response of Russian authorities.[173] Any Hizb ut-Tahrir move into territories such as the Volga, Urals, and western Siberia has an ideological and political logic. Since Tatars are known for their moderate Islamic orientation they could provide a ripe opportunity for an organization that publicly rejects violence to achieve its goals. As Putin's counter-revolution provokes increasing Tatar and even Islamic nationalism, Hizb ut-Tahrir may find Tatar soil increasingly fertile for recruitment.

CONCLUSION

It is clear that the ChRI Islamists' presence in Tatarstan and other Tatar communities is much weaker than in the North Caucasus. At the same time, there is evidence of ties between a small number of Tatar radical nationalists and Islamists, on the one hand, and ChRI and foreign Islamists, on the other. Whether the pool of Tatar Islamists will grow, offering Chechen and foreign Islamists the opportunity to mount a full-scale Islamist revolution across a good part of Russia depends ultimately on whether Tatar national identity emerges as largely secular, nationalist-Islamic and/or Islamist. One thing that is not in question is Tatars' strong desire for self-determination. Whether Tatars perceive self-determination as possible under Russian rule will depend on Moscow's willingness to decentralize: this will be key in determining the content of Tatar national identity. That identity will determine whether and how many Tatars are receptive to appeals for secession, Islamic nationalism, and Islamism.

Today's relative calm should not blind us to the history of violent collective action which abounds with examples of peaceful inter-communal relations suddenly exploding into mass violence.[174] The emergence of violent conflict between Tatars and Russians or the Russian state, would likely be fatal for the Russian state's territorial integrity and, along with the ChRI Islamists' prospective rise to power in a North Caucasus caliphate, would have serious international implications.

Chapter Seven

Conclusions and Security Implications

This chapter summarizes the extent and nature of Russia's Muslim and Islamist challenges and their implications for Russian and international security. The latter is done in the tradition of contingency planning and the post-9/11 call for more imaginative thinking about Islamist terrorism and US national security. I conclude with recommendations for the consideration of Russian, US, and international policymakers.

RUSSIA'S MUSLIM AND ISLAMIST CHALLENGES

There is significant indigenous support for radical Islamic ideas and the Chechen-led revolutionary Islamist network not only in Chechnya but across the North Caucasus Muslim republics and, to a lesser extent, in Tatarstan and Bashkortostan. It is clear from the actions of "moderates" like Maskhadov and Umarov that Sufi Islam can produce jihadism and ally itself with syncretic Islamist jihadists.

It is clear from an analysis of the size and activity of the various republics' jamaats that there is an overall degradation of the network's capacity as one moves away from its ethnic and geographic core in Chechnya. After the Chechens, their fellow Vainakh people, the Ingush, appear to have the most effective combat jamaats and largest network. Ingushetiya had the highest number of known jamaats in 2004–2005, three, in the Ingush, Khalifat, and Amanat Jamaats. The Ingush Jamaat especially has been crucial in many of the ChRI jihadist network's combat and terrorist operations in the North Caucasus, including Beslan and the October 2005 Nalchik raid. After Ingushetiya comes Dagestan, which despite, or more likely because, of its ethnic diversity and geographic proximity to Ingushetiya and Chechnya saw the greatest number of jamaat terrorist attacks in 2005; over a hundred engineered by the Jennet and Shariah Jamaats. Next is the KBR with 'Yarmuk' which, besides Dagestan's Shariat Jamaat, was the second most active outside of Chechnya in terms of operational effectiveness in 2004–2005. The KChR saw few terrorist operations on its territory during this period, but members of its Jamaat Number 3 were involved in attacks elsewhere in the North Caucasus and Moscow. The distant and isolated enclave of Adygeya has seen even less jamaat activity. A sign of the network's viability across ethnicity and geography is the appearance of some indigenous jamaat activity and terrorism in Tatarstan. However, the level there is low, reconfirming a gradient of decline as the ethnic, geographic, and, in this case, theological distance from Chechnya increases. This gradient may persist in the future, but the strength of the network overall and in each republic could grow.

Applying the data presented in previous chapters to Gurr's scale for measuring the level of communal collective action, we come up with a diverse range of scales and, in some cases, high levels of collective action across the six most politicized of the seven Muslim republics besides Chechnya (see Table 12).[1] A striking feature of the variations in scale between them for the three categories of collective action is the contrast between the high levels of anti-government rebellion and/or inter-communal conflict in the North Caucasian republics (Dagestan, Ingushetiya, the KBR, and the KChR) and Tatarstan's low levels for these types of collective action but relatively high level of "anti-government protest." This reflects several factors: Tatarstan's more developed civil society; the leading role of the Soviet-era nomenklatura in the pro-autonomy movement; high levels of urbanization, education, employment, standards of living, and inter-communal (Russian/Tatar) marriage; and the moderating influences of Hanafi Islam and Tatar jadidism. This difference suggests that in the long term Tatarstan has greater potential for organizing a more mass-based, but less violent communalist movement for self-determination. One previously mentioned caveat is that the history of violent collective action is rife with cases of previously peaceful inter-communal relations suddenly exploding into sporadic or even generalized violence.[2] In contrast, the North Caucasian republics show higher levels of violent types of collective action. It should also be added that there appear to be cases of terrorism or battles with Islamists outside Chechnya that go unreported.[3]

Russian Successes

The emerging Chechen-led Islamist jihad has not gone unchallenged by the Russian authorities. The Russians have achieved some recent successes in their efforts to combat it. In the military and security sphere, despite Basaev's May 2005 promise of a "summer of fire" and the *Kavkaz-Tsentr* June commentary titled "The Upcoming Summer Promises to Be Hot," the level of terror in summer 2005 was a marked degree lower than in summer 2004 and saw not one terrorist attack in Moscow and not one mass attack anywhere in the

Table 12. Gurr Scales for Levels of Protest, Rebellion, and Inter-Communal Conflict in
         Russia's Eight Titular Muslim Republics, 2004–2005 (the higher the scale
         number, the higher the level).

REPUBLIC	Level of Protest (Scale = 1–5)	Level of Rebellion (Scale =1–7)	Inter-communal Conflict (Scale = 1–6)
Chechnya	3	7	6
Ingushetiya	3	5	4–5*
Dagestan	3	5–6	4–5*
Kabardino-Balkariya	3	4	3
Karachaevo-Cherkessiya	3**	4	3
Adygeya	4	1	3
Tatarstan	3	1	2–3
Bashkortostan	3	1	2

* Includes conflict with Ossetiyans and North Ossetiya.
** These scales would have been scaled at "3" if not for the fact that the demonstrations and rallies that took place
had a less than clear communalist orientation.

Key for Scales:

Anti-government protest: 0 = none reported; 1 = verbal opposition (public letters,
petitions, posters, publications, agitation, requests by a minority-controlled regional
government for independence); 2 = political organizing activity on a substantial scale,
symbolic resistance or destruction of property and mobilization by a minority-controlled
regional government for autonomy or secession; 3 = one or more demonstrations, rallies,
strikes, and/or riots with total participation of less than 10,000 people; 4 = demonstrations,
rallies, strikes, and/or riots with total participation of between 10,000 and 100,000 people;
and 5 = demonstrations, rallies, strikes, and/or riots with total participation of over 100,000
people.

Anti-government rebellion: 0 = none reported; 1 = political banditry (often the last stage
of guerrilla wars) and sporadic terrorism; 2 = campaigns of terrorism; 3 = local rebellions,
including armed attempts to seize power in a locale, and declarations of independence by a
minority-controlled regional government; 4 = small-scale guerrilla activity (fewer than
1,000 armed fighters, sporadic armed attacks numbering less than six reported per year, and
attacks in a small part of area occupied by the group or in one or two other areas; 5 =
intermediate-scale guerrilla activity (a mix of small- and large-scale traits); 6 = large-scale
guerrilla activity (more than 1,000 armed fighters, frequent armed attacks (more than six)
reported per year, attacks affecting a large part of the area occupied by the group); and 7 =
protracted civil war, fought by rebel military units with base areas.

Inter-communal conflict: 0 = none reported; 1 = individual acts of harassment against
property and persons, no fatalities; 2 = political agitation, campaigns urging the authorities
to impose restrictions on a group, etc.; 3 = sporadic violent attacks by gangs or other small
groups, some of them fatal; 4 = anti-group demonstrations, rallies, and marches; 5 = inter-
communal rioting, armed attacks; and 6 = inter-communal warfare (protracted, large-scale
inter-group violence).

country.[4] On 1 October Russian MVD deputy chief, Colonel-General Aleksandr Chekalin reported that the number of terrorist attacks in the Southern FO had declined by 53 percent in 2005.[5] Russian interior minister Rashid Nurgaliev announced four days later that security forces had "made impossible" and "ruined" the Islamists' planned "Scorching Summer" offensive.[6]

However, claims of continuing successes made by top Russian officials are to some extent exaggerated. The shift in terrorist activities may be explained in some degree by a change in strategy on the jihadists' part from focusing on mass, high-profile terrorist attacks against the "far enemy" in Moscow to targeting police, security, and civilian officials of the "near enemy" in the Caucasus. The MVD's triumphalism was undermined by the jihadist campaign in 2005 in Dagestan, the increase in attacks in Ingushetiya in late summer and early fall, the October raid/uprising in Nalchik, and continuing attacks in Chechnya. Winter 2005–2006 saw the characteristic lull in terrorist activity, dictated by the harsh mountainous terrain and climate in the areas where the bases of the ChRI jihadists and many other global jihadists, including Osama bin Laden, are located.

Nevertheless, Russian forces do seem to have become more successful, even if still rather heavy-handed, in combating the jihadists in urban guerrilla warfare. Basaev admitted in an April 2006 interview that the mujahedin had had a "difficult," "hard winter." ChRI "vice-president" Doku Umarov also acknowledged that the jihad was experiencing new difficulties, including a shortage of finances and weapons, especially in the KBR.[7] There is speculation that the Sufi-oriented Umarov does not have access to the kind of funds from patrons abroad that the Islamist jihadists enjoy.[8] However, the shortages may be affecting the ChRI and global jihad across the board. Al Qaeda has had trouble transferring funds to its affiliates as the US, Russia, and others have cooperated in tightening international banking rules, fighting money-laundering, and coordinating counter-terrorism activities.

Russian forces have become efficient at "beheading" the jihadist network by eliminating its leaders. This suggests improved counter-terrorism intelligence operations. In 2005 alone Russian forces killed ChRI president Maskhadov, the Arab al Qaeda operative Abu Dzeit, the late Maskhadov's deputy successor (after Sadulaev) and Sadulaev's likely designated successor, Shamil-Khadzi Muskiyev,[9] two successive leaders of both Dagestan's notorious Shariah Jamaat and the KBR's Yarmuk, and many other jihadists. In September 2005, Russia's North Caucasus Regional Operational Headquarters (ROSh) reported 13 field commanders killed, 15 "leaders" arrested, 23 emirs killed and 11 arrested since January.[10] Moreover, thousands of Chechen militants have surrendered; hundreds under Moscow's 1999 and 2003 amnesty offers.[11] As estimated in Chapter Three, it appears that in 2005 some 300 jihadists were killed, 1,300 were arrested, and 49 surrendered, meaning the network lost around 1,650 jihadists for the year, or 137.5 a month. Even if one accepts the lower official MVD statistics for 2005, then 49 North Caucasus fighters and terrorists surrendered, 140 were killed, and 311 were taken into custody, making a total annual attrition of 500 militants or nearly 42 per month.[12] In addition, some major figures have surrendered, taking entire units with them; a major blow to morale for those jihadists left out in the field. In March 2004, pro-Moscow Chechen forces convinced Ichkeriya's defense minister Magomed Khambiyev to turn himself in along with forty of his fighters under an amnesty, and in September 2005 Khambiyev announced that he was running for the pro-Moscow regime's parliament in the elections set for 29 November.[13]

Those elections along with the presidential ones, though clearly neither free nor fair, managed to re-establish a relatively loyal Chechen government, and there are some signs that funds for reconstruction are actually now being spent on their designated projects, despite continued fraud and corruption. It remains to be seen, however, whether that government, headed by President Alu Alkhanov and Prime Minister Ramzan Kadyrov, can remain united and deliver good governance. There are signs of tension between the two, and the proliferation of clan-based regional eastern and western "battalions" made up of many former guerrillas risks inter-clan violence and even a new warlordism of the kind that confounded Maskhadov's efforts to establish a stable Chechen regime during the inter-war years. In May 2006 clashes were reported between the Chechen MVD, formerly headed by Alkhanov, and detachments loyal to Kadyrov.

In sum, it remains unclear whether the Ichkeriyan jihad's gambit in spreading its forces thin in order to bring the struggle to Russia's other Muslim lands is viable. Indeed, there remains a question about whether expansion of the jihad was a choice based on the ChRI's sense of its own strength or whether it was an act of desperation dictated by failure in Chechnya and a need to seek manpower elsewhere. In the words of Ansor Astemirov, Yarmuk's new emir and emir of the North Caucasus front's Kabardino-Balkariya sector: "When the same brothers [Basaev and the ChRI mujahedin] turned out to be in a more grave situation, they required help from the Caucasus's Muslims. By help they had in mind introducing partisan war beyond Chechnya's borders."[14] Of course, history knows of acts of desperation that turned out to be strokes of genius leading to victory. If by the end of 2006 we have seen no major operations either in the form of high-profile mass terrorist acts of the kind seen in 2004 or the numerous attacks on local *siloviki* and civilian officials of 2005, we may begin to suspect that the Russians have gained the upper hand

and that the North Caucasus jihad is perhaps unsustainable over the mid- to long term. However, if we see major jihadist activity, the international community will need to conclude the contrary, think more seriously about the broader implications of jihad in Russia, and take them into account in policymaking.

THE IMPLICATIONS FOR INTERNATIONAL SECURITY

At present, political risk and national security assessments do not take much note of Russia's growing Muslim challenge. So far I have laid out the challenge that Russia's multi-ethnic Muslim community and the rise of radicalism and Islamism pose to the Russian state. Now it is necessary to examine the political risks to Western interests and international security. There are five specific real and potential threats:

I. Russia's emerging Islamist network as a recruitment pool for the international Islamist jihad

This is already a reality. Some of Russia's Islamists have already been found participating in the international Islamist network's jihad against the US. Indeed, ethnic Muslims from regions both in the North Caucasus and Volga area were among the Taliban and al Qaeda in Afghanistan arrested by US forces and taken to Guantanamo Bay in 2002. Among the Russian citizens detained at Guantanamo were two Muslims each from the republics of Kabardino-Balkariya (KBR), Tatarstan, and Bashkortostan as well as one each from Chelyabinsk and Tyumen Oblasts. Regarding nationality, at least two were ethnic Tatars and at least one was an ethnic Kabard.[15] More recently, Chechens have turned up fighting in Afghanistan and Iraq against US forces.[16] Indian police uncovered an al Qaeda cell led by a Chechen planning to assassinate Vice-Admiral V. J. Metzger, commander-in-chief of the US Seventh Fleet, during a trip to India.[17] A "Chechen cell" consisting of French nationals who underwent chemical terrorism training and fought in Chechnya and Afghanistan was uncovered in Paris while planning to attack numerous targets in France, including the Russian embassy.[18]

Although many in the West do not subscribe to Samuel Huntington's view regarding a "clash of civilizations," many of the world's Muslims and all Islamists do, including those in Russia. It is instructive to examine the anti-Americanism, anti-Westernism, and anti-Semitism of the Ichkeriyan jihadists, since to a certain extent they are representative of Russia's larger Islamist network and are influencing its operatives as well as their Muslim brothers throughout Russia. Basaev expressed simultaneously his admiration for Osama bin Laden and his disdain for the US in a March 2005 interview:

I have never been acquainted with bin Laden and have had no contact with him, although I would very much like to meet him. . . . One thing I know for certain is that he cannot fundamentally be a villain because his face gives out a strong light in all the photographs which I have been lucky enough to see. From my own experience I know that America and Rusnya [derogatory term for "Russia"] love to decide who the guilty people are and do not allow them even a word to say in order to justify themselves. An example of this is the story of the weapons of mass destruction in Iraq and Saddam, whose overthrow I always supported, but not for the benefit of America, but because I saw in this an advantage for the Muslims.[19]

If this statement does not make the ChRI network's potential to act against the West sufficiently clear, a more strident Basaev comment should: "Scoundrel Western crusaders, bogged down in lechery, and you, hoggish Jews, I have ordered my Muslim brothers and sisters, the Chechens, staying in your filthy countries to annihilate you without taking any compassion on you."[20]

Although Maskhadov generally abstained from making anti-American and anti-Western statements, Sadulaev is less reticent. During the visit to Moscow by Western leaders, including President George Bush, to celebrate the sixtieth anniversary of the Allied victory over Nazi Germany, Sadulaev condemned the visitors as "leader-hypocrites" for their friendly relations with Putin:

> Your words of greeting in the capital of the state aggressor sound like justification for the murder of more than 25 percent of the population of Chechnya. Your handshakes with Putin and other leaders of Russia signify approval of the experience of the fascist concentration camps of Buchenwald and Auschwitz being applied today by the Russian occupiers against Chechens, and your applause at Putin's parade is perceived as excitement for the murder of 45,000 Chechen children.[21]

Such transgressions are punishable by death in Islamist circles. Under Sadulaev, the ChRI website *Kavkaz-Tsentr* published an article accusing the US of another crime: assisting the Russians in killing President Dudaev in 1995 and Chechen field commander Ruslan Gelaev in 2003.[22] Sadulaev further revealed his antagonism toward the West in his August 2005 announcement which dissolved the late Maskhadov's Ichkeriyan government abroad and displaced its foreign representatives: "according to ChRI's special services, future 'Karzais' are being prepared from among them for the Chechen people in prestigious Western institutions of higher education."[23] Sadulaev's derogatory reference to Afghan president Hamid Karzai clearly shows where the Chechen Islamists stand; like other jihadists, the Ichkeriyans view the Afghan president as a US puppet and a traitor to Allah.

Under both Maskhadov and Sadulaev, the Chechen Islamists' propaganda organs have carried blatantly anti-American, anti-Western, and anti-Israeli messages, both produced internally and gleaned from foreign Islamic media sources.[24] The following headlines are typical of *Kavkaz-Tsentr*: "Satanism in Action: 'Skull and Bones' Rules America," "The Americans Burned Woman and Children with White Phosphorous," "The USA Is Sending Murderers of Children to Iraq," "It Looks Like Western 'Freedom' Is Quite Satanized," "To Be Live Cattle – That's Western Democracy," "Moscow's Militia Has Protected the Scarecrow of Putin, Bush, and Blair," and "Toilet Paper with the Image of Putin, Bush, and Blair Has Come Out."[25] A November 2005 article, "Shamil Basaev Bought a Knife," urges jihadists to "break the heads of Bush and Condoleezza Rice."[26]

Another *Kavkaz-Tsentr* article, "Terminological War" equates the US with the USSR and democracy with socialism. Both are the antipodes of the Islamic umma in a bipolar international system defined by the religious element: the Islamic monotheists against the lying kafirs or multi-theists. Consequently, the author of the piece, Said Minkailov, predicts the collapse of American democracy and present-day Russia as comparable parts of the "society of unbelievers" and "the society of lies." Minkailov assures his readers: "Muslims get outraged in vain by the abundance of lies in Russian or Western propaganda. We do not get outraged when a snake emits venom or a pig looks for dirt: such is their nature." In "the war between monotheism and the mendacious world of unbelief . . . America, Western Europe, Russia, and everybody else who has excessive weaponry are cynically and hypocritically using 'human rights' when justifying their aggressions. And as we can see, these so-called 'rights' can be attached to anybody but Muslims."[27]

ChRI jihadists support Iraq's mujahedin, Afghanistan's neo-Taliban, indeed all the jihadist movements around the globe. ChRI websites refer to US and Western forces in Iraq and Afghanistan as "occupiers" and "infidels," while those fighting alongside or working with American and allied forces are "collaborationists" and "puppets."[28] After al Qaeda or other Islamists' terrorist attacks in Iraq, Egypt, and elsewhere, *Kavkaz-Tsentr* produced articles like "Mossad Is Carrying Out Terrorist Attacks in Iraq" and "Mossad May Stand Behind the Terrorist Act in Egypt."[29] The website has a special rubric titled "Their Morals" which features reports on the most decadent, vile, and perverse crimes committed in the West, Russia, and Israel, portraying them as representative of life in "infidel" countries. This sort of propaganda, including the prediction of the inevitable collapse of the US, closely parallels that of Osama bin Laden and Mullah Omar.[30]

Jews and Israel come in for special ire. *Kavkaz-Tsentr* specializes in the standard Islamist/Wahhabist anti-Semitism and support for Israel's destruction with articles like "Award for Abomination: A Jew Completes the Sexual Revolution in America," "Jewish Rabbis Have Forbidden Doctors to Treat Palestinians," "Israel Will Be Destroyed in the Year 2022," "Zionists Are Provoking the War Between Sunnis and Shiites in Iraq," and "Jewish Religious Figure Raped Nine Children."[31] The Ichkeriyan jihadists also are firm deniers of the Holocaust (a word they always put in quotation marks), as seen in *Kavkaz-Tsentr*'s articles "One More Witch-Hunt Trial Against the Next 'Holocaust' Denier in Austria" and "192 Caricatures of the 'Holocaust' Have Aleady Been Entered in the International Competition [contest of Holocaust Denial Art]," among many others.[32] The anti-Western, anti-democratic, anti-Semitic, and Islamo-fascist aspects of the ideology of the ChRI Islamists who now control the Chechen separatist movement should be borne in mind by policymakers.

Worryingly, more moderate Muslims (and non-Muslims) in Russia show a lesser but nonetheless real solidarity with radical foreign Islamic and even Islamist movements in their hateful attitude towards the West. Even the moderate Tatars are producing Americanophobes. As noted earlier, the NChOVTOTs received numerous volunteers to fight US forces in Afghanistan. A February 2003 VTOTS plenum "sharply criticized" US policy in Iraq.[33] During the November 2004 US operation to rid Fallujah of Iraqi Islamists, Tyumen Oblast's leading Muslim cleric, Fatykh Garifullin, an ethnic Tatar, called on his followers to pray for Fallujah's Muslims, commenting:

> There is no limit to the outrage towards the Americans' actions. If the world community does not stop the war in Iraq, the fate of the besieged martyrs in Fallujah awaits all who do not agree to dance to the tune of Bush and his circle . . . . I call upon all Muslims to conduct prayers for their co-believers so that the Almighty will help Iraq's heroic people to save their independence and freedom.[34]

Media controlled by official Muslim organizations produce a constant stream of anti-American, anti-Western, and anti-Israeli propaganda. The KTsMSK's website, Islam.ru routinely carries articles both internally generated and reprinted from foreign Islamic and Islamist media critical of the US, the West, and Israel. Islam.ru, posts commentaries referring to the US "aggression against Afghanistan and Iraq" and US officialdom's "Arabo-phobia," "Islamophobia," "radical Zionism," and "aggressive line in relation to Muslims."[35] Typical pieces charge the US with "sowing injustice, hatred, and crimes against humanity around the world."[36] One article asserted that the US military "teaches its soldiers that all Muslims are terrorists" and that US forces continued to "torture" detainees long after the Abu Ghraib scandal as a matter of course.[37] A typical line of thought is that US policy is controlled by Israel and Jews. Thus, one website posted a 3 November 2003 article from the Saudi Arabian newspaper *al-Watan* purportedly showing that "the USA is hiding Israel's connection with the events of 11 September."[38]

Russia provides al Qaeda with fertile soil for the mobilization of terrorists whose appearance is not particularly "Muslim" and who, therefore, are more easily able to infiltrate the West. First, there is a trend, though still far from a mass one, of ethnic Russians, other Slavs, and other traditionally non-Muslim nationalities in Russia converting to Islam. Although there are no exact figures, it is clear that a Russian/Slavic Islamic community is emerging. According to one report, almost fifty thousand people, mostly ethnic Russians and young women, converted to Islam in Moscow alone between January 2002 and October 2004.[39] Ethnic Russian Muslims have organized their own socio-political organization, the National Organization of Russia's Muslims (NORM), which claims to have about three thousand members.[40]

Second, demographic trends also indicate that the number of mixed Christian–Muslim marriages is on the rise, especially in Moscow and Muslim republics with large Russian minorities like Tatarstan, adding to the stock of Muslims who do not exactly fit the typical "Muslim" physical profile. Some argue that converts and children of inter-faith marriages "are not true Muslims; they remain secular people far removed from true faith."[41] However, ethnic Russian converts have been key participants in several Checheno-Islamist terrorist acts in Russia.[42] Third, traditionally Muslim ethnic groups' population growth rates are much higher than those of ethnic Russians. All of the above will increase the size of Russia's pool of potential Islamists in coming decades.

II. The potential emergence of a Russia-wide terrorist network made up of various Muslim ethnic groups tied to international groups capable of destabilizing the country and sparking civil war in separate regions or across the federation

The al Qaeda model shows that a geographically expansive, ethnically diverse, loosely organized Islamic terrorist network is realizable and viable. The ChRI has gone a long way toward achieving this in the North Caucasus. A mass movement is not needed to achieve many of the goals of Russian and international Islamists. A relatively small network of resourceful operatives implementing an innovative plan can do great damage, as was proven on 9/11. The ChRI jihadist network has already seriously destabilized the North Caucasus. Terrorism abounds and Chechen and Islamist terrorist plots have been uncovered from St. Petersburg to eastern Siberia. Local security organs are in disarray. Republican presidents are being forced to resign with greater frequency. In 2005–06, the presidents of the KBR, Dagestan, and North Ossetiya were all replaced by the Kremlin. There have been hundreds, if not thousands of terrorist attacks and foiled plots in Moscow and across the country.

There is a danger that the Kremlin's policies combined with the Islamists' efforts to appeal across ethnic and territorial boundaries could produce a larger recruitment pool for the Ichkeriyan-led jihadist network. If Russian society begins to treat all ethnic Muslim groups poorly simply because they are Muslim, this is likely to heighten their sense of Muslim identity over their ethnicity and polarize them in opposition to Russia and Russians. Because of the high threat of jihadist terror, general Russian-Muslim tensions are on the rise, which can only assist the Islamists' cause. Finally, Islamists could find allies or make converts among disaffected radical opposition elements, including not only moderate Islamic and ethno-nationalist Muslim groups but also other minority or separatist organizations, the anti-globalization movement, etc.

III. The secession of one or more Muslim republics and the establishment of one or more Islamist caliphates on Russian territory, which become state bases for the global jihadist movement

Islamists could sufficiently destabilize the central Russian state apparatus or even break it up in several ways. One or more of Russia's ethnic Muslim groups could spark a successful secessionist movement, or a Russia-wide Islamist terrorist network could so weaken Russia through war as to precipitate Russia's overall collapse. The separation of Chechnya or other North Caucasus republics and the formation of an independent North Caucasus state (caliphate) would pose grave risks for the US. An independent Chechnya and certainly a North Caucasus caliphate could become a new base for the international jihadists like the one lost in Afghanistan at considerable cost in American lives and coin.

Worse yet, Russia could suffer something approaching a complete collapse. No one could imagine in 1985 that the USSR could break up into fifteen separate states. Few, if any imagine now that Russia could break up, but in fact this remains a distinct possibility, at least until it stabilizes into some form of a functioning federative democracy. The challenge of holding together Russia's vast landmass on the basis of an economy the size of the Netherlands is daunting. Chinese immigration threatens Moscow's hold on the Far East and parts of eastern Siberia, and EU and NATO expansion threatens Russia's hold on Kaliningrad. There are separatist groups in non-Muslim national republics in addition to those in the Muslim republics. Moscow must organize and finance expensive supply lifts to far-flung northern and eastern regions during the long winter months and guard not only its own extremely long border but assist other former Soviet republics in doing so.[43] Drug-trafficking and illegal immigration remains a major problem, making Russia even more vulnerable to international terrorists.

The need to "buy off" separatist titular Muslim republics like Tatarstan and Bashkortostan since the mid-1990s has already caused consternation in other regions. This has drained resources that could have been used to improve the disastrous economic situation in the troublesome North Caucasus and offset centrifugal tendencies in the Far East and Kaliningrad. Moscow continues to preserve some fiscal asymmetry by compensating autonomy-minded republics like Tatarstan through special financing for federal socio-economic development programs.[45] Such imbalances no longer suffice to fully compensate regions for the revenues lost by Putin's centralization of tax revenues, while they anger the governors of "Russian" regions and increase inter-ethnic competition for resources. The need to address security and separatist challenges in the Muslim republics along with problems elsewhere in the federation could overwhelm the Russian state's capacity.

The Tatars and Tatarstan remain an enormous challenge to the Russian state's viability. In the wake of the curtailment of Tatarstan's sovereignty and the adoption of a Chechen constitution promising the war-torn republic autonomy, a treaty that affords Grozny considerable independence in spheres where Kazan has lost it, risks teaching the more numerous Tatars a lesson that war, not compromise, gets results from Moscow. Thus, Moscow is trapped between its anti-federalist state-building policies and its need to normalize Chechnya. It is often argued that a Tatar separatist movement is not viable because Tatarstan lacks an external border. A brief look at the map shows that this argument is weak, especially in a period of state collapse or failure. The Tatars are the second largest nationality in neighboring Bashkortostan, the titular republic of the ethnically and religiously fraternal Bashkirs. A pan-Islamic or "pan-Turkic" Tatar-Bashkir nationalist revolution there could force a bridgehead to an external border less than 100 miles away in Orenburg Oblast.

Furthermore, calls and proposed plans are repeatedly put forward urging the elimination of all the national autonomies, including the republics. Some have even come from high-ranking officials, such as State Duma deputies like Dmitrii Rogozin and Sverdlovsk governor Eduard Rossell.[46] At the 22 June 2005 Tatar Congress in Bashkortostan, the leader of the republic's would-be "orange revolution" and united Tatar-Russian-Bashkir opposition, NKA Committee chairman Ramil Bignov, called for the Tatar community in

Bashkiriya to push for the republic's unification with Orenburg or Samara Oblast.[47] The same proposal emerged in a plan to reduce the number of subjects of the federation from the current eighty-eight to twenty-eight put forward by the influential Council for the Study of Productive Resources (SOPS), a think-tank working for the Russian government. In addition, the plan envisaged: Tatarstan's merger with Ulyanovsk Oblast to create a Volga-Kama Oblast; the merger of Chechnya, Ingushetiya, Dagestan, Kabardino-Balkariya, and North Ossetiya with Stavropol Krai to create a North Caucasus Province; and the incorporation of Adygeya and Karachaevo-Cherkessiya into Krasnodar Krai to create a Prichernomorsk Province.[48] The proposed Adygeya-Krasnodar merger noted earlier could have been a first attempt to implement this plan in the North Caucasus.[49] The political nihilism of such proposals is striking, bordering on state sabotage. They further exacerbate ethno- and even Islamic nationalism while, if implemented, would afford Islamist extremists greater opportunity to travel throughout the North Caucasus in pursuit of recruits, weapons, and vulnerable targets and do part of their work toward forming a united North Caucasus caliphate. Both Tatarstan and Bashkortostan's leaderships have opposed even the vaguest suggestions of any regional merger involving them. If such were ever seriously proposed by Moscow, nationalism would explode in these republics.

IV. With the Russian state's weakening or disintegration, the likelihood that international jihadists would acquire materials and weapons of mass destruction would increase exponentially

Chechen or other Muslim terrorists in Russia could act as intermediaries in international terrorists' acquisition of Russian materials and weapons of mass destruction (MWMDs). Russia remains saturated with MWMDs, including sixteen thousand nuclear warheads located at over two hundred facilities.[50] Both CIA director Porter Goss and Russian Atomic Energy Agency chairman Aleksandr Rumyantsev have stated that they could make no guarantee that nuclear MWMDs might not fall into the hands of terrorists.[51] Russia holds half the world's fissile materials – highly enriched uranium (HEU) and weapons-grade plutonium – stored at hundreds of sites, and forty thousand tons of chemical weapons at seven sites. The full extent of these MWMDs, moreover, is likely not fully declared, and they continue to be developed by the Russian government.[52] Russia also has unknown quantities of various biological weapons and materials located at tens, perhaps even hundreds, of sites.[53]

Proliferation specialists are nearly unanimous in regarding security at Russia's MWMD sites as woefully insufficient, underfunded (including underpaid scientists and other workers), and weakened by corruption and a lax security culture. Terrorists reached Beslan and were able to board two passenger planes and destroy them in mid-air because they paid bribes to police and had inside assistance. A thirty-man terrorist force of the kind that seized the Beslan school in 2004 or the Dubrovka theatre in October 2002 would be sufficient to take possession of many Russian nuclear weapons and fuel sites. The already mentioned June 2004 terrorist attack on the MVD building in Ingushetiya shows that Muslim terrorists are capable of successfully seizing sensitive objects. However, there is no need to actually seize a site. Three or four consignments of nuclear weapons are transported by rail across Russian territory every month.[54] Also, there is no need for such a massive assault or high-profile seizure, which would surely set Russian forces and international community on the terrorists' trail. Using a "micro" approach, exploiting widespread corruption and lax work and security cultures to access small amounts of material at Russia's many MWMD sites, could garner terrorists sufficient materials for a damaging attack, such as one utilizing a "dirty bomb."[55] Indeed, in October 2004, Russian MVD sources stated that three valves costing over $20,000 each were stolen from the Leningrad Nuclear Power Plant and commented that such thefts "happen here often."[56]

Basaev has said he wants nuclear weapons and has engaged in nuclear psychological terror, and terrorists have made several attempts to penetrate nuclear facilities. In 1995 and 1996 he threatened several times to detonate radioactive containers in Russian cities, attack nuclear facilities, and even detonate a nuclear device. At a conference in Shali, Chechnya, he showed off radioactive material containers and informed journalists where he ostensibly had buried such a container: in a Moscow park.[57] Official Russian sources confirm that on four occasions in 2001–02 terrorist teams carried out reconnaissance on two Russian nuclear-warhead storage sites and two nuclear transport trains. Nearly one hundred trespassers, at least some of whom were probably terrorists, were caught in restricted-access areas in 2004. In 2003 there were at least twelve reported cases of trafficking of nuclear, radio-isotope, and dual-use materials, the origins of which were a Russian site.[58] In October 2004, some fifty alleged Dagestanis seized control of a secret, though non-nuclear, military research and development center in the town of Zelenograd near Moscow. However, it remains unclear whether they were terrorists or a group involved in a property dispute.[59] In June 2005, General Igor Valynkin, head of the defense ministry's 12th Main Directorate – the organization in charge of the storage and transport of nuclear weapons – reported that two recent "terrorist attempts to penetrate Russia's nuclear weapons storage facilities [had] been averted."[60] In short, Russian nuclear and other MWMD stockpiles remain vulnerable to terrorist acquisition.[61]

Moreover, poorly secured borders between Russia and other former Soviet republics, whose stockpiles of MWMDs are no more secure than Russia's, add to the potential sources from which Russia-based terrorists could obtain such materials and weapons. In May 2005 two reporters from the London's *Sunday Times* newspaper, posing as middlemen for Islamic terrorists, arranged a meeting in the unrecognized but de facto Russian protectorate of the Transdniestr Republic (Moldova) for the fictive purpose of purchasing a $200,000 a "radio-active" Alazan rocket fitted with a warhead containing up to 400g of caesium-137 and strontium-90. The rocket would reportedly have come from the enormous 50,000-ton Russian weapons stockpile in Kolbasnya, Transdniestr. More disconcertingly, the contact, if not the source, for the sale was a senior officer from the Transdniestr state security ministry, which has close ties to the Russian FSB. The Alazan rocket, with a range of eight miles, is considered a perfect weapon for terrorists.[62] It would be ideal for executing a scenario gamed by the US military in which Islamic terrorists acquire a nuclear warhead, attach it to a Scud missile, place it on a commercial ship, and gain proximity to New York or another major American city by international sea lanes, and when they near their objective fire it, killing hundreds of thousands of Americans.

We know there have been contacts between international and Chechen terrorists involving terrorist acts against the US. Al Qaeda's Ayman al-Zawahiri visited Russia in 1996 to assist the Chechens in their war against Moscow and came away enthusiastic about the prospects for acquiring nuclear materials from Russia or other post-Soviet states.[63] There are also unverified reports of Osama bin Laden trading $3 million and large amounts of opium to Chechens in return for nuclear weapons or material.[64] A nexus of Russian nationalists, mafia, Islamists, and impoverished scientists and other workers could facilitate international terrorists' acquisition of MWMDs.

V. A rising tide of Islamist terrorism and the government's inability to hold onto parts of Russian territory or prevent Russian WMDs from falling into the hands of Islamist terrorists would promote serious domestic instability in Russia and likely create greater public demand for more centralized, dictatorial power to crush the Islamist threat

Any Russian regime that "appeased" or lost out to Islamist separatist revolts and terrorism would be more vulnerable to neo-communist, hardline nationalist forces or be inclined to continue recentralizing power and rolling back democracy to such an extent that it transformed the country into a dictatorship. At present Putin's counter-revolution has brought a rather soft authoritarian form of rule to Russia; a regime carefully calibrated to avoid Western charges of a return to dictatorship as Moscow attempts to implement its belated version of the Chinese economic transition model. De-democratization has been accompanied inevitably by anti-Americanism and anti-Westernism, in line with Russian political culture's deeply ingrained association, indeed suspicion, of democracy and the West. Any move to full-blown dictatorship would be followed by a complete break with the US and the West. This would produce a powerful government opposed to US policies and interests.

Most immediately, any failure to hold onto territories in the North Caucasus or elsewhere could intensify Russian motivation to "take revenge" and challenge growing US influence in the former Soviet Union by fully backing separatism in the various "frozen conflicts" in the post-Soviet space and beyond, in such places as Georgia (Abkhazia and South Ossetia) and Moldova (Transdniestr breakaway region). That the Russians are well aware of the option of playing this secessionist card was reflected in Vladimir Putin's January 2006 press conference. The Russian president conditioned any compromise on Russian opposition to the international community's willingness to grant Kosovo "conditional independence" with the warning that this should then become a general principle of international affairs and be equally applicable to Abkhazia, South Ossetiya, and even Cyprus. Although he did not mention Transdniestr and Nagorno-Karabakh, the same would be supported by Moscow. Russia's loss of Chechnya, the entire North Caucasus, or other regions would be blamed on Western support for the principle, if not the agents, of separatism.

Anti-Americanism among ethnic Russians, though less virulent than Islamist anti-Americanism, has become as fashionable today as pro-Americanism was in the late 1980s and early 1990s before NATO expansion. Opinion surveys suggest that fervent anti-Americanism encompasses around 30 percent of the population. In a survey conducted in December 2005 by the most reliable Russian polling agency, the All-Russian Center for the Study of Public Opinion (VTsIOM), in which respondents were allowed to name up to five sources of threat to Russian national security, 30 percent of those questioned named the United States, more than any other country. China was mentioned by 17 percent. By comparison, Chechnya and the North Caucasus republics occupied fourth place with 5 percent.[65]

A hardline Russian regime would probably attempt to strengthen its strategic relations with a revived and potentially hyper-nationalist China and/or rogue states, with a potentially devastating effect on American international efforts. This would be catastrophic for U.S. national and international security, given the burdens of an ongoing war against terrorism (Iraq, Afghanistan, and elsewhere), the danger of conflict with Iran and North Korea, and other national and international problems. The precursor ideologies – traditional Russian nationalism and the new Eurasianism – for such a regime already predominate among the Russian elite.

Russia's anti-American discourse is reinforced by the "Eurasian school" of Russian nationalism espoused today by Aleksandr Dugin, Aleksandr Panarin, and several Muslim activists including Geidar Dzhemal and Ali Polosin. In the nineteenth century, Eurasianism was an attempt to overcome the rift in the Russian intelligentsia between pro-reform Westernizers and pro-tsarist Slavophiles. Russia's role, Eurasianists argued, was not to imitate Western liberalism and democracy, or to reject it out of hand; rather it was to find from Eurasia's rich diversity a third way, consistent with the culture and traditions of Orthodoxy and Russia but incorporating the best from East and West.

The new post-Soviet Eurasianism contends that Russia's stability and potential as a great power can and should be achieved by bringing Eurasia's ethnicities and civilizations closer together as a counter to globalization.[66] Confessionally, it recommends a "holy alliance" between the Christian Orthodox and Islamic (as well as, for some, the Chinese and Hindu) civilizations against the secular American or "Atlantist" globalizing juggernaut. The eclectic and relatively inclusive nature of the new Eurasianism inevitably creates some strange political bedfellows.[67] Its anti-Westernism is almost wholly anti-American in focus and similar to much of the postmodern left's critique of globalization. America, in this view, is leading the world down a road of unsustainable development, bringing about the destruction of national cultures and non-Western civilizations, and ultimately the death of mankind. Two political strategies for countering American hegemony predominate among the Eurasianists. The more moderate one envisages dividing the West by slicing off Europe from the US-led Atlantic juggernaut, using the points of leverage of the resurgent Germans of Central Europe and perhaps the fraternal Slavs of Eastern Europe. The more radical strategy, supported by Panarin, Dugin, and their Muslim allies, is to rally the forces of the East against the Atlantic civilization.

Publicist and philosopher Aleksandr Panarin's *Revansh istorii* (History's Revenge) represents the most eloquent and sophisticated face of this brand of contemporary Russian Eurasianism. Panarin reflects several strains in Russia's geostrategic and political cultures: anti-Westernism, messianism, and anti-rationalism. Panarin's messianism is represented in his notion that only Russia can ensure Eurasia's stability and the survival of the globe in the teeth of American encroachment and globalization. Russia is uniquely poised to organize an alternative to the techno-economic globalization that threatens the planet's ecology. Only Russia's Orthodox culture can unite the Buddhist, Confucian, and Islamic civilizations, and only a Eurasian civilization can counter the expansion of environmental and cultural pollution and poverty brought to second- and third-world countries by globalization. At the same time, Russia's European and Slavic characteristics make it the logical bridge to a more spiritual and sustainable form of global development, to be offered to Europe as an alternative to the coming American-induced holocaust. According to this view, Russia can be both the reformer of the West and the modernizer of the East. Despite its present economic woes, it is poised to leap over the advanced stage of industrial development and lead the way into a new post-industrial world that rejects the consumerism and homogeneity of the "soulless" American world view. Thus, the new Eurasianism's anti-rationalism rejects the West's reliance on market economics and the social and physical sciences, proposing the spirituality of Russia and the East as the antidote.[68] Like Russian nationalist thinkers from Nikolai Danilevskii to Fyodor Dostoyevsky, Panarin and other Eurasianists believe Russia can save the world.

The Russian authorities' and official Islam's support for the Eurasian movement is considerable. The Eurasian Party, headed by Dugin, has been joined by Muslim activist Geidar Dzhemal and TsDUM chairman Talgat Tadzhuddin. Indeed, the TsDUM's entire leadership board and an overwhelming majority of its members have joined the Eurasia Party. Russian foreign minister Sergei Lavrov's recent statement to the tenth World Russian People's Convocation in April 2006 in Moscow's Christ the Savior Cathedral chaired by Moscow Patriarch Aleksei II reflects Eurasianist sentiment:

> Mankind again has ended up at a critical moment in its development. On one side, there are forces which demand peoples' rejection of their history, culture, and spirituality, since cultural-civilizational differences supposedly lay the bases for contradictions between states. On the other, there are those who insist on their national uniqueness before the press of globalization which is creating a threat to the world's culture-civilizational diversity.[69]

Leading Muslim clergy, such as the KTsMSK's Chairman Mufti Shafik-khadzhi Pshikhachev, and Muslim thinkers such as Geidar Dzhemal and Ali Polosin, proselytize Eurasianism's anti-Western and often anti-Zionist ideas on the KTsMSK's website, Islam.ru.[70] Eurasianists often portray the US and Israel as organizing elaborate conspiracies to turn Russia and Muslims against each other as part of an overall "Zionist" strategy to establish a "new world order." For example, Islam.ru published an article by an ethnic Russian Muslim who found "such a monster" as the United States and Israel to have been the forces behind the Beslan plot: "They want us to ask forgiveness for the actions of those who were brought up by the CIA and Mossad for the implementation of geopolitical provocations against the Islamic world."[71] A Chechen assistant to President Putin implied the same.[72] In Islam.ru's Eurasianist world al Qaeda is nothing but a myth promoted to distract Russians as NATO approaches.[73] The growing popularity of Eurasianism among Russian elites and its propagation in the mass media reinforces both Russian nationalist and Islamic anti-Americanism, anti-Semitism, anti-Westernism, and anti-globalization sentiment among Russia's Muslims and non-Muslims alike.

There are already many Russian nationalist and Eurasianist forces calling for a break with the West and alliances with Islamic states. Hardline Russian nationalist Colonel General Leonid Ivashov has stated that Russia must "search for allies in the Islamic world" in addition to developing "temporary allied relations" with China, India, and Vietnam.[74] A Russian think-tank dominated by intelligence and security agents has called for an alliance of Russia, Iran, China, and India to counterbalance the US-dominated West.[75] Russia's participation in the Shanghai Cooperation Organization (SCO), the observer status and plans for membership of Iran (along with Pakistan, Mongolia, and India) in the SCO, and Russia's observer status and desire to become a full member of the Organization of Islamic States Conference are institutional expressions of Russian Eurasianism. These international organizations position Russia for its break with the West and lay the foundations for an anti-American Eurasian alliance. Such an alliance could eventually include anti-American Arab and/or Muslim states, such as Iran or a post-Musharraf Pakistan, Sudan, and even future Islamist regimes. It will naturally be argued that an Islamist state would be loath to ally with Russia, China, or North Korea even if the latter were in opposition to America and the West. But such a conclusion is based on the mistaken assumption that, unlike all other revolutionary regimes, a new Islamist regime would not lose its revolutionary élan and adopt more realistic policies based on long-range interests. A post-revolutionary practical Islamist state might come to see the benefits of a temporary truce with "infidel states" allied against the West in order to weaken or destroy the "greater Satan."

POLICY RECOMMENDATIONS

Russian, US, and international policymakers need to take steps to reduce the threat to international security that Islamist revolutionary separatism in Russia represents, in particular the danger that international terrorists could acquire MWMDs through Russian Islamist intermediaries. The latter problem must be attacked both from the problem's "supply side" (Russia's MWMDs) and from its "demand side" (the support by Russia's Islamists for the international jihad and their desire to inflict harm on the US and its allies). Specifically, the US government should undertake to:

I. Establish the security of Russian MWMDs as the top priority in Russian-American relations

Only by placing the issue of the security of MWMDs at the top of the US-Russia policy agenda, negotiating hard with the Russians on access to sites, and offering substantially increased funding to remove the threat will US leaders be able to convince the Russians of their seriousness.

II. Increase the scope and effectiveness of the Nunn-Lugar, Proliferation Security Initiative (PSI), and Nuclear Cities Initiative (NCI) programs for destroying and securing Russian MWMDs and providing Russian scientists with employment support[76]

Although these US programs and others dedicated to Russia's chemical and biological weapons and materials sites have been operating for years, the job at nuclear-related sites, where the most extensive programs exist, is not even half-finished and is unlikely to be so within a decade. US-funded "comprehensive upgrades" have been completed at only 10 percent of Russian warhead sites, less comprehensive "rapid upgrades" at 50 percent.[77] Russia's bureaucracy remains highly secretive with regard to its MWMDs and thus a major obstacle to implementation of these programs. Russia has never declared how much highly enriched uranium or weapons-grade plutonium it has, and only a small percentage of nuclear stockpiles are subject to international inspection.[78] Moreover, a significant portion of Russian nuclear, chemical, and biological weapons and materials sites remains outside the jurisdiction of such programs and, as things stand now, will never be subject to such programs. In addition, US officials need to lobby the Russian government hard for greater cooperation and transparency regarding program-funds usage.

III. Increase cooperation between US, Russian, and other intelligence services in the war on terror

This can be implemented on the supply and demand side by jointly tracking scientists working on WMDs and penetrating and destroying terrorist organizations inside Russia as well as outside. Although there are risks in such a policy (unintended intelligence transfer and violation of Russians citizens' rights with the involvement of US agents) and there would be significant resistance from anti-American FSB and GRU officials, a carefully calibrated expansion of cooperation could produce better results. Unusually close US-Russian-UK cooperation brought real dividends in August 2004 when the sale of a Russian shoulder-fired anti-aircraft Igla missile to terrorists was preempted in New Jersey.

In order to address the demand side of the threat from Russia's emerging

Islamist revolution, US policy needs to address the ideological sources and political causes of Russian Muslims' growing radicalization. It is important to:

IV. Encourage a reduction in the cultural divide between a largely secular post-Soviet Russian state and society and Russia's re-Islamizing Muslims by increasing the influence of jadidism and other moderate forms of Islam and Islamic teaching

A recent RAND study proposes using Islamic "modernists" and Sufism against fundamentalists to deradicalize the Muslim world.[79] However, the presence of jihadists in the Sufi-dominated North Caucasus and Indonesia as well as the Algerian Sufi Marabut resistance to French conquerors in 1830–1871 suggests that this prescription will produce only a limited cure. Sufi Islamic brotherhoods had a radicalizing effect on much of the already highly conservative and rigid Islam of the North Caucasus imported from Arabia after the caliphate's military expansion into the southern Caucasus. They played leading roles in the Islamization of the peoples of the North Caucasus and in their resistance to Russian rule. Naqshbandiya Sufi brotherhoods took the lead in proselytizing Islam throughout the North Caucasus and have remained an important religious and political force in the area ever since, despite Russian and especially Soviet efforts to uproot them. The early resistance leaders, first Sheik Mansur Ushurma in the eighteenth century and then Sheik Shamil, who led the mid-nineteenth-century North Caucasus imamate, were murids of the Sufi Naqshbandiya Muslim brotherhood. Imam Hadzhmuddin and Sheik Uzun Hadzhi led the 1920–1921 Dagestan uprising against Soviet rule.[81] The Qadiriya Sufi brotherhood emerged after Russia's defeat of Shamil and the Naqshbandiya brotherhoods in 1865 and inspired, if not led, the Chechen revolts against Soviet power in 1942 as Nazi forces approached the North Caucasus.[82] Many of the ChRI terrorist network's cadres have come from Sufi sects. Basaev, for example, was from a Naqshbandiya tariqat. Indeed, Sufism may actually contribute to the growth of an Islamic revolutionary underground. Sufi brotherhoods are highly structured and hierarchical secretive societies infused with religious rituals. Their adherents or tariqatists consist of masters (murshids) and their adepts (murids). The murshids' authority to teach is based on mystical experiences, which legitimize their claims to knowledge on how to find the path to God. Consequently, the tariqats possess strong organization and discipline and therefore are well-suited for underground terrorist activity.[80]

Moreover, the RAND study ignored the late nineteenth-century Tatar jadidist movement, despite its role in the modernization of Islam and its high potential for influencing it from Central Asia to Turkey. With jadidism's emphasis on moderate religious education, a secular education stressing mathematics and science, respect for secular culture, and orientation on the peaceable sections of the Koran written during the Prophet Mohammed's Meccan period rather than the more jihadist portions from the Medina period – could be a strong antidote to radical politicization, secessionism, and fundamentalist Islam. The US would do well to help Russia's Tatars and other neo-jadidists proselytize throughout the Muslim world the original jadidist luminaries' works (available in Arabic as well as Russian), urge and perhaps assist Russia in doing so inside Russia, and support jadidist-oriented clerics, scholars, and activists inside and outside of Russia's official Islamic circles.[83]

V. Work toward the creation of a multilateral coalition to induce the Russians and the Chechens to declare a ceasefire, including cessation of all terrorist acts, and begin negotiations toward a settlement of the war in Chechnya

The Chechen quagmire is the most immediate cause of expanding radicalism among Russia's Muslims, especially in the North Caucasus. The ongoing war is spawning radicals and helping them and foreign jihadists to mobilize Islamist revolution and war deep inside Russia. The Chechen war has both provided a more fertile recruiting pool among Russia's indigenous Muslims and attracted the attention of international Islamists, leading to their infiltration of the Chechen guerrilla forces and growing influence among Muslims across Russia.

Unfortunately, US-Russian relations are now such that any Chechnya peace plan under sole US sponsorship would be viewed by the Kremlin with suspicion and likely ignored. At the same time, Maskhadov's death at Russian hands in the wake of his ceasefire initiative and the ChRI's subsequent "jihadization" means that any peace plan coming from Russia and/or the US is also unlikely to be welcomed by any of the ChRI's leaders. Therefore, the US should conduct quiet diplomacy to organize an international effort to resolve the Chechen conflict – a joint OIC-OSCE (or G8) initiative. It should stipulate a ceasefire, the designation of chief negotiators by the Russian and Chechen sides, and the beginning of negotiations under joint OIC-OSCE mediation.[84] Any settlement should provide Chechnya with real autonomy in economic affairs, the formation of political institutions, and cultural and language policies. Since late 2003 Chechnya, like Tatarstan and Bashkortostan, has been negotiating a new power-sharing treaty with Moscow, but it remains unclear just how much autonomy it will receive. The international peace plan should provide state-building proposals that combine the general principles of democratic governance with mechanisms that incorporate elements of traditional Chechen institutions. For example, councils of elders based on the traditional Chechen teip or extended family system might form the lower, foundational rungs of a future Chechen democracy. Specifically, the teip-based elders' councils could send deputies or nominate the pool of candidates for election to the districts' and republic's legislatures.

VI. Strongly urge Russian officials to protect Muslims' political, civil, and human rights

The US government and US-based NGOs already have some programs that address the problem of Russia's treatment of its Muslim minorities. However, such programs are funded and operate at levels far below that which the challenge requires. Reports by US government bodies, most importantly the Commission on International Religious Freedom (CIRF), focus inordinately on Russian violations of the rights of the much smaller Jewish and and non-Orthodox Christian groups. Given the gravity of the Islamist threat, the US should lobby for the appointment of a special representative on Muslims rights as it did for addressing anti-Semitism and xenophobia under the OSCE's Office of Democratic Institutions and Human Rights. However, this issue is too important to be left solely to intergovernmental organizations.[85] The overriding importance of Muslims, not just in Russia but globally, for international security suggests that a separate office devoted to the rights of Russia's and other Muslims should be established, perhaps under the CIRF or the National Security Council.

During the Cold War, the US government, using Title VIII funds, helped finance the establishment of numerous research centers for the study of the Soviet Union. Similar funding should be provided for the creation of several new and truly independent research institutes dedicated to producing de-ideologized and de-politicized studies of Islam, Muslims, and politics in Russia from comparative and international perspectives. In addition, the various US-based NGOs focusing on human rights and democracy need more funds for the study of the human, civil, and political rights situation of Russia's Muslims. The goal of these studies should not be the development of talking points about which US officials can lecture Russian politicians, but to provide a clear picture of the political, social, and economic life of Russia's Muslims and assist Russians and Russia's Muslims in coming to an agreement on how to address the country's Muslim and Islamist challenges. To achieve all these goals, government funding for competitive grant-making should be increased substantially in this sphere.[86]

VII. Urge Russian leaders to restore some elements of federalism

Putin's de-federalizing and re-authoritarianizing counter-revolution has increased the democracy deficit of the late Yeltsin era, transforming Russia from a hybrid "managed democracy" to a soft authoritarian regime. This has led to an increase in regional criminality, corruption, arbitrariness, and violations of many innocent Muslims' political, civil, and human rights outside as well as inside Chechnya. Moreover, Putin's revocation of Yeltsin's concessions, perceived as discrimination by many ethnic Muslim and other minority communities, is provoking ethnic and religious communal politicization. In short, Putin's counter-revolution is making Muslims more susceptible to appeals for Islamist revolution and secession, and Russia's vulnerability to radical Islam and terrorism has increased. Therefore, US officials should urge Putin and/or his successor to re-establish at least those federative mechanisms that strengthen democracy and do not run any risk of state disintegration: popular election of governors and Federation Council senators, cultural autonomy (corporate federalism), and strengthened local (sub-regional) democratic governance. To achieve this, the US should increase funding for educating Russian officials and public regarding the merits and various models of federalism. USAID assistance of programs highlighting the advantages of federative governance is at present extremely limited and ineffective. The only program even tangentially related to federalism is on "democratic decentralization." It focuses only on developing local government, ignoring the relations between the regions and the center, Russia's ethno-federalist national-territorial structure, and problems of national self-determination.[87] There is considerable expertise in Russia on comparative federalism at the Tatarstan Academy of Science Institute of History's Kazan Institute for Federalism headed by Rafael Khakimov and funded in part by the John D. and Katherine T. MacArthur Foundation.[88] Maintaining this funding and providing additional money to create similar centers at elite universities in Moscow, St. Petersburg, and the North Caucasus would help familiarize Russian elites with federalism, counter the centralizing tendency that is Russian political culture's natural response to instability, and offer North Caucasian and other Muslim peoples' alternatives to self-determination by secession and Islamist terror.

VIII. Organize an international effort to develop the Chechen and North Caucasus economy

Although the overall level of poverty may not be a reliable predictor of terrorism, relative deprivation between regions or communal groups can help explain why peoples rebel. Russia's poorest regions are most often largely Muslim ones and include most of the North Caucasus. To address abject poverty and widespread youth unemployment in Chechnya and most of the North Caucasus, the US ought to co-sponsor with Russia (under the auspices of the G8) and perhaps the OIC an international conference of the kind that was used to help fund reconstruction in Afghanistan and Iraq in order to secure private and perhaps some state financing for assistance in the reconstruction and development of Chechnya and the North Caucasus. This program should focus on industrial and high-technology development and infrastructure. Perhaps after substantial UN reform, the US and Russia might co-sponsor in the Security Council Chechnya and North Caucasus agricultural reconstruction and development programs to be financed and implemented by the world body.

The implementation of at least some of these measures would reduce the growing threat to international security posed by Russia's emerging Islamist revolution. For all the damage the Ichkeriyan-led North Caucasus jihad has wrought, it is still in its formative stages and therefore remains susceptible to effective security, political, economic, and social measures, especially if they are conducted jointly by Russian, US, and international authorities.

Appendix

Chronology of Terrorism in Dagestan, 2002–2005*

2002

January – An unidentified terrorist group led by Akhmed Magomedov blows up a military vehicle in Makhachkala, killing seven soldiers from the MVD's 106th Internal Troops Brigade.[1]

9 May – Mine detonated under military parade in Kaspiisk.

2003

11 August – Leader of the Union of Russia's Muslims and former Russia State Duma deputy from Dagestan Nadirshakh Khachilaev is killed.

27 August – Magomedsalikh Gusayev, Dagestan's minister of nationalities policy, information, and external relations, is blown up in his car.[2]

From late 2002 to early 2004 – Five assassination attempts target Buinaksk city administration head Abakar Akaev, two using explosive devices.

2004

15 August – An unidentified terrorist cell led by Rustam Abdullayev opens fire on police hitting two passers-by on Sultan Avenue in Makhachkala. One dies on the way to the hospital.[3]

17 August – Abdullayev's cell opens up with automatic weapons at 1030 Zavodskaya Street, Kaspiisk on officers of the Dagestan MVD Administration for Combating Terrorism and an agent from the Russian Federation MVD "T" (counter-terrorism) Center. Lieutenant-Colonel Gadzhi Abdurazakov of the Dagestani MVD, and Russian MVD agent Aleksandr Groshev are killed.

23 August – Abdullayev's cell, hiding out in the region of Talgi, detonates a

radio-controlled mine under a truck carrying members of the Makhachkala OMON (Special-Purpose Police Detachment), wounding eleven.

1 November – Like his predecessor three years earlier, Makhachkala's deputy mayor Akhmed Batalov is killed.[4]

2005
15 January – Makasharipov's Jannat Jamaat and security forces in Makhachkala shoot it out in a fifteen-hour siege. One of five dead militants is thought to be Makasharipov himself. Also, a local jihadist emir in Kaspiisk resists arrest, leading to the deaths of at least six militants and three policemen.[5]

2 February – Jannat or Shariah are likely behind the **killing of Dagestan MVD deputy chief Magomed Omarov and two of his bodyguards from the OMON.**

5–6 February – Again Police and federal troops kill a militant thought to be as Rasul Makasharipov in a large-scale operation in the mountains outside Makhachkala, during which they discover a hiding place used by Makasharipov's fighters, Russian media report. One policeman is killed in a shootout with the militants, and one serviceman is wounded. On 5 February, an attempt to blow up the main gas pipeline in Daghestan fails when the bomb's timing mechanism malfunctions.[6]

13 February – **A car of the traffic patrol service is blown up by a landmine in Stepnyi village on Makhachkala's outskirts, killing one policemen and wounding three seriously.**

Mid-February – Two high-ranking government officials survive a bomb attack in the town of Kizlyar.[7]

16 February – An attempted assassination of Dagestan deputy premier Amuta Amutnov, traveling with Dagestan Security Council chairman Akhmednabi Magdigadzhiev, fails. His driver and two passers-by are killed. A north Caucasian Railroad official is arrested for ordering the attack.

24 February – Deputy head of the Untsukul raion police department, Major Zairbek Aliev, is killed.

1 March – A Kyzylyurt raion state farm chairman is killed.

6 March – A traffic policeman dies of injuries received in a shootout with five militants who open fire from a bus at a checkpoint in the village of Novyi Kyakhulai, on the southern outskirts of Makhachkala. Two militants are injured, and the remaining three apprehended. Dagestan's MVD chief identifies the gunmen as belonging to a group once led by Makarsharipov.[8]

5 April – Police kill two in a shootout near the Dagestan–Chechnya border. Chechen vice-premier Ramzan Khadyrov claims one was emir of Chechnya's Gudermes raion and the other was emir of Dagestan's Khasavyurt raion.[9]

6 April – Shariah Jamaat claims responsibility for killing the chief of the Khasavyurt MVD's Department for Fighting Organized Crime (OBOP), Colonel Saigit Zabitov, who was shot in the head and leg while driving in his car.[10]

7 April – Shariah Jamaat claims responsibility for detonating an 8 kg. bomb packed with nails and bolts and planted near the headquarters of the Russian ministry of defense's 136th Motor-Rifle Brigade in Buinaksk. Shariah claims there were casualties,[11] but other reports claim there were none.[12]

8 April – An explosion shatters windows and causes other minor damage on several floors at police headquarters in Buinaksk.[13]

9 April – Mujahedin and Russian forces engage in a shootout, which according to the latter ends in the deaths of two mujahedin.[14]

13 April – Shariah Jamaat claims responsibility for detonating two explosive devices that killed two law-enforcement officers and wound six others. A third explosion is also registered in the capital.[15]

15 April – Shariah Jamaat claims responsibility for the detonation of three bombs on the roof of the prosecutor's office in Makhachkala.[16]

19 April – NTV, citing Dagestan's interior ministry, reports that two suspected militants were killed when their car blew up in central Makhachkala, apparently as they were preparing an explosive device intended to kill a local prosecutor.[17]

22 April – Shariat Jamaat claims responsibility for blowing up a bus filled beyond capacity with police "infidels" (*kafirs*); the number of casualties is unknown.[18]

2 May – Combat detachments of Dagestani emir Rabbani Khalilov and Akhmad Avdorkhanov engage *spetsnaz* troops in Chechnya's Nozhai-Yurt raion, leaving eleven Russians and five Dagestani and Chechen militants dead, according to the Chechen Islamists' website *Kavkaz-Tsentr*.[19]

10 May – Major Visali Orzumiev of the Khasavyurt raion MVD's Administration for Fighting Organized Crime (UBOP) is killed.

14 May – Police arrest a believed Shariah Jamaat member in possession of a ready-to-use explosive device of the type used in some twenty other bomb attacks.[20]

20 May – Zagir Arukhov, Dagestan's minister of nationalities policy, information and external relations and main ideologist of Dagestan's policy for uprooting Islamists in the republic, and his bodyguard are killed by the detonation of a powerful device planted in his residence's driveway. Shariah Jamaat claims responsibility.[21]

April–May – Several other attacks over the "last month" involving seventeen "casualties" are claimed by Shariah Jamaat.[22]

Late May–June – Shariah Jamaat claims responsibility for the six terrorist attacks on MVD and police in late May and June listed directly below, which, according to the combat jamaat, resulted in four killed and "around 40 wounded" among the "occupiers."[23]

24 May – Sharaiah Jamaat's special "Seifullah" detachment assassinates Buinaksk city MVD investigation department chief Major Magomedkhan Gitinov, the twenty-sixth police officer thought to have been killed by terrorists in 2005.

29 May – Shariah assassinates Buinaksk GOVD criminal investigation chief Asker Askerov.

1 June – Shariah blows up a bus transporting Makhachkala's 2nd militia regiment, resulting in nine casualties.

3 June – Shariah blows up a militia car belonging to Makhachkala's 1st militia regiment, wounding one.

4 June – Shariah Jamaat's special "Dzhundulla" detachment blows up an

automobile carrying militia co-workers in Khasavyurt.

28 June – Political scientist Magomedzagid Varisov, the director of the Center for Strategic Initiatives and Political Technologies based in Dagestan, is killed in his car by Shariah Jamaat machine-gun fire. Varisov, like Arukhov, had worked in Dagestan's ministry of nationalities, external relations and information.[24]

1 July – Two explosive devices detonate below three trucks killing at least ten and wounding at least twenty-one of the MVD's 8th special designation (*spetsnaz*) troops and fourteen civilians in Makhachkala (see below).

2 July – Shariah Jamaat posts a communiqué on the Chechen Islamists' website *Kavkaz-Tsentr* announcing that in accordance with ChRI president and emir Sadulaev's call to shift the war onto Russian territory, it is sending terrorists to Moscow to conduct "sabotage operations."[25]

4 July – Dagestan People's Assembly deputy Zubair Gataev is killed.

5 July – Two police officers are killed in Makhachkala.

6 July – Shariah Jamaat emir Makasharipov and several accomplices are killed by Russian forces, who suffer one fatality and four casualties. Also, an explosion derails a train outside Makhachkala, and a bomb explodes near midnight in the capital. These attacks produce no casualties.[26]

4 August – Mujahedin reportedly under the command of Chechen emir Abubakar engage Russian military intelligence forces (GRU) in an early-morning battle in a forest.[27]

11 August – In an attack bearing the hallmarks of Shariah Jamaat, a roadside device laced with metal shards explodes as a car with two Buinaksk GOVD officers passes by. There are no injuries.[28]

18 August – A device, placed in a zinc bucket, explodes in Makhachkala.[29]

20 August – Three police patrolmen from Stavropol are killed and three others wounded when a bomb, again placed in a zinc bucket, explodes outside a residential building under construction in Makhachkala. A passenger in a passing taxi is also injured by the blast.[30]

25 August – A Shariah Jamaat internet posting claims responsibility for five attacks (likely including the three listed just above) over the previous three weeks, yielding casualties of five dead and twenty-nine wounded.[31]

* Bold-face type indicates that Jannat Jamaat or Shariah Jamaat claimed responsibility. Those events not footnoted are listed in "Khronika Terrora," *Novaya gazeta*, No. 49, 11 July 2005, http://2005.novayagazeta.ru/nomer/2005/49n/n49n-s10.shtml.

Notes

PREFACE

1 Shireen Hunter's *Islam in Russia: The Politics of Identity and Security* (Armonk, N.Y.: M.E. Sharpe, 2002), though offering good analysis of the many political and ideological trends among Russia's Muslims, gives short shrift to the Islamists, who were already a significant factor in the period covered by the book.
2 The only book-length examination of contemporary Chechen jihadists is Paul Murphy's excellent *The Wolves of Islam: Russia and the Faces of Chechen Terror* (Dulles, Va.: Brassey's Inc., 2004). However, Murphy limits his analysis to the Chechen terrorists proper and their terrorist attacks in Moscow, leaving aside their structure, associated combat jamaats, and their attendant ideology. Dmitrii Trenin, Alexei Malashenko, and Anatol Lieven's *Russia's Restless Frontier: The Chechnya Factor in Post-Soviet Russia* (New York: Carnegie Endowment for International Peace, 2004) focuses on the Chechen war's effect on Russian democratization, the military, and foreign policy, and only briefly on inter-ethnic relations.
3 Janusz Bugajski, *Cold Peace: Russia's New Imperialism* (New York: Praeger/CSIS, 2005).
4 Putin and other top Russian officials do acknowledge at times that problems such as the Chechen war, poverty and official crime and corruption in the North Caucasus contributed to the rise of jihad in Russia.
5 "Shamil Basaev: 'Segodnya voyuet ves chechenskii narod,'" Kavkazcenter.net, 17 August 2005, 10:00:42, www.kavkazcenter.net/russ/content/2005/08/17/36759.shtml.

CHAPTER ONE

1 On the complex causality of the fall of the Soviet communist regime and the collapse of the Soviet state, see Gordon M. Hahn, *Russia's Revolution from Above: Reform, Transition, and Revolution in the Fall of the Soviet Communist Regime, 1985–2000* (New Brunswick: Transaction Publishers, 2002).
2 Ibid., Ch. 1.
3 See Robin F. Laird and Erik P. Hoffman, "'The Scientific-Technological Revolution,' 'Developed Socialism,' and Soviet International Behavior," in Robin F. Laird and Erik P. Hoffman, eds., *The Conduct of Soviet Foreign Policy*, Second Edition (Hawthorne, N.Y.: Aldine Publishing Co., 1980), pp. 386–405.
4 For example, see Seweryn Bialer, *The Soviet Paradox* (New York: Knopf, 1986).
5 Also, economic autarchy protected Soviet production from the demands of the market

and deprived it of the investment capital, R&D, and technological innovations available through more open international trade and the burgeoning technological, information, and financial revolutions that were driving the development of its superpower rival, the United States.

6 See Seweryn Bialer, *Stalin's Successors: Leadership, Stability, and Change in the Soviet Union* (Cambridge: Cambridge University Press, 1980), Ch. 10.

7 See Michael Rywkin, *Moscow's Muslim Challenge: Soviet Central Asia* (Armonk, N.Y.: M.E. Sharpe, 1982).

8 Mikhail Bernstam, "Demography of Soviet Ethnic Groups," in Robert Conquest, ed., *The Last Empire: Nationality and the Soviet Future* (Stanford: Hoover Institution Press, 1986), pp. 314–368, at pp. 320 and 332. Although Kazakhstan's urbanization rate increased from 54 to 57 percent between 1979 and 1989, this was largely due to the colonial influx of Russians to the capital Alma-Ata and other cities in the republic. *Pravda,* 29 April 1989, p. 2.

9 Hahn, *Russia's Revolution from Above.*

10 See Ellen Jones, *The Red Army and Society* (Boston: Allen & Unwin, 1985), p. 188; Alexander Bennigsen and S. Enders Wimbush, *Muslims of the Soviet Empire* (Bloomington: Indiana University Press, 1986), p. 28.

11 By "ethnic Muslims" I mean members of those ethnic groups that have traditionally been predominantly Islamic in their religious faith. It is understood that many members of these groups are not religious believers, especially after the Soviets' efforts to quash all religion.

12 For example, it prompted General Secretary Yurii Andropov in 1983 to order a detailed study of these trends and the nationalities problem and to convene a CPSU Central Committee plenum on the issue.

13 On macro-structural crises as precipitants of revolutions, see Theda Skocpol, *States and Revolutions: A Comparative Analysis of France, Russia and China* (Cambridge: Cambridge University Press, 1979).

14 On cruelty and brutality in the nineteenth-century Russo-Caucasian wars see, for example, Moshe Gammer, *The Lone Wolf and the Bear: Three Centuries of Chechen Defiance of Russian Rule* (Pittsburgh: University of Pittsburgh Press, 2006), pp. 30–52.

15 Communalism is defined here as the drive for isolation or self-determination based on ethnic, national, linguistic, religious, or regional identity communities.

16 The studies by Kreuger and Laitin and by Piazza overlook the sub-regional level, however. See Alan B. Kreuger and David Laitin, *Kto Kogo: A Cross-Country Study of the Origins and Targets of Terrorism* (New York: Russel Sage, 2003) and J.A. Piazza, "Rooted in Poverty? Terrorism, Poor Economic Development and Social Cleavages," in *Terrorism and Political Violence,* Vol. 18 (Spring 2006), pp. 159–177.

17 Ted Robert Gurr, *Why Men Rebel* (Princeton: Princeton University Press, 1970).

18 In 2001, President Vladimir Putin divided the Russian Federation's then eighty-nine regions across seven "federal districts" (*federalnyi okuugi*). Two of these are the Southern and Volga FOs.

19 Jack Goldstone has demonstrated the connection between population growth and revolution: *Revolution and Rebellion in the Early Modern World* (Berkeley: University of California Press, 1991).

20 A good overview of other estimates of the number of ethnic Muslims in Russia made before the carrying out of the October 2002 Russian census may be found in A. V. Malashenko, "Islam i politika v sovremennoi Rossii," in Yu. M. Kobishchanov, ed., *Musulmane izmenyayushcheisya Rossii* (Moscow: Russian Political Encyclopedia, 2002), pp. 7–24, at p. 8, and Hunter, *Islam in Russia,* pp. 43–44.

21 This is according to the 2002 Russian census results: Perepis 2002, "Prilozhenie 5 – Naselenie Rossii po natsional'no prinadlezhnosti i vladeniyu russkim yasykom," www.perepis.ru/ct/html/ALL_00_07.htm.

22 For a different though overlapping list of constraining factors, see Matthew Evangelista, *The Chechen Wars: Will Russia Go the Way of the Soviet Union?* (Washington, D.C.: Brookings Institution, 2002), p. 108.

23 In the Southern FO, where the North Caucasus's six titular Muslim republics are located, urbanization of the population is 57.5 percent (higher relative to each of those republics), and in the Volga FO it is 70.8 percent. Perepis 2000, "Prilozhenie 1 – Chislennost' gorodskogo i sel'skogo naseleniya po sub"ektam Rossiiskoi Federatsii," www.perepis2002.ru/ct/html/ALL_00_01.htm.

24 See also the second note in Table 2.

25 Environmental and health problems also reduce reproductive and fertility rates and increase mortality rates.

26 See Yu. M. Kobishchanov, "Musulmane Rossii, korennyie rossiiskie musulmane i russkie musulmane," in Kobishchanov, *Musulmane izmenyayushcheisya Rossii,* pp. 61–112, at p. 107, and Yu. M. Kobishchanov, "Musulmansaya Moskva XXI v.: Musulmane Rossii nakanune XXI veka," *Materialy Mezhdunarodnoi Konferentsii,* Moskva, 6 Sept. 1997 (Moscow, 1998), p. 23.

27 This correlation holds for all ethnic Muslims listed in Table 2 except for the Kyrgyz, Tajhik, and Uzbeks, the groups that are least indigenous to Russia. See Perepis 2002, "Prilozhenie 5."

28 See "Polufabrikat' S. Kazanova schitaet musulman 'nebmenyaemymi i 'sektantami,'" Islam.ru, 28 February 2005, www.islam.ru/press/rus/2005-02-28/#7440.

29 Faisal Devji, *Landscapes of Jihad: Militancy, Morality, Modernity* (Ithaca, N.Y.: Cornell University Press, 2005), pp. 40–60 and 158–164.

30 A 2001 estimate places the number of practicing Muslim believers at 5 percent of the general number of religious believers, who composed 55 percent of Russia's then estimated population of 147 million. This would mean there are approximately 3.7 million Muslim believers. M. Tulskii, "Vakhkhabity v Rossii pobezhdayut umerennykh musulman," *Nezavisimaya gazeta,* 19 June 2001. A 1997 estimate made by the Moscow Sociology Institute put the number of Muslim believers at 6.2 percent of the number of overall religious believers, and 6 percent of Russia's population. This would put the number of Muslim believers at slightly over four million. See Malashenko, "Islam i politika v sovremennoi Rossii," p. 7, citing A. B. Zubov, "Granitsy razlomov i urovni edinstva v segodnyashnei Rossii: Uroki sotsiologicheskogo issledovaniya," in *Dukhovnye osnovy mirovogo soobshestva i mezhdunarodnykh otnoshenii* (Moscow: MGIMO, 2000), p. 270.

31 Neil Buckley, "Russia's Islamic Rebirth Adds Tension," *Financial Times,* 28 Oct. 2005.

32 See "V Nabernykh Chelnakh otkrylas 11 mechet," Islam.ru, 14 Oct. 2005, www.islam.ru/press/rus/ 2005-10-24/#9740, and Georgii N. Engelhardt, "Militant Islam in Russia – Potential for Conflict," Moscow Defense Brief, 4 April 2005, http://mdb.cast.ru/mdb/1-2005/wap/militant_islam/.

33 However, further survey data show that while identification and general belief have risen immensely, the practice of Islamic rituals remains extremely low. In 1990 only 13.9 percent of Muslim believers prayed at home, and 8.3 percent of Muslim believers prayed in a mosque, meaning that 77.8 percent of Muslims never prayed at all. Rosalinda Musina, "Musul'manskaya identichnost' kak forma 'religioznogo natsionalizma' Tatar v kontekste etnosotsial'nykh protsessov i etnopoliticheskoi situatsii v Tatarstane," in M. V. Iordan, R. G. Kuzeev, and S. M. Chervonnaya, eds., *Islam v Yevrazii: sovremennyie etnicheskie i esteticheskie kontseptsii sunnitskogo islama, ikh transformatsiya v massovom soznanii i vyrazhenie v iskusstve musulmanskikh narodov Rossii* (Moscow: Progress-Traditsiya, 2001), pp. 297–301.

34 There have been many more isolated instances of leftist and neo-fascist sabotage and terrorism in Russia, and this has been on the rise under Putin, especially in the form of skinhead attacks on ethnic Muslim as well as Armenian immigrants.

35 On limited illiberal democracy under Yeltsin, see Hahn, *Russia's Revolution from Above*, Ch. 11. On aspects of Putin's soft-authoritarian counter-revolution, see the same author's "Putin's 'Stealth Authoritarianism' and Russia's Second Revolutionary Wave," Radio Free Europe/Radio Liberty Regional Analysis, 21 April 2004, www.regionalanalysis.org/publications/regionalvoices/en/2004/04/616B350A-D9CD-49F59416EC AD7F5F1EAE. ASP and Harley Balzer, "Managed Pluralism: Vladimir Putin's Emerging Regime," *Post-Soviet Affairs*, Vol. 19, No. 3, July–Sept. 2003, pp. 189–227. On the limits of de-democratization, see Leon Aron, "Institutions, and Restoration, and Revolution," *Russia Outlook* (Brookings Institution), 15 April 2005, www.aei.org/docLib/ 20050415_ROInstitutions_g18264.pdf.

36 Alberto Abadie, "Poverty, Political Freedom, and the Roots of Terrorism," National Bureau of Economic Research Working Paper, No. 10589, Oct. 2004, www.nber.org/papers/w10859.

37 See the results of the 2004 Russian presidential elections in Muslim republics as compared to those in other republics in Hahn, "Putin's 'Stealth Authoritarianism' and Russia's Second Revolutionary Wave."

38 The following section is based on Gordon M. Hahn, "Russian Federalism under Putin," in Stephen White, Zvi Gitelman, and Richard Sakwa, eds., *Current Developments in Russian Politics – Vol. 6* (Durham, N.C.: Duke University Press, 2005), pp. 148–67. See also Hahn, "The Past, Present, and Future of the Russian Federal State," *Demokratizatsiya*, Vol. 11, No. 3 (Summer 2003), pp. 343–62; Hahn, "Putin's Federal Reforms: Integrating Russia's Legal Space or Destabilizing Russian Federalism," *Demokratizatsiya*, Vol. 9, No. 4 (Fall 2001), pp. 498–530; Hahn, "The Impact of Putin's Federative Reforms on Democratization in Russia," *Post-Soviet Affairs*, Vol. 19, No. 2 (April–June 2003), pp. 114–153; and Jeffrey Kahn, *Federalism, Democratization, and the Rule of Law in Russia* (Oxford: Oxford University Press, 2002).

39 Kahn, *Federalism, Democratization, and the Rule of Law in Russia*, p. 18 and n. 2.

40 On China's "market-preserving federalism," see Gabriella Montinola, Yinggyi Qian, and Barry Weingast, "Federalism, Chinese Style: The Political Basis for Economic Success," *World Politics*, Vol. 48, No. 1 (1996), pp. 50–81, and Minxin Pei, "Self-Administration and Local Autonomy: Reconciling Conflicting Interests in China," in Wolfgang Danspeckgruber, ed., *The Self-Determination of Peoples: Community, Nation, and State in an Interdependent World* (Boulder, CO: Lynne Reinner Publishers, 2002), pp. 315–32. Moreover, with the reunification of Hong Kong and the mainland's desire to reunite Taiwan, the federalist principle of divided sovereignty as well as political autonomy has been recognized. Michael C. Davis, "The Case for Chinese Federalism," *Journal of Democracy*, Vol. 10, No. 2 (April 1999), pp. 124–137.

41 On traditional federalism, see William H. Riker, *Federalism: Origin, Operation, Significance* (Boston, MA: Little-Brown, 1964) and Carl J. Friedrich, *Trends of Federalism in Theory and Practice* (New York: Praeger, 1968).

42 Other mechanisms have been applied in post-Soviet Russia in a limited way, including "corporate federalism," foreign policy and trade powers for sub-units, and integrative electoral systems. Democratic socialists Otto Bauer and Karl Renner proposed for the Austro-Hungarian Empire a rarely applied "corporate federalism" or non-territorial cultural autonomy for minority communities to allow extra-territorial self-governance on cultural, religious, and linguistic issues. See Freidrich, *Trends of Federalism in Theory and Practice*; Arend Lijphart, *Democracies: Patterns of Majoritarian and Consensus Government in Twenty-One Countries* (New Haven, CN: Yale University Press, 1984), pp. 183–184; and Walker Connor, *The National Question in Marxist-Leninist Theory and Strategy* (Princeton, N.J.: Princeton University Press, 1984), pp. 28–29. Wolfgang Danspeckgruber adds that a combination of regional self-governance and extensive rights in foreign economic and cultural relations, especially intensive

external regional integration, can assuage nationalist aspirations, serving conflict prevention in various multi-ethnic states and conflict resolution in Kashmir, Chechnya, and the former Yugoslavia: "Self-Governance Plus Regional Integration: A Solution to Self-Determination or Secession Claims in the Emerging International System," paper presented to the 2002 Annual Convention of the American Political Science Association, Boston, MA; www.princeton.edu/~ lisd. Donald L. Horowitz proposes "integrative" prescriptions, arguing that the other suggestions outlined above reinforce and may over-institutionalize inter-ethnic and inter-confessional cleavages and thereby weaken state integrity and provoke inter-ethnic tensions and ethno-national/regional separatism: *Ethnic Groups in Conflict* (Berkeley and Los Angeles: University of California Press, 1985). See also Horowitz, "Comparing Democratic Systems," *Journal of Democracy,* Vol. 1, No. 4 (Fall 1990), pp. 73–79; Horowitz, "Democracy in Divided Societies," *Journal of Democracy,* Vol. 4, No. 4 (Fall 1993), pp. 18–38; and Horowitz, "Making Moderation Pay," in Joseph Montville, ed., *Conflict and Peacemaking in Multiethnic Societies* (Lexington, MA: Lexington Books, 1990).

43 Arend Lijphart, "The Puzzle of Indian Democracy: A Consociational Interpretation," *American Political Science Review,* Vol. 90, No. 2 (June 1996), 258–268; Michael Hechter, *Containing Nationalism* (Oxford: Oxford University Press, 2000); and Danspeckgruber, ed., *The Self-Determination of Peoples.* Despite their federative and consensus-based institutions, India and Spain continue to suffer from inter-communal conflict and terrorism in Kashmir, Punjab, Nagaland, and the Basque country. However, there is no evidence that without their federative and consensus-based institutions these inter-communal conflicts would not be greater. Indeed, Spain has seen no violence from non-Basque minorities. India is divided into hundreds of ethno-linguistic groups, but violence tends to occur only between religious elements, which may suggest that confessional communalism is less malleable under the application of ethno-federative and consociational institutions. Finally, it should be noted that there are numerous other cases where such institutional mechanisms correlate with a complete absence of violent conflict if not of tensions, including Belgium, Switzerland, and Canada. Formerly war-torn Bosnia-Herzegovina has remained at peace because a grand coalition under a three-member presidency represents Muslims, Croats, and Serbs alike. Equal representation for these three groups is provided in the parliament's upper house as well.

44 Consociational federative governance may include such mechanisms as special power-sharing rights for national minorities or their regional autonomies, grand inter-communal governing coalitions, or a minority veto so that consensual rule is exercised rather than majority rule. Consensus-based federative mechanisms may be needed in certain communal contexts to preclude tyrannies of communal majorities. See Lijphart, *Democracies* and "The Puzzle of Indian Democracy."

45 David Sisk, "Power Sharing in Multiethnic Societies: Principal Approaches and Practices," in Gail W. Lapidus and Svetlana Tsalik, eds., *Preventing Deadly Conflict: Strategies and Institutions* (New York: Carnegie Corporation, April 1998), pp. 34–67.

46 Hechter, *Containing Nationalism,* pp. 145–149.

47 Horowitz, *Ethnic Groups in Conflict* and "Making Moderation Pay."

48 Aushev was also popular because he permitted local laws allowing bride-kidnapping, polygamy, and other ancient customs in the region. Although Putin's legal harmonization policy forced him to amend or repeal some 150 laws, including those involving these traditional Ingush and, to some extent, North Caucasian practices, he implemented the changes only reluctantly. As a result of Aushev's independence, the Putin administration forced him to resign in 2003. Aushev's resignation was induced through a backroom deal that likely included "sticks", such as *kompromat* (a Russian term for compromising materials relating to a politician's personal or professional

life), and "carrots", such as his appointment to the Federation Council (from which he soon resigned). The Kremlin then deployed federal and republic "administrative resources," including the police and coopted judges, in order to remove all Aushev allies and other viable independent candidates from the Ingush presidential "election" campaign and otherwise rig the election.

49 Ozdoev forced the authorities to release him after declaring a hunger strike and has promised to continue his struggle against Zyazikov.

50 See www.retwa.org during this period. The leader of the Youth Movement of Ingushetiya, Rustam Archakov, stated that such terrorist acts are the logical result of the Ingush authorities' obstruction of, and crackdowns on peaceful protests. RFERL Newsline, Vol. 9, No. 172, 12 Sept. 2005 citing Ingushetiya.ru.

51 On contingency in regime transformations, see Hahn, *Russia's Revolution from Above*, Chs. 1, 8, and 9.

52 Bennigsen and Wimbush, *Muslims of the Soviet Empire*, p. 5.

53 Moreover, Bashkiriya produces only one-third (in 2000) to one-tenth (in 2001) as many Tatar-language teachers as Bashkir- and Russian-language teachers, one-seventh as many Tatar-language journals, and one-ninth as many Tatar books. The Bashkir authorities have also driven the only Tatar-language newspaper from the republic and refused to register the Tatars' "national cultural autonomy" organization allowed by federal law.

54 RFERL Tatar-Bashkir Daily Report, 11 March 2002.

55 For example, Shaimiev's top political advisor, Kazan Institute of History director Rafael Khakimov, theorized that Tatars and Bashkirs are the same people: Tatars. A Bashkir writer proposed that Tatars are actually Bashkirs and that Kazan was historically a Bashkir city. Other Tatar scholars then countered that Bashkirs are actually Tatars. Bashkirs then appealed in a letter to President Putin about Tatar falsifications of Bashkir history and policies. The Tatar and Bashkir World Congresses in 2002 refused to invite their counterparts' representatives and focused on each other's transgressions. On the eve of the census, leading Tatars appealed to both Tatars and Bashkirs to calm down and preserve the two Volga Muslim peoples' historically fraternal relations. "Obrashchenie k Bashkirskomu i Tatarskomu narodam," *Respublika Tatarstan*, 30 Sept. 2002, www.rt-online.ru, 4 Oct. 2002.

56 Days before the census was to begin Bashkiriya raised the ante in the census cold war with Kazan, as Bashkortostan's state radio aired an interview with a leading Kreshen playwright, Necib Asanbaev, who opined that Kreshens or baptized Tatars were not related to Tatars in any way and thus should not be included as Tatars in the census. Perhaps not unwittingly, this coincided with a census-taking policy proposed by Moscow's official Institute for Anthropology and Ethnology of counting Kreshens separately from Tatars. After the census, the Tatar intelligentsia and nationalists charged that Bashkortostan's government had implemented language, education, and cultural policies that discriminated against Tatars and deliberately pressured Tatars to register during the census as Bashkirs to produce a rise in the Bashkir share of the population; a rise that curiously did not emerge among other Bashkir communities or among the Russians and Tatars in the republic. Indeed, Bashkortostan published the results of several surveys prior to the census indicating that the number of the republic's Bashkirs had grown in what seemed an effort to prepare the ground for the result.

57 KChR president Mustafa Batdyiev and the majority of the elite represent the ethnic Karachai group. (Karachais make up only 31 percent of the population. Russians compose 42 percent and Cherkess 10 percent.) Some opposition demonstrations have been led by ethnic Cherkess and Russian groups. See RFERL Newsline, Vol. 8, No. 212, 9 Nov. 2004 and Vol. 8, No. 213, 10 Nov. 2004; RTR Russian TV, 11:00 GMT, 9 Nov. 2004; Sergei Venyavsky, "Russian Government Building Stormed," Associated Press, 9

Nov. 2004; *Nezavisimaya gazeta*, 12 Nov. 2004 cited in RFERL Newsline, Vol. 8, No. 214, 12 Nov. 2004; and Oliver Bullough, "Kremlin Envoy Defuses Caucasus Murder Crisis," *Reuters*, 11 Nov. 2004.

58 See Robert Bruce Ware, Enver Kisriev, Werner J. Patzelt, and Ute Roericht, "Stability in the Caucasus: The Perspective from Dagestan," in *Problems of Post-Communism*, Vol. 50, No. 2 (March–April 2003), pp. 12–23, at pp. 15–17.

59 Igor Zhukov, "The Structure of Teyps and Clans," *Yuzhnyy Reporter* (Rostov-on-Don), 28 Nov. 2005, in Ralph Davis's Chechnya Yahoo Group, 27 Dec. 2005, AltChechnya@yahoogroups.com.

60 Sunnis believe that the leader of the Islamic world must be one who is a successor of the Prophet Mohammed but that he should not be considered as a messenger of Allah. Shiites believe that only one of God's special messengers (an imam) can assume the leadership of the Islamic umma.

61 Kobishchanov, "Musulmane Rossii, korennyie rossiiskie musulmane i russkie musulmane," p. 62.

62 The exceptions are Iraq, Lebanon, and Pakistan, where substantial Shia and Sunni communities co-reside.

63 Bernard Lewis, *Islam and the West* (Oxford: Oxford University Press, 1993), pp. 51–53, and Peter Antes, "Islam v sovremennom mire," in Iordan, Kuzeev, and Chervonnaya, eds., *Islam v Yevrazii*, pp. 38–70, at pp. 45–46 (n.). The relative flexibility of the four maskhabs is determined in part by the number of *hadiths* used by the founders of the four maskhabs. Abu Hanifa used only 17, Malik 300, Abu Abdalakh Mukhammd ibn Ismail al-Bukhari 7,000, and imam Akhmad ibn Hanbal 50,000. Rafael Khakimov, *Gde nasha Mekka?* (Kazan: Magarif, 2003), pp. 17–18.

64 Kobishchanov, "Musulmane Rossii, korennyie rossiiskie musulmane i russkie musulmane," p. 69, and Bennigsen and Wimbush, *Muslims of the Soviet Empire*, p. 13. The Shafi school is also prevalent among ethnic Kurds and has adherents in Egypt, Syria, Bahrain, Indonesia, and Sumatra.

65 The Hanafi school is the basis of Islam in the Astrakhan, Kazan (Bolgar), and Siberian Tatar khanates, much of Central Asia (the emirates of Khorezm and Bukhara), North Africa, and the former Ottoman Empire, which influenced Islam in the Middle Volga, Urals, western Siberia, and, to a lesser extent, the North Caucasus. This school is also well-represented outside the Turkic-language Muslim world, in particular in Afghanistan, Pakistan, and Indonesia. Its presence is relatively limited in the Arab Muslim world.

66 The nephews of leading Naqshbandy Deni Arsanov the "Denievy", Iles-khadzhi and Akhmed, opposed Dudaev. Kobishchanov, "Musulmane Rossii, korennyie rossiiskie musulmane i russkie musulmane," pp. 90–91

67 Hunter, *Islam in Russia*, p. 82.

68 Qadiriya brotherhoods have been strongly revived not only in Chechnya, but also in Ingushetiya. In Dagestan, Russia's most deeply Islamic region, Naqshbandya are reviving and reported to be fighting to hold on to their dominant position. They are particularly strong among the ethnic Kumyks and Dargins who live on the plains. The Qadiriya and, to a lesser extent, Shaziliya brotherhoods are predominant in the mountain areas. The former are strong among the ethnic Andis and Akin-Chechens. The latter are well represented among these same groups but also among the republic's largest nationality, the Avars. In Dagestan, they are credited by some with helping to resolve inter-ethnic disputes. Lesser Sufi revivals are reported in the other titular Muslim republics of the North Caucasus as well as in North Ossetiya and even Tatarstan. Sufi brotherhoods have a limited presence among Tatars outside of Tatarstan (the "internal diaspora"), especially among the 100,000-strong Kasimov Tatars. To some extent they remain present in Bashkiriya. Numerous Naqshbandy have dispersed across Russia's regions, and Qadiry are well represented in Moscow,

Volgograd, and some other large cities. Kobishchanov, "Musulmane Rossii, korennyie rossiiskie musulmane i russkie musulmane," pp. 91–92, and Bennigsen and Wimbush, *Muslims of the Soviet Empire*, pp. 21–22. A casual walk through Russia's New Age bookstores or sections suggests a growing interest among perhaps even ethnic Russian youth in this spiritual experience.

69 See Mufti Ravil Gainutdin, *Islam v sovremennoi Rossii* (Moscow: Fair-Press, 2004), pp. 264–97.

70 Devji, *Landscapes of Jihad*, pp. 40–60 and 158–164.

71 On the assassin sect and its brief state, see I. V. Zhuravlev, S. A. Melkov, and L. I. Shershnev, *Put voinov Allakha: Islam i politika Rossii* (Moscow: Veche, 2004), pp. 212–225, and Bernard Lewis, *The Assassins: A Radical Sect in Islam* (New York: Basic Books, 2002).

72 Devji, *Landscapes of Jihad*, pp. 61–157.

73 Qutb joined the Muslim Brotherhood in 1950 and came to head its propaganda department. Reza Aslan, *No God, But God: The Origins, Evolution, and Future of Islam* (New York: Random House, 2005), pp. 238–40; Rudolph Peters, *Jihad in Classical and Modern Islam* (Princeton, N.J.: Markus Weiner Publishers, 1996), pp. 128–129; and V. I. Maksimenko, "Fundametaliszm i ekstremizm v Islame," in Ye. M. Kozhokin and V. I. Maksimenko, eds., *Islam i Islamizm* (Moscow: Russian Institute of Strategic Studies, 1999), pp. 12–14.

74 See Aslan, *No God But God*, Ch. 5, and Khaled M. Abou El Fadl, *The Great Theft: Wrestling Islam from the Extremists* (San Francisco: Harper, 2005).

75 Kobishchanov, "Musulmane Rossii, korennyie rossiiskie musulmane i russkie musulmane," p. 89.

76 For instance, on 9 April 2005 over the control of the oldest mosque in Russia, Dagestan's Dzhuma mosque located in ancient Derbent. A virtual riot broke out within the mosque itself, involving over three hundred young Muslims from the two sects. Over two hundred were arrested, and tens of young Muslims were seriously injured. "Muftii Dagestana vyekhal v Derbent dlya razbora prichin massovoi draki," Islam.ru, 12 April 2005, www.islam.ru/press/rus/2005-04-12/#7911. NTV reported that over the course of six months the two groups could not come to an agreement on the candidacy of the Dzhuma mosque Sunni imam. NTV, GMT. 10 April 2005, 04:00. Another source reported that there had also been an earlier dispute between the two sides at the Arafat mosque over who should be the imam for a particular Friday prayer service and how the service should be conducted. "Draka v stareishei mecheti Rossii – rezultat provokatsii?" Islam.ru, 11 April 2005, www.islam.ru/press/rus/2005-04-11/#7898.

77 See Hunter, *Islam in Russia*, pp. 54–55 and 58–62.

78 The TsDUM has regional DUMs in twenty-two of Russia's eighty-nine regions as well as the DUMs of the Baltic states, Ukraine, and Belarus, including several regions with large Tatar minorities: the DUMs of Samara, Orenburg, Astrakhan, Chuvashia, Udmurtia, Mari El, Mordovia, Moscow, and Northwest Russia and Leningrad Oblast (which includes St. Petersburg and its large Tatar diaspora).

79 See Aleksandr Dugin, *Osnovy geopolitiki* (Moscow, 1997) and A.S. Panarin, *Revansh istorii* (Moscow: Logos, 1998).

80 The party is the venue for some strange bedfellows. For example, the former Chechen national security minister under first Chechen president Dzhokar Dudaev, Khozh-Akhmed Nukhaev, who rejected participation in the second Chechen war and is now a Chechen peace activist, joined forces with the Russian ultra-nationalist Dugin's Eurasian Party in 2003 at a Moscow conference and established a permanent relationship ostensibly working toward an end to the Chechen war and the unification of Russia and the Muslim world against the "Atlantist" threat. See Ya. A. Goldin, *Rossiya i Chechnya: poiski vykhoda* (St. Petersburg: Zvezda, 2003), pp. 49–51 and 56.

81 The declaration of Haq's founding assembly noted: "The goal of Russia's enemies is not to permit [the Great Russian Power's] economic growth and political influence. For this they want to destroy the historically established complementary 'union of Russians and Tatars' and of Orthodox and right-believers and direct the peoples of our country against each other and provoke centripetal forces." See "Musulmanskii message v otvet na 'putinskii prizyv'," *Islam.ru*, 22 Oct. 2004, www.islam.ru.

Chapter Two

1 See Taimaz Abubakarov, *Rezhim Dzhokhara Dudaeva: pravda i vymysel – zapiski dudaevskogo ministra ekonomi i finansov* (Moscow: INSAN, 1998), pp. 79–80.

2 Similarly, he told a French delegation that Noah's Ark had come to rest in the mountains of Chechnya. Ibid., p. 17.

3 See Valerii Tishkov, *Obshchestvo v vooruzhennom konflikte: etnografiya chechenskoi voiny* (Moscow: RAN, 2001), pp. 462–476, and L. Vakhayev, "Politicheskye fantazii v sovremennoi Chechenskoi respublike," in *Rossiya i Chechnya: obshchestva i gosudarstva* (Moscow, 1998), www.skharov-center.ru/chs/chrus15.1htm.

4 Abubakarov, *Rezhim Dzhokhara Dudaeva: pravda i vymysel*, p. 162.

5 Ibid., pp. 164–165.

6 Khattab's real name is Samir bin Salekh al-Suweilem. His *nomme de guerre* is taken from Umar bin al-Khattab, an associate of the Prophet who is regarded by Sunnis as the second caliph in Islam but by the Shia as an idol-worshiper and a usurper of power from Najaf's Imam Ali, who is known for leading the seventh-century conquests and expansion (which reached the North Caucasus at Derbent in present-day Dagestan) that made Islam a world religion.

7 The possibility that Russian security forces played a role in the Dagestan incursion and the terrorist bombings has been the subject of intense speculation and competing arguments. For a summary see Evangelista, *The Chechen Wars*, pp. 75–85. Basaev contended, unconvincingly, that Dagestani Islamists were intentionally drawn to the republic by Russia's FSB in order in turn to draw his forces into the republic and restart the war. See Andrei Babitskii's interview with Basaev at "Shamil Basaev: 'Segodnya voyuet ves chehchenskii narod!," Kavkaz-Tsentr, 17 Aug. 2005, 10:00:42, www.kavkazcenter.net/russ/content/2005/08/17/36759.shtml.

8 On life in today's Chechnya, see Médecins Sans Frontières, *The Trauma of Ongoing War in Chechnya: Quantitative Assessment of Living Conditions and Psychosocial and General Health Status among the War-Displaced in Chechnya and Ingushetia* (Amsterdam: MSF, Aug. 2004).

9 Both sides' abuses have been documented by numerous independent outside organizations. On the first Chechen war, 1994–96, see the Russian Human Rights Center "Memorial" publication, *Rossiya-Chechnya: tsep' oshibok i prestuplenii* (Moscow: Zvenya, 1998). On the second war, see Human Rights Watch, *The "Dirty War" in Chechnya: Forced Disappearances, Torture, and Summary Executions* (New York: HRW, March 2001); Human Rights Watch, *Swept Under: Torture, Forced Disappearances, and Extrajudicial Killings during Sweep Operations in Chechnya* (New York: HRW, Feb. 2002); US Congress, Commission on Security and Cooperation in Europe, *Democracy and Human Rights Trends in Eurasia and East Europe: A Decade of Membership in the Organization for Security and Cooperation in Europe*, 107th Congress, 2nd Session (Washington, D.C.: Dec. 2002), p. 49; Human Rights Watch, *Human Rights Situation in Chechnya: Briefing Paper to the 59th Session of the UN Commission on Human Rights* (New York: HRW, April 2003); "Russia," in US Department of State, Bureau of Democracy, Human Rights, and Labor, *Country Reports on Human Rights Practices 2003* (Washington, D.C.: Department of State, Feb. 2004); and Human Rights Center "Memorial" *Deceptive Justice: Situation on the*

Investigation of Crimes against Civilians Committed by Members of the Federal Forces in the Chechen Republic during Military Operations, 1999–2003 (Moscow: Memorial, May 2003).

10 See, for example, Olga Allenova, "Chechenskii OMON pochti v karmane: U Akhmata Kadyrova," *Kommersant*, 22 May 2003, p. 5.

11 On this raid and the overall problem of such marauding detachments, see Anna Politkovskaya, "Snova GRU-200," *Novaya gazeta*, No. 45, 27 June 2005, http://2005. novayagazeta.ru/nomer/2005/45n/n45n-s00.shtml.

12 Lieutenant-General Evgenii Abrashin, "Teraktov v Ingushetii i Beslane mozhno bylo ne dopustit,'" *Izvestiya*, 24 Sept. 2004, pp. 1, 3.

13 Denis Kozlov, "Mir bez mira, voina bez pravil: Real'naya Chechnya ne pokhozha na tu, chto my vidim po televizoru," *Nezavisimoe voennoe obozrenie* (Moscow), No. 43 (5 Dec. 2003), pp. 1, 5. Russian soldiers have grown so wary of the loyalties of the Chechen police that they avoid sharing any information about helicopter flights and troop movements. See Paul Quinn-Judge, "No Way Out?," *Time*, 13 Oct. 2003, p. 15.

14 "Za posobnichestvo boevikam zaderzhany militsionery," *Severnaya Ossetiya* (Vladikavkaz), 21 Aug. 2004, p. 1.

15 Comments of Mikhail Lapotnikov, chief of the investigative bureau in the office of the procurator general for the North Caucasus, cited in Vlad Trifonov, "Ingushskie militsionery byly posobnikami Shamilya Basaeva," *Kommersant Daily*, 24 Sept. 2004, p. 5.

16 See S. Pryganov, *Vtorzhenie v Rossii* (Moscow: Eksprint, 2003), pp. 163–85.

17 Evgenii Smyshlyaev, "Vertolety nad Chechnei: Sistemu ekspluatatsii tekhniki reformirovat' v khode konflikta," *Nezavisimoe voennoe obozrenie* (Moscow), No. 38 (13–19 Oct. 2000), p. 6.

18 Mark Kramer, "Guerrilla Warfare, Counterinsurgency, and Terrorism in the North Caucasus: The Military Dimension of the Russian-Chechen Conflict," unpublished paper in the author's archive.

19 Rohan Gunaratna, *Inside al Qaeda: Global Network of Terror* (New York: Columbia University Press, 2002), p. 179.

20 Ibid., pp. 151–152; Vinod Anand, "Export of Holy Terror to Chechnya from Pakistan and Afghanistan," *Strategic Analysis* (New Delhi), Vol. 24, No. 3 (June 2000), pp. 539–51; and Pryganov, *Vtorzhenie v Rossiyu*, pp. 195–196.

21 Gunaratna, *Inside al Qaeda*, p. 180, and Pryganov, *Vtorzhenie v Rossiyu*, pp. 189–190.

22 See Devji, *Landscapes of Jihad*, pp. 130–131. See also Dore Gold, *Hatred's Kingdom: How Saudi Arabia Supports the New Global Terrorism* (Washington, D.C.: Regnery, 2003), p. 137 cited in Jeffrey M. Bale, "The Chechen Resistance and Radiological Terrorism," Center for Nonproliferation Studies, Monterey Institute for International Studies, April 2004, www.nti.org/e_research/e3_47a.html, p. 6.

23 Bale, "The Chechen Resistance and Radiological Terrorism," p. 8.

24 See US National Commission on Terrorist Attacks upon the United States, *The 9/11 Commission Report* (Washington, D.C.: US Government Printing Office, July 2004), pp. 58–59, 64, 109, 125, 149, 160, 165–166, 191, 222, 233, and 524; 30 Oct. 2004 declassified portions of the top-secret US Defense Intelligence Agency report "Intelligence Information Report [deleted]/Swift Knight – Usama Ben Laden's Current and Historical Activities," Oct. 1998; Gunaratna, *Inside al Qaeda*, pp. xl, xlvii, xlviii, 13, 21, 35, 74, 78–79, 85, 91–92, 119, 123, 142, 151–152, 154–155, 179–180, 278; and C. J. Chivers and Steven Lee Myers, "Chechen Rebels Mainly Driven by Nationalism," *The New York Times*, 12 Sept. 2004, pp. 1, 9.

25 David Johnson, "US Agency Sees Global Network for Bomb Making," *The New York Times*, 22 Feb. 2004, pp. 1, 9. On TEDAC, see US Department of Justice, Federal

Bureau of Investigation, *FBI Laboratory 2003 Report* (Quantico, VA: FBI, Jan. 2004), p. 17.

26 On Dubrovka, see Anne Speckherd, Nadejda Tarabrina, Valery Krasnov and Khapta Akhmedova, "Research Note: Observations of Suicidal Terrorists in Action" in *Terrorism and Political Violence*, Vol. 16, No. 2 (Summer 2005), pp. 305–328.

27 On the details of the establishment and operation of Basaev's camps, see the declassified version of the top-secret US Defense Intelligence Agency report, "Intelligence Information Report"; and Tishkov, *Obshchestvo v vooruzhenom konflikte*, pp. 297–303.

28 Aleksandr Ignatenko, "Vakhkhabitskoe kvazigosudarstvo," *Russkii Zhurnal*, www.russ.ru/publish/ 96073701, citing the Chechen militants' website *Kavkaz-Tsentr*, 10 Sept. 2002. The author's attempts in September 2005 to find the *Kavkaz-Tsentr* report cited by Ignatenko produced no results. It should be added that the Chechen websites experience frequent technical problems, some caused by Russian hacking. Ignatenko also refers to an internet videoclip of the meeting. Almost everything else in Ignatenko's account of the meeting is confirmed in a book written by a former US counter-terrorism official. See Murphy, *The Wolves of Islam*, pp. 171–175. Much of it is also confirmed in subsequent reports on *Kavkaz-Tsentr*. See, for example, "President ChRI Sheik Abdul-Khalim. Kto On?," *Kavkaz-Tsentr*, 12 March 2005, 00:59:07 local time, www.kavkazcenter.com/russ/content/2005/ 03/12/31285.shtml. Among others, Basaev himself explicitly confirmed this in a January 2006 interview. "Abdallakh Shamil Abu-Idris: 'My oderzhali strategicheskuyu pobedu,'" *Kavkaz-Tsentr*, 9 Jan. 2006, 08:47:10, www.kavkazcenter.net/russ/content/2006/01/09/40869.shtml.

29 Murphy, *The Wolves of Islam*, pp. 171–175, and Ignatenko, "Vakhkhabitskoe kvazigosudarstvo."

30 *Chechenpress*. org, 22 July 2005, www.chechenpress.com.

31 Abu Omar was regarded by the Russian Islamic scholar Aleksandr Ignatenko as the committee's real leader. Like other foreign mujahedin arriving in the North Caucasus, he soon married a young Dagestani girl from Karamakhi. This was one of the Dagestani villages (along with Chabanmakhi) where Abu Omar and other jihadists established jamaats and sought to establish a bridgehead for a caliphate in the August 1999 Basaev–Khattab invasion that sparked the second post-Soviet Chechen war. In 1997, he took part in Khattab's raid on the Russian military base in Buinaksk, Dagestan. Ignatenko, "Vakhkhabitskoe kvazigosudarstvo," citing *Kavkaz-Tsentr*, 27 Aug. 2002. Again this item was no longer in the site's archive by fall 2005. See also *Kavkaz-Tsentr*, 8 Oct. 2002. According to Murphy, at one time Abu Omar was chairman of the committee of judges and fatwas on the ChRI Shura's Shariah committee and issued fatwas (theologically based legal rulings) in support of carrying out acts of terrorism. According to Russian intelligence, he was an "emissary" of the Muslim Brotherhood and the Al-Haramein Islamist Foundation and arranged foreign financing for terrorism in Moscow (including the October 2002 Dubrovka theatre hostage-taking and the 1999 apartment building bombings), Chechnya, Dagestan, Ingushetiya, and North Ossetiya, including the infamous Belsan school seizure. He is said by Murphy to have made appeals to Muslims for "assistance in the informational, social, and military realms" through *Kavkaz-Tsentr*. Adam Dekkushev, sentenced for participation in the 1999 Moscow apartment building bombings, testified that Abu Omar taught him how to make explosives at his training camp in 1997. Murphy, *Wolves of Islam*, pp. 44–46, 106, 149, 153, 191, and 216. See also "FSB Confirms Death of 'Al-Qaeda's Representative in North Caucasus,'" Retwa.org, 16 Dec. 2005, www.retwa.org/home.cfm? articleId=1556.

32 "Prezident ChRI Sheik Abdul-Khalim. Kto On?"

33 Akhmed Zakaev claimed in March 2005 that Sadulaev was approximately thirty-five

years old. "V Chechnya poyavilsya preemnik Maskhadova – na saite chechenskih separatistov 'Kavkaz-Tsentr novym liderom boevikov nazval Abdul-Khalim Sadulaev,'" *Ekho Moskvy*, 10 March 2005, www.echo.msk.ru/news/ 236585.html. The Chechen rebels' website *Kavkaz-Tsentr* reported that he was born in 1967: "Prezident ChRI Sheik Abdul-Khalim. Kto On?"

34 *Kavkaz-Tsentr* countered probably false Russian media reports that Sadulaev was born in Saudi Arabia by stressing that he has never been outside Chechnya but for his hajj to Mecca. "Prezident ChRI Sheik Abdul-Khalim. Kto On?"

35 Ibid. See also Interfax, 10 March 2005.

36 "V Chechnya poyavilsya preemnik Maskhadova."

37 "Prezident ChRI Sheik Abdul-Khalim. Kto On?"

38 Paul Tumelty, "A Biography of Abdul-Khalim Sadulaev," *The Jamestown Foundation Chechnya Weekly*, Vol. 6, Issue 11 (16 March 2005).

39 Ibid.

40 Utro.ru, 16 March 2004, www.utro.ru.

41 Tumelty, "A Biography of Abdul-Khalim Sadulaev."

42 Paul Tumelty, "Chechnya: A Strategy for Independence," *The Jamestown Foundation Chechnya Weekly*, 3 Aug. 2005.

43 For the interview with Ichkeriyan president Aslan Maskhadov and chairman of the Shariah committee of the republic's state defense committee Abdul-Khalim Sadulaev, see "'My perenosim voinu na territoriyu vraga ... ,'" *Kavkaz-Tsentr*, 1 Aug. 2004, 13:09:21, www.kavkazcenter.com/russ/content/2004/08/01/24101.shtml.

44 Ibid.

45 In a revealing June 2005 interview with Radio Liberty, Sadulaev claimed that just before his death Maskhadov had reinstated Basaev to the ChRI Shura from which he had resigned shortly after he claimed responsibility for the October 2002 "Nord-Ost" theatre hostage-taking in central Moscow. See "A.-Kh. Sadulaev: 'Obeshaem russkim voinu do pobednogo kontsa,'" (Otvety Prezidenta ChRI Abdul-Khalim Sadulaev na voprosy korrespondentov radio "Svoboda," Kavkaz Tsentr, 6 July 2005, 00:30:18, www.kavkazcenter.com/russ/content/2005/07/06/35833.shtml.

46 From the Information-Analytical Center under the president of the ChRI, 3 March 2005, as cited in ChechenPress.co.uk, 4 March 2005, http://chechenpress.co.uk/index.shtml.

47 "Prezident Maskhadov priostanovil voinu," *Kavkaz-Tsentr*, 3 Feb. 2005, 04:03:51, www.kavkazcenter.com/russ/content/2005/02/03/29846.shtml.

48 There were four acts in Dagestan that were of a terrorist character: four assassinations or assassination attempts (of the republic's deputy premier, the deputy OMON chief, a district police chief, and several traffic policemen). However, not one of these was claimed by a ChRI-associated cell or combat jamaat or proven to be the result of Chechen or Islamist activities by Russian law-enforcement organs, and one of them led to the arrest of a local railroad official. "Khronika Terrora," *Novaya gazeta*, No. 49, 11 July 2005, http://2005.novayagazeta.ru/nomer/2005/49n/n49n-s10.shtml.

49 Some disagree with Scheuer on this. Arthur Bluey, "Bin Laden Expert: Muslim Tradition to Offer Truce Before Attack," LibertyPost.org, 21 Jan. 2006, www.libertypost.org/cgi-bin/readart.cgi?ArtNum=125927.

50 "Maskhadov za mir, Putin za voinu," *Kavkaz-Tsentr*, 5 March 2005, 13:41:55, www.kavkazcenter.net/ russ/content/2005/03/05/31101.shtml.

51 "'My perenosim voinu na territoriyu vraga ... .'"

52 Maria Mstislavskaya, "Basaev i Maskhadov pryatalis v odnom bunkere," Lenta.ru, 2 Dec. 2005, http://lenta.ru/articles/2005/12/02/bunker/.

53 See "Prezident Maskhadov priostanovil voinu."

54 Tumelty, "Chechnya: A Strategy for Independence."

55 He pointed to their failure to convince the Parliamentary Assembly of the Council of

Europe to adopt a resolution condemning the killing of Maskhadov and demanding that the Russian authorities hand over his body to his family for burial.

56 "Obrashchenie Prezidenta ChRI A.-Kh. Sadulaeva k chechenckomu narodu," *Kavkaz-Tsentr*, 19 Aug. 2005, 16:55:28, www.kavkazcenter.net/russ/content/2005/08/19/36843.shtml.

57 Ibid.

58 "Prezident ChRI Sadulaev podpisal nivyi ukaz i rasporyazhenie," *Kavkaz-Tsentr*, 11 Sept. 2005, 16:20:57, www.kavkazcenter.net/russ/content/2005/09/11/37432.shtml.

59 "Zayavlenie Administratsii Prezidenta ChRI," Kavkaz-Tsentr, 27 Sept. 2005, 00:59:01, www.kavkazcenter.com/russ/content/2005/09/27/37843.shtml.

60 Kavkaz-Tsentr, 6 July 2005.

61 "A.-Kh. Sadulaev: 'Rossiya ne tolko uidyot iz Chechenii, no i ostavit ves Kavkaz'," Chechen Press.info, 17 Sept. 2005, www.chechenpress.info/events/2005/09/17/10.shtml.

62 "M. Udugov: 'Rossiya dolzhna byt vzyata pod vneshnee upravlenie,'" Kavkaz Tsentr, 20 June 2005, 00:23:42, www.kavkazcenter.net/russ/content/2005/06/20/35635.shtml.

63 "Doku Umarov: 'Russkaya armiya v Chechne vydokhlas,'" Intervyu zhurnalista 'Radio Svoboda' Andreya Babitsskogo s vitse-prezidentom ChRI Doku Umarovym, *Kavkaz-Tsentr*, 15 July 2005, 15:19:31, www.kavkazcenter.net/russ/content/2005/07/15/36133.shtml.

64 "Shamil Basaev: 'Segodnya voyuet ves chechenskii narod.'"

65 The figures for 1997–2003 are from Nataliya Lopashenko, director of the Saratov branch of the Center for Transnational Crime and Corruption at the American University in Washington, D.C., who provided these data in a presentation in Togliatti, Samara Oblast in April 2004. Her report was excerpted in *Russian Regional Report*, Vol. 9, No. 17 (17 Sept. 2004). Lopashenko noted in connection with the data: "The growth trend is not the only negative aspect of Russian terrorism. Terrorists and the acts they commit are becoming more cruel and extreme. In Russia, terrorists have struck at crowded outdoor markets, apartment houses, cemeteries, hospitals, holiday gatherings, popular musicals, and the subway. The cynicism of terrorist attacks is only growing. Given past experience, it is possible to predict that terrorists will attack schools, critical infrastructure (the municipal water system, the electricity grid), and important factories." The figures for 2004 and 2005 come from Igor Dobaev, "Voina na Kavkaz: realii i perspektivy," Novaya Politika, 26 Oct. 2005, www.novopol.ru/article3685.html, as well as my own estimate based on the number of terrorist attacks reported in the first ten months of 2005 (See Table 3). Terrorist attacks continued at a somewhat reduced pace in Dagestan and Ingushetiya in the last two months of 2005.

66 In October FSB chief Aleksandr Patrushev claimed that the security services had prevented more than five hundred terrorist acts in the first nine months of 2004 in Moscow, St. Petersburg, Stavropol, Rostov-on-Don, Kabardino-Balkariya, and Volgograd Oblast, two hundred of which could have had "most serious consequences." Syuzanna Farizova, "Khot' rodni vynosi," *Kommersant-Daily*, 30 Oct. 2004, pp. 1–2, and RFERL Newsline, Vol. 8, No. 190 (6 Oct. 2004).

67 The raid, according to one Ingush source, involved 450 mujahedin and included attacks on eighteen facilities in the republic, including: the headquarters and premises of the OMON and MVD, mobile units of the MVD located in Nazran and Karabulak, the Nazran district MVD headquarters, MVD unit 29483 in the village of Troitskii, and border troops located in Nazran. The attack left 79 dead and 114 wounded, including 57 officers and servicemen of the various *siloviki*. Yevloev, "Problemy borby s terrorizmom na sovremennom etape."

68 "'My perenosim voinu na territoriyu vraga . . . .'"

69 Ibid.

70 Ibid.
71 One of the terrorists involved in the raid claimed that hundreds of young Ingush, alienated by official corruption and the widespread kidnapping of young men in Ingushetiya (at least some of which acts involve the FSB), are joining with Basaev. Liz Fuller, "Chechen Warlord Warns of New Terrorist Attacks," *RFERL Caucasus Report,* Vol. 7, No. 42 (5 Nov. 2004).
72 "Ingushetiya," Ingushetiya.ru, 6 July 2004, 10:00 GMT, www.ingushetiya.ru. Gazeta.ru reported that the militants came to Albogachiev's home during the raid, took the keys to his Mercedes-600 from his wife (the mufti was not there), drove it to the outskirts of town, and burned it. Nadezhda Kevorkova and Svetlana Medvedeva, "Mufti Ingushetii poshel v otstavku," *Gazeta,* 7 July 2004, p. 3.
73 Maskhadov's support for the operation remains unclear. On 6 September, Russian state television broadcast one of the hostage-takers saying "the task was ordered by Maskhadov and Basaev." The latter later claimed responsibility; the former's aides condemned the attack in public. ITAR-TASS, (6 Sept. 2004).
74 RFERL Newsline, Vol. 8, No. 169 (6 Sept. 2004). Early official reports claimed a heavy Arab and even African presence among the hostage-takers. RFERL Newsline, Vol. 8, No. 170 (7 Sept. 2004).
75 Basaev in his 17 September statement claiming responsibility for Beslan stated that two Arabs were among the thirty-three who took part in seizing the hostages. See "Abdallakh Shamil: 'Operatsiya Nord-Vest v Belane.'" Two Algerians, Osman Larussi and Yacine Benalia, were more recently reported to have been among the terrorists. They and another, Basaev's "key aide" Kamel Rabat Bouralha, were active in the Finsbury Park mosque in north London. Jason Burke, "London Mosque Link to Beslan," *The Observer* (London), 3 Oct. 2004.
76 Estimates of the percentage of Muslims among Ossetiyans range from 30 to 40 percent, making the Ossetiyans a people on the cusp of the clash of civilizations inside Russia. Muslims overall make up only 8 percent of North Ossetiya's population. M. N. Yemelyanova, "Islam i kulturnaya traditsiya v Tsentralno-Severnom Kavkaze," in Yu. M. Kobyshanov, *Musul'mane izmenyayusheisya Rossii* (Moscow: ROSSPEN, 2002), pp. 241–260, at pp. 245, 248–249.
77 A linguistic element contributed to the divide between most Ossetiyans, whose language is Iranian, and the region's ethnic Muslims, who speak Turkic and Ibero-Caucasian languages.
78 The deputy mufti in the republic described the republican leadership's attitude toward its Muslims in June 2001, observing: "We cannot but think that they regard us very badly." It should be noted that the perpetrators of the mosque explosion were never determined and that there had been a disagreement between Tatars from Kazan and Muslims in Vladikavkaz over the proprietorship of the mosque. Yemelyanova, "Islam i kulturnaya traditsiya v Tsentralno-Severnom Kavkaze," pp. 248–249.
79 Only twelve thousand Ingush have been resettled. This case of "ethnic cleansing" was abetted by Russian forces who backed their Christian Ossetiyan brethren in the fighting. The conflict is part of an older land dispute. When Stalin deported the Ingush and Chechens, Ingushetiya's Prigorodnyi raion was incorporated into North Ossetiya. In 1957 Stalin's successor, Nikita Khrushchev, rehabilitated the peoples deported by Stalin in 1944, issuing a decree allowing them to return to their homes. When the deported Ingush survivors returned to what had been Ingushetiya, they found Ossetiyans living in their homes in the Prigorodnyi district. In 1991, President Yeltsin signed a law restoring the territorial rights of the Ingush but created no mechanism for resolving the issue, so raising expectations and fueling tensions leading up to the outbreak of violence.
80 The fact that perhaps 70 percent of Beslan's victims might be Muslims, given the ethnic composition of the local population, did not restrain either the terrorists' hand or

ethnic Russians' and Christians' claims that the act was committed by Muslims against Christians. "Musul'mane molyatsya za pogibshchikh v Beslane, osetiny dumayut o mesti," Islam.ru, 13 Oct. 2004, www.islam.ru. (All Islam.ru material cited is in the author's archive, as the website's own archive is incomplete.) In late September former Saudi finance minister Said bin Said visiting Saratov claimed to have been informed (by whom it is unclear) of the same figure of 70 percent for the share of Muslims among Beslan's casualties. "Rossiiskie musulmane privodyat v stranu arabskie investitsii," Islam.ru, 30 Sept. 2004, www.islam.ru.

81 He declared that renewal of the conflict would mean the Chechen terrorists who seized Beslan had achieved their goal. Ekho Moskvy Radio, 9 Oct. 2004, 08:00.

82 Another report claimed one terrorist was Ossetiyan, likely of Islamic faith. Oleg Rubnikovich, Vladimir Varinov, and Margarita Kondratyeva, "Beslan School Seized by Basayev's Guards," *Gazeta*, 6 Sept. 2004, pp. 1, 3. For the Chechens' report on the Ossetiyan jamaat's participation, see "Shkolu v Beslane zakhvatil Osetinskii Dzhamaat?"

83 As one Beslan woman reportedly said: "Ask the people who lost loved ones, their children, their friends, their mothers and fathers. Of course they hate now." "We will fight if we have to," said another. "They brought this evil to our doorstep. Now we have to struggle with it." Another Beslan Ossetiyan stated: "It is the Ingush . . . . They want to kill everyone who is not a Muslim . . . . They do not like anyone who is different from them, they just want to wipe us out. It's all about religion, it's about territory. It's the decades-long problems we've had here." Elizabeth Piper, "Ossetians Fear "Terrorists" Are Their Neighbours," Reuters, 7 Sept. 2004. On the situation in Beslan, North Ossetiya, and Ingushetiya after the tragedy, see "Musul'mane molyatsya za pogibshchikh v Beslane, osetiny dumayut o mesti"; Yelena Rudneva, "Net ni odnogo cheloveka, kotoryi ne vinil by ingushei," Gazeta.ru, 12 Oct. 2004, www.gazeta.ru; Vlad Salugardanov, "KKK Osetii," Gazeta.ru, 12 Oct. 2004, www.gazeta.ru; "Relatives of Victims of Russian School Hostage-taking Protest at Roadblock," AP, 24 Oct. 2004; Sonia Oxley, "Reprisal fears as Russia Death School Mourns," Reuters, 12 Oct. 2004; and David James Smith, "Beslan – the Aftermath," *The Sunday Times* (London), 12 Dec. 2004.

84 "Special Reports on the Beslan Tragedy," *Institute of War and Peace Reporting – Caucasus Reporting Service*, No. 252 (8 Sept. 2004), No. 253 (15 Sept. 2004), and No. 254 (23 Sept. 2004), info@iwpr.net.

85 All but one shell fell short of the academy, and no one was hurt. It remained unclear whether Ossetiyans or Chechen-allied Muslims were behind the attack seeking to provoke an Ossetiyan-Ingush conflict. See the statement of the Ingushetiya State Assembly on its investigation in "Narodnoe Sobranie RI provelo proverku fakta obstrela Gorskogo Kadetskogog corpusa. Spravka o rezul'tatakh proverki," Ingushetia.ru, 18 Nov. 2004, 21:03, www.ingushetia.ru/news/4423.html.

86 Salugardanov, "KKK Osetii."

87 The North Ossetiyan MVD deputy chiefs Mayrbek Mauraov and Vladimir Popov as well as senior officials from the Prigorodnyi district MVD immediately converged on the checkpoint. After two hours of talks the victims' relatives (referred to as "bandits" by Ingushetia.ru) returned home still armed, again according to Ingushetia.ru, and the checkpoint resumed normal work. AP reported that the relatives numbered fifty, while Ingushetia.ru claimed there were seven hundred. See "Relatives of Victims of Russian School Hostage-taking Protest at Roadblock" and Ingushetia.ru, 23 Oct. 2004, www.ingushetia.ru.

88 For example, the patriarch of the Russian Orthodox Church (ROC), Aleksei II, also issued a statement which asserted: "Islam does not teach terrorism and does not teach violence." "Aleksei II prizval ne putat' Islam s terrorizm," Islam.ru, 6 Sept. 2004, www.islam.ru. At a 14 September press conference ROC archbishop Nikon joined the

chairman of the Central Spiritual Board of Muslims, mufti Talgat Tadzhutdin, in an effort to buttress inter-communal comity. Tadzhutdin was also trying to pre-empt the wave of Islamophobia that would sweep across Russia in the coming weeks and months. He denied Islam's responsibility for the crime by reminding Russians that Muslims are neither religiously intolerant nor terrorists and that such a view "is in fact aiding and abetting terrorists who do not have either true faith or nationality in the real sense as they defy all written and unwritten laws." Archbishop Nikon warned that the "enemies of multinational Russia make provocations to compromise Muslims and bring discord in confessional balance." He said that terrorist acts are committed by criminals for political, not religious reasons. RFERL Tatar-Bashkir Daily Report, 15 Sept. 2004.

89 A long-developed cooperation agreement recently signed between North Ossetiya and Ingushetiya was left unimplemented after Beslan. Moreover, North Ossetiya's legislature called for the repeal of the July 1993 Russian law "On the Rehabilitation of Repressed Peoples," prompting a harsh reaction from Ingushetiya's parliament. Deputies of the KChR People's Assembly immediately appealed to President Putin to protect the law. Clearly, North Ossetiya's action was intended as a slap in the face to ethnic Muslims and a way of halting residual immigration to the republic. Ekho Moskvy Radio, 9 Oct. 2004, 08:00 GMT.

90 See Smith, "Beslan – the Aftermath." The Ingushetiya opposition conducted an opinion poll which found that 80 percent of Ingushetiya's population disagreed with Putin's post-Beslan initiatives, in particular the presidential nomination of the regional chief executives. Ingushetiya.ru, 4 Oct. 2004, 06:50 GMT, www.ingushetiya.ru. Beslan and Putin's response also increased anti-Putin sentiments in both republics. Ossetiyans' September 2004 rallies saw anti-Russian and anti-Putin slogans aired. "Special Reports on the Beslan Tragedy," *Institute of War and Peace Reporting – Caucasus Reporting Service*, No. 252 (8 Sept. 2004), No. 253 (15 Sept. 2004), and No. 254 (23 Sept. 2004), info@iwpr.net.

91 Dobaev, "Voina na Kavkaz." Dobaev reported over a hundred in the first nine months, and I counted seven in October. I counted thirty terrorist attacks in Ingushetiya in September–October after only approximately ten in the prior months of 2005. In addition, I estimate some twenty attacks in the RKB in the first ten months of 2005. Terrorist attacks continued at approximately the same pace in November and December in Dagestan and Ingushetiya as in the first ten months. For daily reporting on terrorist attacks and terrorism in Russia, see the websites www.kavkazcenter.net and www.retwa.org.

92 "Ukaz Prezidenta ChRI Abdul-Halima Sadulaeva," ChechenPress.org, 15 March 2005, www.chechenpress.com/events/2005/04/14/ 30.shtml.

93 "Dokku Umarov: 'My nachinaem voinu na territorii Rossii," Chechenpress.com, 9 May 2005, www.chechenpress.com/events/2005/05/09/08.shtml.

94 On 19 June the first salvo was fired when a suicide bomber set off a truck bomb in Chechnya's city of Znamenskoe, killing at least fifteen and wounding more than thirty.

95 See the text of Surkov's speech to Delovaya Rossiya's economic forum at Mosnews.com, 12 July 2005, www.mosnews.com, or at RFERL, 11 July 2005, www.rferl.org.

96 *The Moscow Times*, 21 Sept. 2004, cited in RFERL Newsline, Vol. 8, No. 181 (22 Sept. 2004).

97 RosBalt, 20 Sept. 2004 cited in RFERL Newsline, Vol. 8, No. 181 (22 Sept. 2004.)

98 Viktor Khamrayev, "Motherland Will Seek Dismissal of Government," *Kommersant Daily*, 10 Sept. 2004, p. 2.

99 RFERL Newsline, Vol. 8, No. 201 (29 Oct. 2004). Syuzanna Farizova, "Khot' rodni vynosi," *Kommersant Daily*, 30 Oct. 2004, pp. 1–2.

100 On 20 September Moscow police chief Vladimir Pronin was reported to have

apologized to Tolboev. RFERL Newsline, Vol. 8, No. 173 (10 Sept. 2004) and No. 179 (20 Sept. 2004).

101 "'A teper' musul'mane'. V stolichnom metro provedena etnicheskaya chistka," Islam.ru, 20 Sept. 2004, www.islam.ru, and Sergei Dyupin, "Etot poezd v voine," *Kommersant Daily*, 20 Sept. 2004, www.kommersant.ru/doc.html?docId=506736.

102 Dilyara Saifutdinova, "V Moskve obnaruzhen trup tadzhika s antiislamskimi lozungami," *ASN-News* (also self-labeled the "Russian Tatarsian Islamic News Network," cited henceforth as *ASN-News*), 28 Oct. 2004, 8:45, http://nurlat.kazan.ws/cgi-bin/guide.pl?id_org=78&action=fullnews&id_news=4663.

103 "Putin: Ksenofobskie proyavleniya v Rossii 'oznachayut, chto nasha rabota daet sboi,'" Islam.ru, 19 Oct. 2004, www.islam.ru.

104 A Dagestani family of three, including a four-and-a-half-year-old girl, attempting to fly back home to the North Caucasus, and deputy chairman of the DUM of the Volga Area (DUMP) Suleiman Podarov, scheduled to fly back to Samara, were unable to board their flights when passengers registered suspicions with airline officials. "Paranoiya ili islamofobia?," Islam.ru, 6 Sept. 2004, www.islam.ru, and "Turisty ispugalis' letet' s pomoshchikom imama Povolzh'ua," Islam.ru, 22 Sept. 2004, www.islam.ru. On 23 September some 150 people refused to board a plane at Moscow's Domodedova airport when three "suspicious-looking" men dressed in black and a woman in the Muslim hijab boarded the plane. NTV, 23 Sept. 2004, 03:00 GMT. The RIA news agency reported that the delay was sparked by passengers' fear of two Egyptian women dressed in black, who boarded the plane last because they had been subjected to very strict security checks. RIA (Moscow), 22 Sept. 2004, 22:07 GMT. See also "Aviaislamofobiya stanovitsya normoi," Islam.ru, 23 Sept. 2004, www.islam.ru.

105 Anisimov, "Nizhegorodskim musul'mankam razreshili ne nosit' khidzhab" and "Musul'mankam Nizhnego Novgoroda ne dayut rabotat', Islam.ru, 12 Oct. 2004, www.islam.ru.

106 "Rossiyane vidyat v Islame ugrozu," Islam.ru, 8 Oct. 2004, www.islam.ru and in the author's archive.

107 "Tyumen': obnarodany imena musul'man, obvinyaemyie v ekstremizme," Islam.ru, 13 Sept. 2004, www.islam.ru.

108 Kuraev is a major critic of Putin from the right and an organizer of the Committee of Orthodox Action (Komitet Pravoslavnogo Deistviya or KPD) along with FSB-tied political scientist Stanislav Belkovskii, while Polosin is an ethnic Russian convert to Islam.

109 See "Mitropolit Kirill osudil diakona Kuraeva za islamofobiyu?," Islam.ru, 23 Sept. 2004, www.islam.ru, and *Izvestiya*, 15 Sept. 2004.

110 Ali Vyacheslav Polosin, "Otvet A. Kuraevu. Bibliya, Koran, i Beslan . . . . : Vliyaet li natsionalnost killera na nashu veru v Boga?," Islam.ru, 28 Sept. 2004, www.islam.ru/pressclub/smi/kraevu/?print_page.

111 The site referenced a speech given by a consultant of the State Duma's Committee for Affairs with Public Associations and Religious Organizations Stepan Medvedko in which he reportedly said that behind the scenes Russian Orthodox priests were praising Kuraev. "Chast' svyashchennikov vtaine podderzhivaet islamofoba Kuraev," Islam.ru, 28 Sept. 2004, www.islam.ru, and Polosin, "Otvet A. Kuraevu. Bibliya, Koran, i Beslan."

112 "M. Biibarsov prizvalne vydavat' kriminal'nye razborki na Kavkaze za 'islamskii terrorizm.'" Islam.ru, 27 Oct. 2004, www.islam.ru.

113 Sova designated the following provocateurs: *Moskovskii komsomolets, Argumenty i fakty, Izvestiya*, the Agency for Political Information as well as expert Georgii Engelhardt, deacon Kuraev, and journalists E. Topol' and S. Metelev. "Islamofoby nazvany poimenno," Islam.ru, 25 Oct. 2004, www.islam.ru.

114 Only 18 percent opposed the idea, while 16 percent answered they were not interested

in the issue, 14 percent had not given it any thought, and 8 percent found the question too difficult to answer. See the table from a published interview with Valerii Stepanov from the Institute of Ethnology and Anthropology of the Russian Academy of Sciences in "U Moskvy po-prezhnemu russkoe litso," *Izvestia*, 25 March 2004, p. 5. A 2004 survey found that 42 percent subscribed to the view that "national minorities have too much power in our country." See the results of the survey conducted by the "Ekspertiz" Foundation and Otkrytaya Rossiya summarized in Mark Urnov, "Zhostckaya diktatura nadezhdy," *Moskovskie novosti*, No. 12, 2–8 April 2004, p. 25.

115 The report on the survey was not specific, but one can offer an educated guess that by 'Caucasians' respondents meant Chechens especially, but also other North Caucasus nationalities as well as the Transcaucasian Azeris and Armenians, who have been subject to both state and social repression at times. See the results of the survey conducted by the "Ekspertiz" Foundation and Otkrytaya Rossiya summarized in Georgii Bovt and Georgii Il'ichev, "V chem narod raskhoditsya s prezidentom," *Izvestia*, 19 March 2004, p. 3. Another survey, the results of which were published at about the same time, shows higher support than one would like to see but nevertheless rather limited support in Russia for neo-fascist skinheads, with only 12 percent of respondents in favor of them and two-thirds agreeing that skinheads should be banned. See the results of the Public Opinion Foundation survey in Yelena Rotevkin, "Zaderzhany podozrevaemye v ubiistve tadzhikskikh devochek," *Izvestia*, 19 March 2004, p. 2.

116 The Sova report noted a positive trend in an increase in criminal sentences for racially motivated attacks and extremist propaganda, with 16 guilty verdicts counted in 2005, up from 8 in 2004 and only 3 in 2003. A total of 60 people were found guilty in trials in 2005. See the Sova Center in "Radikal'nyi natsionalizm v Rossii i protivodeistvie emu v 2005 godu," Polit.ru, 9 Feb. 2006, www.polit.ru/research/2006/02/03/year2005.html.

CHAPTER THREE

1 Georgii N. Engelhardt, "Militant Islam in Russia – Potential for conflict," Moscow Defense Brief, 4 April 2005, http://mdb.cast.ru/mdb/1-2005/wap/militant_islam/.
2 This organizational method is described well in John Yoo, "Fighting the New Terrorism," American Enterprise Institute Bradley Lecture, 6 June 2005, www.aei.org/include/pub_print.asp?pubID=22633. html.
3 Gunaratna, *Inside al Qaeda*, p. 112.
4 "Ukaz Prezidenta ChRI Abdul-Khalima Sadulaeva," Chechen Press.org, 15 March 2005, www.chechenpress.com/events/2005/04/14/30.shtml.
5 Oddly enough the article was unsigned and attributed to an organization with a particular infidel-like, even Russian-style title, the Islamic Center for Strategic Research and Political Technologies. Udugov later acknowledged his authorship. See "Razmyshleniya modzhakheda," Kavkaz-Tsentr, 10 Aug. 2005, www.kavkazcenter.com/russ/history/stories/reflections_of_mujahid.shtml.
6 Cases of peaceful attempts to establish Shariah law are noted, including the Islamic party's election victory in Algeria and the subsequent military coup in the early 1990s, the mass demonstrations held in Pakistan and Tajikistan today, Sudan in 1998, and the "temporary failure" of the Afghani Taliban. Ibid.
7 Ibid.
8 "Obrashchenie Prezidenta ChRI A.-Kh. Sadulaeva k chechenskomu narodu," Kavkaz-Tsentr, 19 Aug. 2005, 16:55:28, www.kavkazcenter.Net/russ/content/2005/08/19/36843.shtml.
9 Also, Sadulaev has a very post-Soviet-sounding "presidential administration"headed by Idris Khasanov and a press service headed by Dzhambulat Baskhanov. See

Sadulaev's decree "On the Leader of Press Service of the President of the ChRI", in "Ukazy Prezidenta ChRI A.-Kh. Sadulaev," Kavkaz-Tsentr, 25 Aug. 2005, 14:05:31, www.kavkazcenter.net/russ/content/2005/08/25/37056.shtml.

10 There can be organizational diversity within the international jihad. Thus, according to Sageman, the southeast Asian cluster in the al Qaeda network is structured more hierarchically and engages more in top-down recruitment than is typical of al Qaeda and its affiliates elsewhere. See Marc Sageman, "Understanding Jihadi Networks," Center for Contemporary Conflict's *Strategic Insights,* Issue 4, No. 4, April 2005, www.ccc.nps.navy.mil/si/2005/Apr/sagemanApr05.asp, which is a summary of Sageman's own *Understanding Terror Networks* (Philadelphia: University of Pennsylvania Press, 2004).

11 "Shamil Basaev: 'Segodnya voyuet ves chechenskii narod.'"

12 See "Dzhikhad dlya musulman Kabardino-Balkarii obyazatelen (prodolzhenie)," Kavakaz-Tsentr, 25 March 2004, 18:47, www.kavkazcentre.net/russ/content/2005/03/25/31816.shtml.

13 Mayrbek Vachagaev, "Evolution of the Chechen Jamaat," *The Jamestown Foundation Chechnya Weekly,* Vol. VI, Issue 14, 6 April 2005.

14 Tatyana Gritsenko, "Net takogo slova 'dzhamaat,'" *Vremya novostei,* 22 Feb. 2005, p.2.

15 Vachagaev, "Evolution of the Chechen Jamaat."

16 According to Vachagaev, in 1998–99 the future ChRI president and emir Sadulaev formed a jamaat in Argun in which "violence played absolutely no role." Ibid. However, as already noted in 1999 Sadulaev led the Argun People's Militia, likely little different from a combat jamaat.

17 On the system of safe houses that, for example, helped Basaev move around much of the North Caucasus at will, see Vadim Rechkalov's series of articles "'Pochemu spetssluzhby ne mogut poimat' Shamilya Basaeva," *Izvestiya,* 6–10 Dec. 2004, www.izvestia.ru. On the mobilization (as opposed to the recruitment) model for explaining al Qaeda both before and after 9/11, see Marc Sageman, "Understanding Jihadi Networks" and *Understanding Terror Networks.* On the Islamist safe or guest houses see part one of the interview with Osma bin Laden's former bodyguard Nasir Ahmad Nasir al-Bahri (Abu-Jandal) in *Al-Quds al Arabi* (London), 18 March 2005, translated on Ralph Davis's RMSMC "Chechnya" Yahoo listserve, 22 May 2005; in the author's archive.

18 Engelhardt, "Militant Islam in Russia – Potential for Conflict."

19 FSB deputy head in Chechnya Aleksandr Potapov claims there are 13,500 jamaatists providing various forms of logistical and operational support, in addition to some 1,500 hardcore combatants and terrorists. See Rechkalov, "Pochemu spetssluzhby ne mogut poimat' Shamilya Basaeva," *Izvestiya,* 6 Dec. 2004, www.izvestia.ru/conflict/article793673. One scholar's unsubstantiated estimate put the number of "extremist combatants" the network was capable of mobilizing as of autumn 2004 at more than ten thousand, including no fewer than four thousand from the Volga and Central Russia regions. Engelhardt, "Militant Islam in Russia – Potential for Conflict."

20 "Shamil Basaev: 'Segodnya voyuet ves chechenskii narod.'"

21 "Kadyrov and MVD Disagree on Fighter Numbers," Retwa.org, 18 Jan. 2006, www.retwa.org/home.cfm?articleId=1699.

22 REFERL Newsline, Vol. 9, No. 154 (16 Aug. 2005).

23 The figure of two hundred foreign Islamist fighters comes from the chief of the Russian Armed Forces' General Staff, Yurii Baluevskii. Boris Plugatarev, "2005 god: vyalaya voina s khalifatom," *Nezavisimoe voennoe obozrenie,* No. 49, 23 Dec. 2005, http://nvo.ng.ru/wars/2005-12-23/22005war.html, and "General Staff: 200 Mercenaries Operating in Chechnya," Retway.org, 1 Dec. 2005, www.retwa.org/home.cfm?articleId=1453. The figure of three hundred comes from

Igor Dobaev, "Terroristicheski gruppirovki na Yuge Rossii: novyie tendentsii," Evrazia.org, 12 July 2005, http://evrazia.org/modules.php?name=News&file=article&sid=2558.

24 RIA Novosti, 28 Nov. 2005.

25 These numbers are extrapolated from figures given by the North Caucasus Regional Operational Staff commander, Colonel General Arkadii Yedelyev, for the first eight months of 2005, according to which 231 militants or jihadists were killed and 890 were arrested, though it was unspecified whether the figures regarded the entire North Caucasus or just Chechnya. In light of later figures, they were probably for the entire North Caucasus. In mid-December 2005 deputy commander of the MVD internal troops Lieutenant-General Sergei Topchii cited 85 terrorists killed and 423 arrested during the year on the territory of Chechnya. Plugatarev, "2005 god: vyalaya voina s khalifatom." However, an end-of-year MVD report claimed 140 militants killed, 311 arrested, and 49 surrendered. See "Kadyrov and MVD Disagree on Fighter Numbers."

26 In August 2005 Kavkaz-Tsentr carried an announcement that the Jamagat Jamaat's website was again up and running. Kavkaz-Tsentr claimed that the latter's server had previously been located in the US and had had to relocate because of actions taken by the US authorities. Little is known about Jamagat's operations. "Sait Karachevskogo Dzhamaat 'Jamagat' snova v seti," Kavkaz-Tsentr, 18 Aug. 2005, 00:18:42, www.kavkazcenter.net/russ/content/2005/08/18/36787.shtml.

27 Dobaev, "Terroristicheskie gruppirovki na Yuge Rossii: novyie traditsii."

28 "Ukazom Prezidenta ChRI Sadulaeva sozdan Kavkazskii front," Kavkaz-Tsentr, 16 May 2005, www.kavkazcenter.com/russ/content/2005/05/16/ 33965.shtml. See also "Chechenskie separatisty tozhe ukreplyayut svoyu 'vlastnuyu vertikal,'" Kavkaz-Tsentr, 26 May 2005, 09:24:13, www.kavkazcenter.com/russ/content/2005/05/26/34353.shtml.

29 "Chechenskie separatisty tozhe ukreplyayut svoyu 'vlastnuyu vertical.'"

30 Pryganov, Vtorzhenie v Rossiyu, p.295.

31 "Ukazom Prezidenta ChRI Sadulaeva sozdan Kavkazskii front" and "Chechenskie separatisty tozhe ukreplyayut svoyu 'vlastnuyu vertikal.'"

32 See "Dopolnitelnoe soobsshchenie o sudbe amira Dzhamaata 'Sidik,'" Kavkaz-Tsentr, 22 Dec. 2005, 21:06:59, www.kavkazcenter.com/russ/content/2005/12/22/40436.shtml; "'Emir of Goitinsky Jamaat' and 31 Fighters Killed in Spez-Op," Retwa.org, 7 Sept. 2005, www.retwa.org/hom/cfm?articleId=668; and ITAR-TASS, 8 May 05, 05:12 GMT.

33 Ruslan Bashirov, "Predstoyashee leto obeshaet byt' zharkim," Kavkaz-Tsentr, 4 June 2005, www.kavkazcenter.com/russ/content/2005/06/04/34701.shtml. A very different opinion – that many of the jahidists in Ingushetiya were young, 13–14 years old, and "just beginning" to gain a foothold – has been expressed by commander of the pro-Moscow "Zapad" or Western batallion Said-Magomed Kakiyev in an interview. Yurii Kotenok, "Basaev atakovla palochka Kokha," Utro.ru, 11 Oct. 2005, www.utro.ru/articles/2005/10/11/484902.shtml.

34 N. Yevloev, "Problemy borby s terrorizmom na sovremennom etape," Serdalo, No. 88, 9 Aug. 2005, http://www.ingush.ru/serdalo135_2.asp.

35 "V Ingushetii ubit emir dzhamaat 'Khalifat,'" Kavkazskii uzel, 2 Sept. 2005, www.kavkaz.memo.ru.

36 Dobaev, "Terroristicheskie gruppirovki na Yuge Rossii: novyie traditsii."

37 "V Ingushetii ubit emir dzhamaat 'Khalifat,'"

38 "Shamil Basaev: 'Nalchik atakovalo 217 modzhakhedov," Chechenpress.org, 17 Oct. 2005. www.chechenpress.info/events/2005/10/17/02/shtml.

39 See "Ukazom Prezidenta ChRI Sadulaeva sozdan Kavkazkii front."

40 In May 2005 a truck carrying about a ton of explosives was seized, and a large cache of two toxic substances, one of which was identified as a form of cyanide, was discovered

on the border between Chechyna and Ingushetiya. Mudzhaid was reported by law-enforcement officials to have arranged delivery of the poisons to Amanat Jamaat from Jordan and to be an emissary of al Qaeda and its associated international terrorist organization, the Muslim Brotherhood. "FSB raportuet k 9 maya: svyazannyie c 'Al-Kaidoi' chechenskie terroristy gotovili khimicheskie ataki," NEWSru.com, 6 May 2005, http://palm.newsru.com/russia/06may2005/chemical.html; "Cache of Cyanide, Unknown Substance Discovered on Ingushetian Border," NTV, 5 May 2005, 09:00 GMT, and "Russian Official: Jordan-Born Mercenary Ordered Poison Attacks in North Caucasus," *RIA Novosti,* 5 May 2005, 08:29 GMT.

41 See Sadulaev's decree appointing Digorskii among other emirs, "Ukazom Prezidenta ChRI Sadulaeva sozdan Kavkazkii front." The Chechens posted on their website a report from an "Ingushetiya source" claiming that the Beslan terrorists included "Ossetiyan Jamaat," correctly identifying the attack's leader, Khodov, about whom they naturally had information. "Shukolu v Beslane zakhvatil Osetinskii Dzhamaat?," *Kavkaz-Tsentr,* 2 Sept. 2004, www.kavkazcenter.net/russ/content/2004/09/02/25438. shtml.

42 "Osetinskie modzhakhedy obstrelyali chechenskikh munafikov bliz sela Kardzhi," *Kavkaz-Tsentr,* 4 Oct. 2005, 18:45:52, www.kavkazcenter.net/russ/content/2005/10/04/38126.shtml.

43 Emil Pain director of Moscow's Institute for Ethno-Political Studies, estimates there are ten: "Moscow's North Caucasus Policy Backfires," *Central Asia – Caucasus Analyst,* 29 June 2005. The Moscow Carnegie Center's Alexei Malashenko claims that "now there are more than ten jamaats" in Dagestan, as compared to two or three in the past. "Russian Analyst Sees 'Total Crisis of Power' in Dagestan," Interfax (Moscow), 7 July 2005.

44 Andrei Riskin, "Vakhkhabity pribirayut k rukam yug Rossii," *Nezavisimaya gazeta,* 4 Feb. 2005, p. 4.

45 "Dagestan prisyagnul Sheiku Abdul-Khalimu," *Kavkaz-Tsentr,* 14 March 2005, www.kavkazcenter.net/russ/content/2005/03/14/32304.shtml.

46 See Chapter Four, below.

47 See interview with FSB lieutenant-general Ivan Mironov in *Rossiiskaya gazeta,* 10 Sept. 2002.

48 See Assaf Moghadam, "Palestinian Suicide Terrorism in the Second Intifada: Motivations and Organizational Aspects," *Studies in Conflict and Terrorism,* Vol. 26, No. 2 (Feb.–March 2003), and Moghadam, "The Roots of Suicide Terrorism: A Multi-Causal Approach," Paper presented at the Harrington Workshop on the Root Causes of Suicide Terrorism, University of Texas at Austin, 12–13 May, 2005, p. 13

49 Fatima Tlisova, "Islamist Group Destroyed in Kabardino-Balkariya," IWPR Caucasus Reporting Service, No. 272, 3 Feb. 2005.

50 Oleg Petrovskiy, "Vakhkhabity 'postavili na schetik' Karachayevo-Cherkessiyu," Utro.ru, 7 Oct. 2004, www.utro/ru/articles/2004/10/07/358654.shtml.

51 Aleksandr Zheglov, "Moskovskie terakty organizovalo karachaevskoe pod'pole," *Kommersant – Daily,* 27 Sept. 2004, p. 5.

52 Basaev, after a month-long course of medical treatment in Krasnodar Krai, reportedly married a Kuban Cossack woman there. Chechen authorities rejected the report as propaganda. "Separatisty utverzhdayut, chto Basaev zhenilsya," Kavkazskii uzel, 23 Feb. 2005, www.kavkaz.memo.ru/newstext/news/id/771121.html.

53 "Severnyi Kavkaz v rukakh dzhamaatov," *Kavkaz-Tsentr,* 6 Feb. 2005, 00:24:07, www.kavkazcenter.net/russ/content/2005/02/05/29971.shtml.

54 Ibid.

55 "Abdallakh Shamil Abu-Idris: 'My oderzhali strategicheskuyu pobedu.'"

56 See "M. Udugov: 'Rossiya dolzhna byt vzyata pod vneshnee upravlenie,'" *Kavkaz-Tsentr,* 20 June 2005, 00:23:42,

www.kavkazcenter.net/russ/content/2005/06/20/35635.shtml.
57 Gunaratna, *Inside al Qaeda*, p. 98; Sageman, *Understanding Terrorist Networks;* Sageman, "Understanding Jihadi Networks," p. 6.
58 Al Qaeda in fact developed a detailed set of fourteen requirements, in addition to being a Muslim, for those seeking to join a jihadist military organization: "knowledge of Islam, ideological commitment, maturity, self-sacrifice, discipline, secrecy and concealment of information, good health, patience, unflappability, intelligence and insight, caution and prudence, truthfulness and wisdom, the ability to observe and analyze, and the ability to act." Gunaranta, *Inside al Qaeda*, p. 98.
59 Sageman, *Understanding Terrorist Networks*, pp. 92, 112–113.
60 Sageman, "Understanding Jihadi Networks," p. 6.
61 Gunaratna, *Inside al Qaeda*, p. xxix, and the interview with Nasir Ahmad Nasir al-Bahri (Abu-Jandal) published in *Al-Quds al Arabi*.
62 Sageman, "Understanding Jihadi Networks," p. 5.
63 Tlisova, "Islamist group Destroyed in Kabardino-Balkariya'; Timur Samedov, "Podozrevaemyie iz 'Yarmuka,'" *Kommersant-Daily,* 15 Dec. 2004, p. 4; Tlisova, "Kabardino-Balkariya Fears Spread of Terror" and Ksenya Solyanskaya, "Oni vozneslis na nebo," Gazeta.ru, 28 Jan 2005, www.gazeta.ru/2005/01/28/0a_146501.shtml; and REFERL Newsline, vol. 9, No. 21 (2 Feb 2005). On Kulaev, see Uwe Klussmann, "The Beslan Aftermath: New Papers Critical of Russian Security Forces," *Der Spiegel* (Germany), 4 July 2005.
64 Svetlana Meteleva, "Fizika terrora," *Moskovskii Komsomolets,* 25 Dec. 2004, p. 7.
65 "A.-Kh. Sadulaev: 'Rossiya ne tolko uidyot iz Chechnii, no i ostavit ves Kavkaz.'"
66 Sadulaev did claim that there would be freedom of religion in the Chechen state. "A.-Kh. Sadulaev: 'Obseshaem russkim voinu do pobednogo kontsa.'"
67 "Obrashchenie Prezidenta ChRI Sadulaeva k narodu."
68 "Prezident ChRI Abdul-Khalim. Kto On?"
69 "'My perenosim voinu na territoriyu vraga.'"
70 The investigative groups are to conduct investigations both inside and outside of Chechnya. "A.-Kh. Sadulaev: 'Rossiya ne tolko uidyot iz Chechenii, no i ostavit ves Kavkaz'" and "V voiskakh modzhkhedov Kavkaza vvoditsya institute kadiev (Shariatskikh sudei)," Kavkaz-Tsentr, 11 Sept. 2005, 01:20:51, www.kavkazcenter.net/russ/content/2005/09/11/37421/shtml.
71 Ibid.
72 "M. Udugov: 'Vsyo, chto ne sootvetstvuet Shariatu nelegitimni,'" Kavkaz-Tsentr, www.kavkaz center.net/russprint.php?id=40872. Udugov's article was a response to a critique of his earlier series of articles of a similar nature, "Rasmyshleniya modzhakheda" (Reflections of a Mujahed). The critique, written by one of the last remaining members of the Maskhadov elite in the ChRI leadership, Akhmed Zakaev, defended a policy of complying with international law and working through the UN and Western international organizations such as the OSCE and Council of Europe to defend the ChRI, signaling a fundamental split among the Chechens. "Akhmed Zakaev: 'Zamenchaniya k nekotorym razmyshleniyam i vyskazyvaniyam,'" Kavkaz-Tsentr, 31 Dec. 2005, 21:59:41, www.kavkazcenter.com/russ/content/2005/12/31/40660.shtml.
73 "M. Udugov: 'Vsyo, chto ne sootvetstvuet Shariatu nelegitimni.'"
74 Ibid.
75 Ibid.
76 Ibid.
77 Aslan, *No God But God*, pp. 52–53, 251–266
78 "M. Udugov: 'Vsyo, chto ne sootvetstvuet Shariatu nelegitimni.'"
79 "Razmyshleniya modzhakheda."
80 Sageman, "Understanding Jihadi Networks," p. 2. On bin Laden's break with, and

assassination of, Azzam, see Gunaratna, *Inside al Qaeda*, pp. 2, 24–33.

81 See Anonymous, *Imperial Hubris* (Dulles, VA: Brassey's Inc., 2004) and Bernard Lewis, *The Crisis of Islam: Holy War and Unholy Terror* (New York: Random House, 2003).

82 "Obrashchenie Prezidenta ChRI Sadulaeva k narodu."

83 The ChRI website, *Kavkaz-Tsentr*, made sure to format the appeal in prayer-like form as reproduced here. See "Obrashchenie Prezidenta ChRI Sadulaeva k narodu."

84 "Dzhikhad dlya musulman Kabardino-Balkarii obyazatelen."

85 Ibid.

86 "A.-Kh. Sadulaev: 'Obseshaem russkim voinu do pobednogo kontsa.'" See also "Obrashchenie Prezidenta ChRI Sadulaeva k narodu."

87 See "Dzhikhad dlya musulman Kabardino-Balkarii obyazatelen," *Kavkaz-Tsentr*, 24 March 2004, 13:59, www.kavkazcenter.com/russ/content/2005/03/24/31762.shtml. For similar remarks see Musa's follow-up interview in "Dzhikhad dlya musulman Kabardino-Balkarii obyazatelen (prodolzhenie)," *Kavkaz-Tsentr*, 25 March 2004, 18:47, www.kavkazcenter.net/russ/content/2005/03/25/31816.shtml.

88 See, for example, "Dzhamaat 'Shariat' soobshchayet o boevykh operatsiyakh v Dagestane," *Kavkaz-Tsentr*, 9 April 2005, 14:03:25, www.kavkazcenter.net/russ/content/2005/04/09/32537.shtml and "Dzhamaat 'Shariat': 'Allakh daet nam pravo otvechat van tem zhe,'" *Kavkaz-Tsentr*, 21 May 2005, 13:57:48, www.kavkazcenter.com/russ/content/2005/05/21/34188.shtml.

89 The idea of "bounded rationality" is that terrorist activity, such as suicide bombing, can be a rational act even though it is seemingly at variance with the standard definition of rationality based on the notion that sane individuals act on a calculation of what is in one's self-interest. The idea of bounded rationality envisages how an individual's theology or ideology changes his logic in making such a calculation. Thus, a suicide bomber or other form of martyr may see a greater interest, crudely put, in access to seventy-two virgins, God's protection of one's people, or eternal salvation. See Kenneth D. Wald, Adam I. Silverman, and Kevin S. Fridy, "Making Sense of Religion in Political Life," *Annual Review of Political Science*, Vol. 8, No. 3 (June 2005), pp. 121–43, and Robert A. Pape, "The Logic of Suicide Terrorism," *American Political Science Review*, Vol. 97, No. 3 (Aug. 2003), pp. 343–361.

90 "Zayavlenie Prezidenta ChRI A-Kh. Sadulaeva," Chechen.org, 15 May 2005, 09:07:43, www.chechen. Org/modules.php?name=News&file=article&sid=3406.

91 "M. Udugov: 'Vsyo, chto ne sootvetstvuet Shariatu nelegitimni.'"

92 Sageman, "Understanding Jihadi Networks," p. 2.

93 "Obrashchenie Prezidenta ChRI Sadulaeva k narodu."

94 Dmitrii Verkhoturov and Daniel-bek Tulenkov, "Islamskii vybor Sibiri," *Kavkaz-Tsentr*, 30 Dec. 2005, 16:00:43, www.kavkazcenter.net/russ/content/2005/12/30/40657.shtml.

95 Tumelty, "Chechnya: A Strategy for Independence."

96 "A.-Kh. Sadulaev: 'Rossiyna ne tolko uidyot iz Chechenii, no i ostavit ves Kavkaz.'"

97 "Shamil Basaev: 'U nas est mnogo, chto rasskazat' po Beslanu . . . ,'" *Kavkaz-Tsentr*, 31 Aug. 2005, 00:34:14, www.kavkazcenter.net/russ/content/2005/08/31/37225.shtml.

98 Gunaratna, *Inside al Qaeda*, pp. 29–30.

99 On the terrorist campaign that began in August 2005 in Ingushetiya see RFERL Newsline, Vol. 9, No. 154 (16 Aug. 2005); RFERL Newsline, Vol. 9, No. 159 (23 Aug. 2005); Regnum.ru, 26 Aug. 2005, www.regnum.ru; RFERL Newsline, Vol. 9, No. 162 (26 Aug. 2005); "Respublika Ingushetiya. V Nazrani u zdanii bolnitsy vzorvana bomba: est ubityie i ranenyie," Regions.ru, 22 Aug. 2005, 17:27, www.regions.ru/article/any/id/1869778.html; "V Nazrani unichtozheno i raneno 4 munafika," *Kavkaz-Tsentr*, 23 Aug. 2005, www.kavkazcenter.net/russ/content/2005/08/23/36959.shtml; "Two Bombs Today in Ingushetia," Retwa.org, 6 Sept. 2005, www.retwa.org/home/cfm?articleId=664;

"Roadside Bomb Targets Police in Ingushetia," Retwa.org, 14 Sept. 2005, www.retwa.org/home.cfm?articleId=790; 'Four Kilogram TNT Bomb Found on Busy Street in Nazran," Retwa.org, 07 Sept. 2005, www.retwa.org/home/cfm?articleId=671; "Bombs Target Cellular Tower and Investigating Police," Retwa.org (7 Sept. 2005), www.retwa.org/home.cfm?articleId=673; RFERL Newsline, Vol. 9, No. 172 12 Sept. 2005, "Terrorists' Bombing Marathon Rocks Ingushetia Today," Retwa.org, 16 Sept. 2005, www.retwa.org/home/cfm?articleId=810; "Yesterday's Terrorist Marathon Continued into the Night," Retwa.org, 17 Sept. 2005, www.retwa.org/ home.cfm?arcleId=817; and "Lightning Fast Ambush on Nazran Police at Roadside Café Kills Three," Retwa.org, 21 Sept. 2005, www.retwa.org/home.cfm?articleId=881.

100 Pryganov, *Vtorzhenie v Rossiyu*, pp. 294–296.

101 Klussmann, "The Beslan Aftermath."

102 "North Caucasus Commander Complains about Shortages of Special Equipment for Mountain Trainees," Retwa.org, 14 Sept 2005, www.retwa.org/home.cfm?articleId =793, citing RIA Novosti's Albina Olisayeva.

103 "Press-konferentsiya delegatsii ChRI v Evroparlamente," Kavkaz-Tsentr, 9 July 2005, 00:09:56, www.kavkazcenter.net/russ/content/2005/07/09/35918.shtml.

104 See Yu. A. Levada, "Sotsialno-politicheskaya situatsiya v Rossii v dekyabre 2005g.," Levada-Tsentr, 13 Dec. 2000, www.levada.ru/press/2000121300.html; "Press vypusk #37: O Chechne," Levada-Tsentr, 13 Dec. 2003, www.levada.ru/press/2003121301.html; "Sotsialno-politicheskaya situatsiya v Rossii v dekyabre 2005g.," *Levada-Tsentr*, 29 Dec. 2005, www.levada.ru/press/200122901.html.

105 Gunaratna, *Inside al Qaeda*, pp. 29–31.

106 "A.-Kh. Sadulaev: 'Obeshaem russkim voinu do pobednogo kontsa.'"

107 "M. Udugov: 'Rossiya dolzhana byt vzyata pod vneshnee upravlenie,'" Kavkaz-Tsentr, 20 June 2005, 00:23:42, www.kavkazcenter.net/russ/content/2005/06/20/35635.shtml.

108 "Sh. Basaev: 'Nikto ne mozhet zapretit mne to, chto razreshaet Bog,'" Kavkaz-Tsentr, 21 March 2005, 12:39:05, www.kavkazcenter.net/russ/content/2005/03/21/31642.shtml.

109 On the Russian side (with rare exceptions), grave crimes against humanity and the laws of war usually go unpunished.

110 For example, a group of some forty leading Islamic scholars convened in Lahore, Pakistan on 18 May 2005, and issued at fatwa stipulating that suicide-bombing attacks were only justified in the Kashmire, Palestine, Iraq, and Afghanistan theaters of jihad. "Islamic Scholars Say Suicide Attacks Justified in Palestine, Iraq, Not Pakistan," *Islamabad Khabrain* (Urdu), 19 May 2005, pp. 1, 5, posted on Ralph Davis's "Chechnya" Yahoo Listserve, 19 July 2005.

111 Sadulaev noted that like them the bodies of "the emirs Ruslam Khamzat Gelaev, Rasul Makasharipov, and many other mujahedin of the Caucasus, including also the Chechen fighters who participated in the diversionary acts at Dubrovka and in Beslan," were not returned by the Russian authorities to their families and peoples after their deaths but were interned in unmarked graves at special Russian installations. "Obrashchenie Prezidenta ChRI A.-Kh. Sadulaeva k chechenskomu narodu."

112 Kotenok, "Basaev atakovala Kokha."

113 See Pryganov, *Vtorzhenie v Rossiyu*, pp. 162–185.

114 See Larintseva, Samedov, and Allenova, "Koltso kavkazskoi natsionalnosti," and Rechkalov, "'Eti mestnyie rebyaty, no yavno pobyvali v Chechne.'" See also Samedov, "Prishol, uvidel, i ushol."

115 A possible accomplice of the terrorists, a sixteen-year-old Ingush girl, was arrested in the KBR where she was studying construction at a Nalchik high school. Interfax, 18 Nov. 2004, 08:34 GMT, and *The Moscow Times*, 19 Nov. 2004, p. 3.

116 Borisov, "Pervorot gotovili amiry"; RFERL Newsline, Vol. 5, No. 156 (17 Aug. 2001); and Andrew McGregor, "The Jamaat Movement in Kabardino-Balkaria," *Jamestown*

Foundation Terrorism Monitor, Vol. 3, Issue 7 (7 April 2005).
117 RFERL Newsline, Vol. 9, No. 47 (11 March 2005).
118 Kipkeev was killed after a female suicide bomber prematurely set off her explosives. Shuvayev was arrested on 14 December 2004. Itar-Tass, 15 Dec. 2005 and Aleksandr Zheglov, "Sotrudnik Minusta priyutil terroristov," *Kommersant-Daily,* 16 Dec. 2004, p. 5.
119 Andrei Sharov, "Seriinyie vzryvy so odnim zakazchikom," *Rossiiskaya gazeta,* 13 May 2005, p. 6.
120 Borisov, "Pervorot gotovili amiry" and RFERL Newsline, Vol. 5, No. 156 (17 Aug. 2001).
121 Larintseva, Samedov, and Allenova, "Koltso kavkazskoi natsionalnosti."
122 Rechkalov, "'Eti mestnyie rebyaty, no yavno pobyvali v Chechne.'" See also Samedov, "Prishol, uvidel, i ushol."
123 Vera Postnova, "Vakhkhabity pod nosom u Shaimieva," *Nezavisimaya gazeta,* 22 Sept. 2004, p. 4; Postnova, "Yeshchyo odno vzyatie Kazani," *Nezavisimaya gazeta,* 4 March 2004, p. 4; and Postnova, "Voiny dzhikhada s beregov Kamya," *Nezavisimaya gazeta,* 16 April 2002, p. 4.

CHAPTER FOUR

1 In the early Middle Ages parts of Dagestan were included in smaller entities such as Serir, Khaidak, Lakz, the Country of the Huns, and Derbent. From the sixteenth to the eighteenth centuries, before the beginning of tsarist colonization, it fell under the feudal Kaitag kingdom, Derbent, Kazikumukh, and Avar khanates, and Aksaev, Kostek, and Endirei principalities. Z. S. Arukhov, "Etnokonfessionalnaya struktura Dagestanskogo obshchestva i poiski etnicheskoi i religioznoi identichnosti v usloviakh politizatsii obshchestvennoi zhizni," gleaned from temporary internet posting and in the author's archive, p. 2.
2 Robert F. Baumann, *Russian-Soviet Unconventional Wars in the Caucasus, Central Asia, and Afghanistan,* Leavenworth Papers, No. 20 (Leavenworth, Kansas: Combat Studies Institute, 1993), pp. 1–7.
3 Ibid., p. 9.
4 Ibid., p. 33.
5 See Lewis, *Islam and the West,* pp. 39, 137.
6 Kobishchanov, "Muslumane Rossii, korennyie rossiiskie musulmane i russkie-musulmane," p. 99.
7 Arukhov, "Etnokonfessionalnaya struktura Dagestanskogo obshchestva," p. 1.
8 Seven other nationalities – Aguls, Tsakhurs, Armenians, Azeris, Ukrainians, Tatars, and Jewish Tats – make up the bulk of the remaining 8 percent of the population. Ware, Kisriev, Patzelt, and Roericht, "Stability in the Caucasus," pp. 12–23, at pp. 12–13.
9 Arukhov, "Etnokonfessionalnaya struktura Dagestanskogo obshchestva," p. 2.
10 Ibid., p. 6.
11 Ibid., pp. 2–3. See Robert Bruce Ware and Enver Kisriev, "Political Stability in Dagestan: Ethnic Parity and Religious Polarization," *Problems of Post-Communism,* Vol. 47, No. 2 (March-April 2000), pp. 23–33.
12 The highest rate was recorded among two of Dagestan's three least core ethnic identity groups, the Chechens and Azeris, and at a mere 11.3 and 10.3 percent, respectively. The survey showed that the first points of reference for identity among Dagestan's nine largest ethnic groups, except for Chechens and Russians/Cossacks, were Dagestan first (ranging from 69.2 percent among Azeris to 96.3 percent among Tabasarans) and Russia second (ranging from 69.2 percent among Azeris and 85.2 percent among Tabasarans). Ware, Kisriev, Patzelt, and Roericht, "Stability in the Caucasus," p. 15.

13 Enver Kisriev, "Islam v obshchestvenno-politicheskoi zhiznii Dagestana," in Kobishchanov, *Musulmane izmenyaushcheisya Rossii,* pp. 261–277, at p. 264.
14 Arukhov, "Etnokonfessionalnaya struktura Dagestanskogo obshchestva," p. 9.
15 Ibid.
16 Kisriev, "Islam v obshchestvenno-politicheskoi zhiznii Dagestana," pp. 264, 273.
17 Ibid.
18 Orthodox Christian Russians, Ukrainians, Belorussians, Georgians, and Armenians make up 8 percent of the population, and Tats or mountain Jews compose nearly 1 percent. Enver Kisriev, "Islam v obshchestvenno-politicheskoi zhiznii Dagestana," pp. 261–263.
19 Only 30 percent of respondents regarded inter-ethnic relations as stable, while 51 percent considered that there was inter-ethnic tension. Kobishchanov, "Muslumane Rossii, korennyie rossiiskie musulmane i russkie-musulmane," p. 99.
20 Dagestan's remedy for its ethnic complexities reflected the "consociationalism" suggested by both Lijphart and integrative mechanisms of the kind proposed by Horowitz and discussed in Chapter One. On Dagestan's formerly consociational political system, see Ware and Kisriev, "Political Stability in Dagestan"; Ware and Kisriev, "Ethnic Parity and Democratic Pluralism in Dagestan: A Consociational Approach," *Europe-Asia Studies,* Vol. 53, No. 1 (Jan. 2001); and Kisriev, "Russian Recentralization Arrives in the Republic of Dagestan: Implications for Institutional Integrity and Political Stability," *East European Constitutional Review,* Vol. 10, No. 1 (Winter 2001), pp. 68–75.
21 The system gave Dagestan's fourteen largest nationalities representation in the People's Assembly within at the most two percentage points of their respective shares of the population. Deputies were elected in 121 single-mandate electoral districts, where ethnicity (rather than political party lists and proportional representation as on the federal level and in some Russian regions) structured the voting options. Mono-ethnic "national electoral districts" elected a majority (sixty-six) of the assembly's deputies, while fifty-five districts were multi-ethnic. Although members of all nationalities in the national electoral districts were allowed to vote, they could only vote for candidates from a particular ethnic group. The national electoral districts were distributed among the nationalities as follows: Avar – 12, Kumyk – 12, Russian – 10, Dargin – 7, Tabasaran – 5, Azeri – 5, Lezgin – 4, Chechen – 4, Lak – 3, Tat – 2, Nogai – 1, and Tsakhur – 1. Residency requirements were abandoned, allowing candidates to run in ethnic districts where rules permitted them to stand or gave them a better chance of being elected. Most of the fifty-five multi-ethnic districts were largely confined to the isolated mono-ethnic mountainous regions, which needed no institutional engineering to provide representation for their ethnic groups. The system was amended prior to the March 1995 elections to the first People's Assembly to create special districts for professionals and women. The districts for women were dropped by 1999. Ware and Kisriev, "Political Stability in Dagestan," pp. 29–30. See also Olga Allenova, "Ne synom edinym," *Kommersant-Daily,* 21 Feb. 2006, p. 3.
22 The fourteen largest nationalities in Dagestan are as suggested in the previous note: Avars, Dargins, Kumyks, Russians, Tabasarans, Azeris, Lezgins, Chechens, Laks, Tats, Nogais, and Tsakhurs.
23 Ware and Kisriev, "Political Stability in Dagestan," p. 29.
24 Ibid., p. 28.
25 Sergei Markedonov, "Kto vladeet Dagestanom, tot vladeet Kavkazom," Kavkaz-Forum – Rekonstruktsiya Chechni, 7 July 2005, www.kavkaz-forum.ru/political/10245.html.
26 Such high-profile positions included the mayoralties of the capital Makhachkala, the central city of Kizilyurt, and the republic's third largest city Khasavyurt.
27 Of the more than 400,000 students in general education schools, more than 50 percent

study their native language, and 22 percent of schools conduct studies in indigenous languages. In the majority of schools there are rooms, small libraries, or museums dedicated to the native languages, cultures and traditions of the local ethnic groups. There are journals and newspapers published in the fourteen major ethnic groups' languages, and nearly 30 percent of these receive state funding. There are republic-wide newspapers in twelve different languages. Radio broadcasts exist in eleven languages. Despite these efforts, 9–15 percent of young people do not know their native language. Arukhov, "Etnokonfessionalnaya struktura Dagestanskogo obshchestva," pp. 6–7.

28 Ware and Kisriev, "Ethnic Parity and Democratic Pluralism in Dagestan" and "Russian Recentralization Arrives in the Republic of Dagestan."

29 Arukhov, "Etnokonfessionalnaya struktura Dagestanskogo obshchestva," p. 8, n. 1, and Markedonov, "Kto vladeet Dagestanom, tot vladeet Kavkazom."

30 Markedonov, "Kto vladeet Dagestanom, tot vladeet Kavkazom." Such violence has led to the deaths of several leading politicians, including the republic's finance minister, two People's Assembly deputies, one former and one sitting State Duma deputy, and two district administration heads.

31 Nabi Abdullaev, "Ambivalentnost tselei i sredstv reform Putina v regionalmom kontekste Dagestana," published on the internet, now in the author's archive, pp. 5, 10.

32 "'Rodina' – 0.6%' utochennye dannye po golosovaniyu v Dagestane," Regnum.ru, 8 Dec. 2005, 18:40:08, www.regnum.ru/news/191474.html.

33 Similarly, the prime minister's brother runs the wine producer "Dagvino." The former premier's son owns the textile company "DagTekstil." Dagestan's State Duma deputy, Gadzhi Makhachev, headed "DagNeft," the Dagestan affiliate of the Russian state oil company "RosNeft." Abdullaev, "Ambivalentnost tselei i sredstv reform Putina v regionalnom kontekste Dagestana," p. 5.

34 Official unemployment figures routinely understate the reality. Dagestan's economics minister Ali Nurmagomedov says the unemployment rate is 22 percent. Dagestani experts say it is closer to 33–40 percent. Valerii Vyzhutovich, "Terakty na konveire," *Rossiiskaya gazeta*, 7 July 2005, www.rg.ru/2005/07/07/dagestan-krizis.html. Others, such as Carnegie Moscow Center analyst Alexei Malashenko, cite figures of 60 percent youth unemployment. Shamil Zainalov, a Federation Council member, says that a youth unemployment rate of more than 30 percent in the republic is winning adherents for the religious extremists. Oliver Bullough, "Dagestan, A New Front in Russia's Caucasus War," Reuters, 8 July 2005.

35 A rank-and-file position with the police can cost applicants anywhere from $3,000–5000. Appointment as raion administration head cost one candidate's clan $150,000. Vyzhutovich, "Terakty na konveire."

36 Arukhov, "Etnokonfessionalnaya struktura Dagestanskogo obshchestva," p. 12.

37 Kisriev, "Islam v obshchestvenno-politicheskoi zhiznii Dagestana," p. 263.

38 Arukhov, "Etnokonfessionalnaya struktura Dagestanskogo obshchestva," p. 9.

39 Kisriev, "Islam v obshchestvenno-politicheskoi zhiznii Dagestana," p. 263.

40 Arukhov, "Etnokonfessionalnaya struktura Dagestanskogo obshchestva," p. 9.

41 K. M. Khanbabaev, "Etapi rasprostraneniya vakhkhabizma v Dagestane," *Alimy i uchenyie protiv vakhkhabizma* (Makhachkala, 2001), pp. 105–121.

42 Arukhov, "Etnokonfessionalnaya struktura Dagestanskogo obshchestva," p. 10.

43 Abdullaev, "Ambivalentnost tselei i sredstv reform Putina v regionalmom kontekste Dagestana," pp. 8–9.

44 Arukhov, "Etnokonfessionalnaya struktura Dagestanskogo obshchestva," p. 14.

45 Markedonov, "Kto vladeet Dagestanom, tot vladeet Kavkazom."

46 Kobishchanov, "Muslumane Rossii, korennyie rossiiskie musulmane i russkie-musulmane," p. 101.

47 Some regard Bagautdin and Aktaev to be less radical than more globally focused

jihadist Salafists. Both supported Dagestan's independence from Russia, but the former was more clearly an ally of Basaev. Kobishchanov, "Muslumane Rossii, korennyie rossiiskie musulmane i russkie-musulmane," pp. 101–102 and Kisriev, "Islam v obshchestvenno-politicheskoi zhiznii Dagestana," p. 270.

48 Kobishchanov, "Muslumane Rossii, korennyie rossiiskie musulmane i russkie-musulmane," p. 101.

49 *Nezavisimaya gazeta*, 22 July 1998, cited in Maksimenko, "Fundamentalizm i ekstremizm v Islame," p. 6.

50 Arukhov, "Etnokonfessionalnaya struktura Dagestanskogo obshchestva," pp. 10–11.

51 *Dagestanskaya pravda*, 22 Aug. 1998, cited in Maksimenko, "Fundamentalizm i ekstremizm v Islame," p. 6.

52 *Nezavisimaya gazeta*, 5 Sept. 1999.

53 Arukhov, "Etnokonfessionalnaya struktura Dagestanskogo obshchestva," pp. 10–11.

54 *Nezavisimaya gazeta*, 5 Sept. 1999. In 1998–99, two of the most popular books circulating in the republic were Tagayev's *Our Struggle or the Imam's Insurrection Army* and *Holy War or How to Become Immortal*. Markedonov, "Kto vladeet Dagestanom, tot vladeet Kavkazom."

55 By 1998–99, Kisriev estimates, the number of radical Islamists (in this case, largely Wahhabis) constituted as much as 2–3 percent of those adults in the republic "oriented on Islamic values"; that is, perhaps some twenty thousand of the republic's ethnic Muslims. Kisriev, "Islam v obshchestvenno-politicheskoi zhiznii Dagestana," p. 265. Secretary of Dagestan's Security Council Magomed Tolboev claimed there were twelve thousand "so-called Wahhabis" in numerous districts in the republic, and warned that they were supported by Basaev and Khattab, who had organized a force of some 2,500 jihadists. *Dagestanskaya pravda*, 22 Aug. 1998, cited in Maksimenko, "Fundamentalizm i ekstremizm v Islame," p. 7. Others estimate that the number of Wahhabis in Dagestan has ranged from four to ten thousand over the years. Alexei Malashenko, "The Islamic Factor in Russia," *New Europe Review*, Nov. 2004, www.neweuropereview.com/English/english-malashenko.cfm.

56 The specific villages include: Kirovaul, Komsomolets, Staroe and Novoe Miatli in Khasavyurt raion; Pervomaisk, Mutsalaul, Terechnoe, Sovetskoe in Kazbek raion; Inchkha and Gertma villages in Buinaksk raion; in Karamakhi, Chabanmakhi, Kadar, Buglen in Gubin raion; Kudaly and Sogratl in Karabudakhkent raion; Gubden and Manas in Derebent; and Belidzhi, Zhpedzh, and Khushet in Makhachkala. Kisriev, "Islam v obshchestvenno-politicheskoi zhiznii Dagestana," p. 265.

57 Ibid., pp. 267–268.

58 Ibid., pp. 268–270.

59 Maksimenko, "Fundamentalizm i ekstremizm v Islame," p. 8.

60 Allowed two responses, strong majorities within the surveyed ethnic groups, excluding the Chechens, listed their most important identity references as being first of all Dagestan (ranging from 59.2 percent among Russians and Cossacks to 96.3 percent among Tabasarans, with all the six remaining Muslim ethnic groups above 69 percent) and second Russia (ranging from 52.7 percent among Avars to 88.7 percent among Russians and Cossacks, with all the six remaining ethnic Muslim groups again above 69 percent). The Chechens' low allegiance to Dagestan and Russia, which was reflected in their responses in the same survey at 47.2 and 22.6 percent, respectively, suggests one source from which Basaev and Khattab hoped to receive support. Similarly, allowed two answers, the overwhelming majority of each of Dagestan's main ethnic groups (63.7 percent overall), except for the Chechens, responded that they would trust the Russian leadership in a crisis (more than Dagestan's leadership, party and ethnic movement leaders, religious leaders, and oneself), ranging from 61.2 percent of Kumyks to 81.5 percent of Tabasarans. Finally, the overwhelming majority of each of Dagestan's nine largest ethnic groups, again except for the Chechens, supported closer

relations with Russia. Ware, Kisriev, Patzelt, and Roericht, "Stability in the Caucasus," pp. 14–22.

61 Georgii M. Derluguian, *Bourdieu's Secret Admirer in the Caucasus: A World System Biography* (Chicago: Chicago University Press, 2005), p. 50.

62 Ibid.

63 Kisriev, "Islam v obshchestvenno-politicheskoi zhiznii Dagestana," pp. 271–276.

64 Ware, Kisriev, Patzelt, and Roericht, "Stability in the Caucasus," pp. 15 and 17.

65 Although Dagestan retained the right to appoint the judges of Dagestan's Constitutional Court and justices of the peace, it lost the power of appointment of judges to the republic's Supreme Court and district and municipal courts, whom it now only confirms after nomination by federal bodies. Other amendments subordinated all of the republic's courts to the federal court system by establishing the supremacy of federal court decisions over republican and local court ones. Ware and Kisriev, "Russian Recentralization Arrives in the Republic of Dagestan," pp. 72–73.

66 See Hahn, "Russian Federalism under Putin"; Hahn, "The Impact of Putin's Federative Reforms on Democratization in Russia"; Hahn, "Putin's Federal Reforms" and Kahn, *Federalism, Democratization, and the Rule of Law in Russia.*

67 By May 2000, the Russian Constitutional Court, which had already begun to hear the appeal of a private Dagestan citizen whose brief challenged the constitutionality of the ethnic districts for elections to local councils and to the People's Assembly, appeared to be about to rule against Dagestan's system when Yaraliev requested a delay in the proceedings. The People's Assembly then scrambled to amend the republic's constitution and election laws introducing ethnically open multi-mandate electoral districts. Ballots listed candidates by ethnic category, and a specific number of candidates from each of various ethnic categories was to be elected. Ware and Kisriev, "Russian Recentralization Arrives in the Republic of Dagestan," p. 71.

68 RFERL Newsline, Vol. 9, No. 149 (9 Aug. 2005).

69 In particular, the changes "considerably weaken the influence of the deputies of parliament. Their number is cut to seventy-two. Some people's elected representatives fear they will not get into the new parliament. So they are seeking to find themselves in the ranks of the opposition." Aleksandr Bezmenov, "Kampagn protiv Makhachkaly ne budet," *Rossiyskaya gazeta*, 18 Aug. 2004, pp. 1, 3.

70 Ivan Preobrazhenskii, "Vybory po-Dagestanskii," Politkom.ru, 17 March 2003, www.politkom.ru.

71 Robert Bruce Ware, "The Caucasian Vortex," RFERL Newsline, Vol. 8, No. 163 (26 Aug. 2004).

72 Bezmenov: "Kampagn protiv Makhachkaly ne budet," pp. 1, 3. Besides Umakhanov, Duma deputy Gadzhi Makhachev, who may have his own presidential ambitions, and Nafta-Moskva company head Suleiman Kemirov are considered part of an Avar–Lezgin alliance in opposition to Magomedov and the Dargins. Kemirov financed Makhachev's election campaign in December 2003. Makhachev subtly supported Umakhanov while appearing to take a middle position in his confrontation with Dagestan chairman Magomedov. Vinogradov, Ilichev, and Radzhanov, "Mer poshol protiv prezidenta." Makhachev resembles a kind of Dagestani Ramzan Kadyrov, with his own business interests and armed detachments – one of Dagestan's armed so-called "interbrigades" that have contributed to the criminal, inter-ethnic, and Islamist violence that has mounted under Putin. The emergence of the "interbrigades" was a consequence of the 1999 Basaev-Khattab incursion, when the Dagestan authorities handed out weapons to detachments of volunteers often under the control of ethnic leaders. Afterward, the People's Assembly passed a law which allowed Dagestan citizens to own combat weapons provided they were registered. Subsequently, "interbrigades" were organized for the purpose of protecting the republic's borders and keeping public order. They were subordinated to city and raion administration

heads, who distributed positions within the brigades to members of their families, clans, jamaats, and ethnic groups. Abdullaev, "Ambivalentnost tselei i sredstv reform Putina v regionalmom kontekste Dagestana," p. 6.

73 Maria Bondarenko, "Khasavyurt vstal na zashchitu mera," *Nezavisimaya gazeta,* 23 Aug. 2004, p. 2.

74 Bondarenko, "Khasavyurt vstal na zashchitu mera."

75 Also, Umakhanov's victory in the 6 April 1997 mayoral elections was challenged by ethnic Kumyks, led by Dagestan People's Assembly deputy Abdulla Khasbulatov, and Akin-Chechens, who began to hold daily demonstrations in front of the City Council building and convened a congress which demanded fresh elections. If their demands were not met, they threatened a campaign of civil disobedience and a referendum on the possible secession of Khasavyurt and its unification with then de facto independent Chechnya. The developing uprising was averted when a commission from Makhachkala including members of Dagestan's State Council, Election Commission, and Supreme Court arrived in the city and confirmed the election results and Umakhanov's victory. Kobishchanov, "Muslumane Rossii, korennyie rossiiskie musulmane i russkie-musulmane," p. 100.

76 Magomed Isaev, "Meropresechenie," *Kommersant,* 18 Aug. 2004, p. 1. The Dagestan MVD chief Aldigerei Magomedtagirov then fired Khasavyurt's MVD (GOVD) municipal branch chief Omar Tupaliev and four of his deputies, whereupon the Khasavyurt MVD declared that it would no longer be subordinated to the republican MVD. Magomed Isaev, "Oppozitsiya vnutrennyhk del," *Kommersant,* 17 Aug. 2004, p. 3; Vlad Trifonov and Magomed Isaev, "Militsionery Khasavyurta pereshol na avtonomnyi rezhim," *Kommersant,* 19 Aug. 2004, p. 3; and Mikhail Vinogradov, Goergii Ilichev, and Gadzhimurad Radzhanov, "Mer poshol protiv prezidenta," *Izvestiya,* 17 Aug. 2004, http://main.izvestia.ru/conflict/17-08-04/article277496.

77 Umakhanov also tried to spread the base of his opposition to include Kizlyar and Tsumadin raions, but the demonstrations that were expected did not materialize. "Magomedov nanosit otvetnyi udar," *Kavkaz-Tsentr,* 18 Aug. 2004, 01:48:41, www.kavkazcenter.net/russ/content/2004/08/18/24843.shtml. Gadzhimurad Radzhabov, "Obstanovka v Khasavyurte ne sootvetsvuet konstitutsii," *Izvestiya,* 18 Aug. 2004, http://main.izvestia.ru/conflict/18-08-04/article281538.

78 For Amirov's article in support of Magomedov and in condemnation of Umakhanov see "There Should Be No Forgiveness," *Dagestanskaya pravda,* 18 Aug. 2004.

79 The Southern FO presidential envoy Vladimir Yakovlev characterized Umakhanov's 29 July Khasavyurt demonstration as "not constitutional," opening the way for prosecutors to begin legal proceedings against him. *Dagestanskaya pravda,* 20 Aug. 2004. The Russian government's official daily reported in support of Magomedov that State Council members told him that if he was not involved in Gamidov's assassination, he should appoint the late finance minister's brother to replace him, which Magomedov did. It also implied that Umakhanov's move was "a manifestation of extremism" and was part and parcel of "extremist forces" challenging Magomedov. See Timofei Borisov, "Burnyi avgust," *Rossiiskaya gazeta,* 18 Aug. 2004, www.rg.ru.

80 See the interview with Mayor Umakhanov in *Gazeta,* 18 Aug. 2004, p. 2.

81 Aleksandr Bezmenov: "Kampagn protiv Makhachkaly ne budet," *Rossiyskaya gazeta,* 18 Aug. 2004, pp. 1, 3.

82 Natalya Serova, "War for Dagestan Legacy," *Politkom,* 18 Aug. 2004, www.politkom.ru.

83 Akhmad Ichkeriiskii, "Dagestan likhoradit," *Kavkaz-Tsentr,* 20 Aug. 2004 www.kavkazcenter.net/ russ/content/2004/08/20/24932.shtml.

84 "Magomedov nanosit otvetnyi udar," *Kavkaz-Tsentr,* 18 Aug. 2004, 01:48:41, www.kavkazcenter. net/russ/content/2004/08/18/24843.shtml.

85 Guriya Murklinskaya, "Look Back in Anger," *Dagenstanskaya pravda,* 18 Aug. 2004.

86 RFERL Newsline, Vol. 9, No. 150 (10 Aug. 2005).
87 Kisriev, "Islam v obshchestvenno-politicheskoi zhiznii Dagestana," pp. 269, 271.
88 "Russian Analyst Sees 'Total Crisis of Power' in Dagestan," Interfax (Moscow), 7 July 2005.
89 Ruslan Makhmedov, "After Beslan: Slow Days in Dagestan," *Sobaka*, 23 Oct. 2004.
90 Robert Bruce Ware, "Renewed Terrorist Offensive in Dagestan," unpublished paper.
91 "Saving Captain Bekbulatov," *Novoye delo*, 3 Oct. 2003, Ralph Davis "Chechnya" Listserve, 20 Oct. 2003.
92 Ibid.
93 Rumors were rife that Basaev was in Dagestan during a good part of these combat jamaats' campaign of terror in 2004–2005. In early May 2005, the pro-Moscow Chechnya government deputy prime minister Ramzan Kadyrov reported that Basaev was hiding in Dagestan, though he soon retracted that statement, noting that he had based his claim on rumors, not hard data. Petrovskiy, "'Shariat' Rages in Dagestan."
94 "Dzhamaat 'Shariat': 'Nashi ryady postoyanno uvelichivaetsya," *Kavkaz-Tsentr*, 25 Aug. 2005, 00:40:19, www.kavkazcenter.net/russ/content/2005/08/25/37022.shtml.
95 "Dagestani Rebel Leader Gunned Down," *ISN Security Watch*, 7 July 2005.
96 Itar-Tass, 17 Jan. 2005, 09:59 GMT.
97 "Respublika Dagestan. Pokusheniyana mera Buinaksa priznano teraktom," Regions.ru, 21 Oct. 2004, 11:16, www.regions.ru, and "Respublika Dagestan. Ne zadolgo do pokusheniya glava Buinaksa provyolryad vstrech," Regions.ru, 21 Oct. 2004, 11:27, www.regions.ru.
98 The five were Zaur Bekbulatov, an investigative officer of the Department for combatting Criminal Extremism and Terrorism, deputy chief of the investigations department Shamil Sharudinov, officers of the department Major Tagir Stambulov and Lieutenant Mukhtarpasha Bikeyev, and patrol officer Vagid Esuyev.
99 "Policemen Were Killed As If to Order Russia's Deputy General Prosecutor Suspects", *Kommersant*, 1 Oct. 2003.
100 Ware, "Renewed Terrorist Offensive in Dagestan."
101 Andrei Riskin, "Vakhkhabity pribirayut k rukam yu Rossii," *Nezavisimaya gazeta*, 4 Feb. 2005, p. 4.
102 On 5 April, a section of the pipeline was blown up near the village of Uitash and a nearby section of the Baku–Novorossiisk oil pipeline was damaged. The former runs through Dagestan from the North Ossetiyan town of Mozdok exporting gas to Azerbaijan through the city of Gazimagomed. The latter exports Azeri oil to Europe. Exports of the Dagestani gas company KaspiiskGazProm ceased for several days, as did Azeri oil exports. On 24 May and 8 December, the Mozdok–Gazimagomed pipeline was damaged again. Andrei Smirnov, "Chechen Rebels Are Trying to Damage Russia's Oil-and-Gas Pipeline System," The Jamestown Foundation *Chechen Weekly*, Vol. 5, Issue 46 (15 Dec. 2004).
103 Riskin, "Vakhkhabity pribirayut k rukam yu Rossii," p. 4.
104 "Dagestani Rebel Leader Gunned Down," *ISN Security Watch*, 7 July 2005.
105 Riskin, "Vakhkhabity pribirayut k rukam yu Rossii" and Sergei Migalin, "Boeviki v Dagestane prodolzhayut otstrel silovikov," *Nezavisimaya gazeta*, 4 Feb. 2005, p. 4.
106 Milrad Fatullaev, "Privychka k smerti," *Nezavisimaya gazeta*, 12 May 2005, p. 4.
107 "Dagestan prisyagnul Sheiku Abdul-Khalimu," *Kavkaz-Tsentr*, 14 March 2005, www.kavkazcenter.net/ russ/content/2005/03/14/32304.shtml.
108 Ibid.
109 "Dzhamaat 'Shariat': 'Modzhakhedy budut napravleny v Moskvu,'" *Kavkaz-Tsentr*, 2 July 2005, 00:38:56, www. kavkazcenter.net/ russ/content/2005/07/02/35721.shtml.
110 Fatullaev, "Privychka k smerti," p. 4.
111 "Dzhamaat 'Shariat' soobshchayet o boevykh operatsiyakh v Dagestane."
112 "Dzhamaat 'Shariat': 'Zhdite, i my s vami budem zhdat. . . ,'" *Kavkaz-Tsentr*, 15 July

2005, 11:34:35, www.kavkazcenter.net/russ/content/2005/07/15/36121.shtml.
113 "'Ya vlast ne menyayu, dlya etogo est prezident Rossii,'" *Vremya novostei*, 21 June 2005, www.vremya.ru/2005/108/4/127896.html.
114 See, for example, "Dzhamaat 'Shariat' soobshchayet o boevykh operatsiyakh v Dagestane"; "Dzhamaat Dagestana: 'Prokuratura sgorela vmeste c prokuraturami'"; and "Dzhamaat 'Shariat': 'Provedena uspeshnaya spetsoperatsiya,'" *Kavkaz-Tsentr*, 22 April 2005, 15:51:50, www.kavkazcenter.net/russ/content/2005/04/ 22/33080.shtml.
115 "Dzhamaat 'Shariat': 'Provedena uspeshnaya spetsoperatsiya.'"
116 This is followed directly by an oft-quoted passage from the Koran cited elsewhere here. "Dzhamaat 'Shariat': 'Allakh daet nam pravo otvechat vam tem zhe,'" *Kavkaz-Tsentr*, 21 May 2005, 13:57:48, www.kavkazcenter.com/russ/content/2005/05/21/34188.shtml.
117 "Dzhamaat 'Shariat': 'Pobeda ili Rai! Iz dvukh luchshee!'" *Kavkaz-Tsentr*, 12 July 2005, 03:03:02, www.kavkazcenter.net/russ/content/2005/07/12/36015.shtml.
118 "Dzhamaat 'Shariat': 'Zhdite, i my s vami budem zhdat. . . .'"
119 "Dzhamaat 'Shariat' soobshchayet o boevykh operatsiyakh v Dagestane."
120 "Dzhamaat 'Shariat': 'Zhdite, i my s vami budem zhdat. . . .'"
121 "Dzhamaat 'Shariat' soobshchayet o boevykh operatsiyakh v Dagestane."
122 See the transcript of a videotape by Shariah amir Makasharipov's successor Murad Lakhiyalov and his naib Yasin Rasulov "'My obrashchaemsya ko vsem tem, kto uveroval,'" *Kavkaz-Tsentr*, 21 Nov. 2005, 00:50:57, www.kavkazcenter.com/russ/content/2005/11/21/39551.shtml.
123 See the comments of political scientist Giyar Teimurin in Fatullaev, "Privychka k smerti."
124 "Dzhamaat 'Shariat': 'Allakh daet nam pravo otvechat vam tem zhe.'"
125 "Dzhamaat Dagestana: 'Prokuratura sgorela vmeste c prokuraturami'.'"
126 For example, in a 21 August 2005 interview with the Peshawar-based Afghan Islamic Press agency in which he announced that the Taliban would attack candidates whom it deems "enemies of Islam" and otherwise try to obstruct the elections but would not attack polling stations during Afghanistan's 18 September national and provincial parliamentary elections campaign, neo-Taliban leader mufti Latifullah Hakimi noted: "Even if a candidate, who is the *enemy of Islam*, fails in the elections, we will kill him on charges of being an *enemy of Islam and of the homeland*" (my emphases). He also claimed, like Chechnya's Islamists and its allies, that Taliban forces "have always tried not to hurt civilians." RFERL Newsline, Vol. 9, No. 158 (22 Aug. 2005).
127 "'My obrashchaemsya ko vsem tem, kto uveroval.'"
128 "Dzhamaat Dagestana: 'Prokuratura sgorela vmeste c prokuraturami.'"
129 Ibid.
130 "Dzhamaat 'Shariat': 'Allakh daet nam pravo otvechat vam tem zhe.'"
131 "Dzhamaat 'Shariat' soobshchayet o boevykh operatsiyakh v Dagestane."
132 "Dzhamaat 'Shariat': 'Provedena uspeshnaya spetsoperatsiya.'" See also "Dzhamaat 'Shariat': 'Allakh daet nam pravo otvechat vam tem zhe.'"
133 "Naselenie Dagestana podderzhivaey deistviya modzhakhedov," *Kavkaz-Tsentr*, 8 June 2005, 20:01:39, www.kavkazcenter.net/russ/content/2005/06/08/34863.shtml.
134 Fatullaev, "Privychka k smerti."
135 Ibid.
136 One writer reported that a neighbor came back from a Cossack village to the north with a swollen jaw and said it had come from the village elder's son. This piece of anecdotal evidence fueled rumors that non-Muslims or the "federals" "would do what they did to him to all of us." Makhmedov, "After Beslan: Slow Days in Dagestan."
137 Itar-Tass, 2 Nov. 2004.
138 Dobaev, "Terroristicheskie gruppirovki na Yuge Rossii: novyie tendentsii."
139 Marat Biygishev, "Battle Hits Dagestan Capital," Institute for War and Peace

Reporting [IWPR hereafter] Caucasus Reporting Service, No. 270, 19 Jan. 2005. Another source claims that terrorism in Dagestan in 2004 took sixteen lives and wounded thirty-nine. Dobaev, "Terroristicheskie gruppirovki na Yuge Rossii: novyie tendentsii."

140 Interfax (Moscow), 17 Jan. 2005, 09:35 GMT.

141 "Okupanty priznayut uspekhi modzhakhedov Dagestana," *Kavkaz-Tsentr*, 25 May 2005, 22:35:46, www.kavkazcenter.net/russ/content/2005/05/26/34379.shtml.

142 Andrei Riskin, "V Dagestane nashli strelochnikov," *Nezavisimaya gazeta*, 5 July 2005, p. 4. Another source claims some thirty police officers had been killed in eighty "killings and bomb attacks." RFERL Newsline, Vol. 9, No. 130 (13 July 2005).

143 Salamu Talkhigov, "Svin'y khrukayut, a Dzhikhad idyot!," *Kavkaz-Tsentr*, 5 July 2005, 11:49:16, www.kavkazcenter.com/russ/content/2005/07/05/35815.shtml.

144 Dobaev, "Terroristicheskie gruppirovki na Yuge Rossii: novyie tendentsii."

145 Oleg Petrovskiy, "'Shariat' Rages in Dagestan," Utro.ru, 25 May 2005, www.utro.ru.

146 "Dzhamaat Dagestana: 'Prokuratura sgorela vmeste c prokuraturami'"; "Seriya vzryvov v Makhachkale," Regions.ru, 13 April 2005, 12:49, www.regions.ru/article/any/id/1786050.html; and Petrovskiy, "'Shariat' Rages in Dagestan."

147 "Dzhamaat 'Shariat': 'Provedena uspeshnaya spetsoperatsiya.'"

148 Abdul Suleimanov, "Pokushchenie na militsionerov," *Dagestanskaya pravda*, 22 Aug. 2005, 20:00, www.dagpravda.ru/news.htm#2929.

149 "Dzhamaat Dagestana: 'Prokuratura sgorela vmeste c prokuraturami.'"

150 Two of the "ideologists," Sirazhudin Ramazanov and Adallo Aliev, were given suspended sentences and allowed to return home. "Razryvnaya dolzhnost," *Kommersant*, 21 May 2005, p. 1.

151 Shariah's posting also claimed that Arukhov was a "KGB colonel" recruited by the FSB during his studies at Moscow State University. "Dzhamaat 'Shariat': 'Allakh daet nam pravo otvechat vam tem zhe.'"

152 Murphy, "Makhachkala's War on Terror – A Week in a City under Siege."

153 "Razryvnaya dolzhnost."

154 Ruslan Bashirov, "Predstoyashee leto obeshaet byt zharkim," *Kavkaz-Tsentr*, 4 June 2005, www.kavkazcenter.com/russ/content/2005/06/04/34701.shtml.

155 "Dzhamaat 'Shariat': 'Territoriya Dzhikhada rasshiraetesya."

156 As explained at the beginning of the chapter, it has renamed Makhachkala as Shamilkala and returned Buinaksk its nineteenth-century name, Temirkhan-Shura, and even renamed streets in Makhachkala. Gadzhiev Street was renamed Muslim Street, Lenin Street – Vakkas Street, and Reduktornyi settlement – Zeid settlement after the death of its emir Makasharipov with two of his fellow mujahedin in July 2005. "Dzhamaat 'Shariat': 'Pobeda ili Rai! Iz dvukh luchshee!'"

157 Oliver Bullough, "Dagestan, A New Front in Russia's Caucasus War," Reuters, 8 July 2005.

158 Vyzhutovich, "Terakty na konveiere."

159 Vladimir Mukhin, "Severnyi Kavkaz gotovitsya k bolshoi voine," *Nezavisimaya gazeta*, 13 July 2005, p. 1.

160 See the interview with Dagestan MVD chief Aldigirei Magomedtagirov in "'Ya vlast ne menyayu, dlya etogo est prezident Rossii.'" See also Grani.ru, 8 June 2005 and Newsru.com, 12 June 2005, cited, in Andrei Smirnov and Mikhail Roshchin, "Popular Support Increases for Dagestan Rebels," Jamestown Foundation *Eurasia Daily Monitor*, Vol. 2, No. 122 (23 June 2005).

161 Vyzhutovich, "Terakty na konveire."

162 RFERL Newsline, Vol. 9, No. 132 (15 July 2005).

163 Andrei Riskin, "Ne pomogaet dazhe chrezvychaika," *Nezavisimaya gazeta*, 9 June 2005, p. 1.

164 See "V Makhchkale vzorvano tri gruzovika s okkupanyami," Kavkaz-Tsentr, 1 July

2005, 17:07:57, www.kavkazcenter.net/russ/content/2005/07/01/35707.shtml; "Chislo ranenykh okkupantov v Makhachkale vozroslo do 27"; and Vyacheslav Izmailov, "Terakt v Makhachale," *Novaya gazeta*, No. 47, 4 July 2005, http://2005. novayagazeta.ru/nomer/2005/47n/n47n-s02.shtml. *Kavkaz-Tsentr* attributed the attack to Shariat. Musa Stoun, "Burya dzhikhad usilivaetsya," *Kavkaz-Tsentr*, 2 July 2005, 00:04:15, www.kavkazcenter.com/russ/content/2005/07/02/35720.shtml.

165 Murphy, "Makhachkala's War on Terror."

166 Ibid.

167 "Dagestani Rebel Leader Gunned Down," *ISN Security Watch*, 7 July 2005.

168 See "Russkie soobshchaut o gibeli Amira Rasula Makasharipova," *Kavkaz-Tsentr*, 6 July 2005, 21:24:23, www.kavkazcenter.com/russ/content/2005/07/06/35867.shtml. See also "Boi v Shamilkale zavershilsya. Modzhakhedy prorvali koltso otsepleniya," Kavkaz-Tsentr, 6 July 2005, 11:41:23, www.kavkazcenter.com/russ/content/ 2005/07/06/35852.shtml; "Vozroslo chislo ranennykh v Shamilkhale promoskovskikh militsionerov," Kavkaz-Tsentr, 6 July 2005, 13:27:02, www.kavkazcenter.com/ russ/content/2005/07/06/35854.shtml; and "Novye dannye o boe v Shamilkale (byvshaya Makhachkala)," Kavkaz-Tsentr, 6 July 2005, 14:16:20, www. kavkazcenter.com/russ/content/2005/07/06/ 35855.shtml.

169 In Kaspiisk, a Dagestani special quick reaction (SOBR) unit led by Commander Arzulum Ilyasov moved to detain fifty-year-old radical emir Magomedzagir Akayev in his home during morning prayers. Ilyasov and two SOBR offices were killed. Akayev was also killed, and two of his fighters captured. Marat Biygishev, "Battle Hits Dagestan Capital," Institute of War and Peace Reporting Caucasus Reporting Service, No. 270, 19 Jan. 2005 and Interfax, Moscow, 17 Jan. 2005, 09:35 GMT.

170 Petrovskiy, "'Shariat' Rages in Dagestan."

171 Biygishev, "Battle Hits Dagestan Capital."

172 "Dzhamaat 'Shariat': 'Modzhakhedy budut napravleny v Moskvu.'"

173 Ibid.

174 "Dzhamaat 'Shariat': 'Pobeda ili Rai! Iz dvukh luchshee!'"

175 "Dzhamaat 'Shariat': 'Nashi ryady postoyanno uvelichivaetsya."

176 "Dzhamaat 'Shariat': 'Zhdite, i my s vami budem zhdat . . . ."

177 Aleksandr Khinshtein, "Prodaem Kavkaz. Torg umesten – Sensatsionnyi doklad Kozaka," *Moskovskii Komsomolets*, 16 June 2005, www.mk.ru/numbers/1682/article55887.htm.

CHAPTER FIVE

1 This chapter is adapted and updated from my article previously published as Gordon M. Hahn, "The Rise of Islamist Extremism in Kabardino-Balkariya" *Demokratizatsiya*, Vol. 13, No. 4 (Fall 2005), pp. 543–594.

2 The Circassians are sometimes referred to as the Adygei-Abkhazian or Adygei-Cherkess ethnic group. The designation "Circassian" is the usual English nomenclature. The Circassians include not only the Kabardins, Adygeis, and Cherkess, but also the Abkhaz (largely located in Georgia), Shapsugs and Abazins as well. Shapsug raion in Krasnodar Krai can also be regarded as part of the Circassians' traditional homeland.

3 There is a small community of Christian Kabardins in Mozdok and vicinity in North Ossetiya. Bennigsen and Wimbush, *Muslims of the Soviet Empire*, p. 199.

4 On 30 August 2001, for example, the official Russian news service, Interfax, reported that the leaders and people of Kabardino-Balkariya were marking the eightieth anniversary of their "statehood" granted by the then young Soviet regime and the 444th anniversary of their 1557 "union" with Russia. RFERL Newsline, Vol. 5, No. 166 (31 Aug. 2001).

5 Although Kabardinian society included tribal, clan, and feudal features, its pivotal characteristic was a nine-class structure, ranging from princes to slaves. Bennigsen and Wimbush, *Muslims of the Soviet Empire*, p. 195.

6 Bilal Laipanov, "Islam v istorii i samosoznanii karachaevskogo naroda," in M. V. Iordan, R. G. Kuzeev, and S. M. Chervonnaya, eds., *Islam v Evrazaii: sovremennye etnicheskie i esteticheskie kontseptsii sunnitskogo Islam, ikh transformatsiya v massovom soznanii i vyrazhenie v iskusstve musulmankskikh narodov Rossii* (Moscow: Progress-Traditsiya, 2001), pp. 170–198, at pp. 183–184.

7 "Mezhnatsionalnyie konflikty glavnaya ugroza edinstvu," *Obozrevatel – Rossiya segodnya: Realnyi shans*, www.nasledie.ru/oboz/N21-24_94/013.htm.

8 In addition to the three main Adygei-Abkhazian or Circassian peoples and the Abazins, the Iber-Caucasian linguistic group includes the Chechens, Avars, Lezgins, Dargins, Ingush, Laks, Tabasarans, Rutuls, Tsakhurs, and Aguls. Bennigsen and Wimbush, *Muslims of the Soviet Empire*, pp. 148–149.

9 "Cherkess" is a name of Turkish origin for the three groups. "Kabard" is not an ethnic but a local geographical designation. The traditional English-language designation is "Circassian." Bennigsen and Wimbush, *Muslims of the Soviet Empire*, pp. 190, 197–198.

10 On this and the obstacles precluding the success of any such Adygei national project, see Kobishchanov, "Musulmane Rossii, korennye rossiiskie musulmane i russkie-musumane," p. 96.

11 The prospects for pan-Circassian nationalism, according to some, are constrained by four factors: (1) the absence for some 135 years of an integrated territory populated by the Circassian tribes and their separation into enclaves; (2) the significant concentration of non-Circassian populations on the territories which tie Circassian areas in the KBR, KChR, and Adygeya together; (3) the low birth rates of the Circassian tribes compared to other neighboring ethnic Muslim groups; and (4) the weakness of the Circassian diaspora's movement supporting return to the homeland. Ibid.

12 Bennigsen and Wimbush, *Muslims of the Soviet Empire*, pp. 201–202.

13 Kobishchanov, "Musulmane Rossii, korennye rossiiskie musulmane i russkie-musulmane," pp. 72–74, and Bennigsen and Wimbush, *Muslims of the Soviet Empire*, p. 148. The Balkars (and Karachais) are descendants of the Kuban Bulgars and Kypchak (Polovtsian) tribes who moved up the Caucasian mountains to avoid the Mongol invasion and became vassals of the Kabardins and Adygeis in the fifteenth century. The Balkar and Karachai peoples formed the backbone of the Alan state (Alania is the Ossetiyans' preferred title for the Republic of North Ossetiya) which emerged and expanded in the North Caucasus from the fifth to the thirteenth centuries and was made up of two basic ethno-cultural components: the Karachai-Balkar and Osset-Digor. Laipanov, "Islam v istorii i samosoznanii karachaevskogo naroda," p. 174.

14 Bennigsen and Wimbush, *Muslims of the Soviet Empire*, pp. 201–204.

15 "V KBR pominayut zhertv depotatsii Balkarskogo naroda," Islam.ru, 9 March 2005, www.islam.ru/ press/rus/2005-03-09/#7540.

16 Rajan Menon, "Russia's Quagmire: On Ending the Standoff in Chechnya," *Boston Review*, Summer 2004, www.bostonreview.net.

17 Aleksandr Tsipko, "The Weaknesses and Shortcomings of Putin's State Reforms," *The Jamestown Foundation Prism*, Vol. VI, Issue 10 (Oct. 2000).

18 Bennigsen and Wimbush, *Muslims of the Soviet Empire*, pp. 159, 202.

19 Ibid., p. 7.

20 Kobishchanov, "Musulmane Rossii, korennye rossiiskie musul'mane i russkie-musulmane," pp. 251–253.

21 "Sovet stareishin Verkhnei Balkarii vospitaet molodezh v dukhe Islama," Islam.ru, 25 March 2005, www.islam.ru/press/rus/2005-03-25/#7718.

22 Bennigsen and Wimbush, *Muslims of the Soviet Empire*, p. 159.

23 Ibid., p. 199.

24 Kobishchanov, "Musulmane Rossii, korennye rossiiskie musulmane i russkie-musulmane," pp. 255–56, and Hunter, *Islam in Russia*, p. 65.

25 Oleg Guseinov, "Stroitestvo khrama Marii Magdaliny priostanovlena iz-za otsutsviya sredstv," *Gazeta yuga*, 21 April 2005, www.gazetayuga.ru/archive/2005/16.htm.

26 Kobishchanov, "Musulmane Rossii, korennye rossiiskie musulmane i russkie-musulmane," pp. 254–256.

27 Ibid., p. 259.

28 Irina L. Babich, "Ideologicheskii fundament vozrozhdeniya obychnogo i musulmanskogo prava v Kabardino-Balkarii," IslaminKBR.ru, www.islaminkbr.com/kbr/in.php?mode=004.

29 Liz Fuller, "Balkars Launch New Campaign for Their Own Republic," *RFERL Russian Political Weekly*, Vol. 5, No. 22 (3 June 2005).

30 This has been true for decades. In three censuses of 1959, 1970, and 1979 the ethnic Muslim groups' share of the KBR's population grew from 53.4 to 56.0 percent. Bennigsen and Wimbush, *Muslims of the Soviet Empire*, p. 195.

31 The urban population's percentage of the overall population peaked in the KBR in 1992 at 61.4 percent (481,000) and declined steadily to 57.2 percent (452,400) by 2000, while the overall population increased over the same period from 784,000 to 791,600. According to the October 2002 census results, the urban population's share of the overall population fell to 56.6 percent. For the 2002 census results for KBR, see "Chislennost naseleniya KBR," Elbrusoid.ru, www.elbrusoid.ru/content/kbr/p2688.shtml. For previous years see "Demografiya," Elbrusoid.ru, www.elbrusoid.ru/content/kbr/p524.shtml.

32 Andreas Kappeler and Svetlana Chervonnaya, "Musulmanskie narody Rossii: istoricheskoe vvedenie," in Iordan, Kuzeev, and Chervonnaya, eds., *Islam v Evrazaii*, pp. 98–119, at p. 115.

33 Nikolai Petrov, "Razdelennyi suverenitet po-rossiiski: vzaimootnosheniya Moskvy i regionov," in B. Koppiters, D. Darchiashvili, and N. Akaba, eds., *Poiski alternative dlya Gruzii i Abkhazii* (Moscow: Ves Mir, 1999), pp. 133–171, at pp. 136, 146.

34 Derluguian, *Bordieu's Secret Admirer in the Caucasus*, pp. 236–38, 260–67, 274–81.

35 Robert Orttung, "Separatism Threatens Kabardino-Balkaria," EastWest Institute Russian Regional Report, 27 Oct. 1996, www.isn.ethz.ch/researchpub/rrr/docs/rrr961227.pdf, and "V KBR pominayut zhertv depotatsii Balkarskogo naroda," Islam.ru, 9 March 2005, www.islam.ru/ press/rus/2005-03-09/#7540.

36 Although Bashkortostan's official media organs routinely make the false claim that Ufa's August 1994 treaty with Moscow was the second such agreement, the KBR was in fact the first region after Tatarstan to sign a treaty in 1994. The Russia-KBR power-sharing treaty can be found in M. N. Gobuglo, *Federalizm vlasti i vlasti federalizma* (Moscow: IntelTekh, 1997), pp. 252–258.

37 Ibid., pp. 247–249, 253–255, and 260–261.

38 Ibid., p. 254.

39 "Mezhnatsionalnyie konflikty glavnaya ugroza edinstvu".

40 Fuller, "Balkars Launch New Campaign for Their Own Republic."

41 Igor Nadeinov, "Syn protiv ottsa," *Moskovskie novosti*, No. 27, 23–29 July 2004, p. 15.

42 Hunter, *Islam in Russia*, p. 272, and Petrov, "Razdelennyi suverenitet po-rossiiski: vzaimootnosheniya Moskvy i regionov," p. 137.

43 In a survey of Russian experts the KBR was ranked eighty-fifth out of eighty-eight Russian regions (Chechnya not included in the survey) on its overall level of democracy in the period 1991–2001. On the different levels of democratization in the national republics and the non-national "Russian" regions see Nikolai Petrov's detailed analysis in "Po rezul'tatam issedovanii Permskaya Oblast' okazalas'

demokratichnee Moskvy i Sankt Peterburga," Regions.ru, 16 Oct. 2002, 14:07, www.regions.ru. In an index including various indicators of electoral democracy, 1999–2002, it ranked last of eighty-eight regions (Chechnya again not included). From Nikolai Petrov, "Democracy in Russia's Regions" in Michael McFaul and Nikolai Petrov, eds., *The White Book of Russian Democracy* (Washington, D.C.: Carnegie Endowment of International Peace, 2004). In January 2001 the Moscow-based Glasnost Defense Fund rated the KBR eighty-second out of eighty-seven regions. (Chechnya and Ingushetiya were excluded from the study.) RFERL Russian Federation Report, Vol. 3, No. 5 (31 Jan. 2001).

44 Kokov was and remains the republic's human rights ombudsman, heading its Human Rights Committee. Lyudmilla Maratova, "Kabardino-Balkariya President Continues to Influence Judicial System," *EastWest Institute Russian Regional Report*, Vol. 7, No. 26 (3 Sept. 2003).

45 Orttung, "Separatism Threatens Kabardino-Balkaria."

46 Fuller, "Balkars Launch New Campaign for Their Own Republic."

47 RFERL Newsline, Vol. 1, No. 225 (20 Nov. 1996).

48 Fuller, "Balkars Launch New Campaign for Their Own Republic."

49 Igor Rotar, "Chechen Spark, Caucasian Powderkeg," *Perspective* (Institute for the Study of Conflict, Ideology, and Policy, Boston University), Vol. 10, No. 2 (Nov.–Dec. 1999).

50 "Kabardino-Balkarskaya Respublika: Lider 'Adyge Hase' gotov ko vtoromu sroku," Regions.ru, 10 April 2003, 08:39,
http://www.regions.ru/newsarticle/news/id/1064080.html.

51 "Kabardino-Balkarskaya Respublika: Chinovnik dolzhen znat' vse tri gosudarst-vennykh yazyka," Regions.ru, 7 Aug. 2003, 17:06, www.regions.ru/newsarticle/news/id/1193430.html.

52 "Mezhnatsionalnyie konflikty glavnaya ugroza edinstvu."

53 Itar-Tass, 30 Dec. 2004, 8:48 GMT.

54 In March 2003 the Ataman of the Prokhladnyi Cossack community, Mikhail Koncharenko, managed to get his Cossacks to promise to refrain from calls for redrawing the North Caucasus's borders. However, the same Cossacks rejected a proposal to accept a status as a "sub-ethnos" of the ethnic Russians. See "Kabardino-Balkarskaya Respublika: Kazaki ne khotyat byt' subetnosom," Regions.ru, 6 March 2003, 19:10, www.regions.ru/newsarticle/news/id/1021026.html.

55 Derluguian, *Bourdieu's Secret Admirer in the Caucasus*, pp. 284–285, and Kobishchanov, "Musulmane Rossii, korennye rossiiskie musulmane i russkie-musulmane," p. 96.

56 Kobishchanov, "Musulmane Rossii, korennye rossiiskie musulmane i russkie-musulmane," pp. 257–258.

57 "Shamil Basaev vystupil, chto delaetsya," *Kommersant-Daily*, 5 July 2004, p. 4.

58 At the same time, the amendments included modest gains for democracy, since the supremacy of federal law rendered unconstitutional the KBR's law giving the republic the right to ban demonstrations. RFERL Newsline, 24 July 2001. However, the federal government adopted in 2004 a new law which put some restrictions on the locations where demonstrations could be staged and established rules for registering them with government bodies.

59 Valerii Kalabugin, "Severnyie kadry ne prizhilis na yuge," *Nezavisimaya gazeta*, 2 July 2004, p. 5.

60 The State Council was created as an advisory body composed of the then eighty-nine regions' chief executives as compensation for their loss of seats in the upper house of the Federal Assembly, the Federation Council, after Putin reorganized it. Subsequently, with the merger of Komi-Permyak Autonomous Okrug with Perm Oblast, Russia was left with only eighty-eight regions.

61 Pavel Isaev, "GosSovet obsudil kontseptsiyu reformy, predlozhennoi kommissiei D. Kozaka," *Rossiiskii regionalnyi byulleten* (Institut Vostok-Zapad), T. 4, No. 20 (4 Nov. 2002).

62 Nadeinov, "Syn protiv ottsa."

63 See the KBR website Elbrusoid.ru, www.elbrusoid.ru/content/kbr/p20934.shtml.

64 Election results from the Russian Central Election Commission website, www.cikrf.ru.

65 Hunter, *Islam in Russia*, pp. 100–101.

66 Lyudmila Maratova, "Kokov Lacks Ideas on Fixing Kabardino-Balkaria Economy," *EastWest Institute Russian Regional Report*, Vol. 7, No. 15 (24 April 2002).

67 Maratova, "Kabardino-Balkariya Prepares to Re-Elect Unpopular President."

68 Maratova, "Kokov Lacks Ideas on Fixing Kabardino-Balkariya Economy."

69 *Kabardino-Balkarskaya pravda*, 1 Nov. 2000, cited in Kobishchanov, "Musulmane Rossii, korennye rossiiskie musulmane i russkie-musulmane," pp. 258–259.

70 Valerii Kokov, "Arifmetika sotsialnogo spokoistviya," *Nezavisimaya gazeta*, 15 Feb. 2001, p. 3.

71 On the film, see Yurii Akbashev, "Dokumentalnyi film vyzvalvozmushcheniye," IWPR Caucasus Reporting Service, No. 55, 27 Oct. 2000, www.iwpr.net/index.pl? archive/ cau/cau_200010_55_04_rus.txt. On the protests, see Zarina Kanukova, "Otvet Adygeya," IWPR *Caucasus Reporting Service*, No. 57, 11 Nov. 2000, www.iwpr.net/index.pl? archive/cau/cau_2000 11_57_01_rus.txt.

72 Anna Matveeva, *The North Caucasus: Russia's Fragile Borderland* (London: Royal Institute of International Affairs, 1999), p. 37.

73 RFERL Caucasus Report, 5 Nov. 2004.

74 The other new members were Bashkortostan president Rakhimov, Jewish Autonomous Oblast head Nikolai Volkov, Karelia Republic head Sergei Katanandov, Yaroslavl governor Anatolii Lisitsyn, Omsk governor Leonid Polezhaev, and Khanty-Mansii Autonomous Okrug governor Aleksandr Filipenko. RFERL Newsline, Vol. 5, No. 50 (13 March 2001).

75 The delegation to the OIC, to which Putin proposed Russia's joining the organization under observer status, also included the presidents of Chechnya, Tatarstan, and Bashkortostan as well as Muslim officials in the federal government. RFERL Newsline, Vol. 7, No. 198 (17 Oct. 2003).

76 For example, in January 2002, before the rise of Yarmuk in the KBR, Kokov was ranked sixth among Russia's eighty-nine regional leaders. RFERL Russian Federation Report, Vol. 4, No. 13 (10 April 2002).

77 "DUM Kabardino-Balkarii ishet puti k dialogu s oppozitsionnymi imamami," Islam.ru, 28 Dec. 2004, www.islam.ru/press/rus/2004-12-28/#6932.

78 The Spiritual Center has a mosque, a 1,500-seat auditorium, a wedding hall, conference hall, library, book preservation laboratory, and printing press. Kobishchanov, "Musulmane Rossii, korennye rossiiskie musulmane i russkie-musulmane," p. 255.

79 DUM KBR deputy mufti for ideological issues Khizir Otarov downplayed the gravity of this call, claiming that it was "merely" a protest against the "dirty" state financing of the mosque's construction. "DUM Kabardino-Balkarii ishet puti k dialogu s oppozitsionnymi imamami," Islam.ru, 28 Dec. 2004, www.islam.ru/press/rus/2004-12-28/#6932.

80 "Dzhikhad dlya musulman Kabardino-Balkarii obyazatelen," Kavkaz-Tsentr, 24 March 2004, 13:59, www.kavkazcenter.com/russ/content/2005/03/24/31762.shtml.

81 The imams of the KChR had already been requesting this for six months. Milrad Fatullaev, "Muftiyaty vstayut na kazennoe dovolstvie," *Nezavisimaya gazeta*, 31 Jan. 2005, http://www.ng.ru/regions/2005-01-31/9_caucasus.html, and "Imamy 3 respublik Severnogo Kavkaza prosyat vlasti vzyat' ikh na soderzhanie," Islam.ru, 31 Jan. 2004, www.islam.ru.

82 Nearly a hundred imams in the KBR were forced to undergo retraining in Islamic theology and law at Nalchik's Islamic Institute after an attestation found them wanting. In another, eighty-seven of 150 village imams failed to demonstrate "proper" knowledge of Mohammed's teachings, interpretation of the Koran, and performance of Islamic rites. Islam.ru, 9 Feb., 2005, www.islam.ru/press/rus/2005-02-09/#7266, and "Selskie imamy KBR nauchatsya rabotat s prikhozhanami mechetei," Islam.ru, 16 Feb. 2005, www.islam.ru/press/rus/2005-02-16/#7342.

83 "Kabardino-Balkarskaya Respublika: V Prokhladnenskoi shkole nacali prepodavat' 'Osnovy pravoslavnoi kultury,'" Regions.ru, 26 Sept. 2003, 09:11, www.regions.ru.

84 "Shkolniki Kabardino-Balkarii budet izuchat' Islam," Islam.ru, 23 August 2004, www.islam.ru, and "Kabardino-Balkarskaya Respublika: Pravoslavnaya tserkov' odobrila vvedenie v shkolnuyu programmu novogo predmeta," Regions.ru, 18 Aug. 2005, 15:31, www.regions.ru.

85 Regions.ru, 11 Oct. 2004, cited in "KBR: veryushchie i siloviki poka govoryat na raznykh yaykakh," Islam.ru, 11 Oct. 2004, www.islam.ru and in the author's archive.

86 "Dzhikhad dlya musulman Kabardino-Balkarii obyazatelen."

87 Ibid.

88 Ibid.

89 Fatullaev, "Muftiyaty vstayut na kazennoe dovolstvie" and "Imamy 3 respublik Severnogo Kavkaza prosyat vlasti vzyat' ikh na soderzhanie," Islam.ru, 31 Jan. 2004, www.islam.ru.

90 See "Dzhikhad dlya musulman Kabardino-Balkarii obyazatelen." For his follow-up interview, see "Dzhikhad dlya musulman Kabardino-Balkarii obyazatelen (prodolzhenie)," Kavkaz-Tsentr, 25 March 2004, 18:47, www.kavkazcenter.net/russ/content/2005/ 03/25/31816.shtml.

91 See his comment in Fatima Tlisova, "Islamist Group Destroyed in Kabardino-Balkariya," IWPR Caucasus Reporting Service, No. 272, 3 Feb. 2005.

92 Charles Gurin, "Authorities Suspect Islamists Murdered Drug Agents in Kabardino-Balkaria," The Jamestown Foundation Eurasia Daily Monitor, Vol. 1, Issue 149 (17 Dec. 2004), www.jamestownfoundation.org.

93 Mikhail Roshchin, "The History of Islam in Kabardino-Balkaria," The Jamestown Foundation Chechnya Weekly, Vol. 6, No. 46 (8 Dec. 2005), www.jamestown.org/ publications_details.php?volume_id=409&issue_id=3556&article_id=2370581.

94 See the letter of the new emir of the ChRI North Caucasus front's KBR sector, "Seifullakh," likely Mukozhev's long-time associate Astemirov, in "Amir Seifullakh: 'Pobeda ot Allakha, tak zhe kak i porazhenie,'" Kavkaz-Tsentr, 29 May 2006, 03:34, www.kavkazcenter.net/russ/content/2006/05/29/44895. See also Aleksandr Zhukov, "Religioznyi raskol i politicheskoe reshenie," Polit.ru, 18 May 2006, 08:25, www.polit.ru/analytics/2006/05/18/kanokov.html.

95 "Amir Seifullakh: 'Pobeda ot Allakha, tak zhe kak i porazhenie.'"

96 Roshchin, "The History of Islam in Kabardino-Balkaria."

97 "Amir Seifullakh: 'Pobeda ot Allakha, tak zhe kak i porazhenie.'"

98 Roshchin, "The History of Islam in Kabardno-Balkaria," citing Michael Burdo and Sergei Filatov, eds., Islam in Kabardino-Balkaria Modern Religious Life in Russia, Vol. 3, 2005, pp. 183, 185.

99 "Amir Seifullakh: 'Pobeda ot Allakha, tak zhe kak i porazhenie.'"

100 See the interview with Igor Dobaev, "Pro vakhkhabitov i ne tolko," Religare.ru, 23 Dec. 2004, www.religare.ru.

101 Oleg Guseinov, "Narkontrol' sdali byvshie sotrudniki," Gazeta yuga, 28 April 2005, www.gazetayuga.ru/archive/2005/17.htm.

102 Alexander Raskin and Sergei Kuklev, "Chechnya Metastasis," Newsweek Russia, No. 1, 14 Jan. 2005.

103 "V MVD KBR nedoumevayut, pochemu musul'mane prodolzhayut molit'sya u

zakrytoi mecheti," Islam.ru, 27 April 2005, www.islam.ru/press/rus/2005-04-27/#8075, and Raskin and Kuklev, "Chechnya Metastasis."

104 Roshchin, "The History of Islam in Kabardino-Balkaria."

105 "Amir Seifullakh: 'Pobeda ot Allakha, tak zhe kak i porazhenie.'"

106 Fatima Tlisova, "Kabardino-Balkariya Fears Spread of Terror," IWPR Caucasus Reporting Service, No. 255, 29 Sept. 2004. Astemirov claims Mukozhev's group began with fourteen communities. "Amir Seifullakh: 'Pobeda ot Allakha, tak zhe kak i porazhenie.'"

107 Andrei Alekseyev, "'Est' dannyie o svyazi dzhamaata s Bacaevym,'" Kommersant Vlast, No. 39, 3 Oct. 2005, www.kommersant.ru/k-vlast/get_page.asp?page_id=20053930-7.

108 One Ruslan Odigov was detained by Russian security forces in 2000, accused of supporting the Chechen rebellion, and physically abused for two weeks before being released. He then absconded to Afghanistan where, after initially being distrusted by the Taliban, he was captured by the Northern Alliance, though he insists he was not involved in fighting. Back in the KBR after Guantanamo, Odigov claimed he and other supporters of Mukozhev were on the authorities' extremist list. RFERL Newsline, Vol. 7, No. 60 (28 March 2003); RFERL Russian Federation Report, Vol. 4, No. 14 (17 April 2002); and "Russia's 'Taliban' Faces Uneasy Future after Guantanamo Torment," AFP, 1 Aug. 2004.

109 Oleg Guseinov, "Narkontrol' sdali byvshie sotrudniki."

110 The order also "categorically" banned organizing study for school and pre-school children in mosques, appointing an "assistant" (Khasan Tutovich Khalishov) of the head imam of Chegem to be responsible for enforcing the new regime, and assigning the monitoring of the mosque to the city's administration deputy head. When Chegem's Muslims petitioned the city's prosecutor, he ruled the administration's order a violation of the Russian constitution. However, the city issued a "new" order which differed from the original only in that it reduced the working hours of the mosque by half. R. B. Nakhushev, "O pravovom polozhenii musul'man v Kabardino-Balkarii," IslaminKBR.ru, 5 April 2005, www.islaminkbr.com/kbr/in.php?mode=002.

111 Ibid. and Zhukov, "Religioznyi raskol i politicheskoe reshenie."

112 NTV's Namedni Program and Gazeta, 19 July 2004, cited in "Martial Law Declared in Kabardino-Balkaria," The Jamestown Foundation Eurasia Daily Monitor, Vol. 1, Issue 63 (30 July 2004).

113 Tlisova, "Kabardino-Balkariya Fears Spread of Terror."

114 See "Dzhikhad dlya musulman Kabardino-Balkarii obyazatelen."

115 "Amir Seifullakh: 'Pobeda ot Allakha, tak zhe kak i porazhenie.'"

116 Tlisova, "Kabardino-Balkariya Fears Spread of Terror."

117 On the results of the research conducted by scholars from the KBR government's Institute of Humanitarian Studies and the Russian Academy of Science's Kabardino-Balkariya Science Center and Institute of Ethnology and Anthropology, see Nakhushev, "O pravovom polozhenii musul'man v Kabardino-Balkarii." This article was based on another written by one of the leaders of the field expedition: see Valerii Kazharov, "Etnograficheskaya ekspeditsiya poproblemam islama v KBR," Gazeta yuga, 5 June 2003.

118 "Dzhikhad dlya musulman Kabardino-Balkarii obyazatelen."

119 Musa, described as a spokesman for the IGMKB and a KBR resident (probably Musa Mukozhev), is likely associated with or even a member of Yarmuk Jamaat, since he was setting out what had become a central tenet of Yarmuk statements at the time – that jihad had become obligatory for all Muslims in the KBR and the North Caucasus. See "Dzhikhad dlya musulman Kabardino-Balkarii obyazatelen."

120 Raskin and Kuklev, "Chechnya Metastasis."

121 See the comments of Russian Academy of Sciences Institute of Ethnology and Anthropology scholar Akhmet Yarlykapov in "A. Yarlykapov: Nuzhno seryezno

korrektirovat politiku v otnoshenii Islama na Severnom Kavkaze," Islam.ru, 28 Oct. 2005, www.islam.ru/pressclub/gost/yrlikav/.

122 By November 2000 KBR chief prosecutor Anatolii Tkhagapsoev asserted there were 382 militant Wahhabis in the KBR, with 167 in Nalchik. For the August 2000 KBR DUM chairman Pshikhachev's August 2000 warning and the Council of Muftis of Russia's June 2000 warning about the presence of militant Wahhabism in the republic, see respectively "Vakhkhabizm – eto otritsanie narodnykh obychaev. Otvet mufti KBR Shafiga Pshikhacheva na zayavlenie predstavitelei 'musulmanksikh dzhamaatov'," *Severnyi Kavkaz*, No. 6 Feb. 2001, and Kobishchanov, "Musulmane Rossii, korennye rossiiskie musulmane i russkie-musulmane," pp. 257–259. These accounts were recently confirmed by Astemirov in "Amir Seifullakh: 'Pobeda ot Allakha, tak zhe kak i porazhenie.'"

123 Timur Samedov, "Nad Nalchikom navisla 'oranzhevaya revolyutsiya," *Kommersant-Daily*, 20 Aug. 2004, p. 3.

124 The Federal prosecutors' investigation into the March 2001 car-bomb explosions in Mineralnye Vody, Yessentuki, and the KChR and the 1999 apartment bombings in Moscow and Volgodonsk that helped spark the second Chechen war led to the arrests of eleven alleged Islamic militants and reportedly uncovered a radical Islamist network that the federal prosecutor-general's office stated was planning armed seizures of power in both republics. Timofei Borisov, "Pervorot gotovili amiry," *Rossiiskaya gazeta*, 18 Aug. 2001, p. 1, and RFERL Newsline, Vol. 5, No. 156 (17 Aug. 2001). Newspapers reported that senior security officials in the republics, however, had claimed they had no idea to what the statement referred. See *Izvestiya* and *Nezavisimaya gazeta* on 17 August 2001, cited in RFERL Newsline, Vol. 5, No. 156 (17 Aug. 2001).

125 See Aleksandra Larintseva, Timur Samedov, and Olga Allenova, "Koltso kavkazskoi natsionalnosti," *Kommersant-Vlast*, 29 Sept.–5 Oct. 2003, p. 20; Valerii Khatazhukov, "Kabardino-Balkariya Crackdown on Islamists," IWPR Caucasus Reporting Service, No. 199, August 2003; and Samedov, "Nad Nalchikom navisla 'oranzhevaya revolyutsiya.'" Basaev's presence was revealed to police and security officers during testimony by Zarema Mahadzieva, a Chechen woman who had attempted to blow herself up in Moscow. *Russkiy kurier*, Aug. 2003, cited in "Martial Law Declared in Kabardino-Balkaria." In a November 2004 interview, Basaev himself claimed that he was constantly on the move and mentioned stays in Kabardino-Balkariya. RFERL Caucasus Report, 5 Nov. 2004.

126 See the interview with FSB lieutenant-general Ivan Mironov in *Rossiiskaya gazeta*, 10 Sept. 2002.

127 Tlisova, "Islamist Group Destroyed in Kabardino-Balkariya."

128 According to Valery Kanukov, chief prosecutor in the Elbrus district, Atayev-Seifullah was one of the best students at Kendelen's school, before being accepted to Kabardino-Balkariya University. Ibid. Born in 1974, he reportedly distinguished himself in Gelaev's eyes by his exceptional organizational abilities and good physical condition. Timur Samedov, "Podozrevaemyie iz 'Yarmuka,'" *Kommersant-Daily*, 15 Dec. 2004, p. 4; Tlisova, "Kabardino-Balkariya Fears Spread of Terror"; Ksenya Solyanskaya, "Oni vozneslis na nebo," Gazeta.ru, 28 Jan. 2005, www.gazeta.ru/2005/01/28/ oa_146501.shtml; and RFERL Newsline Vol. 9, No. 21 (2 Feb. 2005).

129 Atayev-Seifullah's telephone number was recorded on the SIM card of one of two mobile telephones discovered in the house in Baksan where Basaev had been hiding and on a mobile telephone found at the scene of the fighting near Chegem. Through this a link was maintained to him via an inhabitant of a Nalchik suburb. Samedov, "Podozrevaemye iz 'Yarmuka.'"

130 Kavkas-Tsentr, 10 March 2005, www.kavkazcenter.net, and "Dzhamaat 'Yarmuk': Prinyat plan boevykh operatsii v KBR na 2005 g.," Kavkaz-Tsentr, 12 March 2005,

www.kavkaz.org.uk/russ/content/ 2005/03/12/31292.shtml.

131 Timur Samedov, "Prishol, uvidel, i ushol," *Kommersant-Daily*, 20 Aug. 2004, pp. 1, 6; Itar-Tass, 19 Aug. 2004, 15:47 GMT; Marina Chernysheva, "Militants Suspected of Killing Tourists Slain in Kabardino-Balkaria," Itar-Tass, 20 Aug. 2004; Vadim Rechkalov, "Eti mestnyie rebyaty, no yavno pobyvali v Chechne," *Izvestiya*, 20 Aug. 2004; and *Nezavisimaya gazeta*, 20 Aug. 2004, cited in RFERL Newsline, Vol. 8, No. 159 (20 Aug. 2004).

132 In a January 2005 operation that ended in the killing of Atayev-Seifullah (a Balkar), his family, and five other members of the jamaat, an unnamed KBR official involved in planning the raid said that there was a thirty-six-hour delay in launching the operation because the militants were Balkars and the republic's leadership feared their deaths would have a negative effect on inter-ethnic relations in the KBR. *Nezavisimaya gazeta*, 28 Jan. 2005, cited in RFERL Newsline, Vol. 9, No. 18 (28 Jan. 2005). Two other insurgents killed during the first major skirmish with Yarmuk fighters near Chegem in summer 2004 were Balkars from Kendelen. *Rossiiskaya gazeta*, 16 Dec. 2004. However, the insurgency network in Kabardino-Balkariya out of which Yarmuk apparently emerged was originally established by two Kabardin brothers who first arranged for Basaev to visit the KBR and were soon killed. Andrei Smirnov, "Who Is Behind Yarmuk Jamaat: Balkars or Kabardins?" The Jamestown Foundation *Eurasia Daily Monitor*, Vol. 2, Issue 23 (2 Feb. 2005).

133 Yarmuk claims that Russian security forces posted a letter purporting to be from Yarmuk announcing that it was planning a Beslan-style siege of a Kabard school. Smirnov, "Who Is Behind Yarmuk Jamaat: Balkars or Kabardins?"

134 Jeremy Page, "Rebel Attacks Spread from Chechnya," *The Times* (UK), 28 Jan. 2005.

135 Andrew McGregor, "The Jamaat Movement in Kabardino-Balkaria," The Jamestown Foundation *Terrorism Monitor*, Vol. 3, Issue 7 (Special Issue on Chechnya), 7 April 2005.

136 See Scheuer, *Imperial Hubris* and Lewis, *The Crisis of Islam*, especially pp. 22–23.

137 "Dzhikhad dlya musulman Kabardino-Balkarii obyazatelen."

138 Members of Yarmuk already had been charged with the July 2004 murder of tourists in Stavropol Krai. Samedov, "Prishol, uvidel, i ushol"; Itar-Tass, 19 Aug. 2004, 15:47 GMT, and Chernysheva, "Militants Suspected of Killing Tourists Slain in Kabardino-Balkaria."

139 Two militants and two members of the security forces were killed and four police were wounded. One report had it that the band had been targeting the *siloviki*, in this case the KBR's MVD chief, Lieutenant-General Khachim Shogenov, whose dacha is not far from the scene of the battle. Other police sources said that 10 kilograms of TNT found in the group's car may have been intended for a terrorist act at Nalchik airport. Samedov, "Prishol, uvidel, i ushol"; Itar-Tass, 19 Aug. 2004, 15:47 GMT; Chernysheva, "Militants Suspected of Killing Tourists Slain in Kabardino-Balkaria"; Rechkalov, "Eti mestnyie rebyaty, no yavno pobyvali v Chechne"; and *Nezavisimaya gazeta*, 20 Aug. 2004, cited in RFERL Newsline, Vol. 8, No. 159 (20 Aug. 2004).

140 Roman Kiloyev, "'Day of Ingushetia' for Kabardino-Balkaria," *Kavkaz-Tsentr*, 22 Aug. 2004, 11:22, www.kavkazcenter.net.

141 The statement was made in clearly Islamist terms: "We may die but others will follow. The Muslims of the Caucasus will live on. Finally, we pay homage to God, the Lord of the worlds. We ask for His help and pray for His forgiveness. God is Great!" It also denied KBR police allegations that elements from Yarmuk were responsible for the murder of tourists in Stavropol. "Kabardino-Balkarskii Jamaat Obyavlyaet Jihad," *Kavkaz-Tsentr*, 23 Aug. 2004, 11:30 GMT, www.kavkazcenter.net.

142 The population reportedly feared another terrorist act and kindergartens, schools, and colleges were frequently closed as a consequence. Parents stopped sending their children to school. Marianna Kalmykova, a journalist and mother in Nalchik, who

kept her son away from School No. 2 for several days, stated: "everybody is waiting for a terrorist attack." Tlisova, "Kabardino-Balkariya Fears Spread of Terror."

143 "Nal'chik. Dzhamaaty sozdayutsya uzhe i v mestakh lisheniya svobody," Regions.ru, 15 Sept. 2004, 20:37, www.regions.ru.

144 "Administratsiya Nal'chika razreshaet lish' odnoi mecehti goroda," Islam.ru, 15 Sept. 2004, www.islam.ru.

145 "Kabardino-Balkariya: vlasti ugrozhayut 'Beslanom,' musul'mane zhaluyutsya na pritesneniya," Islam.ru, 21 Sept. 2004, www.islam.ru.

146 "Deistviya silovikov na Severnom Kavkaze vyzyvayut ozabochennost' musul'man," Islam.ru, 18 Oct. 2004, www.islam.ru and the author's archive.

147 "Zhurnalisty zayavlyayut o narushenii prav cheloveka," Islam.ru, 24 Feb. 2005, www.islam.ru/press/rus/ 2005-02-24/#7417.

148 RFERL Newsline, Vol. 8, No. 190 (6 Oct. 2004).

149 "Napadenie na Upravlenie Narkontrolya KBR sovershila, po versii sledstviya, gruppa 'Yarmuk,'" *Izvestiya*, 14 Dec. 2005, www.izvestia.ru/conflict/article833264, and Oleg Fochkin and Lina Panchenko, "Rasstrel s dalnym pritselom," *Moskovskiy Komsomolets*, 15 Dec. 2004, pp. 1–2. In the attack on the latter MVD colonel Mukhtar Altuyev was seriously wounded but survived. However, his sixteen-year-old son was killed in the attack. Timur Samedov, "Vakhkhabity otomstili svoemu tyuremshchiku," *Kommersant-Daily*, 9 Dec. 2004, p. 6.

150 Gurin, "Authorities Suspect Islamists Murdered Drug Agents in Kabardino-Balkaria." Another source claimed thirty-six machine guns, 136 pistols, and a "large quantity of ammunition" for these were stolen. "Napadenie na Upravlenie Narkontrolya KBR sovershila, po versii sledstviya, gruppa 'Yarmuk.'" See also RFERL Newsline, 15 and 16 Dec. 2004. In a message posted on the Chechen separatist website Daymohk.info on 14 December Yarmuk claimed responsibility for the attack and said that in addition to weapons it came away with sensitive intelligence information and the addresses and hideouts of informers from among the drug addicts. "Kabardino-Balkarskii Dzhamaat Yarmuk provyol spetsoperatsiyu v Nalchike," Daymohk.info, 15 Dec. 2005, http://www.daymohk.info/cgi-bin/archieve/archieve.cgi?choice=15200412. In a later website posting a Yarmuk representative devoted considerable attention to warning potential recruits and supporters to be wary of provocateurs and informants from the Russian security services while organizing guerrilla cells and operations. *Kavkaz-Tsentr*, 16 Dec. 2004, www.kavkazcenter.com and "Dzhikhad dlya musulman Kabardino-Balkarii obyazatelen (prodolzhenie)." This also may have been connected to the surrender to the authorities in November of four Yarmuk activists. Itar-Tass, 15 Dec. 2004.

151 A source close to the investigation when it was still operating under the theory that the attack could also have been undertaken by a drug ring stated that there was "no doubt" that someone from the KBR FSNK's ranks was among the attackers, since the eight to ten militants appeared to have been acquainted with the administration building's layout. It was also reported that guards opened the door casually at the sound of a familiar voice. Fochkin and Panchenko, "Chuzhie sredi svoikh," *Moskovskiy Komsomolets*, 16 Dec. 2004, p. 5, and Gurin, "Authorities Suspect Islamists Murdered Drug Agents in Kabardino-Balkaria." It was later reported that two former lower-ranking FSNK co-workers, who had been fired for membership of a "Wahhabi" organization, informed one of the perpetrators of the attack, twenty-eight-year-old Yarmuk member Anzor Astemirov, regarding the number, location, and security of the weapons and the number of those on duty in the FSNK building. Guseinov, "Narkontrol' sdali byvshie sotrudniki."

152 Guseinov, "Narkontrol' sdali byvshie sotrudniki."

153 "Yarmuk Declares Jihad," The Jamestown Foundation *Chechnya Weekly*, Vol. 6, Issue 2 (13 Jan. 2005), http://www.jamestown.org.

154 Some controversy arose as to whether Atayev-Seifullah's daughter was killed and whether he had a son, and whether he was killed in the siege. See Tlisova, "Islamist Group Destroyed in Kabardino-Balkariya"; Interfax, 27 Jan. 2005, cited in RFERL Newsline, Vol. 9, No. 18 (28 Jan. 2005); Page, "Rebel Attacks Spread from Chechnya"; and RFERL Newsline, Vol. 9, No. 16 (26 Jan. 2005).

155 The site also reported that five Russian troops were killed and ten wounded in the first four hours of the seige. "Dzhamaat 'Yarmuk': 'My prinimaem boi!,'" *Kavkaz-Tsentr*, 26 Jan. 2005, www.kavkazcenter.net/russ/content/2005/01/26/29537.shtml.

156 For the IGMKB's appeals declaring that jihad was now obligatory for all Muslims in the KBR and North Caucasus, see "Dzhikhad v Kabardino-Balkarii prodolzhitsya," Kavkaz-Tsentr, 2 Feb. 2005, www.kavkazcenter.net; RFERL Newsline Vol. 9, No. 21 (2 Feb. 2005); and "Dzhikhad dlya musulman Kabardino-Balkarii obyazatelen."

157 *Kavkaz-Tsentr*, 10 March 2005, 15:53 GMT, www.kavkazcenter.net.

158 "Dzhikhad v Kabardino-Balkarii prodolzhitsya" and RFERL Newsline Vol. 9, No. 21 (2 Feb. 2005).

159 "Dzhamaat 'Yarmuk': Prinyat plan boevykh operatsii v KBR na 2005 g." and "Dvum boevikam, zaderzhannym v Nalchike, predyavleny obvineniya," "Novosti" 5 May 2005, RIA, www.rian.ru/defense_safety/ investigations/20050505/39936220.html.

160 However, Putin also rebuked Nurgaliev for referring to the militants by their preferred designation of "jamaat." RFERL Newsline, Vol. 9, No. 34 (22 Feb. 2005). Muslim leaders and others have cautioned that this term simply means "community" and should not become a synonym for "militant group." Putin's political correctness here, however, cannot compensate for his heavy-handed policies.

161 Vesti newscast, RTR TV, 16 March 2005, 08:00 GMT and Channel One TV, Moscow, 16 March 2005, 06:00. On 15 March the KBR MVD reported that the cache found in this operation included 92 detonators, 92 fuses for VOG-25P fragmentation rounds, 171 electronic explosive devices based on Casio watches using Krona batteries, 2 bags of electric fuses, 41 TNT blocks, over 700 cartridges and a bomb-making lab. Itar-Tass, 16 March 2004, 06:00 GMT.

162 "Grazhdanskuyu oboronu Kabardino-Balkaria perevedut v rezhim voennoro vremeni," *Kavkaz-Tsentr*, 9 April 2005, 00:52, http://www.kavkazcenter.net/russ/content/2005/04/09/32515.shtml.

163 "'Yarmuk' vnov' obezglavlen," *Izvestiya*, 29 April 2005, www.izvestia.ru/conflict/article1703491; "V Nalchike ubit lider bandy 'Yarmuk' i eshyo boevika," Regions.ru, 29 April 2005, 12:02, www.regions.ru/article/any/id/1799883.html; Yelena Denisova, "Prikonchennyi dzhamaat," Smi.ru, 29 April 2005, 14:56, www.smi.ru/05/04/29/3516327.html.

164 "Dvum boevikam, zaderzhannym v Nalchike, predyavleny obvineniya," 5 May 2005, 18:00, www.rian.ru/defense_safety/investigations/20050505/39936220.html. See also Denisova, "Prikonchennyi dzhamaat" and RFERL Newsline, Vol. 9, No. 82 (2 May 2005).

165 "V MVD RF pomnyat o preduprezhdenii 'Yarmuka,'" *Kavkaz-Tsentr*, 7 June 2005, 12:31:39, www.kavkazcenter.com/russ/content/2005/06/07/34807.shtml.

166 "K modzhahedam Kabardino-Balkarii," *Kavkaz-Tsentr*, 5 June 2005, 18:30:52, www.kavkazcenter.com/russ/content/2005/06/05/34742.shtml.

167 Roshchin, "The History of Islam in Kabardino-Balkaria."

168 In October 2005 KBR DUM leader Anas Pshikhachev reiterated the official clergy's dissatisfaction with its relations with the law-enforcement organs. Alekseyev, "'Est dannyie o svyazi dzhamaata s Basaevym'."

169 Regnum.ru cited in "Za chtenie Korana studentok-musulmanok v militsii zastavili zadirat' yubki," Islam.ru, 20 April 2005, www.islam.ru/press/rus/2005-04-20/#7985. The Chechen militants' website, Kavkaz-Tsentr, did not fail to report this as well. See "Militsiya v Nalchike zastablyala muslimanok zadirat' yubki v otmestku za chtenie

Korana," Kavkaz-Tsentr, 21 April 2005, 03:59:49, www.kavkazcenter.net/russ/content/2005/04/21/33024.shtml.

170 "Obstanovku v Nalchike mestnyie musulmane nazyvayut kriticheskoi," Islam.ru, 19 Aug. 2005, www.islam.ru/press/rus/2005-08-19/#9038.

171 "KBR: Musulmanka obratilas v sud za zashchitoi ot militsii," Islam.ru, 13 Oct. 2005, www.islam.ru/press/rus/2005-10-13/#9619.

172 "Musulmane KBR v znak protesta grozyat emigratsiei iz Rossii," Islam.ru, 25 Aug. 2005, www.islam.ru/press/rus/2005-08-25/#9109.

173 "Novyi glava KBR rezko menyaet politiku v otnoshenii Islama," Islam.ru, 30 Sept. 2005, www.islam.ru/press/rus/2005-09-30/#9459.

174 See Basaev's email message "Shamil Basaev: 'Nalchik atakovalo 217 modzhakhedov,'" ChechenPress.org, 17 Oct. 2005, www.chechenpress.info/events/2005/10/17/02.shtml.

175 RFERL Newsline, Vol. 9, No. 195 (17 Oct. 2005). On the Russians' discovery of the weapons cache, see "Huge Explosives Cache Found in Nalchik," Retwa.org, 10 Oct. 2005, www.retwa.org/home.cfm? articleId=1083.

176 "Shamil Basaev: 'Nalchik atakovalo 217 modzhakhedov.'"

177 "Terror Attack at Nalchik Averted," Retwa.org, 8 Oct. 2005, www.retwa.org/home.cfm?articleId= 1066 citing RIA Novosti.

178 For the Russian authorities' figures, see RFERL Newsline, Vol. 9, No. 194 (14 Oct. 2005) and RFERL Newsline, Vol. 9, No. 195 (17 Oct. 2005). For the Islamists' figures see "Shamil Basaev: 'Nalchik atakovalo 217 modzhakhedov'" and "Zayavlenie Dzhamata 'Yarmuk,'" ChechenPress.org, 17 Oct. 2005, www.chechenpress.info/events/2005/10/17/04.shtml.

179 "Zayavlenie Prezidenta ChRI A.-Kh. Sadulaev," ChechenPress.org, 18 Oct. 2005, www.chechenpress.info/events/2005/10/18/01.shtml.

180 For Basaev's message, see "Shamil Basaev: 'Nalchik atakovalo 217 modzhakhedov.'" For Yarmuk's message, see "Zayavlenie Dzhamata 'Yarmuk.'" For the message of Dagestan's Shariah Jamaat, see "V pamyat' o nashikh dagestanskikh bratyakh-mudzhahedakh," ChechenPress.org, 17 Oct. 2005, www.chechenpress.info/events/2005/10/17/16.shtml.

181 Ilya Malyakin, "Reforming the Russian Federation: From 89 to 88," *RFERL Russian Political Weekly*, Vol. 3, No. 5 (30 Jan. 2003).

182 Earlier, in March 2001, members of the Balkar nationalist organization Tere accused the republic's Kabardin-dominated leadership of discrimination and demanded a meeting with President Vladimir Putin to discuss their grievances, but Putin did not respond to their demand. Fuller, "Balkars Launch New Campaign for Their Own Republic."

183 Akhmat Shavayev, "V KBR styanuty rossiiskie okkupanty: Idut repressii protiv balkartsev," Chechen Press.org, 12 March 2005, http://chechenpress.co.uk/news/2005/03/12/08.shtml.

184 Ibid.

185 On 24 May, the KBR Supreme Court dismissed Zokaev's claim that the municipal reform violated the Russian constitution. On 23 May, the Nalchik City Court satisfied a request by the KBR prosecutor to declare as illegal and ban a planned referendum in which the residents of Khasanya would have voted on the village's incorporation into Nalchik. Fuller, "Balkars Launch New Campaign for Their Own Republic."

186 Mariya Bondarenko, "Balkartsy zadumali otdelyatsya," *Nezavisimaya gazeta*, 30 May 2005, www.ng.ru/politics/2005-05-30/1_balkaria.html; RFERL Newsline, Vol. 9, No. 102 (31 May 2005); and Vladlen Maksimov, "Za polshaga do vzryva," *Novyie Izvestiya*, 24 June 2005, www.newizv.ru/news/ 2005-06-24/26911/.

187 Fatima Tlisova, "Zemlya nevoli," *Novaya gazeta*, No. 41, 9 June 2005, http://2005.novayagazeta.ru/nomer/2005/41n/n41n-s27.shtml.

188 Ibid.

189 Ibid., and RFERL Newsline, Vol. 9, No. 107 (7 June 2005), citing Regnum.ru.
190 On 21 July 2005 Camagat.com announced that a KBR "mujahid" had killed two "criminals" from the "so-called militia" and "the illegal armed formations calling themselves the DPS UGIBDD [Traffic Patrol Service] under the MVD." It also charged "head of the Putin puppet regime in Kabardino-Balkariya V. Kokov" with the murder of Khasan village administration head and leader of the revitalized Balkar nationalist movement Artur Zakoev. Camagat.com emphasized that Zakoev was "a well-meaning Muslim and independent politician ... and the only administration head who performed the namaz [Muslim daily prayers] as is proper for a Muslim .... He firmly defended the interests of the Balkar people and openly came out against the genocide of the Chechen people by the Russian occupiers, and for that he was killed." See Abdu Rrakhman, "Vnov poteri sredi nezakonnykh bandformirovanii v Kabardino-Balkarii," Camagat.com, 21 July 2005, www.camagat.com/sitebiz/arhiv/2005/07/07.21/ 20%20unechtojeni%202%20bandita.htm. For a similar report which emphasizes the Balkar factor, see "V Kabardino-Balkarii prokhodit krupnaya terroristicheskaya operatsiya po ustrasheniyu Balkarskogo naroda," Camagat.com, 30 July 2005, www.camagat.com/sitebiz/arhiv/2005/07/07.30/terrer_v_kb.htm.
191 The more Russified Cherkess and the mountain Turkic Karachais went to the brink of civil war in 1999 in the course of presidential elections that pitted candidates representing these two nationalities against one another.
192 The Jamestown Foundation Eurasia Daily Monitor, 9 Aug. 2004.
193 Rafael Uzdenov, "Denying Rumors," Severnyi Kavkaz, 12 Aug. 2004, 00:00 GMT.
194 However, one TV journalist cited as many as two hundred adherents of Wahhabism in the republic. NTV (Moscow), 16 Aug. 2004, 08:00 GMT, www.ntv.ru.
195 NTV (Moscow), 16 Aug. 2004, 08:00 GMT, www.ntv.ru.
196 RFERL Newsline, Vol. 8, No. 181 (22 Sept. 2004).
197 Tlisova, "Kabardino-Balkariya Fears Spread of Terror."
198 Aleksandr Zheglov, "Moskovskie terakty organizovalo karachaevskoe pod'pole," Kommersant-Daily, 27 Sept. 2004, p. 5.
199 Gritsenko, "Net takogo slova 'dzhamaat.'"
200 "V Nalchike ubit lider bandy 'Yarmuk' i eshyo boevika," Regions.ru, 29 April 2005, 12:02, www.regions.ru/ article/any/id/1799883.html, and Solyanskaya, "Oni vozneslis na nebo."
201 One reason Batdyiev went so far in appointing ethnic Karachais to government posts was his low level of support among Karachais (17 percent) in the 2003 presidential election. See Fatima Tlisova, "Prazdnik edeneniya so Vvodom Voisk: KChR: vse soldarnyi – nikto ne prazdnuet," Novaya gazeta, No. 47, 4 July 2005, http://2005.novayagazeta.ru/nomer/2005/47n/n47n-s12.shtml.
202 The news sparked another storming and occupation of Batdyiev's office. Thousands subsequently occupied the adjacent central square in Cherkessk. RFERL Newsline, Vol. 8, No. 212 (9 Nov. 2004), and RFERL Newsline, Vol. 8, No. 213 (10 Nov. 2004.)
203 President Batdyiev noted that he had been subject to threats from criminal groups and that more than two hundred people had been murdered and five hundred had disappeared in the KChR over the past few years. ISN Security Watch, 18 Oct. 2004.
204 Yurii Senatorov, "'Emu khoteli otmstit'. Vitse prem'era Karachaevo-Cherkessii Tebueva rasstrelyali za rabotu v MVD," Izvestiya, 18 Oct. 2004, pp. 1, 6.
205 "The Assassination of a Counterterrorism Leader in the North Caucasus," Stratfor, 19 Oct. 2004, 17:56 GMT, www.stratfor.com.
206 Murat Gukemukhov and Sergey Mashkin, "Karachai kak zvali (Dmitrii Kozak spasaet Mustafa Batdyev ot revolyutsii)," Kommersant-Daily, 22 Oct. 2004. pp. 1, 4. One theory holds that Tebuev knew about the murders and therefore was ordered to be eliminated by Kaitov. Another suggests that Tebuev was himself involved in the conflict. Oleg Tsvetkov, "Crime, Corruption Provoke Crisis in Karachaevo-

Cherkessia," Russian Regional Report, Vol. 9, No. 21 (5 Nov. 2004).

207 This call to federal authorities was made in the speech by the demonstration's leader. See Tlisova, "Prazdnik edeneniya so Vvodom Voisk."

208 RFERL Newsline, Vol. 9, No. 126 (7 July 2005).

209 RFERL Newsline, Vol. 9, No. 128 (11 July 2005).

210 See Tlisova, "Prazdnik edeneniya so Vvodom Voisk."

211 The KBR parliament expressed its dissatisfaction with this trend and characterized the idea as dangerous. One deputy warned that its authors "do not understand that they may wind up with 89 Chechen Republics." Ilya Malyakin, "Reforming the Russian Federation: From 89 to 88."

212 RFERL Newsline, Vol. 9, No. 77 (25 April 2005).

213 RFERL Newsline, Vol. 9, No. 240 (29 Dec. 2005).

214 Liz Fuller, "Adygeya President, Opposition Assail Presidential Envoy," RFERL Caucasus Report, Vol. 9, No. 13 (13 April 2006).

215 It may be that Sovmen was pushed out by the Kremlin for reasons other than facilitation of the merger and that Sovmen's support for the Adygeis' opposition to the merger was purely instrumental ethno-entrepreneurship. See "Pro-Kremlin Party Wins Majority in Adygeya Election," RFERL Newsline, Vol. 10, No. 48 (15 March 2006); "Cherkess Appeal to Council of Europe," RFERL Newsline, Vol. 10, No. 53 (22 March 2006); "Tensions Surface Between Adygeya President, New Parliament," RFERL Newsline. Vol. 10, No. 63 (5 April 2006); "Thousands Demonstrate in Support of Adygeya President," RFERL Newsline, Vol. 10, No. 65 (7 April 2006); and "Thousands Demonstrate in Support of Adygeya President," RFERL Newsline, Vol. 10, No. 68 (12 April 2006).

216 Marieta Kumpilova, "Adygeia's President Confronts Kremlin," IWPR Caucasus Reporting Service, No. 335, 13 April 2006, info@iwpr.net, and Fuller, "Adygeya President, Opposition Assail Presidential Envoy."

217 See "V Adygee militsiya otbiraet u musulman religioznuyu literaturu," Islam.ru, 2 March 2006, www.islam.ru/press/rus/2006-03-02/?single=11163; "V Adygee proshla 'pyatnichnaya zachistka' musulman," Islam.ru, 7 April 2006, www.islam.ru/press/rus/2006-04-07/#11654; "Police Document Local Muslims While Finding Arms and Explosives Caches in Adyegya," Retwa.com, 8 April 2006, www.retwa.org/home.cfm?articleId=2153.

218 "Marat Teuchezhskii ot imeni gruppy musulman adygov, prinyavshchikh reshenie vyiti na Dzhikhad, Dzhikhad – eto sredstvo usmireniya zla," Kavkaz-Tsentr, 4 May 2006, 00:49:55, www.kavkazcenter.com/russ/content/2006/05/04/44253.shtml. Only a few days before the Adygeya group committed itself to jihad, former Maskhadov spokesman Mairbek Vachagaev predicted the emergence of a combat jamaat in Adygeya at a conference in Washington, D.C. See Paul Murphy, "Vachagayev's Predicament," Retwa.org, RETWA Analysis Brief, No. 6, 7 May 2006, www.retwa.org.

219 "Nal'chik. Dzhamaaty sozdayusya uzhe i v mestakh lisheniya svobody," Regions.ru, 15 Sept. 2004, 20:37, www.regions.ru.

220 See Gurin, "Authorities Suspect Islamists Murdered Drug Agents in Kabardino-Balkaria." In other reports police have been quoted as saying that they had information that 437 residents of the KBR were "adherents of radical Islam." See "V MVD KBR nedoumevayut, pochemu musul'mane prodolzhayut molit'sya u zakrytoi mecheti."

221 Milrad Fatullaev, "Na Kavkaze reformy ne zhaluyut," Nezavisimaya gazeta, 15 March 2005, p. 4.

222 Alekseyev, "'Est dannyie o svyazi dzhamaata s Basaevym.'"

223 Jean-Christophe Peuch, "North Caucasus Republics Enter Circle of Violence," Radio Free Europe/Radio Liberty, 23 Feb. 2005, http://www.rferl.org/featuresarticle/2005/02/021f2f06-0c2e-41cb-be1e-2fe3d61e505d.html.

Chapter Six

1 See Ye. O. Khabanskaya, *Tatary o Tatarskom* (Moscow: Natalis, 2006), pp. 16–32, 125–147.

2 I. P. Tagirov, *Istoriya natsionalnoi gosudarstvennosti Tatarskogo naroda i Tatarstana* (Kazan: Tatarskoe knizhnoe izdatelstvo, 2000), pp. 3–148.

3 There were eight nationalist-oriented Tatar revolts encompassing forty-six years of violent conflict in addition to Tatar participation in another twenty-eight peasant uprisings against the Russian imperial state from the sixteenth to the nineteenth centuries. See S. Kh. Alishev, *Ternistyi put borby za svobodu* (Kazan: FEN 1999), pp. 152–154.

4 Ibid.

5 A. N. Yuzeev, "Filisofskaya mysl' kontsa XVIII-XIX vv.," in R. M. Amirkhanov, ed., *Ocherki istorii Tatarskoi obshchestvennoi mysli* (Kazan: Tatarskoe knizhskoe izdatelstvo, 2000), pp. 92–127.

6 Ibid., pp. 97–98.

7 Mikhael Kemper, "Mezhdu Bukharoi i Srednei Volgoi: Stolknovenie Abd An-Nasra Al-Kursavi s ulemami traditsionalistami," *Mir Islama* (Kazan), Vol. 1, No. 1, 1999 pp. 163–174, at pp. 164–168.

8 Yuzeev, "Filisofskaya mysl' kontsa XVIII-XIX vv.," pp. 100–01. Utyz-Imyani and Kursavi's insistence on a return to the holy texts was completely contrary to that of the Salafists, who promoted a literal and selective interpretation in order to claim a monopoly on the holy truth. Similar arguments to those of the pre-jadidists are made by those Muslims around the world today who seek an Islamic reformation. See Aslan, *No God, But God.* See also Giles Kepel, *The War for Muslim Minds: Islam and the West* (Cambridge: Cambridge University Press, 2004); Richard Martin, *Defenders of Reason in Islam* (Oxford: Oxford University Press, 1997); and Abdulazis Abdulhussein Sachedina, *The Islamic Roots of Democratic Pluralism* (Oxford: Oxford University Press, 2001).

9 Yuzeev, "Filisofskaya mysl' kontsa XVIII-XIX vv.," pp. 102–104.

10 Ya. G. Abdullin, "Dzhadidizm kak etap v razvitii Tatarskogo prosvetitelstvo," in Amirkhanov, ed. *Ocherki istorii Tatarskoi obshchestvennoi mysli*, pp. 128–158, at pp. 146–153.

11 Ibid. According to Mukhametshin, 90 percent of all Islamic seminaries and religious schools in Kazan Gubernia employed the jadidist method by 1910. R. M. Mukhametshin, "Islam v Tatarskoi obshchestvennoi mysli nachala XX v.," in Amirkhanov, *Ocherki istorii Tatarskoi obshchestvennoi mysli*, pp. 160–188, at p. 161.

12 The Qadimists opposed all the manifestations of the modern urban Western way of life that jadidists accepted and that some yearned for: science, music, art, theaters, museums, libraries, and the carefree strolling about of youth and, in particular, of liberally dressed women on the streets and other public places. Qadimists even urged tsarist authorities to crack down on the jadidists, informing on them as an ostensibly revolutionary force. Abdullin, "Dzhadidizm kak etap v razvitii Tatarskogo prosvetitelstvo," pp. 154–155.

13 Ibid., pp. 156–57.

14 Mukhametshin, "Islam v Tatarskoi obshchestvennoi mysli nachala XX v.," pp. 180–187.

15 For example, Russian and Austrian scholars Svetlana Chervonnaya and Andreas Koppeler state it is "to a significant extent apolitical." See Koppeler and Chervonnaya, "Musulmanksie narody Rossii: istoricheskoe vvedenie," in Iordan, Kuzeev, and Chervonnaya, eds., *Islam v Yevrazii*, pp. 98–118, at p. 105. Abdullin finds it distinctly national and by implication ethno-political. Other tsarist scholars tended to regard it as nationalist in the sense of chauvinism, as did Soviet propagandists and scholars who added to this charge that jadidism was bourgeois, pan-Turkic, and pan-Islamist. See

Abdullin, "Dzhadidizm kak etap v razvitii Tatarskogo prosvetitelstvo," pp. 129, and 134–142.

16 Abdullin, "Dzhadidizm kak etap v razvitii Tatarskogo prosvetitelstvo," pp. 130–131.

17 Ibid., pp. 133, 135–137.

18 Mukhametshin, "Islam v Tatarskoi obshchestvennoi mysli nachala XX v.," pp. 161–188.

19 Ibid., pp. 178–179.

20 Abdullin, "Dzhadidizm kak etap v razvitii Tatarskogo prosvetitelstvo," p. 140.

21 On the latter point of view see the post-Beslan interview with Tatarstan president Mintimer Shaimiev's top political advisor Rafael Khakimov in Rafael Mirgazizov, "Rafail' Khakimov: Vostok i Zapad sblizhaet idzhtikhad – svobodomyslie," *Respublika Tatarstan*, 7 Oct. 2004, www.rt-online.ru

22 Mona Siddiqui, head of the Department of Theology and Religious Studies at the University of Glasgow in Scotland, finds there are other signs of moderation, too. She notes that, historically, the most widespread form of Sunni Muslim jurisprudence in the region has been the Hanafi maskhab and that among the four schools of Sunni jurisprudence, it is the one most open to new ideas. See Gulnoza Saidazimova, "Central Asia: Region Returns to Muslim Roots," RFERL, 4 Aug. 2005, www.rferl.org.

23 See Hahn, *Russia's Revolution from Above*, Chs. 3–10.

24 See the Tatar sources cited in Harley Balzer, "Rethinking August 1991," *Demokratizatsiya*, Vol. 13, No. 2 (Spring 2005), pp. 193–218, at pp. 202, 216 (n. 28).

25 Aleksei Zverev, "Znachenie opyta Tatarstana dlya Gruzii i Abkhazii," in B. Koppiters, D. Darchiashvili, and N. Akaba, eds., *Poiski alternative dlya Gruzii i Abkhazii: Praktika federalizma* (Moscow: Ves Mir, 1999), pp. 107–132.

26 See Rafael Khakim(ov), "Kto ty, Tatarin," *Vostochnyi ekspress*, Nos. 17–18, 26 April–2 May 2002, and R. S. Khakimov, "Ob osnovakh asimmetrichnosti Rossiiskoi federatsii," in L. M. Drobizheva, ed., *Asimetrichnaya Federatsiya: vzglyad iz tsentra, respublik, i oblastei* (Moscow: Institute of Sociology RAN: 1998), p. 45

27 Matthew Evangelista argues there was no threat of Tatarstan or any other region (except Chechnya) seceding in the early 1990s. Evangelista, *The Chechen Wars*, pp. 6, 8, 102, 190–191.

28 See Dmitrii P. Gorenburg, *Minority Ethnic Mobilization in the Russian Federation* (Cambridge: Cambridge University Press, 2003), pp. 122–124.

29 Evangelista, *The Chechen Wars*, p. 106.

30 Zverev, "Znachenie opyta Tatarstana dlya Gruzii i Abkhazii," p. 120.

31 Evangelista, *The Chechen Wars*, p. 102.

32 Khakimov's *Sumerki Imperii* (Kazan, 1993) is cited in I. K. Kalinin, "Pravo narodov na samoopredelenie," *Zvezda Povolzhya*, 25 Sept. – 1 Oct. 2003, p. 2.

33 Rafik Mukhametshin, "Na putyakh k konfessional'noi politike: Islam v Tatarstane," *Religiya i SMI – Religiya v svetskom mire*, Religare.ru www.religare.ru, p. 14.

34 Mukhametshin, "Na putyakh k konfessional'noi politike: Islam v Tatarstane," p. 14.

35 Khakimov, *Gde nasha Mekka?*. A short version may be found in *Nezavisimaya gazeta – Religiya*, No. 20, 20 Oct. 2004. See also Rafael Khakimov, "Put idzhtikhada," *Otecehestvennyie zapiski*, No. 5, 2003, www.strana-oz.ru/print.php?type=article&id=681&numid=14& article=681, Khakimov, "Islam v Povolzh'e," www.kazanfed.ru/authors/khakimov/.

36 Khakimov, *Gde nasha Mekka?* (page numbers refer to printed internet copy), p. 12.

37 Khakim(ov), "Kto Ty, Tatarin," p. 3 (page numbers refer to printed internet copy).

38 Khakimov, *Gde nasha Mekka?*, p. 20

39 Ibid., pp. 15, 48.

40 Ibid., pp. 4, 39.

41 Ibid., p. 53.

42 Ibid., p. 37.

43 Ibid., pp. 53–54.

44 Ibid., p. 58.
45 "Volga Area News," *Zvezda Povolzhya*, No. 39, 9–15 Oct. 2003, p. 1.
46 "M. Bibarsov sravnil teoretikov 'evroislama' s yenukhami," Islam.ru, 8 Nov. 2005, www.islam.ru/press/rus/2005-11-08/#9930.
47 Valiulla Yakupov, "Religioznyi modernism ili modernizatsiya obshchestva?" *Zvezda Povolzhya*, No. 37, 16–22 Sept. 2003, p. 3.
48 "Oshibka prezidenta. Shaimieva podstavil ego vizir," Islam.ru, 30 Oct. 2004, www.islam.ru/pressclub/tema/shaimiev/; "Dzhadidizm, 'Evroislam,' 'Islamskoe reformatorstvo,'" Islam.ru, 30 Oct. 2004, www.islam.ru/lib/warning/sekty/djaidizm/; Azat Akhunov, "Ne prosto dzhadizm," Islam.ru, 30 Oct. 2004, www.islam.ru/pressclub/histori/jzadidizm/; Renat Bekkin, "'Tatarskii' Islam? Ili: 'A ne zanyatsya li nam idzhtikhadom?'" Islam.ru, 30 Oct. 2004, www.islam.ru/pressclub/analitika/idgtihad/; Abid Ulaz Dzhan, "Mif ob 'umerennom Islame,'" Islam.ru, 30 Oct. 2004, www.islam.ru/pressclub/analitika/new-mif/; "'Tak, Kto zhe Ty, Tatarin?,'" Islam.ru, Oct. 2002, www.islam.ru/pressclub/analitika/hakim_tatarlar/. All Islam.ru articles are in the author's archive, as Islam.ru has no archive link on its site.
49 See Rafik Mukhametshin, "Religiya v svetskom obshchestve – Na putyakh k konfessionalnoi politike: Islam v Tatarstane," Religare.ru, 15 March 2004, www.religare.ru/print8747.htm.
50 Gusman Iskhakov, "Islam v Tatarstane: istoriya i sovremennost'," *Mir Islama*, Vol. 1, Nos. 1–2 (1999), pp. 21–24, at p. 24.
51 Iskhakov, "Islam v Tatarstane: istoriya i sovremennost," p. 23, and Khakim, "Kto Ty, Tatarin," p. 18.
52 Khakim, "Kto Ty, Tatarin?"
53 For example, the main works of Musa Bigiev, a leading Islamic theologian of the jadidist school of thought, have still not been republished, and his lesser works have been published in less than perfect translations. The first volume of Bigiev's works was published only in December 2005. "Vyshel pervyi tom trudov M. Bigieva," Islam.ru, 23 Dec. 2005, www.islam.ru/press/rus/2005-12-23/#10491. See also "Shaimieva podstavil ego vizir,'" Islam.ru, 30 Oct. 2004, www.islam.ru/pressclub/tema/shaimiev.
54 RFERL Russian Federation Report, Vol. 2, No. 42 (15 Nov. 2000).
55 Presidential representative to the Urals Federal District Pyotr Latyshev called for changes in federal legislation on 15 December 2001 and concurred with Shaimiev's view on the advantages of some regional laws and that the federal government ought to change some of its legislation accordingly. Sergei Pushkarev, "Latyshev Seeks Change in Federal Laws," EWI Russian Regional Report, Vol. 7, No. 1 (9 Jan. 2002). Later, President Putin reiterated this point of view, and appears to have urged the federal government to incorporate some of Tatarstan's laws regarding land ownership into federal legislation allowing the limited purchase and sale of urban land plots.
56 RFERL Newsline, Vol. 5, No. 134, Part I (18 July 2001).
57 A 1999 law required that all such contradictions be harmonized by June 2000, and a resolution and finding of the Russian Constitutional Court of 27 June 2000 held that several regions, including Tatarstan, had failed to comply with that law.
58 Only North Ossetiya had endeavored to harmonize its constitution with federal law through amendments, Biryukov noted, but the other four violators, notably three titular Muslim republics (Tatarstan, Bashkortostan, and Adygeya), had not. Yurii Biryukov, "Prokuratura bystrogo reagirovaniya," *Nezavisimaya gazeta*, 28 Feb. 2001, p. 8.
59 Irina Kaisarova, "Chemu soprotivlyaetsya Shaimiev," *Zvezda Povolzhya* 1–7 Feb. 2001, p. 2.
60 "Pochemu vertikal' nravitsya ne vsem," *Rossiiskaya gazeta*, 4 June 2001, www.rg.ru/interview/565.shtm.
61 Presidential envoy in charge of the Central FO Georgii Poltavchenko supports this

view. See Svetlana Sukhova, "'My sotsobyazatel'stb ne beryom . . . ,'" *Segodnya*, 21 March 2001. At least one Russian expert on Russian federalism proposed the same as a member of Yeltsin's advisory Presidential Council. See Leonid Smirnyagin, *Rossiiskii Federalizm: paradoksy, protivorechiya, predrassudki* (Moscow: Moskovskii obshchestvennyi nauchnyi fond, 1998), p. 70. For his critique of Putin's federal reforms, see Smirnyagin, "Federalizm po Putinu ili Putin po federalizmu (zheleznoi pyatoi)?" *Brifing* (Moskovskii Tsentr Karnegi), Vol. 3, No. 3 (March 2001).

62 See the excerpts from Shaimiev's undelivered "Kontseptsiya gosudarstvennoi politiki po razgranicheniyu predmetov vedeniya i polnomochii mezhdu federal'nym, regional'nym i munitsipal'nym urovnyami vlasti" in *Zvezda Povolzhya*, 1–6 March 2001, p. 3, or the full text in *Kazanskii federalist*, Vol. 1, No. 1, (Winter 2002), pp. 105–132.

63 Recall that article 13 of the above mentioned 25 April 1997 Russian federal law "On the Principles and Procedure for Differentiating the Areas of Jurisdiction and Authority between the Organs of State Power of the Russian Federation and the Organs of State Power of the Subjects of the Russian Federation" stipulated that if more than one-third of the subjects' legislatures "speak out against" a draft law before its second reading in the Duma, then a conciliation commission must be set up consisting of Duma deputies and representatives of the opposing federation subjects.

64 Yurii Alaev, "Mintimer Shaimiev budet dobivat'sya polnogo razvoda regionov i tsentra," Strana.ru, www.strana.ru/print/977821979.html. See also East-West Institute Russian Regional Report, Vol. 6, No. 8, (28 Feb. 2001).

65 Tatarstan's old November 1992 constitution can still be found at the official Tatarstan website, Respublika Tatarstan, at www.tatar.ru/append27.html.

66 This was followed by a phrase limiting the republic's sovereignty: "The sovereignty of the Republic of Tatarstan is expressed in the possession of the full range of state power (legislative, executive and judicial) outside the jurisdiction of the Russian Federation and the powers of the Russian Federation under the sphere of joint jurisdiction of the Russian Federation and the Tatarstan Republic and is an inviolable attribute of the Tatarstan Republic." Copy of the May 2002 Tatarstan constitution in the author's archive. See also www.tatar.ru/constitution.html. The force of the word "state" was negated by the absence of the word "sovereignty" and the distribution of powers according to the federal constitution's articles 71–73, which leave the federation's subjects with effectively nil powers should Moscow denude or reject power-sharing treaties and fill the legal field with federal laws which take precedence over regional laws.

67 Postnova, "Tatarstan v grazhdanskom brake s Rossiei."

68 Prosecutor Zvyagintsev also protested against constitutional clauses Moscow regarded to be in violation of Russian citizens' right to be elected regardless of knowledge of a particular language, clauses on the organization and activities of bodies of state power, and clauses on the constitutional responsibility of the president and State Council of Tatarstan. Prosecutors also registered the federal center's dissatisfaction with the Tatarstan constitution's continued emphasis on the power-sharing treaty between Kazan and Moscow as the main document for determining relations between the center and the republic. RFERL Newsline, Vol. 6, No. 118 (13 June 2002) and RFERL Tatar-Bashkir Daily Report, 17 June 2002.

69 "Opyat' konstitutsiyu trebyat," *Vremya i dengi*, 24 Jan. 2003, www.e-vid.ru/?id= 32631.html.

70 The court tried to balance its decision and give something to the republic's leadership by rejecting prosecutors' protests against clauses on the method of recalling deputies to the Tatarstan State Council and on the organization and activities of federal courts and judges' status. Irina Simonova, "Tataria lishilas' suverenitet," *Kommersant*, 1 April 2004, p. 3.

71 It states that Chechnya's sovereignty "is expressed in the possession of the full range of power (legislative, executive, and judicial) outside the competency of the Russian Federation and the joint competencies of the Russian Federation and the Republic of Chechnya and is an inalienable qualitative status of the Chechen Republic."

72 Raisa Shcherbakova, "Farid Mukhametshin: 'My gotovy proiti etot neprostoi put,'" *Respublika Tatarstan*, 19 July 2003, www.rt-online.ru/numbers/analyst/?ID=10517.

73 In November 2002, Tatarstan brought its Administrative Violations Code and numerous related laws into conformity with the federal version adopted earlier in the year. This also involved abolishing or amending numerous Tatarstan laws that pertained to the leveling of fines for various violations of the law as well. This act of legal harmonization involved issues ranging from the environment, housing, welfare violations, the guarding of property, and veterinarian medicine to the maintenance of public order and violations of the law committed by state officials. See "Kodeks Respubliki Tatarstan ob administrativnykh pravonarushenyakh," *Respublika Tatarstan*, 31 Dec. 2002, www.rt-online.ru/documents/laws/?ID=6427&forprint12/30/2002.html, and "Zakon Respubliki Tatarstan 'O vvedenie v deistvie Kodeksa Respubliki Tatarstan ob administrativnykh pravonarushenyakh,'" *Respublika Tatarstan*, 31 Dec. 2002, www.rt-online.ru/documents/laws/?ID=6428&forprint12/30/2002.html. The same occurred in numerous regions across the country that had administrative codes prior to the adoption of the federal version.

74 "Zakony Respubliki Tatarstan i normativnyie akty, ne podlezhashie primeneniyu," *Tatarstan.ru*, 1 August 2003, www.tatarstan.ru.

75 Daniel S. Treisman, *After the Deluge: Regional Crises and Political Consolidation in Russia* (Ann Arbor: University of Michigan Press, 1999).

76 Hahn, "Putin's Federal Reforms," pp. 525–526.

77 Khakim(ov), "Kto Ty, Tatarin," p. 24.

78 See RFERL Tatar-Bashkir Daily Report, 28 and 29 Dec. 2004.

79 Khakim(ov), "Kto Ty, Tatarin," pp. 24, 26.

80 D. Iskhakov, "O deyatelnosti komissii ispolkom VKT . . . ," *Zvezda Povolzhya*, No. 39, 9–15 Oct. 2003, pp. 1–2.

81 See the editorial in Rashid Akhmetov, "Otstuplenie," *Zvezda Povolzhya*, Nos. 30–31, 1–13 Aug. 2003, p. 1.

82 *Zvezda Povolzhya*, 21 Oct. 2004, cited in RFERL Tatar-Bashkir Daily Report, 22 Oct. 2004.

83 Galeev, lamenting Tatarstan's loss of "statehood" as the price of Putin's war with terrorists, argued that if Russia was in a real war as Putin claimed, "then a corresponding legislative act should be adopted." In fact, "a secret military management is being introduced." From an interview with Marat Galeev in the Tatarstan weekly *Zvezda Povolzhya*, 14 Oct. 2004, cited in RFERL Tatar-Bashkir Daily Report, 15 Oct. 2004. Elsewhere, Galeev stated: "This is only ground for the establishment of a unified state. We bade farewell long ago to democracy, since federalism is a part of it. I think supreme federal authorities are not ready for democracy." Vladimir Zhigulskii and Yelena Taran, "Blitz opros: Vernost' reshenii podtverdit lish vremya," *Respublika Tatarstan*, 21 Sept. 2004, www.rt-online.ru/numbers/social/?ID=17929.

84 *Nezavisimaya gazeta*, 13 Oct. 2004, cited in RFERL Tatar-Bashkir Daily Report, 13 Oct. 2004.

85 RFERL Tatar-Bashkir Daily Report, 14 Oct. 2004.

86 RFERL Tatar-Bashkir Daily Report, 25 Oct. 2004.

87 Yekaterina Vorobeva and Alla Barakhova, "Suverenitet proglochen i vozvratu ne podlezhit," *Kommersant -Daily*, 26 Oct. 2004, www.kommersant.ru.

88 "Farid Mukhametshin: Golos Tatarstana dolzhen byt' uslyshan," *Respublika Tatarstan*, 29 Oct. 2004, www.rt-online.ru.

89 Gul'nar Zalyalova, "Na sessii Gosudarstvennogo Soveta," *Respublika Tatarstan*, 26 Oct. 2004, www.rt-online.ru.

90 He added, in what was perhaps a veiled threat to influence the YeR congress's delegate selection process, that in elections of the regions' delegates to the next Yedinaya Rossiya congress that regional party members and parliamentary deputies were demanding that the regional legislatures' opinion be taken into account. "Uchytyvat' mnenie regionov," *Respublika Tatarstan*, 10 Nov. 2004, www.rt-online.ru/numbers/politik/?ID=19314

91 The vote was accompanied by an official commentary from the Tatarstan State Council recommending that the federal bill should not include the presidential power to disband a regional legislature if it rejects his nominee a second time, that FO presidential envoys should not function as mediators between regional chief executives and the Russian president, and that abolition of elections of regional leaders will expire along with Putin's presidential term. RFERL Tatar-Bashkir Daily Report, 26 Oct. 2004.

92 V. N. Lysenko, "Razdelenie vlasti i opyt' Rossiiskoi Federatsii," in M. N. Guboglo, ed., *Federalizm vlasti i vlast' federalizma* (Moscow: IntelTek, 1997), pp. 166–193, at pp. 184–186.

93 See the treaty in Guboglo, *Federalizm vlasti i vlast' federalizma*, p. 247.

94 Ibid., p. 248.

95 Raisa Shcherbakova, "Farid Mukhametshin: 'My gotovy proiti etot neprostoi put,'" *Respublika Tatarstan*, 19 July 2003, www.rt-online.ru/numbers/analyst/?ID=10517.

96 Midkhat Farukshin, "Vlast vykhodit za predely pravogo polya," *Nezavisimaya gazeta*, 28 Jan. 2005, www.ng.ru/politics/2005=01-28/2_chechnya.html.

97 RFERL Tatar-Bashkir Daily Report, 16 Feb. 2005.

98 The subtle game included jockeying for position as well on the part of Shaimiev, who publicly stated his rather dubious reluctance to remain in office. It appears that Shaimiev "agreed" to stay in office to maintain stability in Tatarstan in return for compromises in the new power-sharing treaty.

99 The details regarding natural resources control and management would be specified in inter-governmental agreements which would also need to be submitted to the Russian State Duma for approval. "Mintimer Shaimiev: Nastupilo vremya dlya podpisaniya novogo Dogovora," *Respublika Tatarstan*, 1 Nov. 2005, www.rt-online.ru/numbers/chronicle/?ID=26001.

100 See the official VTOTs statement in *Zvezda Povolzhya*, 1–14 March 2001, p. 2.

101 RFERL Tatar-Bashkir Daily Report, 1 Aug. 2002.

102 RFERL Russian Political Weekly, Vol. 3, No. 8, 21 Feb. 2003, www.rferl.org/reports/rpw/2003/ 02/8-210203.asp.

103 RFERL Tatar-Bashkir Daily Report, 20 Sept. 2004.

104 Ibid.

105 Ovrutskii elaborated: "A historical mission fell on the republics to win over the federation from the empire . . . . Now one can see that the republics did not cope with this task. Policy was not structured in a proper way; there was no foresight in the policy; tactical deceptions were undertaken. [The republics] have not demonstrated to all of Russia that federal relations are most agreeable and useful. Loyalty and federal discipline have not been demonstrated to the federation." RFERL Tatar-Bashkir Daily Report, 19 Oct. 2004.

106 Rashit Akhmetov, "Den' Vovy," *Zvezda Povolzhya*, 16–22 Sept. 2004, p. 1.

107 *Zvezda Povolzhya*, 21 Oct. 2004, cited in RFERL Tatar-Bashkir Daily Report, 22 Oct. 2004.

108 RFERL Tatar-Bashkir Daily Report, 20 Sept. 2004.

109 On the 2003 demonstration, see RFERL Tatar-Bashkir Daily Report, 14 Oct. 2003, www.rferl.org.

110 RFERL Tatar-Bashkir Daily Report, 18 Oct. 2004, www.rferl.org.

111 *Zvezda Povolzhya*, 21 Oct. 2004, cited in RFERL Tatar-Bashkir Daily Report, 22 Oct. 2004.
112 The official Russian Information Agency "Novosti" reported a figure of fifty. RIA "*Novosti*," 23 Oct. 2004. RFERL reported four hundred in attendance. RFERL Tatar-Bashkir Daily Report, 25 Oct. 2004. For comparison, demonstrations held in much larger Moscow on 28 and 29 October attracted 200–300 protesters. Sergei Borisov, "Russia: The Governor of Governors," Transitions Online, 1 Nov. 2004, www.tol.cz.
113 RFERL Tatar-Bashkir Daily Report, 20 Oct. 2004. Liberals at the federal level seemed to reach out to Kazan's democratic, federalist moderate nationalists. For example, State Duma deputy Vladimir Ryzhkov argued in an October *Novaya gazeta* interview that appointing the president of Tatarstan greatly "exceeds the bounds of the constitution and a federative system" because "our republics have sovereignty, though it is limited, and sovereignty is incompatible with the appointment of a head of a republic being, in fact, a state, something that is established in the Russian constitution." Ryzhkov added that "the head of one state cannot appoint the head of another state from above, but this is almost exactly what is being suggested by Putin." *Novaya gazeta*, 18 Oct. 2004, cited in RFERL Tatar-Bashkir Daily Report, 20 Oct. 2004.
114 RFERL Tatar-Bashkir Daily Report, 21 Sept. 2004.
115 Rinat Bilalov, "VTOTS uidyot v podpol'e," *Vostochnyi Ekspress*, 20 Nov. 2004, cited in http://tatarica.yuldash.com/society/article72.
116 See Itar-Tass 2 April 2005, 16:37 GMT.
117 Zverev, "Znachenie opyta Tatarstana dlya Gruzii i Abkhazii," p. 120.
118 Kobishchanov, "Musulmane Rossii, korennye rossiiskie musulmane i russkie-musulmane," p. 79, citing L. Sagitov, "O nekotorykh aspektakh etnokulturnoi spetsifiki sovremennogo tatarskogo obshchestva," *Islam v tatarskom mire*, p. 230.
119 Sergei Kudryavtsev, "TOTs likvidrovan, no . . . ," *Vechernie Chelny*, No. 37, 15 Sept. 2004, www.vechernie–chelny.ru/view.php?viewyear=2004&viewnum=37&viewart=2.
120 Viktor Smirnov, "Glavnoe upravlenie yustitsii RF po RT napravilo v sud zayavlenie o likvidatsii Naberezhnochelninskogo otdeleniya TOTs," Intertat.ru, 2 Aug. 2004, 14:34, www.intertat.ru. According to another source, a representative of the NChOTOTs acknowledged that the branch organization had never attempted to register because by law it was not required to do so. Kudryavtsev, "TOTs likvidrovan, no . . . . "
121 RFERL Tatar-Bashkir Daily Report, 15 Oct. 2004.
122 Vera Postnova, "Naberezhnyi Chelny zachistili," *Nezavsimaya gazeta*, 10 Sept. 2004, p. 4.
123 The statement further declared that it would appeal in the Supreme Courts of Tatarstan and Russia and, if necessary to the International Court at Strasbourg and "defend democracy, justice, freedom of speech, the rights of peoples, and human rights." "Obrashchenie Naberezhnochelninskogo Otdeleniya (NChO) TOTs po povodu usileniya natsional'noi voiny spetssluzhb protov NChOTOTs," *ASN-News*, 23 Oct. 2004, http://nurlat.kazan.ws/cgi-bin/guide.pl?action=article?id_razdel=324&id_article=15476.
124 See the NChOTOTs statement in "Zayavlenie TOTs: Nam nuzhen mezhnatsional'nyi sovet!," *ASN-News*, 2 Aug. 2004, http://nurlat.kazan.ws/cgi-bin/guide.pl?&action=article&id_org=78& id_razdel=1223&id_article=14111.
125 In addition to the arrests of Kashapov and alleged foreign and indigenous Islamists belonging to the Hizb ut-Tahrir Islami revolutionary party discussed further below, one report – although it comes from a source that needs to be approached with caution on this type of issue, the ChRI Islamists' website, *Kavkaz-Tsentr* – claims that the run-up to and aftermath of the August 2005 festivities surrounding the celebration of the thousandth anniversary of Kazan sparked a series of unwarranted arrests in which detainees were beaten and otherwise maltreated. See the report sent to the site from one Ilyas Kadyrov, an ostensible resident of Naberezhnyi Chelny, where most of these arrests supposedly took place, in "Volna novykh repressii protiv musulman

Tatarstana," *Kavkaz-Tsentr*, 3 Oct. 2005, 00:08:26, www.kavkazcenter.net/russ/content/2005/10/03/ 38056.shtml.

126 Boris Bronshtein, "Tatarskoe natsionalnoe dvizhenie soshlo na obochinu," *Novaya gazeta*, 5 Sept. 2005, http://2005.novaya gazeta.ru/nomer/2005/65n/n65n-s09.shtml.

127 RFERL Tatar-Bashkir Daily, 21 Oct. 2005.

128 Group "Pyramid," "Tam, za tumanom," *Zvezda Povolzhya*, No. 1, 13–19 Jan. 2005, pp. 1–2.

129 Chechenpress.com, 4 June 2005, www.chechenpress.com.

130 See Rafis Kashapov, "Tatary trebuyut prekratit' lgat' o 'Kulikovskoi bitve,'" *Kavkaz-Tsentr*, 28 May 2005, www.kavkazcenter.net/russ/content/2005/05/28/34417.shtml.

131 Rafis Kashapov, "Den pamyati tatarskogo naroda," *Kavkaz-Tsentr*, 13 Oct. 2005, 00:16:51, www.kavkazcenter.net/russ/content/2005/10/13/38377.shtml. See also Kashapov, "'Kulikovskaya bitva': Pravda ili vymysel?" *Kavkaz-Tsentr*, 19 Sept. 2005, 00:03:46, www.kavkazcenter.net/russ/content/2005/10/13/37630.shtml.

132 "V Tatarstane proidyt vybory muftiya," Islam.ru, 16 Dec. 2005, wwwislam.ru/press/rus2005-12-26/#10497.

133 See parts 1–6 of Iskhak-khadzhi Lotfullin's Sept.-Oct. 2005 series of articles "V udushayushchikh ob"yatiakh imperii" on *Kavkaz-Tsentr*, (www.kavkazcenter.net/russ/content/2005/09/21/ 37679.shtml, www.kavkazcenter.net/russ/content/2005/09/22/37709.shtml, www.kavkazcenter.net/russ/ content/2005/09/23/37735.shtml, www.kavkazcenter.net/russ/content/2005/09/24/37768.shtml, www.kavkazcenter.com /russ/content/2005/09/26/37816.shtm), and www.kavkazcenter.com/russ/content/2005/09/27/37841.shtml].

134 For example, see "'Tsentrmuskom' prodolzhaet deistvovat," Kavkaz-Tsentr, 2 May 2005, www.kavkazcenter.net/russ/content/2005/05/02/33401.shtml.

135 Mukhametshin, "Na putyakh k konfessional'noi politike: Islam v Tatarstane," p. 15.

136 Yevgenii Aksenov, "A v otvet tishina," *Vechernyaya Kazan*, 9 September 2004, www.evening-kazan.ru.

137 Irina Durnitsyna, "Kak budem zhit' posle Beslana," *Respublika Tatarstan*, 11 Sept. 2004, www.rt-online.ru.

138 Ibid., 12 Sept. 2004, 15:00 GMT.

139 Vera Postnova, "Vakhkhabity pod nosom u Shaimieva," *Nezavisimaya gazeta*, 22 Sept. 2004, p. 4, and "Efir TV," 12 Sept. 2004, 15:00 GMT.

140 Postnova, "Vakhkhabity pod nosom u Shaimieva."

141 It was also reported, citing Kazan's daily *Vostochnyi ekspress*, that Wahhabis were running summer camps in Tatarstan set up with the help of several raion administration heads as claimed by DUMT first deputy chairman Valiulla Yakupov. *Vostochnyi Ekspress*, No. 41, 16 Sept. 2004, cited in Postnova, "Vakhkhabity pod nosom u Shaimieva."

142 Postnova, "Vakhkhabity pod nosom u Shaimieva." See also Postnova, "Yeshchyo odno vzyatie Kazani," *Nezavisimaya gazeta*, 4 March 2002, p. 4, and Postnova, "Voiny dzhikhada s beregov Kamya," *Nezavisimaya gazeta*, 16 April 2002, p. 4.

143 Postnova, "Vakhkhabity pod nosom u Shaimieva."

144 "M. Bibarsov zaveril, chto 'pod nosom u Shaimieva' smertnits net," Islam.ru, 30 Sept. 2004, www.islam.ru and in the author's archive; "Komu-to vygodno ochernyat' islam," *Vechernie Chelny*, No. 39, 22 Sept. 2004, www.vechernie-chelny.ru/view.php?viewyear=2004&viewnum=39&viewart=4; and RFERL Tatar-Bashkir Daily Report, 29 Sept. 2004.

145 "V. Yakupov: korruptsiya sposobstvuet ekstremizmu, prikryvayushchemu Islamom," Islam.ru, 17 Sept. 2004, www.islam.ru and in the author's archive. See also RFERL Tatar-Bashkir Daily Report, 20 Sept. 2004, citing the Tatarstan daily *Vostochnyi ekspress*, 17 Sept. 2004.

146 "V. Yakupov: korruptsiya sposobstvuet ekstremizmu, prikryvayushchemy Islamom."

147 "V Moskve zaderzhan chlen 'Islamskogo dzhamaat,'" *Regnum*, 5 May 2005, www.regnum.ru/news/450313.html, and "Zaderzhannyi v Zelenograde uchastnik ekstremistskoi organizatsii 'Islamskii dzhamaat' pribyl v Moskovskii region dlya podgotovki teraktov v kanun prazdnovaniya Dnya Pobedy," *Prime-Tass*, 6 May 2005, www.prime-tass.ru/news/show.asp?id=502337&ct=news. See also "V Zelenograde zaderzhan activist ekstrimistskoi organizatsii 'Islamskii dzhamaat,' obvinyaemyi v terrorizme," Antiterror.ru, 6 May 2005, www.antiterror.ru/news/85891218 citing RIA "Novosti."

148 "Rossiiskikh talibov primeryayut k teraktu," *Kommersant-Kazan*, 22 April 2005, www.kommersant.ru/region/kazan/main.htm?year=2005&issue=72, and Orkhan Dzhemal, "Rossiiskii Andizhan," *Versiya*, No. 21, 6 June 2005, http//:versiasovsek.ru/material.php?3927.

149 "Uznikov Guantanamo v Bulgume obvinili v terrorizme," *Kommersant*, 14 July 2005, p. 4.

150 "V Tatarii vzorvana opora vysokovoltnoi elektrolinii," Itar-Tass, 1 June 2005, 19:51, www.itar-tass.com/level2.html?NewsID=2094452&PageNum=0.

151 "Mat' pokhishchennogo 'guantanamovtsa' razyskivaet syna," Islam.ru, 1 Sept. 2005, www.islam.ru/press/rus/2005-09-01/#9175, citing the news agency Interfax-Povolzhya.

152 Mansur Mazaev, "Neveroyatnyie prikhucheniya imama, ili v naruchnikakh vokrug sveta," Kavkaz-Tsentr, 3 Oct. 2005 10:55:30, www.kavkazcenter.net/russ/content/2005/10/03/38071.shtml.

153 Vera Postnova, "Chechenskii sled na trassakh Tatarstana," *Nezavisimaya gazeta*, 7 Oct. 2005, p. 4. See also "Strategicheskaya tsel' – sozdanie Islamskogo gosudarstva v Povolzhe," *Kavkaz-Tsentr*, 5 Oct. 2005, 15:57:12, www.kavkazcenter.net/russ/content/2005/10/05/38153.shtml, citing Gazeta.ru.

154 Postnova, "Chechenskii sled na trassakh Tatarstana"; Regnum.ru, 6 Oct. 2005, www.regnum.ru; "Police Capture Two Terrorists in Tatarstan," Retwa.org, 5 Oct. 2005, www.retwa.org/home.cfm?articleId-1043; and "More Details on Arrests of Terrorists in Tatarstan," Retwa.org, 6 October 2005, www.retwa.org/hom.cfm?articleId=1048.

155 It has been identified in Arabic as *Jamaat a-Islami* (Islamic Jamaat) and, in Russian as, *Islamskii Dzhamaat*, as the Tatarstan-based combat jamaat has also been identified. Andrei Skrobot, "Kogo gotova osvozhdat 'Partiya Islamskogo Osvobozhdeniya,'" *Nezavisimaya gazeta*, 25 Jan. 2005, p. 9.

156 Regnum.ru, 30 April 2005, www.regnum.ru cited in RFERL Tatar-Bashkir Daily, 3 May 2005.

157 The official investigation concluded 342 had been injured. RFERL Newsline, Vol. 9, No. 230 (12 Dec. 2005).

158 *Izvestiya*, 24 and 27 Dec. 2004, cited in RFERL Tatar-Bashkir Daily Report, 28 Dec. 2004.

159 "V Ulyanovske FSB ustroila vtoruyu Chechnyu," *Kavkaz-Tsentr*, 19 Dec. 2003, 15:17:12, www.kavkazcenter.net/russ/content/2003/12/19/15097.shtml.

160 "V Ulyanovske prizyazhnyie priznali vinovnymi ekstremistov iz bandy 'Dzhamaat,'" Interfax-Religiya, 21 Dec. 2005, 13:34:00, www.interfax-religion.ru/?act=news&div=8252, and "Seven Islamic Extremists to Be Given Final Plea Friday," Itar-Tass, 30 Dec. 2005.

161 "Seven Islamic Extremists to Be Given Final Plea Friday," Itar-Tass, 30 Dec. 2005.

162 Igor Klin, "Sem mechetei Penzenskoi mekki," *Isvestiya*, 29 Nov. 2005, www.izvestia.ru/special/article3021910.

163 "Penzenskii mufti obvinyaet 'Izvestiya' v klevete i islamofobii," Islam.ru, 3 Dec. 2005, www.islam.ru/pressclub/vslux/ababibars/; "Elyuzanskie musulmane namereny podat v sud na 'Izvestiya,'" Islam.ru, 30 Nov. 2005, www.islam.ru/press/rus/2005-11-30/#10207; and "M Shaimiev seryozno ozabochen antiislamskoi publikatsii v

'Izvestiyakh,'" Islam.ru, 5 Dec. 2005, www.islam.ru/press/rus/2005-12-05/#10262.

164 "Na medrese Srednei Elyuzani zavedeno delo," Islam.ru, 6 Dec. 2005, www.islam.ru/press/rus/2005/11/30/#1-0279.

165 See Hizb ut-Tahrir's website: www.1924.org.

166 Ariel Cohen, "Hizb ut-Tahrir: An Emerging Threat to U.S. Interests in Central Asia," Backgrounder No. 1656, 30 May. 2003, Heritage Foundation, www.heritage.org/Research/RussianandEurasia/BG1656.cfm.

167 "Uznikov Guantanamo v Bulgume obvinili v terrorizme."

168 Cohen, "Hizb ut-Tahrir: An Emerging Threat to U.S. Interests in Central Asia."

169 RFERL Newsline, Vol. 8, No. 228 (7 Dec. 2004) citing, Asia Plus-Blitz, 6 Dec. 2004.

170 Rustam Vafin, "V Kazani zaderzhan glavar' gruppirovki 'Hizb ut-Tahrir Islama,'" *Vechernyaya Kazan'*, 19 Nov. 2004, www.evening-kazan.ru.

171 "V podgotovke terakta podozrevaetsya . . . ," *Vechernie Chelny*, No. 47, 24 Nov. 2004, www.vechernie-chelny.ru/index.php?curyear=2004&curnum=47.

172 See "V podgotovke terakta podozrevaetsya . . . . " "Nizhegorodskie imamy proidut 'kursy povysheniya antiterroristicheskoi kvalifikatsii,'" Islam.ru, 7 Oct. 2004, www.islam.ru; "Chelyabinsk: sovershil namaz – sdai otpechatki pal'tsev," Islam.ru, 13 Oct. 2004, "UFSB Chelyabinska predupreilo musul'man o predstoyashchikh 'zachistkakh,'" Islam.ru, 21 Oct. 2004, www.islam.ru; "'Nursi' i 'Hizb ut-takhrir' – novye 'antiterroristicheskie' brendy?" Islam.ru, 22 Oct. 2004, www.islam.ru; and RFERL Tatar-Bashkir Daily Report, 19 Oct. 2004 and 30 Nov. 2004. HIT has also reportedly been active in Udmurtia, Moscow city, Moscow Oblast, Volgograd, and Astrakhan. Skrobot, "Kogo gotova osvobozhdat 'Partiya Islamskogo Osvobozhdeniya,'" See also Gordon M. Hahn, "Hizb ut-Tahrir's Russia Invasion?" RFERL *Russian Political Weekly*, Vol. 4 No. 48, (16 Dec. 2004), www.rferl.org/reports/rpw/2004/ 12/48-161204.asp.

173 Soon after the arrests in Naberezhnyi Chelny leading Muslims held "an emergency assembly in regard to the wave of arrests." "V podgotovke terakta podozrevaetsya . . . ." In April 2005, a small demonstration in Moscow was organized by the largely ethnic Tatar pro-Muslim Watan party in front of the Russian prosecutor general's office protesting the arrests of Muslims. Placards such as "Stop persecution against Tatars and Muslims," "Freedom of speech," and "Empire, do not trifle with Islam" were seen at the demonstration. RFERL Tatar-Bashkir Daily Report, 26 April 2005.

174 For a groundbreaking examination of this phenomenon, see Charles Tilly, *The Politics of Collective Violence* (Cambridge: Cambridge University Press, 2003).

CHAPTER SEVEN

1. Scales taken from Ted Robert Gurr, *Peoples Versus States: Minorities at Risk in the New Century* (Washington, D.C.: United States Institute of Peace, 2000), p. 31.

2. See Tilly, *The Politics of Collective Violence.*

3 One little-known report, for example, suggests that after many Chechens were forced out of Georgia's Pankisi Gorge they went to forests and caves in Ingushetiya just twelve miles southeast of the capital Nazran where unreported fighting ensued: "For a long time you could only hear about the fighting there from people who had tried to go there and were prevented at their own checkpoints. Officially the fighting was not occurring, except if you were caught in it. The fighting that never happened is over now, but the rebel bands are still there. It's not a loss for the federals because it was not fighting." Makhmedov, "After Beslan: Slow Days in Dagestan."

4 On Basaev's promise of a "summer of fire," see Liz Fuller, "Has the Chechen Resistance Suffered a Major Setback?" RFERL Caucasus Report, Vol. 8, No. 31 (10 Sept. 2005). For the *Kavkaz-Tsentr* commentary, see Bashirov, "Predstoyashee leto obeshaet byt' zharkim."

5 "MVD Says Terror Attacks in Southern Federal Okrug Down 53% in 2005," Retwa.org, 1 Oct. 2005, www.retwa.org/home.cfm?articleId=1013.

6 "Militants' 'Scorching Summer' Terror Plans Dampened," Retwa.org, 5 Oct. 2005, www.retwa.org/ home.cfm?articleId=1036.

7 "Abdallakh Shamil: 'My vocctanovim Islamskoe Gosudarstvo . . . ,'" *Kavkaz-Tsentr*, 19 April 2006, 11:09:57, www.kavkazcenter.com/russ/content/2006/04/19/43858.shtml, and "D. Umarov: 'My bolshe ne predlzhim Rossii mira," *Kavkaz-Tsentr*, 18 April 2006, 03:01:06, www.kavkazcenter.com/russ/content/ 2006/04/18/43822.shtml.

8 See Russian political analyst Alexei Makarkin's comments in Liz Fuller, "Chechnya: Separatist Leaders Admit to Logistical, Financial Problems," RFERL, 21 April 2006, www.rferl.org/featuresarticle/2006/4/ 6911B99E-B492-425D-B4F1-DDB31C87780A.html.

9 "Ramzan Kadyrov: Saidullayev's Right Hand Man Killed," Retwa.org, 14 Sept. 2005, www.retwa.org/home.cfm?articleId=791.

10 ROSh also reported: 20 large field bases destroyed; 1,143 secret caches of arms and explosives destroyed; 5 anti-aircraft missile launchers destroyed; 162 terror attacks have been prevented; and 600 homemade explosive devices disarmed. "Russia Publishes North Caucasus 2005 Anti-Terror Statistics," Retwa.org, 12 Sept. 2005, www.retwa.org/home.cfm?articleId=770.

11 In 1999 and again in 2003 Russia's State Duma passed legislation offering amnesty to Chechen fighters who laid down their weapons. According to Radio Liberty, 150 fighters were amnestied during the first period, and some two hundred fighters during the second. Putin has noted that nearly 50 percent of the Chechen police force consists of former Chechen militants. RFERL Newsline, Vol. 10, No. 24 (8 Feb. 2006).

12 See "Kadyrov and MVD Disagree on Fighter Numbers," Retwa.org, (18 Jan. 2006), www.retwa.org/ home.cfm?articleId=1699.

13 "Former Ichkeria Defense Minister to Run for Parliament," Retwa.org, 22 Sept. 2005, www.retwa.org/home.cfm?articleId=945. Also, ChRI "Brigadier General" Khizir Khachukayev voluntarily surrendered to police in November 2005, disbanded his armed formation, and publicly called upon other fighters to lay down their arms. "An Ichkerian Brigadier General Turns Himself In," Retwa.org, 23 Nov. 2005, www.retwa.org/home.cfm?articleId=1389. In March 2006, the former Chairman of Chechnya's State Security Adminstration under President Dudaev, Sultan Geliskhanov, turned himself in and was reported by Russian law enforcement as likely to be amnestied. "Eks-glavy departmenta gosbezopasnosti Ichkerii, vozmozhno, amnistiruyut," Kavkazskii uzel, 29 March 2006, www.kavkaz.memo.ru/news/news/date/20060329.html.

14 "Amir Seifullakh: 'Pobeda ot Allakha, tak zhe kak i porazhenie.'"

15 The eight prisoners are Shamil Khadzhiev and Ravil Gumarov from Bashkortostan, Rasul Kudaev and Ruslan Odizhev from the KBR, Ravil Mingazov and Airat Vakhitov from Tatarstan, Rustam Akmetov from Chelyabinsk, and Timur Ishmuradov from Tyumen Oblast. The biography of one of them is instructive. KBR native Ruslan Odizhev is a Sunni Muslim of the southern Caucasus's Kabard ethnic group, who upon returning from Islamic study in Saudi Arabia in the 1990s was recruited by radical KBR imam Musa Mukozhev. Odizhev was detained by Russian security forces in 2000, accused of supporting the Chechen rebellion, and physically abused for two weeks before being released. He then went to Afghanistan where, after initially being distrusted by the Taliban, he was captured by the Northern Alliance, though he insists he was not involved in fighting. Regions.ru, 27 March 2003, www.regions.ru; RFERL Newsline, Vol. 7, No. 60 (28 March 2003); RFERL Russian Federation Report, Vol. 4, No. 14 (17 April 2002); and "Russia's 'Taliban' Faces Uneasy Future after Guantanamo Torment," *AFP*, 1 Aug. 2004

16 This is according to Iraqi interior minster Falah al-Naqib. See "Iraq's Al-Naqib – 'Terrorists' From Chechnya, Sudan, and Syria Killed Arrested," Beirut LBC SAT

Television, 13:00 GMT, 30 Jan. 2005.

17 See Gunaratna, *Inside al Qaeda*, p. 292.

18 See Murphy, *The Wolves of Islam*, pp. 206, 212–214. See also "Trial of 'Chechen Network' Members Begins in Paris," Retwa.org, 21 March 2006, www.retwa.com/home.cfm?articleId=2025.

19 See Basaev's interview "Sh. Basaev: 'Nikto ne mozhet zapretit mne to, chto razreshaet Bog."

20 This was in an email purportedly sent by Basaev to the Institute for War and Peace Reporting on 27 August 2004, just days before Beslan. See Tom de Waal, "Basayev and Maskhadov under Pressure," *IWPR Caucasus Reporting Service*, No. 252, 8 Sept. 2004.

21 "Prezident ChRI Sadulaev vystupil s obrashheniem," *Kavkaz-Tsentr*, 9 May 2005, www.kavkazcenter. net/russ/content/2005/05/09/33702.shtml.

22 "Voina protiv Islama i rech Busha," *Kavkaz-Tsentr*, 10 Oct. 2005, 00:35:37, www.kavkazcenter.net/ russ/content/2005/10/10/38307.shtml.

23 "ObrashcheniePrezidenta ChRI A.-Kh. Sadulaeva k chechenckomu narodu," *Kavkaz-Tsentr*, 19 Aug. 2005, 16:55:28, www.kavkazcenter.net/russ/content/2005/08/19/36843.shtml.

24 Islam.ru posted excerpts from Iranian chief ayatollah Ali Khomeini's speech on the twenty-sixth anniversary of the 1979 revolution, another anti-American tirade. See "Poslanie dukhovnogo lidera Irana musulmanam mira," Islam.ru, www.islam.ru/pressclub/analitika/poslanie/.

25 Musa Stoun, "Satanizm v deistvii: 'Cherep ikosti' pravyat Amerikoi," *Kavkaz-Tsentr*, 13 April 2006, 00:48:10, www.kavkazcenter.com/russ/content/2006/04/13/43682.shtml; "Amerikantsy szhigali irakskikh zhenshchin i detei belym fosforom," *Kavkaz-Tsentr*, 8 Nov. 2005, 06:32:02, www.kavkazcenter.net/russ/content/2005/11/08/39130.shtml; "SShA otpravlyayut v Irak ubiits detei," *Kavkaz-Tsentr*, 10 Oct. 2005, 13:57:23, www.kavkazcenter.net/russ/content/2005/10/10/38329.shtml; "Pokhozhe, chto zapadnaya 'svoboda' sovsem osatanela," *Kavkaz-Tsentr*, 14 April 2006, 18:42:23, www.kavkazcenter.com/russ/content/2006/04/14/43744.shtml; "Byt' zhivotnoi skotinoi – eto zapadnaya demokratiya," *Kavkaz-Tsentr*, 5 March 2006, 02:18:01, www.kavkazcenter.com/russ/ content/2006/03/05/42580.shtml; "Moskovskaya militsiya otstoyala chuchela Putina, Busha i Blera," *Kavkaz-Tsentr*, 5 March 2006, 20:37:03, www.kavkazcenter.com/russ/content/2006/03/05/42606.shtml; and "Vypushchena tualetnaya bumaga s izobrazheniem Putina, Busha, i Blera," *Kavkaz-Tsentr*, 10 Oct. 2005, 11:05:21, www.kavkazcenter.net/russ/content/2005/10/10/38319.shtml.

26 Andrei Novikov, "Shamil Basaev kupil nosh," Kavkaz-Tsentr, 23 Nov. 2005, 22:13:40, www.kavkazcenter.com/russ/content/2005/11/23/39653.shtml.

27 Said Minkailov, "Terminologicheskaya voina," *Kavkaz-Tsentr*, 18 June 2004, www.kavkazcenter.net/russ/content/2004/06/18/22366.shtml. See also Said Minkailov, "Vtoraya Mirovaya voina glazami chechenskikh modzhahedov," *Kavkaz-Tsentr*, 11 April 2005, www.kavkazcenter.net/russ/content/2005/04/11/32959.shtml.

28 See "V Irake rasstrelyany 10 kollaboratsionistov," *Kavkaz-Tsentr*, 20 April 2005, 18:37:55, www.kavkazcenter.net/russ/content/2005/04/20/33012.shtml; "Taliban: Dzhikhad prodolzhaetsya," *Kavkaz-Tsentr*, 10 Oct. 2005, 00:03:14, www.kavkazcenter. net/russ/content/2005/10/10/38310.shtml; "V 2005 godu v Afganistane bylo unichtozheno 655 amerikanskikh soldat," *Kavkaz-Tsentr*, 11 March 2006, 17:24:49, www.kavkazcenter.com/russ/content/2006/03/11/42763.shtml; "V Bagdade unich-tozheny 5 munafikov," *Kavkaz-Tsentr*, 25 March 2006, 11:47:06, www.kavkazcenter. com/russ/content/2006/03/25/43133.shtml.

29 See "Mossad provodit terakty v Irake," *Kavkaz-Tsentr*, 2 May 2006, 15:56:48, www.kavkazcenter.com/ russ/content/2006/05/02/44225.shtml, and "Za teraktom v Egypte mozhet stoyat' 'Mossad,'" *Kavkaz-Tsentr*, 25 April 2006, 12:49:34,

www.kavkazcenter.com/russ/content/2006/04/25/44038.shtml.

30 See *The 9/11 Commission Report,* p. 123.

31 "Premiya za merzost. Yevrei sovershili seksualnuyu revolyutsiyu v Amerike," *Kavkaz-Tsentr,* 11 Jan. 2006, 23:47:59, www.kavkazcenter.net/russ/content/2006/01/11/40946.shtml; "Yevreiskie ravviny zapretili vracham lechit' palestintsev," *Kavkaz-Tsentr,* 15 April 2006, 16:26:34, www.kavkazcenter.com/russ/content/2006/04/15/43766.shtml; "Religioznyi yereiskii deyatel' iznasiloval 9 detei," *Kavkaz-Tsentr,* 7 April 2006, 14:32:40, www.kavkazcenter.com/russ/content/2006/04/07/43537. shtml; "Israel budet razrushen v 2022 godu?," *Kavkaz-Tsentr,* 14 April 2006, 17:38:38, www.kavkazcenter.com/russ/content/2006/04/14/43739.shtml; and "Sionisty provot-siruyut v Irake voinu mezhdu sunnitami i shiitami," *Kavkaz-Tsentr,* 11 March 2006, 02:03:33, www.kavkazcenter.com/russ/content/2006/03/11/42749.shtml.

32 Yeshchyo odin 'protsess ved'm' protiv ocherednogo otritsatelysa 'kholokosta' v Avstrii," *Kavkaz-Tsentr,* 5 March 2005, 10:56:21, www.kavkazcenter.com/russ/content/2006/03/05/42597.shtml, and "Na Mezhdunarodnyi konkurs postupilo uzhe 192 karikatury o 'kholocoste,'" *Kavkaz-Tsentr,* 12 March 2006, 17:10:55, www.kavkazcenter.com/russ/content/2006/03/12/42793.shtml.

33 RFERL Russian Political Weekly, Vol. 3, No. 8 (21 Feb. 2003), www.rferl.org/reports/rpw/2003/02/8-210203.asp.

34 "Glava Tyumenskogo kazyyata prizval molitsya za musulman Falludzhi v Noch Predopredeleniya," Islam.ru, 9 Nov. 2004, www.islam.ru/press/rus/2004-11-09/.

35 See, for example, "Blizhnemu Vostoku Vashington gotovit Pletku," Islam.ru, 29 Nov. 2004, www.islam.ru/pressclub/tema/pletka, and "Normalizatsiya ili imitatsiya. SShA khotyat druzhit s musulmanami," Islam.ru, www.islam.ru/pressclub/analitika/friendship/.

36 Abid Ulakh Dzhan, "Moment istiny dlya Ameriki," Islam.ru, 11 Dec. 2004, www.islam.ru/pressclub/tema/moment/?print_page.

37 "V Amerikanskoi armii soldat uchat tomu, chto vse musulmane – teroristy," Islam.ru, 14 Dec. 2004, www.islam.ru/press/world/2004-12-14/#6796.

38 "SShA skryvayut svyaz Izraelya s sobytiyami 11 sentyabrya," Islam-info.ru, 13 April 2004, www.islam-info.ru/?a=255.

39 This occurred at a growing rate, moreover. In the first nine months of 2004, some 20,000 people converted to Islam in Moscow, as compared to 15,300 in 2003 and 12,450 in 2002. Some 60 percent of the noted converts were ethnic Russians who had not previously been adherents of any faith, and 75 percent were reportedly women between seventeen and twenty-one years of age. Although the numbers in such reports can be questioned, especially given the source, the existence of this small trend is nonetheless beyond question. The figures come from a posting on a Qatar-based website, IslamOnLine citing an anonymous source from the Council of Muftis of Russia in "S 2002 Islam v Moskve prinyali pochti 50 tys. chelovek," Islam.ru, 7 Oct. 2004, www.islam.ru/press/rus/2004/10/07/. An ethnic Russian Muslim community emerged in Omsk in 2004. Aleksei Malashenko, "Shadow of Islam over Europe," *International Affairs* (Moscow), Vol. 50, No. 5 (Sept.-Oct. 2004), pp. 65–74, at p. 70.

40 Aleksandr Ignatenko, "Krovavaya doroga v rai," *Nezavisimaya gazeta-religiya,* No. 12, 16 July 2003, p. 1, and Dmitrii Sokolov-Mitrich, "Russkii Ben Laden," *Izvestiya,* 21 Jan. 2005, www.izvestia.ru/conflict/1043323_print. Another organization, Direct Path is headed by Muslim journalist and ex-Orthodox priest Ali Polosin. Dagestan has set up a committee for converts to Islam. Just as the Afghan war produced Soviet converts to Islam, there are cases of Russian soldiers who fought in Chechnya converting to Islam. Malashenko, "Shadow of Islam over Europe," p. 70.

41 Malashenko, "Shadow of Islam over Europe," p. 70.

42 For example, the organizer of the 6 February 2004 Moscow metro bombing, Pavel Kosolapov, was an ethnic Russian. See Sokolov-Mitrich, "Russkii Ben Laden."

Also, the Chechen insurgents' first suicide bombers in summer 2000 were ethnic Russian Muslims. Vadim Rechkalov, "Ya odnazhdi sprosila, kak mozhno stat' shakhidom," *Izvestiya*, 18 June 2004, pp.1, 4.

43 Fiona Hill and Clifford G. Gaddy, *The Siberian Curse: How Communist Planners Left Russia Out in the Cold* (Washington, D.C.: Brookings Institution, 2003).

44 Treisman, *After the Deluge.*

45 For example, in 2002 Moscow's financing of Kazan's socio-economic program exceeded by a factor of ten the funds for programs to all regions in the Far East FO together.

46 The most recent such call came on 26 May 2005 from powerful Sverdlovsk Oblasts's governor, Eduard Rossel just a week after the aforementioned mass demonstrations in Adygeya in opposition to its incorporation into surrounding Krasnodar Krai. See Mikhail Vyugin, "Rossiya dlya rossiyan," *Vremya MN*, 27 May 2005, p. 4.

47 The congress did include the proposal in its resolutions. RFERL Tatar-Bashkir Daily, 23 June 2005.

48 See *Argumenty i fakty*, No. 15, April 2006, cited in Viktor Yasmann, "The Future Of Russias 'Ethnic Republics,'" RFERL, 21 April 2006, www.rferl.org.

49 The Pro-Moscow Chechen State Council chairman has twice proposed merging Chechnya, Ingushetiya, Daghestan, Kabardino-Balkariya, and Stavropol Krai into a single region, arguing that it is more difficult to cross internal borders between North Caucasian republics than the frontier "between the former USSR and a capitalist country." RFERL Newsline, Vol. 8, No. 219 (22 Nov. 2004), and Interfax, 21 April 2005, cited in RFERL Newsline, Vol. 9, No. 77, 25 April 2005.

50 Matthew Bunn and Anthony Weir, *Securing the Bomb*, Nuclear Threat Initiative, Belfer Center for Science and International Affairs, John F. Kennedy School of Government, Harvard University, May 2005, www.nti.org/e_research/report_cnwmupdate2005.pdf, p. 34.

51 Goss added that he could not guarantee that it has not already happened. Ibid., pp. 12, 15.

52 US Department of Defense, *Proliferation: Threat and Response 2001*, www.defenselink.mil/pubs/ptr20010110.pdf, p. 57, US Department of Defense, *Proliferation: Threat and Response 1997*, www.defenselink.mil/pubs/prolif97/fsu.html#russia.

53 Russian defector Kanatjan Alibekov (Kenneth Alibek), former deputy director of the Soviet/Russian biological warfare development program, named the following biological agents as weaponized or researched by the Soviet/Russian program: the African swine fever virus, anthrax, Argentinian hemorrhagic fever, brucellosis, the Ebola virus, glanders, Japanese encephalitis, Lassa fever, the Machupo virus, the Marburg virus, ornithosis, plague, psittacosis, Q-fever, riceblast, the rinderpest virus, Russian spring-summer encephalitis, smallpox, tularemia, typhus, Venezuelan equine encephalomyelitis, wheat stem rust, and yellow fever. See Dr. Kenneth Alibek, Statement before the Joint Economic Committee, US Congress, Joint Economic Committee, "Terrorism and Intelligence Operations: Hearing before the Joint Economic Committee," 105th Congress, Second Session, 20 May, 1998, www.house.gov/jec/hearings/intell/alibek.htm.

54 Dmitrii Litovkin, "Predotvrashcheny dve popytki yadernogo terrorizma," *Izvestiya*, 23 June 2005, http://main.izvestia.ru/armia2/23-06-05/article2014237.

55 Many Russian MWMD sites remain guarded by undermanned security forces. Low pay and alcoholism produce a "security culture" in which doors are propped open and loud security alarms are shut off. Poorly paid Russian scientists and workers at such sites are susceptible to bribery. Russian officers and officials have been charged in the past with selling conventional weapons to the Chechens. Bunn and Weir, *Securing the Bomb*, pp. 13–30.

56 The location of the sites and train routes are state secrets but were secured by the terrorists. Ibid., pp. 12–14.

57 Bale, "The Chechen resistance and Radiological Terrorism," pp. 11–12.

58 See "Summary of Reported Nuclear, Radioisotope, and Dual-Use Materials Trafficking Incidents Involving the NIS (January-December 2003)" of the joint Nuclear Threat Initiative/Center for Non-Proliferation Studies (Monterey Institute for International Studies) database, www.nti.org/db/nistraff/tables/2003_all.htm.

59 Bunn and Weir, *Securing the Bomb*, pp. 12–14.

60 General Valynkin, however, did not specify at which sites the attempts occurred or who had been responsible. Litovkin, "Predotvrashcheny dve popytki yadernogo terrorizma."

61 On attempts by terrorists to acquire nuclear, chemical, and biological materials in Russia and around the world through 2002, see Wayne Turnbull and Praveen Abhayaratne, "2002 WMD Terrorism Chronology: Incidents Involving Sub-National Actors and Chemical, Biological, Radiological, and Nuclear Materials," Center for Non-Proliferation Studies, 2003, http://cns.miis.edu.

62 See Brian Johnson Thomas and Mark Franchetti, "Radioactive Rockets 'For Sale' in Breakaway Soviet Republic," *The Sunday Times* (London), 8 May 2005, www.timesonline.co.uk/article/02087160360200. html.

63 Smita P. Nordwall, "Detainee Said to Link al-Qaeda, 'Dirty Bomb,'" *USA Today*, 23 April 2002, p. A8.

64 Adam Dolnik, "America's Worst Nightmare? Osama bin Laden and Weapons of Mass Destruction," PIR Center, 12 Sept. 2001, www.ceip.org/files/projects/npp/resources/America's%20 Worst%20Nightmare%20%20/Osama%20bin%20Laden%20and%20 Weapons%20of%20Mass%20Destruction.pdf, 11 April 2005.

65 Chechnya and the North Caucasus came just behind Japan (6 percent) and just ahead of the "Middle East and Arab countries" (3 percent). "Rossiya – mezhdu Zapadom i Vostokom," VTsIOM, Press-Vypusk No. 361, 19 Dec. 2005, www.wciom.ru/?pt=9&article=2129.

66 See, for example, Dugin, *Osovy geopolitiki* and Panarin, *Revansh istorii.*

67 The Eurasianists' political party, the Eurasian Party, includes Russian Orthodox members, and both ethnic Russian Muslims and traditionally Muslim nationalities. A former Chechen official under first Chechen president Dzhokar Dudaev, Khozh-Akhmed Nukhaev, who rejected participation in the second Chechen war, and has been a Chechen activist for an end to the war, joined forces with Dugin's Eurasian Party in 2003 at a Moscow conference that established a permanent relationship ostensibly working toward an end to the war and the unification of the Russian and Muslim worlds against the "Atlantist" threat. See Goldin, *Rossiya i Chechnya: Poiski vykhod*, pp. 49–51, 56. In 2005, Russian police accused Nukhaev of organizing the murder of American journalist Paul Khlebnikov.

68 Panarin, *Revanshlistorii.*

69 "S. Lavrov: Rossiyu pytayutsya stolknut' s islamskoi tsivilizatsiei," Islam.ru, 5 April 2006, www.islam.ru/press/rus/2006-04-05/#11627.

70 This can be seen in many of the statements surrounding the creation of Haq. Haq board member Sergei Komkov told Haq's founding assembly: "Forces antagonistic to Russia as well as to the Muslim world lobby Islamophobia which serves as one of the levers for the Russia's destruction." See "Musul'manskii message v otvet na 'putinskii prizyv.'"

71 Artur Yastrebov, "Tragediya Beslana i perspektivy russkikh musul'man," Islam.ru, 22 Sept. 2004, www.islam.ru. See similar Islam.ru commentary in David Merkhav, "Za chto pogibli nashi deti?" Islam.ru, 22 Sept. 2004, www.islam.ru/pressclub/histori/ziokhronic/ and by Muslim Eurasianist Geidar Dzhemal in "Eksperty rassuzhdali, Khazam 'lomal komediyu', a Porokhova opyat vykinula syurpriz," Islam.ru, 15 Oct.

2004, www.islam.ru/press/rus/2004-10-15/.

72 "Pomoshchnik V. Putina fakticheski obvinil SShA v organizatsii teraktov v Rossii," Islam.ru, 7 Sept. 2004.

73 See "Mify ob 'al-Kaide' oslepili 77% rossian," Islam.ru, 25 Oct. 2005, www.islam.ru/press/rus/2004-10-25/.

74 Andrei Baranov, Maksim Chizhikov, and Yegenii Umerenkov, "Amerika obyavit Rossii vtoruyu 'kholodnuyu voinu'?" *Komsomolskaya pravda*, 28 April 2006, www.kp.ru/daily/23698.4/52546/.

75 I. V. Zhuravlev, S. A. Melkov, and L. I. Shershnev, *Put voinov Allakha: Islam i politika Rossii* (Moscow: Veche, 2004), pp. 306–354.

76 On obstacles in Russia to dismantling its chemical arms stockpiles, see "Russia's Chemical Weapons Aresenal Is a Ticking Time Bomb," RIA "Novosti," 4 Nov. 2004.

77 Bunn and Weir, *Securing the Bomb*, pp. v, vii.

78 Ibid. pp. vi, 31.

79 Cheryl Benard, *Civil Democratic Islam: Partners, Resources, and Strategies* (Santa Monica, CA: Rand Corporation, 2003), pp. 46–48, 61–64, http://www.rand.org/publications/MR/MR1716/MR1716.pdf.

80 Bennigsen and Wimbush, *Muslims of the Soviet Empire*, p. 21.

81 Naqshbandy led many revolts against Russian rule in Central Asia as well. Naqshbandy murshid Ishan Madali led the 1897 Andizhan (Uzbekistan) revolt and other murshids and murids led the Basmachi revolts against Soviet power in Central Asia in 1918–1919. Ibid.

82 Ibid.

83 This should be done using the strategy and tactics laid out by Bernard, *Civil Democratic Islam.*

84 It is important that negotiations begin in winter, as summer and early autumn are periods when the Chechen terrorist have typically undertaken major terrorist acts.

85 See the US Commission on International Religious Freedom Annual Report, May 2005, www.uscirf.gov/countries/publications/currentreport/2005annualRpt.pdf#page=1, pp. 79, 91–92.

86 The underfunding of this issue is symbolized by the aforementioned arrest of the brother of mufti Shangareev, who briefed the CIRF in February 2005 on the situation with regard to Muslims' rights in Russia. Ibid., p. 93.

87 See the USAID Europe/Eurasia's web page at www.usaid.gov/locations/europe_eurasia/ or view "Democracy and Governance" programs at www.usaid.gov/our_work/democracy_and_governance/gov.html. USAID does support the Moscow School of Political Studies which has conducted three seminars in Russia on federalism in recent years and most recently an April 2005 seminar in the US on "American Federalism and Public Policy" for some thirty Russian lawmakers. "Members of Congress to Address Russian Federal and Regional Leaders at Moscow School of Political Studies Seminar; Annual Event to Focus on Federalism, Intergovernmental Relations, and U.S.-Russia Relations," PRNewswire, 7 April 2005, http://news.findlaw.com/prnewswire/20050407/07apr2005151208.html. However, the US model has limited value for constructing a system of federative governance for a Russian system that inherited an ethno-federal national-territorial administrative structure from the USSR and has tens of large nationalities living in concentrated groups on their historical lands, some of which had independent states in the past.

88 See the Kazan Institute for Federalism website: at http://federalmcart.ksu.ru/.

APPENDIX

1 Magomedov was arrested for his attack and sentenced to imprisonment by the Supreme Court of Dagestan for a series of crimes. Svetlana Meteleva, "Fizika terrora,"

Koskovskii Komsomolets, 25 Dec. 2004, p. 7.

2 "Razryvnaya dolzhnost," *Kommersant,* 21 May 2005, p.1.

3 The source for this and the 17 and 23 August 2004 Abdullayev attacks is Meteleva, "Fizika terrora."

4 RFERL Newsline, 3 Nov. 2004, www.rferl.org/newsline/2004/12/1-rus/rus-031204.asp.

5 In Kaspiisk, a Dagestani special quick reaction (SOBR) unit led by commander Arzulum Ilyasov moved to detain fifty-year-old radical emir Magomedzagir Akayev in his Kaspiisk home during morning prayers. Ilyasov and two SOBR offices were killed. Akayev was also killed, and two of his fighters were captured. Marat Biygishev, "Battle Hits Dagestan Capital," IWPR Caucasus Reporting Service, No. 270, 19 Jan. 2005, and Interfax, Moscow, 17 Jan. 2005, 09:35 GMT.

6 Interfax reported. RFERL Newsline, Vol. 9, No. 24, 7 February 2005.

7 Jean-Christophe Peuch, "North Caucasus Republics Enter Circle of Violence," Radio Free Europe/Radio Liberty, 23 Feb. 2005, www.rferl.org/featuresarticle/2005/02/021f2f06-0c2e-41cb-bele-2fe3d61e505d.html.

8 RFERL Newsline, Vol. 9, No. 43 (7 March 2005).

9 "V Khasavyurte unichtozhili dvoikh boevikov," *Dagestanskaya pravda,* 5 April 2005, www.dagpravda.ru/news/htm,citing Interfax, 5 April 2005, 23:30.

10 "Dzhamaat 'Shariat' soobshchayet o boevykh operatsiyakh v Dagestane."

11 Ibid.

12 Oleg Petrovskiy, "'Shariah' Rages in Dagestan," Utro.ru, 25 may 2005, www.utro.ru.

13 Interfax, 8 April 2005.

14 The website reports no communiqué was received from Shariah Jamaat or other Dagestan mujahedin. "V Makhachkala prizoshla perestrelka," *Kavkaz-Tsentr,* 9 April 2005, 15:52, www.kavkazcenter.net/russ/content/2005/04/09/32545.shtml.

15 "Dzhamaat Dagestana: 'Prokuratura sgorela vmeste c prokuraturami'"; "Seriya vzryvov v Makhachkale," Regions.ru, 13 April 2005, 12:49, www.regions.ru/article/any/id/1786050.html; and Petrovskiy, "'Shariah' Rages in Dagestan."

16 "Dzhamaat Dagestana: 'Prokuratura sgorela vmeste c prokuraturami.'"

17 See NTV and Associated Press, 19 April 2005.

18 "Dzhamaat 'Shariat': 'Provedena uspeshnaya spetsoperatsiya.'"

19 "Chechenskie separatisty tozhe ukreplyayut svoyu 'vlastnuyu vertikal,'" *Kavkaz-Tsentr,* 26 May 2005. www.kavkazcenter.com/russ/content/2005/05/26/34353.shtml.

20 NTV, 14 May 2005, 06:00 GMT.

21 "Dzhamaat 'Shariat': 'Allakh daet nam pravo otvechat vam tem zhe.'"

22 Explosions in Makhachkala of two militia cars, one traffic patrol car, and one militia school car, and the liquidation of an "especially active" militia officer of the Kirov raion section of the MVD (ROVD), as well as the explosion of the car of the Untsukyl ROVD chief and of a truck of Russian "infidels" of the 136 Motor-Rifle Brigade in Buinaksk. The attacks could possibly include only the 10 and 14 May attacks listed above. "Dzhamaat 'Shariat': Allakh daet nam pravo otvechat vam tem zhe.'"

23 "Dzhamaat 'Shariat': 'Territoriya Dzhikhada rasshiraetesya," *Kavkaz-Tsentr,* 30 June 2005, 00:34:49, www.kavkazcenter.com/russ/content/2005/06/30/35646.shtml.

24 Gunmen opened fire with a machine gun at his car as it was passing by the building of General School No. 36 on Mayakovsky Street in Makhachkala. Varisov had previously also worked in the Dagetsan People's Assembly Information and Analysis Department. Itar-Tass, 28 June 2005. Shariah claimed responsibility for Varisov's assassination in "Dzhamaat 'Shariat': 'Territoriya Dzhikhada rasshiraetesya.'"

25 "Dzhamaat 'Shariat': 'Modzhakhedy budut napravleny v Moskvu.'"

26 Paul Murphy, "Makhachkala's War on Terror – A Week in a City under Siege," posting on Johnson's Russia List, Center for Defense Information, 12 July 2005, www.cdi.org.

27 "V Dagestane mudzhakhidy vstupili v boi c banditami iz GRU," Camagat.com, 8 Aug.

2005, www.camagat.com/sitebiz/arhiv/2005/08/08.08/boy_v_dage.htm, and "Dagestan: V lesnom massive proizoshlo boesyolknovenie s terroristami iz GRU, ChechenPress.org, 7 Aug. 2005, www.chechenpress.org/events/2005/08/08/05.shtml, citing Daymohk.ru, 7 Aug. 2005. www.daymohk.ru.

28 "Dagestan: Na okraine Buinakska proizoshyol vzryv ryadom s militseiskom UAZom," ChechenPress.org, 11 Aug. 2005, www.chechenpress.org/events/2005/08/11/07.shtml.

29 REFERL Newsline, Vol. 9, No. 158 (22 Aug. 2005).

30 Ibid. A perhaps additional attack occurred on the same day. Although press reports were similar to this one, the remotely detonated explosive device was said to have been placed not in a zinc bucket, but in a large plastic bottle. Abdul Suleimanov, "Pokushchenie na militsionerov," *Dagestanskaya pravda*, 22 Aug. 2005, 20:00, www.dagpravda.ru/news.html#2929.

31 "Dzhamaat 'Shariat': 'Nashi ryady postoyanno uvelichivaetsya,'" *Kavkaz-Tsentr*, 25 Aug. 2005, 00:40:19, www.kavkazcenter.net/russ/content/2005/08/25/37022.shtml

Bibliography

BOOKS

Abubakarov, Taimaz. *Rezhim Dzhokhara Dudaeva: pravda i vymysel – zapiski dudaevskogo ministra ekonomi i finansov* (Moscow: INSAN, 1998).

Amirkhanov, R. M., ed. *Ocherki istorii Tatarskoi obshchestvennoi mysli* (Kazan: Tatarskoe knizhskoe izdatelstvo, 2000).

Aslan, Reza. *No God, But God: The Origins, Evolution, and Future of Islam* (New York: Random House, 2005).

Baumann, Robert F. *Russian-Soviet Unconventional Wars in the Caucasus, Central Asia, and Afghanistan*, Leavenworth Papers, No. 20 (Leavenworth, Kansas: Combat Studies Institute, 1993).

Bennigsen, Alexander, and Wimbush, S. Enders. *Muslims of the Soviet Empire* (Bloomington: Indiana University Press, 1986).

Bialer, Seweryn. *The Soviet Paradox* (New York: Knopf, 1986).

_____. *Stalin's Successors: Leadership, Stability, and Change in the Soviet Union* (Cambridge: Cambridge University Press, 1980).

Bugajski, Janusz. *Cold Peace: Russia's New Imperialism* (New York: Praeger/CSIS, 2005).

Connor, Walker. *The National Question in Marxist-Leninist Theory and Strategy* (Princeton, N.J.: Princeton University Press, 1984).

Conquest, Robert, ed. *The Last Empire: Nationality and the Soviet Future* (Stanford, CA: Hoover Institution Press, 1986).

Danspeckgruber, Wolfgang, ed. *The Self-Determination of Peoples: Community, Nation, and State in an Interdependent World* (Boulder, CO: Lynne Reinner Publishers, 2002).

Derluguian, Georgi M. *Bourdieu's Secret Admirer in the Caucasus: A World-System Biography* (Chicago: Chicago University Press, 2005).

Devji, Faisal. *Landscapes of Jihad: Militancy, Morality, Modernity* (Ithaca. N.Y.:

Cornell University Press, 2005).

Dugin, Aleksandr. *Osnovy geopolitiki* (Moscow, 1997).

El Fadl, Khaled M. Abou. *The Great Theft: Wrestling Islam from the Extremists* (San Francisco: Harper, 2005).

Evangelista, Matthew. *The Chechen Wars: Will Russia Go the Way of the Soviet Union?* (Washington, D.C.: Brookings Institution, 2002).

Freidrich, Carl J. *Trends of Federalism in Theory and Practice* (New York: Praeger, 1968).

Gainutdin, Mufti Ravil. *Islam v sovremennoi Rossii* (Moscow: Fair-Press, 2004).

Gammer, Moshe. *The Lone Wolf and the Bear: Three Centuries of Chechen Defiance of Russian Rule* (Pittsburgh: University of Pittsburgh Press, 2006).

Gobuglo, M. N. *Federalizm vlasti i vlasti federalizma* (Moscow: IntelTekh, 1997).

Gold, Dore. *Hatred's Kingdom: How Saudi Arabia Supports the New Global Terrorism* (Washington, D.C.: Regnery, 2003).

Goldin, Ya. A. *Rossiya i Chechnya: poiski vykhoda* (St. Petersburg: Zvezda, 2003).

Goldstone, Jack. *Revolution and Rebellion in the Early Modern World* (Berkeley: University of California Press, 1991).

Gorenburg, Dmitrii P. *Minority Ethnic Mobilization in the Russian Federation* (Cambridge: Cambridge University Press, 2003).

Gunaratna, Rohan. *Inside al Qaeda: Global Network of Terror* (New York: Columbia University Press, 2002).

Gurr, Ted Robert. *Peoples Versus States: Minorities at Risk in the New Century* (Washington D.C.: United States Institute of Peace, 2000).

_____. *Why Men Rebel* (Princeton, N.J.: Princeton University Press, 1970).

Hahn, Gordon M. *Russia's Revolution from Above: Reform, Transition, and Revolution in the Fall of the Soviet Communist Regime, 1985–2000* (New Brunswick: Transaction Publishers, 2002).

Hechter, Michael. *Containing Nationalism* (Oxford: Oxford University Press, 2000).

Hill, Fiona, and Gaddy, Clifford G. *The Siberian Curse: How Communist Planners Left Russia Out in the Cold* (Washington, D.C.: Brookings Institution, 2003).

Horowitz, Donald L. *Ethnic Groups in Conflict* (Berkeley and Los Angeles: University of California Press, 1985).

Human Rights Center "Memorial." *Deceptive Justice: Situation on the Investigation of Crimes against Civilians Committed by Members of the Federal Forces in the Chechen Republic during Military Operations,*

1999–2003 (Moscow: Memorial, May 2003).

Human Rights Watch, *The "Dirty War" in Chechnya: Forced Disappearances, Torture, and Summary Executions* (New York: HRW, March 2001).

____. *Swept Under: Torture, Forced Disappearances, and Extrajudicial Killings during Sweep Operations in Chechnya* (New York: HRW, Feb. 2002).

____. *Human Rights Situation in Chechnya: Briefing Paper to the 59th Session of the UN Commission on Human Rights* (New York: HRW, April 2003).

Hunter, Shireen. *Islam in Russia: The Politics of Identity and Security* (Armonk, N.Y.: M.E. Sharpe, 2002).

Iordan, M. V., Kuzeev, R.G., and Chervonnaya, S. M., eds. *Islam v Yevrazii: sovremennyie etnicheskie i esteticheskie kontseptsii sunnitskogo islama, ikh transformatsiya v massovom soznanii i vyrazhenie v iskusstve musulmanskikh narodov Rossii* (Moscow: Progress-Traditsiya, 2001).

Jones, Ellen. *The Red Army and Society* (Boston, MA: Allen & Unwin, 1985).

Kahn, Jeffrey. *Federalism, Democratization, and the Rule of Law in Russia* (Oxford: Oxford University Press, 2002).

Kepel, Giles. *The War for Muslim Minds: Islam and the West* (Cambridge: Cambridge University Press, 2004).

Khakimov, Rafael. *Gde nasha Mekka?* (Kazan: Magarif, 2003).

Kobishchanov, Yu. M., ed. *Musulmane izmenyayushcheisya Rossii* (Moscow: Russian Political Encyclopedia, 2002).

Koppiters, B., Darchiashvili, D., and Akaba, N., eds., *Poiski alternative dlya Gruzii i Abkhazii* (Moscow: Ves Mir, 1999).

Kozhokin, Ye. M. and Maksimenko, V. I., eds. *Islam i Islamizm* (Moscow: Russian Institute of Strategic Studies, 1999).

Kreuger, Alan B., and Laitin, David. *Kto Kogo: A Cross-Country Study of the Origins and Targets of Terrorism* (New York: Russel Sage, 2003).

Laird, Robin F., and Hoffman, Erik P., eds. *The Conduct of Soviet Foreign Policy*, 2nd edn. (Hawthorne, N.Y.: Aldine Publishing Co., 1980).

Lapidus, Gail W., and Tsalik, Svetlana, eds. *Preventing Deadly Conflict: Strategies and Institutions*, Proceedings of a Conference in Moscow, Russian Federation, 14–16 August 1996 (New York: Carnegie Corporation, April 1998).

Lewis, Bernard. *The Assassins: A Radical Sect in Islam* (New York: Basic Books, 2002).

____. *The Crisis of Islam: Holy War and Unholy Terror* (New York: Random House, 2003).

____. *Islam and the West* (Oxford: Oxford University Press, 1993).

Lijphart, Arend. *Democracies: Patterns of Majoritarian and Consensus Government in Twenty-One Countries* (New Haven, CT: Yale University Press, 1984).

McFaul, Michael, and Petrov, Nikolai, eds. *The White Book of Russian Democracy* (Washington, D.C.: Carnegie Endowment of International Peace, 2004).

Martin, Richard. *Defenders of Reason in Islam* (Oxford: Oxford University Press, 1997).

Matveeva, Anna. *The North Caucasus: Russia's Fragile Borderland* (London: Royal Institute of International Affairs, 1999).

Médecins Sans Frontières. *The Trauma of Ongoing War in Chechnya: Quantitative Assessment of Living Conditions and Psychosocial and General Health Status among the War-Displaced in Chechnya and Ingushetia* (Amsterdam: MSF, Aug. 2004).

Montville, Joseph, ed. *Conflict and Peacemaking in Multiethnic Societies* (Lexington, Mass.: Lexington Books, 1990).

Murphy, Paul. *The Wolves of Islam: Russia and the Faces of Chechen Terror* (Dulles, VA: Brassey's Inc., 2004).

Panarin, A. S. *Revansh istorii* (Moscow: Logos, 1998).

Peters, Rudolph. *Jihad in Classical and Modern Islam* (Princeton, N.J.: Markus Weiner Publishers, 1996).

Pryganov, S. *Vtorzhenie v Rossii* (Moscow: Eksprint, 2003).

Riker, William H. *Federalism: Origin, Operation, Significance* (Boston, MA: Little-Brown, 1964).

Rossiya-Chechnya: tsep' oshibok i prestuplenii (Moscow: Zvenya, 1998).

Rywkin, Michael. *Moscow's Muslim Challenge: Soviet Central Asia* (Armonk, N.Y.: M.E. Sharpe, 1982).

Sachedina, Abdulazis Abdulhussein. *The Islamic Roots of Democratic Pluralism* (Oxford: Oxford University Press, 2001).

Sageman, Marc. *Understanding Terror Networks* (Philadelphia: University of Pennsylvania Press, 2004).

Scheuer, Michael (Anonymous). *Imperial Hubris* (Dulles, VA: Brassey's Inc., 2004).

Skocpol, Theda. *States and Revolutions: A Comparative Analysis of France, Russia, and China* (Cambridge: Cambridge University Press, 1979).

Smirnyagin, Leonid. *Rossiiskii Federalizm: paradoksy, protivorechiya, predrassudki* (Moscow: Moskovskii obshchestvennyi nauchnyi fond, 1998).

Tagirov, I. P. *Istoriya natsionalnoi gosudarstvennosti Tatarskogo naroda i Tatarstana* (Kazan: Tatarskoe knizhnoe izdatelstvo, 2000).

Tilly, Charles. *The Politics of Collective Violence* (Cambridge: Cambridge University Press, 2003).

Tishkov, Valerii. *Obshchestvo v vooruzhennom konflikte: etnografiya chechenskoi voiny* (Moscow: RAN, 2001).

Treisman, Daniel S. *After the Deluge: Regional Crises and Political Consolidation in Russia* (Ann Arbor: University of Michigan Press, 1999).

Trenin, Dmitrii, Malashenko, Alexei, and Lieven, Anatol. *Russia's Restless Frontier: The Chechnya Factor in Post-Soviet Russia* (New York: Carnegie Endowment for International Peace, 2004).

US Congress Commission on Security and Cooperation in Europe. *Democracy and Human Rights Trends in Eurasia and East Europe: A Decade of Membership in the Organization for Security and Cooperation in Europe*, 107th Congress, 2nd Session (Washington, D.C.: Dec. 2002).

US Defense Intelligence Agency. Report, "Intelligence Information Report [deleted]/Swift Knight – Usama Ben Laden's Current and Historical Activities" (Washington, D.C.: October 1998).

US Department of Justice, Federal Bureau of Investigation. *FBI Laboratory 2003 Report* (Quantico, VA: FBI, Jan. 2004).

US National Commission on Terrorist Attacks upon the United States. *The 9/11 Commission Report* (Washington, D.C.: US Government Printing Office, July 2004).

White, Stephen, Gitelman, Zvi, and Sakwa, Richard, eds. *Current Developments in Russian Politics – Vol. 6* (Durham, N.C.: Duke University Press, 2005).

Zhuravlev, I. V., Melkov, S. A., and Shershnev, L. I. *Put voinov Allakha: Islam i politika Rossii* (Moscow: Veche, 2004).

MAJOR ARTICLES AND OTHER WORKS FROM BOOKS, JOURNALS, NEWSPAPERS, AND WEBSITES

Abadie, Alberto. "Poverty, Political Freedom, and the Roots of Terrorism," National Bureau of Economic Research Working Paper, No. 10589, Oct. 2004, www.nber.org/papers/w10859.

"A.-Kh. Sadulaev: 'Obeshaem russkim voinu do pobednogo kontsa,'" Otvety Prezidenta ChRI Abdul-Khalim Sadulaev na voprosy korrespondentov radio "Svoboda," *Kavkaz Tsentr*, 6 July 2005, 00:30:18, www.kavkaz center.com/russ/content/2005/07/06/35833.shtml.

"A.-Kh. Sadulaev: 'Rossiya ne tolko uidyot iz Chechenii, no i ostavit ves Kavkaz,'" Chechen Press.info, 17 Sept. 2005, www.chechenpress.info/events/2005/09/17/10.shtml.

"Abdallakh Shamil Abu-Idris: 'My oderzhali strategicheskuyu pobedu,'" *Kavkaz-Tsentr*, 9 Jan. 2006, 08:47:10, www.kavkazcenter.net/russ/content/2006/01/09/40869.shtml.

Abdullin, Ya. G. "Dzhadidizm kak etap v razvitii Tatarskogo prosvetitelstvo," in R. M. Amirkhanov, ed., *Ocherki istorii Tatarskoi obshchestvennoi mysli*

(Kazan: Tatarskoe knizhskoe izdatelstvo, 2000), pp. 128–158.

"Akhmed Zakaev: 'Zamenchaniya k nekotorym razmyshleniyam i vyskazyvaniyam,'" *Kavkaz-Tsentr*, 31 Dec. 2005, 21:59:41, www.kavkaz center.com/russ/content/2005/12/31/40660. shtml.

Akhunov, Azat. "Ne prosto dzhadizm," Islam.ru, 30 Oct. 2004, www.islam.ru/pressclub/histori/jzadidizm/.

Alekseyev, Andrei. "'Est' dannyie o svyazi dzhamaata s Bacaevym,'" *Kommersant Vlast*, No. 39, 3 Oct. 2005, www.kommersant.ru/k-vlast/get_page.asp?page_id=20053930-7.

Alibek, Dr. Kenneth. "Terrorism and Intelligence Operations: Hearing before the Joint Economic Committee," Statement before the Joint Economic Committee, US Congress, Joint Economic Committee, 105th Congress, Second Session, 20 May 1998, www.house.gov/jec/hearings/intell/alibek.htm.

Alishev, S. Kh. *Ternistyi put borby za svobodu* (Kazan: FEN, 1999).

"Amerikantsy szhigali irakskikh zhenshchin i detei belym fosforom," *Kavkaz-Tsentr*, 8 Nov. 2005, 06:32:02, www.kavkazcenter.net/russ/content/2005/11/08/39130.shtml.

Anand, Vinod. "Export of Holy Terror to Chechnya from Pakistan and Afghanistan," *Strategic Analysis* (New Delhi), Vol. 24, No. 3 (June 2000), pp. 539–551.

Antes, Peter. "Islam v sovremennom mire," in M. V. Iordan, R. G. Kuzeev, and S. M. Chervonnaya, eds., *Islam v Yevrazii: sovremennyie eticheskie i esteticheskie kontseptsii sunnitskogo Islama, ikh transformatsiya v massovom soznanii i vyrazhenie v iskusstve musulmanskikh narodov Rossii* (Moscow: Progress-Traditsiya, 2001), pp. 38–70.

Aron, Leon. "Institutions, and Restoration, and Revolution," *Russia Outlook* (Brookings Institution), 15 April 2005, www.aei.org/docLib/20050415_ROInstitutions_g18264.pdf.

Arukhov, Z. S. "Etnokonfessionalnaya struktura Dagestanskogo obshchestva i poiski etnicheskoi i religioznoi identichnosti v usloviakh politizatsii obshchestvennoi zhizni," gleaned from temporary internet posting and now in the author's archive.

Babich, Irina L. "Ideologicheskii fundament vozrozhdeniya obychnogo i musulmanskogo prava v Kabardino-Balkarii," IslaminKBR.ru, www.islaminkbr.com/kbr/in.php?mode=004.

Bale, Jeffrey M. "The Chechen Resistance and Radiological Terrorism," Center for Nonproliferation Studies, Monterey Institute for International Studies, April 2004, www.nti.org/e_research/e3_47a.html.

Balzer, Harley. "Managed Pluralism: Vladimir Putin's Emerging Regime," *Post-Soviet Affairs*, Vol. 19, No. 3 (July–Sept. 2003), pp. 189–227.

_____. "Rethinking August 1991," *Demokratizatsiya*, Vol. 13, No. 2 (Spring 2005), pp. 193–218.

Bekkin, Renat. "'Tatarskii' Islam? Ili: 'A ne zanyatsya li nam idzhtikhadom?'" Islam.ru, 30 Oct. 2004, www.islam.ru/pressclub/analitika/idgtihad/.

Benard, Cheryl. *Civil Democratic Islam: Partners, Resources, and Strategies* (Santa Monica, CA: Rand Corporation, 2003), http://www.rand.org/publications/MR/MR1716/MR1716.pdf.

Bernstam, Mikhail. "Demography of Soviet Ethnic Groups," in Robert Conquest, ed., *The Last Empire: Nationality and the Soviet Future* (Stanford, CA: Hoover Institution Press, 1986), pp. 314–368.

Bilalov, Rinat. "VTOTS uidyot v podpol'e," *Vostochnyi Ekspress*, 20 Nov. 2004, cited in http://tatarica.yuldash.com/society/article72.

Bluey, Arthur. "Bin Laden Expert: Muslim Tradition to Offer Truce before Attack," LibertyPost.org, 21 Jan. 2006, www.libertypost.org/cgi-bin/readart.cgi?ArtNum=125927.

Bovt, Georgii, and Il'ichev, Georgii. "V chem narod raskhoditsya s prezidentom," *Izvestiya*, 19 March 2004, p. 3.

Bunn, Matthew, and Weir, Anthony. *Securing the Bomb,* Nuclear Threat Initiative, Belfer Center for Science and International Affairs, John F. Kennedy School of Government, Harvard University, May 2005, www.nti.org/e_ research/report_cnwmupdate2005.pdf.

"Byt' zhivotnoi skotinoi – eto zapadnaya demokratiya," *Kavkaz-Tsentr*, 5 March 2006, 02:18:01, www.kavkazcenter.com/russ/content/2006/03/05/42580.shtml.

"Chechenskie separatisty tozhe ukreplyayut svoyu 'vlastnuyu vertikal,'" *Kavkaz-Tsentr*, 26 May 2005, 09:24:13, www.kavkazcenter.com/russ/content/2005/05/26/34353.shtml.

"Chislennost naseleniya KBR," Elbrusoid.ru, www.elbrusoid.ru/content/kbr/p2688.shtml.

"Chislo ranenykh okkupantov v Makhachkale vozroslo do 27," *Kavkaz-Tsentr*, 2 July 2005, 09:32:23, www.kavkazcenter.net/russ/content/2005/07/02/35728.shtml.

Cohen, Ariel. "Hizb ut-Tahrir: An Emerging Threat to U.S. Interests in Central Asia," Backgrounder No. 1656, 30 May 2003, Heritage Foundation, www.heritage.org/Research/ RussiaandEurasia/BG1656.cfm.

"Dagestan prisyagnul Sheiku Abdul-Khalimu," *Kavkaz-Tsentr*, 14 March 2005, www.kavkazcenter.net/russ/content/2005/03/14/32304.shtml.

Danspeckgruber, Wolfgang. "Self-Governance Plus Regional Integration: A Solution to Self-Determination or Secession Claims in the Emerging International System," paper presented to the 2002 Annual Convention of the American Political Science Association, Boston, MA;

www.princeton.edu/~lisd.

Davis, Michael C. "The Case for Chinese Federalism," *Journal of Democracy*, Vol. 10, No. 2 (April 1999), pp. 124–137.

"Demografiya," Elbrusoid.ru, www.elbrusoid.ru/content/ kbr/p524.shtml.

Dobaev, Igor. "Terroristicheskie gruppirovki na Yuge Rossii: novyie tendentsii," Evrazia.org, 12 July 2005, http://evrazia.org/modules. php?name=News&file=article&sid=2558.

———. "Voina na Kavkaz: realii i perspektivy," *Novaya Politika*, 26 Oct. 2005, www.novopol.ru/article3685.html.

"Doku Umarov: 'My nachinaem voinu na territorii Rossii," ChechenPress.com, 9 May 2005, www.chechenpress.com/events/2005/ 05/09/08.shtml.

"Doku Umarov": 'Russkaya armiya v Chechne vydokhlas,'" Intervyu zhurnalista "Radio Svoboda" Andreya Babitsskogo s vitse-prezidentom ChRI Doku Umarovym, *Kavkaz-Tsentr*, 15 July 2005, 15:19:31, www.kavkazcenter.net/russ/content/2005/07/15/36133.shtml. Interview of Radio Liberty journalist Andrei Babotskii, with ChRI Vice President Doku Umarov.

Dolnik, Adam. "America's Worst Nightmare? Osama bin Laden and Weapons of Mass Destruction," PIR Center, 12 Sept. 2001, at www.ceip.org/files/ projects/npp/resources/America's%20Worst%20Nightmare%20%20Os ama%20bin%20Laden%20and%20Weapons%20of%20Mass%20Destr uction.pdf, 11 April 2005.

"Dzhadidizm, 'Evroislam', 'Islamskoe reformatorstvo,'" Islam.ru, 30 Oct. 2004, www.islam.ru/lib/warning/sekty/djaidizm/.

"Dzhamaat Dagestana: 'Prokuratura sgorela vmeste c prokuraturami,'" ChechenPress, 17 April 2005, www.chechenpress.com/news/2005/04/ 17/06.shtml.

"Dzhamaat 'Shariat': 'Allakh daet nam pravo otvechat vam tem zhe,'" *Kavkaz-Tsentr*, 21 May 2005, 13:57:48, www.kavkazcenter.com/russ/content/ 2005/05/21/34188.shtml.

"Dzhamaat 'Shariat': 'Modzhakhedy budut napravleny v Moskvu,'" *Kavkaz-Tsentr*, 2 July 2005, 00:38:56, www.kavkazcenter.net/russ/content/ 2005/07/02/35721.shtml.

"Dzhamaat 'Shariat': 'Nashi ryady postoyanno uvelichivaetsya,'" *Kavkaz-Tsentr*, 25 Aug. 2005, 00:40:19, www.kavkazcenter.net/russ/content/ 2005/08/25/37022.shtml.

"Dzhamaat 'Shariat': 'Pobeda ili Rai! Iz dvukh luchshee!'" *Kavkaz-Tsentr*, 12 July 2005, 03:03:02, www.kavkazcenter.net/russ/content/2005/07/12/ 36015.shtml.

"Dzhamaat 'Shariat': 'Provedena uspeshnaya spetsoperatsiya'," *Kavkaz-*

Tsentr, 22 April 2005, 15:51:50, www.kavkazcenter.net/russ/content/
2005/04/22/33080.shtml.

"Dzhamaat 'Shariat': soobshchayet o boevykh operatsiyakh v Dagestane"
Kavkaz-Tsentr, 9 April 2005, 14:03:25, www.kavkazcenter.net/russ/
content/2005/04/09/32537.shtml.

"Dzhamaat 'Shariat': 'Territoriya Dzhikhada rasshiraetesya," *Kavkaz-Tsentr*,
30 June 2005, 00:34:49, www.kavkazcenter.com/russ/content/
2005/06/30/35646.shtml.

"Dzhamaat 'Shariat': 'Zhdite, i my s vami budem zhdat' . . . ,'" *Kavkaz-Tsentr*,
15 July 2005, 11:34:35, www.kavkazcenter.net/russ/content/2005/
07/15/36121.shtml.

"Dzhamaat 'Yarmuk': 'My prinimaem boi!,'" *Kavkaz-Tsentr*, 26 Jan. 2005,
www.kavkazcenter.net/russ/content/2005/01/26/29537.shtml.

"Dzhamaat 'Yarmuk': Prinyat plan boevykh operatsii v KBR na 2005 g.,"
Kavkaz-Tsentr, 12 March 2005, www.kavkaz.org.uk/russ/content/
2005/03/12/31292.shtml.

Dzhan, Abid Ulaz. "Mif ob 'umerennom Islame,'" Islam.ru, 30 Oct. 2004,
www.islam.ru/pressclub/analitika/new-mif/.

"Dzhikhad dlya musulman Kabardino-Balkarii obyazatelen," *Kavkaz-Tsentr*,
24 March 2004, 13:59, www.kavkazcenter.com/russ/content/2005/03/24/
31762.shtml.

"Dzhikhad dlya musulman Kabardino-Balkarii obyazatelen (prodolzhenie),"
Kavkaz-Tsentr, 25 March 2004, 18:47, www.kavkazcenter.net/russ/
content/2005/ 03/25/31816.shtml.

Engelhardt, Georgii N. "Militant Islam in Russia – Potential for Conflict,"
Moscow Defense Brief, 4 April 2005, http://mdb.cast.ru/mdb/1-
2005/wap/militant_islam/.

Hahn, Gordon M. "The Impact of Putin's Federative Reforms on
Democratization in Russia," *Post-Soviet Affairs*, Vol. 19, No. 2 (April-
June 2003), pp. 114–153.

_____. "The Past, Present, and Future of the Russian Federal State,"
Demokratizatsiya, Vol. 11, No. 3 (Summer 2003), pp. 343–362.

_____. "Putin's Federal Reforms: Integrating Russia's Legal Space or
Destabilizing Russian Federalism," *Demokratizatsiya*, Vol. 9, No. 4 (Fall
2001), pp. 498–530.

_____. "Putin's 'Stealth Authoritarianism' and Russia's Second Revolutionary
Wave," Radio Free Europe/Radio Liberty *Regional Analysis*, 21 April
2004, www.regionalanalysis.org/publications/regionalvoices/en/2004/
04/616B350A-D9CD-49F59416 ECAD7F5F1EAE.ASP.

_____. "Russian Federalism under Putin," in Stephen White, Zvi Gitelman, and
Richard Sakwa, eds., *Current Developments in Russian Politics – Vol. 6*

(Durham, NC: Duke University Press, 2005), pp. 148–167.

Horowitz, Donald L. "Comparing Democratic Systems," *Journal of Democracy*, Vol. 1, No. 4 (Fall 1990), pp. 73–79.

____. "Democracy in Divided Societies," *Journal of Democracy*, Vol. 4, No. 4 (Fall 1993), pp. 18–38.

____. "Making Moderation Pay" in Joseph Montville, ed., *Conflict and Peacemaking in Multiethnic Societies* (Lexington, MA.: Lexington Books, 1990).

Ignatenko, Aleksandr. "Krovavaya doroga v rai," *Nezavisimaya gazeta-religiya*, No. 12, 16 July 2003, p. 1.

____. "Vakhkhabitskoe kvazigosudarstvo," *Russkii Zhurnal*, www.russ.ru/publish/96073701.

Interview with Osama bin Laden's former body guard Nasir Ahmad Nasir al-Bahri (Abu-Jandal), *Al-Quds al Arabi* (London), 18 March 2005, translated on Ralph Davis's "Chechnya" Yahoo listserve, 22 May 2005, in the author's archive.

Iskhakov, Gusman. "Islam v Tatarstane: istoriya i sovremennost'," *Mir Islama*, Vol. 1, Nos. 1–2 (1999), pp. 21–24

"Israel budet razrushen v 2022 godu?" *Kavkaz-Tsentr*, 14 April 2006, 17:38:38, www.kavkazcenter.com/russ/content/2006/04/14/43739.shtml.

"Kabardino-Balkarskii Dzhamaat Yarmuk provyol spetsoperatsiyu v Nalchike," Daymohk.info, 15 Dec. 2005, http://www.daymohk.info/cgi-bin/archieve/archieve.cgi?choice=15200412.

Kappeler, Andreas, and Chervonnaya, Svetlana. "Musulmanskie narody Rossii: istoricheskoe vvedenie," in M. V. Iordan, R. G. Kuzeev, and S. M. Chervonnaya, eds., *Islam v Yevrazii: sovremennyie etnicheskie i estetich-eskie kontseptsii sunnitskogo islama, ikh transformatsiya v massovom soznanii i vyrazhenie v iskusstve musulmanskikh narodov Rossii* (Moscow: Progress-Traditsiya, 2001), pp. 98–119.

Kashapov, Rafis. "Den pamyati tatarskogo naroda," *Kavkaz-Tsentr*, 13 Oct. 2005, 00:16:51, www.kavkazcenter.net/russ/content/2005/10/13/38377.shtml.

____. "'Kulikovskaya bitva': Pravda ili vymysel?" *Kavkaz-Tsentr*, 19 Sept. 2005, 00:03:46, www.kavkazcenter.net/russ/content/2005/10/13/37630.shtml.

____. "Tatary trebuyut prekratit' lgat' o 'Kulikovskoi bitve,'" *Kavkaz-Tsentr*, 28 May 2005, www.kavkazcenter.net/russ/content/2005/05/28/34417.shtml.

Kemper, Mikhael. "Mezhdu Bukharoi i Srednei Volgoi: Stolknovenie Abd An-Nasra Al-Kursavi s ulemami traditsionalistami," *Mir Islama* (Kazan), Vol. 1, No. 1, 1999, pp. 163–174.

Khakim(ov), Rafael. "Kto ty, Tatarin," *Vostochnyi ekspress,* Nos. 17–18, 26 April–2 May 2002.

Khakimov, Rafael. "Islam v Povolzhe," www.kazanfed.ru/authors/khakimov/.

____. "Ob osnovakh asimmetrichnosti Rossiiskoi federatsii," in L. M. Drobizheva, ed., *Asimetrichnaya Federatsiya: vzglyad iz tsentra, respublik, i oblastei* (Moscow: Institute of Sociology RAN: 1998).

____. "Put idzhtikhada," *Otecehestvennyie zapiski,* No. 5, 2003, www.strana-oz.ru/print.php?type=article&id=681&numid=14&article=681.

Khanbabaev, K. M. "Etapi rasprostraneniya vakhkhabizma v Dagestane," *Alimy i uchenyie protiv vakhkhabizma* (Makhachkala, 2001).

Khinshtein, Aleksandr. "Prodaem Kavkaz. Torg umesten – Sensatsionnyi doklad Kozaka," *Moskovskii Komsomolets,* 16 June 2005, www.mk.ru/numbers/1682/article55887.htm.

Kisriev, Enver. "Islam v obshchestvenno-politicheskoi zhiznii Dagestana" in Yu. M. Kobishchanov, *Musulmane izmenyayushcheisya Rossii* (Moscow: Russian Political Encyclopedia, 2002), pp. 261–277.

Klussmann, Uwe. "The Beslan Aftermath: New Papers Critical of Russian Security Forces," *Der Spiegel* (Germany), 4 July 2005.

Kobishchanov, Yu. M. "Musulmansaya Moskva XXI v.: Musulmane Rossii nakanune XXI veka," Materialy Mezhdunarodnoi Konferentsii, Moskva, 6 September 1997 (Moscow, 1998).

____. "Musulmane Rossii, korennyie rossiiskie musulmane i russkie musulmane," in Kobishchanov, *Musulmane izmenyayushcheisya Rossii* (Moscow: Russian Political Encyclopedia, 2002), pp. 61–112.

"Kodeks. Respubliki Tatarstan ob administrativnykh pravonarushenyakh," *Respublika Tatarstan,* 31 Dec. 2002, www.rt-online.ru/documents/laws/?ID=6427&forprint12/30/2002.html.

"Kontseptsiya gosudarstvennoi politiki po razgranicheniyu predmetov vedeniya i polnomochii mezhdu federal'nym, regional'nym i munitsipal'nym urovnyami vlasti," *Zvezda Povolzhya,* 1–6 March 2001, p. 3.

Kozlov, Denis. "Mir bez mira, voina bez pravil: Real'naya Chechnya ne pokhozha na tu, chto my vidim po televizoru," *Nezavisimoe voennoe obozrenie,* No. 43, 5 Dec. 2003, pp. 1, 5.

Kramer, Mark. "Guerilla Warfare, Counterinsurgency, and Terrorism in the North Caucasus: The Military Dimension of the Russian-Chechen Conflict," unpublished paper in the author's archive.

Laipanov, Bilal. "Islam v istorii i samosoznanii karachaevskogo naroda," in M. V. Iordan, R. G. Kuzeev, and S. M. Chervonnaya, eds., *Islam v Evrazaii: sovremennye etnicheskie i esteticheskie kontseptsii sunnitskogo Islam, ikh transformatsiya v massovom soznanii i vyrazhenie v iskusstve musulmankskikh narodov Rossii* (Moscow: Progress-Traditsiya, 2001), pp. 170–198.

Laird, Robin F., and Hoffman, Erik P. "'The Scientific-Technological Revolution,' 'Developed Socialism,' and Soviet International Behavior," in Laird and Hoffman, eds., *The Conduct of Soviet Foreign Policy*, 2nd edn. (Hawthorne, N.Y.: Aldine Publishing Co., 1980), pp. 386–405.

Levada, Yu. A. "Sotsialno-politicheskaya situatsiya v Rossii v dekyabre 2005g.," Levada-Tsentr, 13 Dec. 2000, www.levada.ru/press/2000 121300.html.

Lijphart, Arend. "The Puzzle of Indian Democracy: A Consociational Interpretation," *American Political Science Review*, Vol. 90, No. 2 (June 1996), pp. 258–268.

Lopashenko, Nataliya. "Rise in Terrorism in Russia," *Russian Regional Report*, Vol. 9, No. 17 (17 Sept. 2004).

Lotfullin, Iskhak-khadzhi. Sept.–Oct. 2005 series of articles "V udushayush-chikh ob"yatiakh imperii" at Kavkaz-Tsentr, www.kavkazcenter.net/russ/content/2005/09/21/37679.shtml, www.kavkazcenter.net/russ/content/2005/09/22/37709.shtml, www.kavkazcenter.net/russ/content/2005/09/23/37735.shtml, www.kavkazcenter.net/russ/content/2005/09/24/37768.shtml, www.kavkazcenter.com/russ/content/2005/09/26/37816.shtml, and www.kavkazcenter.com/russ/content/2005/09/27/37841.shtml.

Lysenko, V. N. "Razdelenie vlasti i opyt' Rossiiskoi Federatsii," in M. N. Guboglo, ed., *Federalizm vlasti i vlast' federalizma* (Moscow: IntelTek, 1997), pp. 166–193.

"M. Udugov: 'Rossiya dolzhna byt vzyata pod vneshnee upravlenie'," *Kavkaz-Tsentr*, 20 June 2005, 00:23:42, www.kavkazcenter.net/russ/content/2005/06/20/35635.shtml.

"M. Udugov: 'Vsyo, chto ne sootvetstvuet Shariatu nelegitimni'," *Kavkaz-Tsentr*, www.kavkazcenter.net/russprint.php?id=40872.

McGregor, Andrew. "The Jamaat Movement in Kabardino-Balkaria," The Jamestown Foundation *Terrorism Monitor*, Vol. 3, Issue 7 (Special Issue on Chechnya), (7 April 2005).

Maksimenko, V. I. "Fundametaliszm i ekstremizm v Islame," in Ye. M. Kozhokin and V. I. Maksimenko, eds., *Islam i Islamizm* (Moscow: Russian Institute of Strategic Studies, 1999).

Malashenko, A. V. "Islam i politika v sovremennoi Rossii," in Yu. M. Kobishchanov, ed., *Musulmane izmenyayushcheisya Rossii* (Moscow: Russian Political Encyclopedia, 2002), pp. 7–24.

——. "The Islamic Factor in Russia," *New Europe Review*, Nov. 2004, www.neweuropereview.com/English/english-malashenko.cfm.

——. "Shadow of Islam over Europe," *International Affairs* (Moscow). Vol.

50, No. 5 (Sept.–Oct. 2004), pp. 65–74.

Markedonov, Sergei. "Kto vladeet Dagestanom, tot vladeet Kavkazom," Kavkaz-Forum – Rekonstruktsiya Chechni, 7 July 2005, www.kavkaz-forum.ru/politic/10245.html.

"Members of Congress to Address Russian Federal and Regional Leaders at Moscow School of Political Studies Seminar; Annual Event to Focus on Federalism, Intergovernmental Relations, and U.S.-Russia Relations," PRNewswire, 7 April 2005, http://news.findlaw.com/prnewswire/20050407/07apr2005151208.html.

Menon, Rajan. "Russia's Quagmire: On Ending the Standoff in Chechnya," *Boston Review*, Summer 2004, www.bostonreview.net.

"Mezhnatsionalnyie konflikty glavnaya ugroza edinstvu," *Obozrevatel – Rossiya segodnya: realnyi shans*, Nasledie www.nasledie.ru/oboz/N21-24_94/013.htm.

Minkailov, Said. "Terminologicheskaya voina," *Kavkaz-Tsentr*, 18 June 2004, www.kavkazcenter.net/russ/content/ 2004/06/18/22366.shtml.

_____. "Vtoraya Mirovaya voina glazami chechenskikh modzhahedov." *Kavkaz-Tsentr*, 11 April 2005, www.kavkazcenter.net/russ/content/2005/04/11/32959.shtml.

Mirgazizov, Rafael. "Rafail' Khakimov: Vostok i Zapad sblizhaet idzhtikhad – svobodomyslie," *Respublika Tatarstan*, 7 Oct. 2004, www.rt-online.ru.

Moghadam, Assaf. "Palestinian Suicide Terrorism in the Second Intifada: Motivations and Organizational Aspects," *Studies in Conflict and Terrorism*, Vol. 26, No. 2 (Feb.–March 2003).

_____. "The Roots of Suicide Terrorism: A Multi-Causal Approach," paper presented for the Harrington Workshop on the Root Causes of Suicide Terrorism, University of Texas at Austin, 12–13 May 2005.

Montinola, Gabriella, Qian, Yinggyi, and Weingast, Barry. "Federalism, Chinese Style: The Political Basis for Economic Success," *World Politics*, Vol. 48, No. 1 (1996), pp. 50–81.

"Mossad provodit terakty v Irake," *Kavkaz-Tsentr*, 2 May 2006, 15:56:48, www.kavkazcenter.com/russ/content/2006/05/02/44225.shtml.

Mukhametshin, Rafik. "Islam v Tatarskoi obshchestvennoi mysli nachala XX v.," in R. M. Amirkhanov, ed., *Ocherki istorii Tatarskoi obshchestvennoi mysli* (Kazan: Tatarskoe knizhskoe izdatelstvo, 2000), pp. 160–188.

_____. "Na putyakh k konfessional'noi politike: Islam v Tatarstane," *Religiya i SMI – Religiya v svetskom mire*, www.religare.ru.

_____. "Religiya v svetskom obshchestve – Na putyakh k konfessionalnoi politike: Islam v Tatarstane," Religare.ru, 15 March 2004, www.religare.ru/print8747.htm.

Murphy, Paul. "Makhachkala's War on Terror – A Week in a City under

Siege," posting on Johnson's Russia List, Center for Defense Information, 12 July 2005, www.cdi.org.

Musina, Rosalinda. "Musul'manskaya identichnost' kak forma 'religioznogo natsionalizma' Tatar v kontekste etnosotsial'nykh protsessov i etnopoliticheskoi situatsii v Tatarstane," in M. V. Iordan, R. G. Kuzeev, and S. M. Chervonnaya, eds., *Islam v Yevrazii: sovremennyie etnicheskie i esteticheskie kontseptsii sunnitskogo islama, ikh transformatsiya v massovom soznanii i vyrazhenie v iskusstve musulmanskikh narodov Rossii* (Moscow: Progress-Traditsiya, 2001), pp, 297–301.

"'My obrashchaemsya ko vsem tem, kto uveroval,'" *Kavkaz-Tsentr*, 21 Nov. 2005, 00:50:57, www.kavkazcenter.com/russ/content/2005/11/21/39551.shtml.

"'My perenosim voinu na territoriyu vraga . . . ,'" *Kavkaz-Tsentr*, 1 Aug. 2004, 13:09:21, www.kavkazcenter.com/russ/content/2004/08/01/24101.shtml.

Nakhushev, R. B. "O pravovom polozhenii musul'man v Kabardino-Balkarii," IslaminKBR.ru, 5 April 2005, www.islaminkbr.com/kbr/in.php?mode=002.

"Obrashchenie Prezidenta ChRI A.-Kh. Sadulaeva k chechenckomu narodu," Kavkaz-Tsentr, 19 Aug. 2005, 16:55:28, www.kavkazcenter.net/russ/content/2005/08/19/36843.shtml.

"Obrashchenie Prezidenta ChRI Sadulaeva k narodu," *Kavkaz-Tsentr*, 25 June 2005, 00:25:45, www.kavkazcenter.com/russ/content/2005/06/25/35478.shtml.

"Osetinskie modzhakhedy obstrelyali chechenskikh munafikov bliz sela Kardzhi," *Kavkaz-Tsentr*, 4 Oct. 2005, 18:45:52, www.kavkazcenter.net/russ/content/2005/10/04/38126.shtml.

"Oshibka prezidenta. Shaimieva podstavil ego vizir," Islam.ru, 30 Oct. 2004, www.islam.ru/pressclub/tema/shaimiev/.

Pain, Emil "Moscow's North Caucasus Policy Backfires," *Central Asia – Caucasus Analyst*, 29 June 2005.

Pape, Robert A. "The Logic of Suicide Terrorism," *American Political Science Review*, Vol. 97, No. 3 (Aug. 2003), pp. 343–361.

Pei, Minxin. "Self-Administration and Local Autonomy: Reconciling Conflicting Interests in China," in Wolfgang Danspeckgruber, ed., *The Self-Determination of Peoples: Community, Nation, and State in an Interdependent World* (Boulder, CO: Lynne Reinner Publishers, 2002), pp. 315–332.

Perepis 2002, "Prilozhenie 5 – Naselenie Rossii po natsional'no prinadlezhnosti i vladeniyu russkim yasykom," www.perepis.ru/ct/html/ALL_00_07.htm.

Petrov, Nikolai. "Democracy in Russia's Regions," in Michael McFaul and

Nikolai Petrov, eds., *The White Book of Russian Democracy* (Washington, D.C.: Carnegie Endowment of International Peace, 2004).

_____. "Po rezul'tatam issedovanii Permskaya Oblast' okazalas' demokratichnee Moskvy i Sankt Peterburga," Regions.ru, 16 Oct. 2002, 14:07, www.regions.ru.

_____. "Razdelennyi suverenitet po-rossiiski: vzaimootnosheniya Moskvy i regionov," in B. Koppiters, D. Darchiashvili, and N. Akaba, eds., *Poiski alternative dlya Gruzii i Abkhazii* (Moscow: Ves Mir, 1999), pp. 133–171.

Piazza, J. A. "Rooted in Poverty? Terrorism, Poor Economic Development and Social Cleavages," *Terrorism and Political Violence*, Vol. 18, No. 1 (Spring 2006), pp. 159–177.

Plugatarev, Boris. "2005 god: vyalaya voina s khalifatom," *Nezavisimoe voennoe obozrenie*, No. 49, 23 Dec. 2005, http://nvo.ng.ru/wars/2005-12-23/2_2005war.html.

Polosin, Ali Vyacheslav. "Otvet A. Kuraevu. Bibliya, Koran, i Beslan . . . : Vliyaet li natsionalnost killera na nashu veru v Boga?," Islam.ru, 28 Sept. 2004, www.islam.ru/pressclub/smi/kraevu/?print_page.

Preobrazhenskii, Ivan. "Vybory po-Dagestanskii," Politkom.ru, 17 March 2003, www.politkom.ru.

"Press vypusk #37: O Chechne," Levada-Tsentr, 13 Dec. 2003, www.levada.ru/press/2003121301.html.

"Prezident ChRI Sadulaev podpisal novyi ukaz i rasporyazhenie," *Kavkaz-Tsentr*, 11 Sept. 2005, 16:20:57, www.kavkazcenter.net/russ/content/2005/09/11/37432.shtml.

"Prezident ChRI Sheik Abdul-Khalim. Kto On?" *Kavkaz-Tsentr*, 12 March 2005, 00:59:07, www.kavkazcenter.com/russ/content/2005/03/12/31285.shtml.

"Radikal'nyi natsionalizm v Rossii i protivodeistvie emu v 2005 godu," Polit.ru, 9 Feb. 2006, www.polit.ru/research/2006/02/03/year2005.html.

Rechkalov, Vadim. "'Pochemu spetssluzhby ne mogut poimat' Shamilya Basaeva," *Izvestiya*, 6–10 Dec. 2004, www.izvestia.ru.

"Religioznyi yevreiskii deyatel' iznasiloval 9 detei," *Kavkaz-Tsentr*, 7 April 2006, 14:32:40, www.kavkazcenter.com/russ/content/2006/04/07/43537.shtml.

Roshchin, Mikhail. "The History of Islam in Kabardino-Balkaria," *Jamestown Foundation Chechnya Weekly*, Vol. 6, No. 46 (8 Dec. 2005), www.jamestown.org/publications_details.php?volume_id=409&issue_id=3556&article_id=2370581.

"Rossiya – mezhdu Zapadom i Vostokom," VTsIOM, Press-Vypusk, No. 361, 19 Dec. 2005, www.wciom.ru/?pt=9&article=2129.

Rotar, Igor. "Chechen Spark, Caucasian Powderkeg," *Perspective* (Institute for the Study of Conflict, Ideology, and Policy, Boston University), Vol. 10, No. 2 (Nov.–Dec. 1999).

"Russia" in US Department of State, Bureau of Democracy, Human Rights, and Labor, *Country Reports on Human Rights Practices 2003* (Washington, D.C.: Department of State, Feb. 2004).

Sageman, Marc. "Understanding Jihadi Networks," Center for Contemporary Conflict's Strategic Insights, Issue 4, No. 4, April 2005, www.ccc.nps.navy.mil/si/2005/Apr/ sagemanApr05.asp

"Shamil Basaev: 'Nalchik atakovalo 217 modzhakhedov,'" Chechenpress.info, 17 Oct. 2005, www.chechenpress.info/events/2005/10/17/02.shtml.

"Shamil Basaev: 'Segodnya voyuet ves chechenskii narod,'" *Kavkaz-Tsentr*, 17 Aug. 2005, 10:00:42, www.kavkazcenter.net/russ/content/2005/08/17/ 36759.shtml.

"Shkolu v Beslane zakhvatil Osetinskii Dzhamaat?," *Kavkaz-Tsentr*, 2 Sept. 2004, www.kavkazcenter.net/russ/content/2004/09/02/25438.shtml.

Sisk, David. "Power Sharing in Multiethnic Societies: Principal Approaches and Practices," in Gail W. Lapidus and Svetlana Tsalik, eds., *Preventing Deadly Conflict: Strategies and Institutions*, Proceedings of a Conference in Moscow, Russian Federation, 14–16 Aug. 1996 (New York: Carnegie Corporation, April 1998), pp. 34–67.

Smirnov, Andrei. "Who Is Behind Yarmuk Jamaat: Balkars or Kabardins?" *The Jamestown Foundation Eurasia Daily Monitor*, Vol. 2, Issue 23 (2 Feb. 2005).

Smirnyagin, Leonid. "Federalizm po Putinu ili Putin po federalizmu (zheleznoi pyatoi)?" *Brifing* (Moskovskii Tsentr Karnegi), Vol. 3, No. 3 (March 2001).

Sokolov-Mitrich, Dmitrii. "Russkii Ben Laden," *Izvestiya*, 21 Jan. 2005, www.izvestia.ru/conflict/1043323_print.

"Sotsialno-politicheskaya situatsiya v Rossii v dekyabre 2005g.," Levada-Tsentr, 29 Dec. 2005, www.levada.ru/press/2005122901.html.

"Special Reports on the Beslan Tragedy," *IWPR – Caucasus Reporting Service*, No. 252 (8 Sept. 2004), No. 253 (15 Sept. 2004), and No. 254 (23 Sept. 2004), info@iwpr.net.

"SShA otpravlyayut v Irak ubiits detei," *Kavkaz-Tsentr*, 10 Oct. 2005, 13:57:23, www.kavkazcenter.net/russ/content/2005/10/10/38329.shtml.

"SShA skryvayut svyaz Izraelya s sobytiyami 11 sentyabrya," Islam-info.ru, 13 April 2004, www.islam-info.ru/?a=255.

Stoun, Musa. "Satanizm v deistvii: 'Cherep ikosti' pravyat Amerikoi," *Kavkaz-Tsentr*, 13 April 2006, 00:48:10, www.kavkazcenter.com/russ/content/ 2006/04/13/43682.shtml.

"Strategicheskaya tsel' – sozdanie Islamskogo gosudarstva v Povolzhe,"

Kavkaz-Tsentr, 5 Oct. 2005, 15:57:12, www.kavkazcenter.net/russ/content/2005/10/05/38153.shtml.

"Summary of Reported Nuclear, Radioisotope, and Dual-Use Materials Trafficking Incidents Involving the NIS (January–December 2003)" of the joint Nuclear Threat Initiative/Center for Non-Proliferations Studies (Monterey Institute for International Studies) database, www.nti.org/db/nistraff/tables/2003_all.htm.

"'Tak, Kto zhe Ty, Tatarin?,'" Islam.ru, Oct. 2002, www.islam.ru/pressclub/analitika/hakim_tatarlar/.

Tsipko, Aleksandr. "The Weaknesses and Shortcomings of Putin's State Reforms," *The Jamestown Foundation Prism*, Vol. 6, Issue 10 (Oct. 2000).

Tumelty, Paul. "A Biography of Abdul-Khalim Sadulaev," *The Jamestown Foundation Chechen Weekly*, Vol. 6, Issue 11 (16 March 2005).

____. "Chechnya: A Strategy for Independence," *The Jamestown Foundation Chechnya Weekly*, 3 Aug. 2005.

Turnbull, Wayne, and Abhayaratne, Praveen. "2002 WMD Terrorism Chronology: Incidents Involving Sub-National Actors and Chemical, Biological, Radiological, and Nuclear Materials," Center for Non-Proliferation Studies, 2003, http://cns.miis.edu.

Udugov, Movladi. "Razmyshleniya modzhakheda," *Kavkaz-Tsentr*, 10 Aug. 2005, www.kavkazcenter.com/russ/history/stories/reflections_of_mujahid.shtml.

"Ukaz Prezidenta ChRI Abdul-Halima Sadulaeva," ChechenPress.com 15 March 2005, www.chechenpress.com/events/2005/04/14/30.shtml.

"Ukazom Prezidenta ChRI Sadulaeva sozdan Kavkazskii front," Kavkaz-Tsentr, 16 May 2005, www.kavkazcenter.com/russ/content/2005/05/16/33965.shtml.

"Ukazy Prezidenta ChRI A.-Kh. Sadulaev," *Kavkaz-Tsentr*, 25 Aug. 2005, 14:05:31, www.kavkazcenter.net/russ/content/2005/08/25/37056. shtml.

Urnov, Mark. "Zhostckaya diktatura nadezhdy," *Moskovskie novosti*, No. 12, 2–8 April 2004, p. 25.

US Commission on International Religious Freedom Annual Report, May 2005, www.uscirf.gov/countries/publications/currentreport/2005annualRpt.pdf# page=1.

US Department of Defense, *Proliferation: Threat and Response 1997*, www.defenselink.mil/pubs/prolif97/fsu.html#russia.

US Department of Defense, *Proliferation: Threat and Response 2001*, www.defenselink.mil/pubs/ptr20010110. pdf.

Vachagaev, Mayrbek. "Evolution of the Chechen Jamaat," *Jamestown Foundation Chechnya Weekly*, Vol. 6, Issue 14 (6 April 2005).

Vakhayev, L. "Politicheskye fantazii v sovremennoi Chechenskoi respublike," in *Rossiya i Chechnya: obshchestva i gosudarstva* (Moscow, 1998), www.skharov-center.ru/chs/chrus15.1htm.

Wald, Kenneth D., Silverman, Adam L., and Fridy, Kevin S. "Making Sense of Religion in Political Life," *Annual Review of Political Science*, Vol. 8, No. 3 (June 2005), pp. 121–143.

Ware, Robert Bruce. "Renewed Terrorist Offensive in Dagestan," unpublished paper in the author's archive.

Ware, Robert Bruce, and Kisriev, Enver. "Ethnic Parity and Democratic Pluralism in Dagestan: A Consociational Approach," *Europe-Asia Studies*, Vol. 53, No. 1 (Jan. 2001).

_____. "Political Stability in Dagestan: Ethnic Parity and Religious Polarization," *Problems of Post-Communism*, Vol. 47, No. 2 (March–April 2000), pp. 23–33.

_____. "Russian Recentralization Arrives in the Republic of Dagestan: Implications for Institutional Integrity and Political Stability," *East European Constitutional Review*, Vol. 10, No. 1 (Winter 2001), pp. 68–75.

Ware, Robert Bruce, Kisriev, Enver, Patzelt, Werner J., and Roericht, Ute. "Stability in the Caucasus: The Perspective from Dagestan," *Problems of Post-Communism*, Vol. 50, No. 2 (March–April 2003), pp. 12–23.

Yakupov, Valiulla. "Religioznyi modernism ili modernizatsiya obshchestva?" *Zvezda Povolzhya*, No. 37, 16–22 Sept. 2003, p. 3.

Yemelyanova, M. N. "Islam i kulturnaya traditsiya v Tsentralno-Severnom Kavkaze," in Yu. M. Kobyshanov, *Musul'mane izmenyayusheisya Rossii* (Moscow: ROSSPEN, 2002), pp. 241–260.

"Yeshchyo odin 'protsess ved'm' protiv ocherednogo otritsatelysa 'kholokosta' v Avstrii," *Kavkaz-Tsentr*, 5 March 2005, 10:56:21, www.kavkazcenter.com/russ/content/2006/03/05/.shtml.

Yevloev, N. "Problemy borby s terrorizmom na sovremennom etape," *Serdalo*, No. 88, 9 Aug. 2005, http://www.ingush.ru/serdalo135_2.asp.

"Yevreiskie ravviny zapretili vracham lechit' palestintsev," *Kavkaz-Tsentr*, 15 April 2006, 16:26:34, www.kavkazcenter.com/russ/content/2006/04/15/43766.shtml.

Yoo, John. "Fighting the New Terrorism," American Enterprise Institute Bradley Lecture, 6 June 2005, www.aei.org/include/pub_print.asp?pubID=22633. html.

Yuzeev, A. N. "Filisofskaya mysl' kontsa XVIII-XIX vv.," in R. M. Amirkhanov, ed., *Ocherki istorii Tatarskoi obshchestvennoi mysli* (Kazan: Tatarskoe knizhskoe izdatelstvo, 2000), pp. 92–127.

Zakon Respubliki Tatarstan 'O vvedenie v deistvie Kodeksa Respubliki Tatarstan ob administrativnykh pravonarushenyakh, *Respublika Tatarstan*, 31 Dec. 2002, www.rt-online.ru/documents/laws/?ID=

6428&forprint12/30/2002.html.

"Zakony Respubliki Tatarstan i normativnyie akty, ne podlezhashie primeneniyu," Tatarstan.ru, 1 Aug. 2003, www.tatarstan.ru.

"Zayavlenie Administratsii Prezidenta ChRI," Kavkaz-Tsentr, 27 Sept. 2005, 00:59:01, www.kavkazcenter.com/russ/content/2005/09/27/37843.shtml.

"Zayavlenie Dzhamaata 'Yarmuk'", ChechenPress.info, 17 Oct. 2005, www.chechenpress.info/events/2005/10/17/04.shtml.

"Zayavlenie Prezidenta ChRI A-Kh. Sadulaeva," Chechen.org, 15 May 2005, 09:07:43,

www.chechen.org/modules.php?name=News&file=article&sid=3406.

Zhukov, Igor. "The Structure of Teyps and Clans," *Yuzhnyy Reporter* (Rostov-on-Don), 28 Nov. 2005, in Ralph Davis's Chechnya Yahoo Group, 27 Dec. 2005, AltChechnya@yahoogroups.com.

Zubov, A. B. "Granitsy razlomov i urovni edinstva v segodnyashnei Rossii: Uroki sotsiologicheskogo issledovaniya," in *Dukhovnyie osnovy mirovogo soobshestva i mezhdunarodnykh otnoshenii* (Moscow: MGIMO, 2000).

Zverev, Aleksei. "Znachenie opyta Tatarstana dlya Gruzii i Abkhazii," in B. Koppiters, D. Darchiashvili, and N. Akaba, eds., *Poiski alternative dlya Gruzii i Abkhazii: Praktika federalizma* (Moscow: Ves Mir, 1999), pp. 107–132.

RUSSIAN-LANGUAGE NEWSPAPERS, JOURNALS, AND INTERNET WEBSITES

Antiterror.ru (www.antiterror.ru)

Camagat.com (www.camagat.com)

ChechenPress.org (http://chechenpress.co.uk)

Dagestanskaya pravda (www.dagpravda.ru)

Daymohk.ru (www.daymohk.ru)

"Ekho Moskvy" Radio (www.echo.msk.ru)

Elbrusoid.ru (www.elbrusoid.ru)

Gazeta

Gazeta.ru (www.gazeta.ru)

Gazeta yuga (www.gazetayuga.ru)

Ingushetia.ru (www.ingushetia.ru)

Ingushetiya.ru (www.ingushetiya.ru)

Intertat.ru (www.intertat.ru)

Islam.ru (www.islam.ru)

IslaminKBR.ru (www.islaminkbr.com)

Itar-Tass (www.itar-tass.com)

Izvestiya (www.izvestia.ru)

Kavkazskii uzel (www.kavkaz.memo.ru)
Kavkaz-Tsentr (www.kavkazcenter.net, www.kavkazcenter.com)
Kazanskii federalist
Kommersant(-Daily) (www.kommersant.ru)
Kommersant-Kazan (www.kommersant.ru/region/kazan)
Kommersant-Vlast
Komsomolskaya pravda (www.kp.ru)
Mir Islama (Kazan)
Moskovskie novosti
Moskovskii Komsomolets (www.mk.ru)
Mosnews.com (www.mosnews.com)
NEWSru.com (http://palm.newsru.com)
Nezavisimaya gazeta (www.ng.ru)
Nezavisimaya gazeta-religiya
Nezavisimoe voennoe obozrenie
Novaya gazeta (www.novayagazeta.ru)
Novoye Delo
NTV (www.ntv.ru)
Perepis.ru (www.perepis.ru)
Polit.ru (www.polit.ru)
Politkom.ru (www.politkom.ru)
Pravda
Prime-Tass (www.prime-tass.ru)
Regions.ru (www.regions.ru)
Regnum.ru (www.regnum.ru)
Religare.ru, (www.religare.ru)
Respublika Tatarstan (www.rt-online.ru)
Rossiiskaya gazeta (www.rg.ru)
Russian Central Election Commission website (www.cikrf.ru)
Russian Information Agency 'Novosti' (www.rian.ru)
Russkii Zhurnal (www.russ.ru)
Segodnya
Severnaya Ossetiya (Vladikavkaz)
Smi.ru (www.smi.ru)
Sobaka
Strana.ru (www.strana.ru)
Tatarica (http://tatarica. yuldash.com)
Tatarstan.ru (www.tatarstan.ru)
Utro.ru (www.utro.ru)
Vechernie Chelny (Naberez.nye Chelny, Tatarstan) (www.vechernie-chelny.ru)
Vechernyaya Kazan (www.evening-kazan.ru)

Vostochni ekspress
Vremya i dengi (www.e-vid.ru)
Vremya MN
Vremya novostei
Zvezda Povolzhya (Kazan)

ENGLISH-LANGUAGE NEWSPAPERS, INTERNET WEBSITES, AND NEWSLETTERS

EastWest Institute Russian Regional Report (www.isn.ethz.ch)
The Financial Times
Hizb ut-Tahrir's website (www.1924.org)
Institute for War and Peace Reporting (IWPR) Caucasus Reporting Service
    (www.iwpr.org)
The Jamestown Foundation *Chechen Weekly* (www.jamestown.org)
The Jamestown Foundation *Eurasia Daily Monitor* (www.jamestown.org)
The Jamestown Foundation *Terrorism Monitor* (www.jamestown.org)
The Moscow Times
The New York Times
Newsweek Russia
The Observer (London)
Radio Free Europe/Radio Liberty (RFERL) (www.rferl.org)
RFERL Caucasus Report (www.rferl.org)
RFERL Russian Federation Report (www.rferl.org)
RFERL Russian Political Weekly (www.rferl.org)
RFERL Tatar-Bashkir Daily Report (www.rferl.org)
Ralph Davis's Chechnya Yahoo Listserve
Reuters (www.reuters.com)
Russian and Eurasian Terrorism Watch (www.retwa.com, www.retwa.org)
Stratfor (www.stratfor.com)
The Sunday Times (London)
Transitions Online (www.tol.cz)
USA Today

Index

Note: Bold page numbers indicate tables. Endnotes are indicated by *n* or *nn*; only those notes which give significant information are indexed.